Professional Review Guide for the CCS-P Examination
2010 Edition

Patricia J. Schnering, RHIA, CCS
Toni Cade, MBA, RHIA, CCS, FAHIMA
Lisa M. Delhomme, MHA, RHIA

PRG Publishing, Inc.
Professional Review Guides, Inc.

DELMAR
CENGAGE Learning

**Professional Review Guide for the CCS-P
Examination, 2010 Edition**
Patricia J. Schnering, RHIA, CCS
Toni Cade, MBA, RHIA, CCS, FAHIMA
Lisa M. Delhomme, MHA, RHIA

Vice President, Career and Professional Editorial:
Dave Garza

Director of Learning Solutions:
Matthew Kane

Managing Editor:
Marah Bellegarde

Senior Acquisitions Editor:
Rhonda Dearborn

Product Manager:
Jadin Babin-Kavanaugh

Vice President, Career and Professional:
Jennifer McAvey

Executive Marketing Manager:
Wendy Mapstone

Senior Marketing Manager:
Nancy Bradshaw

Marketing Coordinator:
Erica Ropitzky

Production Director:
Carolyn Miller

Senior Content Project Manager:
James Zayicek

Senior Art Director:
Jack Pendleton

2010 Current Procedural Terminology © 2009 American Medical Association. ALL RIGHTS RESERVED.

For product information and technology assistance, contact us at
Cengage Learning Customer & Sales Support,
1-800-354-9706
For permission to use material from this text or product, submit
all requests online at **www.cengage.com/permissions**
Further permissions questions can be emailed to
permissionrequest@cengage.com

Library of Congress Cataloging-in-Publication Data : 2010920474
ISBN 10: 1-1111-2797-2
ISBN 13: 978-1-1111-2797-8

Delmar
Executive Woods
5 Maxwell Drive
Clifton Park, NY 12065-2919
USA

Cengage Learning products are represented in Canada by Nelson Education, Ltd.

For your course and learning solutions, visit **delmar.cengage.com**

Purchase any of our products at your local college store or visit our corporate website at **cengage.com**

Notice to the Reader

Printed in United States of America
1 2 3 4 5 13 12 11 10

ABOUT THE AUTHORS

Patricia J. Schnering, RHIA, CCS

Patricia J. Schnering was the founder of PRG Publishing, Inc. and Professional Review Guides, Inc. Mrs. Schnering is a 1995 graduate of the Health Information Management program at St. Petersburg College in St. Petersburg, Florida. In 1998, she was certified as a CCS and in 1999 she received her RHIA certification. Her education also includes a Bachelor's degree from the University of South Florida in Tampa, Florida, with a major in Business Administration. Her HIM experiences include working in health information services supervisory positions, as a HIM consultant, and as an adjunct HIM instructor at St. Petersburg College. She has been active in her local and state HIM associations. Mrs. Schnering was awarded the Florida Health Information Management Association (FHIMA) Literary Award in 2000 and 2005.

Lisa M. Delhomme, MHA, RHIA

Lisa M. Delhomme is an instructor in the Health Information Management Department at the University of Louisiana at Lafayette, located in Lafayette, Louisiana. She has a Bachelor's degree in Health Information Management and a Master's degree in Health Services Administration. She teaches several courses including CPT coding, legal aspects of healthcare, and computers in healthcare organizations. Prior to teaching, she held a management position at a physician practice and ambulatory surgery center. Mrs. Delhomme has been an active member of the American Health Information Management Association for 10 years. Additionally, she has been involved with committees and projects for the Louisiana Health Information Management Association and Louisiana Medical Group Management Association.

Toni Cade, MBA, RHIA, CCS, FAHIMA

Toni Cade is a tenured Associate Professor in the Health Information Management Department at the University of Louisiana at Lafayette. She teaches several courses including healthcare reimbursement methodologies (MS-DRGs, APCs, RUGs, etc.), hospital statistics, case management, performance improvement, medical terminology, and healthcare risk management. She is also the Management Internship Site Coordinator responsible for coordinating affiliation sites throughout the United States.

Mrs. Cade has 30 years experience with previous positions, including Data Analyst for the QIO, Utilization Review Supervisor, and Coding Supervisor in a large acute care hospital. Mrs. Cade holds a Bachelor's degree (B.S.) in Medical Record Science and a Master's degree (MBA) in Business Administration. Her credentials include RHIA (Registered Health Information Administrator) and CCS (Certified Coding Specialist). She was also awarded the designation of Fellow (FAHIMA) by the American Health Information Management Association.

She is listed in Marquis' *Who's Who in Medicine and Health Care*. Mrs. Cade serves on the Editorial Advisory Board of *Health Information Management Manual* and *For the Record*. She has reviewed and authored publications on topics including medical terminology, billing and reimbursement, and healthcare statistics.

As an independent consultant, Mrs. Cade has extensive experience conducting seminars in coding and reimbursement. She also consults at acute care hospitals and works with attorneys involved in medical malpractice cases as an expert healthcare data analyst and expert witness.

Mrs. Cade has served AHIMA in various positions including delegate, Nominating Committee member, and Fellowship Review Committee member. She was nominated for AHIMA's Champion Award and Educator's Award. She has served her state association, the Louisiana Health Information Management Association (LHIMA), in many capacities, including serving on the Board of Directors and as President, Secretary, and Project Manager of various projects. She was awarded the Distinguished Member Award in 2003. She also received the Outstanding Volunteer Award for her efforts as Coding Roundtable Coordinator in Louisiana in 2003–2004. In 2009, she received the Outstanding Volunteer Award for her efforts in creating a Central Office Coordinator position for LHIMA.

ACKNOWLEDGMENTS

First and foremost, I wish to express my gratitude to the authors who collaborated on the book. They are the educators and clinical coding experts who worked diligently to provide comprehensive coverage of coding procedures. I am very grateful to have such seasoned professionals working with me on the book.

I would like to express my gratitude to all of the authors who have worked on the educational materials PRG Publishing has produced. They are seasoned professionals and excellent educators. They inspire me to work harder to produce better products. Each one of these educators presents a facet of HIM practice necessary to view the HIM arena as a whole.

There are very special people in my family who always knew I could do it when I was not sure I could. My husband, Bob, as always, continues to keep me grounded when I tend to spin off in space as I become engrossed in working on the books. He graciously listens to me go on and on about the work's progress throughout the process. And, I could never forget the encouragement my mother provides. Mom, you are always there for me! My mother is my role model for perseverance leading to success. She embodies grace, courage, strength, and endurance.

And, of course, I appreciate all the help from my family at Delmar Learning. They have all the answers and have been extremely helpful in guiding me through the publishing system. Thank you all very much!

My special reward is knowing that the materials you study here may assist you in preparing for the challenge of the CCS-P Examination. Thank you for the letters and words of encouragement.

I wish you the very best now and throughout your career.

Until we meet....

Patricia J. Schnering, RHIA, CCS

PJSPRG@AOL.COM

TABLE OF CONTENTS

Introduction

Patricia J. Schnering, RHIA, CCS

INTRODUCTION TO THE PROFESSIONAL REVIEW GUIDE FOR THE CCS-P EXAMINATION

This examination review guide represents a renewed effort to provide materials for HIM students and professionals. In reviewing the results of past examinations, we found that it would be beneficial for examination candidates to have additional practice in answering multiple-choice questions and coding medical cases. We have selected questions and cases to cover the broad topic of categories necessary for sitting the CCS-P Certification Examination. Researching the questions and cases as you study should increase your knowledge such that, when you encounter similar questions and cases, you can arrive at the correct answer. We believe that this review material will jog your memory and build on information you have already gained through your education and professional experiences. This book provides you with a mix of coding questions and case exercises to both increase your coding skills and provide you with testing that mimics the exam format.

The beginning of this book offers suggestions for studying and test-taking strategies. The book is then divided into two additional sections. The first section is a coding review section containing multiple-choice questions and coding case studies. The second section contains a mock examination for Part I of the exam with sixty (60) multiple-choice questions and mock cases to code for Part II of the exam. The back of the book contains appendices with information on pharmacology and laboratory testing.

The questions in this examination review guide are based on the broad competencies listed in the AHIMA Candidate Handbook for the CCS_P Examination. Review the latest Candidate Handbook when preparing for the exam.

Table 1 displays the major content areas of this book by sections.

Table 1 CCS-P Content areas for the Professional Review Guide for the CCS-P Examination

Professional Review Guide for the CCS-P Examination Content Areas	
Introduction	
Examination Study Strategies and Resources	
Coding Review	
Section 1 of the book includes the following chapters	NUMBER OF QUESTIONS/CASES
Health Data Content, Requirements, and Standards	89
Medical Sciences	111 Questions
Classification Systems and Secondary Data Sources	79 Questions
Medical Billing and Reimbursement Systems	59 Questions
ICD-9-CM Coding	198 Questions
CPT Coding	233 Questions
CCS-P Case Study Coding Review	42 Cases
Section 2 of the book includes the following Mock Exams	
Part I Mock Examination Questions	60 Questions
Part II Mock Examination Cases	16 Cases
Appendices	
Appendix A Pharmacology	
Appendix B Laboratory Testing	
Official Coding Guidelines effective October 1, 2009	

ABOUT THE COMPETENCIES FOR THE CCS-P EXAMINATION

We suggest that you start by examining the competencies for the Certified Coding Specialist-Physician Based Examination (CCS-P). They are listed as domains and task statement competencies. The competencies were created to reflect the necessary skill level for professional practice. A detailed list of the competencies is provided in the AHIMA Candidate Handbook for the Certification Examinations.

It is the responsibility of the American Health Information Management Association's (AHIMA) Council on Certification (COC) to assess what job tasks are frequently executed by newly certified practitioners. Additionally, the COC determines the job tasks that are critical to the practice—in other words, the job tasks that, if done incorrectly, could create a negative impact. The Task Statements are also referred to as the test specifications.

The process of identifying those critical job functions was accomplished by conducting a job analysis. The objective was to determine how the practice is evolving and to develop the test specifications and a certification examination to correspond with changes that are occurring in the field. The data that were collected as a result of this research provided the essential elements necessary to establish the test specifications for the certifying exam. The COC is responsible for developing and administering the certification examination and for determining the eligibility of applicants to write the exam. The task statements for the Certified Coding Specialist-Physician-based are grouped into seven domains. These domains are divided further into task statements. Weights for each domain are assigned; however, weights were not assigned to the task statements. Each weight correlates to the degree of emphasis, or importance, given to each domain statement as it relates to the current health information practice. Table 2 displays the domains you will be responsible for on the examination.

Crosswalks between the competencies for the CCS-P Certification Examination and the questions in the chapters are provided in Table 3. In addition to the competencies, the questions are written in three cognitive levels of testing, which are explained after Table 3.

Table 2 CCS-P Part I Examination Content with Percentage of Questions by Domain

CCS-P Part I Examination Content with Percentage Questions by Domain		
Domains	Number of Questions	Percentage of Exam
Domain 1: Health Information Documentation	11	18%
Domain 2: ICD-9-CM Diagnosis Coding	14	24%
Domain 3: CPT and HCPCS II Coding	14	24%
Domain 4: Reimbursement	5	8%
Domain 5: Data Quality and Analysis	6	10%
Domain 6; Information and Communication Technologies	4	6%
Domain 7: Compliance and Regulatory Issues	6	10%
TOTAL	60	100%

Reminder: Monitor AHIMA's Web site for updates on the testing information.

Table 3 Crosswalk of the CCS-P Examination Competencies and the Questions in the Chapters

Crosswalk of CCS-P Competencies to Chapter

Chapter Name	Competency Domain							Total
	1	2	3	4	5	6	7	
Health Data Content and Standards	23	0	0	2	11	26	27	89
Medical Science	111	0	0	0	0	0	0	111
Classification Systems and Secondary Data Sources	10	34	24	0	4	5	2	79
Medical Billing and Reimbursement Systems	1	0	5	46	1	1	5	59
ICD-9-CM Coding	0	198	0	0	0	0	0	198
CPT Coding	0	0	233	0	0	0	0	233
CCS-P Mock Examination Part 1	4	7	35	2	7	2	3	60
Total CCS-P Questions	150	241	300	54	28	40	44	829

About the Cognitive Levels of Testing for Part I of the CCS-P Examination

These examination questions test your knowledge on three cognitive levels: recall (RE), application (AP), and analysis (AN). The recall level tests your memory of basic facts, such as being able to identify terms, methods, and procedures. The application level tests your ability to interpret data and information, to be able to apply concepts and principles, recognize relationships among data, and calculate mathematical problems. The analysis level measures your ability to solve specific problems by evaluating, comparing, and selecting appropriate solutions for action; and to evaluate information and perform multiple calculations to assemble various elements into a total picture.

The general format of Part I of the exam is primarily designed to engage your problem-solving and critical thinking skills. These types of questions require you to translate what you have learned and apply it to a situation. There are sample questions provided on the AHIMA Web site (http://www.AHIMA.org) so that you can experience the testing situation.

CCS-P EXAMINATION CONTENTS

The CCS-P examination is in a computer-based format. Carefully read the latest Candidate Handbook for the CCS-P Examination and continue to monitor AHIMA's Web site to look for updated information on the examination format. The handbook is available for downloading in PDF format on the AHIMA Web site (http://www.AHIMA.org).

Part I of the examination has 60 multiple-choice questions. Fifty of the questions are counted toward your test score. The remaining 10 questions are unscored items. These unscored items included in the examination will be used to "test" the questions before using them in a future examination. The unscored questions are scrambled randomly throughout the examination. They do not count toward your score. However, you will have no way of knowing which is a scored question or which is an unscored question. You will be expected to answer the multiple-choice questions without use of your references and code books. The time constraint is ninety (90) minutes.

Part II of the examination has a total of 16 cases to code using your CPT and HCPCS Level II code books (for procedural coding), and ICD-9-CM code books (for diagnostic coding). Cases from the Hospital, Emergency Room, Operating Room, and Physician Office/Clinic setting will be used. The time allotted for completing Part II of the examination is 3 hours (180 minutes). Review the CCS-P Examination content as shown in Table 4.

The key to success on the exam is a thorough knowledge of procedural coding in CPT and HCPCS Level II, and coding for diagnoses using ICD-9-CM, which can only be achieved through extensive use and familiarity with the code books. Having to use the code books to answer questions will help increase your speed in the use of both coding books.

This book is only one of many tools available to you to prepare. Use a variety of review methodologies (multiple-choice questions, case studies, review of theory, mock exams, etc.) as an effective means of reviewing. These tools can help prepare you for the challenge of the CCS-P coding exam.

Table 4 CCS-P Examination Content

CCS-P Examination Content	
PART I	
Number of multiple-choice questions	60
Amount of time for questions	90 minutes
Average time to answer each question	1.5 minutes per question
PART II	
CPT E&M Chapter Cases	6
CPT Surgery Chapter Cases	6
CPT Medicine Chapter Cases	3
Case from remaining CPT Chapters and HCPCS Level II	1
Total number of cases	16
Amount of time for cases	150 minutes
Average time to code each case	9.38 minutes per case
Total time for examination	4 hours

Reminder: Monitor AHIMA's Web site for the latest updates on the testing information.

ADDITIONAL INSIGHTS ABOUT THE CCS-P EXAMINATION

1. **Computerized Testing.** You will be able to review questions on the computer screen and check your answers before you close the exam file on the computer.

2. **On-Screen Information.** Any additional information needed to complete the questions in Part I of the examination will be available on the screen in the testing software.

3. **Medical Sciences.** These questions tend to be interspersed throughout other topic categories. Medical terminology, pathophysiology, and anatomy and physiology are a part of the general knowledge base for Health Information Management, coding, and reimbursement.

4. **National Exam.** Keep in mind that this is a national examination. Concentrate on federal legislation, statutes and legal issues that would be appropriate nationally in all 50 states.

5. **Be prepared to shift gears quickly throughout the exam.** Questions on the examinations are scrambled and change topics from question to question. Therefore, you may have a CPT coding question, followed by a reimbursement question, followed by an ICD-9-CM question, etc.

6. **You will need to bring your ICD-9-CM coding book, the AMA CPT-4 code book, and the HCPCS coding book to the test for use in Part II of the exam.** Practicing coding using your coding books will help increase your speed in finding the codes by the book. Remember, the test is timed. The faster you code, the more time you have to choose your answers. It may make the difference in being able to successfully complete the examination in the time allotted.
   - Part I of the examination: You will not be allowed to use your code books to answer the questions or verify the answer you choose. The multiple-choice questions in Part I of the exam are in a narrative form and any necessary codes and/or code narratives will be supplied in the answer options on the computer screen for you to choose from.
   - Part II of the examination: You will be using the coding books in Part II of the examination.

7. **The focus is on critical concepts.** Our major focus is on covering the concepts and competencies in the body of knowledge for the Certified Coding Specialist-Physician Based (CCS-P). The questions and cases on the examination may combine several concepts into one question that may increase the level of difficulty in the question or case.

8. **Review the latest candidate handbook.** The AHIMA Candidate Handbook for the Certification Examinations contains information on the exam, how to apply for the examination, what to bring, and other pertinent information you need.

9. **Make sure that you have the necessary items for admission for testing.** Again, review your AHIMA Candidate Handbook for specific information on what you will need to bring with you to the examination center. You will need to bring your Authorization to Test (ATT) and two forms of identification (review the accepted forms of identification listed in your handbook). You will need code books for Part II of the exam. Bring the ICD-9-CM Coding book Volumes 1–2, the CPT code book (reminder: only AMA's CPT books may be used on the exam), and the HCPCS Level II National Code Book. You may also bring a medical dictionary for use in Part II of the examination.

I. Examination Study Strategies and Resources

Patricia J. Schnering, RHIA, CCS

STUDY STRATEGIES AND RESOURCES

How to Use This Book

We suggest you answer the multiple-choice questions and code the case studies in the review section of the book before taking the mock examination. It will give you a baseline to begin your CCS-P Examination preparation. Your strengths and weaknesses will become more apparent, allowing you to plan your study time more effectively and focus on your problem areas.

After working through the review questions and case studies in the book, take the mock examination. It will provide you with an opportunity to assess your speed in answering multiple-choice questions and in coding cases.

Study Strategies

Preparing for a major examination is similar to preparing for a marathon athletic event. The time allotted for the examination is a total of 4 hours. One suggestion is to use your study process to slowly build up your concentration time until you can focus your energy for several hours at a time. This is like the runner who begins jogging for 30 minutes and builds up to one hour, then one and a half hours, etc., and gradually increases the endurance time to meet the demands of the race. This strategy could work for you.

Everyone has his or her particular study style. Some people prefer to study alone and others work best in a group. Regardless of your preference, we strongly recommend that you take advantage of studying with a group at least some of the time. Studying with others can prove very helpful when working through your areas of weakness. Each member of the study team will bring strengths and weaknesses to the table and all can benefit from the collaboration. Even if you are a solitary learner, you may occasionally want to work with a group on those topics you find more challenging. If you do not have easy access to a study group for the examination, you may want to study with other HIM professionals over the Internet. The HIM AHIMA communities of practice (CoP) on the Internet is an excellent avenue for finding others who are in the same position.

Theoretically, material learned thoroughly after one study session will fade predictably with time. After one day, the average person retains only 80% of what was learned; ultimately he or she will remember about 30% of the material originally learned. That is why you are relearning information that you have acquired over a period of years. Your aim is to achieve maximum recall through effective review.

Make your study process a systematic review of all coding topic categories, followed by achieving mastery of strategically selected subjects within the topic categories. To facilitate this effort, we recommend that you design a 10-week study program. Plan on spending an average of 10 to 12 hours per week studying. The idea is to study smart, not to bulldoze through tons of material in a haphazard way.

BEGIN BY BUILDING YOUR STUDY STRATEGIES

First, you must get organized.
You must be deliberate about making sure that you develop and stick to a regular study routine. Find a place where you can study, either at home or at the library.

How you schedule your study time during the week is an individual decision. However, we recommend that you avoid all-nighters and other unreasonably long study sessions. The last thing you want to do is burn yourself out by working too long and too hard at one time. Try to do a little bit at a time and maintain a steady pace that is manageable for you.

Second, develop your individual study program.
Write the exam topics and subjects in a list. Outline the chapters in your coding textbooks and review the sections in your code books. Pinpoint your weakest subjects. Pause at each chapter outline and recall basic points. Do you draw a blank, recall them more or less, or do you feel comfortable with your recall? By using this approach, you can see where you stand.

Then, weigh the importance of each subject.
How are the topics emphasized in the examination competencies, textbooks, professional journal articles, coding guidelines, and coding books? Take a look at the APCs. Try to pick out concepts that would make good examination questions.

Make a list of the topics in the order that you plan to study them.
Avoid trying to make a head-on attack by giving equal time and attention to all topics. Use the outline you have made to identify your weakest topics. Determine which topics you believe will require a significant amount of study time and which will only require a brief review. Your list will give you a clear mental picture of what you need to do and will keep you on track.

There are three additional advantages to a list. One, it builds your morale as you steadily cross off items that you have completed as you monitor your progress. Two, glancing back at the list from time to time serves to reassure you that you are on target. And three, you can readily see that you are applying your time and effort where they are most needed.

Keep the list conspicuously in view. Carefully plan your pre-exam study time and stick to your plan. Go to the exam like a trained and disciplined runner going to a marathon event!

A Summary of Tips for Organizing Your Time and Materials

1. Review the major CPT, HCPCS II and ICD-9-CM coding topic categories and determine which areas you are strong in and which areas you need improvement in.

2. Set up a realistic study schedule. Customize the sample schedule provided in this book to meet your needs.

3. Spend more time and energy studying your areas of weakness. Remember, every question counts toward that passing grade.

4. Organize and review all of the following items:
    a. The latest AHIMA Candidate Handbook for the CCS-P Examinations
    b. Official Coding Guidelines
    c. Official Outpatient coding guidelines
    d. coding textbooks and any coding course syllabi, outlines, class notes, and tests
    e. coding books
    f. *Coding Clinic* from the past 3–4 years
    g. *CPT Assistant* from the past 3–4 years
    h. professional journal articles on documentation, reimbursement, and coding issues
    i. list of pertinent Web sites for research and review

5. Enter valuable coding information directly into your code books. You will not be allowed to have loose materials in your books. However, any information that is permanently attached or written into the code book is acceptable.

6. One of the best ways to study for an examination is to take tests. Practice answering questions and working coding cases as much as possible. Time yourself so that you become accustomed to taking, on the average, less than 1 minute per each multiple-choice question and around an average of 13 to 14 minutes for coding cases. Work with your watch in front of you. When working coding cases, be sure to follow the coding procedures that will be used in the examination. These procedures are listed in the Candidate Handbook from AHIMA.

7. Carefully read the latest Candidate Handbook from AHIMA. If anything in the handbook is not clear, seek assistance from AHIMA. You are held accountable for the important information, deadlines, and instructions addressed in this material.

Sample Study Schedule

Week 1   Use your references to review Health Data Content and Structure concepts listed in domain 1, 5, 6, and 7 of the competencies for the CCS-P exam.
- Domain 1: Health Information Documentation
- Domain 5: Data Quality and Analysis
- Domain 6: Information and Communications Technologies
- Domain 7: Compliance and Regulatory Issues

Answer the questions in the Health Data Content and Structure chapter in this book.

Use your references to review pathophysiology and medical terminology as a refresher before beginning your ICD-9-CM and CPT coding review. These questions fall into Domain 1. Answer the questions in the Medical Science chapter.

Week 2   Use your references to review for tasks in Domains 2, 3, 4, and 5.
Study the Coding Review section on ICD-9-CM and CPT coding concepts in this book.
Answer the questions in the Billing and Reimbursement chapter.
Answer the questions in the Classification and Secondary Data Sources chapter.

Week 3   Gather and review references for tasks in Domains 2 and 4: ICD-9-CM Diagnosis Coding.
Answer the questions in the ICD-9-CM Coding chapter.

Week 4   Gather and review references for tasks in Domain 3: CPT and HCPCS II Coding.
Review the CPT Coding rules.
Review the CPT Evaluation and Management Guidelines in your coding materials.
Review the CPT Surgery section and remaining CPT sections, including using modifiers.
Answer the questions in the CPT Coding chapter.

Week 5 &   Work the case studies provided after the CPT Coding chapter.
Week 6

Week 7 &   Continue your review of CPT, HCPCS Level II and ICD-9-CM materials.
Week 8   Answer the questions in the Mock Examinations for Part I of the CCS-P examination.
Work the cases in the Mock Examination Part II.

Week 9   Continue your review of CPT, HCPCS Level II and ICD-9-CM materials.
Look over areas of weakness for a final review

Week 10   Do an overall review of the tasks in the domains and plan your attack for the coming test.

STUDY RESOURCES

Don't spend time trying to memorize something you do not understand. The main issue is to understand the materials so you can use the knowledge in a practical way. Search for additional information that will help make the subject clearer to you. There are four basic sources of information: books, people, educational programs/colleges, and Internet resources.

Books and other written resources

➢ A different textbook may use another style of presentation that you are more receptive to and may be all you need to gain a better insight into the subject. It can offer a fresh point of view, provide relief from boredom, and encourage critical thinking in the process of comparing the texts. There are a variety of books and workbooks available to use in studying for your coding certification.

➢ Periodical literature in the field provides well-written articles that may open up the subject to you and turn your study into an adventure in learning. AHIMA publishes authoritative and insightful information on every aspect of coding. In addition to the ongoing coding articles in the *Journal of AHIMA*, *Advance for Health Information Professionals* has a special series of articles called "CCS Prep!" The journal, For the Record, has articles on coding in each issue. Sometimes an article can help put the subject material into practical perspective and pull it together so that you gain a deeper understanding. Don't forget to use the *Coding Clinics* and *CPT Assistant* to refresh your memory and learn more about specific coding guidelines. HIM journals will help you keep updated on new information on coding issues that may be incorporated into the exams.

➢ Take advantage of the local college library by using reserved materials specifically set aside for HIM student study purposes.

Your HIM community

➢ Interaction with others can be truly beneficial in keeping you motivated and on track.

➢ Professional contacts can also be helpful in your study effort. Most people in our field are eager to share their knowledge and are flattered by appeals for information. Schedule a conference with the director of the HIM/Coding program at your local college. These educators may have current information and resources you are not aware of. Talking to those who have recently taken the examination can also be of great assistance.

➢ Collaboration with other test applicants can reveal fresh viewpoints, stimulate thought by disagreement, or at least let you see that you are not alone in your quest. Organize study groups and set aside specific times to work together. This interaction can be truly beneficial in keeping you motivated and on task.

Classes, workshops, and seminars and Coding Teleconferences present opportunities to learn and review the subject matter in a new light and keep you updated on changes. Take advantage of any coding review sessions available in your area.

Internet Resources

➢ Use the Internet to connect with others who are preparing for the examination. AHIMA is online for members. Using the coding Communities of Practice (CoP) on AHIMA's Web site is an excellent way to get connected with professionals and peers. You may find other examination applicants to work with using e-mail. Use AHIMA Body of Knowledge, available on the AHIMA Web site at: AHIMA.ORG Sample question and cases are available on AHIMA's Web site under certification for you to use as test examples.

➢ There are innumerable resources for coding and reimbursement on the Internet. Just be aware that you may want to verify the information as it is only as good as the source.

Some Suggested Study Resources Include

1. **MANDATORY**: AHIMA *Candidate Handbook for the CCS and CCS-P Examinations*
2. **MANDATORY**: Current ICD-9-CM Code Book, volume 1 & 2 including updates
3. **MANDATORY**: Current AMA CPT Code Book
4. **MANDATORY:** Current HCPCS Level II Code Book
5. "Official ICD-9-CM Guidelines for Coding and Reporting" is available online at http://www.cdc.gov/nchs/icd/icd9cm or http://www.ahacentraloffice.org
6. *Coding Clinic* for ICD-9-CM (past issues from the last 3 to 4 years)
7. "Documentation Guidelines for Evaluation and Management Services", *CPT Assistant* (May 1995) and "Documentation Guidelines for Evaluation and Management Services", *CPT Assistant* (May 1997), as well as information in other *CPT Assistant* issues
8. Professional journal articles on coding
   Journal of AHIMA
   Advance for Health Information Professionals
   For the Record
9. Medical Dictionaries (Check for latest edition.)
10. Coding class, seminar, workshop notes, and tests
11. Study groups/partners
12. On-the-job experience
13. Examination review sessions
14. Review books written for the CCS-P examinations
18. Various online resources. For online coding practice sites, as well as those for information and Internet interaction with others, visit the following examples:
    www.AHIMA.org
    www.CMS.hhs.gov
    www.ICD-9-CM.org
    http://www.hospitalconnect.com
    http://www.medlearn/icd9code.asp

Those resources marked **MANDATORY** will be essential for you to have in order to prepare for the examination.

Contact Information for Resources for CCS-P Examination Review Studies

AMA CPT Code Book 2010
American Medical Association (AMA) Phone: (800) 621-8335 Fax: (312) 464-5600
INGENIX ICD-9-CM Phone: (800) 464-3649
5032 W. Amelia Earhart Drive Salt Lake City, UT 84116

HCPCS II, Code Book 2010
American Medical Association: Phone: (800) 621-8335

AMA CPT Assistant
American Medical Association: Phone: (800) 621-8335 Fax: (312) 464-5600
Documentation Guidelines for E & M Coding
Published May 1995 and revised November 1997
American Medical Association (AMA) and HCFA
Printed in the *CPT Assistant* May 1995 and November 1997.
Online at: http://www.cms.hhs.gov/medlearn/emdoc.asp
This Web site is part of the Centers for Medicare and Medicaid Services Web site:
http://www.cms.hhs.gov/

ICD-9-CM Code Book with October 1, 2009 updates
Channel Publishing, Ltd. P. O. Box 70723 Reno, NV 89570 Phone: (800) 248-2882
INGENIX ICD-9-CM Phone: (800) 464-3649
5032 W. Amelia Earhart Drive Salt Lake City, UT 84116

Official ICD-9-CM Guidelines for Coding and Reporting
Central Office on ICD-9-CM of the American Hospital Association (AHA)
Phone: (312) 422-3000 or it can be accessed online at the
Web site for National Center for Health Statistics (NCHS) http://www.cdc.gov/nchs

Coding Clinic for ICD-9-CM
American Hospital Association: Phone: (312) 422-3000
Phone: (800) 242-2626 FAX: (312) 951-8491

Delmar Cengage Publishing has a number of excellent HIM and Coding books (see the examples below)
3-2-1 Code It! by Michelle Green
Understanding ICD-9-CM: A Worktext by Mary Jo Bowie and Regina Schaffer
Understanding Medical Coding: A Comprehensive Guide (2ⁿᵈ ed) by Sandra L. Johnson and Connie S. McHugh
*Understanding Procedural Coding: A Worktex*t by Mary Jo Bowie and Regina Schaffer
For a complete list contact:
Cengage Learning, Inc.
P O Box 6904   Florence, KY 41022-6904
Email: esales@cengage.com
Web site: http://www.cengage.com/delmar
Phone: (800) 487-6904

AHIMA has developed a series of HIM and coding resources.
To place an order: call (800) 335-5535.
Visit the AHIMA Web site at http://www.ahima.org for additional resources and information about the coding certification examinations.

Ingenix has an array of coding, reimbursement, and compliance products.
Contact them at 1-800-INGENIX
Visit their Web site at www.ingenixonline.com.

THE DAY BEFORE AND THE MORNING OF THE EXAM

1. **Know the exam location.**
   If there are several testing sites, make sure you have the correct directions to the correct center. Going to the wrong address for a test and then having to hustle to get to the right testing center is very stressful.

2. **Avoid studying the night before the exam.**
   Last minute studying tends to increase your anxiety level. However, you may want to allocate a small amount of time to review any information that you feel you must look at one more time.

3. **Organize in advance all the materials you need to take with you to the exam.**
   Review the candidate handbook carefully and be sure to have all the items that are required, especially the admission card, proof of identity, and your code books.

4. **Get a good night's sleep.**
   Taking a 4-hour test with little rest the night before may prevent you from having the energy and stamina you need to complete the exam.

5. **Have a healthy meal before your exam.**
   Four hours is a long time to go on an empty stomach. Try to eat a nutritious meal, for instance, cereal and fruit, bagel and fruit or juice, or a meal with protein such as cheese and crackers or eggs and toast. You need something to give you energy to keep going. Take a healthy snack bar to munch on if you get hungry and need to take a short break at the testing center.

6. **Dress comfortably.**
   Plan for possible variations in room temperature. Dressing in layers may prove helpful if the room is too cold or too hot for you.

7. **Arrive early.**
   Allow yourself plenty of time so that you arrive at the test site early. Take a practice drive. If the exam site is a great distance from your home, spend the night before the examination in a nearby hotel or motel.

TAKING THE EXAMINATION

You have stuck to your study schedule and have conditioned yourself to be in the best physical and mental shape possible. Now comes the "moment of truth": the examination pops up on the screen before your eyes. Every paratrooper knows that, in addition to having a parachute, one must know how to open it. You have mastered the major topics; you have the parachute. Now, you need to utilize good test-taking techniques to apply the knowledge you have gained; open the parachute!

Part I of the Examination (60 multiple-choice questions)

1. **Taking the practice test.** Prior to starting the exam, you will be given a chance to practice taking an examination on the computer. Time will be allotted for this practice test; however, you may quit the practice test and begin the actual exam when you are comfortable with the computerized testing process.

2. **Read all directions and questions carefully.** Try to avoid reading too much into the questions. Be sensible and practical in your interpretation. Read ALL of the possible answers, because the first one that looks good may not be the best one.

3. **Scan the screen quickly for general question format.** Like the marathon runner, pace yourself for the distance. A good rule of thumb is 1 to 1.5 minutes per each multiple-choice question. You may wish to keep the timer displayed on the computer to check your schedule throughout the exam. For example, at question 30, about one half hour will have elapsed, etc.

4. **Coming back to questions.** Some people answer all questions that they are certain of first. Then they go back through the exam a second time to answer any questions they were uncertain about. Others prefer not to skip questions, but make their best choice on encountering each question and go on. Both can be good approaches; choose the one that works best for you. You can "mark" questions that you have left unanswered and/or those questions you may want to review. Before you sign off of the exam or run out of time, you have the ability to go back to those questions for a final review.

5. **Answer all the questions.** There are no penalties for guessing, but entering no answer is definitely a wrong answer.

6. **Process of elimination.** Use deductive reasoning and the process of elimination to arrive at the most correct answer. Some questions may have more than one correct answer. You will be asked to select the "best" possible answer based on the information presented.

7. **Determine what is being asked.** If the question is written in a scenario format, first identify the question being asked and then review the entire question for the information needed to determine the correct answer.

8. **Use all the time available to recheck your answers.** However, avoid changing your answers unless you are absolutely certain it is necessary. Second-guessing yourself often results in a wrong answer.

9. **You must pass the multiple-choice question part of the examination** as well as the coding portion in order to receive your certification. All of that practice in taking multiple-choice exams will pay off here.

Part II of the Examination: Coding Scenarios

1. **Taking the Practice Test.** Prior to starting the exam, you will be given a chance to practice taking an examination on the computer. Time will be allotted for this practice test; however, you may quit the practice test and begin the actual exam when you are comfortable with the computerized testing process.

2. **Follow the procedures given in the Candidate Handbook for coding the test cases.** Do not use hospital, regional, or insurance standards that may differ from those used in the national examination directions. The test will be scored using the coding procedures given.

3. **Read all abstracts completely.** Identify the qualifying words and statements.

4. **Try to avoid reading too much into the information given.** Be sensible and practical in your interpretation. Points are deducted for inappropriate codes.

5. **Carefully review ancillary reports.** Ancillary reports may or may not contain information that is pertinent to the coding of the case. Do not assign codes for abnormal findings listed on ancillary reports unless the physician documents clinical significance.

6. **Only the codes themselves are considered in scoring.** Narrative descriptions will be ignored in scoring the examination. Carefully check the answer form to verify that you have entered the codes for a given case abstract into the space provided for that case.

7. **Use all the time available** to recheck your codes and make sure your answer form has been filled in correctly. However, avoid changing your answers unless you are absolutely certain it is necessary. Second-guessing yourself often results in a wrong answer.

8. **The sequencing of diagnoses and operative procedures is not considered in scoring Part II of the exam.** List any diagnoses that are appropriate. Just remember, you will be penalized for inappropriate codes or for missing necessary codes.

9. **Procedures will be supplied with each section of Part II of the exam.** The test will be scored using these procedures.

10. **Modifiers and linking diagnoses to procedures are not tested in Part II of the exam.** Then list any additional diagnoses that are appropriate. The additional diagnoses do not need to be in any special order.

11. **Again, you MUST pass both Part I and Part II** of the examination in order to receive your certification.

After the Examination

A huge advantage to taking the computerized exam is that, before you leave the testing center, you will be able to get your final test score instead of having to wait up to 6 weeks to receive the score by mail.

After taking the examination, it is time to reclaim your life and focus on your career. Plan a special reward for yourself at some point after the exam. Schedule a family vacation or a relaxing weekend get-away. Just find some way of being good to yourself. You certainly deserve it! You have worked hard, so relish your success.

PAT'S EXAM EXPERIENCE

The CCS examination was a moment of truth for me. Some people asked me what I was going to do if I failed the examination. Now there is something to give you nightmares—to co-author an exam review book and then FLUNK the exam! That was when I decided to borrow a line from the movie *True Lies*, "fear is not an option," and adapted it for my own motto—"failure is not an option."

There were many days and nights when I doubted that I had what it takes. When I felt really fearful and uncomfortable, I made myself look back over the years of going to classes and all of the coding practice. I had completed all the courses required. I had studied hard and long in each one of them. I had made good grades. In fact, I graduated with honors. I was studying virtually every day to prepare for the exam. What more could I do? ABSOLUTELY NOTHING! Therefore, if I had done the best I could and I was doing the best I could, then the worry was just taking up space in my head.

I told myself there was no way I could fail the exam. This was a routine that I had to repeat, sometimes several times a day when the doubt would creep in. Positive attitudes can and will make the pre-test jitters disappear. If you feel you can't do this, tell yourself that you have done it and that *this is just one more test!* I had prepared myself. I had taken many, many, many tests successfully before. This one is JUST ONE MORE!

The night before the test, I tried to study just a little, but I just could not concentrate. I gave up trying to cram more information into my head and went to bed.

The next morning at the testing center, I had coffee while we waited for the room to be prepared. One of the students milling around commented that she had failed the CCS examination twice before and hoped to pass it this time. I was really nervous then, because this person had over 10 years of experience of coding in a hospital setting next to my measly experience. There were a lot of very nervous people there.

I had to remind myself to keep thinking: "I think I can. I think I can." I tried my best not to panic. After waiting what seemed like forever to start the exam, we were finally told to open the booklet for Part I and begin. I panicked at the first question. I could not understand what it asked. I had to stop, take a deep breath, and relax. I went to the next question, and was able to answer it quickly. I went back to the first question and it looked simple! I found myself going down the page breezing along and answering the questions. Then, I gasped as I thought, "What if I am not going fast enough?" I stopped, looked at the question number, checked the time and figured that I was answering them in about 1 minute each. Right on schedule. So, I calmed myself down and got back to business.

When I took the examination, it was still paper and pencil with fill-in answer bubbles. About halfway through the exam, I had another thought: "What if I am putting the answers in the wrong answer bubble?" After catching my breath, I looked at the question number and checked the answer bubble. Both were the same. I told myself to just relax and do the work at hand. Before I knew it, I had answered all the questions. I even had enough time to go back and review the ones I was not sure about.

One of the most difficult parts of the exam is the length of time sitting. I did take one break in the middle of the exam to use the restroom and walk around for a minute to clear my head.

Part I was the easy part. I was very adept at taking multiple-choice question exams. Part II with the coding cases was my hardest section. I found that I wasn't completing the cases in 13 to 14 minutes, so I needed to speed up to finish the exam. It was really hard for me not to mull over each case.

When the exam was over, I was relieved, to say the least. For months it had been hanging over my head and now IT WAS OVER! I left not knowing if I had passed the examination or not. But, no matter what the results were, I had done the best I could and I was still a winner! Do the best you can and you will past the exam too. YOU CAN DO IT!

Affirmation: "I can handle anything on the exam—one question at a time." ~ Kathy DeAngelo, 1995

II. Coding Review

Toni Cade, MBA, RHIA, CCS, FAHIMA

Lisa Delhomme, MHA, RHIA

HEALTH RECORD CODING REVIEW
CODING PROCESS

Fine-tune your coding skills by seeking complete documentation and selecting the most detailed codes.

1. Assess the case by performing a quick review of the record's demographic information and the first few lines of the History and Physical.

2. Get an overview of key reports because they contain valuable detailed information.
    A. The discge summary sums up the patient's hospital course and confirms conditions or complications. In ambulatory records, look at the final progress note and/or discharge instructions.
    B. Review the physician orders for treatment protocols. The orders may indicate chronic or acute conditions for which the patient is receiving treatment.
    C. Review the history and physical to complete the clinical picture. Social and family history, as well as past and present illnesses, may have clinical implications.
    D. Read the progress notes to track the course of hospitalization or outpatient treatment. These provide information concerning daily status, reactions, or post-operative complications.
    E. Study the operative reports. Additional procedures may be identified in the body of the operative report.

3. Check all data from clinical reports.
    A. Laboratory reports may show evidence of conditions such as anemia, renal failure, infections, and metabolic imbalances.
    B. Radiology reports may confirm diagnosis of pneumonia, COPD, CHF, degenerative joint diseases, and traumatic injuries.
    C. Respiratory therapy notes document the use of mechanical ventilation and describe severity of respiratory disorders.
    D. Physical therapy reports detail useful information for coding musculoskeletal dysfunctions.
    E. Dietary reports describe nutritional deficiencies (e.g., malnutrition).
    F. Speech pathology reports give information on dysphasia, aphasia, and other speech-related conditions.
    G. Pathology reports are essential for accurate coding of conditions where excised tissue has been submitted for interpretation.

4. Perform a coding evaluation.
    A. Establish the principal diagnosis and formulate secondary diagnoses codes.
    B. Exclude all conditions not relevant to the case. Abnormal lab and x-ray findings and previous conditions having no effect on current management of patient are not coded.

5. Take time to review and refine your coding.
    A. Review all diagnoses and procedures to confirm the selections of appropriate principal and secondary diagnoses and all procedure codes.
    B. For inpatient records, determine if each diagnosis was present on admission (POA) to adequately identify the POA indicator.
    C. Refine code assignments, where necessary, to make changes to more accurately classify the diagnoses and procedure codes selected.

Some Additional Tips for Coding

1. When a patient is admitted with, or develops a condition during his or her stay, look to see if there is documentation to differentiate if the co-morbidity or complication is acute, chronic, or both acute and chronic.

2. When a patient presents with or develops infectious conditions, seek documentation of any positive cultures (urine, wound, sputum, blood) pertaining to that condition. If the positive cultures are available for that condition (e.g., sepsis due to Pseudomonas) it will help in being more specific in coding the diagnoses, and may increase reimbursement in some cases. For example, in a case of pneumonia due to Pseudomonas, the MS-DRG may increase considerably. According to coding guidelines, if the culture is not documented, even though present in laboratory reports, the condition is to be coded as unspecified, which can decrease reimbursement. Examples: sepsis, cellulitis, UTI, pneumonia, etc.

3. If a condition is due to surgery, ask the physician to verify that it is due to the procedure. If the patient has been discharged, and you are not sure, but believe it was due to the procedure, seek verification that it is possibly due to the procedure by querying the physician.

4. If the patient is in for day surgery for removal of a lesion, look for documentation of the size of the lesion that may have been removed. It should be documented in your operative report.

   The key to proper and entitled reimbursement for patient care in the Prospective Payment System for Medicare outpatients (APC) is complete and sufficient documentation. The American Medical Association's publication, *CPT Assistant* (issues from Fall 1995 and August 2000) states, "Since the physician can make an accurate measurement of the lesion(s) at the time of the excision, the size of the lesion should be documented in the OP (operative) report. A pathology report is likely to contain a less accurate measurement due to the shrinking of the specimen or the fact that the specimen may be fragmented."

   Reimbursement is based on the diameter of lesion(s). Even 1 millimeter (mm) off in the diameter calculation can mean fewer dollars for the hospital and the physician. The documentation in the record ensures appropriate reimbursement.

5. Look for documentation in the final diagnoses in the discharge summary for clarification or to differentiate whether specific conditions are currently present, or if the patient only has a history of the condition.

   Examples: 1. Acute CVA versus history of CVA
   2. Current drug or alcohol abuse versus history of drug or alcohol abuse
   3. Current neoplasm being treated versus history of malignancy

6. Verify if a condition is a manifestation of an existing condition.

   Example: CRF secondary to DM or CRF due to HTN

7. Look for documentation of conditions that are secondary to previous conditions.

   Examples: 1. Quadriplegia due to fall
   2. Dysphagia due to previous CVA

8. When coding charts of discharged patients:

   1. <u>Rule out</u> conditions are coded as confirmed for inpatients. The condition is still considered to be a possibility if stated as possible, probable, likely, questionable, or suspected. According to coding guidelines, rule out diagnoses are coded as established, based on the fact that the diagnostic work-up and initial therapeutic approach would have addressed this condition even though a final determination was not made.

   2. <u>Ruled out</u> conditions are not coded for inpatients. The condition originally considered is no longer a possibility. Documentation should clarify if the condition was ruled out.

Commonly Missed Complications and Co-morbidities (CCs)

Depending on the patient's principal diagnosis, this list of commonly missed complications co-morbidities (CCs) may or may not help the MS-DRG when documented and coded. If any of these conditions are being managed while the patient is being hospitalized, it may help to improve the MS-DRG. Some MS-DRGs will not change even if these are present. The MS-DRG may or may not change if the patient has a major procedure performed. Some of these conditions may be considered CCs, while some may be considered Major CCs.

Acidosis

Alcoholism acute/chronic

Alkalosis

Anemia due to blood loss, acute/chronic (e.g. from GI bleed, or surgery, etc.)

Angina pectoris (stable or unstable angina)

Atrial fibrillation/flutter

Atelectasis

Cachexia

Cardiogenic shock

Cardiomyopathy

Cellulitis, when patient also has this or develops as a complication (e.g., 2° to PEG tube, etc.)

CHF

Combination of both Acidosis/Alkalosis

COPD

Decubitus ulcer, not usually common, but if present and being treated

Dehydration (volume depletion)

Diabetes If DM is uncontrolled (type I or II)

Electrolyte imbalance

Hematuria

Hematemesis

Hypertension (HTN) Accelerated or Malignant HTN only qualifies (not uncontrolled, hypertensive urgency or hypertensive crisis)

Hypertensive heart disease with CHF

Hyponatremia ($\downarrow$ Na)

Hypernatremia ($\uparrow$ Na)

Hypochloremia ($\downarrow$ Cl)

Hyperchloremia ($\uparrow$ Cl)

Hyperpotassemia ($\uparrow$ K) (not $\downarrow$ K, Hypo-K is not a CC)

Malnutrition

Melena

Pleural effusion (especially if it has to be treated by procedure, e.g., thoracentesis)

Pneumonia

Pneumothorax

Postoperative complications

Renal failure, acute or chronic (not renal insufficiency)

Respiratory failure

Septicemia

Urinary retention

UTI (e.g., Urosepsis): If urosepsis is documented, it will be coded as a UTI unless otherwise specified.

Please Note: This is not an all-inclusive listing of possible complications and co-morbidities.

International Classification of Diseases,
Ninth Revision, Clinical Modification, Sixth Edition
Coding Guidelines and Updates Effective October 1, 2009

Information regarding ICD-9-CM Coding Guidelines and updates effective October 1, 2009 may be found at: http://www.cdc.gov/nchs/icd/icd9cm_addenda_guidelines.htm

ICD-9-CM Guidelines. 112 pages. (PDF)
Note: These guidelines were created on08/31/2009 and are effective as of 10/01/2009.

Conversion table

ICD-9-CM Code Conversion Table. 64 pages (10/01/2009) (PDF)

A conversion table for diagnostic and procedural code changes between 1986 and 2009 is provided to assist users in data retrieval. The table shows the date the new code became effective and its previously assigned code equivalent. New codes effective October 1, 2009, are shown in bold.
Note: This conversion table was updated on 06/03/2009.

Addenda

ICD-9-CM Index Addenda. 48 pages (10/01/2009) (PDF)

ICD-9-CM Tabular Addenda. 53 pages (10/01/2009) (PDF)

The annual update to ICD-9-CM is provided as addenda changes to the index and tabular list of ICD-9-CM, effective October 1, 2009. In the index, additions are marked with bold and underlining, revisions are marked with bold, underlining, and italic, while deletions are marked with bold and strikeout.
Note: These addenda were created on06/03/2009.

ICD-9-CM Index Addenda Errata. 2 pages (10/01/2009) (PDF)

ICD-9-CM Tabular Addenda Errata. 1 page. (10/01/2009) (PDF)
Note: These addenda were created on 07/20/2009.

ICD-9-CM CODE BOOK CONTENTS

Three Volumes of ICD-9-CM are:
- Vol. 1: Tabular List
- Vol. 2: Index of Diseases
- Vol. 3: Tabular List and Index for Procedures

Special Alphanumeric Codes

V-codes Used for patient encounters that influence health status other than for disease or injury
E-codes Describe external causes of injury, poisoning, or other adverse reactions
M Codes Used to report the morphology of the neoplasms

CONVENTIONS USED IN <u>TABULAR LIST</u>

Abbreviations

NEC - Not Elsewhere Classifiable (other specified)
1. Ill-defined terms
2. Terms for which a more specific code does not exist.
3. Used only when the coder lacks the information necessary to code the term to a more specific category

NOS: Not Otherwise Specified (unspecified)
1. Use when the information in the medical record is insufficient to assign a more specific code

Punctuation

[Brackets] Brackets enclose synonyms, alternative wordings, or explanatory phrases.
{Braces} Braces enclose a series of terms, each of which is modified by the statement appearing at the right of the brace.
[Brackets Slanted] Codes in slanted brackets are always listed as secondary codes because they are manifestations (results) of another condition.
(Parentheses) Parentheses enclose supplementary words that may be present or absent in the statement of a disease or procedure without affecting the code assigned (nonessential modifiers).
Colon: Colons are used in the Tabular List after an incomplete term that needs one or more of the modifiers that follow in order to make it assignable to a given category.

Symbols

[] Lozenge symbol in the left margin preceding the disease code indicates that contents of a 4th digit category have been moved or modified, so that it is not the same as in ICD-9.
§ Section mark symbol preceding a code denotes the placement of a note at the top of the page which is applicable to all subdivisions in that category.

Other Conventions

Bold typeface is used for all codes and titles in the Tabular List.
Italicized typeface is used for
1. all exclusion notes, and
2. to identify those subcategories that are not to be used for primary tabulation of diseases. (Italicized codes must always follow the code for the underlying cause of the disease.)
Format: indented format for ease in reference.

Instructional Notations

Includes further defines, or gives example of, the contents of the category. It appears immediately under a two or three digit code title to further define, or give examples of, the content of the category.

Excludes terms following the word excludes are to be coded elsewhere as indicated in each case.

Inclusion terms is a list of terms is included under certain four or five digit codes. It lists conditions for which that code number is to be used. The terms may be synonyms and are not necessarily exhaustive.

"Use Additional Code" - placed in Tabular List where use of an additional code may give a more complete picture of the diagnosis or procedure.

Code first underlying disease - used in categories not intended to be used as a principal diagnosis. Requires that the underlying disease etiology be recorded first and the particular manifestation recorded second. This notation appears only in the disease Tabular List.

Code also - used in Tabular List of procedures (Volume 3) as an instruction to code:
1. each component of a procedure accomplished at the same time.
2. the use of special adjunctive (accompanying) procedures or equipment.

Omit code - used in Alphabetical Index of procedures (Volume 3) as an instruction to omit coding of incisions made only for the purpose of performing further surgery.

Code if applicable, any causal condition first - a code with this note may be the principal diagnosis if no casual condition is applicable or known.

CONVENTIONS USED IN ALPHABETICAL INDEX

Main Terms

The Alphabetic Index is organized by "main terms" printed in bold type face for ease of reference.
1. Diseases (e.g., influenza, bronchitis)
2. Conditions (e.g., fatigue, fracture, injury)
3. Nouns (e.g., disease, disorder, and syndrome)
4. Adjectives (e.g., double, large, kink)
5. Anatomical sites are not used for main terms. Look under the condition or disease term.

Conditions may be found in more than one place in the Alphabetical Index.
1. Obstetrical conditions may be found under the name of the condition and under entries for: delivery, pregnancy, and puerperal.
2. Complications of medical and surgical care are indexed under the name of the condition and/or under Complications.
3. Late effects (e.g., of infections, injury) will be found under late effects.
4. V-codes can be found under admission, examination, history of, observation, problem with, status, vaccination, and screening.
5. Main terms that are general adjectives, such as acute, chronic, or lymphoid and references to anatomical site, such as leg or limb, appear as main terms, but they have only a "see condition" reference.

Eponyms

Diseases or syndromes named for persons are listed both as main terms in their appropriate alphabetic sequence and under the main terms "Disease" or "Syndrome." A description of the disease or syndrome is usually included in parentheses following the eponym.

Abbreviations

NEC – Not Elsewhere Classifiable (other specified) Used when a specific code is not available for a condition, therefore the Alphabetical Index directs the coder to the "other specified" code in the Tabular List.

Punctuation

[Brackets] – Brackets are used to identify manifestation codes.
(Parentheses) – Parentheses enclose supplementary words that may be present or absent in the statement of the disease or procedure without affecting the code assigned (nonessential modifiers).

Special Main Terms for V-codes

Abnormal
Admission
Aftercare
Anomaly
Attention to
Boarder
Care of
Carrier
Checking
Complication
Contraception
Counseling
Delivery
Dialysis
Donor
Examination
Exposure to
Fitting of
Follow-up

Foreign Body
Healthy
History (family)
History (personal)
Maintenance
Maladjustment
Observation
Problem with
Procedure (surgical)
Prophylactic
Replacement
Screening
Status
Supervision (of)
Test
Transplant
Unavailability of medical facilities
Vaccination

Joined Main Terms

Two main terms may be joined together by combination terms listed in the Alphabetic Index as subterms (e.g., associated with, complicated [by], due to, following, in, secondary to, with, without). These terms advise the coder to use one or two codes depending on the condition. The terms are also often indented under subterms in the Alphabetic Index. Combination codes may identify all of the components of a diagnosis. These codes are provided for terms that occur together frequently (e.g., hypertensive heart and renal disease), and must be used whenever a patient has both conditions rather than assigning codes from both categories.

Cross References Shows possible modifiers for a term or its synonyms
1. "see" directs user to look elsewhere. Used for anatomical sites and general adjective modifiers not normally used in the Alphabetic Index for reference to the appropriate main term under which information concerning a specific disease will be found, e.g., Ache(s) – see Pain.
2. "see also" directs the user to look under another main term if all the information sought cannot be located under the first main entry.
   Example: Blueness - (see also Cyanosis) 782.5
3. "see category" directs the user to Volume 1 Diseases: Tabular List for important information governing the use of the specific code.

Notes Certain main terms that are followed by notes used to define terms and give coding instructions (e.g., Amputation Note—Complicated includes traumatic amputation with delayed healing, delayed treatment, foreign body, or major infection). Notes are also used to list the fifth-digit subclassifications for those categories. The user must refer to the note following the main term to obtain the appropriate fifth-digit subclassification. Example: Note – Use the following fifth-digit subclassification with category 493:

> 0 unspecified
> 1 with status asthmaticus
> 2 with (acute) exacerbation

Etiology and Manifestation of Diseases For certain conditions it is important to record both the etiology (cause) and the manifestation (demonstration of sign, symptom, or alteration) of the disease. 1. Accomplished with a single 5-digit code (e.g., syphilitic myocarditis 093.82). 2. The two facets of the disease are coded individually and the Alphabetic Index lists both codes. The codes must be recorded in the same sequence used in the Alphabetic Index. Example: Diabetic retinopathy 250.5 [362.01]. The first code represents the etiology, and the code in brackets represents the manifestation.

Some Areas of Special Interest

Abortions

- The primary axis for coding abortion is the type of abortion: spontaneous, legally induced, illegally induced, or failed abortion.
- Fourth digits are used with categories 634–638 to indicate whether a complication is present and the general type of complication.
- The fifth-digit subclassification is used to indicate whether the abortion was unspecified (0), incomplete (1), or complete (2).
- When a patient is readmitted because of a complication subsequent to an abortion, a code from category 639 is assigned.
- If the re-admission is for the purpose of dealing with retained products of conception, following a spontaneous or legally induced abortion, a code from category 634 or 635 with a fifth digit of "1" (incomplete) is assigned rather than 639.
- Codes from categories 640–648 and 651–659 can be assigned as additional codes to indicate the complication that necessitated the abortion.
- When an abortion results in a live birth, the code for early onset of delivery (644.21) is used rather than the abortion code with an appropriate code from category V27.

Adhesions

- When minor adhesions are present, but do not cause symptoms or increase the difficulty of an operative procedure, coding a diagnosis of adhesions and a lysis procedure is inappropriate.
- When adhesions are dense or strong or create problems during a surgical procedure, it is appropriate to code both the diagnosis of adhesions and the operative procedure to lyse the adhesions.

Adverse Effects/Poisonings

Adverse effects: caused when medication is correctly prescribed and properly administered.
- Code the manifestation of the adverse reaction.
- Assign the drug's E-code from the "Therapeutic Use" column. (Do not use an E code from the "Therapeutic Use" column for a poisoning.)
- It is mandatory to report E-codes for all conditions identified as adverse effects.

Poisoning: caused when substance is not used according to a physician's instructions.
- Locate the drug or agent in the Table of Drugs and Chemicals and assign the code from the poisoning column.
- Code the specified effect of the poisoning.
- Assign the E-code for the appropriate cause.

Late effects: caused by a previous adverse effect or poisoning.
- When the condition being coded is a late effect of an adverse effect, a code is assigned for the residual condition with code 909.5 assigned as an additional code. An E-code is used to identify the drug.
- When the condition being coded is a late effect of a poisoning; the residual is coded first with code 909.0 or 909.1 used as an additional code. A late effect E-code should be used.

Anemia

- The coder must distinguish between chronic blood loss anemia and acute blood loss anemia because the two conditions are assigned to different category codes.
- Acute blood loss anemia occurring after surgery may or may not be a complication of surgery. The physician must clearly identify postoperative anemia as a complication of the surgery in order to use the complication code.

Asthma

- Asthma is classified to category 493 with a fourth digit indicating the type of asthma. A fifth digit is used with codes 493.0 to 493.2 and 493.9 indicating whether status asthmaticus is present (1), unspecified (0), or with acute exacerbation (2).
- Terms suggesting status asthmaticus include: intractable asthma; refractory asthma; severe, intractable wheezing; airway obstruction not relieved by medication.
- The coder must not assume status asthmaticus is present. The physician must document the condition in order to code it.
- It is inappropriate to assign an asthma code with the fifth digit 2 with acute exacerbation, together with an asthma code with fifth digit 1, with status asthmaticus. Only the fifth digit 1 should be assigned.

Burns

- Sequence the highest degree burn first. Code different degrees of the same local site to the highest degree (only) of burn documented.
- Nonhealing burns are coded as acute burns.
- Multiple burns: assign separate codes for each site (to the highest degree only of each site).
- Necrosis of burned skin is coded as a non-healed burn.
- Posttraumatic wound infection, NOS, should be reported as an additional diagnosis for documented infected burn site.

Cellulitis

- Coders must not assume that documentation of redness at the edges of a wound represents cellulitis. Rely on physician documentation of cellulitis.
- Coding of cellulitis with an injury or burn requires one code for the injury and one for the cellulitis. Sequencing will depend on the circumstances of admission.
- When the patient is seen primarily for treating the original injury, sequence that code first. When the patient is seen primarily for treatment of the cellulitis, the code for cellulitis is the principal diagnosis.

COPD

- A general term used to describe a variety of conditions that result in obstruction of the airway.
- It can appear as chronic obstructive asthma (493.2x), obstructive chronic bronchitis (491.2x), emphysema (492.8), or obstructive chronic bronchitis without exacerbation (with emphysema) (491.20).
- When the diagnosis is stated only as COPD, the coder should review the record to see if a more definite diagnosis can be made.

Coronary Artery Bypass Graft (CABG)
- A coronary artery bypass is a surgery that is performed to bypass blood around the clogged arteries in the heart.
- The axis for coding coronary artery bypass grafts is the number of arteries involved.
- An internal mammary bypass graft is done by loosening the mammary artery from the normal position and using it to bring blood to the heart.
- The axis for coding internal mammary bypass grafts is whether one or both internal mammary arteries are used.

Debridement
- Excisional debridement is the surgical removal or cutting away of tissue.
- It may be performed by a physician or other health care practitioner.
- Nonexcisional debridement is the nonsurgical brushing, irrigating, scrubbing, or washing of tissue.

Diabetes Mellitus
- Uncontrolled or Out of Control: The physician must specifically document this in order to use the fifth digits of 2 (type II or unspecified type, uncontrolled) or 3 (type I –juvenile type-uncontrolled).
- Diabetes with a manifestation or complication requires documentation of a causal relationship to be coded.
- Even if the patient is taking insulin, it does not necessarily mean that the patient is type 1.
- If the type of diabetes mellitus is not documented in the medical record, the default is type 2.
- Most type 1 diabetics develop the condition before reaching puberty. For this reason type 1 diabetes mellitus is also referred to as juvenile diabetes.
- For type 2 patients who routinely use insulin, code V58.67 (long-term, current use of insulin) should also be assigned.
- An underdose of insulin due to an insulin pump failure should be assigned 996.57, Mechanical complications due to insulin pump.
- The first listed code for an encounter due to an insulin pump malfunction resulting in an overdose of insulin would also be assigned 996.57 with an additional code of 962.3, which is poisoning by insulins and antidiabetic agents and the appropriate diabetes mellitus code.

Dysplasia of the Vulva and Cervix
- A diagnosis of cervical intraepithelial neoplasia (CIN) III or vulvar intraepithelial neoplasia (VIN) III is classified as carcinoma in situ of the site.
- A diagnosis of CIN III or VIN III is made only on the basis of pathological evaluation of tissue.

E-Codes
- Never used as a principal diagnosis.
- If two or more events caused separate injuries, an E-code is assigned for each. The code for the most direct cause is listed first.
- When the condition code for the diagnosis is a late effect, a late effect E-code must be used.
- E-codes for adult and child abuse take precedence over all other E-codes.
- The only E codes that are required are codes from the E93.0–E949 series to identify the causative substance for an adverse effect of drug, medicinal, and biological substances, correctly prescribed and properly administered, though most hospitals also collect E codes for injuries and poisoning.

Elevated Blood Pressure vs. Hypertension
- A diagnosis of high or elevated blood pressure without a firm diagnosis of hypertension is reported using code 796.2.
- This code is never assigned on the basis of review of blood pressure readings; the physician must document elevated blood pressure/hypertension.

Fracture
- An open fracture is one in which there is communication with the bone. The following terms indicate open fracture: compound, infected, missile, puncture, and with foreign body.
- A closed fracture does not produce an open wound. Some types of closed fractures are: comminuted, depressed, elevated, greenstick, spiral, and simple.
- When a fracture is not identified as open or closed, the code for a closed fracture is used.
- The most common fracture treatment is "reduction." The first axis for coding reductions is whether the reduction is open or closed. The second axis identifies the use of internal fixation.
- Internal fixation devices include screws, pins, rods, staples, or plates.
- External fixation devices include casts, splints, or traction device (Kirschner wire) (Steinman pin).
- V-codes are used to identify encounters or admissions for orthopedic aftercare.
- V-codes can also be used to indicate an orthopedic status if it is appropriate to the episode of care.

Gastrointestinal Hemorrhage
- Patients may be admitted for an endoscopy after a history of GI bleeding. It is acceptable to use a code for GI hemorrhage even if there is no hemorrhage noted on the current encounter.

Heart Failure
- All codes for heart failure include pulmonary edema.
- Fifth digits specify whether the heart failure is acute (1), chronic (2), acute on chronic (3), or unspecified (0).
- Right-sided failure secondary to left-sided failure is classified as congestive heart failure (428.0).
- Codes for both right-sided failure and left-sided failure are never used on the same chart.

Hematuria
- Many conditions in the genitourinary system have hematuria as an integral associated symptom and therefore the hematuria is not coded separately unless it is excessive and has been documented as such by the physician.
- Blood in the urine discovered on a urinalysis is not coded as hematuria, but is coded to 791.2, Hemoglobinuria.
- Hematuria following a urinary procedure is not considered a postoperative complication.

Hemiplegia
- Hemiplegia is often a consequence of a CVA. When it is transient and resolves before discharge, it is not coded separately. When the hemiplegia is still present at discharge, it is coded.

HIV

- 042: Patients with symptomatic HIV disease or AIDS.
- V08: Patients with physician-documented asymptomatic HIV infection who have never had an HIV-related illness.
- 795.71: Patients with inconclusive HIV test results, but on definitive diagnosis or manifestation of the illness.
- Patients admitted with an HIV-related condition are assigned code 042 followed by additional diagnosis codes for all reported HIV-related conditions.
- For patients admitted for a condition unrelated to the HIV (such as traumatic injury), the condition should be sequenced first, followed by 042.
- Documentation of HIV infection as "suspected," "possible," "likely," or "questionable": physician should be queried for clarification. Code only confirmed cases of HIV infection.
- When an obstetric patient has the HIV infection, a code from subcategory 647.6X is sequenced first with either code 042 (symptomatic) or V08 (asymptomatic) used as an additional code.

Hypertension

Hypertension Table Found under the main term Hypertension and contains a complete listing of all conditions due to or associated with hypertension. These conditions are classified as malignant, benign, and unspecified. If the physician does not specify the hypertension as malignant or benign, it is classified as unspecified.

- 402.xx: Hypertensive heart disease. Physician must document causal relationship between hypertension and heart disease (425.8, 429.0-429.3, 429.8, 429.9). Use an additional code from category 428 to identify the type of heart failure if present.
- 403.xx: Hypertensive chronic kidney disease. ICD-9-CM assumes a causal relationship between HTN and kidney disease (585). There is no causal relationship with acute renal failure.
- 404.xx: Hypertensive heart and chronic kidney disease. Physician must document causal relationship with the heart disease, but assume a causal relationship with kidney disease. Assign an additional code for category 482 to identify the type of heart failure. More than one code for category 428 may be assigned if the patient has systolic or diastolic failure and CHF.

Ischemic Heart Disease (Chronic)

- Category 414 includes forms of chronic heart diseases such as atherosclerosis.
- Code 414.0x includes arteriosclerotic heart disease, coronary arteriosclerosis, coronary stricture, and coronary atheroma.
- Fifth digits provide information about the type of coronary artery involved such as native, vein bypass, or artery bypass.

Kidney Disease

- Chronic kidney disease (CKD) develops as a complication of other diseases.
- Both chronic kidney disease and end stage renal disease are classified to 585.x.
- Chronic kidney disease is identified as the correct terminology rather than chronic renal failure.
- Category 585, chronic kidney disease, has been expanded at the fourth digit level for further specification of the severity (stages) of CKD.

Late Effects
- A late effect is a residual condition that remains after the acute phase of the illness or injury has passed.
- There is no set time period before a condition is considered a late effect.
- Coding of late effects requires two codes: one code for the residual condition and a code to identify the cause of the residual late effect.

Late Effects of Cerebrovascular Disease
- Codes in category 438, Late effect of cerebrovascular disease, are combination codes which indicate the residual as well as the "late effect" of the CVA.
- Codes from 438 are used for remaining deficits when the patient is admitted at a later date following a cerebrovascular injury.

Mechanical Ventilation
- Codes for mechanical ventilation indicate whether the patient was on the ventilator for less than 96 consecutive hours or more than 96 consecutive hours.
- Codes for intubation or tracheostomy should also be assigned
- It is possible for a patient to be placed back on mechanical ventilation, thus necessitating two codes for mechanical ventilation on the same admission.

Myocardial Infarction (MI)
- A MI that is documented as acute or with a duration of 8 weeks or less is coded to category 410, Acute MI.
- Fourth digits indicate the area or wall that is involved.
- Fifth digits indicate whether the encounter is for the initial episode of care (1), for a subsequent episode of care (2), or unspecified (0).
- Fifth digit 1 is used for the initial or first encounter for care after an infarction. It can be used by more than one facility when the patient is transferred from one hospital or another.
- Fifth digit 2 is used when the patient is seen for further care of a previously treated MI (within 8 weeks) or for an unrelated condition.
- When a patient has a second infarction at the time of the encounter for the original infarction, both should be coded.

Neoplasms *Listed in the Alphabetic Index in two ways:*
1. The Table of Neoplasms appears in the Alphabetic Index. It gives the code numbers for neoplasms by anatomic site. For each site, there are six possible code numbers according to whether the behavior of the neoplasm is Malignant primary, Malignant secondary, Malignant in situ, Benign, Of Uncertain Behavior, or of Unspecified Nature.
2. Histological terms for neoplasms (e.g., adenoma, adenocarcinoma, and sarcoma) are listed as main terms in the appropriate alphabetical sequence and are usually followed by a cross reference to the neoplasm table. Each morphological term (form and structure of the neoplasm) will appear with its morphology code from ICD-Oncology (ICD-0), e.g., Adenoma (sessile M8141/0—See also Neoplasm, by site, benign).
   - Morphology codes (M codes) identify the histological type of tumor and its behavior (benign, malignant, etc.). M codes are optional.
   - In sequencing neoplasms, when the treatment is directed toward the malignancy, then the malignancy of that site is designated as the principal diagnosis.
   - When the patient has a secondary neoplasm and treatment is directed toward the secondary site, the secondary site can be sequenced as the principal diagnosis.

Neoplasms (continued)

- When a patient is admitted solely for chemotherapy, immunotherapy, or radiation therapy, a code from category V58 is assigned as the principal diagnosis.
- Codes from category V10 are used when the primary neoplasm is totally eradicated and the patient is no longer having treatment.
- When a patient is admitted for pain management associated with the malignancy, code 338.3 as the principal diagnosis followed by the appropriate code for the malignancy.
- When a patient is admitted for management of an anemia associated with the malignancy, and the treatment is only for anemia, code the anemia code (such as code 285.22) as the principal diagnosis followed by the appropriate code for the malignancy.
- When a patient is admitted for management of dehydration associated with the malignancy or the therapy, or both, and only the dehydration is being treated (intravenous rehydration), the dehydration is sequenced first, followed by the code(s) for the malignancy.

Newborn
- A code from categories V30 to V39 is assigned as the principal diagnosis for any live birth.
- The fourth digit indicates whether the birth occurred in the hospital (0) or born before admission to hospital (1) or born outside hospital and not hospitalized (2).
- For live births in the hospital, a fifth digit indicates whether the delivery was with or without mention of c-section.
- Other diagnoses may be coded for significant conditions noted after birth.
- Insignificant or transient conditions that resolve without treatment are not coded.
- Codes are provided to indicate immaturity or prematurity. Fifth digits indicate birth weight. There is no time limit for using these codes. Immaturity and prematurity may continue to be coded, as long as the physician indicates that the birth weight is an issue.
- A code from V29, Observation and evaluation of newborns and infants for suspected condition not found is used when a healthy baby is evaluated for a suspected condition that proves to not exist. These codes are used when the baby exhibits no signs or symptoms.
- Codes from Chapter 14, Congenital Anomalies, can be reported for patients of any age. Many congenital anomalies do not manifest any symptoms until much later in life.

Obstetrics
- Chapter 11 codes take precedence over other chapter codes. Codes from other chapters may be assigned to provide further specificity as needed.
- Principal diagnosis is determined by the circumstances of the encounter or admission.
- Complications: Any condition that occurs during pregnancy, childbirth, or the puerperium is considered to be a complication unless the physician specifically documents otherwise.
- A code from category V27 is assigned as an additional code to indicate the outcome of delivery.
- Code 650, normal delivery, is used only when a delivery is perfectly normal and results in a single live birth. No abnormalities of labor or delivery or postpartum conditions can be present. V27.2, single liveborn, is the only outcome of delivery code appropriate for use with 650.
- V-Code categories V22, V23, and V24 are used when no obstetric complications are present.
- Code 677 is assigned when an initial complication of a pregnancy or delivery develops a residual or sequela at a late date. As with other late effect codes, residual is sequenced first followed by code 677.

Open Wounds

- Open wounds are considered complicated when the following conditions are present: delayed healing, delayed treatment, foreign body in wound, or infection.

Pain

- Use a code from Category 338 in addition to other codes to provide more detail about whether the pain is acute, chronic, or neoplasm-related pain.
- If pain is not specified as acute or chronic, do not assign a code from Category 338 except for post-thoracotomy pain, post-operative pain, neoplasm-related pain, or central pain syndrome.
- A code from Category 338 can be the principal or first-listed diagnosis code when pain control or management is the reason for the admission or encounter. Code the underlying cause of the pain as an additional diagnosis.

Pathological Fractures

- Pathological fractures are fractures caused by disease rather than trauma.
- These may be described as "spontaneous."
- When the term "compression" fracture is used, the coder should review the record for evidence of disease or trauma. If in doubt, query the physician.
- Pathological fractures are coded to 733.1x, with the fifth digit indicating the bone involved when the fracture is newly diagnosed.

Pleural Effusion

- Pleural effusion is almost always integral to the underlying condition and therefore is usually not coded.
- When the effusion is addressed and treated separately, it can be coded.
- Pleural effusion noted only on an x-ray is not coded.

Pneumonia

- There are many combination codes that describe the pneumonia and the infecting organism.
- In some situations, the pneumonia is a manifestation of an underlying condition. In this situation, two codes are needed—one for the underlying condition and one for the pneumonia.
- Lobar pneumonia does not refer to the lobe of the lung that is affected. It is a particular type of pneumonia.
- Gram-negative pneumonias are much more difficult to treat than gram-positive pneumonias. If the findings suggest a gram-negative pneumonia, and it is not documented as such, contact the physician.
- Signs of gram-negative pneumonia include: worsening of cough, dyspnea, fever, purulent sputum, elevated leukocyte count, and patchy infiltrate on chest x-ray.

Post-operative Complications

- Physician must document that a condition is a complication of the procedure before assigning a code from 996–999.
- "Expected" conditions occur in the immediate post-op period. These are not reported unless they exceed the usual post-op period and meets criteria for reporting as an additional diagnosis.

Procedures

- The UHDDS requires that all significant inpatient procedures be coded.
- A significant procedure is one that is surgical in nature, carries an anesthetic or surgical risk, or requires specialized training.
- The principal procedure is described as the one performed for definitive treatment.
- The operative approach is not coded separately when a definitive procedure has been performed.
- When only a diagnostic procedure is performed such as a biopsy, the operative approach is coded.
- When a laparoscopic, thoracoscopic, or arthroscopic procedure is converted to an open one, only the open procedure is coded. A code from V64.4x is used to describe this situation.
- Closed biopsies are those performed percutaneously by needle, brush, aspiration, or endoscopy.
- An open biopsy generally involves an incision into the body part.
- When a procedure is cancelled after admission, a code from category V64, Persons encountering health services for specific procedures not carried out, should be used as an additional code. The principal diagnosis code is still the reason for admission. If the cancellation is due to a complication, the complication should be coded.
- When a planned procedure is begun, but cannot be completed, it is coded to the extent that it was performed. If an incision only is made, code to incision of the site. If an endoscopic approach is used, but the physician is unable to reach the site, code the endoscopy only. If the cavity or space was entered, code to exploration of site.

Pulmonary Edema

- Pulmonary edema can be cardiogenic or non-cardiogenic.
- Pulmonary edema is a manifestation of heart failure and, as such, is included in heart failure, hypertension, or rheumatic heart disease. Therefore it is not coded separately.
- Non-cardiogenic acute pulmonary edema occurs in the absence of heart failure or other heart disease.

Respiratory Failure

- Careful review of the medical record is required for the coding and sequencing of respiratory failure.
- When a patient is admitted with respiratory failure and another acute condition, the principal diagnosis will depend on the individual patient's condition and the chief (main) reason that caused the admission of the patient to the hospital.

Septicemia

- A diagnosis of bacteremia (790.7) refers to the presence of bacteria in the bloodstream following relatively minor injury or infection.
- Septicemia is a systemic condition associated with pathogenic microorganisms or toxins in the blood which can include bacteria, viruses, fungi, or other organisms. Most septicemia is classified to category 038. Fourth and fifth digits identify the infecting organism. Additional codes are assigned for any manifestations, if present.
- Negative blood cultures do not preclude a diagnosis of septicemia or sepsis. Query the physician. A code for septicemia is used only when the physician documents a diagnosis of septicemia.
- Urosepsis is assigned to 599.0. The coder should verify with the physician that this is the appropriate code instead of the more serious septicemia.

- <u>Systemic Inflammatory Response Syndrome (SIRS)</u> refers to the systemic response to infection or trauma, burns, or other insult (such as cancer) with symptoms such as fever, tachycardia, tachypnea, and leukocytosis.
- <u>Septic shock</u> is defined as sepsis with hypotension, which is a failure of the cardiovascular system. Septic shock is used as an additional code when the underlying infection is present.
- <u>Sepsis</u> generally refers to SIRS due to infection.
- Severe sepsis <u>generally refers to sepsis with associated acute organ dysfunction.</u>
- <u>If sepsis or severe sepsis is present on admission, the systemic infection code (such as 038.xx or 112.5) should be coded first, followed by code 995.91 sepsis, or 995.92 severe sepsis. Codes from subcategory 995.9 can never be assigned as a principal diagnosis.</u>
- <u>For all cases of septic shock, code the systemic infection first (such as 038.xx or 112.5) followed by codes 995.95 and 785.52. Any additional codes for other acute organ dysfunction should also be assigned.</u>

Substance Abuse
- Substance abuse and dependence are classified as mental disorders in ICD-9-CM.
- Alcohol dependence is classified to category 303 and nondependent alcohol use is coded to category 305.
- Drug dependence is classified to category 304 and nondependent drug use is classified to category 305.
- For both abuse and dependence codes, the fifth digit represents the pattern of abuse as unspecified (0), continuous (1), episodic (2), or in remission (3). The physician documentation must indicate the pattern of use.
- There are codes for alcohol withdrawal and drug withdrawal symptoms. These codes are used in conjunction with the dependence codes.
- When a patient is admitted in withdrawal or when withdrawal develops after admission, the withdrawal code is principal.
- There are procedure codes for rehabilitation, detoxification, and combination rehabilitation and detoxification for both alcohol and drug dependence.

V-codes
- Some V-codes can only be principal diagnosis/first-listed codes, some may only be additional codes, and others may be principal/first-listed or additional.
- Aftercare V-codes (V51-V58) are used when the initial treatment of the disease or injury has ended, but the patient requires continued care.
- A code from V67 is used as the reason for encounter when a patient is admitted for follow-up or surveillance purposes after treatment for a disease or injury.
- There are V-codes to indicate a personal or family history of various conditions.
- When a condition is still present or still under treatment, the personal history code should not be reported.
- Category V09 is used to identify infections that are resistant to the various medications. It is always coded in addition to the code for the infection.
- A code from category V71, Observation and evaluation for suspected conditions not found, is assigned when a patient is admitted or has an encounter for work-up for a suspected condition when there are no signs or symptoms present.

Sample 10 Step Inpatient ICD-9-CM coding process
1. **Locate and write down Admitting Date, Admitting Dx, Attending Physician, and the Patient's Age and Sex.**
2. **Locate and write down the Discharge Date and Discharge Status (Disposition).**   **For example:**   **01**: Home   **20**: Expired   **02**: Acute Care Hospital   **30**: Still patient or expected to return for OPt services   **03**: SNF   **61**: Swing bed   **04**: ICF   **62**: Inpatient rehab facility or distinct rehab unit   **05**: Other type of institution   **63**: Long term care hospital   **06**: Home Health   **65**: Psychiatric hospital or distinct psych unit   **07**: AMA   **66**: Critical access hospital
3. **List Consultants** as you go through the consults.   **Write down pertinent diagnoses** (histories and present illnesses).
4. **Locate and list all procedures:**   Include date, physician, anesthesiologist, and description of each procedure performed with the date performed.
5. **Go through the physician orders:**   This is where you will find any admission errors (e.g., pt, status, admission date).
6. **Read the H&P, ER record, and progress notes**.   **Write down all diagnoses that meet criteria for principal and secondary diagnosis:**   If a diagnosis is ruled out, just cross it off the list.
7. **Select the Principal Diagnosis (PDx)**   UHDDS Definition: The condition established *after study* to be chiefly responsible for occasioning the admission of the patient to the hospital for care.
8. **Select Other Diagnoses (ODx) and indicate whether each was present on admission (POA) or not. Up to 17 ODx may be included on the UB-04.**   <u>UHDDS Definition:</u> All conditions that co-exist at the time of admission, that develop subsequently, or that affect the treatment received and/or the length of stay. Diagnoses that relate to an earlier episode of care which have no bearing on the current hospital stay are to be excluded.   **Complication** UHDDS Definition: A condition arising during hospitalization, which increases the patient's length of stay by one day in 75% of cases.   **Co-morbidity** UHDDS Definition: Condition present at admission, in addition to the principal diagnosis, which increases the patient's length of stay by one day in 75% of cases.
9. **Principal Procedure (PPx)**   UHDDS Definition: One performed for definitive treatment (rather than performed for diagnostic or exploratory purposes) or one that was necessary to care for a complication. If two or more procedures appear to meet the definition, then the one most closely related to the principal diagnosis should be selected as the PPx.

10. **Other Procedures (OPx). Up to 5 may be included on the UB-04.**
UHDDS Definition for significant procedures: One that meets any of the following conditions: is surgical in nature, carries an anesthetic risk, carries a procedural risk, or requires specialized training.

ICD-9-CM Coding for Outpatient Diagnostic Tests

The following are instructions to use in determining the use of ICD-9-CM codes for coding diagnostic test results. Note that physicians are responsible for the accuracy of the information submitted on a bill.

A. Determining the Appropriate first listed ICD-9-CM Diagnosis Code for Diagnostic Tests Ordered Due to Signs and/or Symptoms
    1. If the physician has confirmed a diagnosis based on the results of the diagnostic test, the physician interpreting the test should code that diagnosis. The signs and/or symptoms that prompted the order for the test may be reported as additional diagnoses if they are not fully explained or related to the confirmed diagnosis.
    2. If the diagnostic test did not provide a diagnosis or was normal, the interpreting physician should code the sign(s) or symptom(s) that prompted the treating physician to order the study.
    3. If the results of the diagnostic test are normal or non-diagnostic, and the referring physician records a diagnosis preceded by words that indicate the uncertainty (e.g., probable, suspected, questionable, rule out, or working), then the interpreting physician should not code the referring diagnosis. Rather, the interpreting physician should report the sign(s) or symptom(s) that prompted the study. Diagnoses labeled as uncertain are considered by the ICD-9-CM Coding Guidelines as unconfirmed and should not be reported. This is consistent with the requirement to code the diagnosis to the highest degree of certainty.

B. Instructions to Determine the Reason for the Test: The referring physicians are required to provide diagnostic information to the testing entity at the time the test is ordered. All diagnostic tests "must be ordered by the physician who is treating the beneficiary." An order by the physician may include the following forms of communication:
    - A written document signed by the treating physician/practitioner, which is hand delivered, mailed, or faxed to the testing facility.
    - A telephone call by the treating physician/practitioner or his or her office to the testing facility.
    - An electronic mail by the treating physician or practitioner or his or her office to the testing facility.
      NOTE: Telephone orders must be documented by both the treating physician or practitioner office and the testing facility.

If the interpreting physician does not have diagnostic information as to the reason for the test, and the referring physician is unavailable, it is appropriate to obtain the information directly from the patient or patient's medical record. Attempt to confirm any information obtained from the patient by contacting the referring physician.

C. Incidental Findings: Incidental findings should never be listed as first listed diagnoses. They may be reported as secondary diagnoses by the physician interpreting the diagnostic test.

D. Unrelated/Co-existing Conditions/Diagnoses: Unrelated and co-existing conditions/diagnoses may be reported as additional diagnoses by the physician interpreting the diagnostic test.

E. Diagnostic Tests ordered in the Absence of Signs and/or Symptoms (e.g., screening tests): When a diagnostic test is ordered in the absence of signs/symptoms or other evidence of illness or injury, the physician interpreting the diagnostic test should report the reason for the test (e.g., screening) as the first listed ICD-9-CM diagnosis code. The results of the test, if reported, may be recorded as additional diagnoses.

F. Use of ICD-9-CM to the Greatest Degree of Accuracy and Completeness: Code the ICD-9-CM code that provides the highest degree of accuracy and completeness for the diagnosis resulting from the test or for the sign(s)/symptom(s) that prompted the ordering of the test.

Resource: CMS Publication 60AB, Transmittal AB-01-144, Date: September 26, 2001
Tips for Outpatient ICD-9-CM Coding

ICD-9-CM Outpatient/Ambulatory Coding Guidelines

Note: This is a brief overview. ICD-9-CM codes are used for diagnoses. CPT Codes are used for procedures for billing purposes.

1. Documentation should include specific diagnoses, as well as symptoms, problems, and reasons for visits.

2. Codes from 001.0 to V89 must be provided to identify the reason for encounter/visit.

3. Codes from 001.0 to 999.9 identify diseases and injuries and are most frequently used.

4. Signs and symptoms may be coded if no diagnosis is made.

5. Codes V01.0 to V89 are used for reasons for encounters other than for a disease or injury.

6. Fourth and fifth digits must be assigned where available. If not, the code is considered invalid.

7. Primary diagnosis is listed first with other codes following.

8. Qualified diagnoses should not be coded (such as "suspected"). Code instead the signs and symptoms.

9. Chronic diseases may be coded as long as the patient receives treatment.

10. Code all documented conditions that co-exist at the time of the visit and are treated or affect treatment. History codes may be used if they impact treatment.

11. Diagnosis coding for Diagnostic Services: Code the diagnosis chiefly responsible for the service. Secondary codes may follow.

12. Diagnosis coding for Therapeutic Services: Code the diagnosis chiefly responsible for the service. Secondary codes may follow.

13. Exception to 12: For chemotherapy, radiation therapy, and rehabilitation, the V-code for the service is listed first and the diagnosis chiefly responsible for the service is listed second.

14. Diagnosis coding for Preoperative Evaluations: Sequence first a code from V72.8x. Then assign a code for the condition that is the reason for surgery. Code also any resulting findings.

15. Diagnosis coding for Ambulatory Surgery. Code the diagnosis for which surgery was done. Use the postoperative diagnosis if it is available and more specific.

Sample 10 Step Outpatient ICD-9-CM coding process:
Never code only from the index. Always consult the Tabular List.
Coding must accurately reflect provider's diagnostic statement as well as coding rules.

General Conventions are summarized earlier in this section of the book.
Indentations are used for all subterms below the term to which they apply.

Caution is advised in following the several levels of indentations of subterms.

1. **Main Term** (conditions) are boldface type and are followed by the code number.

   Qualified Diagnosis is a working diagnosis that is not yet proven or established. Do not code diagnoses with terms such as *suspected*, *rule out, ruled out, possible, probably, questionable*, etc. Code the sign(s) and/or symptom(s) that are documented.

   Special Main Terms should be reviewed and considered. See list in text.
   See Condition indicates a descriptive term was looked up rather than the condition.
   See directs the coder to a more specific term.
   See Also refers to an index entry that may provide additional information.

2. **(Nonessential Modifiers) do not have to be included in the diagnostic statement.**
   These subterms clarify or qualify the main term and are enclosed in parentheses.

3. **Essential Modifiers/Subterms that MUST BE included in the dx statement** are indented below the main term in alphabetical order (except "with" and "without"). They clarify the main term listing alternative sites, etiology, or clinical status.

4. **Select Preliminary Code** before turning to the Tabular List.

5. **Locate Preliminary Code** number and review the code descriptions.
   See Category refers to the Tabular List category (3-digit code).

6. **Includes Notes** appears with 3-digit categories and further defines or adds clarification.
   Excludes Notes directs the coder to another location for proper code assignment.
   Return to the Index of Diseases for other possible code selections if the code description in the Tabular List does not appear to fit the condition or reason for visit.

   NEC or "not elsewhere classified" identifies codes to be assigned when information needed to assign a more specific code cannot be located in the code book.
   NOS or "not otherwise specified" indicates that the code lacks specificity and the provider should be asked for a more specific diagnosis before assigning a code.

7. **Assign 4th or 5th Digit** if one is available. Instructional notes about additional digits are found below the category or subcategory description.

8. **Use Additional Code** indicates a second code is required to add necessary detail.

9. **First Listed Diagnosis** is the most significant condition for which services and/or procedures were provided and is sequenced first.
   Secondary Diagnosis co-exists with the first listed diagnosis, has the potential to affect treatment of the primary condition, and is a condition being actively managed.
   Code First Underlying Condition indicates the code is to be sequenced as a secondary code. The code, title, and instructions are italicized.

10. **Record Final Code(s).**

OUTPATIENT PROCEDURE CODING REVIEW

CMS (Centers for Medicare and Medicaid Services, formerly HCFA, Health Care Financing Administration) administers Medicare and Medicaid.

HCPCS (Healthcare Common Procedure Coding System)
- A coding system describing the physician and non-physician patient services covered by the government's Medicare and Medicaid programs
- Designed by CMS and used primarily to report reimbursable services rendered to the patient
- Has two levels of HCPCS codes for ambulatory (outpatient) patients

LEVEL I - CPT (Current Procedural Terminology) is a coding system developed by the American Medical Association (AMA) to convert descriptions of medical, surgical, and diagnostic services rendered by health care providers into five-digit numerical codes. The codes are updated annually by AMA.

The CPT coding system:
- Provides uniform language to accurately designate medical, surgical, and diagnostic services
- Provides effective means of reliable, nationwide communication between physicians, patients, and third-party payers
- Allows for ability to compare reimbursements for procedures

Justification for listing of a procedure:
- The procedure is commonly performed by physicians nationally.
- The procedure must be consistent with modern medical practice.

LEVEL II -National Codes
- Updated annually by CMS
- 5-digit alphanumeric codes

Rules for Coding CPT

1. Determine the service provided by analyzing the statement provided by the physician.
2. Identify the main term(s) in the Alphabetic Index.

   To locate a code in the index, the coder should first look up the procedure or service provided. If the procedure is not listed, look under the anatomic site involved, the condition, synonym, or eponym. Follow the guidance of the index in locating the code most accurately describing the service.

3. Write down or note the code number(s) found for the term.
   - If a single code number is given, locate the code in the body of the CPT book. Verify the code and its description against the statement assuring they match.
   - If two or more codes separated by a comma are given, locate each code in the body of the CPT book. Read the description of each and select the appropriate code matching the statement.
   - If a range of codes is given, locate the range of codes in the body of the CPT book. Review the description of each entry prior to selecting a code.

4. NEVER code from the Alphabetic Index; look up the codes to verify accuracy.
5. Read all notes that apply to the code selected.

   Notes may appear at the beginning of a section, subsection, before or after a code or within the code description. Notes are utilized throughout the CPT, requiring special attention and review by the coder. Some of these notes define terms, such as simple, intermediate, and complex wound repair. Other notes provide specific coding instruction, applicable to specific codes.

6. Select the appropriate modifier, if applicable to complete the code description.
7. Code multiple procedures from highest resource intensive to lowest (most complicated to least complicated).

Common Errors That Prevent Payment to Physicians

1. No documentation or incomplete documentation for services billed
2. Missing signatures
3. Consistently assigning the same level of services
4. Billing of a consult instead of an office visit
5. Using invalid codes in the bill due to use of old coding resources or forms
6. Unbundling procedure codes
7. Not listing the chief complaint
8. Abbreviations that are misinterpreted
9. Billing of services included in global fee as a separate professional fee
10. Not using a modifier or use of an inappropriate modifier for accurate payment of a claim

CPT Code Book Format Information

Guidelines provide specific instructions about coding for each section. The guidelines contain definitions of terms, explanations of notes, subsection information, unlisted services, and special reports information.

Sections: There are eight major areas into which all CPT codes and descriptions are categorized. CPT codes are arranged in numerical order in each section. The first 6 sections are comprised of 5-digit numerical codes. The codes in the last two sections, Category II and Category III Codes, are comprised of 5-digit codes: 4 numbers and a letter.

> Evaluation and Management
> Anesthesia
> Surgery
> Radiology
> Pathology/Laboratory
> Medicine
> Category II Codes
> Category III Codes

Category II Codes are optional tracking codes used to measure performance.

Category III Codes are temporary codes for emerging technology, services, and procedures. These codes can be used for data collection purposes or possibly in the FDA approval process. If a Category III code is available, this code must be reported instead of a Category I unlisted code.

Subsections, subcategories, and headings divide the sections into smaller units, based on anatomy, procedure, condition, description, or approach.

Symbols used in CPT coding: The following symbols are special guides that help the coder compare codes and descriptors with the previous year's CPT edition, or that provide additional coding guidance.

•   Bullet is used to indicate a new procedure or service code added since the previous edition of the CPT manual.

▲   Triangle indicates that the code has been changed or modified since the last CPT manual edition.

+   A plus sign is used to indicate an add-on code.

⊘   Null symbol is used to identify a modifier -51 exempt code

►◄   A right and left triangle indicate the beginning and end of the text changes.

⊙   A circled bullet indicates the code includes moderate sedation

⊕   Reference to CPT Assistant, Clinical Examples in Radiology and CPT Changes

\#   **The number sign is used to identify codes that have been resequenced and are not placed numerically.**

Modifiers: Two-character codes added to CPT codes to supply more specific information about the services provided.

Special Reports: Detailed reports that include adequate definitions or descriptions of the nature, extent, and need for the procedure, and the time, effort, and equipment necessary to provide the service.

Unlisted procedures: Procedures that are considered unusual, experimental, or new and do not have a specific code number assigned. Unlisted procedure codes are located at the end of the subcategories, or headings and may be used to identify any procedure that lacks a specific code.

CPT Index: Located at the back of the CPT manual and arranged alphabetically. To locate terms in the alphabetical index, look under the

> Service/procedure
>
> Anatomic site/body organ
>
> Condition/disease/problem
>
> Synonym
>
> Eponym (procedure named after someone)
>
> Abbreviation or acronym (e.g., CBC)

Notations:

> "see" sends you to a more appropriate section.
>
> "see also" cross-reference to refer to another main term.

CPT Appendices in back section of the CPT manual:

> Appendix A: Lists all modifiers with complete explanations for use
>
> Appendix B: Contains a complete list of additions to, deletions from, and revisions of the previous year's edition
>
> Appendix C: Provides clinical examples of Evaluation and Management (E&M) codes
>
> Appendix D: Contains a listing of the CPT add-on codes
>
> Appendix E: Contains a list of modifier -51 exempt codes
>
> Appendix F: Contains a list of modifier -63 exempt codes
>
> Appendix G: Summary of CPT codes that include moderate (conscious) sedation
>
> Appendix H: Alphabetic index of performance measures by clinical condition or topic
>
> Appendix I: Genetic testing code modifiers
>
> Appendix J: Electrodiagnostic medicine listing of sensory, motor, and mixed nerves
>
> Appendix K: Product pending FDA approval
>
> Appendix L: Vascular families
>
> Appendix M: Crosswalk to Deleted CPT Codes
>
> Appendix N: Summery of resequenced CPT codes

General E&M Coding Guidelines

1. Determine place of service: e.g., office, emergency room, or nursing home.
2. Determine type of service: consult, admission, newborn.
3. Determine patient status: new unless seen in last 3 years by the physician or another physician of the same specialty in the same group.
4. Determine the level of each of the 3 key components:
    1. **History:** problem focused, expanded problem focused, detailed, comprehensive
    2. **Physical examination:** problem focused, expanded problem focused, detailed, comprehensive
    3. **Medical decision making:** straightforward, low, moderate, high
        - New patients, consultations, emergency department services, and initial care: generally require all 3 key components
        - Established patients and subsequent care: usually require 2 of the 3 key components
        - Some codes are based on time: critical care, prolonged services
5. Read Critical Care guidelines carefully. Watch for the procedures that are included in the codes.
6. Read Inpatient Neonatal and Pediatric Critical Care Services and intensive (non-critical) low birth weight services guidelines carefully. Watch for procedures that are inclusive in this area.
7. Be sure to read the coding guidelines for E&M coding carefully.
8. Review definition for "consultations" and determine when consult codes are more appropriate than office visit codes.
9. There are specific codes used for hospital observation services (initial care, discharge services) and codes for same day admissions and discharges.
10. When a patient is admitted as an inpatient on the same day services are provided at another site (office, ER, observation, etc.), only the inpatient services are reported. The E&M services provided in these outpatient settings can be used to determine the level of inpatient services provided.
11. Preventive Care codes are based on the patient's age.

Some Additional Areas of Interest When Coding with CPT

Abortion

"Incomplete Abortions" and "Miscarriages" are alternate terms for missed and spontaneous abortions.

Spontaneous abortion that occurs during any trimester and is completed surgically, assign 59812.

Missed abortion that occurs during the first trimester, assign 59820.

Induced abortion, which combines curettage and evacuation, assign 59851.

Induced abortion by dilation and evacuation, code 59841.

Induced abortion by dilation and curettage, code 59840. Code 58120 is used for a non-obstetrical D&C.

Angioplasty

Determination of the site and whether it is open or percutaneous.

Open transluminal angioplasty of renal or other visceral arteries, aortic, iliac, femoral-popiteal, brachiocephalic, tibioperoneal trunk, and branches, or venous sites code from 35450–35460.

Percutaneous transluminal angioplasty of renal or other visceral arteries, aortic, iliac, femoral-popiteal, brachiocephalic, tibioperoneal trunk or branches, or venous sites code from 35470–35476.

PTCA: Percutaneous transluminal coronary angioplasty assign code appropriately from 92982 and 92984.

Percutaneous transluminal angioplasty of the peripheral arteries and visceral arteries:
- 75962–75968 (Radiology Section) for the radiological supervision and interpretation

Codes 92980 and 92981 for stent placement include the PTCA and thus the PTCA is not coded separately.

Appendectomy

There are several codes that are used to describe appendectomies: open surgical appendectomy (including incidental), laparoscopic appendectomy, appendectomy done for a ruptured appendix, and appendectomy done for a specified purpose at the time of other major surgery.

Auditory

Simple mastoidectomy also called a transmastoid antrotomy (69501).

Apicetomy is the excision of the tip of the petrous bone. This is often performed with a radical mastoidectomy (69530). It would be inappropriate to code 69511 in addition.

Tympanostomy (requiring insertion of ventilating tube). Code 69436, Tympanostomy (requiring insertion of ventilating tube) general anesthesia and 69433, Tympanostomy (requiring insertion of ventilating tube), local or topic anesthesia are used for "insertion of tubes."

Removal of impacted cerumen from one or both ears, use code 69210.

Some Additional Areas of Interest When Coding with CPT

Bronchoscopy and Biopsy

Surgical bronchoscopy includes a diagnostic bronchoscopy.

Code appropriate endoscopy for each anatomic site examined.

Endobronchial biopsy, code 31625.

Review for types of specimen collection:

- **Biopsy** forceps used to remove tissue.
- **Bronchial brush** used to obtain surface cells.
- **Bronchial alveolar lavage (BAL)** used to collect cells from peripheral lung tissue.
- **Cell washings** used to exfoliate cells from crevices.
- NOTE: Cell washings or brushings are NOT biopsies.

Transbronchial biopsy is performed by positioning the scope in the bronchus nearest to the lesion. A hole is punctured through the bronchus into the lung tissue where the lesion is located. The lesion is then biopsied. Transbronchial lung biopsy is reported with code 31628.

Transbronchial needle aspiration biopsy (31629)

Catheter aspiration of tracheobronchial tree at bedside (31725)

CABG

To report combined arterial-venous grafts, it is necessary to report 2 codes:

1. The appropriate combined arterial-venous graft code (33517–33523); and
2. The appropriate arterial graft code (33533–33536).

Procurement of the saphenous vein graft is included in the description of the work for 33517–33523 and is not reported separately.

Procurement of an upper extremity artery is reported separately.

Casting and Strapping

Services in the musculoskeletal system include the application or removal of the first cast or traction device only. Subsequent replacement of casts, traction devices, or removals are reported using codes from the 29000–29750 series of codes.

The codes in the 29000–29750 series of codes have very specific guidelines directing the use of the codes.

Endoscopy

Codes specify the purpose and site of application.

Dx endoscopy is coded only if a surgical procedure was not done. Surgical endoscopy always includes a diagnostic endoscopy.

Code as far as the scope is passed.

Stomach endoscopy is included with UGI endoscopy, not separately.

Multiple codes may be necessary to cover one endoscopic episode.

Removal of gastrostomy tube by endoscopy, code 43247.

Colonoscopy: first determine the route the procedure follows (via colostomy, colotomy, or rectum).

Colonoscopy with dilation of rectum or anorectum, code 45999.

Biliary endoscopy (47550) is only used with 47420 or 47610.

EGDs are coded to 43235–43259.

Some Additional Areas of Interest When Coding with CPT

Eye and Ocular

Preliminary iridectomy is not coded separately if performed as part of a cataract extraction or prior to lens extraction. It is included in the code for the lens extraction.

Two types of cataract extraction:
- ICCE: Intracapsular cataract extraction
- ECCE: Extracapsular cataract extraction

Do not code medication injections used in conjunction with cataract surgery. Injections are considered part of the procedure.

Cataract removal includes the following in codes 66830–66984.

DO NOT CODE THE FOLLOWING PROCEDURES SEPARATELY: anterior capsulotomy, enzymatic zonulysis, iridectomy, iridotomy, lateral canthotomy, pharmacological agents, posterior capsulotomy, viscoelastic agents, subconjunctival, and sub-tenon injections.

Female Genital System

Codes 57452–57461 are used to report various cervical colposcopic procedures.

Code 57455 describes colposcopy with single or multiple biopsies of the cervix.

Code 58150 describes total abdominal hysterectomy with or without removal of tube(s) or ovary(s).

Code 58611 is an add-on code that describes tubal ligation or transection when done at the time of cesarean delivery or intra-abdominal surgery.

Fractures/Dislocations

- Treatment of fractures/dislocations can be open or closed.
- Closed treatment means that the fracture or dislocation site is not surgically opened. It is used to describe procedures that treat fractures by three methods: without manipulation, with manipulation, and with or without traction.
- Open treatment implies that the fracture is surgically opened and the fracture is visualized to allow treatment.
- Skeletal fixation is neither open nor closed treatment. Usually pins are placed across the fracture using x-ray guidance.
- Manipulation is used to indicate the attempted reduction or restoration of a fracture or dislocation.

Genitourinary

Many of the procedures in the urinary system are performed endoscopically—cystoscopy, urethroscopy, cystourethroscopy, ureteroscopy, pyeloscopy, and renal endoscopy.

Most cystourethroscopy codes are unilateral. When a cysto is performed bilaterally modifier -50 should be appended.

Codes in the 52320–52355 series include the insertion and removal of a temporary stent during diagnostic or therapeutic cystourethroscopic intervention(s).

Cystourethroscopy with removal of a self-retaining/indwelling ureteral stent, planned or staged during the associated normal postoperative follow-up period of the original procedure, is reported by means of code 52310 or 52315 with the -58 appended as appropriate.

Be careful to differentiate between codes for ureteral and urethral procedures.

Some Additional Areas of Interest When Coding with CPT

GI Biopsy

Code only the biopsy if a single lesion is biopsied but not excised.

Code only the biopsy and list only one time if multiple biopsies are done (from the same or different lesions) and none of the lesions are excised.

Code only the excision if a biopsy of a lesion is taken and the balance of the same lesion is then excised.

Code both the biopsy and excision if both are performed and if the biopsy is taken from a lesion different from that which is excised; AND the code for the excision does not include the phrase "with or without biopsy." If such a phrase is in the code narration, then a separate biopsy code should not be used.

Surgical endoscopy always includes a diagnostic endoscopy.

Modifier -59 may be used to explain unusual circumstances when coding both biopsy and removal of a different lesion.

Hernia Repair

- Hernia repair codes are categorized by type (inguinal, femoral, etc.).
- Hernias are further categorized as "initial" or "recurrent" based on whether or not the hernia has required previous repair.
- Age and clinical presentation (reducible versus strangulated)
- Code 49568 is used only with nonlaparscopic incisional or ventral hernia repairs.

Immunizations

Codes 90465–90474 are used to report the administration of vaccines/toxoids.

Codes 90476–90749 identify the vaccine PRODUCT alone.

If a combination vaccine code is provided (MMR) it is not appropriate to report each component of the combination vaccine separately.

When the physician provides face-to-face counseling of the patient and family during the administration of a vaccine, report codes 90465–90468.

Do not append modifier-51 to the vaccine/toxoid product codes 90476–90749.

Integumentary

Three types of repairs: Add lengths of repairs together and use one code for repairs of the same location and same type.

- **Simple:** Superficial wound involving skin and/or subcutaneous tissues and requiring simple suturing.
- **Intermediate:** Involving skin, subcutaneous tissues, and fascia, or muscle, and requiring layer closure. May also be used when a single closure requires intensive debridement.
- **Complex** repairs requiring reconstructive surgery or time-consuming or complicated closures.

Debridement is coded separately: When gross contamination requires cleaning, when appreciable amounts of devitalized or contaminated tissue are removed, and when debridement is carried out separately without primary closure.

Lesion size is best found on the operative report.

Benign or malignant lesion(s): Code each lesion excised separately; simple closure after excision of lesion(s) is included in the code.

Adjacent tissue transfers include excision of tissues, including lesions.

Free skin grafts: Identify by size and location of the defect (recipient area) and the type of graft; includes simple debridement of granulations or recent avulsion.

Use 15002–15005 for initial wound preparation.

Repair of donor site requiring skin graft or local flaps is to be added on as an additional procedure.

Some Additional Areas of Interest When Coding with CPT

Report excision of lesion(s) separately.

Excisional biopsy is used when the entire lesion, whether benign or malignant, is removed.

Breast lesion excisions performed after being identified by pre-op radiological marker (localization wires) code 19125 and 19126.

Placement of needle localization wires prior to biopsies, excisions, and other breast procedures, use additional codes 19290 and 19291.

Laryngoscopy

Many of the codes used to report laryngoscopies include the use of an operating microscope. Therefore, code 69990, Microsurgical techniques, requiring the use of operating microscope (list separately in addition to code primary procedure) would not be used with any codes that include the use of the microscope.

Maternity Care and Delivery

Antepartum care or services provided above the normally expected care (as defined in the CPT book) should be coded separately.

Medical problems complicating labor and delivery management may require additional resources and should be identified by using E&M codes in addition to the codes for maternity care.

For surgical complications of pregnancy, see services in the surgery section.

If a physician provides all or part of the antepartum and/or postpartum patient care, but does not perform delivery due to termination of pregnancy by abortion or referral to another physician for delivery, see the antepartum and postpartum care codes 59425–59426 and 59430.

Patients who have had previous cesarean delivery and now present with the expectation of a vaginal delivery are coded using codes 59610–59622. If the patient has a successful vaginal delivery after a previous cesarean delivery (VBAC), use codes 59610–59614. If the attempt is unsuccessful and another cesarean delivery is carried out, use codes 59618–59622.

Nasal Hemorrhage

Was it anterior or posterior?

- If anterior, was the hemorrhage simple or complex?
- If posterior, was the control of hemorrhage an initial or subsequent procedure?

Anterior nasal hemorrhage has likely occurred if the physician inserts gauze packing or anterior packing or performs cauterization.

Posterior nasal hemorrhage has likely occurred if the physician inserts nasal stents, tampons, balloon catheters, or posterior packing, or if the patient is taken to the OR for ligation of arteries to control bleeding.

Nosebleed subsequent to initial one (30906).

Some Additional Areas of Interest When Coding with CPT

Neurology/Spine Surgery

The spinal and spinal cord injection codes reflect the specific spinal anatomy, such as subarachnoid or epidural, the level of the injection (cervical, thoracic, lumbar, or sacral), and the types of substances injected, such as anesthetic steroids, antispasmodics, phenol, etc.

Injection of contrast material during fluoroscopic guidance is included in the codes 62263–62264, 62267, 62270–62273, 62280–62282, and 62310–62319. The fluoroscopic guidance itself is reported by code 77003. Code 62263 describes treatment involving injections of various substances over a multiple day period. Code 62263 is not reported for each individual injection, but is reported once to describe the entire series of injections or infusions.

Code 62264 describes multiple treatments performed on the same day.

Other codes in this section refer to laminectomies, excisions, repairs, and shunts. A basic distinction among the codes is the condition, such as herniated disk, as well as the approach used, such as anterior or posterior or costovertebral.

Lumbar punctures (62270) are also called spinal taps and are used to obtain cerebrospinal fluid by inserting a needle into the subarachnoid space in the lumbar area.

When coding surgery on the spine, there are many sets of guidelines for the coder to review, including those at the beginning of the subsection as well as throughout the subsection.

Co-surgery is common in spinal surgeries. When two surgeons work together, both as primary surgeons, each surgeon should report his or her distinct operative work by adding modifier -62 to the procedure code and any associated add-on codes for that procedure as long as both surgeons continue to work together as primary surgeons.

Additional codes for coding procedures on the spine and spinal cord are found in the nervous system subsection of the surgery section.

Spinal instrumentation is used to stabilize the spinal column during repair procedures. There are two types: segmental and nonsegmental.

- Segmental instrumentation involves attachment at each end of the spinal area and at least one intermittent fixation.
- Nonsegmental instrumentation involves attachment at each end and may span several vertebral segments without intermittent fixation.

Pacemakers

1. Is it permanent or temporary?
2. What was the approach (transvenous or epicardial)?
3. What type of device (electrodes and/or pulse generator)?
4. Where were the electrodes placed (atrial, ventricle, or both)?
5. Is this an insertion, revision, removal, or a replacement?
6. Was revision of the skin pocket done?

Sentinel Nodes

Sentinel node procedures utilize injection of a radiotracer or blue dye. After absorption of dye, the physician can visualize the node(s). Code 38792 is used for identification of sentinel nodes. For excision of sentinel nodes, see 38500–38542.

Use appropriate lymph node excision codes to report the excision.

A second sentinel node from a different lymphatic chain excised from a separate incision, report the excision and add modifier -59.

Lymphoscintigraphy, code 78195.

Injection for gamma probe node detection with imaging code 38790.

Some Additional Areas of Interest When Coding with CPT

Thyroid

Recall the thyroid has two lobes, one on each side of the trachea. The procedure may only be unilateral (60220), but it is still considered to be a total lobectomy.

Thyroidectomy may be:

- Total or Complete (60240), removing both lobes and the isthmus. It is not necessary to list the code twice.
- Partial lobectomy (60210), unilateral, with or without insthmusectomy.

Thyroidectomy with neck dissection (60252 and 60254). Do not assign these codes if an isolated lymph node is excised or biopsied.

Tonsillectomy and Adenoidectomy

Separate codes describe: tonsillectomy and adenoidectomy; tonsillectomy alone, whether primary or secondary; adenoidectomy alone, primary; adenoidectomy alone, secondary.

Separate codes are reported for procedures performed on patients under age 12, and age 12 or older.

A primary procedure is one in which no prior tonsillectomy or adenoidectomy has been performed. A secondary procedure is one that is performed to remove residual or regrowth of tonsil or adenoid tissue.

Wound Exploration

Wound exploration codes (20100–20103) are used when repair of a penetrating wound requires enlargement of the existing defect for exploration, cleaning, and repair.

If the wound does not need to be enlarged, then only repair codes from the integumentary section are used.

III. Health Data Content, Requirements, and Standards

Patricia J. Schnering, RHIA, CCS

1. A coder who needed to locate the microscopic description of tissue excised during surgery would be most likely to find this information within the
   A. recovery room record
   B. pathology report.
   C. operative report.
   D. discharge summary.

   REFERENCE: Abdelhak, p 110
                 Green & Bowie, p 156
                 Johns, p 66
                 Odom-Wesley, p 171
                 LaTour and Eichenwald-Maki, p 200

2. Patient data collection requirements vary according to the health care setting. A data element you would expect to be collected in the MDS, but NOT in the UHDDS, would be
   A. personal identification.
   B. level of cognition.
   C. procedures and dates.
   D. principal diagnosis.

   REFERENCE: Abdelhak, p 134–135
                 Green & Bowie, p 114, 243
                 Johns, p 164–168
                 Davis and LaCour, p 148–149
                 LaTour and Eichenwald-Maki, p 168

   Uniform Disch. Hosp. Disch. Data Set

   MDS - minimum Data Set

3. A good first step toward protecting the security of data contained in a health information computer system would be to
   A. transcribe reports that are important or that require a higher level of security.
   B. develop policies defining different levels of security for different types of information.
   C. provide remote terminals for improved access to the record.
   D. monitor the clinical pertinence of documentation on a quarterly basis.

   REFERENCE: Abdelhak, p 294
                 Johns, p 338

4. In the number "09-0001" listed in a tumor registry accession register, what does the prefix "09' represent?
   A. the number of primary cancers reported for that patient
   B. the year the patient was entered into the database of the registry
   C. the sequence number of the case
   D. the stage of the tumor based upon the TNM system of staging

   REFERENCE: Johns, p 400–403
                 LaTour and Eichenwald-Maki, p 332

5. For continuity of care, ambulatory care providers are more likely than providers of acute care services to rely on the documentation found in the
   A. interdisciplinary patient care plan.
   B. pharmacy consultations.
   C. transfer record.
   D. problem list.

   REFERENCE: Abdelhak, p 133
                 Green & Bowie, p 79
                 Johns, p 79
                 Davis and LaCour, p 71, 73
                 Odom-Wesley, p 326–327
                 LaTour and Eichenwald-Maki, p 202

6. As part of a quality improvement study you have been asked to provide information on the menstrual history, number of pregnancies, and number of living children on each OB patient from a stack of obstetrical records. The best place in the record to locate this information is the

    A. antepartum record.
    B. labor and delivery record.
    C. postpartum record.
    D. discharge summary.

REFERENCE: Abdelhak, p 110–111
               Green & Bowie, p 172
               Odom-Wesley, p 180–186

7. A risk manager needs to locate full documentation of a patient's fall from his bed, including witness reports and probable reasons for the fall. She would most likely find this information in the

    A. doctors' progress notes.
    B. integrated progress notes.
    C. incident report.
    D. nurses' notes.

REFERENCE: Abdelhak, p 456
               Green & Bowie, p 88
               Johns, p 528
               LaTour and Eichenwald-Maki, p 302
               McWay (2003), p 109–110
               McWay, 110
               Davis and LaCour, p 299–301
               Odom-Wesley, p 54

8. As a concurrent record reviewer for an acute care facility, you have asked Dr. Miller to provide an updated history and physical for one of his recent admissions. Dr. Miller pages through the medical record to a copy of an H&P performed in his office a week before admission. You tell Dr. Miller

    A. a new H&P is required for every inpatient admission.
    B. that you apologize for not noticing the H&P he provided.
    C. the H&P copy is acceptable as long as he documents any interval changes.
    D. Joint Commission standards cannot be met unless he documents an H&P after each admission.

REFERENCE: Abdelhak, p 105
               Green & Bowie, p 136
               Odom-Wesley, p 367
               LaTour and Eichenwald-Maki, p 196

- Every surgery needs an H&P B.4 surgery
- must be on chart 24 hrs prior to surgery

9. You have been asked to identify every reportable case of cancer from the previous year. A key resource will be the facility's

    A. disease index.
    B. number control index.
    C. physicians' index.
    D. patient index.

REFERENCE: Abdelhak, p 267
               Johns, p 401
               LaTour and Eichenwald-Maki, p 332
               McWay, p 116

10. The performance of <u>qualitative analysis</u> is an important tool in ensuring data quality through accurate health records. These reviews evaluate
   A. quality of care through the use of pre-established criteria.
   B. adverse effects and contraindications of drugs utilized during hospitalization.
   C. potentially compensable events.
   D. completeness, adequacy, and quality of documentation.

REFERENCE: Abdelhak, p 124
               Johns, p 851
               LaTour and Eichenwald-Maki, p 214
               Odom-Wesley, p 251–256
               Davis and LaCour, p 294–298

11. Discharge summary documentation must include
   A. a detailed history of the patient.
   B. a note from social services or discharge planning.
   C. significant findings during hospitalization.
   D. correct codes for significant procedures.

REFERENCE: Abdelhak, p 109
               Green & Bowie, p 134–135
               Johns, p 68–72
               LaTour and Eichenwald-Maki, p 201
               Odom-Wesley, p 200–205
               Davis and LaCour, p 98

12. The foundation for communicating all patient care goals in long-term care settings is the
   A. legal assessment.   C. interdisciplinary patient care plan.
   B. physical exam.   D. Uniform Hospital Discharge Data Set.   UHDDS

REFERENCE: Abdelhak, p 138, 142
               Johns, p 83–84
               LaTour and Eichenwald-Maki, p 203
               Odom-Wesley, p 371

13. As the privacy officer of your facility, you have been charged with developing policies and procedures for protecting the confidentiality and security of the clinical data collected in your computerized system. One of the first steps you will take is to judge the value of information processed by your system and classify it. Another step you will need to take is to
   A. authorize access to information collected based on level of data sensitivity.
   B. prevent all nonclinicians' access to any confidential information in the system.
   C. establish firewalls to protect aggregate data collected within your facility.
   D. establish passwords for all customers, both internal and external, who request access to the information in your system.

REFERENCE: Green & Bowie, p 136
               Johns, p 820
               LaTour and Eichenwald-Maki, p 255
               Davis and LaCour, p 329

14. A qualitative review of a health record reveals that the history and physical for a patient admitted on June 26 was performed on June 30 and transcribed on July 1. Which of the following statements regarding the history and physical is true in this situation? Completion and charting of the H&P indicates

    Has to be done w/in 24hrs of admission

    A. non-compliance with Joint Commission standards.
    B. compliance with Joint Commission standards.
    C. compliance if consistent with medical staff bylaws.
    D. compliance with Joint Commission standards for non-surgical patients.

    REFERENCE: Abdelhak, p 92
                   Odom-Wesley, p 367
                   Johns, p 684
                   LaTour and Eichenwald-Maki, p 191

15. When developing a data collection system, the most effective approach first considers
    A. the end user's needs.   C. hardware requirements.
    B. applicable accreditation standards. D. facility preference.

    What using it for?

    REFERENCE: Johns, p 144–145
                   Odom-Wesley, p 230

16. Based upon the following documentation in an acute care record, where would you expect this excerpt to appear?

    "With the patient in the supine position, the right side of the neck was appropriately prepped with betadine solution and draped. I was able to pass the central line which was taped to skin and used for administration of drugs during resuscitation."

    A. Physician progress notes
    B. Operative record
    C. Nursing progress notes
    D. Physical examination

    REFERENCE: Johns, p 62
                   Abdelhak, p 110
                   Davis and LaCour, p 100
                   Odom-Wesley, p 164

17. For each report of care rendered to a patient, the health record entry should include the date plus the provider's name and
    A. department.   *Who Is he*   C. initials.
    B. discipline.   *MD*   D. supervising physician.

    REFERENCE: Green and Bowie, p 111
                   Johns, p 92
                   LaTour and Eichenwald-Maki, p 301
                   Odom-Wesley, p 113, 115

18. A key item you would expect to find recorded on an <u>ER record</u>, but would probably NOT see in an <u>acute care record</u> is the
   A. physical findings.
   B. lab and diagnostic test results.
   C. time and means of arrival.
   D. instructions for follow-up care.

REFERENCE: Abdelhak, p 111
               Peden, p 31
               Johns, p 78
               LaTour and Eichenwald-Maki, p 202
               Odom-Wesley, p 171
               Davis and LaCour, p 165

19. In 1987, OBRA helped shift the focus in long-term care to patient outcomes. As a result, core assessment elements are collected on each resident as defined in the
   A. UHDDS.
   B. MDS.   *minimum Data set*
   C. Uniform Clinical Data Set.
   D. Uniform Ambulatory Core Data.

minimum Data Set

REFERENCE: Abdelhak, p 134
               Green & Bowie, p 243
               Johns, p 83
               LaTour and Eichenwald-Maki, p 166
               Peden, p 337
               Odom-Wesley, p 365, 368–378
               Davis and LaCour, p 175

20. Under which of the following conditions can an original patient health record be physically removed from the hospital?
   A. when the patient is brought to the hospital emergency department following a motor vehicle accident and, after assessment, is transferred with his health record to a trauma designated emergency department at another hospital
   B. when the director of health records is acting in response to a subpoena duces tecum and takes the health record to court
   C. when the patient is discharged by the physician, and at the time of discharge is transported to a long-term care facility with his health record
   D. when the record is taken to a physician's private office for a follow-up patient visit postdischarge

REFERENCE: Abdelhak, p 527
               Johns, p 685
               McWay (2003), p 139

21. An example of an <u>objective entry</u> in the health record supplied by a health care practitioner is the

   A. past medical history.
   B. physical assessment.
   C. chief complaint.
   D. review of systems.

REFERENCE: Abdelhak, p 107
               Green & Bowie, p 138–139
               Johns, p 54–55
               LaTour and Eichenwald-Maki, p 195–196, 204
               Odom-Wesley, p 217, 331–332
Davis and LaCour, p 96–97

22. One essential item to be captured on the <u>physical exam</u> is the
  A. objective survey of body systems.   C.   family history.
  B. chief complaint.   D.   subjective review of systems.

REFERENCE: Abdelhak, p 107
                Green & Bowie, p 139–141
                Johns, p 55
                LaTour and Eichenwald-Maki, p 195–197
                Odom-Wesley, p 108–111
                Davis and LaCour, p 94–95

23. Using the SOAP style of documenting progress notes, choose the "subjective" statement from the following:
  A. Sciatica unimproved with hot pack therapy.   *Assessment*
  B. Patient moving about very cautiously, appears to be in pain.   *Objective*
  C. Adjust pain medication; begin physical therapy tomorrow.   *Plan*
  D. Patient states low back pain is as severe as it was on admission.

REFERENCE: Abdelhak, p 115
                Green & Bowie, p 92
                LaTour and Eichenwald-Maki, p 204
                Odom-Wesley, p 217, 331–332
                Davis and LaCour, p 96–97

24. One distinct advantage of the EHR over paper-based health records is the
  A. ease of developing screen designs over form designs.
  B. accessibility of the record by multiple data users.
  C. standardized format.
  D. ease of data collection.

REFERENCE: Johns, p 116
                LaTour and Eichenwald-Maki, p 231
                Davis and LaCour, p 366

25. The Data Security Officer for your institution plans to implement a log-on process for electronic signing that is LEAST susceptible to improper delegation of use. The method you would recommend is
  A. password assigned by system administrator.
  B. password assigned by user.
  C. biometrics-based identifier.   *finger/ eye scan*
  D. encryption.

REFERENCE: Green and Bowie, p 26
                LaTour and Echenwald-Maki, p 79

26. You notice on the admission H&P that Mr. McKahan, a Medicare patient, was admitted to repair a retinal detachment, but the progress notes indicate that due to some heart irregularities, he may not be a good surgical risk. Because of your knowledge of COP regulations, you expect that a(n) _____will be added to his health record.

    Conditions of Participation

    A. interval summary
    B. consultation report
    C. advance directive
    D. interdisciplinary care plan

    REFERENCE: Abdelhak, p 109
                    Green & Bowie, p 142
                    Davis and LaCour, p 91
                    Odom-Wesley, p 117–118
                    LaTour and Eichenwald-Maki, p 198

27. Joint Commission standards require that a complete history and physical be documented on the health records of operative patients. Does this report carry a time requirement?
    A. yes, within 8 hours post surgery
    B. no, as long as it is dictated ASAP
    C. yes, prior to surgery   *after*
    D. yes, within 24 hours post surgery

    REFERENCE: Abdelhak, p 110
                    Green & Bowie, p 153
                    LaTour and Eichenwald-Maki, p 196
                    Odom-Wesley, p 108
                    Davis and LaCour, p 94

28. You have been asked by a peer review committee to print a list of the medical record numbers of all patients who had EGDs performed in the past year at your facility. Which secondary data source could be used to quickly gather this information?
    A. disease index
    B. physician index
    C. master patient index
    D. operation index   *What operations performed*

    REFERENCE: Johns, p 376–377
                    LaTour and Eichenwald-Maki, p 331

29. An important element of data quality is security in preventing unauthorized access, corruption, misuse, and loss of data. Both technical and procedural methods will be used with the CPR to control and manage confidential information. An example of a procedural method for protecting data is

    CPR > Computerized patient record

    A. having confidentiality statements signed by all staff.
    B. limiting access of certain screens based on the staff's need to know.
    C. auditing capability of the system to track data access.
    D. using computer back-up systems.

    REFERENCE: Green & Bowie, p 271
                    Johns, p 850

30. Reviewing a medical record to ensure that all diagnoses are justified by documentation throughout the chart is an example of
    A. peer review.
    B. quantitative review.
    C. qualitative analysis.
    D. legal analysis.

    quality of record

    REFERENCE: Abdelhak, p 127
    Green & Bowie, p 102
    LaTour and Eichenwald-Maki, p 214
    McWay, p 104
    Odom-Wesley, p 251–252
    Davis and LaCour, p 298

31. The health care providers at your hospital do a very thorough job of periodic open record review to ensure the completeness of record documentation. A qualitative review of surgical records would likely include checking for documentation regarding
    A. the presence or absence of such items as preoperative and postoperative diagnosis, description of findings, and specimens removed.
    B. whether a postoperative infection occurred and how it was treated.
    C. the quality of follow-up care.
    D. whether the severity of illness and/or intensity of service warranted acute level care.

    REFERENCE: Abdelhak, p 110
    Green & Bowie, p 153
    Johns, p 62
    LaTour and Eichenwald-Maki, p 200
    Davis and LaCour, p 296–298
    Odom-Wesley, p 251–256

32. In developing procedures for the medical record staff of a new home health agency, you recommend that the staff routinely check to verify that a summary on each patient is provided to the attending physician so that he or she can review, update, and recertify the patient as appropriate. The time frame for requiring this summary is at least every
    A. week.
    B. month.
    C. 60 days.
    D. 90 days.

    REFERENCE: Abdelhak, p 138
    Johns, p 85
    Peden, p 425
    Odom-Wesley, p 401–402

33. The one document in your facility that will spell out the documentation requirements for patient records, designate the time frame for completion by the active medical staff, and indicate the penalties for failure to comply with these record standards is the
    A. information management plan.
    B. quality management plan.
    C. Joint Commission accreditation manual.
    D. medical staff rules and regulations.

    REFERENCE: Green & Bowie, p 16
    Johns, p 620
    LaTour and Eichenwald-Maki, p 542
    Odom-Wesley, p 43

34. Which method of identification of authorship or authentication of entries would be inappropriate to use in a patient's health record?
    A. written signature of the provider of care
    B. identifiable initials of a nurse writing a nursing note
    C. a unique identification code entered by the person making the report
    D. delegated use of computer key by radiology secretary

Authenticated By Physician

REFERENCE: Abdelhak, p 114
              Green & Bowie, p 80–82
              LaTour and Eichenwald-Maki, p 213

35. Though you work in an integrated delivery network, not all systems in your network communicate with one another. As you meet with your partner organizations, you begin to sell them on the concept of an important development intended to support the exchange of health information across the continuum within a geographical community. You are promoting that your organization join a
    A. data warehouse.
    B. regional health information organization.
    C. continuum of care.
    D. data retrieval portal group.

REFERENCE: Abdelhak, p 82–83
              LaTour and Eichenwald-Maki, p 51
              McWay, p 181
              Davis and LaCour, p 263
              Odom-Wesley, p 15

36. Accreditation by Joint Commission is a voluntary activity for a facility and it is
    A. considered unnecessary by most health care facilities.
    B. required for state licensure in all states.
    C. conducted in each facility annually.
    D. required for reimbursement of certain patient groups.

REFERENCE: Abdelhak, p 15
              Odom-Wesley, p 299
              LaTour and Eichenwald-Maki, p 280
              Davis and LaCour, p 24

37. Which of the following indices might be protected from unauthorized access through the use of unique identifier codes assigned to members of the medical staff?
    A. disease index   C. master patient index
    B. procedure index   D. physician index

REFERENCE: Green & Bowie, p 230
              Johns, p 377
              LaTour and Eichenwald-Maki, p 331

38. Which of the four distinct components of the problem-oriented record serves to help index documentation throughout the record?
    A. database   C. initial plan
    B. problem list   D. progress notes

REFERENCE: Abdelhak, p 114–115
              Green and Bowie, p 89–90
              Johns, p 91–99
              Odom-Wesley, p 215–216
              Davis and LaCour, p 71–74

39. The information security officer is revising the policies at your rehabilitation facility for handling all patient clinical information. The best resource for checking out specific accreditation standards and guidelines is the
    A. Conditions of Participation for Rehabilitation Facilities
    B. Medical Staff Bylaws, Rules, and Regulations
    C. Joint Commission manual
    D. CARF manual   *Commission on Accreditation Rehab facilities*

REFERENCE: Green & Bowie, p 30
              Johns, p 87–88
              LaTour and Eichenwald-Maki, p 36
              Odom-Wesley, p 191–196
              Davis and LaCour, p 25–26, 286

40. Which of the following is a secondary data source that would be used to quickly gather the health records of all juvenile patients treated for diabetes within the past 6 months?
    A. disease index   C. pediatric census sheet
    B. patient register   D. procedure index

REFERENCE: Green & Bowie, p 230
              Johns, p 376–377
              LaTour and Eichenwald-Maki, p 331

41. A primary focus of screen format design in a health record computer application should be to ensure that
    A. programmers develop standard screen formats for all hospitals.
    B. the user is capturing essential data elements.
    C. paper forms are easily converted to computer forms.
    D. data fields can be randomly accessed.

REFERENCE: Abdelhak, p 116Johns, p 370
              LaTour and Eichenwald-Maki, p 216
              Odom-Wesley, p 230
              Davis and LaCour, p 75–78

42. The purpose of the notice of privacy practices is to
    A. notify the patient of uses of PHI   C. report incidents to the OIG
    B. notify patient of audits   *Protected Health Infor.*   D. notify researchers of allowable data use

REFERENCE: McWay, p 60
              Krager and Krager, p 43
              Odom-Wesley, p 99
              Davis and LaCour, p 331
              LaTour and Eichenwald-Maki, p 92, 94

43. Your organization is sending confidential patient information across the Internet using technology that will transform the original data into unintelligible code that can be re-created by authorized users. This technique is called
    A. a firewall.   C. a call-back process.
    B. validity processing.   D. data encryption.

REFERENCE: Abdelhak, p 297
              McWay, p 321
              Green & Bowie, p 286

44. An example of a primary data source is the
    A. physician index.
    B. health record.
    C. cancer registry.
    D. hospital statistical report.

REFERENCE: LaTour and Eichenwald-Maki, p 288
                  Abdelhak, p 474
                  Johns, p 398
                  McWay, p 115
                  Davis and LaCour, p 240
                  LaTour and Eichenwald-Maki, p 330
                  Odom-Wesley, p 83

45. Which of the following statements would be found in the laboratory report section of the health record?
    A. BUN reported as 20 mg   *Blood/urea/nitrogen*
    B. morphine sulfate gr. 1/4 q.4h. for pain
    C. IV sodium Pentothal 1% started at 9:05 AM   *Temp/pulse/Resp*
    D. TPR recorded q.h. for 12 hr.

REFERENCE: Abdelhak, p 112
                  Green and Bowie, p 158–159
                  LaTour and Eichenwald-Maki, p 181

46. The medical record is generally accepted as being the property of the
    A. patient's guardian.
    B. court.
    C. institution.   *provider*
    D. patient.

REFERENCE: Green & Bowie, p 75–76
                  LaTour & Eichenwald-Maki, p 251–252
                  McWay, p 61
                  McWay (2003), p 90   Servais, p 54

47. The ownership of the information contained in the physical medical/health record is considered to belong to the
    A. patient.
    B. hospital.
    C. physician.
    D. insurance company.

REFERENCE: Green & Bowie, p 75–76
                  LaTour & Eichenwald-Maki, p 251–252
                  McWay (2003), p 90; 100

48. If the patient record is involved in litigation and the physician requests to make a change to that record, what should the HIM professional do?   *HIM : Health Infor mgment*
    A. Refer request to legal counsel.
    B. Allow the change to occur.
    C. Notify the patient.
    D. Say the record is unavailable.

REFERENCE: Green & Bowie, 84–85
                  Servais, p 30–32

49. HIM professionals are bound to protect the confidentiality of patient information under the
    A. Patient Bill of Rights.
    B. AHIMA's Code of Ethics.
    C. Hippocratic oath.
    D. Joint Commission standards.

REFERENCE: Green & Bowie, p 337–338
               LaTour & Eichenwald-Maki, p 274
               McWay, p 83

50. One of the greatest threats to the confidentiality of health data is
    A. when medical information is reviewed as a part of quality assurance activities.
    B. disclosure of information for purposes not authorized in writing by the patient.
    C. lack of written authorization by the patient.
    D. when medical information is used for research or education.

REFERENCE: Green & Bowie, p 261
               LaTour & Eichenwald-Maki, p 273–274
               Servais, p 52–55
               McWay, p 59–60
               McWay (2003), p 116–121

51. In order to determine which information should be considered confidential, a health information manager should consider and answer yes to all the following questions EXCEPT:
    A. Is there a patient-provider relationship?
    B. Is the information needed to treat or diagnose the patient?
    C. Was the information in question exchanged through the professional relationship?
    D. Is there a need for all health care providers to access the patient information?

Need to Know Basis

REFERENCE: Green & Bowie, p 261
               McWay, p 59–60
               Servais, p 7, 53–55

52. While performing routine quantitative analysis of a record, a medical record employee finds an incident report in the record. The employee brings this to the attention of her supervisor. The supervisor should
    A. remove the incident report and send it to the patient.
    B. tell the employee to leave the report in the record.
    C. remove the incident report and have nursing personnel transfer all documentation from the report to the medical record.
    D. refer this record to the Risk Manager for further review and removal of the incident report.

REFERENCE: Green & Bowie, p 88
               LaTour & Eichenwald-Maki, p 266
               McWay, p 110

TPO - Treatment, Payment, Operations

53. Which of the following agencies is empowered to implement the law governing Medicare and Medicaid?
    A. Centers for Medicare & Medicaid Services (CMS) formerly known as Health Care Financing Administration (HCFA)
    B. Joint Commission
    C. Institutes of Health
    D. Department of Health and Human Services

REFERENCE: Green & Bowie, p 68–69
                LaTour & Eichenwald-Maki, p 346
                McWay, p 50, 69

54. Internal disclosures of patient information for patient care purposes should be granted
    A. to legal counsel.
    B. on a need to know basis.
    C. to any physician on staff.
    D. to a family member who is an employee.

REFERENCE: Green & Bowie, p 124, 126
                LaTour & Eichenwald-Maki, p 257
                McWay, p 62

55. Which of the following acts was passed to stimulate the development of standards to facilitate electronic maintenance and transmission of health information?
    A. Health Insurance for the Aged
    B. Health Insurance Portability and Accountability Act
    C. Conditions of Participation
    D. Hospital Survey and Construction Act

REFERENCE: Green & Bowie, p 11, 312
                LaTour & Eichenwald-Maki, p 250
                McWay, p 360

56. The facility has a policy that states, "Original medical records may be removed from the Medical Record Department jurisdiction only by court order." Which situation would be a violation of the policy?
    A. A physician wishes to have the record sent to the physician lounge in the OR suite for final signatures.
    B. The Risk Manger requests the record for review by physicians at a quality assurance meeting.
    C. A lawyer has subpoenaed the record for deposition.
    D. The physician has been sued and wants to study the original record at home prior to his deposition.

REFERENCE: LaTour & Eichenwald-Maki, p 263
                Green & Bowie, p 260–261, 268

57. Which of the following measures should a health care facility incorporate into its institution-wide security plan to protect the confidentiality of the patient record?
    A. verification of employee identification
    B. locked access to data processing and record areas
    C. use unique computer passwords, key cares, or biometric identification
    D. all of the above

REFERENCE: Green & Bowie, p 272
                LaTour & Eichenwald-Maki, p 263
                Servais, p 42–46

58. The process of comparing the outcomes of HIM abstracting functions at your facility with those of comparable departments of superior performance in other health care facilities to help improve accuracy and quality is referred to as
    A. focused review.
    B. benchmarking.
    C. peer review.
    D. occurrence screening.

REFERENCE: McWay, p. 148
               Abdelhak, p 446–447, 613
               Shaw, p 16
               Johns, p 481
               LaTour and Eichenwald-Maki, p 491, 679

Answer Key for Health Data Content, Requirements, and Standards

ANSWER   EXPLANATION

1. B   (C and D) Although a gross description of tissue removed may be mentioned on the operative note or discharge summary, only the pathology report will contain a microscopic description.

2. B   Answers A, C, and D represent items collected on Medicare inpatients according to UHDDS requirements. Only B represents a data item collected more typically in long-term care settings and required in the MDS.

3. B   Information of a higher sensitivity (e.g., substance abuse, psychiatric treatment, etc.) should be defined in release of information policies and special measures taken to protect against `unauthorized access to this information. In computer-based systems, control is often achieved by limiting access to authorized personnel via ID/passwords.

4. B   Every case entered into the registry is assigned a unique accession number preceded by the accession year, or the year the case is entered into the database.

5. D   (A, B, and C) Patient care plans, pharmacy consultations, and transfer summaries are likely to be found on the records of long-term care patients.

6. A   The antepartum record should include a comprehensive history and physical exam on each OB patient visit with particular attention to menstrual and reproductive history.

7. C   Factual summaries investigating unexpected facility events should not be treated as part of the patient's health information and therefore would not be recorded in the health record.

8. C   Joint Commission and COP allow a legible copy of a recent H&P done in a doctor's office in lieu of an admission H&P as long as interval changes are documented in the record upon admission. In addition, when the patient is readmitted within 30 days for the same or a related problem, an interval history and physical exam may be completed if the original H&P is readily available.

9. A   The major sources of case finding for cancer registry programs are the pathology department, the disease index, and the logs of patients treated in radiology and other outpatient departments. B. The number index identifies new health record numbers and the patients to whom they were assigned. C. The physicians' index identifies all patients treated by each doctor. D. The patient index links each patient treated in a facility with the health number under which the clinical information can be located.

10. D   A and B deal with issues directly linked to quality of care reviews. C deals with risk management. Only D points to a review aimed at evaluating the quality of documentation in the health record.

11. C   A. Some reference to the patient's history can be found in the discharge summary, but not a detailed history. B. The attending physician records the discharge summary. D. Codes are usually recorded on a different form in the record.

12. C   Unlike the acute care hospital where most health care practitioners document separately, the Patient Care Plan is the foundation around which patient care is organized in long-term care facilities because it contains the unique perspective of each discipline involved.

Answer Key for Health Data Content, Requirements, and Standards

ANSWER   EXPLANATION

13. A   Highly sensitive information (e.g. psychiatric records) should be defined as sensitive and special measures should be taken to protect against unauthorized access. In computer-based information systems, control is often achieved by limit of access to authorized personnel through the designated use of ID/passwords or access denial of certain information types.

14. A   Joint Commission specifies that H&Ps must be completed within 24 hours.

15. A   The needs of the end user are always the primary concern when designing systems.

16. B   This entry is typical of a surgical procedure.

17. B   All health record signatures should be identified by a minimum of name and discipline, e.g., "J. Smith, P. T." Other types of authentication other than signature (such as written initials or computer entry) must be uniquely identifiable.

18. C   Answers A, B, & D are required items in BOTH acute and ER records.

19. B   OBRA mandates comprehensive functional assessments of long-term care residents using the Minimum Data Set for Long-term Care.

20. B   A and C. In these situations a transfer summary or pertinent copies from the inpatient health record may accompany the patient, but the original record stays on the premises.

21. B   The medical history, including a review of systems and chief complaint, is information supplied by the patient. A physical assessment adds objective data to the subjective data provided by the patient in the history.

22. A   The medical history, including the chief complaint, a history of present illness, past medical history, personal history, family history, and a review of systems is provided by the patient or the most knowledgeable available source. The physical examination adds objective data to the subjective data provided by the patient. The exam includes all body systems.

23 D   A. represents the assessment statement, B. the objective, and C. the plan.

24. B   The average health record is viewed by approximately 150 end users, yet the paper-based health record can be viewed by only one at a time. In contrast, the EHR can be accessed by multiple users simultaneously in remote locations.

25. C   Biometrics is a type of identifier that measures a borrower's unique physical characteristics, such as fingerprints or a retinal scan, and compares it to a stored digital template to identify the borrower.

26. B   COP requires a consultation report on patients who are not a good surgical risk, as well as those with obscure diagnoses, patients whose physicians have doubts as to the best therapeutic measure to be taken, and patients for whom there is a question of criminal activity.

27. C   Joint Commission standards require the surgeon to document the history and physical examination prior to surgery.

28. D   A. The disease index is a listing in diagnostic code number order. B. The physician index is a listing of cases in order by physician name or number. C. The MPI cross-references the patient name and medical record number.

Answer Key for Health Data Content, Requirements, and Standards

ANSWER   EXPLANATION

29. A   Answers B, C, and D all represent technical methods of protecting computerized data. Additional procedural techniques include developing policies, procedures, and educational training that address confidentiality.

30. C   A. Peer review typically involves quality of care issues rather than quality of documentation issues. D. Legal analysis ensures that the record entries would be acceptable in a court of law.

31. A   B represents an appropriate job for the infection control officer. Answer C represents the clinical care evaluation process, rather than the review of quality documentation. Answer D is a function of the utilization review program.

32. C   This 60-day time frame is often referred to as the patient's certification period. Recertification can continue every 62 days until the patient is discharged from home health services.

33. D   Although the medical staff bylaws reflect general principles and policies of the medical staff, the rules and regulations outline the details for implementing these principles, including the process and time frames for completing records, and the penalties for failure to comply.

34. D   Written signatures, identifiable initials, unique computer codes, and rubber stamp signatures may all be allowed as legitimate means of authenticating an entry. However, the use of codes and stamped signatures MUST be confined to the owners and are never to be used by anyone else.

35. B   Regional health information organizations are intended to support health information exchange within a geographic region.

36. D   A. Advantages of accreditation are numerous and include financial and legal incentives. B. State licensure is required for accreditation, but not the reverse. C. Joint Commission conducts unannounced on-site surveys approximately every 3 years.

37. D   Because information contained in the physicians' index is considered confidential, identification codes are often used rather than the physicians' names.

38. B   In a POMR, the database contains the history and physical; the problem list includes titles, numbers, and dates of problems and serves as a table of contents of the record; the initial plan describes diagnostic, therapeutic, and patient education plans; and the progress notes document the progress of the patient throughout the episode of care, summarized in a discharge summary or transfer note at the end of the stay.

39. D   The manual published by the Commission on Accreditation of Rehabilitation Facilities will have the most specific and comprehensive standards for a rehabilitation facility.

40. A   The disease index is compiled as a result of abstracting patient code numbers into a computer database, allowing a variety of reports to be generated.

41. B   Both paper-based and computer-based records share similar forms and view design considerations. Among these are the selection and sequencing of essential data items

42. A

43. D

44. B

Answer Key for Health Data Content, Requirements, and Standards

ANSWER	EXPLANATION

45. A

46. C

47. A

48. A

49. B

50. B

51. D

52. D The incident or occurrence report should not be treated as part of the patient's record. They are to be used by the risk management department and/or attorneys to investigate incidents that have the potential to become claims against the organization or individual provider. They are also used in the quality improvement process to identify shortcomings and suggesting possible solutions.

53. A

54. B

55. B

56. D

57. D

58. B

REFERENCES

Abdelhak, M., Grostick, S., Hanken, M. A., and Jacobs, E. (Eds.). (2007). *Health information: Management of a strategic resource* (3rd ed.). Philadelphia: W. B. Saunders.

Davis and LaCour. (2007). *Health information technology* (2nd ed.). Maryland, MO: Elsevier (Saunders).

Green, M. A., and Bowie, J. (2006). *Essentials of health information management: Principles and practices.* Clifton Park, NY: Thomson Delmar Learning.

Horton, L. (2010). *Calculating and reporting health care statistics* (3rd ed.) Chicago: American Health Information Management Association (AHIMA).

Johns, M. L. (2006). *Health information management technology: An applied approach* (2nd ed.). Chicago: American Health Information Management Association (AHIMA).

Koch, G. (2008). *Basic allied health statistics and analysis* (3rd ed.). Clifton Park, NY: Thompson Delmar Learning.

LaTour, K., & Eichenwald-Maki, S. (2009). *Health information management: Concepts, principles and practice* (3rd ed.). Chicago: American Health Information Management Association (AHIMA).

McWay, D. C. (2003). *Legal aspects of health information management.* Clifton Park, NY: Thompson Delmar Learning.

McWay, D. C. (2008). *Today's health information management: An integrated approach.* Clifton Park, NY: Thompson Delmar Learning.

Odom-Wesley, B., Brown, D., and Meyers, C. (2009). *Documentation for medical records.* Chicago: American Health Information Management Association (AHIMA).

Peden, A. H. (2005). *Comparative health information management* (2nd ed.). Clifton Park, NY: Thompson Delmar Learning.

Servais, C., Olderman, N. and Trahan, K. (2008) *The legal health record*. Chicago: American Health Information Management Association.

Shaw, P. (2006). *Quality and performance improvement in healthcare: A tool for programmed learning* (3rd ed.). Chicago: American Health Information Management Association (AHIMA)

Competencies for the CCS-P Health Data Chapter

Question	CCS-P Domain						
	1	2	3	4	5	6	7
1	X						
2	X						
3						X	
4	X						
5	X						
6	X						
7	X						
8	X						
9	X						
10					X		
11	X						
12	X						
13							X
14							X
15						X	
16					X		
17	X						
18	X						
19							X
20							X
21	X						
22	X						
23	X						
24						X	
25							X
26	X						
27							X
28						X	
29							X
30					X		
31					X		
32					X		
33							X
34							X
35						X	
36							X

Question	CCS-P Domain						
	1	2	3	4	5	6	7
37						X	
38	X						
39							X
40						X	
41						X	
42							X
43						X	
44						X	
45	X						
46							X
47							X
48							X
49							X
50							X
51							X
52							X
53							X
54							X
55							X
56							X
57							X
58					X		

IV. Medical Science

Patricia Schnering, RHIA, CCS

pernicious anemia

1. The cause of aplastic anemia is
   A. acute blood loss.
   B. bone marrow failure.
   C. chronic blood loss.
   D. inadequate iron intake.

REFERENCE: Jones, p 311
                     Neighbors & Tannehill-Jones, p 117
                     Scott & Fong, p 250

2. The most common cause of dementia in the United States is
   A. autism.
   B. Alzheimer's disease.
   C. alcohol abuse.
   D. anxiety disorder.

REFERENCE: Jones, p 946
                     Neighbors & Tannehill-Jones, p 273

3. Dr. Zambrano ordered a CEA test for Mr. Logan. Dr. Zambrano may be considering a diagnosis of
   A. cancer.
   B. carpal tunnel syndrome.
   C. cardiomyopathy.
   D. congestive heart failure.

Carcino Embryonic Antigen

REFERENCE: Moisio, p 219–220

4. The prevention of illness through vaccination occurs due to the formation of
   A. helper B cells.
   B. immunosurveillance.
   C. mast cells.
   D. memory cells.

REFERENCE: Jones, p 329
                     Scott & Fong, p 338

5. A bee stung little Bobby. He experiences itching, erythema, and respiratory distress caused by laryngeal edema and vascular collapse. In the emergency department, Bobby is diagnosed with
   A. allergic rhinitis.
   B. allergic sinusitis.
   C. anaphylactic shock.
   D. asthma.

REFERENCE: Jones, p 329–330
                     Neighbors & Tannehill-Jones, p 69

6. Genital warts are caused by
   A. HAV.
   B. HIV.
   C. HPV.
   D. VZV.

REFERENCE: Jones, p 663
                     Scott & Fong, p 468

7. A patient's history includes the following documentation:

   - Small ulcers (chancres) appeared on the genitalia and disappeared after 4 to 6 weeks
   - Elevated temperature, skin rash, and enlarged lymph nodes

   Which procedure will be used to initially diagnose the patient?
   A. bone marrow test
   B. chest x-ray
   C. serology test
   D. thyroid scan

REFERENCE: Jones, p 668
                     Moisio, p 114–115
                     Neighbors & Tannehill-Jones, p 329

8. What cells produce histamine in a type I hypersensitivity reaction?
   A. lymphocyte
   B. macrophages
   C. mast cells
   D. neutrophils

REFERENCE: Jones, p 100
               Neighbors & Tannehill-Jones, p 47
               Rizzo, p 104

9. Which one of the following cells produces antibodies?
   A. A cells
   B. cytotoxic T cells
   C. helper T cells
   D. plasma cells

REFERENCE: Neighbors & Tannehill-Jones, p 64
               Rizzo, p 349, 350, 352
               Scott & Fong, p 338

10. Which of the following conditions is NOT a predisposing risk associated with essential hypertension?
    A. age
    B. cigarette smoking
    C. low dietary sodium intake
    D. obesity

REFERENCE: Jones, p 374–375
               Neighbors & Tannehill-Jones, p 134
               Scott & Fong, p 300–301

11. A patient, who is HIV positive, has raised lesions, red or purple in color appearing on the skin, in the mouth, or anywhere on the body. What is the stage of his disease process in today's medical terminology?   *Kaposi Sarcoma*
    A. ARC
    B. AIDS
    C. AZT   *meds*
    D. HIV positive

REFERENCE: Jones, p 660–661
               Neighbors & Tannehill-Jones, p. 78

12. Each of the following pertains to COPD EXCEPT
    A. chronic bronchitis.
    B. emphysema.
    C. pneumonia.
    D. smoking.

REFERENCE: Neighbors & Tannehill-Jones, p 160–161
               Rizzo, p 407
               Scott & Fong, p 368

13. Which of the following is a lethal arrhythmia?
    A. atrial fibrillation
    B. atrial tachycardia
    C. bradycardia
    D. ventricular fibrillation

REFERENCE: Jones, p 382
               Neighbors & Tannehill-Jones, p 144

14. The drug commonly used to treat bipolar mood swings is
    A. Lanoxin.
    B. Lasix.
    C. lithium carbonate.
    D. lorazepam.

REFERENCE: Neighbors & Tannehill-Jones, p 417
               Nobles, p 526
               Woodrow, p 357–358

15. A vision-related pathology that is caused by diabetes is
    A. retinal detachment.
    C. retinopathy.
    B. retinoblastoma.
    D. rhabdomyosarcoma.

REFERENCE: Jones, p 525, 560, 1009
                Neighbors & Tannehill-Jones, p 254–255, 289, 294–295, 300
                Scott & Fong, p 195, 231–232

16. Penicillin is effective in the treatment of all the following diseases EXCEPT
    A. Lordosis.
    C. strep throat.
    B. Lyme disease.
    D. syphilis.

REFERENCE: Jones, 167, 213–214, 418, 664
                Neighbors & Tannehill-Jones, p 89–90, 190, 345, 325
                Rizzo, 459

17. Impetigo can
    A. spread through autoinoculation.
    C. be caused by *Staphlococcus aureus.*
    B. be caused by *Streptococcus.*
    D. either A or B..

REFERENCE: Jones, p, 115, 800, 1069
                Neighbors & Tannehill-Jones, p 344, 393
                Scott & Fong, p 78–79

18. Diagnostic testing for meningitis usually involves
    A. blood cultures.
    C. stool C&S.
    B. cerebrospinal fluid analysis.
    D. testing urine.

    REFERENCE: Jones, p 264
                    Neighbors & Tannehill-Jones, p 266

19. Which disease is a malignancy of the lymphatic system?
    A. cystic fibrosis
    C. neutropenia
    B. Hodgkin's disease
    D. von Willebrand's disease

REFERENCE: Jones, p 333
                Neighbors & Tannehill-Jones, p 114, 119,121, 380
                Rizzo, p 354
                Scott & Fong, p 312

20. Which of the following is a hereditary disease of the cerebral cortex?
    A. Huntington Chorea.
    C. Bell's Palsy.
    B. Lou Gehrig's disease.
    D. Guillain-Barre syndrome.

REFERENCE: Jones, p 390
                Neighbors & Tannehill-Jones, p 280
                Scott & Fong, p 481

21. Which of the following autoimmune diseases affects tissues of the nervous system?
    A. Goodpasture's syndrome
    C. myasthenia gravis
    B. Hashimoto's disease
    D. rheumatoid arthritis

REFERENCE: Jones, p 265–266, 333–334
                Neighbors & Tannehill-Jones, p 72, 107
                Scott & Fong, p 139

22. Pain is a symptom of which of the following conditions?
    A. first-degree burn (superficial)
    B. second-degree burn (partial thickness)
    C. third-degree burn (full thickness)
    D. A and B

REFERENCE: Jones, p 110–111
                Neighbors & Tannehill-Jones, p 356
                Scott & Fong, p 81–82

23. A 75-year-old patient has a sore tongue with tingling and numbness of the hands and feet. She has headaches and is fatigued. Following diagnostic workup, the doctor orders monthly injections of vitamin B12. This patient mostly likely has which of the following conditions?
    A. aplastic anemia   C. pernicious anemia   ← Ins. will pay for this one
    B. autoimmune hemolytic anemia   D. sickle cell anemia

REFERENCE: Jones, p 312
                Neighbors & Tannehill-Jones, p 116
                Scott & Fong, p 250

24. Which one of the following is NOT a pathophysiological factor in anemia?
    A. excessive RBC breakdown   C. loss of bone marrow function
    B. lack of RBC maturation   D. loss of spleen function

REFERENCE: Jones, p 310–312
                Neighbors & Tannehill-Jones, p 116
                Rizzo, p 308
                Scott & Fong, p 250–251

25. Many bacterial diseases are transmitted directly from person to person. Which of the diseases listed below is a bacterial disease that is transmitted by way of a tick vector?
    A. Legionnaires' disease   C. tetanus
    B. Lyme disease   D. tuberculosis

REFERENCE: Jones, p 213–214
                Neighbors & Tannehill-Jones, p 345
                Scott & Fong, p 335

26. Necrosis extending down to the underlying fascia is characteristic of a decubitus ulcer in stage
    A. one.   Skin   C. three. fascia
    B. two.   subcutaneous   D. four.   bone

REFERENCE: Scott & Fong, p 83

27. Scabies, a highly contagious condition that produces intense pruritus and rash, is caused by
    A. head lice.   C. jock itch.
    B. itch mites.   D. ringworm.

REFERENCE: Jones, p 119
                Neighbors & Tannehill-Jones, p 347

28. A physician prescribes a diuretic for his patient. He could be treating any of the following disorders EXCEPT
    A. congestive heart failure.   C. pneumonia.
    B. mitral stenosis.   D. pulmonary edema.

REFERENCE: Neighbors & Tannehill-Jones, p 162
                Scott & Fong, p 274, 366

29. All of the following are examples of direct transmission of a disease EXCEPT
   A. contaminated foods.
   B. coughing or sneezing.
   C. droplet spread.
   D. physical contact.

   REFERENCE: Neighbors & Tannehill-Jones, p 5–6
                  Scott & Fong, p 332–336

30. _Basal cell_ is the most common type of skin cancer and ____malignant____ is the most deadly type of skin cancer?
   A. malignant melanoma, basal cell carcinoma
   B. basal cell carcinoma, malignant melanoma
   C. oat cell carcinoma, squamous cell carcinoma
   D. squamous cell carcinoma, oat cell carcinoma

   REFERENCE: Jones, p 111, 872, 988
                  Neighbors & Tannehill-Jones, p 351
                  Rizzo, p 132
                  Scott & Fong, p 81
                  Sormunen, p 262

31. John Palmer was in a car accident and sustained severe chest trauma resulting in a tension pneumothorax. Manifestations of this disorder include all of the following EXCEPT
   A. severe chest pain.
   B. dyspnea.
   C. shock.
   D. clubbing.

   REFERENCE: Jones, p 422
                  Neighbors & Tannehill-Jones, p 166

32. Cancer derived from epithelial tissue is classified as a(n)
   A. adenoma.
   B. carcinoma.
   C. lipoma.
   D. sarcoma.

   REFERENCE: Jones, p 870
                  Neighbors & Tannehill-Jones, p 26
                  Rizzo, p 90
                  Sormunen, p 262

33. Sex-linked genetic diseases
   A. are transmitted during sexual activity.
   B. involve a defect on a chromosome.
   C. occur equally between males and females.
   D. occur only in males.

   REFERENCE: Neighbors & Tannehill-Jones, p 14
                  Rizzo, p 457
                  Scott & Fong, p 480–485

34. A stapedectomy is a common treatment for   chronic progressive deafness
   A. atherosclerosis. arteriosclerosis
   B. multiple sclerosis.
   C. otosclerosis.
   D. scoliosis.

   REFERENCE: Jones, p 584
                  Neighbors & Tannehill-Jones, p 298
                  Scott & Fong, p 201

35. In systemic circulation which of the following veins carry oxygenated blood?
    A. right vena cava
    B. renal veins
    C. varicose veins
    D. pulmonary veins

REFERENCE: Jones, p 353
                  Neighbors & Tannehill-Jones, p 128
                  Rizzo, p 322, 335
                  Scott & Fong, p 286–287, 295
                  Sormunen, p 188

36. Which of the following sequences correctly depicts the flow of blood through the heart to the lungs?
    A. right atrium, right ventricle, lungs, pulmonary artery
    B. right atrium, right ventricle, pulmonary artery, lungs
    C. right ventricle, right atrium, lungs, pulmonary artery
    D. right ventricle, right atrium, pulmonary artery, lungs

REFERENCE: Jones, p 353–354
                  Neighbors & Tannehill-Jones, p 128
                  Rizzo, p 322, 325
                  Scott & Fong, p 286–288, 295
                  Sormunen, p 188

To expand

37. Diastole occurs when
    A. cardiac insufficiency is present.
    B. the atria contracts.
    C. the ventricles contract.
    D. the ventricles fill.

REFERENCE: Jones, p 357
                  Neighbors & Tannehill-Jones, p 130
                  Rizzo, p 333
                  Scott & Fong, p 295
                  Sormunen, p 189

38. The most fatal type of lung cancer is
    A. adenocarcinoma.
    B. large cell cancer.
    C. small cell cancer.
    D. squamous cell cancer.

REFERENCE: Scott & Fong, p 368–369

39. Gas exchange in the lungs takes place at the
    A. alveoli.
    B. bronchi.
    C. bronchioles.
    D. trachea.

REFERENCE: Neighbors & Tannehill-Jones, p 154
                  Rizzo, 402–404
                  Scott & Fong, p 358
                  Sormunen, p 314

40. Oxygen is carried in the blood
    A. bound to hemoglobin.
    B. in the form of carbonic acid.
    C. plasma.
    D. serum.

REFERENCE: Neighbors & Tannehill-Jones, p 112
                  Rizzo, p 408, 413
                  Sormunen, p 223, 230

41. Which of the following anatomical parts is involved in both the respiratory and digestive systems?
    A. larynx *voice Box*
    B. nasal cavity
    C. pharynx
    D. trachea *throat*

REFERENCE: Rizzo, p 371
                Scott & Fong, p 355–356
                Sormunen, p 313

42. A disease of the ear that causes vertigo is
    A. labyrinthitis.
    B. mastoiditis.
    C. Meniere's disease.
    D. A and C

REFERENCE: Neighbors & Tannehill-Jones, p 300–301
                Scott & Fong, p 201

43. _____ causes of softening of the bone in children.
    A. Raynaud's disease
    B. Reye's syndrome
    C. Rickets
    D. Rubella

REFERENCE: Neighbors & Tannehill-Jones, p 92
                Scott & Fong, p 112
                Rizzo, p 147

44. A pathological diagnosis of transitional cell carcinoma is made. The examined tissue was removed from the
    A. bladder.
    B. esophagus.
    C. oral cavity.
    D. pleura.

REFERENCE: Rizzo, p 102–103
                Neighbors & Tannehill-Jones, p 235

45. Most carbon dioxide is carried in the
    A. blood as CO_2 gas.
    B. blood bound to hemoglobin.
    C. blood plasma in the form of carbonic acid.
    D. red blood cells.

REFERENCE: Scott and Fong, p 243
                Rizzo, p 408, 413
                Sormunen, p 223

46. The key diagnostic finding for typical pneumonia is
    A. abnormal blood electrolytes.
    B. elevated WBC.
    C. lung consolidation x-ray.
    D. positive sputum culture.

REFERENCE: Neighbors & Tannehill-Jones, p 162

47. The presence of fluid in the alveoli of the lungs is characteristic of
    A. COPD.
    B. Crohn's disease.
    C. pneumonia.
    D. tuberculosis.

REFERENCE: Neighbors & Tannehill-Jones, p 163
                Rizzo, p 407

48. Full-blown AIDS sets in as
    A. CD4 receptors increase.
    B. helper T-cell concentration decreases.
    C. HIV virus concentration decreases.
    D. immunity to HIV increases.

REFERENCE: Scott & Fong, p 321–324
                Sormunen, p 239

49. Which of the following BEST describes tuberculosis?
    A. a chronic, systemic disease whose initial infection is in the lungs
    B. an acute bacterial infection of the lung
    C. an ordinary lung infection
    D. a viral infection of the lungs

REFERENCE: Neighbors & Tannehill-Jones, p 49, 392–393
                Scott & Fong, p 366
                Sormunen, p 240, 323

50. Treatments for sensorineural hearing loss include
    A. cochlear implants.   C. removal of impacted cerumen.
    B. myringotomy.   D. stapedectomy.

REFERENCE: Jones, p 580
                Scott & Fong, p 202

51. Mary Mulholland has diabetes. Her physician has told her about some factors that put her more at risk for infections. Which of the following factors would probably NOT be applicable?
    A. hypoxia   C. increased blood supply
    B. increased glucose in body fluids   D. A and C

REFERENCE: Neighbors & Tannehill-Jones, p 253–257

52. Most of the digestion of food and absorption of nutrients occurs in the
    A. ascending colon.   C. small intestine.
    B. esophagus.   D. stomach.

REFERENCE: Neighbors & Tannehill-Jones, p 185
                Rizzo, p 377–378
                Scott & Fong, p 385–386
                Sormunen, p 339, 341

53. The Phalen's wrist flexor test is a noninvasive method for diagnosing
    A. carpal tunnel syndrome.   C. severe acute respiratory syndrome.
    B. Down syndrome.   D. Tourette's syndrome.

REFERENCE: NINDS

54. Ulcerations of the small intestine are characteristic of
    A. appendicitis.   C. diverticulitis.
    B. Crohn's disease.   D. Graves' disease.

REFERENCE: Neighbors & Tannehill-Jones, p 193, 198
                Rizzo, p 381
                Sormunen, p 351

55. The patient's pathology report revealed the presence of Reed-Sternberg cells. This is indicative of
    A. Hodgkin's disease.
    B. leukemia.
    C. non-Hodgkin's lymphoma.
    D. sarcoma.

REFERENCE: Neighbors & Tannehill-Jones, p 119

56. The most common rickettsial disease in the U.S. is   *intracellular parasites (bacteria)*
    A. Hantavirus. *rodents*
    B. Lyme disease. *ticks*
    C. Rocky Mountain spotted fever.
    D. syphilis. *spirochettes/STD*

REFERENCE: Neighbors & Tannehill-Jones, p 57
               Scott & Fung, 331–332

57. Early detection programs apply screening guidelines to detect cancers at an early stage, which provides the likelihood of increased survival and decreased morbidity. Which of the following would NOT be a diagnostic or screening test for colorectal cancer?
    A. double contrast barium enema
    B. sigmoidoscopy
    C. fecal occult blood test
    D. upper GI x-ray

REFERENCE: ACS (1)
               Neighbors & Tannehill-Jones, p 200
               Scott & Fong, p 399

58. Prevention programs identify risk factors and use strategies to modify attitudes and behaviors to reduce the chance of developing cancers. Which of the following would NOT be an identified risk factor for colorectal cancer?
    A. alcohol use
    B. physical inactivity
    C. high-fiber diet
    D. obesity

REFERENCE: ACS (2)

59. In general, excessive RBC breakdown could result in
    A. Crohn's disease.
    B. elevated BUN. *Blood Urea Nitrogen*
    C. high bilirubin levels.
    D. peptic ulcers.

REFERENCE: Neighbors & Tannehill-Jones, p 209
               NLM (2)
               Labtestsonline (1)

60. The most common bloodborne infection in the United States is
    A. Helicobacter pylori.
    B. hepatitis A.
    C. hepatitis C.
    D. hemophilia.

REFERENCE: Scott & Fong, p 397

61. The first stage of alcoholic liver disease is
    A. alcoholic hepatitis.
    B. cirrhosis.
    C. fatty liver.
    D. jaundice.

REFERENCE: Neighbors & Tannehill-Jones, p 211

62. Portal hypertension can contribute to all of the following EXCEPT
    A. ascites. *abnormal accumulation of fluid in peritoneal cavity*
    B. dilation of blood vessels lining the intestinal tract.
    C. esophageal varices. *little swollen veins in esophagus*
    D. kidney failure.

REFERENCE: Mayo Clinic (1)
               Neighbors & Tannehill-Jones, p 211–214

63. Which of the following is a liver function test?
    A. AST (SGOT) *Aspartate amino transferase*   C. ECG   *Electrocardiogram*
    B. BUN *Blood urea Nitrogen*   D. TSH   *Thyroid Stim. Hormone*

REFERENCE: Neighbors & Tannehill-Jones, p 211–214
                Sormunen, p 348–349

64. Which of the following is a risk factor involved in the etiology of gallstones?
    A. being overweight   C. low-fat diets
    B. being an adolescent   D. presence of peptic ulcer

REFERENCE: Rizzo, p 215

65. A serum potassium level of 2.8 would indicate
    A. Addison disease.   C. diabetic ketoacidosis.
    B. anemia.   D. hyperkalemia.   *excessive amt. of potassium in blood*

REFERENCE: Mayo Clinic (2)
                NLM (4)

66. A procedure performed with an instrument that freezes and destroys abnormal tissues (including seborrheic keratoses, basal cell carcinomas, and squamous cell carcinomas) is
    A. cryosurgery.   C. phacoemulsification.
    B. electrodesiccation.   D. photocautery.

REFERENCE: Rizzo, p 81, 469

67. Which of the organs listed below has endocrine and exocrine functions?
    A. kidney   C. lung
    B. liver   D. pancreas

REFERENCE: Neighbors & Tannehill-Jones, p 252
                Rizzo, p 282–283, 274
                Scott & Fong, p 386

68. Which of the following is an effect of insulin?
    A. decreases glycogen concentration in liver
    B. increases blood glucose
    C. increases the breakdown of fats
    D. increases glucose metabolism

REFERENCE: Neighbors & Tannehill-Jones, p 244, 252–256
                Rizzo, p 274–276, 282, 284–285
                Scott & Fong, p 225–226, 233, 504
                Sormunen, p 499

69. The causative organism for severe acute respiratory syndrome (SARS) is a
    A. bacterium.   C. fungus.
    B. coronavirus.   D. retrovirus.

REFERENCE: Neighbors & Tannehill-Jones, p 165
                Scott & Fong, p 366

[handwritten: pertaining to any chromosome other than sex X & Y]

70. Before leaving the hospital, all newborns are screened for an autosomal recessive genetic disorder of defective enzymatic conversion in protein metabolism. With early detection and a protein-restricted diet, brain damage is prevented. This disease is
    A. cystic fibrosis.
    B. hereditary hemochromatosis.
    C. phenylketonuria. *[handwritten: PKU test]*
    D. Tay-Sachs disease.

REFERENCE: Neighbors & Tannehill-Jones, p 378
Scott & Fong, p 481

71. Diabetic microvascular disease occurs *[handwritten: smallest arterioles & venules & capillary networks of the body]*
    A. as a direct result of elevated serum glucose.
    B. as a result of elevated fat in blood.
    C. due to damage to nerve cells.
    D. only in type 1 diabetics.

REFERENCE: Neighbors & Tannehill-Jones, p 254–255
Rizzo, p 284–285
Scott & Fong, p 231–232

72. Older age, obesity, family history of diabetes are all characteristics of
    A. type I diabetes. *[handwritten: juvenile onset]*
    B. type II diabetes.
    C. type III diabetes.
    D. type IV diabetes. *[handwritten: not exist]*

REFERENCE: Rizzo, p 284–285
Scott & Fong, p 232

73. An elevated serum amylase would be characteristic of
    A. acute pancreatitis.
    B. gallbladder disease.
    C. post renal failure.
    D. pre renal failure.

REFERENCE: Neighbors & Tannehill-Jones, p 219

74. Clinical manifestations of this disease include polydipsia, polyuria, weight loss, and hyperglycemia. Which of the following tests would be ordered to confirm the disease? *[handwritten: excessive thirst excessive urination]*
    A. fasting blood sugar
    B. glucagon
    C. glucose tolerance test
    D. postprandial blood sugar

REFERENCE: Neighbors & Tannehill-Jones, p 253–254
Rizzo, p 84–85
Scott & Fong, p 231, 235

75. Common kidney stone treatments that allow small particles to be flushed out of the body through the urinary system include all of the following EXCEPT
    A. extracorporeal shock wave lithotripsy.
    B. fluid hydration.
    C. ureteroscopy and stone basketing.
    D. using medication to dissolve the stone(s).

REFERENCE: Neighbors & Tannehill-Jones, p 229

76. When a decubitus ulcer has progressed to a stage in which osteomyelitis is present, the ulcer has extended to the
    A. bone.
    B. fascia.
    C. muscle.
    D. subcutaneous tissue.

REFERENCE: Neighbors & Tannehill-Jones, p 92–93
Scott & Fong, p 83–84

77. The patient has no visible bleeding, but remains anemic. Her physician is concerned about possible gastrointestinal bleeding. Which of the following tests might be ordered?
    A. DEXA scan
    B. guaiac smear test
    C. Pap smear test
    D. prostatic-specific antigen test

    REFERENCE: Estridge & Reynolds, p 694–695
                   Sormunen, p 37

78. Which of the following tests is NOT part of a liver panel?
    A. albumin
    B. alkaline phosphatase
    C. bilirubin
    D. creatinine

    REFERENCE: Estridge & Reynolds, p 519–520

79. Maria Giovanni is in the hospital recovering from surgery. Based on her symptoms, her doctors are concerned about the possibility that she has developed a pulmonary embolism. Which of the following procedures will provide the definitive diagnosis?
    A. chest x-ray
    B. lung scan
    C. pulmonary angiography
    D. none of the above

    REFERENCE: Neighbors & Tannehill-Jones, p 168
                   Scott & Fong, p 369

80. A condition that involves the fifth cranial nerve, also known as "tic douloureux," causes intense pain in either the eye and forehead; lower lip, the section of the cheek closest to the ear, and the outer segment of the tongue; or the upper lip, nose, and cheek.
    A. Bell palsy
    B. thrush
    C. trigeminal neuralgia
    D. Tourette disorder

    REFERENCE: Jones, p 272
                   Scott & Fong, p 182

81. Which of the following is a congenital condition that is the most severe neural tube defect?
    A. meningocele
    B. myelomeningocele
    C. severe combined immunodeficiency
    D. spina bifida occulta

    REFERENCE: Neighbors & Tannehill-Jones, p 374

82. Which of the following tubes conveys sperm from the seminal vesicle to the urethra?
    A. ejaculatory duct
    B. epididymis
    C. oviduct
    D. vas deferens

    REFERENCE: Neighbors & Tannehill-Jones, p 481
                   Rizzo, p 444

83. The most common type of vaginitis is
    A. yeast.
    B. protozoan.
    C. viral.
    D. A & B.

    REFERENCE: Neighbors & Tannehill-Jones, p 315

84. The childhood viral disease that unvaccinated pregnant women should avoid because it may be passed to the fetus, causing congenital anomalies such as mental retardation, blindness, and deafness, is
    A. rickets.
    B. rubeola.
    C. rubella.
    A. tetanus.

    REFERENCE: Neighbors & Tannehill-Jones, p 389

85. In _____ anemia the red blood cells become shaped like elongated, crescents in the presence of low oxygen concentration.
   A. aplastic
   B. folic acid
   C. sickle cell
   D. vitamin B_{12}

REFERENCE: Jones, p 312
                Rizzo, p 308
                Scott & Fong, p 250–251

86. _____ is usually the first symptom of benign prostate hyperplasia.
   A. Abdominal pain
   B. Burning pain during urination
   C. Difficulty in urinating
   D. Pelvic pain

REFERENCE: Neighbors & Tannehill-Jones, p 322–324
                Rizzo, 444
                Scott & Fong, p 467–468

87. The hypothalamus, thalamus, and pituitary gland are all parts of the
   A. brainstem.
   B. cerebellum.
   C. exocrine system.
   D. limbic system.

REFERENCE: Rizzo, p 157–158

88. Which of the following BEST summarizes the current treatment of cervical cancer?
   A. A new three-shot vaccination series protects against the types of HPV that cause most cervical cancer cases.
   B. All stages have extremely high cure rates.
   C. Early detection and treatment of cervical cancer does not improve patient survival rates.
   D. Over 99 percent of cases are linked to long-term HPV infections.

REFERENCE: CDC (1)

89. Children at higher risk for sudden infant death syndrome (SIDS) include those
   A. with sleep apnea.
   B. with respiratory problems
   C. who are premature infants.
   D. all of the above

REFERENCE: Jones, p 423, 809
                Neighbors & Tannehill-Jones, p 395
                Scott & Fong, p 369

90. Decrease in blood pressure, salivation, and heart rate are examples of
   A. automatic nervous system responses.
   B. higher brain function.
   C. parasympathetic nervous system responses.
   D. sympathetic nervous system responses.

parasympath. helps sympathetic

REFERENCE: Jones, p 235, 247
                Rizzo, p 227, 251
                Scott & Fong, p 177–179
                Sormunen, p 530

91. Photophobia or visual aura preceding a headache is characteristic of
   A. malnutrition.
   B. mastitis.
   C. migraines.
   D. myasthenia gravis.

REFERENCE: Jones, p 259–260
                Neighbors & Tannehill-Jones, 271
                Scott & Fong, p 163

92. Graves' disease
    A. is an autoimmune disease.
    B. most commonly affects males.
    C. usually cannot be treated.
    D. usually affects the elderly.

REFERENCE: Jones, p 517–518
                Neighbors & Tannehill-Jones, p 248
                Rizzo, p 280, 285
                Scott & Fong, p 228

93. "Pill-rolling" tremor is a characteristic symptom of
    A. epilepsy.
    B. Guillain-Barre syndrome.
    C. myasthenia gravis.
    D. Parkinson disease.

REFERENCE: Jones, p 267
                Neighbors & Tannehill-Jones, p 281
                Scott & Fong, p 162–164

94. Rheumatoid arthritis typically affects the
    A. intervertebral disks.
    B. hips and shoulders.
    C. knees and small joints of the hands and feet.
    D. large, weight-bearing joints.

REFERENCE: Jones, p 215
                Neighbors & Tannehill-Jones, p 71–72, 94–95
                Rizzo, p 183
                Scott & Fong, p 110–111

95. Henry experienced sudden sharp chest pain that he described as heavy and crushing. His pain and past medical history caused Dr. James to suspect that Henry was having a myocardial infarction. Which of the following tests is a more specific marker for a MI?
    A. AST *Aspartate Aminotransferase*
    B. CK-MB
       Creatinine Kinase – minimal brain ?
    C. LDH1
    D. troponin I   *(3 levels)*

REFERENCE: labtestsonline (2)

96. Bone mineral density (BMD) is a useful diagnostic test for
    A. osteoarthritis.
    B. osteomyelitis.
    C. osteoporosis.
    D. rheumatoid arthritis.

REFERENCE: Jones, p 173
                Neighbors & Tannehill-Jones, p 90–92
                Scott & Fong, p 113

97. A patient is on Coumadin therapy. Which of the following tests is commonly ordered to monitor the patient's Coumadin levels?
    A. bleeding time
    B. blood smear
    C. partial thromboplastin time
    D. prothrombin time
       clotting time

REFERENCE: Jones, p 318
                Labtestsonline (3)
                Neighbors & Tannehill-Jones, p 235

98. A toxic goiter has what distinguishing characteristic?
    A. iodine deficiency *causes*
    B. parathyroid involvement
    C. presence of muscle spasm
    D. thyroid hyperfunction

REFERENCE: Neighbors & Tannehill-Jones, p 247–248
                Rizzo, p 280
                Sormunen, p 511

99. How can Graves' disease be treated?
   A. antithyroid drugs
   B. radioactive iodine therapy
   C. surgery
   D. all of the above

REFERENCE: Jones, p 517
             Neighbors & Tannehill-Jones, p 247–248
             Rizzo, p 285
             Sormunen, p 511

100. Fractures occur in patients with osteoporosis due to
   A. falling from loss of balance.
   B. fibrous joint adhesions tearing apart small bones.
   C. loss of bone mass.
   D. tendency to fall from lack of joint mobility.

REFERENCE: Jones, p 163
             Neighbors & Tannehill-Jones, p 90–92
             Scott & Fong, p 113

101. United States health care providers are concerned about a possible pandemic of avian flu because
   A. there is no vaccine currently available.
   B. it is caused by a group of viruses that mutate very easily.
   C. the causative virus is being spread around the world by migratory birds.
   D. all of the above

REFERENCE: CDC (2)

102. A sweat test was done on a patient with the following symptoms: frequent respiratory infections, chronic cough, and foul-smelling bloody stools. Which of the following diseases is probably suspected?
   A. cystic breast disease
   B. cystic fibrosis
   C. cystic lung disease
   D. cystic pancreas

REFERENCE: Neighbors & Tannehill-Jones, p 380

103. Margaret Vargas needs to have her mitral valve replaced. Her surgeon will discuss which of the following issues with her before the surgery?
   A. A mechanical valve will require that she take a "blood thinner" for the rest of her life.
   B. A biological valve (usually porcine) will last 10 to 15 years.
   C. A mechanical valve increases the risk of blood clots that can cause stroke.
   D. all of the above

REFERENCE: NHLBI

104. Cervical cerclage is a procedure used to help prevent
   A. breathing restrictions.
   B. miscarriage.
   C. torsion. *twisting*
   D. torticollis. *Stiff neck - spasms*

REFERENCE: Jones, p 746

105. Sam Spade has been injured in a MVA. The organ in his body, situated at the upper left of his abdominal cavity, under the ribs, that is part of his lymphatic system has been ruptured and he is bleeding internally. Sam needs a surgical procedure known as a

A. sequestrectomy.
B. sialoadenectomy.
C. sigmoidoscopy.
D. splenectomy.

REFERENCE: Jones, p 324
               Rizzo, p 346
               Sormunen, p 229, 242

106. Henrietta Dawson presents with a chief complaint of pain and weakness in her arms and neck. After an H&P and review of diagnostic tests that include a myelogram, her doctor diagnoses a herniated nucleus pulposus at the _____ level of her spine.

A. cervical
B. lumbar
C. sacral
D. thoracic

REFERENCE: Jones, p 64, 149, 213, 261,
               Neighbors & Tannehill-Jones, p 103
               Rizzo, p157, 170
               Scott & Fong, p 99, 112
               Sormunen, p 119, 120, 135

107. Ingrid Anderson presents with a skin infection that began as a raised itchy bump, resembling an insect bite. Within 1 to 2 days it developed into a vesicle. Now it is a painless ulcer, about 2 cm in diameter, with a black necrotic area in the center. During the history, her doctor learns that she has recently returned from an overseas vacation and becomes concerned that she may have become infected with anthrax. He will prescribe an

A. antibiotic.
B. antineoplastic.   cancer
C. antiparasitic.
D. antiviral.

REFERENCE: Scott & Fong, p 342, 366–367

108. Etiologies of dementia include

A. brain tumors.
B. ischemia.
C. trauma.
D. all of the above.

REFERENCE: Neighbors & Tannehill-Jones, p 414
               Rizzo, p 937, 946
               Scott & Fong, p 164
               Sormunen, p 539

109. Carpal tunnel syndrome is caused by entrapment of the

A. medial nerve.
B. radial nerve.
C. tibial nerve.
D. ulnar nerve.

REFERENCE: Jones, 254,
               Neighbors & Tannehill-Jones, p 104
               Rizzo, p 182
               Sormunen, p 134

110. The organism transmitted by a mosquito bite that causes malaria is a
    A. bacteria.
    C. protozoa.
    B. prion.
    D. virus.

REFERENCE: Neighbors & Tannehill-Jones, p 54–55, 57
              Rizzo, p 309
              Scott & Fong, p 309

111. Contributing factors of mental disorders include
    A. heredity.
    C. trauma.
    B. stress.
    D. all of the above.

REFERENCE: Jones, p 933
              Neighbors & Tannehill-Jones, p 408

Answer Key for Medical Science

1.	B	49.	A	97.	D
2.	B	50.	A	98.	D
3.	A	51.	C	99.	D
4.	D	52.	C	100.	C
5.	C	53.	A	101.	D
6.	C	54.	B	102.	B
7.	C	55.	A	103.	D
8.	C	56.	C	104.	B
9.	D	57.	D	105.	D
10.	C	58.	C	106.	A
11.	B	59.	C	107.	A
12.	C	60.	C	108.	D
13.	D	61.	C	109.	A
14.	C	62.	D	110.	C
15.	C	63.	A	111.	D
16.	A	64.	A		
17.	D	65.	D		
18.	B	66.	A		
19.	B	67.	D		
20.	A	68.	D		
21.	C	69.	B		
22.	D	70.	C		
23.	C	71.	A		
24.	D	72.	B		
25.	B	73.	A		
26.	C	74.	C		
27.	B	75.	C		
28.	C	76.	A		
29.	A	77.	B		
30.	B	78.	D		
31.	D	79.	C		
32.	B	80.	C		
33.	B	81.	B		
34.	C	82.	A		
35.	D	83.	D		
36.	B	84.	C		
37.	D	85.	C		
38.	C	86.	C		
39.	A	87.	D		
40.	A	88.	A		
41.	C	89.	D		
42.	D	90.	C		
43.	C	91.	C		
44.	A	92.	A		
45.	D	93.	D		
46.	C	94.	C		
47.	C	95.	D		
48.	B	96.	C		

REFERENCES

American Cancer Society (ACS). http://www.cancer.org (accessed 9/29/09)

> ACS (1).
> http://www.cancer.org/docroot/CRI/content/CRI_2_4_3X_Can_colon_and_rectum_cancer_be_found_early.asp?rnav=cri (accessed 9/29/09)

> ACS (2).
> http://www.cancer.org/docroot/CRI/content/CRI_2_4_2X_What_are_the_risk_factors_for_colon_and_rectum_cancer.asp?rnav=cri(accessed 9/29/09)

American Medical Association. (2003) *Complete medical encyclopedia.* Chicago: American Medical Association (AHIMA).

Centers for Disease Control and Prevention (CDC). http://www.cdc.gov/index.htm

> CDC (1)
> http://www.cdc.gov/std/Hpv/STDFact-HPV-vaccine-young-women.htm#why (accessed 9/29/09)

> CDC (2)
> http://www.cdc.gov/flu/avian/gen-info/pdf/avian_facts.pdf (accessed 9/29/09)

Damjanov, I. (2006). *Pathology for the health professions.* (3rd ed.). Philadelphia: W. B. Saunders.

Estridge, B. H. and Reynolds, A. P., (2008). *Basic Clinical Laboratory Techniques).* Clifton Park, NY: Delmar Cengage Learning.

Jones, B.D. (2008). *Comprehensive medical terminology. (3rd ed.).* Clifton Park, NY. Delmar Cengage Learning.

Labtestsonline. http://www.labtestsonline.org

> Labtestsonline (1).
> http://www.labtestsonline.org/understanding/analytes/bilirubin/glance.html (accessed 9/29/09)

> Labtestsonline (2).
> http://www.labtestsonline.org/understanding/analytes/troponin/related.html (accessed 9/29/09)

> Labtestsonline (3).
> http://www.labtestsonline.org/understanding/analytes/pt/test.html (accessed 9/29/09)

Mayo Clinic. http://www.mayoclinic.com
> Mayo Clinic (1).
> http://www.mayoclinic.com/print/esophageal-varices/DS00820/ (accessed 9/29/09)
> Mayo Clinic (2).
> http://www.mayoclinic.com/health/diabetic-ketoacidosis/DS00674 (accessed 10-10-09)

The Merck manual of diagnosis and therapy. (18th ed.) (2007). Rahway, NJ: Merck.

Mosby's medical, nursing, & allied health dictionary. (8th ed.). (2009). St. Louis, MO:. Elsevier

NHLBI—National Heart Lung and Blood Institute. http://www.nhlbi.nih.gov
http://www.nhlbi.nih.gov/health/dci/Diseases/hvd/hvd_treatments.html (accessed 10/7/09)

NINDS—National Institute of Neurological Disorders and Stroke.
http://www.ninds.nih.gov/disorders/carpal_tunnel/detail_carpal_tunnel.htm(Accessed 10/10/09)

National Library of Medicine. http://www.nlm.nih.gov/medlineplus/
NLM (1).
http://www.nlm.nih.gov/medlineplus/ency/article/000433.htm (accessed 10/6/09)
NLM (2).
http://www.nhlbi.nih.gov/health/dci/Diseases/ha/ha_diagnosis.html (accessed 9/29/09)
http://www.nlm.nih.gov/medlineplus/ency/article/003479.htm (accessed 9/29/09)
NLM (3).
http://www.nlm.nih.gov/medlineplus/ency/article/003652.htm (accessed 9/29/09)
NLM (4)
http://www.nlm.nih.gov/medlineplus/ency/article/003498.htm (accessed 9/29/09)

Nobles, S. *Delmar's drug reference for health care professionals.* (2002). Clifton Park, NY: Delmar Cengage Learning.

Scott, A. S., & Fong, P E. (2009). *Body structures and functions* (11th ed.) Clifton Park, NY: Delmar Cengage Learning.

Sormunen, C. (2003). *Terminology for allied health professionals* (5th ed.) Clifton Park, NY: Delmar Cengage Learning.

Woodrow, R. (2007). *Essentials of pharmacology for health occupations* (5th ed.). Clifton Park, NY: Delmar Cengage Learning.

Medical Sciences Competencies

Question	CCS-P Domain						
	1	2	3	4	5	6	7
ALL	111						

V. Classification Systems and Secondary Data Sources

Lisa M. Delhomme, MHA, RHIA

1. Robert Thompson was seen in the outpatient department with a chronic cough and the record states "rule out lung cancer." What should be coded as the patient's diagnosis?
   A. chronic cough
   B. observation and evaluation without need for further medical care
   C. diagnosis of unknown etiology
   D. lung cancer

REFERENCE: Frisch, p 134
Green, p 206
Hazelwood and Venable, p 4–5
Johnson and McHugh, p 31
Schraffenberger (2010), p 599

2. Which of the following is a valid ICD-9-CM principal diagnosis code?
   A. V27.2   Outcome of delivery, twins, both live born
   B. V30.00   Single live born, born in hospital   *Goes on babies/infan*
   C. E867   Accidental poisoning by gas distributed by pipeline   *External cause*
   D. M9010/0   Fibroadenoma, NOS

REFERENCE: Frisch, p 150–151
Green, p 174
Johnson and McHugh, 16, 45, 60
Brown, p 270–272, 314, 375–376, 401

3. A physician performed an outpatient surgical procedure on the eye orbit of a Medicare patient. Upon searching the CPT codes and consulting with the physician, the coder is unable to find a code for the procedure. The coder should assign
   A. an unlisted Evaluation and Management code from the E/M section.
   B. an unlisted procedure code located in the eye and ocular adnexa section.   *Send documentation*
   C. a HCPCS Level II (alphanumeric) code.
   D. an ophthalmologic treatment service code.

REFERENCE: AMA (2010), p 53–54
Green, p 304, 430
Frisch, p 254
Smith, p 23

4. A system of preferred terminology for naming disease processes is known as a
   A. set of categories.
   B. classification system.
   C. medical nomenclature.
   D. diagnosis listing.

REFERENCE: Green, p 10
Green and Bowie, p 294
McWay, p 125–128
Abdelhak, p 201
Johns, p 194
LaTour and Eichenwald-Maki, p 348, 192

meclizine hydrochloride antihistamine

5. A patient who is taking the drug Antivert may have a diagnosis of
   A. dizziness.
   B. urinary tract infection.
   C. arthritis.
   D. congestive heart failure.

REFERENCE: Nobles, p 543

6. Which of the following classification systems was designed with computer systems in mind and is currently being used for medical research studies, clinical trials, disease surveillance, and consumer health information services?
   A. SNOMED CT
   B. SNDO
   C. ICDPC-2
   D. GEM

REFERENCE: Abdelhak, p 204–205
               LaTour and Eichenwald-Maki, p 356–357
               McWay, p 127

7. In reviewing the medical record of a patient admitted for a left herniorrhaphy, the coder discovers an extremely low potassium level on the laboratory report. In examining the physician's orders, the coder notices that intravenous potassium was ordered. The physician has not listed any indication of an abnormal potassium level or any related condition on the discharge summary. The best course of action for the coder to take is to
   A. confer with the physician and ask him or her to list the condition as a final diagnosis if he or she considers the abnormal potassium level to be clinically significant.
   B. code the record as is.
   C. code the condition as an abnormal blood chemistry.
   D. code the abnormal potassium level as a complication following surgery.

REFERENCE: Bowie and Shaffer (2010), p 67
               Green, p 209
               Johnson and McHugh, p 31, 578
               Brown, p 33

8. The patient is diagnosed with congestive heart failure. A drug of choice is
   A. ibuprofen.   C. haloperidol.
   B. oxytocin.   D. digoxin.

REFERENCE: Nobles, p 329

9. The local safety council requests statistics on the number of head injuries occurring as a result of skateboarding accidents during the last year. To retrieve this data, you will need to have the correct
   A. CPT code.
   B. Standard Nomenclature of Injuries codes.
   C. E-codes and ICD-9-CM codes.
   D. HCPCS Level II codes.

REFERENCE: Bowie and Shaffer (2010), p 346–351
               Frisch, p 150–151
               Green, p 186
               Johnson and McHugh, p 16, 60–63
               McWay, p 130
               Brown, p 399–400
               Schraffenberger, (2010), p 302

10. The Unified Medical Language System (UMLS) is a project sponsored by the
    A. National Library of Medicine.
    B. CMS.
    C. World Health Organization.
    D. Office of the Inspector General.

REFERENCE: Green and Bowie, p 296
               Johns, p 228–229
               LaTour and Eichenwald-Maki, p 364
               McWay, p 127

11. The use of radioactive sources placed into a tumor-bearing area to generate high intensity radiation is termed
    A. stereotactic radiation treatment.
    B. proton beam treatment.
    C. brachytherapy.
    D. external beam radiation.

REFERENCE: Bowie and Shaffer (2008), p 328
               Johnson and McHugh, p 392–393
               Smith, p 155–156

12. In general, all three key components (history, physical examination, and medical decision making) for the E/M codes in CPT should be met or exceeded when
    A. the patient is established.
    B. a new patient is seen in the office.
    C. the patient is given subsequent care in the hospital.
    D. the patient is seen for a follow-up inpatient consultation. *No such thing*

REFERENCE: AMA (2010), p 10
               Bowie and Shaffer (2008), p 36–50
               Green, p 341–342
               Johnson and McHugh, p 126–127

13. A direction to "code first underlying disease" should be considered
    A. only when coding inpatient records.
    B. a mandatory instruction.
    C. mandatory dependent upon the code selection.
    D. a suggestion only.

REFERENCE: Bowie and Shaffer (2010), p 46–47
               Frisch, p 130
               Green, p 80, 101
               Brown, p 18–19
               Schraffenberger (2010), p 23
               Hazelwood and Venable, p 22

14. According to the UHDDS, a procedure that is surgical in nature, carries a procedural or anesthetic risk, or requires special training is defined as a
    A. principal procedure. *relates to diagnosis*
    B. significant procedure.
    C. operating room procedure. *probably*
    D. therapeutic procedure. *aren't cound*

REFERENCE: Brown, p 65
               Green, p 111
               Johnson and McHugh, p 573–574
               Schraffenberger, (2010), p 44–45

15. The "cooperating party" responsible for maintaining the ICD-9-CM disease classification is the
    A. Centers for Medicare and Medicaid Services (CMS).
    B. National Center for Health Statistics (NCHS).
    C. American Hospital Association (AHA).
    D. American Health Information Management Association (AHIMA).

REFERENCE: Green, p 35
               Johns, p 197
               Johnson and McHugh, p 12
               LaTour and Eichenwald-Maki, p 349

16. An encoder that prompts the coder to answer a series of questions and choices based on the documentation in the medical record is called a(n)
    A. logic-based encoder.   C. grouper.
    B. automated codebook.   D. automatic code assignment.

REFERENCE: McWay, p 132
               LaTour and Eichenwald-Maki, p 400

17. Prolonged pregnancy is a pregnancy that has advanced beyond _____ completed weeks of gestation.
    A. 39   C. 41
    B. 40 normal gestation period   D. 42   p 476

REFERENCE: Hazelwood and Venable, p 205–206
               Schraffenberger (2010), p 209

18. Jane Moore was admitted to the ambulatory care unit of the hospital for a planned cholecystectomy for cholelithiasis. Shortly before surgery, Jane developed tachycardia, and the surgery was canceled. After a thorough workup for the tachycardia, Jane was discharged. This outpatient admission should be coded in the following sequence:

    A. V code for canceled surgery, tachycardia, cholelithiasis.
    B. tachycardia, V code for canceled surgery, cholelithiasis.
    C. cholelithiasis, V code for canceled surgery.
    D. cholelithiasis, V code for canceled surgery, tachycardia.

REFERENCE: Bowie and Shaffer (2010), p 363
               Brown, p 72–73
               Green, p 108–109
               Schraffenberger (2010), p 40–41

19. A patient has a total abdominal hysterectomy with bilateral salpingectomy. The coder selected the following codes:

> 58150 Total abdominal hysterectomy (corpus and cervix), with or without removal of tube(s) with or without removal of ovary(s)
>
> 58700 Salpingectomy, complete or partial unilateral or bilateral (separate procedure)

is included in the procedure

This type of coding is referred to as
A. upcoding.
B. unbundling.
C. maximizing.
D. optimization.

REFERENCE: Bowie and Schaffer (2008), p 92–93
Frisch, p 235–240, 341
Green, p 13
Johnson and McHugh, p 559
McWay, p 67, 356
Smith, p 52–53

20. Code 402, Hypertensive Heart Disease, would appropriately be used in which of the following situations?
A. left heart failure with benign hypertension
B. congestive heart failure; hypertension
C. hypertensive cardiovascular disease with congestive heart failure
D. cardiomegaly with hypertension

REFERENCE: Bowie and Schaffer (2010), p 189–190
Brown, p 347
Frisch, p 146–147
Green, p 141
Hazelwood and Venable, p 147–148
Johnson and McHugh, p 279–280
Schraffenberger (2010), p 141–142

21. Your physician had a patient admitted to the hospital 6 weeks post myocardial infarction with severe chest pains. Which is the correct code?
A. 414.8 chronic MI *@ symptoms after 8wks of MI*
B. 410.1x acute MI *8wks or less*
C. 412 old MI
D. 413.0 angina

REFERENCE: Bowie and Schaffer (2010), p 193–194
Brown, p 333–334
Hazelwood and Venable, p 149–151
Johnson and McHugh, p 38–39
Schraffenberger (2010), p 145–148

22. Which of the following is classified as a poisoning in ICD-9-CM?
    A. syncope due to Contac pills and a three martini lunch
    B. digitalis intoxication
    C. reaction to dye administered for pyelogram
    D. idiosyncratic reaction between various drugs

REFERENCE: Bowie and Schaffer (2010), p 193–194
               Brown, p 333–334
               Hazelwood and Venable, p 149–151
               Johnson and McHugh, p 38–39
               Schraffenberger (2010), p 145–148

23. Susan Dawn is status post mastectomy (6 weeks) due to carcinoma of the breast. She is admitted to the outpatient clinic for chemotherapy. What is the correct sequencing of the codes?
    A. V58.11   chemotherapy; 174.9 malignant neoplasm of breast
    B. V58.11   chemotherapy; V10.3 personal history of neoplasm of the breast
    C. V67.00   follow-up exam after surgery; V58.11 chemotherapy
    D. V10.3   personal history of neoplasm of the breast; V58.11 chemotherapy

REFERENCE: Bowie and Schaffer (2010), p 117–118
               Brown, p 388
               Frisch, p 153
               Green, p 129
               Hazelwood and Venable, p 90–91
               Johnson and McHugh, p 56–57
               Schraffenberger (2010), p 81–82

24. Which of the following is coded as an adverse effect in ICD-9-CM?
    A. mental retardation due to intracranial abscess   *late effect*
    B. rejection of transplanted kidney   *complication*
    C. tinnitus due to allergic reaction after administration of eardrops   *adverse effect*
    D. nonfunctioning pacemaker due to defective soldering   *mechanical complication*

REFERENCE: Bowie and Schaffer (2010), p 326–327, 347–349, 599
               Brown, p 435
               Frisch, p 149–150
               Green, p 165–167, 170
               Hazelwood and Venable, p 262–263
               Johnson and McHugh, p 70
               Schraffenberger (2010), p 284–286

25. A service provided by a physician whose opinion or advice regarding evaluation and/or management of a specific problem is requested by another physician is referred to as
    A. a referral.   C. risk factor intervention.
    B. a consultation.   D. concurrent care.

REFERENCE: AMA (2010), p 16–17
               Bowie and Shaffer (2008), p 56–57
               Frisch, p 77
               Green, p 353–364
               Johnson and McHugh, p 165–168, 595
               Smith, p 189

medicare does not recognize consultations as of 2010

26. A patient with leukemia is admitted for chemotherapy 5 weeks after experiencing an acute myocardial infarction. How will the MI be coded?
    A. acute MI with 5th digit 1—initial episode of care
    B. acute MI with 5th digit 2—subsequent episode of care *pg 369 ICD-9*
    C. history of MI
    D. chronic MI

REFERENCE: Bowie and Schaffer (2010), p 193–194
                      Brown, p 333–334
                      Hazelwood and Venable, p 149–151
                      Johnson and McHugh, p 38–39
                      Schraffenberger (2010), p 145–148

27. The most widely discussed and debated unique patient identifier is the
    A. patient's date of birth.
    B. patient's first and last names.
    C. patient's Social Security number.
    D. Unique Physician Identification Number (UPIN).

REFERENCE: LaTour and Eichenwald-Maki, p 179–180

28. The Central Office on ICD-9-CM, which publishes *Coding Clinic,* is maintained by the
    A. National Center for Health Statistics.
    B. Centers for Medicare and Medicaid Services. *Hospital uses*
    C. American Hospital Association.
    D. American Health Information Management Association.

REFERENCE: Johnson and McHugh, p 12
                      Schraffenberger (2007), p 13

29. A nomenclature of codes and medical terms that provides standard terminology for reporting physicians' services for third-party reimbursement is
    A. Current Medical Information and Terminology (CMIT).
    B. Current Procedural Terminology (CPT).
    C. Systematized Nomenclature of Pathology (SNOP).
    D. Diagnostic and Statistical Manual of Mental Disorders (DSM).

REFERENCE: Bowie and Schaffer (2008), 1–2, 6–7
                      Frisch, p 5
                      Green, p 10
                      Johnson and McHugh, p 103
                      Schraffenberger (2007), p 8–9

30. The Level II (national) codes of the HCPCS coding system are maintained by the
    A. American Medical Association.
    B. CPT Editorial Panel.
    C. local fiscal intermediary.
    D. Centers for Medicare and Medicaid Services.

REFERENCE: Bowie and Schaffer (2008), p 6–7
                      Green and Bowie, p 24
                      Johnson and McHugh, p 85–86

31. A patient is admitted in alcohol withdrawal suffering from delirium tremens. The patient is a chronic alcoholic and cocaine addict. Which of the following is the principal diagnosis?
    A. alcoholic withdrawal
    B. chronic alcoholism #2
    C. cocaine dependence
    D. delirium tremens #1

REFERENCE: Bowie and Schaffer (2010), p 155–158
               Brown, p 143–144
               Frisch, p 132
               Schraffenberger (2010), p 120–121

32. The Level I (CPT) codes of the HCPCS coding system are maintained by the
    A. American Medical Association.   wrote
    B. American Hospital Association.
    C. local fiscal intermediary.
    D. Centers for Medicare and Medicaid Services.

REFERENCE: Bowie and Schaffer (2008), p 1–2, 6
               Frisch, p 5
               Green, p 10
               Green and Bowie, p 24, 297–298
               Johnson and McHugh, p 103–104
               McWay, p 127–130

33. A physician excises a 3.1 cm malignant lesion of the scalp which requires full-thickness graft from the thigh to the scalp. In CPT, which of the following procedures should be coded?
    A. full-thickness skin graft to scalp only
    B. excision of lesion; full-thickness skin graft to scalp
    C. excision of lesion; full-thickness skin graft to scalp; excision of skin from thigh
    D. code 15004 for surgical preparation of recipient site; full-thickness skin graft to scalp

REFERENCE: AMA, CPT Assistant, vol. 7, no. 9, Sept. 1997, p 1–3
               Green, p 446–447
               Johnson and McHugh, p 224, 229–230
               Smith, p 55–57, 65–67

34. A patient is seen by a surgeon who determines that an emergency procedure is necessary. Identify the modifier that may be reported to indicate that the decision to do surgery was made on this office visit.
    A. -25   B. -55   C. -57   D. -58

REFERENCE: AMA (2010), p 530
               Bowie and Schaffer (2008), p 18
               Frisch, p 18–19
               Green, p 310
               Smith, p 186

35. A patient develops difficulty during surgery and the physician discontinues the procedure. Identify the modifier that may be reported by the physician to indicate that the procedure was discontinued.
    A. -52   B. -53   C. -73   D. -74

REFERENCE: AMA (2010), p 530
               Bowie and Schaffer (2008), p 16–17
               Frisch, p 18
               Green, p 310
               Johnson and McHugh, p 117
               Smith, p 42

36. A patient has major surgery and sees the surgeon 10 days later for an unrelated E/M service. Indicate the modifier that should be attached to the E/M code for the service provided.

A. -24   B. -25   C. -59   D. -79 *Unrelated proced. by same DR. during postop period*

E/m same dr same day   unbundling

REFERENCE: AMA (2010), p 529
Bowie and Schaffer (2008), p 14
Frisch, p 15, 30
Green, p 309
Johnson and McHugh, p 115
Smith, p 185

medicare has incentive for DR's if they change to automated

37. A barrier to widespread use of automated code assignment is
A. inadequate technology.   C. resistance by physicians.
B. poor quality of documentation.   D. resistance by HIM professionals.

REFERENCE: McWay, p 136
LaTour and Eichenwald-Maki, p 400–401

38. In assigning E/M codes, three key components are used. These are
A. history, examination, counseling.
B. history, examination, time.
C. history, nature of presenting problem, time.
D. history, examination, medical-decision making.

REFERENCE: AMA (2010), p 6
Bowie and Schaffer (2008), p 36–37
Frisch, p 12
Green, p 335
Johnson and McHugh, p 127–142
Smith, p 171

39. Mrs. Jones had an appendectomy on November 1. She was taken back to surgery on November 2 for evacuation of a hematoma of the wound site. Identify the modifier that may be reported for the November 2 visit.
A. -58   B. -76   C. -78   D. -79

REFERENCE: AMA (2010), p 530–531
Bowie and Schaffer (2008), p 20
Frisch, p 22, 240
Green, p 312, 307
Johnson and McHugh, p 119–120
Smith, p 44

40. A pregnant patient was admitted to the hospital with uncontrolled diabetes mellitus. She is a type I diabetic and was brought under control and subsequently discharged. The following code was assigned:

> 648.03 Other current condition in the mother classifiable elsewhere but complicating pregnancy, childbirth of the puerperium, diabetes mellitus

Which of the following describe why the coding is in error?
A. The incorrect fifth digit was used.
B. The condition should have been coded as gestational diabetes because she is pregnant.
C. An additional code describing the diabetes mellitus should be used.
D. Only the code for the diabetes mellitus should have been used.

REFERENCE: Bowie and Schaffer (2010), p 250–251
              Brown, p 276–277
              Frisch, p 130
              Green, p 152
              Johnson and McHugh, p 43–44, 339–340
              Schraffenberger (2010), p 215–216

41. A secondary data source that houses and aggregates extensive data about patients with a certain diagnosis is a
A. disease index.
B. master patient index.
C. disease registry.
D. admissions register.

REFERENCE: Green and Bowie, p 230, 232–233
              LaTour and Eichenwald-Maki, p 331–332
              McWay, p 116–117

42. After reviewing the following excerpt from CPT, code 27646 would be interpreted as

27645	Radical resection of tumor, bone; tibia
27646	fibula
27647	talus or calcaneus

A. 27646   radical resection of tumor, bone; tibia and fibula.
B. 27646   radical resection of tumor, bone; fibula.
C. 27646   radical resection of tumor, bone; fibula or tibia.
D. 27646   radical resection of tumor, bone; fibula, talus or calcaneus.

REFERENCE: Bowie and Schaffer (2008), p 3–5
              Green, p 301
              Smith, p 18–19

everything up to the ; is included then indent add the

43. A patient was admitted to the hospital with hemiplegia and aphasia. The hemiplegia and aphasia were resolved before discharge and the patient was diagnosed with cerebral thrombosis. What is the correct coding and sequencing?
    A. hemiplegia; aphasia
    B. cerebral thrombosis
    C. cerebral thrombosis; hemiplegia; aphasia
    D. hemiplegia; cerebral thrombosis; aphasia

REFERENCE: Brown, p 344
                Hazelwood and Venable, p 157
                Schraffenberger (2010), p 157

44. A 36-year-old woman was admitted to the hospital for an obstetrical delivery of her third child. During the admission, a sterilization procedure was performed for contraceptive purposes. The V25.2 code for sterilization would be
    A. assigned as a principal diagnosis.
    B. assigned as a secondary diagnosis.
    C. not assigned because this was the patient's third child.
    D. not assigned because it is the same admission as the delivery.

Delivery principal diagnosis

REFERENCE: Brown, p 283–284
                Schraffenberger (2010), p 328

45. According to ICD-9-CM, which one of the following is NOT a mechanical complication of an internal implant?
    A. erosion of skin by pacemaker electrodes –
    B. inflammation of urethra due to indwelling catheter
    C. leakage of breast prosthesis –
    D. IUD embedded in uterine wall –

REFERENCE: Brown, p 449–450
                Hazelwood and Venable, p 279–280
                Johnson and McHugh, p 71–72
                Schraffenberger (2010), p 293–294

46. Given the diagnosis "carcinoma of axillary lymph nodes and lungs, metastatic from breast," what is the primary cancer site(s)?
    A. axillary lymph nodes   C. breast
    B. lungs   D. both A and B

REFERENCE: Bowie and Schaffer (2010), p 109–110
                Brown, p 379
                Frisch, p 142–144
                Green, p 124–126
                Hazelwood and Venable, p 97
                Johnson and McHugh, p 55–58
                Schraffenberger (2010), p 90

47. In the diagnosis "first-, second-, and third-degree burns of the chest wall," a code is required for
    A. the first-degree burn only.
    B. the second-degree burn only.
    C. the third-degree burn only.
    D. for each first-, second-, and third-degree burn.

REFERENCE: Bowie and Schaffer (2010), p 323–326
                Brown, p 426–427
                Frisch, p 140–141
                Hazelwood and Venable, p 252
                Johnson and McHugh, p 65–67, 214–215, 236–237
                Schraffenberger (2010), p 275–276

48. When is it appropriate to use category V10, history of malignant neoplasm?
    A. primary malignancy recurred at original site and adjunct chemotherapy is directed at the site
    B. primary malignancy has been eradicated and no adjunct treatment is being given at this time
    C. primary malignancy eradicated and the patient is admitted for adjunct chemotherapy to primary site
    D. primary malignancy is eradicated; adjunct treatment is refused by patient even though there is some remaining malignancy

Once no Rad or Chemo is being used cancer still active

REFERENCE: Bowie and Schaffer (2010), p 112–113, 335
                Frisch, p 142–144
                Green, p 128–130
                Johnson and McHugh, p 55–58
                Schraffenberger (2010), p 81–82, 324–325

49. According to CPT, in which of the following cases would an established E/M code be used?
    A. A home visit with a 45-year-old male with a long history of drug abuse and alcoholism. The man is seen at the request of Adult Protective Services for an assessment of his mental capabilities.
    B. John and his family have just moved to town. John has asthma and requires medication to control the problem. He has an appointment with Dr. You and will bring his records from his previous physician.
    C. Tom is seen by Dr. X for a sore throat. Dr. X is on-call for Tom's regular physician, Dr. Y. The last time that Tom saw Dr. Y was a couple of years ago.
    D. A 78-year-old female with weight loss and progressive agitation over the past 2 months is seen by her primary care physician for drug therapy. She has not seen her primary care physician in 4 years.

REFERENCE: AMA (2010), p 4–5
                AMA, CPT Assistant, vol. 8, no. 10, Oct 1998
                Bowie and Schaffer (2008), p 32–33
                Frisch, p 49–50
                Green, p 332–333
                Smith, p 170

50. In order to use the inpatient CPT consultation codes, the consulting physician must
   A. order diagnostic tests.
   B. document his findings in the patient's medical record.
   C. communicate orally his opinion to the attending physician.
   D. use the term "referral" in his report.

REFERENCE: AMA (2010), p 16–17
               Bowie and Schaffer (2008), p 56–57
               Frisch, p 77–78
               Green, p 353–355
               Smith, p 189

Consult:
Request
Review
Report

51. The attending physician requests a consultation from a cardiologist. The cardiologist takes a detailed history, performs a detailed examination, and utilizes moderate medical decision making. The cardiologist orders diagnostic tests and prescribes medication. He documents his findings in the patient's medical record and communicates in writing with the attending physician. The following day the consultant visits the patient to evaluate the patient's response to the medication, to review results from the diagnostic tests, and to discuss treatment options. What codes should the consultant report for the two visits?
   A. an initial inpatient consult and a follow-up consult
   B. an initial inpatient consult for both visits
   C. an initial inpatient consult and a subsequent hospital visit
   D. an initial inpatient consult and initial hospital care

REFERENCE: Bowie and Schaffer (2008), p 56–57
               Frisch, p 82–86
               Green, p 353–355
               Smith, p 189

inpatient consult
or
outpatient consult
DR. refers to
specialist
then pat. is new pat.

52. According to the American Medical Association, medical decision making is measured by all of the following except
   A. number of diagnoses or management options.
   B. amount and complexity of data reviewed.
   C. risk of complications.
   D. specialty of the treating physician.

REFERENCE: AMA (2010), p 10
               Bowie and Schaffer (2008), p 47–50
               Frisch, p 322
               Green, p 337–341
               Johnson and McHugh, p 133
               Smith, p 178–179

53. CPT provides Level I modifiers to explain all of the following situations except
    A. when a service or procedure is partially reduced or eliminated at the physician's discretion.
    B. when one surgeon provides only postoperative services.
    C. when a patient sees a surgeon for follow-up care after surgery.
    D. when the same laboratory test is repeated multiple times on the same day.

REFERENCE: AMA (2010), p 529–533
                Bowie and Schaffer (2008), p 13–22
                Frisch, p 13–23
                Green, p 306–316
                Johnson and McHugh, p 113–120

54. The best place to ascertain the size of an excised lesion for accurate CPT coding is the
    A. discharge summary.   C. operative report.
    B. pathology report.   D. anesthesia record.

REFERENCE: Green, p 435–439
                Johnson and McHugh, p 221
                Smith, p 56–57

55. Which of the following contains a list of coding edits developed by CMS in an effort to promote correct coding nationwide and to prevent the inappropriate unbundling of related services?
    A. National Coverage Determination (NCD)
    B. National Correct Coding Initiative (NCCI)
    C. CPT Assistant
    D. Healthcare Common Procedure Coding System (HCPCS)

REFERENCE: Bowie and Schaffer (2008), p 91–93
                Frisch, p 235–240
                Green, p 317–318 1
                Smith, p 53
                Johnson and McHugh, p 556

56. To gather statistics for surgical services provided on an outpatient basis, which of the following codes are needed?
    A. ICD-9-CM codes
    B. Evaluation and Management Codes
    C. HCPCS Level II Codes
    D. CPT codes

REFERENCE: Schraffenberger (2007), p 8–9
                Green and Bowie, p 230
                McWay, p 116

57. In regard to quality of coding, the degree to which the same results (same codes) are obtained by different coders or on multiple attempts by the same coder refers to
   A. reliability.
   B. validity.
   C. completeness.
   D. timeliness.

REFERENCE: LaTour and Eichenwald-Maki, p 399

58. In regards to quality of coding, the degree to which the codes selected accurately reflect the diagnoses and procedures refers to
   A. reliability.
   B. validity.
   C. completeness.
   D. timeliness.

REFERENCE: Green and Bowie, p 247–248
              LaTour and Eichenwald-Maki, p 399

59. When coding free skin grafts, which of the following is NOT an essential item of data needed for accurate coding?
   A. recipient site
   B. donor site
   C. size of defect
   D. type of repair

REFERENCE: Bowie and Schaffer (2008), p 103–104
              Green, p 445–448
              Johnson and McHugh, p 231, 233–234
              Smith, p 66–67

60. In CPT, Category III codes include codes
   A. to describe emerging technologies.
   B. to measure performance.
   C. for use by nonphysician practitioners.
   D. for supplies, drugs, and durable medical equipment.

REFERENCE: AMA (2010), p 519
              Bowie and Schaffer (2008), p 7
              Green, p 294
              Johnson and McHugh, p 103, 112, 327–328
              Smith, p 3

61. In the ICD-9-CM classification system, shooting pain in the right eye due to the presence of an intact, correctly positioned permanent contact lens would be coded as a(n)
   A. current injury.
   B. late effect.
   C. mechanical complication of an internal prosthetic device.
   D. abnormal reaction of the body to the presence of an internal prosthetic device.

REFERENCE: Brown, p 449–450
              Hazelwood and Venable, p 279–280
              Schraffenberger (2010), p 293–294

62. In the ICD-9-CM classification system, severe shock due to third-degree burns sustained in an industrial accident would be coded as a(n)
    A. current injury.
    B. late effect.
    C. mechanical complication of an internal prosthetic device.
    D. abnormal reaction of the body to the presence of an internal prosthetic device.

REFERENCE: Bowie and Schaffer (2010), p 323–327
                    Brown, p 428–429
                    Frisch, p 137
                    Johnson and McHugh, p 74–7

63. In the ICD-9-CM classification system, a nonfunctioning pacemaker due to the disintegration of the electrodes (leads) would be coded as a(n)
    A. current injury.
    B. late effect.
    C. mechanical complication of an internal prosthetic device.
    D. abnormal reaction of the body to the presence of an internal prosthetic device.

REFERENCE: Brown, p 449–450
                    Hazelwood and Venable, p 279–280
                    Johnson and McHugh, p 71
                    Schraffenberger (2010), p 293–294

64. In the ICD-9-CM classification system, an esophageal stricture due to a burn received in a house fire several years ago would be coded as a(n)
    A. current injury.
    B. late effect.
    C. mechanical complication of an internal prosthetic device.
    D. abnormal reaction of the body to the presence of an internal prosthetic device.

REFERENCE: Bowie and Schaffer (2010), p 61–63
                    Brown, p 418
                    Hazelwood and Venable, p 54–55
                    Schraffenberger (2010), p 313–314

65. Dizziness and blurred vision following ingestion of prescribed Allegra and a glass of wine at dinner would be reported as a(n)
    A. poisoning.
    B. adverse reaction to a drug.
    C. late effect of a poisoning.
    D. late effect of an adverse reaction.

REFERENCE: Bowie and Schaffer (2010), p 326–327, 347–349, 600
                    Brown, p 436
                    Frisch, p 149–150
                    Green, p 165–167
                    Hazelwood and Venable, p 265
                    Johnson and McHugh, p 68–69
                    Schraffenberger (2010), p 289–290

66. Tachycardia after taking a correct dosage of prescribed Lortab would be reported as a(n)
    A. poisoning.
    B. adverse reaction to a drug.
    C. late effect of a poisoning.
    D. late effect of an adverse reaction.
REFERENCE: Bowie and Schaffer (2010), p 326–327, 347–349, 599
                Brown, p 435
                Frisch, p 149–150
                Green, p 170
                Hazelwood and Venable, p 262–263
                Johnson and McHugh, p 70
                Schraffenberger (2010), p 284–285

67. Blindness due to an allergic reaction to ampicillin administered 6 years ago would be reported as a(n)
    A. poisoning.   C. late effect of a poisoning.
    B. adverse reaction to a drug.   D. late effect of an adverse reaction.

REFERENCE: Bowie and Schaffer (2010), p 323, 326–327
                Brown, p 443
                Frisch, p 134–135
                Green, p 170
                Hazelwood and Venable, p 263–264
                Johnson and McHugh, p 72
                Schraffenberger (2010), p 288

68. The patient underwent bypass surgery for life-threatening coronary artery disease. With the aid of extracorporeal circulation, the right internal mammary artery was taken down to the left anterior descending artery and saphenous vein grafts were brought from the aorta to the diagonal, the right coronary artery, and the posterior descending artery. What is the correct ICD-9-CM coding for this procedure?
    A. single internal mammary artery bypass; aortocoronary artery bypass of three vessels
    B. aortocoronary bypass of three coronary arteries
    C. aortocoronary bypass of four coronary arteries
    D. single internal mammary artery bypass; aortocoronary bypass of three vessels, extracorporeal circulation

REFERENCE: Brown, p 360–362
                Schraffenberger (2010), p 163–164

69 Which code represents an HCPCS Level II National Code?
    A. W0166   no w's   C. D0417   Dental
    B. 99281   D. 66690

REFERENCE: Green, p 258–259
                Johns, p 208–209
                Johnson and McHugh, p 85–87
                Smith, p 4

70. A radiologist is asked to review a patient's CT scan that was taken at another facility. The modifier -26 attached to the code indicates that the physician is billing for what component of the procedure?

   A. professional   C. global

   B. technical   D. confirmatory

REFERENCE: Bowie and Schaffer (2008), p 15

                      Frisch, p 14, 16

                      Green, p 307, 315, 657

71. When coding neoplasms, topography means

   A. cell structure and form.   C. variation from normal tissue.

   B. site.   D. extent of the spread of the disease.

REFERENCE: Abdelhak, p 477

72. According to CPT, antepartum care includes all of the following except

   A. initial and subsequent history.   C. monthly visits up to 36 weeks.

   B. physical examination.   D. routine chemical urinalysis.

REFERENCE: Green, p 607

                      Johnson and McHugh, p 343, 351

                      Smith, p 126

73. A list or collection of clinical words or phrases with their meanings is a

   A. data dictionary.   C. medical nomenclature.

   B. language.   D. clinical vocabulary.

REFERENCE: Green, p 8

                      Green and Bowie, p 294

                      McWay, p 125–128

74. A patient was discharged from the acute care hospital with a final diagnosis of bronchial asthma. As the coder reviews the record, she notes that the patient was described as having prolonged and intractable wheezing, airway obstruction that was not relieved by bronchodilators and the lab values showed decreased respiratory function. The coder queried the physician to determine whether the code for _____ is appropriate to be added to the final diagnoses.

   A. acute and chronic bronchitis

   B. chronic obstructive pulmonary disease

   C. respiratory failure

   D. status asthmaticus

REFERENCE: Bowie and Schaffer (2010), p 209

                      Brown, p 186–187

                      Frisch, p 139

                      Green, p 145

                      Hazelwood and Venable, p 170–171

                      Schraffenberger (2010), p 172–173

75. A patient is undergoing hemodialysis for end-stage renal disease in the outpatient department of an acute care hospital. The patient develops what is believed to be severe heartburn, but is sent to observation for several hours, at which time the patient is admitted to inpatient care for further workup. The cardiologist diagnoses the patient's problem as unstable angina. What is the principal diagnosis for the acute hospital stay?
   A. complications of hemodialysis   C. unstable angina
   B. heartburn   D. renal disease

REFERENCE: Bowie and Schaffer (2010), p 64
             Green, p 202–203
             Johnson and McHugh, p 570–571
             Schraffenberger (2010), p 598–599

76. A patient is seen in the emergency room of an acute care hospital with tachycardia and hypotension. The patient had received an injection of tetanus toxoid (correct dosage) earlier at his primary care physician's office. Which of the following is the appropriate sequencing for this encounter?
   A. hypotension; tachycardia; accidental poisoning E code (tetanus toxoid)
   B. unspecified adverse reaction to tetanus toxoid; undetermined cause E code (tetanus toxoid)
   C. hypotension; tachycardia; therapeutic use E code (tetanus toxoid)
   D. poisoning code (tetanus toxoid); hypotension; tachycardia; accidental poisoning E code (tetanus toxoid)

REFERENCE: Bowie and Schaffer (2006), p 273–274, 293–295, 493
             Frisch, p 149–150
             Green, p 160–162
             Johnson and McHugh, p 68–69
             Schraffenberger (2009), p 278–279
             Hazelwood and Venable, p 259–261
             Brown, p 365–368

77. A rare malignant tumor often associated with AIDS is
   A. Kaposi's sarcoma.   C. pheochromocytoma.
   B. glioblastoma multiforme.   D. melanoma.

REFERENCE: Hazelwood and Venable, p 81–82
             Schraffenberger (2010), p 71–73

78. A PEG procedure would most likely be done to facilitate
   A. breathing.   C. urination.
   B. eating.   D. none of the above

REFERENCE: Johnson and McHugh, p 194
             Schraffenberger (2010), p 189

PEG Percutaneous endoscopic gastrostomy

79. What ICD-9-CM coding scheme is used to show that a therapeutic abortion resulted in a live fetus?
   A. spontaneous abortion; V30 code to show a newborn birth
   B. code 644.21, early onset of delivery; V27 code (outcome of delivery)
   C. abortion by type; V27 code (outcome of delivery)
   D. therapeutic abortion

REFERENCE: Bowie and Schaffer (2010), p 249
               Brown, p 297
               Green, p 154
               Hazelwood and Venable, p 205
               Johnson and McHugh, p 340
               Schraffenberger (2010), p 207

Answer Key for Classification Systems and Secondary Data Sources

NOTE: Explanations are provided for those questions that require mathematical calculations and questions that are not clearly explained in the references that are cited.

	ANSWER	EXPLANATION
1.	A	
2.	B	M codes and E codes are never principal diagnosis codes and, in fact, are optional for coding. V codes to describe the outcome of delivery are always secondary codes on the mother's chart.
3.	B	
4.	C	
5.	A	Antivert is used for the management of nausea and dizziness associated with motion sickness and in vertigo associated with diseases affecting the vestibular system.
6.	A	
7.	A	A coder should never assign a code on the basis of laboratory results alone. If findings are clearly outside the normal range and the physician has ordered additional testing or treatment, it is appropriate to consult with the physician as to whether a diagnosis should be added or whether the abnormal finding should be listed.
8.	D	Digoxin is used for maintenance therapy in congestive heart failure, atrial fibrillation, atrial flutter, and paroxysmal atrial tachycardia. Ibuprofen is an anti-inflammatory drug. Oxytocin is used to initiate or improve uterine contractions at term, and haloperidol is used to manage psychotic disorders.
9.	C	HCPCS codes (Levels I and II) would only give the code for any procedures that were performed and would not identify the diagnosis code or cause of the accident. The correct name of the nomenclature for athletic injuries is the Standard Nomenclature of Athletic Injuries and is used to identify sports injuries. It has not been revised since 1976.
10.	A	
11.	C	
12.	B	All three key components (history, physical examination, and medical decision making) are required for new patients and initial visits. At least two of the three key components are required for established patients, and subsequent visits.
13.	B	
14.	B	
15.	B	
16.	A	
17.	D	
18.	D	There are V codes that indicate various reasons for canceled surgery. Review codes V64.0x, V64.1, V64.2, and V64.3. As usual, the principal diagnosis is always the reason for admission, in this case, the cholelithiasis. The contraindication (the tachycardia) should also be coded.
19.	B	

Answer Key for Classification Systems and Secondary Data Sources

ANSWER		EXPLANATION

20. C In order to use category 402 there must be a cause and effect relationship shown between the hypertension and the heart condition. "With" does not show this relationship, nor does the fact that both conditions are listed on the same chart. The term "hypertensive" indicates a cause and effect relationship.

21. B An acute MI is considered to be anything under 8 weeks' duration from the time of initial onset. A chronic MI is considered anything over 8 weeks with symptoms. An old MI is considered anything over 8 weeks with NO symptoms.

22. A A reaction due to mixing drugs and alcohol is coded as a poisoning.

23. A The patient is admitted for chemotherapy (V58.11) and, because the breast cancer is still actively being treated, it is still coded as current.

24. C Mental retardation is a late effect, rejection of the kidney is a complication, and a nonfunctioning pacemaker is a mechanical complication.

25. B

26. B

27. C

28. C

29. B

30. D

31. D

32. A

33. B

34. C

35. B

36. A

37. B

38. D

39. C

40. C

41. C

42. B

43. B

44. B

45. B

46. C

47. C

48. B

49. C

50. B

51. C The first visit would be an inpatient consult. Because the physician continued to treat the patient and participate in his care, all subsequent visits are considered as subsequent hospital care and are no longer consults.

Answer Key for Classification Systems and Secondary Data Sources

ANSWER		EXPLANATION

52. D

53. C Modifier -52 can be used if a physician elects to partially reduce or eliminate a service or procedure. Modifier -55 is used by a physician who only provides postoperative services. Modifier -91 is used when a laboratory test is repeated multiple times on the same day. CPT code 99024 is used to report a follow-up visit after surgery.

54. C

55. B

56 D

57. A

58. B

59. B

60. A

61. D

62. A

63. C

64. B

65. A

66. B

67. D

68. D The procedure described includes one internal mammary artery, which is not considered an aortocoronary bypass. There were three aortocoronary bypasses: aorta to diagonal, aorta to right coronary artery, and aorta to the posterior descending artery. The description states that extracorporeal circulation was used.

69. C HCPCS Level I codes are five-digit (numeric) codes found in the CPT book. HCPCS Level II National Codes are alphanumeric starting with letters A-V. HCPCS Level III Local Codes are alphanumeric starting with a letter W-Z. Level III codes were eliminated as of December 31, 2003.

70. A With CPT radiology codes, there are three components that have to be considered. These are the professional, technical, and global components. The professional component describes the services of a physician who supervises the taking of an x-ray film and the interpretation with report of the results. The technical component describes the services of the person who uses the equipment, the film, and other supplies. The global component describes the combination of both professional and technical components. If the billing radiologist's services include only the supervision and interpretation component, the radiologist bills the procedure code and adds the modifier -26 to indicate that he or she did only the professional component of the procedure.

71. B

72. C

73. D

Answer Key for Classification Systems and Secondary Data Sources

	ANSWER	EXPLANATION
74.	D	
75.	C	
76.	C	
77.	A	
78.	B	
79.	B	

REFERENCES

Abdelhak, M., Grostick, S., Hanken, M. A., and Jacobs, E. (Eds.). (2007). *Health information: management of a strategic resource* (3rd ed.). St. Louis: Saunders Elsevier.

American Hospital Association. *Coding clinic.* Chicago: American Hospital Association (AHA).

American Medical Association. *CPT assistant.* Chicago: American Medical Association (AMA).

American Medical Association. (2010). *Physicians' current procedural terminology (CPT) 2010, Professional Edition.* Chicago: American Medical Association (AMA).

Bowie, M. J., and Schaffer, R. (2010). *Understanding ICD-9-CM: A worktext.* Clifton Park, NY: Delmar Cengage Learning.

Bowie, M. J., and Schaffer, R. (2008). *Understanding procedural coding: A worktext.* Clifton Park, NY: Delmar Cengage Learning.

Brown, F. (2010). *ICD-9-CM coding handbook 2010 with answers.* Chicago: American Hospital Association (AHA).

Centers for Disease Control and Prevention. *Draft ICD-10-CM official guidelines for coding and reporting for acute short-term and long-term hospital inpatient and physician office and other outpatient encounters effective October 1, 2009.* Accessed 11/16/2009 from

http://www.cdc.gov/nchs/icd/icd10cm.htm#09update

ftp://ftp.cdc.gov/pub/Health_Statistics/NCHS/Publications/ICD10CM/2009/

Frisch, B. (2007). *Correct coding for Medicare, compliance, and reimbursement.* Clifton Park, NY: Delmar Cengage Learning.

Green, M. (2010). *3-2-1 code it* (2nd ed.), Clifton Park, NY: Delmar Cengage Learning.

Green, M. A., and Bowie, M. J. (2005). *Essentials of health information management: Principles and practices.* Clifton Park, NY: Delmar Cengage Learning.

Hazelwood, A. C., and Venable, C. A. (2010). *ICD-9-CM diagnostic coding and reimbursement for physician services.* Chicago: American Health Information Management Association (AHIMA).

ICD-9-CM. (2010) *Code book professional edition.* Salt Lake City: INGINEX.

Johns, M. (2007). *Health information management technology: An applied approach* (2nd ed.). Chicago: American Health Information Management Association (AHIMA).

Johnson, S. L., and McHugh, C. S. (2006). *Understanding medical coding: A comprehensive guide* (2nd ed.) Clifton Park, NY: Delmar Cengage Learning.

LaTour, K., and Eichenwald-Maki, S. (2010). *Health information management: Concepts, principles and practice* (3rd ed.). Chicago: American Health Information Management Association (AHIMA).

McWay, D. C. (2008). *Today's health information management: an integrated approach.* Clifton Park, NY: Delmar Cengage Learning.

Nobles, S. (2002). *Delmar's drug reference for health care professionals.* Clifton Park, NY: Delmar Cengage Learning.

Schraffenberger, L. A., and Kuehn, L. (2007). *Effective management of coding services* (3rd ed.). Chicago: American Health Information Management Association (AHIMA).

Schraffenberger, L. A. (2010). *Basic ICD-9-CM coding.* Chicago: American Health Information Management Association (AHIMA).

Smith, G. (2009). *Basic current procedural terminology and HCPCS coding 2009.* Chicago: American Health Information Management Association (AHIMA).

CCS-P Competencies for the Classification Systems and Secondary Data Sources Chapter

Question	CCS-P Domain						
	1	2	3	4	5	6	7
1		X					
2		X					
3			X				
4	X						
5	X						
6						X	
7	X						
8	X						
9					X		
10						X	
11			X				
12			X				
13		X					
14		X					
15							X
16						X	
17	X						
18		X					
19			X				
20		X					

Question	CCS-P Domain						
	1	2	3	4	5	6	7
21		X					
22		X					
23		X					
24		X					
25	X						
26		X					
27							X
28	X						
29	X						
30			X				
31		X					
32			X				
33			X				
34			X				
35			X				
36			X				
37						X	
38			X				
39			X				
40		X					
41						X	
42			X				
43		X					
44		X					

Question	CCS-P Domain						
	1	2	3	4	5	6	7
45		X					
46		X					
47		X					
48		X					
49		X					
50			X				
51			X				
52			X				
53			X				
54			X				
55			X				
56					X		
57					X		
58					X		
59			X				
60			X				
61		X					
62		X					
63		X					
64		X					

Question	CCS-P Competency						
	1	2	3	4	5	6	7
65		X					
66		X					
67		X					
68		X					
69			X				
70			X				
71		X					
72			X				
73	X						
74		X					
75		X					
76		X					
77		X					
78	X						
79		X					

VI. Medical Billing and Reimbursement Systems

Toni Cade, MBA, RHIA, CCS, FAHIMA

1. Under the RBRVS, each HCPCS/CPT code contains 3 components, each having assigned relative value units. These 3 components are

   A. geographic index, wage index, and cost of living index.
   B. fee-for-service, per diem payment, and capitation.
   C. conversion factor, CMS weight, and hospital-specific rate.
   D. physician work, practice expense, and malpractice insurance expense.

   REFERENCE: Frisch, p 185–186, 235
                  Green, p 795–796

2. A patient was seen by Dr. Zachary. The charge for the office visit was $125. The Medicare beneficiary has already met his deductible. The Medicare fee schedule amount is $100. Dr. Zachary does not accept assignment. The office manager will apply a practice termed as "balance billing," which means that the patient is

   A. financially liable for the Medicare fee schedule amount.
   B. financially liable for charges in excess of the Medicare fee schedule.
   C. not financially liable for any amount.
   D. financially liable for only the deductible.

   REFERENCE: Green and Rowell, p 52, 294, 366–367, 437
                  Johns, p 308
                  LaTour and Eichenwald-Maki, p 405

3. The _____ is a statement sent to the provider to explain payments made by third-party payers.

   A. remittance advice   C. attestation statement
   B. advance beneficiary notice   D. acknowledgement notice

   REFERENCE: Frisch, p 188–192
                  Green, p 813–814
                  Green and Rowell, p 6, 69–71, 73
                  Kuehn, p 11
                  Rimmer, p 95

4. Under ASCs, when multiple procedures are performed during the same surgical session, a payment reduction is applied. The procedure in the highest level group is reimbursed at _____ (percent) and all remaining procedures are reimbursed at _____ (percent).

   A. 50%, 25%   C. 100%, 25%
   B. 100%, 50%   D. 100%, 75%

   REFERENCE: Casto and Layman, p 191
                  Green, p 793

5. The _____ refers to a statement sent to the patient to show how much the provider billed, how much Medicare reimbursed the provider, and what the patient must pay the provider.

   A. Medicare summary notice   C. health care claims transaction
   B. remittance advice   D. coordination of benefits

   REFERENCE: Green and Rowell, p 294–295, 447–448
                  Johns, p 294
                  LaTour and Eichenwald-Maki, p 401–403

6. Currently, which prospective payment system is used to determine the payment to the physician for outpatient surgery performed on a Medicare patient?

    A. MS-DRGs   C. RBRVS
    B. APGs   D. ASCs

REFERENCE: Schraffenberger and Kuehn, p 144
                Green, p 796–797

7. Which of the following best describes the situation of a provider who agrees to accept assignment for Medicare Part B services?

    A. The provider is reimbursed at 15% above the allowed charge.
    B. The provider is paid according to the Medicare physician fee schedule (MPFS) plus 10%.
    C. The provider cannot bill the patients for the balance between the MPFS amount and the total charges.
    D. The provider is a non-participating provider.

REFERENCE: Green and Rowell, p 52
                Green, p 795–796

8. According to the Federal Register, the definition of a "new" patient when assigning a CPT Evaluation and Management (medical visit) code to a Medicare hospital outpatient under the prospective payment system is a patient that has

    A. not seen the physician within the last 3 years.
    B. not seen the physician within the last 5 years.
    C. not already been assigned a medical record number.
    D. never seen the physician before.

REFERENCE: Federal Register, April 7, 2000, p 18451
                Green, p 332

9. Under ASCs, bilateral procedures are reimbursed at _____ (percent) of the payment rate for their group

    A. 50%   C. 200%
    B. 100%   D. 150%

REFERENCE: Casto and Layman, p 191

10. These are assigned to every HCPCS/CPT code under the Medicare hospital outpatient prospective payment system, to identify how the service or procedure described by the code would be paid.

    A. geographic practice cost indices   C. minimum data set
    B. major diagnostic categories   D. payment status indicator

REFERENCE: Green and Rowell, p 286–287
                Casto and Layman, p 175–176

11. _____ is the term used to indicate that the service or procedure is reasonable and necessary for the diagnosis or treatment of illness or injury consistent with generally accepted standards of care.

A. Peer review
B. Optimization
C. Benchmarking
D. Medical necessity

REFERENCE: Green and Rowell, p 3, 97, 125
                       Green, p 14–15

12. If the Medicare non-PAR approved payment amount is $128.00 for a proctoscopy, what is the total Medicare approved payment amount for a doctor who does not accept assignment, applying the limiting charge for this procedure?

A. $ 140.80
B. $ 143.00
C. $ 192.00
-D. $ 147.20

REFERENCE: Green and Rowell, p 292–294, 437–439

13. Home health agencies (HHAs) utilize a data entry software system developed by the Centers for Medicare and Medicaid Services (CMS). This software is available to HHAs at no cost through the CMS Web site or on a CD-ROM.

A. PACE (Patient Assessment and Comprehensive Evaluation)
- B. HAVEN (Home Assessment Validation and Entry)
C. HHASS (Home Health Agency Software System)
D. PEPP (Payment Error Prevention Program)

REFERENCE: Green & Bowie, p 281
                       Johns, p 285
                       LaTour & Eichenwald-Maki, p 395

14. In a global payment methodology, which is sometimes applied to radiological and similar types of procedures that involve professional and technical components, all of the following are part of the "technical" components EXCEPT

A. radiological equipment.
B. physician services.
C. radiological supplies.
D. support services.

REFERENCE: Johns, p 272
                       LaTour and Eichenwald-Maki, p 387
                       Green, p 656–657

15. This prospective payment system replaced the Medicare physician payment system of "customary, prevailing, and reasonable (CPR)" charges whereby physicians were reimbursed according to historical record of the charge for the provision of each service.

A. Medicare Physician Fee Schedule (MPFS)
B. Medicare Severity Diagnosis Related Groups (MS-DRGs)
C. Medicare Case Mix Index
D. MEDISGRPS

REFERENCE: Green, p 795–796
                       Green and Rowell, p 292–298
                       Frisch, p 185–189
                       Kuehn, p 77–78

16. The occurrence of an OCE (outpatient code editor) edit can result in one of _____ different dispositions, which helps to ensure that the fiscal intermediaries in all parts of the country are following similar claims processing procedures. An example of one of these dispositions is "claim rejection."

    A. 100   C. 3
    B. 50   ~D. 6

REFERENCE: Green and Rowell, p 251
               Jones, p 61–62
               Kuehn, p 67

17. The hospital outpatient prospective payment system for Medicare applies to all of the following, EXCEPT

    A. professional services, such as physician fees.
    B. facility reimbursement for outpatient hospital clinic visits.
    C. facility reimbursement for emergency department visits.
    D. facility reimbursement for hospital-based ambulatory surgery.

REFERENCE: Casto and Layman, p 171
               Green and Rowell, p 286–287
               Green, p 796–797

18. The Correct Coding Initiative (CCI) edits contain a listing of codes under two columns titled, "comprehensive codes" and "component codes." According to the CCI edits, when a provider bills Medicare for a procedure that appears in both columns for the same beneficiary on the same date of service

    A. code only the component code.
    B. do not code either one.
    ~C. code only the comprehensive code.
    D. code both the comprehensive code and the component code.

REFERENCE: Frisch, p 236–237
               Green, p 806–809
               Green and Rowell, p 105–109, 251–253

19. LCDs and NCDs are review policies that describe the circumstances of coverage for various types of medical treatment. They advise physicians which services Medicare considers reasonable and necessary and may indicate the need for an advance beneficiary notice. They are developed by the Centers for Medicare and Medicaid Services (CMS), Medicare carriers, or fiscal intermediaries. LCD and NCD are acronyms that stand for

    A. local covered determinations and non-covered determinations.
    B. local coverage determinations and national coverage determinations.
    C. list of covered decisions and non-covered decisions.
    D. local contractor's decisions and national contractor's decisions.

REFERENCE: Frisch, p 167
               Scott, p 23
               Green and Rowell, p 330
               Green, p 277

20. The limiting charge is a percentage limit on fees specified by legislation that the non-participating physician may bill Medicare beneficiaries above the non-PAR fee schedule amount. The limiting charge is

A. 10%.   C. 20%.
- B. 15%.   D. 50%.

REFERENCE: Green and Rowell, p 292–294, 437–439

Use the following case scenario to answer questions #21 – #25.

> A Medicare patient is seen in the physician's office.
> The total charge for this office visit is $250.00.
> The patient has previously paid his deductible under Medicare Part B.
> The Par Medicare fee schedule amount for this service is $200.00.
> The non-PAR Medicare fee schedule amount for this service is $190.00.

21. The patient is financially liable for the coinsurance amount which is

A. 80%.   C. 20%.
B. 100%.   D. 15%.

REFERENCE: Green and Rowell, p 291–294, 436–439
                    Rizzo, p 187

22. If this physician is a participating physician who accepts assignment for this claim, the total amount he will receive is

A. $200.00.   C. $218.50.
B. $250.00.   D. $190.00.

REFERENCE: Green and Rowell, p 291–294, 436–439
                    Rizzo, p 187

23. If this physician is a non-participating physician who does NOT accept assignment for this claim, the total amount he will receive is

A. $250.00.   - C. $218.50.
B. $200.00.   D. $190.00.

REFERENCE: Green and Rowell, p 291–294, 436–439
                    Rizzo, p 187

24. If this physician is a participating physician who accepts assignment for this claim, the total amount of the patient's financial liability (out-of-pocket expense) is

A. $200.00. _PAR medicare_   C. $160.00.
B. $40.00.   D. $30.00.

REFERENCE: Green and Rowell, p 291–294, 436–439
                    Rizzo, p 187

25. If this physician is a non-participating physician who does not accept assignment for this claim, the total amount of the patient's financial liability (out-of-pocket expense) is

A. $66.50.   C. $190.00.
B. $38.00.   D. $152.00.

REFERENCE: Green and Rowell, p 291–294, 436–439
                    Rizzo, p 187

26. Under APCs, payment status indicator "X" means

    A. ancillary services.
    B. clinic or emergency department visit (medical visits).
    C. significant procedure, multiple procedure reduction applies.
    D. significant procedure, not discounted when multiple.

REFERENCE: Casto and Layman, p 176
                LaTour and Eichenwald-Maki, p 393

27. Under APCs, payment status indicator "V" means

    A. ancillary services.
    B. clinic or emergency department visit (medical visits).
    C. inpatient procedure.
    D. significant procedure, not discounted when multiple.

REFERENCE: Casto and Layman, p 176
                LaTour and Eichenwald-Maki, p 393

28. Under APCs, payment status indicator "S" means

    A. ancillary services.
    B. clinic or emergency department visit (medical visits).
    C. multiple procedure reduction applies.
    D. significant procedure, not discounted when multiple.

REFERENCE: Green and Rowell, p 286
                Casto and Layman, p 176
                Green, p 793
                LaTour and Eichenwald-Maki, p 393

29. Under APCs, payment status indicator "T" means

    A. ancillary services.
    B. clinic or emergency department visit (medical visits).
    C. significant procedure, multiple procedure reduction applies.
    D. significant procedure, not discounted when multiple

REFERENCE: Green and Rowell, p 286
                Green, p 796
                LaTour and Eichenwald-Maki, p 393
                Casto and Layman, p 176

30. Under APCs, payment status indicator "C" means

    A. ancillary services.
    B. inpatient procedures.
    C. significant procedure, multiple procedure reduction applies.
    D. significant procedure, not discounted when multiple.

REFERENCE: Casto and Layman, p 176
                LaTour and Eichenwald-Maki, p 393

31. This is a ten-digit, intelligence-free numeric identifier designed to replace all previous provider legacy numbers. This number identifies the physician universally to all payers. This number is issued to all HIPAA-covered entities. It is mandatory on the CMS-1500 and UB-04 claim forms.

   A. National Practitioner Databank (NPD)
   B. Universal Physician Number (UPN)
   C. Master Patient Index (MPI)
   D. National Provider Identifier (NPI)

REFERENCE: Frisch, p 198
                Rimmer, p 45–46
                Green, p 866
                Green and Rowell, p 365–366

32. In the managed care industry, there are specific reimbursement concepts, such as "capitation." All of the following statements are true in regards to the concept of "capitation," EXCEPT

   A. each service is paid based upon the actual charges.
   B. the volume of services and their expense does not affect reimbursement.
   C. capitation means paying a fixed amount per member per month.
   D. capitation involves a group of physicians or an individual physician.

REFERENCE: Casto and Layman, p 87
                Green and Rowell, p 334

33. When billing for the admitting physician for a patient who is admitted to the hospital as an inpatient, one must use a CPT Evaluation and Management code based upon the level of care provided.

   These are the codes to be selected from for initial hospital care.
   99221   Initial hospital care, per day, for the evaluation and management of a patient, which requires these 3 key components:
   -   a detailed or comprehensive history,
   -   a detailed or comprehensive examination, and
   -   medical decision making that is straightforward or of low complexity
   99222   Initial hospital care, per day, for the evaluation and management of a patient, which requires these 3 key components:
   -   a comprehensive history,
   -   a comprehensive examination, and
   -   medical decision making of moderate complexity
   99223   Initial hospital care, per day, for the evaluation and management of a patient, which requires these 3 key components:
   -   a comprehensive history,
   -   a comprehensive examination, and
   -   medical decision making of high complexity
   The following statement is true.

   A. This code can be used only once per hospitalization.
   B. This code can be used by the admitting physician or consulting physician.
   C. This code can be used for patients admitted to observation status.
   D. This code can be used by the hospital to bill for facility services.

REFERENCE: Frisch, p 60
                Rimmer, p 73–74

34. This document is published by the Office of Inspector General (OIG) every year. It details the OIG's focus for Medicare fraud and abuse for that year. It gives health-care providers an indication of general and specific areas that are targeted for review. It can be found on the Internet on CMS' Web site.

    A. The OIG's Evaluation and Management Documentation Guidelines
    B. The OIG's Model Compliance Plan
    C. The Federal Register
    - D. The OIG's Workplan

REFERENCE: Frisch, p 341

35. Accounts Receivable (A/R) refers to

    A. cases that have not yet been paid.
    B. the amount the hospital was paid.
    C. cases that have been paid.
    D. denials that have been returned to the hospital.

REFERENCE: Green and Bowie, p 76
                Schraffenberger and Kuehn, p 355
                Rimmer, p 118

36. An Advance Beneficiary Notice (ABN) is a document signed by the

    A. utilization review coordinator indicating that the patient stay is not medically necessary.
    B. physician advisor indicating that the patient's stay is denied.
    · C. patient indicating whether he/she wants to receive services that Medicare probably will not pay for.
    D. provider indicating that Medicare will not pay for certain services.

REFERENCE: LaTour and Eichenwald-Maki, p 405–406
                Green, p 276, 319

37. Which modifier indicates that a signed ABN is on file?

    A. AB   C. GY
    · B. GA   D. GZ

REFERENCE: Frisch, p 175

38. Under Medicare Part B, all of the following statements are true and are applicable to non-participating physician providers, EXCEPT

    A. providers must file all Medicare claims.
    B. non-participating providers have a higher fee schedule than that for participating providers.
    C. fees are restricted to charging no more than the "limiting charge" on non-assigned claims.
    D. collections are restricted to only the deductible and co-insurance due at the time of service on an assigned claim.

REFERENCE: Green and Rowell, p 292–295

39. Under the APC methodology, discounted payments occur when

    A. there are two or more (multiple) procedures that are assigned to status indicator "T."
    B. there are two or more (multiple) procedures that are assigned to status indicator "S."
    C. modifier -73 is used to indicate a procedure is terminated after the patient is prepared, but before anesthesia is started.
    D. both A and C

REFERENCE: Green and Bowie, p 286
              Schraffenberger and Kuehn, p 142–143

40. This information is published by the Medicare contractors to describe when and under what circumstances Medicare will cover a service. The ICD-9-CM and CPT/HCPCS codes are listed in the memoranda.

    A. LCD (Local Coverage Determinations)
    B. CCI (Correct Coding Initiatives)
    C. OSHA (Occupational Safety and Health Administration)
    D. PEPP (Payment Error Prevention Program)

REFERENCE: Green and Bowie, p 330
              Schraffenberger and Kuehn, p 170

41. The term "hard coding" refers to

    A. HCPCS/CPT codes that are coded by the coders.
    B. HPCS/CPT codes that appear in the hospital's chargemaster and will be included automatically on the patient's bill.
    C. ICD-9-CM codes that are coded by the coders.
    D. ICD-9-CM codes that appear in the hospital's chargemaster.

REFERENCE: Schraffenberger and Kuehn, p 156–157

42. This is the amount collected by the facility for the services it bills.

    A. costs   C. reimbursement
    B. charges   D. contractual allowance

REFERENCE: Green, p 24–25
              Schraffenberger and Kuehn, p 335

43. Assume the patient has already met his or her deductible and that the physician is a Medicare participating (PAR) provider. The physician's standard fee for the services provided is $120.00. Medicare's PAR fee is $60.00. How much reimbursement will the physician receive from Medicare?

    A. $120.00   C. $48.00
    B. $60.00   D. $96.00

REFERENCE: Green and Rowell, p 292, 294, 437–439

44. This accounting method attributes a dollar figure to every input required to provide a service.

    A. cost accounting   C. reimbursement
    B. charge accounting   D. contractual allowance

REFERENCE: Schraffenberger and Kuehn, p 334

45. This is the amount the facility actually bills for the services it provides.

    A. costs
    B. charges
    C. reimbursement
    D. contractual allowance

    REFERENCE: Green and Rowell, p 58–59
                  Schraffenberger and Kuehn, p 334

46. This is the difference between what is charged and what is paid.

    A. costs
    B. charges
    C. reimbursement
    D. contractual allowance

    REFERENCE: Schraffenberger and Kuehn, p 334

47. When appropriate, under the outpatient PPS, a hospital can use this CPT code in place of, but not in addition to, a code for a medical visit or emergency department service.

    A. CPT Code 99291 (critical care)
    B. CPT Code 99358 (prolonged evaluation and management service)
    C. CPT Code 35001 (direct repair of aneurysm)
    D. CPT Code 50300 (donor nephrectomy)

    REFERENCE: Green, p 357–359
                  Jones, p 34–35

48. To monitor timely claims processing in a hospital, a summary report of "patient receivables" is generated frequently. Aged receivables can negatively affect a facility's cash flow; therefore, to maintain the facility's fiscal integrity, the HIM manager must routinely analyze this report. Although this report has no standard title, it is often called the

    A. remittance advice
    B. periodic interim payments
    C. DNFB (discharged, no final bill)
    D. chargemaster

    REFERENCE: LaTour and Eichenwald-Maki, p 794

49. Assume the patient has already met his or her deductible and that the physician is a non-participating Medicare provider, but does accept assignment. The standard fee for the services provided is $120.00. Medicare's PAR fee is $60.00 and Medicare's non-PAR fee is $57.00. How much reimbursement will the physician receive from Medicare?

    A. $120.00
    B. $60.00
    C. $57.00
    D. $45.60

    REFERENCE: Green and Rowell, p 292, 294, 437–439

50. This program, formerly called CHAMPUS (Civilian Health and Medical Program of the Uniformed Services), is a health care program for active members of the military and other qualified family members.

    A. TRICARE
    B. CHAMPVA
    C. Indian Health Service
    D. workers' compensation

    REFERENCE: Green and Rowell, p 502–505
                  Johns, p 258–259

51. Under Medicare Part B, Medicare participating providers

    A. will be able to collect his or her total charges.
    B. agrees to charge no more than 15% (limiting charge) over the allowed charge from the non-PAR fee schedule.
    C. accepts, as payment in full, the allowed charge from the non-PAR fee schedule.
    D. agrees to charge no more than 10% (limiting charge) over the allowed charge from the non-PAR fee schedule.

REFERENCE: Green and Rowell, p 292, 294, 437–439

52. If the physician's standard fee for a service is $210.00 and the Medicare PAR fee is $115.00, what is the limiting charge for a non-participating (non-PAR) provider?

    A. $241.50   C. $132.25
    B. $109.25   D. $125.63

REFERENCE: Green and Rowell, p 292, 294, 437–439

53. In calculating the fee for a physician's reimbursement, the three relative value units are each multiplied by

    A. geographic practice cost indices.
    B. national conversion factor.
    C. usual and customary fees for the service.
    D. the cost of living index for the particular region.

REFERENCE: Green, p 795–796
                Frisch, p 186
                Green and Rowell, p 23

54. If a participating provider's usual fee for a service is $700.00 and Medicare's allowed amount is $450.00, what amount is written off by the physician?

    A. none of it is written off   C. $340.00
    B. $250.00   D. $391.00

REFERENCE: Green and Rowell, p 292, 294, 437–439

55. Health plans that use _____ reimbursement methods issue lump-sum payments to providers to compensate them for all the health care services delivered to a patient for a specific illness and/or over a specific period of time.

    A. episode-of-care (EOC)   C. fee-for-service
    B. capitation   D. bundled

REFERENCE: Johns, p 270

56. Fee schedules are updated by third-party payers

    A. monthly.   C. annually.
    B. weekly.   D. semi-annually.

REFERENCE: Johns, p 308

57. Commercial insurance plans usually reimburse health care providers under some type of _____ payment system, where as the federal Medicare program uses some type of _____ payment system

    A. prospective, retrospective   C. retrospective, prospective
    B. retrospective, concurrent   D. prospective, concurrent

REFERENCE: Green and Rowell, p 275–276, 281
                       Green, p 843–845
                       Johns, p 268

58. The difference between a rejected claim and a denied claim is that
    A. A rejected claim is sent back to the provider, errors may be corrected and the claim resubmitted.
    B. A denied claim is sent back to the provider, errors may be corrected and the claim resubmitted.
    C. A rejected claim may be appealed, but a denied claim may not be appealed.
    D. If a procedure or service is unauthorized, the claim will be rejected, not denied.

REFERENCE: Rimmer, p 105–109
                       Green and Rowell, p 73–76, 78–79

59. Some services are performed by a nonphysician practitioner (such as a Physician Assistant). These services are an integral yet incidental component of a physician's treatment for illness or injury. A physician must have personally performed an initial visit and must remain actively involved in the continuing care to the patient. Medicare requires direct supervision for these services to be billed.
    A. "technical component" billing
    B. "assignment" billing
    C. "incident to" billing
    D. "assistant" billing

REFERENCE: Frisch, p 114
                Green and Bowie, p 297–298

Answer Key for Medical Billing and Reimbursement Systems

	ANSWER	EXPLANATION

1. D

2. B

3. A

4. B

5. A

6. C

7. C The Medicare Physician Fee Schedule (MPFS) amounts are 5% higher for participating (PAR) providers than for non-participating (non-PAR) providers. Only non-PAR physicians are subject to the "limiting" charge.

8. C The definition of "new patient" in the CPT Code Book is "one who has not received any professional services from the physician or another physician of the same specialty who belongs to the same group practice within the past three years". This definition is used by physicians. In the April 7, 2000 Federal Register (page 18451) CMS defined "new patient" as "one who does not already have a medical record number." This definition is used by hospitals under the outpatient prospective payment system (APCs).

9. D

10. D

11. D

12. D The limiting charge is 15% above Medicare's approved payment amount for doctors who do NOT accept assignment ($128.00 × 1.15 = $147.20).

13. B

14. B

15. A The Medicare Physician Fee Schedule (MPFS) reimburses providers according to predetermined rates assigned to services.

16. D The six dispositions are claim rejection, claim denial, claim return to provider, claim suspension, line item rejection, and line item denial.

17. A

18. C

19. B

20. B

21. C

22. A If a physician is a participating physician who accepts assignment, he will receive the lesser of the total charges or the PAR Medicare fee schedule amount. In this case, the Medicare fee schedule amount is less; therefore, the total received by the physician is $200.00.

Answer Key for Medical Billing and Reimbursement Systems

ANSWER   EXPLANATION

23. C   If a physician is a non-participating physician who does not accept assignment, he can collect a maximum of 15% (the limiting charge) over the non-PAR Medicare fee schedule amount. In this case, the non-PAR Medicare fee schedule amount is $190.00 and 15% over this amount is $28.50; therefore, the total that he can collect is $218.50.

24. B   The PAR Medicare fee schedule amount is $200.00. The patient has already met the deductible. Of the $200.00, the patient is responsible for 20% ($40.00). Medicare will pay 80% ($160.00). Therefore the total financial liability for the patient is $40.00.

25. A   If a physician is a non-participating physician who does not accept assignment, he may collect a maximum of 15% (the limiting charge) over the non-PAR Medicare fee schedule amount.

   $190.00 = non-PAR Medicare schedule amount.

   $190.00 × .20 = $38.00 = patient liable for 20% coinsurance

   $190.00 − $38.00 = $152.00 = Medicare pays 80%

   $190.00 × .15 = $28.50 = 15% (limiting charge) over non-PAR Medicare fee schedule amount

   Physician can balance bill and collect from the patient the difference between the non-PAR Medicare fee schedule amount and the total charge amount. Therefore, the patient's financial liability is $38.00 + $28.50 = $66.50.

26. A   Under the APC system, there exists a list of status indicators (also called service indicators, payment status indicators, or payment indicators). This indicator is provided for every HCPCS/ CPT code and identifies how the service or procedure would be paid (if covered) by Medicare for hospital outpatient visits.

27. B   Under the APC system, there exists a list of status indicators (also called service indicators, payment status indicators, or payment indicators). This indicator is provided for every HCPCS/ CPT code and identifies how the service or procedure would be paid (if covered) by Medicare for hospital outpatient visits.

28. D   Under the APC system, there exists a list of status indicators (also called service indicators, payment status indicators, or payment indicators). This indicator is provided for every HCPCS/ CPT code and identifies how the service or procedure would be paid (if covered) by Medicare for hospital outpatient visits.

29. C   Under the APC system, there exists a list of status indicators (also called service indicators, payment status indicators, or payment indicators). This indicator is provided for every HCPCS/ CPT code and identifies how the service or procedure would be paid (if covered) by Medicare for hospital outpatient visits.

30. B   Under the APC system, there exists a list of status indicators (also called service indicators, payment status indicators, or payment indicators). This indicator is provided for every HCPCS/ CPT code and identifies how the service or procedure would be paid (if covered) by Medicare for hospital outpatient visits.

   31   D

   32.   A

   33.   A

Answer Key for Medical Billing and Reimbursement Systems

ANSWER   EXPLANATION

34. D

35. A

36. C

37. B   GA indicates that a waiver of liability statement is on file. GZ indicates that an item or service is expected to be denied as not reasonable and necessary, but the physician's office does not have a signed ABN. GY indicates that an item or service is statutorily excluded or does not meet the definition of a Medicare benefit.

38. B   Under Medicare Part B, Congress has mandated special incentives to increase the number of health care providers signing PAR (participating) agreements with Medicare. One of those incentives includes a 5% higher fee schedule for PAR providers than for non-PAR (non-participating) providers.

39. D   Discounts are applied to those multiple procedures identified by CPT codes with status indicator "T" and also those CPT codes assigned with the modifier -73.

40. A   Local coverage determinations (LCDs) were formerly called local medical review policies (LMRPs).

41. B

42. C

43. C   The physician receives 80% of the MPFS amount ($48.00) from Medicare. (The remaining 20% ($12.00) is paid by the patient to the physician. The total amount paid is $60.00.)

44. A

45. B

46. D

47. A   When a patient meets the definition of critical care, the hospital must use CPT Code 99291 to bill for outpatient encounters in which critical care services are furnished. This code is used instead of another E&M code.

48. C

49. D   The Medicare non-PAR fee is 5% less than the Medicare PAR fee, which is $57.00 ($60.00 × .95 = $57.00).

           The physician then receives 80% ($57.00 × .80) of the non-PAR fee, which is $45.60 from Medicare. He will also collect 20% from the patient, which is $11.40.

50. A

51. C

Answer Key for Medical Billing and Reimbursement Systems

ANSWER   EXPLANATION

52.	D	Physician's standard fee	$210.00	
		Medicare fee	$115.00	
		Medicare PAR fee	$109.25	(115.00 × .95)
		Limiting charge	$125.63	(109.25 × 1.15)

53. A

54. B   The participating physician agrees to accept Medicare's fee as payment in full, therefore the physician would collect $450.00. The remainder ($700.00 − $450.00 = $250.00) is written off.

55. A

56. C

57. C

58. A

59. C

REFERENCES

Casto, A.B., and Layman, E. (2009). *Principles of healthcare reimbursement* (2nd edition). Chicago: American Health Information Management Association (AHIMA).

CMS Web site: http://www.cms.hhs.gov/home/Medicare.asp (This Web site provides links to pages containing official informational materials on all of the Medicare Fee-For-Service Payment Systems.)

Diamond, M. S. (2007) *Understanding hospital coding and billing a worktext.* Clifton Park, NY: Delmar Cengage Learning.

Federal Register, Department of Health and Human Services-Center for Medicare and Medicaid Services, Vol. 65 No. 68. Medicare Program, *"Prospective Payment System for Hospital Outpatient Services; Final Rule."* Friday, April 7, 2000.

Frisch, Belinda. (2007). *Correct coding for Medicare, compliance, and reimbursement.* Clifton Park, NY: Thomson Delmar Learning.

Green, Michelle A. (2010). *3-2-1- Code it!* (2nd ed.). Clifton Park, NY: Delmar Cengage Learning.

Green, M. A., & Rowell, J. C. (2008). *Understanding health insurance: A guide to billing and reimbursement* (9th ed.). Clifton Park, NY: Delmar Cengage Learning.

Johns, M.L. (2007). *Health Information Management Technology: An Applied Approach* (2nd edition). Chicago: American Health Information Management Association (AHIMA).

Jones, L. (2005). Coding and *reimbursement for hospital outpatient services.* Chicago: American Health Information Management Association (AHIMA).

Kuehn, L. (2009). *A practical approach to analyzing healthcare data.* Chicago: American Health Information Management Association (AHIMA).

LaTour, K., and Eichenwald-Maki, S. (2010). *Health information management: Concepts, principles, and practice* (3rd ed.). Chicago: American Health Information Management Association (AHIMA).

Rimmer, M. (2009). *Medical billing 101.* Clifton Park, NY: Thomson Delmar Learning.

Rizzo, Christina (2000). *Uniform billing: a guide to claims processing.* Albany, NY: Delmar Thomson Learning.

Schraffenberger, L.A., and Kuehn, L. (2007). *Effective management of coding services* (3rd edition.). Chicago: American Health Information Management Association (AHIMA).

Scott, K. (2009). *Coding and reimbursement for hospital inpatient services* (2nd ed.). Chicago: American Health Information Management Association (AHIMA).

Competencies for the Medical
Billing and Reimbursement Chapter

Question	CCS-P Domain						
	1	2	3	4	5	6	7
1			X				
2				X			
3				X			
4				X			
5				X			
6				X			
7				X			
8			X				
9				X			
10				X			
11							X
12				X			
13						X	
14				X			
15				X			
16				X			
17				X			
18				X			
19				X			
20				X			
21				X			
22				X			
23				X			
24				X			

Question	CCS-P Domain						
	1	2	3	4	5	6	7
25				X			
26				X			
27				X			
28				X			
29				X			
30				X			
31							X
32				X			
33			X				
34							X
35				X			
36				X			
37				X			
38				X			
39				X			
40							X
41			X				
42				X			
43				X			
44				X			
45				X			
46				X			
47			X				
48					X		
49							X

Question	CCS-P Domain						
	1	2	3	4	5	6	7
50	X						
51				X			
52				X			
53				X			
54				X			
55				X			
56				X			
57				X			
58				X			
59				X			

VII. ICD-9-CM Coding

Toni Cade, MBA, RHIA, CCS, FAHIMA

Infectious and Parasitic Diseases

1. Patient presents with a left ankle fracture. Patient also has AIDS with Kaposi's sarcoma of the skin.
    A. 042, 176.0, 824.8
    B. 824.8, 176.0, V08
    C. 176.1, 824.8, V08
    D. 824.8, 042, 176.0

    REFERENCE: Brown, p 115–116, 407–408, 410–411
                    Schraffenberger, p 70–73

2. Septicemia due to methicillin-resistant *Staphylococcus aureus*. Patient also has septic shock and decubitus ulcer of the sacrum.
    A. 038.19, 785.59, 707.02
    B. 038.11, V09.0, 707.03, 995.92, 707.20, 785.52
    C. 707.00, 038.11, 785.59
    D. 038.11, 785.59, 995.92

    REFERENCE: Bowie and Shaffer, p 89–92
                    Brown, p 109–113, 241–242
                    Lovaasen and Schwerdtfeger, p 167–168
                    Schraffenberger, p 68–70

3. Nephropathy due to tuberculosis (confirmed histologically) of the kidney.
    A. 016.05, 583.81
    B. 583.81, 016.0
    C. 016.02, 583.81

    REFERENCE: Brown, p 108–109, 220–222
                    Eid, p 217
                    Lovaasen and Schwerdtfeger, p 164–165
                    Schraffenberger, p 66

4. A patient presents with fever and severe headache. Diagnostic workup revealed viral meningitis. Patient also has asthma with acute exacerbation and hypertension, both of which are treated.
    A. 047.9, 780.60, 784.0, 493.90, 401.9
    B. 047.8, 493.92, 401.1
    C. 047.9, 493.92, 401.9
    D. 780.60, 784.0, 047.9, 493.90, 401.9

    REFERENCE: Brown, p 107, 161–162, 186–187, 346–348
                    Schraffenberger, p 66, 140–142, 172–176

5. Nurse Jones suffered a needlestick and presented for HIV testing. She saw her physician for the test results and counseling.
    A. V72.60, 795.71
    B. 795.71, V65.8
    C. V08, V72.60, V65.44
    D. V73.89, V65.44, V01.79

    REFERENCE: Brown, p 115–116
                    Lovaasen and Schwerdtfeger, 158
                    Schraffenberger, p 73

6. Right arm paralysis due to poliomyelitis that patient suffered as a child.
    A. 045.11, 342.81
    B. 138, 344.41
    C. 344.40, 138
    D. 138, 344.41

    REFERENCE: Brown, p 108–109

Neoplasms

7. Patient presents for chemotherapy for treatment of breast cancer with liver metastasis. Patient had a mastectomy 4 months ago.
   A. 197.7, V10.3
   B. 174.9, 197.7
   C. V58.11, V10.3, 197.7
   D. V58.11, 174.9, V45.71, 197.7

   REFERENCE: Bowie & Schaffer, p 107
   Brown, p 376–377, 379–381, 386–390
   Schraffenberger, p 78–82

8. Patient with a history of malignant neoplasm of the lung presents with seizures. Workup revealed metastasis of the lung cancer to the brain.
   A. 780.39, V10.11 198.3
   B. 162.9, V10.11, 198.3, 780.39
   C. 198.3, 780.39, V10.11
   D. 198.3, 780.39, 162.9

   REFERENCE: Bowie and Schaffer, p 113–114
   Brown, p 376–377, 379–381
   Schraffenberger, p 91–93

9. Patient presents for treatment of dehydration following chemotherapy as treatment for ovarian cancer.
   A. 276.51, 183.0
   B. 183.0, 276.51
   C. 276.50, 183.0

   REFERENCE: Bowie and Schaffer, p 116
   Brown, p 386–390

10. Malignant melanoma, skin of back.

    A. 173.5
    B. 172.5

    REFERENCE: Brown, p 373
    Schraffenberger, p 78

11. Patient presented with abdominal pain. Needle biopsy of the liver revealed secondary malignancy of the liver. Primary site was unknown at time of discharge.
    A. 197.7, 199.1, 789.00
    B. 197.7, 789.00
    C. 197.7, 199.1

REFERENCE: Brown, p 379–381

12. Patient with a history of cancer of the colon and status post-colostomy presents for closure of the colostomy. Patient is also being treated for chronic obstructive pulmonary disease and diastolic heart failure.
    A. 153.2, 496, 428.30
    B. V55.3, 496, V10.05, 428.30
    C. V55.3, 496, V10.05, 428.0
    D. V10.05, 492.8, 428.30

    REFERENCE: Brown, p 186, 339–340, 391
    Schraffenberger, p 324, 335–336

Endocrine, Nutritional, and Metabolic Disorders and Immunity Disorders

13. Female, 68 years old, presents with type II diabetes mellitus with a diabetic ulcer of the left heel.
    A. 250.80, 707.14
    B. 707.14, 250.80
    C. 250.81, 707.13
    D. 250.82, 707.14

REFERENCE: Brown, p 119–126, 242–243
                Lovaasen and Schwerdtfeger, p 241–245
                Schraffenberger, p 100–102, 228

14. Sixty-seven-year-old presents with acute dehydration that needs treatment, secondary to nausea and vomiting that is due to acute gastroenteritis.
    A. 558.9, 787.01, 276.51
    B. 276.51, 558.9
    C. 276.51, 787.01, 558.9
    D. 276.51, 558.9

REFERENCE: Schraffenberger, p 104, 184

15. Patient was found at home in a hypoglycemic coma. This patient had never been diagnosed as being diabetic.
    A. 250.30
    B. 251.0
    C. 251.1
    D. 251.2

REFERENCE: Brown, p 128

16. Aplastic anemia secondary to chemotherapy administered for multiple myeloma.
    A. 284.89, 203.00, E933.1
    B. 203.00, 284.81, E933.1
    C. 284.9, 203.00, E933.1
    D. 203.01, 284.89, E933.1

REFERENCE: Bowie and Schaffer, p 143
                Brown, p 153–154, 437–438

17. Male patient presents with gastrointestinal hemorrhage resulting in acute blood loss anemia. Source of bleed unknown.
    A. 285.9, 578.1
    B. 578.1, 285.1
    C. 578.9, 285.1
    D. 578.9, 280.0

REFERENCE:
                Brown, p 152–153, 199–200

18. Patient presents with severe malnutrition.
    A. 263.9
    B. 261
    C. 263.8

REFERENCE: Brown, p 129
                Lovaasen and Schwerdtfeger, p 251

Diseases of the Blood and Blood-Forming Organs

19. Patient presents with thrombocytopenia, purpura.
    A. 287.4
    B. 287.8
    C. 287.9
    D. 287.30

REFERENCE: Lovaasen and Schwerdtfeger, p 192–193
                Schraffenberger, p 110

20. Sickle cell anemia with crisis
    A. 282.61
    B. 282.62
    C. 282.63
    D. 282.69

REFERENCE: Brown, p 154
                  Lovaasen and Schwerdtfeger, p 187–188
                  Schraffenberger, p 108

21. Sickle cell pain crisis
    A. 282.62
    B. 282.60
    C. 282.5
    D. 282.42

REFERENCE: Bowie and Schaffer, p 143
                  Brown, p 154
                  Eid, p 223
                  Schraffenberger, p, 108

22. Cooley's anemia
    A. 282.41
    B. 282.0
    C. 282.49
    D. 282.42

REFERENCE: Brown, p 151
                  Schraffenberger, p 108

23. Anemia due to end-stage renal disease, treatment was focused on the anemia.
    A. 285.8
    B. 285.21, 585.6
    C. 285.22, 585.6
    D. 285.9

REFERENCE: Brown, p 151
                  Schraffenberger, p 109

24. Pernicious anemia
    A. 280.9
    B. 280.8
    C. 281.1
    D. 281.0

REFERENCE: Brown, p 151
                  Schraffenberger, p 107–108

Mental Disorders

25. Mild mental retardation due to old viral encephalitis
    A. 319, 049.8
    B. 317, 326
    C. 317, 047.8
    D. 317, 139.0

REFERENCE: Brown, p 108

26. Anxiety with depression
    A. 300.11, 311
    B. 300.4
    C. 309.28
    D. 300.00, 311

REFERENCE: Brown, p 139
                  Lovaasen and Schwerdtfeger, p 560–561

27. Delirium tremens with alcohol dependence
  A. 291.0, 303.90
  B. 303.91, 291.0
  C. 291.3, 303.90
  D. 291.0, 303.00
REFERENCE: Brown, p 141–142
               Schraffenberger, p 115, 119–121

28. Latent schizophrenia, chronic with acute exacerbation
  A. 295.52
  B. 295.55
  C. 295.54
  D. 295.53
REFERENCE: Bowie and Schaffer, p 156
               Brown, p 137

29. Chronic paranoia due to continuous cocaine dependence.
  A. 301.0, 305.61
  B. 297.1, 304.21
  C. 297.1, 305.61
REFERENCE: Brown, p 143
               Schraffenberger, p 115, 119–121

30. Psychogenic paroxysmal tachycardia
  A. 427.2, 316
  B. 306.2, 427.1
  C. 427.1, 306.2
  D. 316, 427.2
REFERENCE: Brown, p 139

Diseases of the Nervous System and Sense Organs

31. A 5-year-old female presents to ambulatory surgery with chronic otitis media.
  A. 381.20
  B. 381.3,
  C. 382.9
  D. 381.89
REFERENCE: Schraffenberger, p 133

32. Patient is a type II diabetic with a diabetic cataract.
  A. 250.51, 366.42
  B. 250.50, 366.41
  C. 250.52, 366.41
  D. 366.41, 250.50
REFERENCE: Brown, p 125, 172
               Schraffenberger, p 100–102, 132

33. Epilepsy and paraplegia as residuals of a head injury suffered 5 years ago
  A. 345.90, 344.1, 907.0
  B. 345.91, 344.1, 907.0
  C. 959.01, 345.90, 344.1
  D. 345.81, 344.2, 907.0
REFERENCE: Brown, p 164–165
               Lovaasen and Schwerdtfeger, p 585–586
               Schraffenberger, p 126–130

34. Alzheimer's disease with dementia
    A. 331.0, 294.8
    B. 294.8
    C. 331.0, 294.10
    D. 331.0

REFERENCE: Brown, p 136

35. Meningitis sarcoidosis
    A. 321.2, 136.1
    B. 135, 321.4
    C. 136.1, 321.2
    D. 321.4, 135

REFERENCE: Brown, p 162

36. Carpal tunnel syndrome
    A. 354.0
    B. 354.1

REFERENCE: Brown, p 167

Diseases of the Circulatory System

37. Patient presents with carotid artery disease and acute cerebral infarction with left hemiparesis, dysphagia, and aphasia. Dysphagia and aphasia have resolved by discharge, but residual hemiparesis remains.
    A. 433.11, 342.90
    B. 433.11, 434.91, 342.90, 784.3, 787.20
    C. 436, 342.90, 784.3, 787.20
    D. 433.11, 342.90, 784.3, 787.20

REFERENCE: Brown, p 342–344
              Schraffenberger, p 157

38. Hypertensive kidney disease, congestive heart failure, and acute systolic heart failure
    A. 593.9, 401.9, 482.0, 428.21
    B. 404.11, 428.0, 428.21
    C. 403.90, 428.0, 428.21
    D. 404.91

REFERENCE: Brown, p 347–348
              Schraffenberger, p 142, 152–1539

39. Acute inferior wall myocardial infarction with unstable angina. Patient also has coronary artery disease and atrial fibrillation.
    A. 410.41, 411.1, 414.01, 427.31
    B. 410.41, 414.00, 411.1, 427.31
    C. 410.40, 414.00, 427.31
    D. 410.41, 414.00, 427.31

REFERENCE: Bowie and Schaffer, p 192–194
              Brown, p 333–339
              Eid, p 226
              Schraffenberger, p 145–150, 154

40. Patient with a diagnosis of aortic valve stenosis and mitral valve regurgitation presents for aortic valve replacement. Patient is also under treatment for congestive heart failure.
    A. 396.2, 398.91
    B. 424.1, 424.0, 428.0
    C. 396.2, 428.0

REFERENCE: Brown, p 329–332
              Lovaasen and Schwerdtfeger, p 302
              Schraffenberger, p 139

41. Atherosclerotic peripheral vascular disease of the lower leg with claudication.
    A. 440.20   C. 444.22
    B. 440.21   D. 443.9

REFERENCE: Brown, p 350–351

Diseases of the Respiratory System

42. Patient presents to the outpatient department for a chest x-ray. Physician order lists the following reasons for the chest x-ray: fever and cough, rule out pneumonia. Radiologist reports the chest x-ray is positive for pneumonia.
    A. 486   C. 780.61, 786.2
    B. 486, 780.61, 786.2, V72.5   D. V72.5, 780.60, 786.2

REFERENCE: Brown, p 179–184
                Schraffenberger, p 171

43. Aspiration pneumonia with pneumonia due to *Staphylococcus aureus*. Patient also has emphysema.
    A. 507.0, 482.9, 496   C. 507.0, 491.21
    B. 507.0, 482.41, 496   D. 507.0, 482.41, 492.8

REFERENCE: Brown, p 179–183
                Schraffenberger, p 169, 171

44. Acute respiratory failure due to congestive heart failure.
    A. 518.81, 428.0
    B. 428.0, 518.83
    C. 428.0, 518.81

REFERENCE: Brown, p 157–159, 189–191, 339–340
                Lovaasen and Schwerdtfeger, p 266–277
                Schraffenberger, p 152–153, 174–177

45. Hypertrophic tonsillitis
    A. 463
    B. 474.00
    C. 474.02

REFERENCE: Schraffenberger, p 169

46. Chronic obstructive pulmonary disease with an exacerbation of acute bronchitis
    A. 491.22   C. 466.0, 496
    B. 496, 466.0   D. 491.22, 466.0

REFERENCE: Brown, p 186–187
                Schraffenberger, p 169

47. Extrinsic asthma with status asthmaticus
    A. 493.11   C. 493.91
    B. 493.90   D. 493.81

REFERENCE: Brown, p 186–188
                Schraffenberger, p 172–174
                Lovaasen and Schwerdtfeger, p 274–275

48. Exacerbation of myasthenia gravis resulting in acute respiratory failure.
    A. 358.00, 518.81   C. 358.00, 581.89
    B. 518.81, 358.01   D. 518.82, 358.00
REFERENCE: Brown, p 189–191, 194–195
                 Schraffenberger, p 174–177

Disease of the Digestive System

49. Patient presents to the hospital for repair of ventral hernia. Surgery is canceled after chest x-ray revealed lower lobe pneumonia. Patient is placed on antibiotics to treat the pneumonia.
    A. 553.20, 486, V64.1   C. 486, 553.20
    B. 486, 553.20, V64.3   D. 553.20, 486

REFERENCE: Brown, p 72–73, 181–182, 208–210
                 Schraffenberger, p 40, 171, 183

50. Gastric ulcer with hemorrhage resulting in acute blood-loss anemia..
    A. 531.20, 285.1   C. 531.40, 280.0
    B. 285.1, 531.20   D. 531.40, 285.1

REFERENCE: Bowie and Schaffer, p 218–219
                 Brown, p 116–117, 203
                 Schraffenberger, p 109, 182

51. Diverticulitis large bowel with abscess
    A. 562.10
    B. 562.11
    C. 562.11, 569.5

REFERENCE: Brown, p 205

52. Acute and chronic cholecystitis with cholelithiasis.
    A. 574.00, 574.10, V64.41   C. 574.00
    B. 574.00, 574.10   D. 574.00, V64.41

REFERENCE: Brown, p 206–207
                 Eid, p 230
                 Lovaasen and Schwerdtfeger, p 543
                 Schraffenberger, p 184

53. Bleeding esophageal varices with alcoholic liver cirrhosis and portal hypertension. Patient is alcohol dependent.
    A. 456.20, 571.2, 303.90   C. 572.3, 571.2, 303.90, 456.20
    B. 571.2, 456.20, 303.90, 280.0 D. 303.90, 456.20, 303.90

REFERENCE: Brown, p 141–145, 203

54. Patient presented for workup for melena. Laboratory results revealed chronic blood loss anemia. Colonoscopy with biopsy revealed Crohn's disease of the descending colon.
    A. 578.1, 555.1
    B. 555.1
    C. 555.1, 578.1

REFERENCE: Brown, p 151
                 Schraffenberger, p 184

Diseases of the Genitourinary System

55. Acute urinary tract infection due to *E. coli*
    A. 599.0, 041.4
    B. 599.0
    C. 041.4, 599.0
    D. 590.2, 041.4

REFERENCE: Brown, p 112
               Schraffenberger, p 194

56. Patient presents with complaint of gross hematuria. Diagnosis of benign prostatic hypertrophy is made.
    A. 600.01
    B. 600.00
    C. 600.00, 599.71

REFERENCE: Brown, p 225–226
               Lovaasen and Schwerdtfeger, p 207

57. Male patient presents to the ER in acute renal failure; he is also being treated for hypertension
    A. 410.00, 586
    B. 401.9, 584.9
    C. 585.9, 401.1
    D. 584.9, 401.9

REFERENCE: Brown, p 219–221

58. Hemorrhagic cystitis
    A. 595.9
    B. 595.9, 041.4
    C. 595.82
    D. 596.7

REFERENCE: Brown, p 217
               Schraffenberger, p 195

59. Chronic kidney disease due to hypertension and type I diabetes mellitus
    A. 250.41, 403.90, 585.9
    B. 250.40, 403.10, 585.1
    C. 403.90, 250.41, 585.9, V58.67
    D. 403.10, 250.41, 585.2

REFERENCE: Brown, p 220

60. End-stage kidney disease which resulted from malignant hypertension
    A. 403.01, 585.6
    B. 585.9, 401.0
    C. 403.00
    D. 401.0, 585.9

REFERENCE: Brown, p 219–220
               Schraffenberger, p 142–194

Obstetrics

61. Vaginal delivery of a full-term liveborn infant. Patient had post delivery elective tubal ligation.
    A. 650, V25.2, V27.0
    B. 648.91, V27.0
    C. 650, V27.0

REFERENCE: Bowie and Schaffer, p 253–254
               Brown, p 269–271, 282–283
               Schraffenberger, p 212–214

62. Incomplete spontaneous abortion complicated by excessive hemorrhage.
    A. 634.12
    B. 634.12, 285.1
    C. 634.11
    D. 634.91

REFERENCE: Brown, p 293–295
               Lovaasen and Schwerdtfeger, p 395–396
               Schraffenberger, p 204–206

63. Patient had obstructed labor due to breech presentation; a single liveborn was delivered via Cesarean section. (Not necessary to code ICD-9-CM procedure code for cesarean section delivery)
    A. 660.81
    B. 660.01, 652.21, V27.0
    C. 660.01, V27.0
    D. 660.81, 652.21

REFERENCE: Brown, p 269–271, 283

64. Patient delivered a single newborn at 43 weeks' gestation.
    A. 650, V27.0
    B. 645.20, V27.0
    C. 644.21, V27.0
    D. 645.21, V27.0

REFERENCE: Brown, p 279–282
               Schraffenberger, p 213–214

65. Female, 26 weeks' pregnancy is treated for a fractured distal radius and ulna.
    A. 813.44
    B. 648.93, 813.44
    C. 813.44, V22.2
    D. V22.2, 813.44

REFERENCE: Brown, p 269–270
               Schraffenberger, p 215, 265

66. Patient diagnosed with tubal pregnancy.
    A. 633.20
    B. 633.11
    C. 633.00
    D. 633.10

REFERENCE: Brown, p 298–299
               Schraffenberger, p 210–212

Diseases of the Skin and Subcutaneous Tissue

67. Abscess with cellulitis of the abdominal wall. Culture is positive for Staph aureus.
    A. 682.8, 041.11
    B. 682.2, 041.11
    C. 682.2, 707.8
    D. 682.2

REFERENCE: Brown, p 241–242
               Schraffenberger, p 226

68. Patient had a cholecystectomy 6 days ago and is now coming back with evidence of staphylococcal cellulitis at the site of operative incision.
    A. 958.3, 682.2, 041.19
    B. 998.51, 682.8, 041.11
    C. 958.3, 682.8, 041.11
    D. 998.59, 682.2, 041.10

REFERENCE: Brown, p 242–243
               Eid, p 233

69. Chronic ulcers of the calf and back.
    A. 707.12, 707.8
    B. 707.8

REFERENCE: Brown, p 242–244
                Lovaasen and Schwerdtfeger, p 606–607
                Schraffenberger, p 228, 230–231

70. Dermatitis due to prescription topical antibiotic cream used as directed by physician
    A. 692.4   C. 692.3
    B. 692.3, E930.9   D. 692.3, E930.1

REFERENCE: Brown, p 239–240
                Lovaasen and Schwerdtfeger, p 604–605
                Schraffenberger, p 226

71. Boil, left face.
    A. 680.0   C. 680.9
    B. 680.8   D. 682.9

REFERENCE: Brown, p 239

72. Abscessed pilonidal cyst
    A. 685.1   C. 685.0
    B. 686.09   D. 686.01

REFERENCE: Brown, p 239

Diseases of the Musculoskeletal System and Connective Tissue

73. Pathological fracture of the femur due to metastatic bone cancer. Patient has a history of lung cancer.
    A. 198.5, 733.14, V10.11   C. 733.19, 198.5, V10.11
    B. 733.14, 198.5, V10.11   D. 821.00, 162.9

REFERENCE: Brown, p 255
                Lovaasen and Schwerdtfeger, p 436–438
                Schraffenberger, p 92, 235–236

74. Herniated lumbar intervertebral disc with paresthesia
    A. 722.11
    B. 839.20
    C. 722.10

REFERENCE: Brown, p 251–252
                Schraffenberger, p 234

75. Pyogenic arthritis of the hip due to Group A streptococcus
    A. 716.95, 041.01   C. 711.05, 041.01
    B. 715.95, 041.01   D. 711.05

REFERENCE: Brown, p 253
                Schraffenberger, p 67–68, 234

76. Bunion left foot and hammertoe right foot.
    A. 727.1, 735.4   C. 727.2, 735.4
    B. 727.1, 735.8   D. 727.1, 735.3

REFERENCE: Schraffenberger, p 234–235

77. Malunion of humeral fracture (original injury occurred 1 year ago).
    A. 812.20   C. 733.81, 905.2
    B. 733.82, 905.2   D. 733.94, 905.2

REFERENCE: Schraffenberger, p 235–236

78. Recurrent internal derangement of the left knee.
    A. 715.96
    B. 718.36
    C. 836.2

REFERENCE: Brown, p 254

Congenital Anomalies

79. Liveborn infant, born in hospital, cleft palate and lip
    A. 749.00, 749.10   C. V30.00, 749.20
    B. 749.20   D. V30.00, 749.00, 749.10

REFERENCE: Bowie and Schaffer, p 290–291
                   Brown, p 307, 314
                   Schraffenberger, p 241, 244, 330–331

80. Newborn, born in hospital with tetralogy of Fallot
    A. 745.8   C. 745.2
    B. V30.01, 746.09   D. V30.00, 745.2

REFERENCE: Brown, p 307, 314

81. Newborn infant transferred to Manasota Hospital for treatment of esophageal atresia. Code for Manasota Hospital.
    A. V30.00   C. V30.00, 750.3
    B. 750.3   D. 750.3, V30.00

REFERENCE: Brown, p 307

82. Cervical spina bifida with hydrocephalus
    A. 741.02   C. 741.01
    B. 741.93   D. 741.91

REFERENCE: Brown, p 307
                   Eid, p 235
                   Schraffenberger, p 240–241

83. Infant with clubfoot.
    A. 754.70   C. 736.71
    B. 754.71   D. 736.79

REFERENCE: Brown, p 307
                   Schraffenberger, p 245–246

84. Full-term infant, born in hospital. Diagnosed with polycystic kidneys.
 A. 753.12
 B. V30.00, 753.12
 C. V30.00
 D. 753.12, V30.00

REFERENCE: Brown, p 307, 314
             Schraffenberger, p 241, 244–245, 330–331

Certain Conditions Originating in the Perinatal Period

85. Full-term newborn, born in hospital. Mother is addicted to cocaine; however, infant tested negative.
 A. V30.00, 760.75
 B. 779.5 V29.8
 C. V30.00, 779.5
 D. V30.00, V29.8

REFERENCE: Brown, p 314, 318–319
             Schraffenberger, p 241, 330

86. Preterm infant born via Cesarean section presents at Children's Hospital for severe birth asphyxia
 A. V30.01, 765.10, 768.5
 B. 765.10, 768.5, V30.01
 C. 768.5, 765.10
 D. 768.5

REFERENCE: Brown, p 315–316

87. Neonatal jaundice in preterm infant born in hospital.
 A. V30.00, 774.2
 B. 774.2
 C. V30.00

REFERENCE: Brown, p 314

88. One-week-old infant presents for admission to the hospital with diagnosis of urinary tract infection contracted prior to birth. Urine culture positive for E. coli.
 A. V30.00, 599.0
 B. 599.0, 041.4
 C. V30.00, 599.0, 041.4
 D. 771.82, 041.4

REFERENCE: Brown, p 107, 319

89. Hypoglycemia in infant with diabetic mother
 A. 251.2
 B. 775.1
 C. 775.0
 D. 251.1

REFERENCE: Brown, p 313, 320–321

90. Full-term infant born in hospital. Birth complicated by cord compression which affected newborn.
 A. V30.00, 762.5
 B. V30.00
 C. 762.5
 D. 762.6, V30.00

REFERENCE: Bowie and Schaffer, p 300–301
             Brown, p 314, 319
             Schraffenberger, p 241, 330–331

Symptoms, Signs, and Ill-Defined Conditions

91. Patient presented with abdominal pain. Discharge diagnosis is listed as abdominal pain due to gastroenteritis or diverticulosis.
    - A. 789.00
    - B. 562.10, 558.9
    - C. 789.00, 558.9, 562.10
    - D. 558.9, 562.10, 789.00

REFERENCE: Bowie and Schaffer, p 309–310
Brown, p 97–99
Schraffenberger, p 184, 254–255

92. Lung mass.
    - A. 518.89
    - B. 786.6
    - C. 793.1

REFERENCE: Brown, p 97–99

93. Pap smear with cervical high-risk human papillomavirus (HPV) DNA test positive
    - A. 795.05
    - B. 795.09
    - C. 795.04
    - D. 795.02

REFERENCE: Brown, p 97–99

94. Patient presents to the emergency room with ascites.
    - A. 789.30
    - B. 789.51
    - C. 789.59
    - D. 782.3

REFERENCE: Brown, p 97–99

95. Patient presented with fever due to bacteremia.
    - A. 780.61, 790.7
    - B. 038.9
    - C. 780.61
    - D. 790.7, 780.61

REFERENCE: Brown, p 97–99
Eid, p 236–237
Lovaasen and Schwerdtfeger, p 136–137

96. Patient presents with urinary retention
    - A. 788.21
    - B. 788.29
    - C. 788.20

REFERENCE: Brown, p 97–99

Injury and Poisoning

97. Fracture of the medial malleolus due to fall down steps.
    - A. 824.1, E880.9
    - B. 824.0, E880.9
    - C. 824.0
    - D. 824.1, E880.1

REFERENCE: Bowie and Schaffer, p 317–320
Brown, p 407–408, 410
Schraffenberger, p 265–267

98. Closed head injury, patient was a passenger in a motor vehicle involved in a head-on collision with another motor vehicle.
    A. 959.01, E812.1   C. 959.01, E813.1
    B. 959.09, E812.2   D. 959.09, E813.1

REFERENCE: Brown, p 399–402
                    Schraffenberger, p 279–280

99. Gunshot wound to abdomen with moderate laceration of liver. Patient was assaulted with a pistol.
    A. 864.00, E965.1   C. 864.13, E965.1
    B. 864.10, E965.0   D. 864.13, E965.0

REFERENCE: Brown, p 399–402
                    Schraffenberger, p 271–272

100. Patient has third-degree burn of upper back which involved 20% of his body surface. There was an explosion and fire at his home.
    A. 942.25, 948.22, E890.2   C. 942.34, 948.22, E890.3
    B. 942.44, 948.21, E895   D. 942.24, 949.3, E897

REFERENCE: Brown, p 425–428
                    Schraffenberger, p 275–277

101. Third-degree burn to thigh and second-degree burn to foot. Patient was burned by hot liquid.
    A. 945.36, 945.22, E924.0   C. 945.22, E924.0
    B. 945.22, 945.36, E924.0   D. 945.29, 945.39, E924.0

REFERENCE: Brown, p 425–428
                    Lovaasen and Schwerdtfeger, p 493–494
                    Schraffenberger, p 275–277

102. Laceration of left wrist with injury to radial nerve as a result of an accident with embedded glass.
    A. 881.02   C. 955.3, E920.8
    B. 881.12, E920.8   D. 881.12, 955.3, E920.8

REFERENCE: Brown, p 399–402, 414
                    Schraffenberger, p 264

103. Female, 76 years old, presents with tachycardia due to theophylline toxicity.
    A. 785.0, E942.1   C. 785.0, E944.1
    B. 995.20, E942.1   D. 995.20, E944.1

REFERENCE: Brown, p 435–438
                    Lovaasen and Schwerdtfeger, p 497–499
                    Schraffenberger, p 254–255

104. Patient suffered dizziness as a result of taking prescribed phenobarbital. Patient took medication with beer.
    A. 780.4, 980.0, E860.0
    B. 967.0, 980.0, 780.4, E851, E860.0
    C. 967.0, 708.4, E851
    D. 780.4, E851, E860.0

REFERENCE: Brown, p 435–438
                    Eid, p 262–263
                    Schraffenberger, p 290–291

105. Pain in hip due to displaced hip prosthesis.
    A. 996.49
    B. 996.77
    C. 719.45
    D. 996.49, 719.45

REFERENCE: Schraffenberger, p 293–295

106. Post-operative hemorrhage resulting in acute blood-loss anemia
    A. 997.72, 285.1
    B. 999.1, 285.1
    C. 998.11, 285.1
    D. 998.11

REFERENCE: Brown, p 152, 453
              Schraffenberger, p 296

V-Codes

107. Admission for colostomy takedown.
    A. V44.3
    B. 569.60
    C. 997.4
    D. V55.3

REFERENCE: Brown, p 83–85
              Schraffenberger, p 335–336

108. The patent presents for a preoperative EKG on an outpatient basis. He is scheduled to have an elective cholecystectomy tomorrow for chronic cholecystitis and cholelithiasis. EKG reveals atrial flutter.
    A. 574.10
    B. V72.81, 51.23
    C. V72.81, 574.10, 427.32
    D. 427.32

REFERENCE: Brown, p 88
              Schraffenberger, p 345–347

109. Screening examination for lung cancer
    A. V72.82
    B. 162.9
    C. V72.5
    D. V76.0

REFERENCE: Brown, p 89
              Eid, p 238
              Lovaasen and Schwerdtfeger, p 145
              Schraffenberger, p 347

110. Patient presents for observation for head injury following a fall. Patient also suffered a minor laceration to the forehead. Head injury was ruled out.
    A. V71.4, 873.42, E888.9
    B. 873.42, E888.9
    C. 959.01, 873.42, E888.9
    D. V71.4, E888.9

REFERENCE: Brown, p 86–87
              Lovaasen and Schwerdtfeger, p 145–146
              Schraffenberger, p 272–273, 345

When the question has the ICD-9-CM codes and their respective narrative description, you should practice answering the diagnoses in the question without using your coding book.

111. Elderly man presents to the emergency department for severe urinary retention. Upon study, it was determined that his hypertension was uncontrolled (215/108). Prior medical records show admission 8 weeks ago for the same problem. As per conditions on previous admission, his BPH is complicated by acute cystitis. He is noncompliant with medications. Medication for the hypertension was immediately started and his hypertension was quickly brought under control.

401.0	Essential hypertension, malignant
401.9	Essential hypertension, unspecified
595.0	Acute cystitis
595.9	Cystitis, unspecified
600.00	Hypertrophy, (benign) of prostate without urinary obstruction and other lower urinary tract symptoms (LUTS)
600.01	Hypertrophy (benign) of prostate with urinary obstruction and other lower urinary tract symptoms (LUTS)
600.3	Cyst of prostate
788.20	Retention of urine, unspecified
V15.81	Non-compliance with medical treatment

A. 600.01, 595.0, 788.20, 401.9, V15.81
B. 600.3, 595.0, 401.0, V15.81
C. 600.00, 595.9, 788.20, 401.9, V15.81
D. 600.3, 595.0, 788.20, 401.0, V15.81

REFERENCE: Brown, p 83–84, 97–98, 346–347
Schraffenberger, p 140–141, 195–196, 254–255

112. A 32-year-old female known to be HIV positive presents with lesions of the anterior trunk. The skin lesions were positive for Kaposi's sarcoma. Further examination revealed thrush.

042	Human Immunodeficiency Virus (HIV) Disease
112.0	Candidiasis of mouth
176.0	Kaposi's sarcoma of skin
528.9	Other and unspecified diseases of the oral soft tissues
686.00	Pyoderma, unspecified
795.71	Non-specific serological evidence of Human Immunodeficiency Virus (HIV)

A. 042, 686.00, 112.0
B. 042, 176.0, 112.0
C. 795.71, 176.0, 528.9
D. 795.71, 686.00, 528.9

REFERENCE: Brown, p 115–117
Schraffenberger, p 70–73

113. A female patient presents with uncontrolled type II diabetes. Patient also had an abscessed diabetic ulcer of the foot with growth of *Staphylococcus aureus,* methicillin resistant. Patient is on oral as well as injectional insulin for control of diabetes.

041.11	Bacterial infection in conditions classified elsewhere and of unspecified site, methicillin susceptible staphylococcus aureus (MSSA)
041.19	Bacterial infection in conditions classified elsewhere and of unspecified site, other staphylococcus
250.82	Diabetes mellitus with other specified manifestation, type II or unspecified type uncontrolled
250.83	Diabetes mellitus with other specified manifestation, type I (juvenile type) uncontrolled
682.7	Other cellulitis and abscess of foot, except toes
682.8	Other cellulitis and abscess of other specified sites
707.00	Chronic ulcer of skin, pressure ulcer, unspecified site
707.15	Ulcer of lower limbs, except pressure ulcer, of other part of foot (toes)
707.8	Chronic ulcer of other specified sites
V09.0	Infection with microorganisms resistant to penicillins

   A.   250.83, 682.8, V09.0
   B.   682.7, 682.87, 707.15, 041.19
   C.   682.8, 041.19, 250.82, 707.00
   D.   250.82, 682.7, 707.15, 041.11, V09.0

REFERENCE: Brown, p 112, 121–16, 239–242
                          Schraffenberger, p 67–68, 100–102, 226, 228

114. Patient presents from the nursing home in acute respiratory failure due to congestive heart failure. Patient also has pulmonary edema.

428.0	Congestive heart failure, unspecified
428.1	Left heart failure
428.20	Systolic heart failure, unspecified as to acute, chronic, or acute on chronic
518.4	Acute edema of lung, unspecified
518.81	Acute respiratory failure
518.84	Acute and chronic respiratory failure

   A.   428.1, 518.84, 518.4
   B.   428.20, 428.0, 518.81, 518.4
   C.   518.81, 428.0
   D.   428.0, 518.4

REFERENCE: Brown, p 189–192, 194–195
                          Lovaasen and Schwerdtfeger, p 312–313
                          Schraffenberger, p 152–153, 175–177

115. The patient has hypertensive heart disease and nephrosclerosis with end stage renal disease.

404.92	Hypertensive heart and chronic kidney disease, unspecified as malignant or benign, without heart failure and with chronic kidney disease Stage V or end stage renal disease
404.93	Hypertensive heart and chronic kidney disease unspecified as malignant or benign with heart failure and chronic kidney disease Stage V or end stage renal disease
585.6	End stage renal disease
585.9	Chronic kidney disease, unspecified
V56.0	Extracorporeal dialysis

   A. 404.93, 585.9   C. 404.93, 585.6
   B. 404.92, 585.6   D. 404.92, 585.9

REFERENCE: Brown, p 221–222
                   Lovaasen and Schwerdtfeger, p 303–304

116. The patient has had abnormal heavy uterine bleeding and abdominal pain. There was bright red blood in the vagina and the right adnexa was enlarged. The woman had a right follicular ovarian cyst. A laparoscopic ovarian cystectomy was performed. Following surgery she was transfused two units of packed red blood cells for acute blood-loss anemia.

(Code for diagnoses only)

280.0	Iron deficiency anemia secondary to blood loss (chronic)
285.1	Acute posthemorrhagic anemia
620.0	Follicular cyst of ovary

   A. 620.0, 285.1
   B. 620.0, 280.0

REFERENCE: Brown, p 153
                   Schraffenberger, p 109, 197

117. Jane is 6 weeks post mastectomy for carcinoma of the breast. She presents for chemotherapy. What is the correct sequencing of the codes?

   A. V58.11 (chemotherapy), 174.9 (malignant neoplasm of the breast), V45.71 (acquired absence of breast)
   B. V58.11 (chemotherapy), V10.3 (personal history of malignant neoplasm of breast), V45.71 (acquired absence of breast)
   C. V67.00 (follow-up exam after surgery), V58.11 (chemotherapy)
   D. V10.3 (personal history of malignant neoplasm of breast)

REFERENCE: Brown, p 386–390
                   Schraffenberger, p 333–334, 337–338

118. The patient presents due to increasingly severe pain in his right arm, shoulder, and neck for the past 6 weeks due to herniation of the C5–C6 disc. The patient is currently being treated for COPD and CAD with a history of a PTCA.

414.00	Coronary atherosclerosis of unspecified type of vessel, native or graft
414.01	Coronary atherosclerosis of native coronary artery
492.8	Other emphysema
496	Chronic airway obstruction, not elsewhere classified
722.0	Displacement of cervical intervertebral disc without myelopathy
722.11	Displacement of thoracic intervertebral disc without myelopathy
V45.82	Percutaneous transluminal coronary angioplasty status

    A. 722.0, 492.8, 414.01, V45.82
    B. 722.11, 496, 414.01, V45.82
    C. 722.11, 492.8, 414.00
    D. 722.0, 496, 414.01, V45.82

REFERENCE: Brown, p 186, 251–252, 337, 354
                    Schraffenberger, p 149–151, 174, 234, 333–334

119. A 75-year-old man presents with acute cerebral embolism with infarction. He had hemiplegia and dysphagia. Dysphagia was resolved at the time of discharge

342.90	Hemiplegia, unspecified, affecting unspecified side
434.11	Cerebral embolism with cerebral infarction
787.20	Dysphagia, unspecified

    A. 434.11, 342.90
    B. 434.11, 342.90, 787.20

REFERENCE: Bowie and Schaffer, p 196
                    Brown, p 342–343
                    Schraffenberger, p 129, 157

Infectious Diseases

120. Patient presents to St. Mary's Hospital emergency room with hyperthermia, tachycardia, hypoxemia, and altered mental status. Urinalysis is positive for E. coli and blood cultures are negative. Patient is immediately started on broad-spectrum IV antibiotics. Physician documents urosepsis as the final diagnosis. The coder should
    A. report 599.0 (UTI) and 041.4 (E. coli).
    B. report 038.42 (septicemia due to E. coli) and 995.91 (SIRS-sepsis).
    C. report 038.42 (septicemia due to E. coli), 599.0 (UTI) and 995.91 (SIRS-sepsis).
    D. confer with physician for reporting 038.9 (unspecified septicemia) based upon the clinical findings with 041.4 (E. coli) and 995.91 (SIRS-sepsis).

REFERENCE: Brown, p 109–110
                    Schraffenberger, p 68–70

121. Six-year-old Alex attended a birthday party where hot dogs and potato salad were served for lunch. Several hours after returning home, Alex began vomiting and having severe diarrhea. Alex presented to the hospital emergency room for treatment of his vomiting and diarrhea and was diagnosed with Salmonella food poisoning. Alex was given IV fluids for dehydration. Alex also has asthma, so he was given respiratory treatments while in the hospital.

003.9	Salmonella infection, unspecified
005.9	Food poisoning, unspecified
276.51	Dehydration
493.90	Asthma, unspecified, unspecified as to with status athmaticus or with acute exacerbation
787.03	Vomiting alone
787.91	Diarrhea

A. 003.9, 276.51, 493.90

C. 005.9, 276.51, 493.90

B. 005.9, 003.9, 276.51, 493.90

D. 005.9, 003.9, 267.51, 787.03, 787.91, 493.90

REFERENCE: Schraffenberger, p 65–66, 104, 172–174

122. A patient presents to the hospital emergency room with listlessness, fever, and persistent cough. Work-up reveals HIV infection with HIV-related pneumonia. The patient is treated for pneumonia.

042	Human Immunodeficiency Virus (HIV) disease
486	Pneumonia, organism unspecified
795.71	Nonspecific serologic evidence of Human Immunodeficiency Virus (HIV)
V08	Asymptomatic Human Immunodeficiency Virus (HIV) infection status

A. 486, 042

C. 486, 795.71

B. 042, 486

D. 486, V08

REFERENCE: Brown, p 115
Schraffenberger, p 70–73, 171

123. David presented with complaints of experiencing chronic fatigue and was experiencing flulike symptoms. Workup indicated that he had hepatitis C.

070.41	Acute hepatitis C with hepatic coma
070.51	Acute hepatitis C without mention of hepatic coma
487.1	Influenza with other respiratory manifestations
780.79	Other malaise and fatigue

A. 070.51, 487.1, 780.79

C. 070.51, 487.1

B. 070.41

D. 070.51

REFERENCE: Brown, p 70–71, 107
Schraffenberger, p 66

124. A 40-year-old female suddenly develops a painful rash and the physician reveals she has shingles. She is experiencing a great amount of anxiety and stress, so her physician prescribes medication for the shingles and for the anxiety that occurred as a reaction to the stress.

053.8	Herpes zoster with unspecified complication
053.9	Herpes zoster without mention of complication
300.00	Anxiety state, unspecified
308.0	Predominant disturbance of emotions
308.3	Other acute reactions to stress

A. 053.9, 308.0
B. 053.9, 308.3, 300.00

C. 053.8, 300.00
D. 053.8, 308.0

REFERENCE: Brown, p 107, 139–140
Schraffenberger, p 66, 115

Neoplasms

125. James presents to the hospital emergency room for severe anemia that is a result of the chemotherapy treatments he is receiving for metastatic prostate cancer to bone.

185	Malignant neoplasm of prostate
198.5	Secondary malignant neoplasm, bone and bone marrow
285.22	Anemia in neoplastic disease
E933.1	Adverse effect of antineoplastic and immunosuppressive drugs

A. 185, 198.5, 285.22, E933.1
B. E933.1, 285.22

C. 285.22, E933.1
D. 285.22, 185, 198.5, E933.1

REFERENCE: Brown, p 151, 153, 379–381
Schraffenberger, p 87–95, 109

126. Mary had resection of the large bowel for carcinoma of the colon. She presents for further staging of her cancer.

153.9	Malignant neoplasm of colon, unspecified
V10.05	Personal history of malignant neoplasm of large intestine
V58.0	Admission for radiotherapy
V67.09	Follow-up examination following other surgery

A. 153.9
B. V58.0, V10.05

C. V67.09, V58.0
D. V10.05, V58.0

REFERENCE: Brown, p 378–379, 386–387

127. Jackie has developed a lesion on her right shoulder. Result of a biopsy was positive for malignant melanoma.

172.6	Malignant melanoma of skin, upper limb, including shoulder
173.5	Other malignant neoplasm of skin of trunk, except scrotum
173.6	Other malignant neoplasm of skin of upper limb, including shoulder

A. 172.6
B. 172.5
C. 173.5

REFERENCE: Brown, p 243, 373–375
Schraffenberger, p 87

128. Sophia has been diagnosed with metastatic carcinoma of lung, primary site breast. Simple mastectomy performed 2 years ago. What is the principal diagnosis?
   A. metastatic carcinoma of lung
   B. carcinoma of breast
   C. history of carcinoma of breast
   D. status post mastectomy

REFERENCE: Brown, p 378–381
               Schraffenberger, p 92–93

129. Given the following diagnosis: "Carcinoma of axillary lymph nodes and lungs, metastatic from breast." What is the primary cancer site(s)?
   A. axillary lymph nodes   C. breast
   B. lungs   D. both A and B

REFERENCE: Brown, p 378–381, 383
               Schraffenberger, p 91–93

130. When is it appropriate to use category V10, history of malignant neoplasm?
   A. Primary malignancy recurred at original site and adjunct chemotherapy is directed at the site.
   B. Primary malignancy has been eradicated and no adjunct treatment is being given at this time.
   C. Primary malignancy eradicated and the patient presents for adjunct chemotherapy to primary site.
   D. Primary malignancy is eradicated; adjunct treatment is refused by patient even though there is some remaining malignancy.

REFERENCE: Brown, p 89–90
               Lovaasen and Schwerdtfeger, p 362–365
               Schraffenberger, p 86–87

Endocrine/Nutritional/Metabolic

131. Ralph is a 96-year-old nursing home resident with malnutrition. Ralph has suffered a previous stroke that has left him with dysphagia. Ralph is treated for malnutrition with hyperalimentation. Ralph was also found to have hypokalemia that was treated with IV potassium replacement. (Code diagnoses only.)

263.9	Unspecified protein-calorie malnutrition
276.8	Hypopotassemia (Hypokalemia)
438.82	Dysphagia, late effect of cerebrovascular disease
787.20	Dysphagia, unspecified

   A. 438.82, 263.9, 787.20   C. 263.9, 276.8, 438.82
   B. 787.20, 276.8   D. 263.9, 787.20, 276.8

REFERENCE: Brown, p 129, 342–343
               Schraffenberger, p 100, 104, 158

132. Jessica has been diagnosed with hyperthyroidism due to toxic multinodular goiter with crisis. She also has hypertension and has a history of sick sinus syndrome with pacemaker insertion.

240.9	Goiter, unspecified
241.1	Non-toxic multinodular goiter
242.21	Toxic multinodular goiter with mention of thyrotoxic crisis or storm
401.0	Essential hypertension, malignant
401.9	Essential hypertension, unspecified
427.81	Sinoatrial node dysfunction
V45.01	Other post-procedural states, cardiac pacemaker

   A. 240.9, 401.0, 427.81
   B. 242.21, 401.9, 427.81, V45.01
   C. 240.9, 242.21, 401.9. V45.01
   D. 242.21, 401.9. V45.01

REFERENCE: Brown, p 346
                   Lovaasen and Schwerdtfeger, p 238–240
                   Schraffenberger, p 99–100, 140–141, 333–334

133. Laura is 7 years old and has acute bronchitis and cystic fibrosis.

277.00	Cystic fibrosis without mention of meconium ileus
277.01	Cystic fibrosis with mention of meconium ileus
466.0	Acute bronchitis

   A. 466.0, 277.00
   B. 466.0, 277.01
   C. 277.00

REFERENCE: Brown, p 129
                   Schraffenberger, p 105, 169

134. Estelle has had nausea and vomiting and is unable to eat. She develops dehydration..

276.51	Dehydration
787.01	Nausea with vomiting
787.02	Nausea alone
787.03	Vomiting alone

   A. 276.51, 787.01   C. 276.51, 787.02
   B. 276.51   D. 276.51, 787.02, 787.03

REFERENCE: Schraffenberger, p 104

135. A patient presents for treatment of peripheral vascular disease, renal failure, and diabetes mellitus. The coder would
   A. assign codes for PVD, renal failure, and diabetes.
   B. assign codes for diabetes with peripheral vascular and renal manifestations.
   C. query physician for causal relationship between the PVD, renal failure, and diabetes.
   D. assign codes of diabetes with PVD and a code for renal failure.

REFERENCE: Brown, p 123–126

136. Lucy is in a diabetic coma. She is a type II diabetic with nephritic syndrome and gangrene of her toes, all due to her diabetes.

250.30	Diabetes mellitus with other coma, type II or unspecified type, not stated as uncontrolled
250.31	Diabetes mellitus with other coma, type I (juvenile type), not stated as uncontrolled
250.40	Diabetes mellitus with renal manifestations, type II or unspecified type, not stated as uncontrolled
250.41	Diabetes mellitus with renal manifestations, type I (juvenile type), not stated as uncontrolled
250.70	Diabetes mellitus with peripheral circulatory disorders, type II or unspecified type, not stated as uncontrolled
581.81	Nephrotic syndrome in diseases classified elsewhere
785.4	Gangrene

A. 250.30, 250.40, 581.81, 250.70, 785.4
B. 250.31, 581.81, 785.4
C. 250.30, 250.40, 581.81
D. 250.30 250.41, 785.4

REFERENCE: Brown, p 121–126
Schraffenberger, p 100–102, 194

137. George is a type II diabetic who is in a coma with a blood glucose of 876. He is diagnosed with diabetic ketoacidosis. George also has a diabetic cataract.

250.10	Diabetes mellitus with ketoacidosis, type II or unspecified type, not stated as uncontrolled
250.11	Diabetes mellitus with ketoacidosis, type I (juvenile type), not stated as uncontrolled
250.30	Diabetes mellitus with other coma, type II or unspecified type, not stated as uncontrolled
250.31	Diabetes mellitus with other coma, type I (juvenile type), not stated as uncontrolled
250.32	Diabetes mellitus with other coma, type II or unspecified type, uncontrolled
250.50	Diabetes mellitus with ophthalmic manifestations, type II or unspecified type, not stated as uncontrolled
250.51	Diabetes mellitus with ophthalmic manifestations, type I (juvenile type), not stated as uncontrolled
250.52	Diabetes mellitus with ophthalmic manifestations, type II or unspecified type, uncontrolled
366.41	Diabetic cataract
366.9	Unspecified cataract

A. 250.11, 250.31, 366.9
B. 250.10, 250.30, 250.50, 366.9
C. 250.32, 250.52, 366.41
D. 250.31, 250.51, 366.41

REFERENCE: Brown, p 121–126
Lovaasen and Schwerdtfeger, p 241–245
Schraffenberger, p 100–102, 132

138. Spencer has hypercholesterolemia that is treated with medication.

272.0	Pure hypercholesterolemia
272.1	Pure hyperglyceridemia
272.3	Hyperchylomicronemia
272.8	Other disorders of lipoid metabolism

A. 272.0
B. 272.1
C. 272.3
D. 272.8

REFERENCE: Schraffenberger, p 99

139. Edward is diagnosed with syndrome of inappropriate antidiuretic hormone with resultant electrolyte imbalance.

253.6	Other disorders of neurohypophysis (syndrome of inappropriate secretion of antidiuretic hormone-ADH)
272.9	Unspecified disorder of lipoid metabolism
276.50	Volume depletion, unspecified
276.8	Hypopotassemia (hypokalemia)
276.9	Electrolyte and fluid disorders, not elsewhere classified

A. 276.50
B. 276.9, 272.9
C. 253.6, 276.9
D. 253.6. 276.8

REFERENCE: Schraffenberger, p 99, 104

Blood and Blood-Forming Organs

140. Ruth presents with chronic lymphadenitis. She is on medication for gout and atrial fibrillation.

274.9	Gout, unspecified
289.1	Chronic lymphadenitis
289.2	Nonspecific mesenteric lymphadenitis
427.31	Atrial fibrillation

A. 289.1, 274.9, 427.31
B. 274.9, 289.2, 427.31
C. 289.1, 427.31
D. 289.1, 427.31, 274.9

REFERENCE: Brown, p 70–71
                Schraffenberger, p 104, 111, 154

141. Elizabeth has a history of von Willebrand's disease and frequently requires transfusions for chronic blood loss anemia associated with her condition. She presents to the outpatient department for routine blood transfusion. (Code diagnoses only)

280.0	Iron deficiency anemia secondary to blood loss (chronic)
280.1	Iron deficiency anemia secondary to inadequate dietary iron intake
285.1	Acute posthemorrhagic anemia
286.4	Von Willebrand's disease
286.7	Acquired coagulation factor deficiency

A. 285.1, 286.4
B. 286.7, 286.4
C. 286.4, 280.1
D. 280.0, 286.4

REFERENCE: Brown, p 151–153
                Schraffenberger, p 108–110

142. Steven, a 7 year old, is seen in the emergency department with severe joint pain. Following work-up it is discovered that he is having a severe crisis due to sickle cell anemia.

282.61	Sickle-cell disease (Hb-SS disease without crisis)
282.62	Sickle-cell disease (Hb-SS disease with crisis)
282.63	Sickle-cell /Hb-C disease without crisis
282.69	Other sickle-cell disease with crisis

A. 282.61
B. 282.62
C. 282.63
D. 282.69

REFERENCE: Bowie and Schaffer, p 143
Brown, p 154
Schraffenberger, p 108

143. Angela has just undergone orthopedic surgery. Documentation indicates that she lost 700 cc of blood during surgery. Her hemoglobin and hematocrit are monitored following surgery. Subsequently she is transfused. The physician documents anemia as a secondary diagnosis. In coding the diagnoses, the coder would
A. query the physician to clarify the type of anemia as acute blood loss.
B. assign a code for unspecified anemia.
C. assign a code for acute blood loss anemia.
D. not assign a code for anemia.

REFERENCE: Brown, p 152

144. Liza has been diagnosed with anemia. The pathology report indicates that she has iron-deficiency anemia.

280.0	Iron deficiency anemia secondary to blood loss (chronic)
280.8	Other specified iron deficiency anemias
280.9	Iron deficiency anemia, unspecified

A. 280.0
B. 280.9
C. 280.8

REFERENCE: Bowie and Schaffer, p 141–142
Brown, p 151

145. Peggy has thymic dysplasia with immunodeficiency.

254.0	Persistent hyperplasia of thymus
254.8	Other specified diseases of thymus gland
254.9	Unspecified disease of thymus gland
279.2	Combined immunity deficiency (thymic dysplasia with immunodeficiency)
279.3	Unspecified immune deficiency

A. 279.3, 254.8
B. 254.0
C. 279.2
D. 279.2, 254.9

REFERENCE: Brown, p 130

146. Aaron has suffered a hypoglycemic reaction due to alcohol intoxication. His hypoglycemia is treated.

250.80	Diabetes mellitus with other specified manifestations, type II or unspecified type, not stated as uncontrolled
251.2	Hypoglycemia, unspecified
303.90	Other and unspecified alcohol dependence, unspecified
305.00	Alcohol abuse, unspecified
995.29	Unspecified adverse effect of other drug, medicinal and biological substance

A. 251.2, 305.00
B. 251.2, 303.90

C. 995.29, 303.90
D. 250.80, 305.00

REFERENCE: Brown, p 128, 141–142

Mental Disorders

147. Joe is being admitted for treatment of chronic alcoholism. As a result of Joe's drinking he also has chronic alcoholic gastritis for which he receives medication.

303.01	Acute alcoholic intoxication, continuous
303.90	Other and unspecified alcohol dependence, unspecified
303.91	Other and unspecified alcohol dependence, continuous
535.00	Acute gastritis without mention of hemorrhage
535.30	Alcoholic gastritis without mention of hemorrhage
535.31	Alcoholic gastritis with mention of hemorrhage

A. 303.01, 535.00
B. 303.91, 535.00

C. 303.90, 535.30
D. 303.01, 303.90, 535.30

REFERENCE: Brown, p 141–142, 201
                        Schraffenberger, p 123, 182–183

148. Sheila has paranoid alcoholic psychosis with chronic alcoholism, continuous.

291.5	Alcohol induced psychotic disorder with delusions
303.91	Other and unspecified alcohol dependence, continuous

A. 291.5, 303.91
B. 303.91, 291.5
C. 303.91

REFERENCE: Brown, p 135, 141–142
                        Lovaasen and Schwerdtfeger, p 557–558
                        Schraffenberger, p 115, 120

149. Sybil arrives at Shady Acres Psychiatric facility for treatment of schizophrenia. Sybil is also manic depressive and has been noncompliant with her medications.

295.40	Schizophreniform disorder, unspecified
295.41	Schizophreniform disorder, subchronic
295.90	Unspecified schizophrenia, unspecified
296.7	Bipolar I disorder, most recent episode (or current) unspecified
296.80	Bipolar disorder, unspecified
296.89	Other bipolar disorders (manic-depressive psychosis, mixed type)
V15.81	Personal history, presenting hazards to health (noncompliance with medical treatment)

A. V15.81, 296.89, 295.40
B. 296.89, 295.41, V15.81

C. 296.7, 295.90
D. 295.90, 296.80, V15.81

REFERENCE: Brown, p 137

150. Allen is addicted to Vicodin. He has stopped taking the drug and is now having withdrawal symptoms. Allen has chronic back pain for which he has been prescribed the medication. Allen presents for treatment of his withdrawal symptoms.

292.0	Drug withdrawal
292.11	Drug-induced psychotic disorder with delusions
292.2	Pathological drug intoxication
304.00	Drug dependence, opioid type dependence, unspecified
304.91	Unspecified drug dependence, continuous
724.5	Backache, unspecified

A. 292.2, 724.5
B. 292.11, 292.2, 304.91

C. 292.0, 304.00, 724.5
D. 292.11, 304.91, 724.5

REFERENCE: Brown, p 141–142
Schraffenberger, p 115, 119–120

151. Acute epileptic twilight state with delirium

293.0	Delirium due to conditions classified elsewhere (epileptic twilight state)
293.1	Subacute delirium
294.0	Amnestic disorder in conditions classified elsewhere
345.00	Generalized nonconvulsive epilepsy without mention of intractable epilepsy
780.02	Transient alteration of awareness

A. 293.0
B. 780.02

C. 293.1
D. 294.0, 345.00

REFERENCE: Brown, p 164–165

152. Sally has been diagnosed with panic attacks and is prescribed Xanax. She has been taking the medication as prescribed by her physician for 3 days and is now having hallucinations. Her physician advises her to stop taking the medication and her symptoms abate. Her doctor determines that the hallucinations were due to the Xanax.

292.12	Drug-induced psychotic disorder with hallucinations
300.01	Panic disorder without agoraphobia
E939.4	Benzodiazepine-based tranquilizers

A. 292.12, E939.4, 300.01   C. E939.4, 292.12
B. 292.12   D. 300.01, 292.12

REFERENCE: Brown, p 435–438
              Schraffenberger, p 115

153. Lou has profound mental retardation due to mongolism.

317	Mild mental retardation
318.0	Moderate mental retardation
318.2	Profound mental retardation
758.0	Down's syndrome
759.0	Anomalies of spleen

A. 318.2, 758.0   C. 758.0, 318.2
B. 318.0, 759.0   D. 317, 758.0

REFERENCE: Lovaasen and Schwerdtfeger, p 565–566
              Schraffenberger, p 115, 240

Diseases of the Nervous System and Sense Organs

154. Mark has a long history of epilepsy. He is brought to the emergency department with intractable epileptic seizures. Mark's epilepsy is the result of a head injury he suffered several years ago.

345.11	Generalized convulsive epilepsy with intractable epilepsy
345.10	Generalized convulsive epilepsy, without mention of intractable epilepsy
345.3	Grand mal status
345.91	Epilepsy, unspecified, with intractable epilepsy
780.39	Other convulsions
907.0	Late effect of intracranial injury without mention of skull fracture

A. 780.39, 907.0   C. 345.3
B. 345.91, 907.0   D. 345.10, 780.39

REFERENCE: Brown, p 59–60, 164–165
              Schraffenberger, p 129–130

155. Jeff was in a car accident when he was 25 years old and suffered a spinal cord injury. As a result, he is a paraplegic and has neurogenic bladder. Jeff also has chronic ulcers of the buttocks. He is being seen for evaluation of his paraplegia. (Code diagnoses only)

344.1	Paraplegia
344.60	Cauda equina syndrome without mention of neurogenic bladder
596.53	Paralysis of bladder
596.54	Neurogenic bladder, not otherwise specified
707.00	Chronic pressure ulcer of skin, unspecified site
707.8	Chronic ulcer of other specified sites
907.2	Late effect of spinal cord injury

A. 344.1, 907.2, 596.54, 707.8   C. 344.1, 596.53, 907.2
B. 344.60, 596.53, 707.00, 907.2   D. 344.1, 596.54, 707.8

REFERENCE: Brown, p 60, 418

156. Josephine has developed senile cataracts in both eyes.

366.10	Senile cataract, unspecified
366.9	Unspecified cataract

A. 366.9
B. 366.10

REFERENCE: Brown, p 172
              Schraffenberger, p 132

157. Diabetic macular or retinal edema

250.50	Diabetes mellitus with ophthalmic manifestations, type II or unspecified type, not stated as uncontrolled
250.51	Diabetes mellitus with ophthalmic manifestations, type I (juvenile type), not stated as uncontrolled
362.01	Background diabetic retinopathy
362.02	Proliferative diabetic retinopathy
362.07	Diabetic macular edema

A. 250.51, 362.07, 360.02   C. 250.50, 362.07, 362.01
B. 362.07, 250.51, 362.02   D. 362.02, 362.07, 250.50

REFERENCE: Schraffenberger, p 100–102, 131–132

158. Bilateral sensorineural conductive hearing loss

389.20	Mixed hearing loss, unspecified
389.21	Mixed hearing loss, unilateral
389.22	Mixed hearing loss, bilateral
389.9	Unspecified hearing loss

A. 389.22   C. 389.9
B. 389.21   D. 389.20

REFERENCE: Schraffenberger, p 133

Diseases of the Circulatory System

159. Madeline is diagnosed with bilateral carotid stenosis. She also has Parkinson's disease and glaucoma.

332.0	Paralysis agitans (Parkinson's disease)
365.9	Unspecified glaucoma
433.30	Occlusion and stenosis of precerebral arteries, multiple and bilateral, without mention of cerebral infarction

A. 433.30
B. 433.30, 332.0, 365.9

REFERENCE: Brown, p 172–173, 342–343
Schraffenberger, p 127, 132, 157

160. Bleeding prolapsed internal hemorrhoids and chronic constipation. Patient presents for rubber band ligation of the internal hemorrhoids.

455.1	Internal thrombosed hemorrhoids
455.2	Internal hemorrhoids with other complication
564.09	Other constipation

A. 455.1, 564.09   C. 455.2, 564.09
B. 455.1   D. 455.1, 455.2

REFERENCE: Schraffenberger, p 182

161. Frank has been diagnosed with sick sinus syndrome. Frank also has type II diabetes on oral medication as well as insulin regimen.

250.00	Diabetes mellitus without mention of complication, type II or unspecified type, not stated as uncontrolled
250.01	Diabetes mellitus without mention of complication, type I (juvenile type), not stated as uncontrolled
427.81	Sinoatrial node dysfunction
V58.67	Long-term (current) use of insulin

A. 427.81, 250.00, V58.67   C. 427.81
B. 427.81, 250.01   D. 427.81, 250.00, 250.01

REFERENCE: Brown, p 121–122, 357

162. Patient presents with congestive heart failure with pleural effusion.

428.0	Congestive heart failure, unspecified
511.9	Unspecified pleural effusion

A. 511.9
B. 428.0
C. 428.0, 511.9

REFERENCE: Brown, p 189, 339–340
Schraffenberger, p 152–154

163. Patient presents to the emergency room complaining of a severe headache. Work-up revealed a ruptured berry aneurysm.

430	Subarachnoid hemorrhage
437.3	Cerebral aneurysm, nonruptured
784.0	Headache

A. 430   C. 784.0, 430
B. 784.0   D. 437.3

REFERENCE: Brown, p 342–343

Diseases of the Respiratory System

164. Joseph has had cough, fever, and painful respirations for 2 days. He also has congestive heart failure and COPD. Joseph presents to the emergency department with severe shortness of breath, using accessory muscles to assist with breathing. Upon examination, Joseph is diagnosed with acute respiratory failure, congestive heart failure, pneumonia, and exacerbation of COPD.

428.0	Congestive heart failure, unspecified
486	Pneumonia, organism unspecified
491.21	Obstructive chronic bronchitis with (acute) exacerbation
496	Chronic airway obstruction, not elsewhere classified
518.81	Acute respiratory failure

A. 428.0, 486, 496, 518.81   C. 486, 428.0, 518.81, 491.21
B. 518.81, 428.0, 491.21   D. 518.81, 486, 428.0, 491.21

REFERENCE: Bowie and Schaffer, p 210
Brown, p 189–191, 194–195, 339–340
Schraffenberger, p 152–154, 171, 174–177

165. Ronald presents with stenosis of his tracheostomy. He is a quadriplegic, C1–C4 secondary to spinal cord injury suffered in a diving accident. He has chronic respiratory failure and is maintained on mechanical ventilation.

344.00	Quadriplegia, unspecified
344.01	Quadriplegia, C1–C4, complete
518.83	Chronic respiratory failure
519.02	Mechanical complication of tracheostomy
519.09	Other tracheostomy complications
907.2	Late effect of spinal cord injury
V46.11	Dependence on respirator status

A. 518.83, 519.09, 907.2
B. 344.01, 518.83, 519.02, V46.11
C. 519.02, 344.01, 518.83, 907.2, V46.11
D. 519.02, 518.83, 907.2

REFERENCE: Brown, p 189–191, 194–195
Schraffenberger, p 129, 174–177, 334

166. Jennifer presents to the emergency department with severe chest pain and shortness of breath. Chest x-ray revealed a spontaneous pneumothorax. Jennifer also has acute bronchitis.

466.0	Acute bronchitis
491.20	Obstructive chronic bronchitis without exacerbation
491.21	Obstructive chronic bronchitis with (acute) exacerbation
512.0	Spontaneous tension pneumothorax
512.1	Iatrogenic pneumothorax
512.8	Other spontaneous pneumothorax

A. 512.8, 466.0
B. 512.0, 491.21
C. 466.0, 491.21, 512.1
D. 491.20, 466.0, 512.8

REFERENCE: Schraffenberger, p 169–170

167. Agnes presented with cough, fever, and dysphagia. Chest x-ray showed infiltrates in both lower lobes. Sputum culture was positive for Staph aureus. Swallow study indicated that Agnes aspirates. Physician documented aspiration pneumonia and Staph aureus pneumonia. As a coder, you would assign codes for the following and with correct sequencing order.
A. Staph aureus pneumonia, dysphagia
B. Staph aureus pneumonia, aspiration pneumonia
C. Aspiration pneumonia, dysphagia
D. Aspiration pneumonia, Staph aureus pneumonia, dysphagia

REFERENCE: Bowie and Schaffer, p 206
Brown, p 181–183
Schraffenberger, p 171, 174

168. This patient has pneumonia. She also has acute exacerbation of COPD.

486	Pneumonia, organism unspecified
491.20	Obstructive chronic bronchitis, without exacerbation
491.21	Obstructive chronic bronchitis, with (acute) exacerbation

A. 491.21
B. 486, 491.21
C. 491.20, 486
D. 486

REFERENCE: Brown, p 181–182, 186
Schraffenberger, p 171

169. Acute and chronic maxillary sinusitis.

461.0	Acute maxillary sinusitis
461.2	Acute ethmoidal sinusitis
473.0	Chronic maxillary sinusitis

A. 461.0
B. 473.0
C. 461.0, 473.0
D. 461.2

REFERENCE: Schraffenberger, p 169

Diseases of the Digestive System

170. Grace had been having abdominal pain for several weeks and had been vomiting blood for 2 days. Her physician performed an esophagogastroduodenoscopy and biopsied a lesion in the duodenum. The pathology report indicates Grace has acute and chronic gastritis.

532.00	Acute duodenal ulcer with hemorrhage without mention of obstruction
535.01	Acute gastritis with hemorrhage
535.11	Chronic (atrophic) gastritis with hemorrhage
789.00	Abdominal pain, unspecified site

   A. 532.00, 789.00   C. 535.01, 535.11, 789.00
   B. 535.01, 789.00   D. 535.01, 535.11

REFERENCE: Brown, p 201

171. Mary presents to the emergency department with complaints of chest pain. Myocardial infarction is ruled out, however gastrointestinal studies indicate Mary is suffering from gastroesophageal reflux disease (GERD). Mary is given medication to relieve her symptoms and instructed to follow up with her physician.

410.91	Acute myocardial infarction, unspecified site, initial episode of care
530.81	Gastroesophageal reflux (GERD)
786.50	Chest pain, unspecified

   A. 530.81   C. 530.81, 410.91
   B. 786.50   D. 410.91, 786.50

REFERENCE: Brown, p 203
                        Lovaasen and Schwerdtfeger, p 536

172. Crystal has been vomiting for 24 hours with complaint of right lower quadrant pain. Examination is suspicious for acute appendicitis. Crystal is taken to surgery and laparoscopic appendectomy is carried out. Pathological diagnosis is consistent with acute appendicitis. Crystal developed post-operative paralytic ileus. (Code for diagnoses only)

540.0	Acute appendicitis with generalized peritonitis
540.9	Acute appendicitis, without mention of peritonitis
560.1	Paralytic ileus
997.4	Digestive system complications, not elsewhere classified

   A. 540.0, 997.4   C. 540.9, 997.4, 560.1
   B. 997.4, 560.1, 540.9   ,

REFERENCE: Brown, p 210–211
                        Lovaasen and Schwerdtfeger, p 539

173. Patient presents with intestinal obstruction due to adhesions. Peripheral vascular disease and chronic urinary tract infections, both conditions are being treated with oral medication.

443.9	Peripheral vascular disease, unspecified
560.81	Intestinal or peritoneal adhesions with obstruction (postoperative) (post infection)
560.89	Other specified intestinal obstruction
560.9	Unspecified intestinal obstruction
599.0	Urinary tract infection, site not specified

A. 560.81, 443.9, 599.0
B. 560.9
C. 560.9, 443.9, 599.0
D. 560.89, 443.9, 599.0

REFERENCE: Brown, p 208, 217

174. This patient has chronic diarrhea associated with Crohn's disease. She also has protein-calorie malnutrition.

263.9	Unspecified protein-calorie malnutrition
555.1	Regional enteritis, large intestine (Crohn's disease)
556.9	Ulcerative colitis, unspecified
787.91	Diarrhea

A. 556.9, 263.9
B. 555.1, 263.9
C. 555.1, 787.91, 263.9

REFERENCE: Schraffenberger, p 184

175. Hepatic coma with ascites due to Laennec's cirrhosis

71.2	Alcoholic cirrhosis of liver (Laennec's cirrhosis)
572.2	Hepatic encephalopathy (hepatic coma)
789.59	Other ascites

A. 572.2, 571.2, 789.59
B. 571.2, 789.59
C. 789.59, 572.2
D. 789.59, 572.2, 571.2

REFERENCE: Schraffenberger, p 182

Diseases of the Genitourinary System

176. Infertility secondary to pelvic peritoneal adhesions.

614.6	Pelvic peritoneal adhesions, female (postoperative) (post infection)
628.2	Infertility, female, of tubal origin

A. 628.2, 614.6
B. 628.2, 54.21
C. 614.6

REFERENCE: Brown, p 208

177. Chronic pelvic inflammatory disease with dysmenorrhea. Patient undergoes a diagnostic laparoscopy.

| 614.4 | Chronic or unspecified parametritis and pelvic cellulitis |
| 625.3 | Dysmenorrhea |

A. 625.3
B. 614.4

C. 625.3, 614.4
D. 614.4, 625.3

REFERENCE: Schraffenberger, p 197

178. Chronic interstitial cystitis

595.1	Chronic interstitial cystitis
595.2	Other chronic cystitis
599.0	Urinary tract infection, site not specified

A. 599.0
B. 595.1

C. 595.2
D. 595.1, 599.0

REFERENCE: Brown, p 217

179. Fibrocystic disease of the breast

610.1	Diffuse cystic mastopathy (fibrocystic disease of breast)
610.2	Fibroadenosis of breast
610.3	Fibrosclerosis of breast
610.9	Benign mammary dysplasia, unspecified

A. 610.1
B. 610.3

C. 610.2
D. 610.9

REFERENCE: Brown, p 229

Obstetrics

180. Intrauterine pregnancy, twins, 33 weeks. Premature rupture of membranes. Spontaneous delivery of premature twins, vertex presentation, both live born.

644.21	Early onset of delivery, delivered, with or without mention of antepartum condition
644.22	Early onset of delivery, delivered, with mention of postpartum complication
644.23	Early onset of delivery, antepartum condition or complication
651.01	Twin pregnancy, delivered, with or without mention of antepartum condition
651.02	Twin pregnancy, delivered, with mention of postpartum complication
658.11	Premature rupture of membranes, delivered, with or without mention of antepartum condition
659.11	Failed medical or unspecified induction, delivered, with or without mention of antepartum condition
V27.2	Outcome of delivery, twins, both liveborn

A. 644.21, 658.11, 651.01, V27.2
B. 644.22, 659.11, V27.2
C. 644.23, 658.11, 651.02
D. 658.11, 651.01, V27.2

REFERENCE: Brown, p 269–275
Schraffenberger, p 207, 214, 219

181. A pregnant patient presents with uncontrolled diabetes mellitus. She is a type I diabetic and was brought under control. The following code was assigned:

> 648.03   Other current conditions in the mother classifiable elsewhere but complicating pregnancy, childbirth or the puerperium, diabetes mellitus, antepartum condition, or complication

Which of the following describe why the coding is in error?
A.   The incorrect fifth digit was used.
B.   The condition should have been coded as gestational diabetes because she is pregnant.
C.   An additional code describing the diabetes mellitus should be used.
D.   Only the code for the diabetes mellitus should be used.

REFERENCE: Brown, p 126–127, 276–277
                Schraffenberger, p 100–103

Skin

182. Max is 80% bald. Max is also treated for congestive heart failure and hypertension for which he is on medication.

> 401.9   Essential hypertension, unspecified
> 402.91   Hypertensive heart disease unspecified as to malignant or benign, with heart failure, unspecified
> 428.0   Congestive heart failure, unspecified
> 704.00   Alopecia, unspecified
> 704.8   Other specified diseases of hair and hair follicles

A.   704.00, 402.91   C.   704.00, 401.9, 428.0
B.   704.8, 401.9, 428.0   D.   704.8, 402.91

REFERENCE: Brown, p 277, 339–340
                Schraffenberger, p 140–141, 152–153, 225

183. Melissa is status post mastectomy due to breast cancer. There has been no recurrence of the disease. Encounter for insertion of unilateral breast implant.

> 174.9   Malignant neoplasm of breast (female), unspecified
> V10.3   Personal history of malignant neoplasm of breast
> V45.71   Acquired absence of breast and nipple
> V51.0   Encounter for breast reconstruction following mastectomy
> V58.42   Aftercare following surgery for neoplasm

A.   V51.0, V10.3   C. V45.71, 174.9
B.   V58.42, V51.0, V45.71, V10.3   D. V51.0, V45.71, V10.3

REFERENCE: Brown, p 83–84, 89–90

184. Roscoe is 57-years old and has been diagnosed with gynecomastia. Roscoe also is on medication for temporal arteritis.

446.5	Giant cell arteritis
611.1	Hypertrophy of breast

A. 611.1
B. 446.5
C. 611.1, 446.5

REFERENCE: Brown, p 453–454
              Schraffenberger, p 196–197, 226, 296–297

185. Brandon has an infected ingrown toenail..

681.11	Onychia and paronychia of toe
703.0	Ingrowing nail

A. 703.0
B. 681.11

REFERENCE: Schraffenberger, p 225

Musculoskeletal

186. Julia is an 80-year-old female with osteoporosis. She presents to the emergency department complaining of severe back pain. X-rays revealed pathological compression fractures of several vertebrae.

721.90	Spondylosis of unspecified site without mention of myelopathy
733.00	Osteoporosis, unspecified
733.13	Pathological fracture of vertebrae
805.8	Fracture of vertebral column without mention of spinal cord injury, unspecified, closed

A. 733.13, 733.00
B. 805.8, 733.00
C. 721.90, 733.13
D. 733.00, 733.13

REFERENCE: Brown, p 255–256, 409
              Lovaasen and Schwerdtfeger, p 436–437
              Schraffenberger, p 235–236

187. Scott has a deformity of his left ring finger, due to an old tendon injury.

727.82	Calcium deposits in tendon and bursa
736.20	Unspecified deformity of finger (acquired)
834.02	Closed dislocation of finger, interphalangeal (joint), hand
905.8	Late effect of tendon injury

A. 727.82
B. 736.20, 905.8
C. 834.02

REFERENCE: Schraffenberger, p 235

188. Sara has Dupuytren's contracture of the right middle finger.

728.6	Contracture of palmar fascia (Dupuytren's contracture)
728.71	Plantar fascial fibromatosis
728.86	Necrotizing fasciitis

A. 728.6   C. 728.86
B. 728.71

REFERENCE: Schraffenberger, p 234–235

189. Cheryl has had chronic worsening pain of her left knee from rheumatoid arthritis.

714.0	Rheumatoid arthritis
714.31	Polyarticular juvenile rheumatoid arthritis, acute
715.96	Osteoarthrosis, unspecified whether generalized or localized, low leg

A. 715.96   C. 714.31
B. 714.0

REFERENCE: Brown, p 218, 251–252, 256–257
                Schraffenberger, p 194–195, 233

Injury and Poisoning

190. A patient who is HIV positive and currently asymptomatic presents with a compound fracture of the tibia. The patient was treated previously for pneumocystis carinii pneumonia. Given the following codes, which is the correct coding and sequencing?

042	Human Immunodeficiency Virus (HIV) disease
136.3	Pneumocystosis (pneumonia due to Pneumocystis carinii)
V08	Asymptomatic HIV infection status
823.80	Fracture of tibia alone, unspecified part, closed
823.90	Fracture of tibia alone, unspecified part, open

A. 823.90, V08   C. 823.80, V08, 136.3
B. 823.90, 042   D. 823.80, 042

REFERENCE: Brown, p 115–116
                Schraffenberger, p 72–73, 265

191. The diagnosis reads "first-, second-, and third-degree burns of the right arm." You would code
    A. the first degree only.   C. the third degree only.
    B. the second degree only.   D. each degree of burn separately.

REFERENCE: Brown, p 115–116
                Schraffenberger, p 72–73, 265

And Just A Few More Coding Questions for Practice

192. A physician lists the final diagnosis as diarrhea and constipation due to either irritable bowel syndrome or diverticulitis. The following codes are assigned:

562.10	Diverticulosis of colon without mention of hemorrhage
562.11	Diverticulitis of colon without mention of hemorrhage
564.00	Constipation, unspecified
564.1	Irritable bowel syndrome
787.91	Diarrhea

    A. 564.1, 562.11   C. 564.00, 787.91, 564.1, 562.11
    B. 562.10, 564.1   D. 564.1, 562.10, 564.00, 787.91

REFERENCE: Brown, 28–29
                  Schraffenberger, p 182, 254–255

193. Codes from category 655, known or suspected fetal abnormality affecting the mother, should
    A. be assigned if the fetal conditions are documented.
    B. be assigned at the discretion of the physician.
    C. be assigned when they affect the management of the mother.
    D. never be assigned.

REFERENCE: Brown, p 276

194. There are a limited number of late effect codes in ICD-9-CM. When coding a residual condition where there is no applicable late effect code, one should code
    A. the residual condition followed by its cause.
    B. the cause followed by the residual condition.
    C. only the residual condition.
    D. only the cause of the residual condition.

REFERENCE: Brown, p 59–60

195. A diabetic patient presents with acute gastrointestinal hemorrhage due to ulcer disease. In this case, the diabetes would be
    A. the first listed diagnosis.
    B. a comorbid condition.
    C. a complication.
    D. irrelevant and not coded.

REFERENCE: Brown, p 27–28
                  Schraffenberger, p 49

196. Which of the following are considered late effects regardless of time?
    A. congenital defect
    B. nonunion, malunion, scarring
    C. fracture, burn
    D. poisoning

REFERENCE: Brown, p 418

197. When a patient arrives in respiratory failure due to a chronic nonrespiratory condition,
     A. the respiratory failure is the principal diagnosis.
     B. the chronic nonrespiratory problem is the principal diagnosis.
     C. only the respiratory failure is coded.
     D. only the chronic nonrespiratory condition is coded.

REFERENCE: Brown, p 189–191
                Schraffenberger, p 175–177

198. Robert presents with diagnoses of congestive heart failure with acute pulmonary edema. You're coding Robert's record and you will code
     A. the CHF only.
     B. the edema only.
     C. both the CHF and the edema; sequence the CHF first.
     D. both the CHF and the edema; sequence the edema first.

REFERENCE: Brown, p 27, 31

Answer Key for ICD-9-CM Coding

1. D	46. A
2. B	47. C
3. A	48. B
4. C	49. A
5. D	50. D
6. C	51. C
7. D	52. B
8. C	53. C
9. A	54. B The physician should be asked if the blood loss should be added as a discharge diagnosis.
10. B	
11. C	
12. B	55. A
13. A	56. C
14. D	57. D
15. B	58. A
16. A	59. C
17. C	60. A
18. B	61. A
19. D	62. C
20. B	63. B
21. A Pain is a symptom that is integral to the sickle cell crisis and therefore is not coded.	64. D
	65. B
	66. D
22. C	67. B
23. B	68. D
24. D	69. A
25. D	70. B
26. B	71. A
27. A	72. C
28. C	73. B
29. B	74. C
30. D	75. C
31. C	76. A
32. B	77. C
33. A	78. B
34. C	79. C
35. B	80. D
36. A	81. B Newborn V-code is not assigned by the receiving facility when a newborn is transferred.
37. A	
38. C	
39. D	82. C
40. A	83. A
41. B	84. B
42. A	85. D
43. D	86. C
44. A	87. A
45. B	88. D

Answer Key for ICD-9-CM Coding

89. C
90. A
91. C
92. B
93. A
94. C
95. D
96. C
97. B
98. A
99. D
100. C
101. A
102. D
103. C
104. B
105. A
106. C
107. D
108. C
109. D
110. A
111. A
112. B
113. D
114. C
115. B
116. A
117. A
118. D
119. A
120. D
121. A
122. B
123. D   Fatigue and flulike symptoms/signs of hepatitis would not be coded.

124. A
125. D
126. A
127. A
128. A
129. C
130. B
131. C

132. D   SSS would not be reported as a current condition because the pacemaker would have taken care of this condition.

133. A
134. B
135. C   The coder cannot assume a causal relationship between the diabetes and conditions that are usually related to the diabetes unless a physician confirms this relationship.

136. A
137. C   Diabetic ketoacidosis by definition is uncontrolled.

138. A
139. C
140. A
141. D
142. B
143. A
144. B
145. C
146. A
147. C   The term "continuous" refers to daily intake of large amounts of alcohol, or regular heavy drinking on weekends or days off. The coder should not assume to use the fifth digit 1 unless documented as continuous.

148. A
149. D
150. C
151. A
152. A
153. A.
154. B
155. A
156. B
157. C
158. A
159. B
160. C
161. A
162. C
163. A

Answer Key for ICD-9-CM Coding

164. D COPD (496) is a general term. It will present as chronic obstructive bronchitis.
165. C
166. A
167. D
168. B
169. C The alphabetic index is misleading and directs the coder to use one code for acute and chronic sinusitis. The Tabular List, however, directs the coder to use two separate codes.
170. D
171. A
172. C The note under category 997 instructs the coder to "use additional code to identify complication."
173. A
174. B
175. A
176. A
177. D
178. B
179. A
180. A
181. C
182. C
183. B
184. C
185. A
186. A
187. B
188. A
189. B
190. B A "compound" fracture is considered an "open" fracture.
191. C Code the highest degree burn ONLY of the same site.
192. C
193. C
194. C
195. B
196. B
197. A
198. A

REFERENCES

Bowie, M., and Schaffer, R. (2010). *UnderstandingICD-9-CM: A worktext.* Clifton Park, NY: Delmar Cengage Learning.

Brown, F. (2010). *ICD-9-CM coding handbook with answers.* Chicago: American Hospital Association (AHA).

Channel Publishing, Ltd. (2010). *The educational annotation of ICD-9-CM.* Reno, NV: Channel Publishing, Ltd.

Eid, D. (2008). *Applying coding concepts: encoder workbook.* Clifton Park, NY: Delmar Cengage Learning.

Ingenix. (2009). *ICD-9-CM Expert for hospitals*, Vol. 1, 2 & 3. St. Louis, MO: Ingenix.

Lovaasen, K., and Schwerdtfeger, J. (2009). *ICD-9-CM coding: theory and practice.* St. Louis, MO: Saunders Elsevier.

Schraffenberger, L. A. (2010). *Basic ICD-9-CM coding.* Chicago: American Health Information Management Association (AHIMA).

ICD-9-CM Chapter Competencies

Question	CCS-P Domain						
	1	2	3	4	5	6	7
		198					

VIII. CPT Coding

Lisa Delhomme, MHA, RHIA

Evaluation and Management

1. Patient is admitted to the hospital with acute abdominal pain. The attending medical physician requests a surgical consult. The consultant agrees to see the patient and conducts a comprehensive history and physical examination. The physician ordered lab work to rule out pancreatitis, along with an ultrasound of the gallbladder and abdominal x-ray. Due to the various diagnosis possibilities and the tests reviewed, a moderate medical decision was made.
    A. 99244
    B. 99222
    C. 99254
    D. 99204

    REFERENCE: Frisch, p 82–85
                  Green, p 353–355
                  Johnson & McHugh, p 165–167
                  Smith, p 189
                  AMA (6th ed), p 66

2. An established patient returns to the physician's office for follow-up on his hypertension and diabetes. The physician takes the blood pressure and references the patient's last three glucose tests. The patient is still running above normal glucose levels, so the physician decides to adjust the patient's insulin. An expanded history was taken and a physical examination was performed.
    A. 99213
    B. 99232
    C. 99202
    D. 99214

    REFERENCE: Frisch, p 53–55
                  Johnson & McHugh, p 127–128
                  Green, p 347–348
                  Smith, p 188
                  AMA (6th ed), p 54

3. Patient arrives in the emergency room via a medical helicopter. The patient has sustained multiple life-threatening injuries due to a multiple car accident. The patient goes into cardiac arrest 10 minutes after arrival. An hour and 30 minutes of critical care time is spent trying to stabilize the patient.
    A. 99285; 99288; 99291
    B. 99291; 99292
    C. 99291; 99292; 99285
    D. 99282

    REFERENCE: Frisch, p 27–29
                  Green, p 357–359
                  Johnson & McHugh, p 170–171
                  Smith, p 190–191
                  AMA (6th ed), p 70–71

4. The physician provided services to a new patient who was in a rest home for an ulcerative sore on the hip. A problem-focused history and physical examination were performed and a straightforward medical decision was made.
    A. 99304
    B. 99325
    C. 99324
    D. 99334

    REFERENCE: Johnson & McHugh, p 174
                  Green, p 361
                  AMA (6th ed), p 76–77
                  Smith, p 191

5. A doctor provides critical care services in the emergency department for a patient in respiratory failure. He initiates ventilator management and spends an hour and 10 minutes providing critical care for this patient.
    A. 99281, 99291, 99292, 94002
    B. 99291, 99292, 94002
    C. 99291, 94002
    D. 99291

REFERENCE: Green, p 357–359
     Johnson & McHugh, p 168–171
     AMA (6th ed), p 68–71
     Smith, p 190–191

6. Services were provided to a patient in the emergency room after the patient twisted her ankle stepping down from a curb. The emergency room physician ordered x-rays of the ankle, which came back negative for a fracture. A problem-focused history and physical examination were performed and ankle strapping was applied. A prescription for pain was given to the patient. Code the emergency room visit only.
    A. 99201   C. 99281
    B. 99282   D. 99211

REFERENCE: Frisch, p 71–72
     Green, p 355–357
     AMA (6th ed), p 66–68
     Johnson & McHugh, p 168
     Smith, p 190

7. An established patient was seen in her primary physician's office. The patient fell at home and came to the physician's office for an examination. Due to a possible concussion, the patient was sent to the hospital to be admitted as an observation patient. A detailed history and examination were performed and the medical decision was low complexity. The patient stayed overnight and was discharged the next afternoon.
    A. 99214; 99234   C. 99218
    B. 99214; 99218; 99217   D. 99218; 99217

REFERENCE: AMA, 2010
     Green, p 350
     AMA (6th ed), p 54–56
     Frisch, p 69–71
     Johnson & McHugh, p 162–163
     Smith, p 188

8. An out-of-town patient presents to a walk-in clinic to have a prescription refilled for a nonsteroidal anti-inflammatory drug. The physician performs a problem-focused history and physical examination with a straightforward decision.
    A. 99211   C. 99212
    B. 99201   D. 99202

REFERENCE: Frisch, p 49–51
                Johnson & McHugh, p 126–128
                AMA (6th ed), p 52–53
                Green, p 347–348
                Smith, p 188

9. An office consultation is performed for a post-menopausal woman who is complaining of spotting in the past 6 months with right lower quadrant tenderness. A detailed history and physical were performed with a low-complexity medical decision.
    A. 99242   C. 99253
    B. 99243   D. 99254

REFERENCE: Frisch, p 77–81
                Green, p 353–355
                AMA (6th ed), p 64–65
                Johnson & McHugh, p 167–168
                Smith, p 189

Anesthesia

10. Code anesthesia for upper abdominal ventral hernia repair
    A. 00832   C. 00752
    B. 00750   D. 00830

REFERENCE: Green, p 282–283
                Johnson & McHugh, p 196–197
                AMA (6th ed), p 99–101
                Smith, p 219–220

11. Code anesthesia for total hip replacement
    A. 01210   C. 01230
    B. 01402   D. 01214

REFERENCE: Green, p 382–383
                Smith, p 219–220
                AMA (6th ed), p 99–101

12. Code anesthesia for vaginal hysterectomy
    A. 00846   C. 00840
    B. 00944   D. 01963

REFERENCE: Green, p 382–383
                Smith, p 219–220
                AMA (6th ed), p 99–101

13. Code anesthesia for placement of vascular shunt in forearm
    A. 01844
    B. 01850
    C. 00532
    D. 01840

REFERENCE: Green, p 382–383
               Smith, p 219–220
               AMA (6th ed), p 99–101

14. Code anesthesia for decortication of left lung
    A. 01638-LT
    B. 00542-LT
    C. 00546-LT
    D. 00500-LT

REFERENCE: Green, p 382–383
               Smith, p 219–220
               AMA (6th ed), p 99–101

15. Code anesthesia for total shoulder replacement
    A. 01760
    B. 01630
    C. 01402
    D. 01638

REFERENCE: Green, p 382–383
               Smith, p 219–220
               AMA (6th ed), p 99–101

16. Code anesthesia for cesarean section
    A. 00840
    B. 01961
    C. 00940
    D. 01960

REFERENCE: Green, p 382–383
               Smith, p 219–220
               AMA (6th ed), p 99–101

17. Code anesthesia for procedures on bony pelvis
    A. 00400
    B. 01170
    C. 01120
    D. 01190

REFERENCE: Green, p 382–383
               Smith, p 219–220
               AMA (6th ed), p 99–101

18. Code anesthesia for corneal transplant
    A. 00144
    B. 00140
    C. 00147
    D. 00190

REFERENCE: Green, p 382–383
               Smith, p 219–220
               AMA (6th ed), p 99–101

Surgery—Integumentary System

19. Patient presents to the hospital for skin grafts due to previous third-degree burns. The burn eschar of the back was removed. Once the eschar was removed, the defect size measured 10 cm x 10 cm. A skin graft from a donor bank was placed onto the defect and sewn into place as a temporary wound closure.
    A. 15170, 15002
    B. 15300
    C. 15002, 15200
    D. 15002, 15300

REFERENCE: Green, p 446–448
             Smith, p 64–67
             AMA (6th ed), p 133–136

20. Patient presents to the operating room for excision of a 4.5 cm malignant melanoma of the left forearm. A 6 cm x 6 cm rotation flap was created for closure.
    A.   14021
    B. 11606; 14020
    C. 14301
    D. 11606; 15100

REFERENCE: Green, p 445
             Smith, p 65
             AMA 2010
             AMA (6th ed), p 132–133

21. Female patient has a percutaneous needle biopsy of the left breast lesion in the lower outer quadrant. Following the biopsy frozen section results, the physician followed this with an excisional removal of the same lesion.
    A. 19100; 19125
    B. 19100; 19120-LT
    C. 19120-LT
    D. 19100; 19120; 19120

REFERENCE: Green, p 455
             Smith, p 70–71
             AMA (6th ed), p 42–43

22. Patient presents to the emergency room with lacerations of right lower leg that involved the fascia. Lacerations measured 5.0 cm and 2.7 cm.
    A. 11406; 11403
    B. 12034
    C. 12032; 12031
    D. 12032

REFERENCE: Smith, p 60–61
             AMA (6th ed), p 131

23. Ten sq cm epidermal autograft to the face from the back
    A. 15110
    B. 15115
    C. 15110, 15115
    D. 15120

REFERENCE: AMA 2010
             AMA (6th ed), p 134

24. Nonhuman graft for temporary wound closure. Patient has a 5 cm defect on the scalp.
    A. 15335   C. 15420
    B. 15400   D. 15430

REFERENCE: AMA 2010
               Green, p 446
               AMA (6th ed), p 134–136
               Smith, p 66–67

25. Patient is admitted for a blepharoplasty of the left lower eyelid and a repair for a tarsal strip of the left upper lid.
    A. 67917-E1; 15822-E2   C. 67917-E1
    B. 67917-E1; 15820-E2   D. 67917-E1; 15823-E2

REFERENCE: CPT Assistant, January 2005, p 46
               AMA (6th ed), p 300

26. Patient presents to the emergency room with lacerations sustained in an automobile accident. Repairs of the 3.3 cm skin laceration of the left leg that involved the fascia, 2.5 cm and 3.0 cm lacerations of the left arm involving the fascia, and 2.7 cm of the left foot, which required simple sutures, were performed. Sterile dressings were applied.
    A. 12032; 12032-51; 12031-51; 12002-51   C. 12034, 12002-51
    B. 12002, 12002-51   D. 13150; 12032-51, 12032-51, 12001-51

REFERENCE: Green, p 443–445
               Smith, p 60–61
               AMA (6th ed), p 126, 131

27. Patient presents to the operating room for excision of three lesions. The 1.5 cm and 2.0 cm lesions of the back were excised with one excision. The 0.5 cm lesion of the hand was excised. The pathology report identified both back lesions as squamous cell carcinoma. The hand lesion was identified as seborrheic keratosis.
    A. 11604; 11420   C. 11403; 11642; 11462
    B. 11402; 11420; 11403   D. 11602; 11402

REFERENCE: CPT Assistant, Nov. 2002, p 5–6, 8
               Green, p 435–439
               Smith, p 57
               AMA (6th ed), p 124, 126, 128, 132–133

28. Patient presents to the radiology department where a fine-needle aspiration of the breast is performed utilizing computer tomography.
    A. 19120; 77012   C. 19125
    B. 19102   D. 10022, 77012

REFERENCE: Green, p 454
               CPT Assistant, November 2002, p 2–3
               AMA (6th ed), p 110, 380

29. Patient presents to the operating room where a 3.2 cm malignant lesion of the shoulder was excised and repaired with simple sutures. A 2.0 cm benign lesion of the cheek was excised and was repaired with a rotation skin graft.
   A. 11604; 11442; 14040; 12001   C. 15002; 15120
   B. 14040; 11604   D. 17264; 17000; 12001

REFERENCE: CPT Assistant, November 2002, p 5–8
             CPT Assistant, August 2002, p 5
             CPT Assistant, July 1999, p 3–4
             Green, p 435–439, 445
             AMA (6th ed), p 126, 128, 131–133
             Smith, p 65

30. Patient was admitted to the hospital for removal of excessive tissue due to massive weight loss. Liposuction of the abdomen and bilateral thighs was performed.
   A. 15830   C. 15877; 15879–50
   B. 15830; 15833; 15833   D. 15839

REFERENCE: AMA 2010

Surgery—Musculoskeletal

31. Patient presents to the hospital with ulcer of the right foot. Patient is taken to the operating room where a revision of the right metatarsal head is performed.
   A. 28104-RT   C. 28288-RT
   B. 28111-RT   D. 28899-RT

REFERENCE: AMA 2010

32. Patient presents to the emergency room following a fall. X-rays were ordered for the lower leg and results showed a fracture of the proximal left tibia. The emergency room physician performed a closed manipulation of the fracture with skeletal traction.
   A. 27532-LT   C. 27530-LT
   B. 27536-LT   D. 27524-LT

REFERENCE: Green, 466–469
             Smith, p 74–75

33. Trauma patient was rushed to the operating room with multiple injuries. Open reduction with internal fixation of intertrochanteric femoral fracture; open reduction of the tibial and fibula shaft with internal fixation was performed.
   A. 27245; 27759   C. 27248; 27756
   B. 20690   D. 27244; 27758

REFERENCE: Green, p 466–467
             Smith, p 74–75

34. Open I&D of a deep abscess of the cervical spine
   A. 22010   C. 10060
   B. 22015   D. 10140

REFERENCE: AMA 2010

35. Patient presents to the emergency room following an assault. Examination of the patient reveals blunt trauma to the face. Radiology reports that the patient suffers from a fracture to the frontal skull and a blow-out fracture of the orbital floor. Patient is admitted and taken to the operating room where a periorbital approach to the orbital fracture is employed and an implant is inserted.
   A. 21407; 21275
   B. 21387; 61330
   C. 21390
   D. 61340; 21401

REFERENCE: Smith, p 74–75
              AMA (6th ed), p 263–264

36. Patient presents with a traumatic partial amputation of the second, third, and fourth fingers on the right hand. Patient was taken to the operating room where completion of the amputation of three fingers was performed with direct closure.
   A. 26910-F6; 26910-F7; 26910-F8
   B. 26843-RT
   C. 26951-F6; 26951-F7; 26951-F8
   D. 26550-RT

REFERENCE: AMA 2010

37. Patient is brought to the emergency room following a shark attack. The paramedics have the patient's amputated foot. The patient is taken directly to the operating room to reattach the patient's foot.
   A. 28800
   B. 28200; 28208
   C. 28110
   D. 20838

REFERENCE: AMA 2010

38. Patient presents to the hospital with a right index trigger finger. Release of the trigger finger was performed.
   A. 26060-F7
   B. 26055-F6
   C. 26170-F6
   D. 26110

REFERENCE: AMA 2010

39. Patient had been diagnosed with a bunion. Patient was taken to the operating room where a simple resection of the base of the proximal phalanx along with the medial eminence was performed. Kirschner wire was placed to hold the joint in place.
   A. 28292
   B. 28290
   C. 28293
   D. 28298

REFERENCE: CPT Assistant, December 1995, p 5–7
              AMA 2010

              AMA (6th ed), p 116–117, 166

Surgery—Respiratory

40. Patient has a bronchoscopy with endobronchial biopsies of three sites.
   A. 31625; 31625; 31625
   B. 31625
   C. 31622; 31625
   D. 31622; 31625; 31625; 31625

REFERENCE: CPT Assistant, June 2004, p 11
              Green, p 497–498
              Smith, p 85–86
              AMA (6th ed), p 178

41. Patient presents to the surgical unit and undergoes unilateral endoscopy, partial ethmoidectomy, and maxillary antrostomy.
   A. 31254; 31256-51
   B. 31201; 31225-51
   C. 31290; 31267-51
   D. 31233; 31231-51

REFERENCE: Green, p 493–494   CPT Assistant, January 1997, p 4–6
             Smith, p 81
             AMA (6th ed), p 270

42. Patient has been diagnosed with metastatic laryngeal carcinoma. Patient underwent subtotal supraglottic laryngectomy with radical neck dissection.
   A. 31540
   B. 31367
   C. 31365
   D. 31368

REFERENCE: Green, p 494–495

43. Patient was involved in an accident and has been sent to the hospital. During transport the patient develops breathing problems and, upon arrival at the hospital, an emergency transtracheal tracheostomy was performed. Following various x-rays, the patient was diagnosed with traumatic pneumothorax and a thoracentesis with insertion of tube was performed.
   A. 31603; 31612
   B. 31610; 32421
   C. 31603; 32422
   D. 31603; 32421

REFERENCE: AMA 2010
             AMA (6th ed), p 142

44. Patient with laryngeal cancer has a tracheoesophageal fistula created and has a voicebox inserted.
   A. 31611
   B. 31580
   C. 31395
   D. 31502

REFERENCE: AMA 2010

45. Upper lobectomy of the right lung with repair of the bronchus
   A. 32480
   B. 32486
   C. 32320
   D. 32480, 32501

REFERENCE: Green, p 500
             AMA (6th ed), p 180–181

46. Patient with a deviated nasal septum that was repaired by septoplasty
   A. 30400
   B. 30620
   C. 30520
   D. 30630

REFERENCE: AMA 2010

47. Lye burn of the larynx repaired by laryngoplasty
   A. 31588
   B. 16020
   C. 31360
   D. 31540

REFERENCE: AMA 2010

48. Bronchoscopy with multiple transbronchial right upper and right lower lobe lung biopsy with fluoroscopic guidance
    A. 31628-RT; 76000-RT
    B. 31717-RT; 31632-RT
    C. 32405-RT
    D. 31628-RT; 31632-RT

    REFERENCE: CPT Assistant, March 1999, p 3
                  Green, p 497–498
                  Smith, p 85–86
                  AMA (6th ed), p 178

49. Patient has recurrent spontaneous pneumothorax which has resulted in a chemical pleurodesis by thoracoscopy.
    A. 32650
    B. 32310; 32601
    C. 32605
    D. 32960

    REFERENCE: AMA 2010
                  AMA (6th ed), p 79–80

50. Laryngoscopic stripping of vocal cords for leukoplakia of the vocal cords
    A. 31535
    B. 31540
    C. 31541
    D. 31570

    REFERENCE: Smith, p 83–84
                  Green, p 496
                  AMA (6th ed), p 175

Surgery—Cardiovascular System

51. Patient returns to the operating room following open-heart bypass for exploration of blood vessel to control postoperative bleeding in the chest.
    A. 35820
    B. 20101
    C. 35761
    D. 35905

    REFERENCE: AMA 2010

52. Patient undergoes construction of apical aortic conduit with an insertion of a single-ventricle ventricular assist device.
    A. 33400
    B. 33975
    C. 33977
    D. 33975; 33404

    REFERENCE: CPT Assistant, January 2004, p 28

53. Patient presents to the operating room where a CABG x 3 is performed using the mammary artery and two sections of the saphenous vein.
    A. 33534; 33511
    B. 33534; 33518; 33511
    C. 33535
    D. 33533; 33518

    REFERENCE: Green, p 519–520
                  Smith, p 89
                  AMA (6th ed), p 195–198

54. Patient complains of recurrent syncope following carotid thromboendarterectomy. Patient returns 2 weeks after initial surgery and undergoes repeat carotid thromboendarterectomy.
   A. 33510
   B. 35301
   C. 35201
   D. 35301; 35390

REFERENCE: CPT Assistant, Winter 1993, p 3

55. Patient is admitted with alcohol cirrhosis and has a TIPS procedure performed.
   A. 35476; 36011; 36481
   B. 37183
   C. 37182
   D. 37140

REFERENCE: CPT Assistant, December 2003, p 1–3

56. Eighty-year-old patient has carcinoma and presents to the operating room for placement of a tunneled implantable centrally inserted venous access port.
   A. 36558
   B. 36571
   C. 36561
   D. 36481

REFERENCE: CPT Assistant, February 1999, p 1–5
           CPT Assistant, November 1999, p 19–20
           Green, p 534–536
           Smith, p 95–97

57. Patient presents to the operating room and undergoes an endovascular repair of an infrarenal abdominal aortic aneurysm utilizing a unibody bifurcated prosthesis.
   A. 34800; 34813
   B. 34802
   C. 34804
   D. 35081

REFERENCE: CPT Assistant, September 2002, p 4;
           CPT Assistant, February 2003, p 2–4, 16   Green, p 526–527
           AMA (6th ed), p 200

58. The physician punctures the left common femoral to examine the right common iliac.
   A. 36245
   B. 36246
   C. 36247
   D. 36140

REFERENCE: AMA 2010
           AMA (6th ed), p 198, 335

59. Patient has a history of PVD for many years and experiences chest pains. The patient underwent Doppler evaluation which showed a common femoral DVT. Patient is now admitted for thromboendartectomy.
   A. 35371
   B. 35372
   C. 35456
   D. 35256

REFERENCE: AMA 2010

60. Patient presents to the hospital with a diagnosis of femoral artery atherosclerotic disease. The patient is taken to the operating room and undergoes an aortofemoral popliteal bypass.
   A. 35551
   B. 35651
   C. 35556
   D. 35656

REFERENCE: AMA 2010

Surgery—Hemic and Lymphatic Systems, Mediastinum, and Diaphragm

61. Patient has breast carcinoma and is now undergoing sentinel node biopsy. Patient was injected for sentinel node identification and two deep axillary lymph nodes showed up intensely. These two lymph nodes were completely excised. Path report was positive for metastatic carcinoma.
    A. 38525; 38790
    B. 38589
    C. 38308; 38790
    D. 38525; 38792
    REFERENCE: CPT Assistant, November, 1998 p 15–16
                              CPT Assistant, July 1999, p 6–12
                              Green, p 542–543

62. Patient has a history of hiatal hernia for many years, which has progressively gotten worse. The decision to repair the hernia was made and the patient was sent to the operating room where the repair took place via the thorax and abdomen.
    A. 39545
    B. 39530
    C. 39502
    D. 39503

    REFERENCE: Green, p 577
                              Smith, p 112
                              AMA (6th ed), p 229

63. Patient has a bone marrow aspiration of the iliac crest and of the tibia.
    A. 38220, 38220–59
    B. 38221
    C. 38230
    D. 38220

    REFERENCE: CPT Assistant, January 2004, p 26
                              Green, 542
                              AMA (6th ed), p 156, 374

64. Trauma patient is rushed to the operating room with multiple injuries. The patient had his spleen removed due to massive rupture with repair of lacerated diaphragm.
    A. 38115; 39501
    B. 38120; 39599
    C. 38102; 39540
    D. 38100; 39501

    REFERENCE: AMA 2010

65. Laparoscopic retroperitoneal lymph node biopsy
    A. 38570
    B. 38780
    C. 49323
    D. 38589

    REFERENCE: AMA 2010

66. Excision of mediastinal cyst
    A. 11400
    B. 39200
    C. 17000
    D. 39400

    REFERENCE: AMA 2010

67. Patient diagnosed with cystic hygroma of the axilla, which was excised.
    A. 38555
    B. 11400
    C. 38550
    D. 38300

    REFERENCE: AMA 2010

68. Laparoscopy with multiple biopsies of retroperitoneal lymph nodes
    A. 38570
    B. 38571
    C. 38570-22
    D. 38572

REFERENCE: AMA 2010

69. Cannulation of the thoracic duct
    A. 38794
    B. 36810
    C. 36260
    D. 38999

REFERENCE: AMA 2010

70. Patient has been on the bone marrow transplant recipient list for 3 months. A perfect match was made and the patient came in and received peripheral stem cell transplant.
    A. 38242
    B. 38230
    C. 38241
    D. 38240

REFERENCE: Green, p 541–542

Surgery—Digestive System

71. Laparoscopic gastric banding
    A. 43842
    B. 43843
    C. 43770
    D. 43771

REFERENCE: AMA 2010

72. Patient presents with a history of upper abdominal pain. Cholangiogram was negative and patient was sent to the hospital for ERCP. During the procedure the sphincter was incised and a stent was placed for drainage.
    A. 43260; 43262; 43264
    B. 43262; 43269
    C. 43267
    D. 43262; 43268

REFERENCE: CPT Assistant, Spring 1994, p 5–7

73. Patient presents to the emergency room with right lower abdominal pains. Emergency room physician suspects possible appendicitis. Patient was taken to the operating room where a laparoscopic appendectomy was performed. Pathology report was negative for appendicitis.
    A. 44950
    B. 44950; 49320
    C. 44970
    D. 44901

REFERENCE: AMA 2010
              AMA (6th ed.), p 214

74. Morbidly obese patient comes in for vertical banding of the stomach.
    A. 43848
    B. 43659
    C. 43842
    D. 43999

REFERENCE: CPT Assistant, May 1998, p 5–6

75. Patient underwent anoscopy followed by colonoscopy. The physician examined to colon to 60cm.
    A. 46600; 45378
    B. 46600; 45378-59
    C. 45378
    D. 45999

REFERENCE: Green, p 571–572
             Smith, p 102, 104–105
             AMA (6th ed.), p 216

76. Injection snoreplasty for treatment of palatal snoring.
    A. 42299
    B. 42145
    C. 42999
    D. 40899

REFERENCE: CPT Assistant, December 2004, p 19

77. Patient arrives to the hospital and has a Nissen fundoplasty done endoscopically.
    A. 43410
    B. 43415
    C. 43502
    D. 43280

REFERENCE: AMA 2010

78. Young child presents with cleft lip and cleft palate. This is the first attempt of repair, which includes major revision of the cleft palate and unilateral cleft lip repair.
    A. 42200; 40701
    B. 42225; 40700
    C. 42220; 40720
    D. 42215; 40700

REFERENCE: AMA 2010

79. Patient has a history of chronic alcohol abuse with portal hypertension. Patient has been vomiting blood for the past 3 days and presented to his physician's office. Patient was sent to the hospital for evaluation and an EGD was performed. Biopsy findings showed gastritis, esophagitis and bleeding esophageal varices, which were injected with sclerosing solution.
    A. 43235; 43244; 43204
    B. 43239; 43244
    C. 43239; 43243
    D. 43239; 43243; 43204

REFERENCE: Green, p 562–565
             Smith, p 102
             AMA (6th ed.), p 216–217, 220

Surgery—Urinary System

80. Patient is admitted for contact laser vaporization of the prostate. The physician performed a TURP and transurethral resection of the bladder neck at the same time.
    A. 52648
    B. 52648; 52450; 52500
    C. 52450; 53500
    D. 52648; 52450

REFERENCE: CPT Assistant, July 2005, p 15
             AMA (6th ed.), p 242

81. Patient comes to the hospital with a history of right flank pain. Urine tests are negative. Radiology examination reveals that the patient has renal cysts. Patient is now admitted for laparoscopic ablation of the cysts.
    A. 50541
    B. 50390
    C. 50280
    D. 50920

REFERENCE: CPT Assistant, November 1999, p 25
              CPT Assistant, May 2000, p 4
              CPT Assistant, October 2001, p 8
              CPT Assistant, January 2003, p 19
              AMA (6th ed.), p 234

82. Patient has extensive bladder cancer. She underwent a complete cystectomy with bilateral pelvic lymphadenectomy and creation of ureteroileal conduit.
    A. 51575; 50820
    B. 50825; 51570; 38770
    C. 51595
    D. 51550; 38770

REFERENCE: AMA 2010

83. Patient presents to the hospital with right ureteral calculus. Patient is taken to the operating room where a cystoscopy with ureteroscopy is performed to remove the calculus.
    A. 52353
    B. 52310
    C. 51065
    D. 52352

REFERENCE: Green, p 583–585
              Smith, p 117

84. Female with 6 months of stress incontinence. Outpatient therapies are not working and the patient decides to have the problem fixed. Laparoscopic urethral suspension was completed.
    A. 51992
    B. 51990
    C. 51840
    D. 51845

REFERENCE: CPT Assistant, November 1999, p 26
              CPT Assistant, May 2000, p 4
              CPT Changes: An Insider's View, 2000
              AMA (6th ed.), p 245

85. Patient has ovarian vein syndrome and has ureterolysis performed.
    A. 58679
    B. 58660
    C. 52351
    D. 50722

REFERENCE: AMA 2010

86. Male patient has been diagnosed with benign prostatic hypertrophy and undergoes a transurethral destruction of the prostate by radiofrequency thermotherapy.
    A. 52648
    B. 53852
    C. 52601
    D. 53850

REFERENCE: CPT Assistant, November 1997, p 20
              CPT Assistant, April 2001, p 4
              AMA (6th ed.), p 242

87. Nephrectomy with resection of half of the ureter.
    A. 50220
    B. 50234
    C. 50230; 50650
    D. 50546

REFERENCE: Green, p 579
              AMA (6th ed.), p 234

88. Male with urinary incontinence. Sling procedure was performed 6 months ago and now the patient has returned for a revision of the sling procedure.
    A. 53449
    B. 53442
    C. 53440
    D. 53431

REFERENCE: AMA 2010

89. Excision of 2.5 cm bladder tumor with cystoscopy.
    A. 51550
    B. 51530
    C. 52235
    D. 51060

REFERENCE: Green, p 583–582
              Smith, p 117
              AMA (6th ed.), p 238–239

90. Closure of ureterocutaneous fistula
    A. 50930
    B. 50920
    C. 57310
    D. 50520

REFERENCE: AMA 2010

Surgery—Male Genital System

91. Removal of nephrostomy tube with fluoroscopic guidance
    A. 50387
    B. 50389
    C. 99212
    D. 99213

REFERENCE: AMA 2010
              AMA (6th ed.), p 232, 240

92. Patient has been diagnosed with prostate cancer. Patient arrived in the operating room where a therapeutic orchiectomy is performed.
    A. 54560
    B. 54530
    C. 55899
    D. 54520

REFERENCE: CPT Assistant, October 2001, p 8

93. Patient undergoes laparoscopic orchiopexy for intra-abdominal testes.
    A. 54650
    B. 54699
    C. 54692
    D. 55899

REFERENCE: CPT Assistant, November 1999, p 27
              CPT Assistant, May 2000, p 4
              CPT Assistant, October 2001, p 8

94. Scrotal wall abscess drainage
    A. 55100
    B. 55150
    C. 54700
    D. 55110

REFERENCE: AMA 2010

95. Hydrocelectomy of spermatic cord
    A. 55500
    B. 55000
    C. 55041
    D. 55520

REFERENCE: CPT Assistant, October 2001, p 8

96. Patient has been followed by his primary care physician for elevated PSA. Patient underwent prostate needle biopsy in the physician office 2 weeks ago and final pathology was positive for carcinoma. Patient is admitted for prostatectomy. Frozen section of the prostate and one lymph node is positive for prostate cancer with metastatic disease to the lymph node. Prostatectomy became a radical perineal with bilateral pelvic lymphadenectomy.
    A. 55845
    B. 55815
    C. 55815; 38562
    D. 38770

REFERENCE: Smith, p 121–122
              Green, p 598

97. Male presented to operating room for sterilization by bilateral vasectomy.
    A. 55200
    B. 55400
    C. 55250
    D. 55450

REFERENCE: CPT Assistant, June 1998, p 10
              CPT Assistant, July 1998, p 10
              AMA (6th ed.), p 242

98. Laser destruction of penile condylomas
    A. 54057
    B. 17106
    C. 17270
    D. 54055

REFERENCE: AMA 2010
              Smith, p 121

99. First-stage repair for hypospadias with skin flaps
    A. 54300
    B. 54308; 14040
    C. 54322
    D. 54304

REFERENCE: AMA 2010

100. Priapism operation with spongiosum shunt
    A. 54450
    B. 54352
    C. 54430
    D. 55899

REFERENCE: AMA 2010

Surgery—Female Genital System

101. Patient was admitted to the hospital with sharp pelvic pains. A pelvic ultrasound was ordered and the results showed a possible ovarian cyst. The patient was taken to the operating room where a laparoscopic destruction of two corpus luteum cysts was performed.
    A. 49321
    B. 58925
    C. 58561
    D. 58662

REFERENCE: AMA 2010

102.Patient was admitted with a cystocele and rectocele. An anterior colporrhaphy was performed.
  A. 57250   C. 57240
  B. 57260   D. 57110

REFERENCE: AMA 2010

103. Patient has a Bartholin's gland cyst that was marsupialized.
  A. 54640   C. 58999
  B. 10060   D. 56440

REFERENCE: AMA 2010

104. Patient is at a fertility clinic and undergoes intrauterine embryo transplant.
  A. 58679   C. 58323
  B. 58322   D. 58974

REFERENCE: AMA 2010
                AMA (6th ed.), p 244

105. Patient has been diagnosed with carcinoma of the vagina and she has a radical vaginectomy with
     complete removal of the vaginal wall.
  A. 57107   C. 58150
  B. 57110   D. 57111

REFERENCE: AMA 2010
                AMA (6th ed.), p 244

106. Patient has been diagnosed with uterine fibroids and undergoes a total abdominal hysterectomy
     with bilateral salpingo-oophorectomy.
  A. 58200   C. 58262
  B. 58150   D. 58150; 58720

REFERENCE: Green, p 604
                Johnson and McHugh, p 370–371
                Smith, p 126
                AMA (6th ed.), p 116, 246, 249, 250

107. Hysteroscopy with D&C and polypectomy
  A. 58563   C. 58120; 58100; 58555
  B. 58558   D. 58558; 58120

REFERENCE: Green, p 604
                Smith, p 125–126
                AMA (6th ed.), p 250

108. Laparoscopic tubal ligation utilizing Endoloop
  A. 58670   C. 58671
  B. 58615   D. 58611

REFERENCE: Green, p 605
                AMA (6th ed.), p 249, 250–251

109.Laser destruction extensive herpetic lesions of the vulva
    A. 17106   C. 56515
    B. 17004   D. 56501

REFERENCE: AMA 2010
                     AMA (6th ed.), p 243

110. Patient undergoes hysteroscopy with excision uterine fibroids
    A. 58545   C. 58561
    B. 58140   D. 58140; 49320

REFERENCE: Green, p 604
                     Smith, p 125–126
                     AMA (6th ed.), p 249–250

Surgery—Maternity Care and Delivery

111. Attempted vaginal delivery in a previous cesarean section patient, which resulted in a repeat cesarean section.
    A. 59409   C. 59620
    B. 59612   D. 59514

REFERENCE: Green, p 610
                     Smith, p 126–127
                     AMA (6th ed.), p 255

112. Patient is admitted to the hospital following an ultrasound at 25 weeks which revealed fetal pleural effusion. A fetal thoracentesis was performed.
    A. 59074   C. 32422
    B. 32421   D. 76815

REFERENCE: CPT Assistant, May 2004, p 3–4
                     AMA (6th ed.), p 252

113. Patient in late stages of labor arrives at the hospital. Her OB physician is not able to make the delivery and the house physician delivers the baby vaginally. Primary care physician resumes care after delivery. Code the delivery.
    A. 59409   C. 59620
    B. 59612   D. 59400

REFERENCE: Green, p 606–610
                     Smith, p 126
                     AMA (6th ed.), p 255–257

114. Patient is 24 weeks' pregnant and arrives in the emergency room following an automobile accident. No fetal movement or heartbeat noted. Patient is taken to the OB ward where prostaglandin is given to induce abortion.
    A. 59200   C. 59821
    B. 59855   D. 59410

REFERENCE: Green, p 610

115.Patient is 6 weeks' pregnant and complains of left-sided abdominal pains. Patient is suspected of having an ectopic pregnancy. Patient has a laparoscopic salpingectomy with removal of the ectopic tubal pregnancy.

A. 59120   C. 59121
B. 59200   D. 59151

REFERENCE: AMA 2010
        AMA (6th ed.), p 252

116. Cesarean delivery with antepartum and postpartum care

A. 59610   C. 59400
B. 59514   D. 59510

REFERENCE: Green, p 606–610
        Smith, p 126
        AMA (6th ed.), p 252

117. A pregnant patient has an incompetent cervix which was repaired using a vaginal cerclage.

A. 57700   C. 59320
B. 57531   D. 59325

REFERENCE: AMA 2010
        AMA (6th ed.), p 253

118. A D&C is performed for postpartum hemorrhage.

A. 59160   C. 58558
B. 58120   D. 58578

REFERENCE: AMA 2010

119. Hysterotomy for hydatidifom mole and tubal ligation

A. 58285; 58600   C. 51900; 58605
B. 58150; 58605   D. 59100; 58611

REFERENCE: AMA 2010
        AMA (6th ed.), p 250

120. D&C performed for patient with diagnosis of incomplete abortion at 8 weeks.

A. 59812   C. 58120
B. 59820   D. 59160

REFERENCE: Green, p 610
        AMA (6th ed.), p 258

Surgery—Endocrine System

121. Patient comes in for a percutaneous needle biopsy of the thyroid gland.

A. 60000   C. 60699
B. 60270   D. 60100

REFERENCE: CPT Assistant, June 1997, p 5

122. Laparoscopic adrenalectomy, complete

A. 60650   C. 60659
B. 60650-50   D. 60540

REFERENCE: AMA 2010

123.Left carotid artery excision for tumor of carotid body
  A. 60650
  B. 60600
  C. 60605
  D. 60699

REFERENCE: AMA 2010

124. Patient undergoes total thyroidectomy with parathyroid autotransplantation.
  A. 60240; 60512
  B. 60520; 60500
  C. 60260; 60512
  D. 60650; 60500

REFERENCE: Green, p 611–612

125. Unilateral partial thyroidectomy
  A. 60252
  B. 60210
  C. 60220
  D. 60520

REFERENCE: Green, p 611–612

Surgery—Nervous System

126. Patient comes in through the emergency room with a wound that was caused by an electric saw. Patient is taken to the operating room where two ulna nerves are sutured.
  A. 64837
  B. 64892; 69990
  C. 64836; 64837
  D. 64856; 64859

REFERENCE: AMA 2010

127. Laminectomy and excision of intradural lumbar lesion
  A. 63272
  B. 63267
  C. 63282
  D. 63252

REFERENCE: AMA 2010
              AMA (6th ed.), p 154

128. Patient comes in for steroid injection for lumbar herniated disk. Marcaine and Aristocort were injected into the L2–L3 space.
  A. 64520
  B. 64483
  C. 62311
  D. 64714

REFERENCE: CPT Assistant, September 1997, p 10
              Smith, p 131–132
              AMA (6th ed.), p 276, 279, 286, 288

129. Patient with Parkinson's disease is admitted for insertion of a brain neurostimulator pulse generator with one electrode array.
  A. 61885
  B. 61850; 61863
  C. 61888
  D. 61867; 61870

REFERENCE: CPT Assistant, April 2001, p 8–9
              CPT Assistant, June 2000, p 4, 12
              AMA (6th ed.), p 272–273

130. Patient has rhinorrhea which requires repair of the CSF leak with craniotomy.
  A. 63707
  B. 63709
  C. 62100
  D. 62010

REFERENCE: AMA 2010
              AMA (6th ed.), p 274

131. Patient has metastatic brain lesions. Patient undergoes stereotactic radiosurgery gamma knife of two lesions.
  A. 61533
  B. 61500
  C. 61796; 61797
  D. 61796

REFERENCE: AMA 2010
              AMA (6th ed.), p 269–270

132. Patient has right sacroiliac joint dysfunction and requires a right S2–S3 paravertebral facet joint anesthetic nerve block with image guidance.
  A. 62311
  B. 64493
  C. 64490
  D. 64520

REFERENCE: AMA 2010

133. Patient requires repair of a 6 cm meningocele.
  A. 63700
  B. 63709
  C. 63180
  D. 63702

REFERENCE: AMA 2010
              AMA (6th ed.), p 273

134. Patient comes in through the emergency room with a laceration of the posterior tibial nerve. Patient is taken to the operating room where the nerve requires transposition and suture.
  A. 64856
  B. 64831; 64832; 64876
  C. 64840; 64874
  D. 64834; 64859; 64872

REFERENCE: AMA 2010
              AMA (6th ed.), p 310

Surgery—Eye and Ocular Adnexa

135. Patient returns to the physician's office complaining of obscured vision. Patient has had cataract surgery 6 months prior. Patient requires laser discission of secondary cataract.
  A. 66821
  B. 66940
  C. 67835
  D. 66830

REFERENCE: Smith, p 136–137
              AMA (6th ed.), p 297

136. Patient undergoes enucleation of left eye and muscles were reattached to an implant.
  A. 65135-LT
  B. 65105-LT
  C. 65730-LT
  D. 65103-LT

REFERENCE: AMA 2010
              AMA (6th ed.), p 310

137. Patient suffers from strabismus and requires surgery. Recession of the lateral rectus (horizontal) muscle with adjustable sutures was performed.
   A. 67340; 67500
   B. 67314; 67320
   C. 67332; 67334
   D. 67311; 67335

REFERENCE: AMA 2010
CPT Assistant, Summer 1993, p 20
CPT Assistant, March 1997, p 5
CPT Assistant, November 1998, p 1
CPT Assistant, September 2002, p 10
Smith, p 137–138
AMA (6th ed.), p 300–301

138. Radial keratotomy
   A. 92070
   B. 65855
   C. 65767
   D. 65771

REFERENCE: Green, p 628
AMA (6th ed.), p 409

139. Correction of trichiasis by incision of lid margin
   A. 67840
   B. 67830
   C. 67835
   D. 67850

REFERENCE: AMA 2010

140. Patient undergoes ocular resurfacing construction utilizing stem cell allograft from a cadaver.
   A. 67320
   B. 66999
   C. 68371
   D. 65781

REFERENCE: CPT Assistant, May 2004, p 9–11

141. Aphakia penetrating corneal transplant
   A. 65755
   B. 65730
   C. 65750
   D. 65765

REFERENCE: AMA 2010
AMA (6th ed.), p 296–297, 409

142. Lagophthalmos correction with implantation using gold weight
   A. 67912
   B. 67911
   C. 67901
   D. 67121

REFERENCE: CPT Assistant, May 2004, p 12

143. Lacrimal fistula closure
   A. 68760
   B. 68761
   C. 68700
   D. 68770

REFERENCE: AMA 2010
AMA (6th ed.), p 302

Surgery—Auditory

144. Patient comes into the office for removal of impacted earwax.
    A. 69210   C. 69222
    B. 69200   D. 69000

REFERENCE: Green, p 634
               AMA (6th ed.), p 305

145. Patient with a traumatic rupture of the eardrum. Repaired with tympanoplasty with incision of the mastoid. Repair of ossicular chain not required.
    A. 69641   C. 69642
    B. 69646   D. 69635

REFERENCE: AMA 2010
               AMA (6th ed.), p 307

146. Patient came in for excision of a middle ear lesion.
    A. 11440   C. 69552
    B. 69540   D. 69535

REFERENCE: AMA 2010

147. Patient with chronic otitis media requiring eustachian tube catheterization
    A. 69400   C. 69421
    B. 69424   D. 69405

REFERENCE: AMA 2010
               AMA (6th ed.), p 304–305

148. Modified radical mastoidectomy
    A. 69511   C. 69635
    B. 69505   D. 69641

REFERENCE: AMA 2010

149. Decompression internal auditory canal
    A. 69979   C. 69970
    B. 69915   D. 69960

REFERENCE: AMA 2010
               AMA (6th ed.), p 304, 308

150. Myringoplasty
    A. 69620   C. 69610
    B. 69635   D. 69420

REFERENCE: CPT Assistant, March 2001, p 10
               AMA (6th ed.), p 306

151. Insertion of cochlear device inner ear
    A. 69711   C. 69930
    B. 69949   D. 69960; 69990

REFERENCE: AMA 2010
               AMA (6th ed.), p 157, 159, 175, 264, 268, 280, 293, 304–305, 308, 310

152. Patient with Bell's palsy requiring a total facial nerve decompression
   A. 64742
   B. 64771
   C. 69955
   D. 64864

REFERENCE: AMA 2010
             AMA (6th ed.), p 304, 308

153. Drainage of simple external ear abscess
   A. 69000
   B. 69100
   C. 10060
   D. 69020

REFERENCE: CPT Assistant, October 1997, p 11
             CPT Assistant, October 1999, p 10
             AMA (6th ed.), p 304

Radiology

154. Administration of initial oral radionuclide therapy for hyperthyroidism
   A. 78015
   B. 77402
   C. 78099
   D. 79005

REFERENCE: Green, p 687
             AMA (6th ed.), p 326

155. Patient comes into the outpatient department at the local hospital for an MRI of the cervical spine with contrast. Patient is status post automobile accident.
   A. 72156
   B. 72142
   C. 72149
   D. 72126

REFERENCE: Smith, p 150–151
             AMA (6th ed.), p 328

156. Obstetric patient comes in for a pelvimetery with placental placement.
   A. 74710
   B. 76946
   C. 76805
   D. 76825

REFERENCE: AMA 2010

157. Patient comes into his physician's office complaining of wrist pain. Physician sends the patient to the hospital for an arthrography. Code the complete procedure.
   A. 73115
   B. 73100
   C. 73110
   D. 25246; 73115

REFERENCE: AMA 2010
             AMA (6th ed.), p 329

158. Patient has carcinoma of the breast and undergoes proton beam delivery of radiation to the breast with a single port.
   A. 77523
   B. 77432
   C. 77520
   D. 77402

REFERENCE: Green, p 680–682
             Smith, p 153–154
             AMA (6th ed.), p 349

159. CT scan of the head with contrast
    A. 70460
    B. 70542
    C. 70551
    D. 70470

REFERENCE: Smith, p 150–151
              AMA (6th ed.), p 268, 323

160. Patient undergoes x-ray of the foot with three views.
    A. 73620
    B. 73610
    C. 73630
    D. 27648; 73615

REFERENCE: Smith, p 150–151

161. Unilateral mammogram with computer-aided detection with further physician review and interpretation
    A. 77055, 77032
    B. 77055-22
    C. 77056-52, 77051
    D. 77055, 77051

REFERENCE: AMA 2010
              Green, p 676–677
              AMA (6th ed.), p 342–343

162. Pregnant female comes in for a complete fetal and maternal evaluation via ultrasound.
    A. 76856
    B. 76805
    C. 76811
    D. 76810

REFERENCE: Green, p 675
              AMA (6th ed.), p 340

163. Ultrasonic guidance for the needle biopsy of the liver. Code the complete procedure.
    A. 47000; 76942
    B. 47000; 76937
    C. 47000; 76999
    D. 47000; 77002

REFERENCE: Green, p 675–676
              AMA (6th ed.), p 142, 150, 220, 239, 320, 332–333, 380

Pathology and Laboratory

164. What code is used for a culture of embryos less than 4 days?
    A. 89251
    B. 89272
    C. 89268
    D. 89250

REFERENCE: CPT Assistant, April 2004, p 2
              CPT Assistant, May 2004, p 16
              CPT Assistant, June 2004, p 9
              AMA (6th ed.), p 389

165. Basic metabolic panel (calcium, total) and total bilirubin
    A. 80048; 82247
    B. 80053
    C. 80100
    D. 82239; 80400; 80051

REFERENCE: Green, p 705–706
              Smith, p 164
              AMA (6th ed.), p 361–362

166. Huhner test and semen analysis
    A. 89325   C. 89310
    B. 89258   D. 89300

REFERENCE: CPT Assistant, November 1997, p 36
                        CPT Assistant, July 1998, p 10
                        CPT Assistant, October 1998, p 1
                        CPT Assistant, April 2004, p 3

167. Chlamydia culture
    A. 87110   C. 87118
    B. 87106   D. 87109; 87168

REFERENCE: Green, p 713

168. Partial thromboplastin time utilizing whole blood
    A. 85732   C. 85245
    B. 85730   D. 85246

REFERENCE: Green, p 709–711
                        Smith, p 165
                        AMA (6th ed.), p 374

169. Pathologist bills for gross and microscopic examination of medial meniscus.
    A. 88300   C. 88325
    B. 88302; 88311   D. 88304

REFERENCE: Green, p 717–718
                        Smith, p 165
                        AMA (6th ed.), p 383–389

170. Cytopathology of cervical Pap smear with automated thin-layer preparation utilizing computer screening and manual rescreening under physician supervision.
    A. 88175   C. 88160; 88141
    B. 88148   D. 88161

REFERENCE: Green, p 714
                        CPT Assistant, July 2003, p 9
                        CPT Assistant, March 2004, p 4
                        AMA (6th ed.), p 377–379

171. Pathologist performs a postmortem examination including brain of an adult. Tissue is being sent to the lab for microscopic examination.
    A. 88309   C. 88099
    B. 88025   D. 88028

REFERENCE: Green, p 714
                        Smith, p 165

172. Clotting factor VII
    A. 85220   C. 85362
    B. 85240   D. 85230

REFERENCE: Green, p 709–711
                        Smith, p 165

Medicine Section

173. IV push of one anti-neoplastic drug
   A. 96401
   B. 96409
   C. 96411
   D. 96413

REFERENCE: Green, p 758–759
            Smith, p 213–214
            AMA (6th ed.), p 465

174. One-half hour of IV chemotherapy by infusion followed by IV push of a different drug
   A. 96413
   B. 96413; 96411
   C. 96413; 96409
   D. 96409; 96411

REFERENCE: Green, p 758–759
            Smith, p 213–214
            AMA (6th ed.), p 464–466

175. Caloric vestibular test using air
   A. 92543; 92700
   B. 92543; 92543
   C. 92700
   D. 92543

REFERENCE: CPT Assistant, November 2004, p 10
            AMA (6th ed.), p 417

176. Patient presents to the emergency room with chest pains. The patient is admitted as a 23-hour observation. The cardiologist orders cardiac workup and the patient undergoes left heart catheterization via the left femoral artery with visualization of the coronary arteries and left ventriculography. The physician interprets the report. Code the heart catheterization.
   A. 36245; 93514; 93545; 93540; 93555
   B. 93524; 93545; 93542; 93555; 93556
   C. 93510; 93545; 93543; 93555; 93556
   D. 93511; 93539; 93541; 93545; 93555

REFERENCE: Green, p 745–748
            Smith, p 207–209
            AMA (6th ed.), p 432–433,

177. Mother brings her 1-year-old in for the influenza split virus vaccine. Physician discusses merits of the vaccine with the mother.
   A. 90658; 90472
   B. 90657; 90465
   C. 90703
   D. 90657

REFERENCE: CPT Assistant, April 2005, p 2–3
            Green, p 732–733
            Smith, p 200
            AMA (6th ed.), p 394–395

178. Patient with hematochromatosis had a therapeutic phlebotomy performed on an outpatient basis.
    A. 99195
    B. 36522
    C. 36514
    D. 99199

REFERENCE: CPT Assistant, June 1996, p 10
              AMA (6th ed.), p 360

179. A physician performs a PTCA with drug-eluting stent placement in the left anterior descending artery and angioplasty only in the right coronary artery.
    A. 92996; 92980
    B. 92980-LD; 92984-RC
    C. 93510; 92980; 92981
    D. 92982; 92996; 92981

REFERENCE: CPT Assistant, April 2005, p 14
              Smith, p 205–206
              AMA (6th ed.), p 419–423

180. Transesophageal echocardiography (TEE) with probe placement, image, and interpretation and report.
    A. 93307
    B. 93303; 93325
    C. 93312; 93313; 93314
    D. 93312

REFERENCE: CPT Assistant, December 1997, p 5
              CPT Assistant, January 2000, p 10
              AMA (6th ed.), p 429–430

181. Which code listed below would be used to report an esophageal electrogram during an EPS?
    A. 93600
    B. 93615
    C. 93612
    D. 93616

REFERENCE: CPT Assistant, April 2004, p 9
              Smith, p 210
              AMA (6th ed.), p 437, 440

182. Cardioversion of cardiac arrhythmia by external forces
    A. 92961
    B. 92950
    C. 92960
    D. 92970

REFERENCE: CPT Assistant, Summer 1993, p 13
              CPT Assistant, November 1999, p 49
              CPT Assistant, June 2000, p 5
              CPT Assistant, November 2000, p 9
              CPT Assistant, July 2001, p 11
              AMA (6th ed.), p 418

183. Osteopathic manipulative treatment to three body regions.
    A. 98926
    B. 98941
    C. 97110
    D. 97012

REFERENCE: Green, p 760–761

184. Patient presents to the Respiratory Therapy Department and undergoes a pulmonary stress test. CO_2 production with O_2 uptake with recordings was also performed.
    A. 94450
    B. 94620
    C. 94002
    D. 94621

REFERENCE: CPT Assistant, November 1998, p 35
              CPT Assistant, January 1999, p 8CPT Assistant, August 2002, p 10

185. IV infusion of chemotherapy for 3 hours
    A. 96422, 96423, 96423
    B. 96409, 96411
    C. 96413, 96415, 96415
    D. 96413, 96413, 96413

REFERENCE: Green, p 758–759
              Smith, p 213–214
              AMA (6th ed.), p 464, 466

For the following questions, you will be utilizing the codes provided for the scenarios. You will need to code appropriate ICD-9-CM and CPT-4 codes.

186. Patient presents to the hospital for debridement of a diabetic ulcer of the left ankle. The patient has a history of recurrent ulcers. Medication taken by the patient includes Diabeta and the patient was covered in the hospital with insulin sliding scales. The decubitus ulcer was debrided down to the bone.

250.70	Diabetes with peripheral circulatory disorders, type II, or unspecified
250.71	Diabetes with peripheral circulatory disorders, type I
250.80	Diabetes with other specified manifestations, type II, or unspecified
250.81	Diabetes with other specified manifestations, type I
707.06	Decubitus ulcer, ankle
707.09	Decubitus ulcer other site
707.20	Pressure ulcer unspecified stage
707.24	Pressure ulcer stage IV, Pressure ulcer with necrosis of soft tissues through to underlying muscle, tendon, or bone
11043	Debridement, skin, subcutaneous tissue and muscle
11044	Debridement, skin, subcutaneous tissue, muscle and bone

    A. 250.81, 707.06, 707.20, 11044
    B. 250.71, 707.24, 11043
    C. 250.80, 707.06, 707.24, 11044
    D. 250.81, 250.70, 707.09, 707.20, 11044

REFERENCE: AMA 2010
              Brown, p 121–126

187. Patient presents to the emergency room following a fall from a tree. X-rays were ordered for the left upper arm which showed a fracture of the humerus shaft. The emergency room physician performed a closed reduction of the fracture and placed the patient in a long arm spica cast. Code the diagnoses and procedures, excluding the x-ray.

812.21	Fracture humerus, shaft, closed
812.31	Fracture, humerus, shaft, open
E000.9	unspecified external cause status
E030	Unspecified activity
E884.9	Other fall from one level to another
24500	Closed treatment of humeral shaft fracture; without manipulation
24505	Closed treatment of humeral shaft fracture; with manipulation, with or without skeletal traction
24515	Open treatment of humeral shaft fracture with plate/screws, with or without cerclage
29065	Application, cast; shoulder to hand (long arm)
LT	Left side

A. 812.21, E884.9, E030, E000.9, 24505-LT
B. 812.21, 24515-LT
C. 812.21, E884.9, E030, E000.9, 24505-LT, 29065
D. 812.31, 24500-LT

REFERENCE: Brown, p 407–408
Green, p 466–469
Smith, p 74–75
AMA (6th ed.), p 169–170

188. Patient was admitted with hemoptysis and underwent a bronchoscopy with transbronchial lung biopsy. Following the bronchoscopy the patient was taken to the operating room where a left lower lobe lobectomy was performed without complications. Pathology reported large cell carcinoma of the left lower lobe.

162.5	Malignant neoplasm of the lower lobe of the lung
162.8	Malignant neoplasm of other parts of bronchus or lung
162.9	Malignant neoplasm of the bronchus and lung, unspecified
31625	Bronchoscopy with biopsy, with or without fluoroscopic guidance
31628	Bronchoscopy with transbronchial lung biopsy, with or without fluoroscopic guidance
32405	Biopsy, lung or mediastinum, percutaneous needle
32440	Removal of lung, total pneumonectomy
32480	Removal of lung, other than total pneumonectomy, single lobe (lobectomy)
32484	Removal of lung, other than total pneumonectomy, single segment (segmentectomy)

A. 162.9, 31625
B. 162.5, 31628, 32480
C. 162.9, 32405, 32484
D. 162.8, 32440

REFERENCE: CPT Assistant, June 2001, p 10
CPT Assistant, September 2004, p 9
CPT Assistant, June 2002, p 10
Green, p 500
Smith, p 85–86
AMA (6th ed.), p 177–178, 180–181

189. Patient was admitted for right upper quadrant pain. Workup included various x-rays that showed cholelithiasis. Patient was taken to the operating room where a laparoscopic cholecystectomy was performed. During the procedure, the physician was unable to visualize through the ports and an open cholecystectomy was elected to be performed. Intraoperative cholangiogram was performed. Pathology report states acute and chronic cholecystitis with cholelithiasis.

574.00	Calculus of gallbladder with acute cholecystitis without obstruction
574.10	Calculus of gallbladder with other cholecystitis without obstruction
789.01	Abdominal pain of the right upper quadrant
V64.41	Laparoscopic procedure converted to open procedure
47605	Cholecystectomy with cholangiography
47563	Laparoscopy, surgical; cholecystectomy with cholangiography

A. 789.01, 574.10, 47563
B. 789.01, 574.00, 574.10, 47563, 47605
C. 574.00, 574.10, V64.41, 47605
D. 574.00, 47563, 47605

REFERENCE: Brown, p 206
Hazelwood & Venable, p 185–186
Green, p 576
AMA (6th ed.), p 225

190. Patient came to the hospital from a local nursing home for a PEG tube placement via EGD. Patient had neurogenic dysphagia and dominant hemiplegia due to prior CVA.

436	Acute, but ill-defined, cerebrovascular disease
438.21	Late effect of CVA with hemiplegia affecting dominant side
438.81	Late effect of CVA with apraxia
438.82	Late effect of CVA with dysphagia
787.29	Dysphagia, neurogenic
43219	Esophagoscopy, rigid or flexible with insertion of plastic tube or stent
43246	Upper gastrointestinal endoscopy of esophagus, stomach, and either the duodenum and/or jejunum with directed placement of percutaneous gastrostomy tube
44372	Small intestine endoscopy, enteroscopy beyond second portion of duodenum with placement of percutaneous jejunostomy tube

A. 438.81, 43219
B. 438.82, 438.21, 787.29, 43246
C. 436, 787.29, 44372
D. 436, 43246

REFERENCE: Brown, p 342–344
Hazelwood & Venable, p 157–158
Smith, p 102
AMA (6th ed.), p 220, 228

191. Patient presents to the emergency room complaining of right forearm/elbow pain after racquetball last night. Patient states that he did not fall, but overworked his arm. Past medical history is negative and the physical examination reveals the patient is unable to supinate. A four-1view x-ray of the right elbow is performed and is negative. The physician signs the patient out with right elbow sprain. Prescription of Motrin is given to the patient.

841.2	Sprain of radiohumeral joint
841.8	Sprain of other specified sites of the elbow and forearm
841.9	Sprain of unspecified site of the elbow and forearm
E000.8	External cause status
E008.2	Activities involving racquet and hand sports
E927.2	Excessive physical exertion from prolonged activity
E928.9	Unspecified accident
73040	X-ray of shoulder, arthrography radiological supervision and interpretation
73070	X-ray of elbow, two views
73080	X-ray of elbow, complete, minimum of three views
99281	E/M visit to emergency room—problem-focused history, problem-focused exam, straightforward medical decision.
99282	E/M visit to emergency room—expanded problem-focused history, expanded problem-focused exam, and medical decision of low complexity
-25	Significant, separately identifiable evaluation and management service by the same physician on the same day of the procedure or other service.

A. 841.8, 73080
B. 841.9, E928.9, 99281, 73070, E000.8, E008.2
C. 841.2, 73080, 99282, 73040
D. 841.9, E927.2, 99281-25, E000.8, E008.2, 73080

REFERENCE: Brown, p 400–402
AMA 2010
Smith, p 150–151, 190
AMA (6th ed.), p 326

192. A physician orders a lipid panel on a 54-year-old male with hypercholesterolemia, hypertension, and a family history of heart disease. The lab employee in his office performs and reports the total cholesterol and HDL cholesterol only.

272.0	Pure hypercholesterolemia
401.9	Essential hypertension, unspecified
402.90	Hypertensive heart disease, unspecified, without heart failure
V17.49	Family history of other cardiovascular disease
80061	Lipid panel; This panel must include the following: Cholesterol, serum, total (82465); Lipoprotein, direct measurement, high density cholesterol (HDL cholesterol) (83718); Triglycerides (84478)
82465	Cholesterol, serum or whole blood, total
83718	Lipoprotein, direct measurement; high density cholesterol (HDL cholesterol)
84478	Triglycerides
52	Reduced services

    A. 272.0, 80061-52
    B. 272.0, 401.9, V17.49, 80061-52
    C. 272.0, 401.9, V17.49, 82465, 83718
    D. 272.0, 402.90, 82465, 83718

REFERENCE: Green, p 705–706
                Smith, p 164
                AMA (6th ed.), p 361

193. Chronic nontraumatic rotator cuff tear. Arthroscopic subacromial decompression with mini-open rotator cuff repair.

726.10	Disorders of bursae and tendons in shoulder region, unspecified
727.61	Complete rupture of rotator cuff, nontraumatic
840.4	Sprains and strains of rotator cuff (capsule)
23410	Repair of ruptured musculotendinous cuff (e.g., rotator cuff); open, acute
23412	Repair of ruptured musculotendinous cuff (e.g. rotator cuff) open; chronic
29821	Arthroscopy, shoulder, surgical; synovectomy, complete
29823	Arthroscopy, shoulder, surgical; debridement, extensive
29826	Arthroscopy, shoulder, surgical; decompression of subacromial space with partial acromioplasty, with or without coracoacromial release
29827	Arthroscopy, shoulder, surgical; with rotator cuff repair
-59	Distinct procedural service

    A. 840.4, 726.10, 29823   C. 840.4, 29826, 29821
    B. 727.61, 23412, 29826-59   D. 727.61, 23410

REFERENCE: Smith, p 77
                    AMA (6th ed.), p 498

194. The patient is on vacation and presents to a physician's office with a lacerated finger. The physician repairs the laceration and gives a prescription for pain control and has the patient follow up with his primary physician when he returns home. The physician fills out the superbill as a problem-focused history and examination with straightforward medical decision making. Also checked is a laceration repair for a 1.5 cm finger wound.

99201	New patient office visit with a problem-focused history, problem-focused examination and straightforward medical decision making
99212	Established patient office visit with a problem-focused history, problem-focused examination and straightforward medical decision making
12001	Simple repair of superficial wounds of scalp, neck, axillae, external genitalia, trunk and/or extremities (including hands and feet); 2.5 cm or less
13131	Repair, complex, forehead, cheeks, chin, mouth, neck, axillae, genitalia, hands and/or feet; 1.1 cm to 2.5 cm

A. 99212; 13131
B. 12001

C. 99212; 12001
D. 99201; 12001

REFERENCE: Green, p 347, 443–444
Smith, p 188
AMA (6th ed.), p 54, 295

195. A 69-year-old established female patient presents to the office with chronic obstructive lung disease, congestive heart failure, and hypertension. The physician conducts a comprehensive history and physical examination and makes a medical decision of moderate complexity. Physician admits the patient from the office to the hospital for acute exacerbation of CHF.

428.0	Congestive heart failure, unspecified
402.91	Hypertensive heart disease, with congestive heart failure
401.9	Essential hypertension, unspecified
401.1	Essential hypertension, benign
496	Chronic obstructive pulmonary disease
99212	Established office visit for problem-focused history and exam, straightforward medical decision making
99214	Established office visit for a detailed history and exam, moderate medical decision making
99222	Initial hospital care for comprehensive history and exam, moderate medical decision making
99223	Initial hospital care for comprehensive history and exam, high medical decision making

A. 402.91; 496; 99214
B. 428.0; 496; 401.1; 99223

C. 428.0; 496; 401.9; 99222
D. 402.91; 496; 401.1; 99212

REFERENCE: Brown, p 346–347
Green, p 347
Smith, p 188–189
AMA (6th ed.), p 58

196. Established 42-year-old patient comes into your office to obtain vaccines required for his trip to Sri Lanka. The nurse injects intramuscularly the following vaccines: hepatitis A and B vaccines, cholera vaccine, and yellow fever vaccine. As the coding specialist, what would you report on the CMS 1500 form?
    A. office visit, hepatitis A and B vaccine, cholera vaccine and yellow fever vaccine
    B. office visit, intramuscular injection; HCPCS Level II codes
    C. office visit; administration of two or more single vaccines; vaccine products for hepatitis A and B, cholera, and yellow fever
    D. Administration of two or more single vaccines; vaccine products for hepatitis A and B, cholera, and yellow fever.

REFERENCE: Green, p 732–733

              Smith, p 200
              AMA (6th ed.), p 394–398

197. Patient presents to the operating room where the physician performed, using imaging guidance, a percutaneous breast biopsy utilizing a rotating biopsy device.

19000	Puncture aspiration of cyst of breast
19103	Biopsy of breast; percutaneous, automated vacuum assisted or rotating biopsy device, using imaging guidance
19120	Excision of cyst, fibroadenoma, or other benign or malignant tumor, aberrant breast tissue, duct lesion, nipple or areolar lesion (except 19300), open, male or female, one or more lesions
19125	Excision of breast lesion identified by preoperative placement of radiological marker, open; single lesion
19295	Image guided placement, metallic localization clip, percutaneous, during breast biopsy (List separately in addition to code for primary procedure)

    A. 19103   C. 19120
    B. 19125; 19295   D. 19000

REFERENCE: CPT Assistant, Jan 2001, p 10–11
              Green, p 454–455
              Smith, p 70–71
              AMA (6th ed.), p 142

198. Facelift utilizing the SMAS flap technique

15788	Chemical peel, facial; epidermal
15825	Rhytidectomy; neck with platysmal tightening (platysmal flap, P-flap)
15828	Rhytidectomy; cheek, chin, and neck
15829	Rhytidectomy; superficial musculoaponeurotic system (SMAS) flap

    A. 15825   C. 15829
    B. 15788   D. 15828

REFERENCE: Green, p 450
              AMA, 2010

199. Patient presents to the operating room for a secondary Achilles tendon repair.

27599	Unlisted procedure, femur or knee
27650	Repair, primary, open or percutaneous, ruptured Achilles tendon
27654	Repair, secondary, Achilles tendon, with or without graft
27698	Repair, secondary, disrupted ligament, ankle, collateral (e.g., Watson-Jones procedure)

A. 27599   C. 27650
B. 27654   D. 27698

REFERENCE: AMA, 2010

200. Tracheostoma revision with flap rotation

31613	Tracheostoma revision; simple, without flap rotation
31614	Tracheostoma revision; complex, with flap rotation
31750	Tracheoplasty; cervical
31830	Revision of tracheostomy scar

A. 31830   C. 31614
B. 31750   D. 31613

REFERENCE: AMA, 2010

201. Patient complains of frequent temporal headaches and the physician suspects temporal arteritis. Patient underwent temporal artery biopsy.

784.0	Headache
446.5	Giant cell arteritis
37600	Ligation; external carotid artery
37609	Ligation or biopsy, temporal artery
37615	Ligation, major artery (e.g., post-traumatic, rupture); neck

A. 784.0; 37615   C. 446.5; 37600
B. 784.0; 37609   D. 446.5; 37609

REFERENCE: AMA, 2010

202. Blood transfusion of three units of packed red blood cells

36430	Transfusion, blood or blood components
36455	Exchange transfusion; blood, other than newborn
36460	Transfusion, intrauterine, fetal

A. 36430   C. 36460
B. 36430; 36430; 36430   D. 36455

REFERENCE: AMA, 2010
AMA (6th ed.), p 92

203. Two-year-old patient returns to the hospital for cleft palate repair where a secondary lengthening procedure takes place.

40720	Plastic repair of cleft lip/nasal deformity; secondary, by recreation of defect and reclosure
42145	Palatopharyngoplasty
42220	Palatoplasty for cleft palate; secondary lengthening procedure
42226	Lengthening of palate, and pharyngeal flap

A. 40720
B. 42220

C. 42226
D. 42145

REFERENCE: AMA, 2010

204. Tonsillectomy on a 14-year-old

42820	Tonsillectomy and adenoidectomy; under age 12
42821	Tonsillectomy and adenoidectomy; age 12 or over
42825	Tonsillectomy, primary or secondary; under age 12
42826	Tonsillectomy, primary or secondary; age 12 or over

A. 42820
B. 42821

C. 42825
D. 42826

REFERENCE: Green, p 560–561
              AMA (6th ed.), p 210

205. Laparoscopic repair of umbilical hernia

49580	Repair umbilical hernia, under age 5 years, reducible
49585	Repair umbilical hernia, age 5 years or over, reducible
49652	Laparoscopy, surgical, repair, ventral, umbilical, spigelian or epigastric hernia (includes mesh insertion when performed); reducible
49654	Laparoscopy, surgical, repair, incisional hernia (includes mesh insertion when performed); reducible

A. 49580
B. 49654

C. 49585
D. 49652

REFERENCE: AMA 2010
              AMA (6th ed.), p 230

206. Excision of simple internal and external hemorrhoids

46221	Hemorrhoidectomy, internal, by rubber band ligation(s)
46255	Hemorrhoidectomy, internal and external, single column/group
46260	Hemorrhoidectomy, internal and external, two or more columns/groups
46945	Hemorrhoidectomy, internal, by ligation other than rubber band, single hemorrhoid, column/group

A. 46255   C. 46221
B. 46945   D. 46260

REFERENCE: AMA 2010,
                       AMA (6th ed.), p 225

207. Ureterolithotomy completed laparoscopically

50600	Ureterotomy with exploration or drainage (separate procedure)
50945	Laparoscopy, surgical ureterolithotomy
52325	Cystourethroscopy; with fragmentation of ureteral calculus
52352	Cystourethroscopy, with urethroscopy and/or pyeloscopy; with removal or manipulation of calculus (ureteral catheterization is included)

A. 52352   C. 50600
B. 52325   D. 50945

REFERENCE: CPT Assistant, November 1999, p 26
                       CPT Assistant, May 2000, p 4
                       CPT Assistant, October 2001, p 8

208. Patient undergoes partial nephrectomy for carcinoma of the kidney.

50220	Nephrectomy, including partial ureterectomy, any open approach including rib resection
50234	Nephrectomy with total ureterectomy and bladder cuff; through same incision
50240	Nephrectomy, partial
50340	Recipient nephrectomy (separate procedure)

A. 50234   C. 50340
B. 50220   D. 50240

REFERENCE: Green, p 579
                       AMA (6th ed.), p 234

209. Patient presents to the operating room for fulguration of bladder tumors. The cystoscope was inserted and entered the urethra which was normal. Bladder tumors measuring approximately 1.5 cm were removed.

50957	Ureteral endoscopy through established ureterostomy, with or without irrigation, instillation, or ureteropyelography, exclusive of radiologic service; with fulguration and/or incision, with or without biopsy
51530	Cystotomy; for excision of bladder tumor
52214	Cystourethroscopy, with fulguration of trigone, bladder neck, prostatic fossa, urethra, or periurethral glands
52234	Cystourethroscopy, with fulguration (including cryosurgery or laser surgery) and/or resection of small bladder tumor(s) (0.5 up to 2.0 cm)

A. 52234
B. 50957
C. 52214
D. 51530

REFERENCE: Smith, p 117
Green, p 583–584
AMA (6th ed.), p 237

210. Excision of Cowper's gland

53220	Excision or fulguration of carcinoma of urethra
53250	Excision of bulbourethral gland (Cowper's gland)
53260	Excision or fulguration; urethral polyp(s), distal urethra
53450	Urethromeatoplasty, with mucosal advancement

A. 53250
B. 53450
C. 53260
D. 53220

REFERENCE: AMA, 2010

211. Placement of double-J stent

52320	Cystourethroscopy (including ureteral catheterization); with removal of ureteral calculus
52330	Cystourethroscopy; with manipulation, without removal of ureteral calculus
52332	Cystourethroscopy with insertion of indwelling ureteral stent (e.g. Gibbons or double-J type)
52341	Cystourethroscopy, with treatment of ureteral stricture (e.g. balloon dilation, laser electrocautery, and incision)

A. 52341
B. 52320
C. 52330; 52332
D. 52332

REFERENCE: Green, p 583–584
Smith, p 117
AMA (6th ed.), p 237, 239

212. Closure of traumatic kidney injury.

13100	Repair, complex trunk, 1.1 cm to 2.5 cm
50400	Pyeloplasty (Foley Y-pyeloplasty), plastic operation on renal pelvis, with or without plastic operation on ureter, nephropexy, nephrostomy, pyelostomy or ureteral splinting; simple
50500	Nephrorrhaphy, suture of kidney wound or injury
50520	Closure of nephrocutaneous or pyelocutaneous fistula

A. 50520   C. 50500
B. 13100   D. 50400

REFERENCE: AMA, 2010

213. Litholapaxy, 3.0 cm calculus

50590	Lithotripsy, extracorporeal shock wave
52317	Litholapaxy, simple or small (less than 2.5 cm)
52318	Litholapaxy, complicated or large (over 2.5 cm)
52353	Cystourethroscopy, with ureteroscopy and/or pyeloscopy; with lithotripsy

A. 52353   C. 52318
B. 50590   D. 52317

REFERENCE: AMA, 2010

214. Patient presented to the operating room where an incision was made in the epigastric region for a repair of ureterovisceral fistula.

50520	Closure of nephrocutaneous or pyelocutaneous fistula
50525	Closure of nephrovisceral fistula, including visceral repair; abdominal approach
50526	Closure of nephrovisceral fistula including visceral repair; thoracic approach
50930	Closure of ureterovisceral fistula (including visceral repair)

A. 50526   C. 50520
B. 50930   D. 50525

REFERENCE: AMA, 2010

215. Amniocentesis

57530	Trachelectomy, amputation of cervix (separate procedure)
57550	Excision of cervical stump, vaginal approach
59000	Amniocentesis, diagnostic
59200	Insertion of cervical dilator (separate procedure)

A. 59000   C. 57550
B. 59200   D. 57530

REFERENCE: AMA, 2010
             AMA (6th ed.), p 252

216. Excision of thyroid adenoma

60100	Biopsy thyroid, percutaneous core needle
60200	Excision of cyst or adenoma of thyroid, or transection of isthmus
60210	Partial thyroid lobectomy, unilateral; with or without isthmusectomy
60280	Excision of thyroglossal duct cyst or sinus

A. 60210
B. 60200

C. 60280
D. 60100

REFERENCE: AMA, 2010

217. Patient is admitted to the hospital with facial droop and left-sided paralysis. CT scan of the brain shows subdural hematoma. Burr holes were performed to evacuate the hematoma.

432.1	Subdural hemorrhage
852.20	Subdural hemorrhage following injury without mention of open intra-cranial wound, unspecified state of unconsciousness
61150	Burr hole(s) or trephine; with drainage of brain abscess or cyst
61154	Burr hole(s) with evacuation and/or drainage of hematoma, extradural or subdural
61156	Burr hole(s); with aspiration of hematoma or cyst, intracerebral
61314	Craniectomy or craniotomy for evacuation of hematoma, infratentorial; extradural or subdural

A. 852.20; 61156
B. 432.1; 61314

C. 432.1; 61154
D. 852.20; 61150

REFERENCE: Brown, 406–407
              Green, p 615–616

218. Spinal tap

62268	Percutaneous aspiration, spinal cord cyst or syrinx
62270	Spinal puncture, lumbar diagnostic
62272	Spinal puncture, therapeutic, for drainage of cerebrospinal fluid (by needle or catheter)
64999	Unlisted procedure, nervous system

A. 62272
B. 64999

C. 62268
D. 62270

REFERENCE: AMA, 2010
              AMA (6th ed.), p 92, 276, 490, 508

219. Injection of anesthesia for nerve block of the brachial plexus

64413	Injection, anesthetic agent; cervical plexus
64415	Injection, anesthetic agent; brachial plexus, single
64510	Injection, anesthetic agent; stellate ganglion (cervical sympathetic)
64530	Injection, anesthetic agent; celiac plexus, with or without radiologic monitoring

A. 64415
B. 64413
C. 64530
D. 64510

REFERENCE: Green, p 623
AMA (6th ed.), p 285, 492

220. Repair of retinal detachment with vitrectomy

67040	Vitrectomy, mechanical, pars plana approach; with endolaser panretinal photocoagulation
67105	Repair of retinal detachment, one or more sessions; photocoagulation, with or without drainage of subretinal fluid
67108	Repair of retinal detachment; with vitrectomy, any method, with or without air or gas tamponade, focal endolaser photocoagulation, cryotherapy, drainage of subretinal fluid, scleral buckling, and/or removal of lens by same technique
67112	Repair of retinal detachment; by scleral buckling or vitrectomy, on patient having previous ipsilateral retinal detachment repair(s) using scleral buckling or vitrectomy techniques

A. 67112
B. 67105
C. 67108
D. 67040

REFERENCE: CPT Assistant, October 2002, p 8
AMA (6th ed.), p 298

221. SPECT bone imaging

77080	Dual energy x-ray absorptiometry (DXA), bone density study, one or more sites; axial skeleton (e.g. hips, pelvis, spine)
76977	Ultrasound bone density measurement and interpretation, peripheral site(s), any method
78300	Bone and/or joint imaging; limited area
78320	Bone and/or joint imaging; tomographic (SPECT)

A. 76977
B. 78320
C. 77080
D. 76977

REFERENCE: AMA, 2010
CPT Assistant, June 2003, p 11
AMA (6th ed.), p 355

222. Vitamin B$_{12}$

82180	Ascorbic acid (vitamin C), blood
82607	Cyanocobalamin (vitamin B12)
84590	Vitamin A
84591	Vitamin, not otherwise specified

A. 84590
B. 82180

C. 84591
D. 82607

REFERENCE: Green, p 709–710
Smith, p 165
AMA (6th ed.), p 362, 365, 372

223. Hepatitis C antibody.

86803	Hepatitis C antibody
86804	Hepatitis C antibody; confirmatory test (e.g., immunoblot)
87520	Infectious agent detection by nucleic acid (DNA or RNA); hepatitis C, direct probe technique
87522	Infectious agent detection by nucleic acid (DNA or RNA); hepatitis C, quantification

A. 86804
B. 86803

C. 87522
D. 87520

REFERENCE: Green, p 711–712
AMA (6th ed.), p 376

224. Creatinine clearance.

82550	Creatine kinase (CK), (CPK); total
82565	Creatinine; blood
82575	Creatinine; clearance
82585	Cryofibrinogen

A. 82550
B. 82565

C. 82575
D. 82585

REFERENCE: Green, p 709–710
Smith, p 165

225. Comprehensive electrophysiologic evaluation (EPS) with induction of arrhythmia.

93618	Induction of arrhythmia by electrical pacing
93619	Comprehensive electrophysiologic evaluation with right atrial pacing and recording, right ventricular pacing and recording, His bundle recording, including insertion and repositioning of multiple electrode catheters, without induction or attempted induction of arrhythmia
93620	Comprehensive electrophysiologic evaluation including insertion and repositioning of multiple electrode catheters with induction or attempted induction of arrhythmia; with right atrial pacing and recording, right ventricular pacing and recording, His bundle recording
+93623	Programmed stimulation and pacing after intravenous drug infusion (List separately in addition to code for primary procedure.)
93640	Electrophysiologic evaluation of single- or dual-chamber pacing cardioverter-defibrillator leads including defibrillation threshold evaluation (induction of arrhythmia, evaluation of sensing and pacing for arrhythmia termination) at time of initial implantation or replacement

A. 93618; 93620
B. 93620

C. 93640; 93623
D. 93619; 93620

REFERENCE: CPT Assistant, Summer 1994, p 12
CPT Assistant, August 1997, p 9
CPT Assistant, October 1997, p 10
CPT Assistant, July 1998, p 10
AMA (6th ed.), p 438–439

226. Patient presents to the hospital for a two-view chest x-ray for a cough. The radiology report comes back negative. What would be the correct codes to report to the insurance company?

786.2	Cough
786.3	Hemoptysis
V72.5	Radiology examination, not elsewhere classified
71010	Radiologic examination, chest; single view, frontal
71020	Radiologic examination, chest, two views, frontal and lateral
71035	Radiologic examination, chest, special views

A. V72.5; 71020
B. 786.2; 71020

C. V72.5; 71035
D. 786.2; 786.3, 71010

REFERENCE: Schraffenberger, p 598
AMA 2010
AMA (6th ed.), p 69, 511

227. Patient presents to the hospital for a three-view x-ray of the right shoulder. The diagnosis is shoulder pain and the radiology report states the patient has a dislocated shoulder. What would be the correct codes to report to the insurance company?

719.41	Shoulder pain
831.00	Closed dislocation shoulder, unspecified
831.01	Closed dislocation shoulder, anterior
73020	Radiologic examination, shoulder; one view
73030	Radiologic examination, shoulder; complete, minimum of two views
73060	Radiologic examination; humerus, minimum of two views
RT	Right side

A. 831.00; 73060-RT
B. 719.41; 73020-RT

C. 831.01; 73030-RT
D. 831.00; 73030-RT

REFERENCE: Brown, p 97–98
                AMA 2010
                AMA (6th ed.), p 326

And Now a Few More CPT Visits to Code with Your CPT Book

228. A 32-year-old patient has a colonoscopy with removal of three polyps by snare. Moderate sedation was used and provided by the physician. The intraservice time was 30 minutes
A. 45385; 45385-51; 45385-51
B. 45385; 99144

C. 45385
D. 45385, 45385-51, 45385-51, 99144

REFERENCE: CPT Assistant, February 2006, p 9–10
                AMA, 2010
                AMA (6th ed.), p 216, 224

229. High-energy ESW of the lateral humeral epicondyle using general anesthesia
A. 0019T
B. 0101T

C. 0102T
D. 28890

REFERENCE: CPT Assistant, March 2006 p 2
                AMA (6th ed.), p 24

230. Laparoscopic gastric restrictive procedure and placement of adjustable gastric band
A. 43770
B. 43800

C. 43845
D. 43846

REFERENCE: CPT Assistant, April 2006, p 2
                AMA (6th ed.), p 221–222

231. Laparoscopic takedown of the splenic flexure and a partial colectomy with anastomosis
A. 44140, 44213
B. 44204

C. 44213
D. 44204, 44213

REFERENCE: CPT Assistant, April 2006, p 19
                AMA (6th ed.), p 214

232. Laryngoscopic submucosal removal of non-neoplastic lesion of the vocal cord with graft reconstruction. An operating microscope was used.
    A. 31546, 69990
    B. 31546, 20926
    C. 31546
    D. 31546, 20926-51

REFERENCE: CPT Assistant, May 2006, p 16–17
             AMA (6th ed.), p 310

233. Laparoscopic removal and replacement of both a gastric band and the subcutaneous port components
    A. 43774, 43659
    B. 43659
    C. 43773
    D. 43848

REFERENCE: CPT Assistant, June 2006, p 16
             AMA (6th ed.), p 215

Answer Key for CPT-4 Coding

1.	C	51.	A
2.	A	52.	B
3.	B	53.	D
4.	C	54.	B
5.	D	55.	C
6.	C	56.	C
7.	D	57.	C
8.	B	58.	A
9.	B	59.	A
10.	C	60.	B
11.	D	61.	D
12.	B	62.	B
13.	A	63.	A
14.	B	64.	D
15.	D	65.	A
16.	B	66.	B
17.	C	67.	C
18.	A	68.	A
19.	D	69.	A
20.	C	70.	D
21.	C	71.	C
22.	B	72.	D — Radiology codes would be used for the supervision and interpretation.
23.	B		
24.	C		
25.	B	73.	C
26.	C	74.	C
27.	A	75.	C
28.	D	76.	A
29.	B	77.	D
30.	C	78.	D
31.	D	79.	C
32.	A	80.	A
33.	D	81.	A
34.	A — Codes 10060 and 10140 are used for I&Ds of superficial abscesses.	82.	C
		83.	D
		84.	B
35.	C	85.	D
36.	C	86.	B
37.	D	87.	A
38.	B	88.	B
39.	A	89.	C
40.	B	90.	B
41.	A	91.	B
42.	D	92.	D
43.	C	93.	C
44.	A	94.	A
45.	D	95.	A
46.	C	96.	B
47.	A	97.	C
48.	D	98.	A
49.	A		
50.	B		

Answer Key for CPT-4 Coding

99.	D		146.	B	
100.	C		147.	D	
101.	D		148.	B	
102.	C		149.	D	
103.	D		150.	A	
104.	D		151.	C	
105.	D		152.	C	
106.	B		153.	A	
107.	B		154.	D	
108.	C		155.	B	
109.	C		156.	A	
110.	C		157.	D	
111.	C		158.	C	
112.	A		159.	A	
113.	A		160.	C	
114.	B		161.	D	
115.	D		162.	C	
116.	D		163.	A	
117.	C		164.	D	
118.	A		165.	A	
119.	D	When tubal ligation is performed at the same time as hysterotomy, use 58611 in addition to 59100	166.	D	
			167.	A	
			168.	B	
			169.	D	
120.	A		170.	A	
121.	D		171.	B	
122.	A		172.	D	
123.	C		173.	B	
124.	A		174.	B	
125.	B		175.	C	Code 92543 is for use when an irrigation substance is used.
126.	C				
127.	A		176.	C	
128.	C		177.	B	
129.	A		178.	A	
130.	C		179.	B	Physicians use codes 92980 or 92981 for placement of drug eluting stents. Hospitals report placement of drug eluting stents with HCPCS Level II codes (G0290 or G0291)
131.	C				
132.	B				
133.	D				
134.	C				
135.	A				
136.	B				
137.	D		180.	D	
138.	D		181.	B	
139.	B		182.	C	
140.	D		183.	A	
141.	C		184.	D	
142.	A		185.	C	
143.	D		186.	C	
144.	A		187.	A	Casting is included in the surgical procedure.
145.	D		188.	B	

Answer Key for CPT-4 Coding

189. C

190. B

191. D

192. C   In order to use the code for the panel, every test must have been performed.

193. B   Code both the arthroscopic procedure and the open procedure. Both need to be reported because there were two separate procedures. Modifier -59 must be added to code 29826 because it is a component of the comprehensive procedure 23412. That is allowed if an appropriate modifier is used per NCCI edits.

194. D

195. C   According to CPT guidelines, when a patient is admitted to the hospital on the same day as an office visit, the office visit is not billable. Code rules do not allow the use of 402.91 because the scenario given does not state that the patient has hypertensive heart disease.

196. D   According to the CPT coding guidelines for vaccines, only a separate identifiable Evaluation and Management code may be billed in addition to the vaccine. In this scenario, the patient was seen only for his vaccines. This guideline immediately eliminates all the other answers.

197. A

198. C

199 B

200. C

201. B

202. A   Report this code only once no matter how many units were given.

203. B

204. D

205. D

206. A

207. D

208. D

209. A

210. A

211. D

212. C

213. C

214. B

215. A

216. B

217. C   Codes starting with 852 are considered to be traumatic injuries. No injury was stated in the case, so 432.1, non-traumatic subdural hematoma, would be the appropriate code.

218. D

219. A

220. C

221. B

222. D

223. B

224. C

225. B

226. B

227. D

228. C   CPT designates certain procedures as including moderate sedation; therefore moderate sedation is included in the code for the removal of polyps.

229. C

230. A

231. D

232. C

233. B

REFERENCES

American Medical Association. *CPT assistant.* Chicago American Medical Association (AMA).

American Medical Association. (2010). *Physician's Current Procedural Terminology (CPT) 2010, Professional Edition.* Chicago: American Medical Association (AMA).

Brown, F. (2010). *ICD-9-CM coding handbook 2010 with answers.* Chicago: American Hospital Association (AHA).

Frisch, B. (2007). *Correct coding for Medicare compliance and reimbursement.* Clifton, NY: Delmar Cengage Learning.

Green, M. (2010). *3-2-1 Code It.* (2nd ed.). Clifton, NY: Delmar Cengage Learning.

Hazelwood, A., & Venable, C. (2010). *ICD-9-CM coding and reimbursement for physician services.* Chicago: American Health Information Management Association (AHIMA).

Johnson, S.L., & McHugh, C. S. (2006) *Understanding medical coding: A comprehensive guide* (2nd ed.) Clifton, NY: Delmar Cengage Learning.

Schraffenberger, L.A. (2010). *Basic ICD-9-CM Coding.* Chicago: American Health Information Management Association (AHIMA).

Smith, G. (2009). *Basic CPT/HCPCS coding, 2009 edition.* Chicago: American Health Information Management Association (AHIMA).

CPT Competencies

Question	CCS-P Domain						
	1	2	3	4	5	6	7
			233				

IX. CCS-P Case Study Coding Review

CCS-P CODING INSTRUCTIONS

Refer to the latest AHIMA candidate handbook for updated coding instructions for coding the cases in Part II of the CCS-P Certification Examination. Visit AHIMA online at www.AHIMA.org for additional information on the electronic testing process.

1. You will record up to four ICD-9-CM diagnoses and seven CPT and/or HCPCS Level II procedural codes in the spaces provided on-screen at the end of each coding case. Do not forget that, on the certification examination, points are deducted for inappropriate codes and failure to list a required code. You will be typing the codes on an answer form screen on the computer.

2. Select diagnoses, conditions, problems, or other reasons for care that require ICD-9-CM coding in a physician-based encounter/visit, either in a physician's office, clinic, outpatient area, emergency room, ambulatory surgery, or other ambulatory care setting. Apply ICD-9-CM instructional notations and conventions and current approved "Basic Coding Guidelines for Outpatient Services" and "Diagnostic Coding and Reporting Requirements for Physician Billing" (*Coding Clinic for ICD-9-CM*, Fourth Quarter, 1995). In addition, the latest updated Coding Guidelines for Outpatient Services are in the back of this book. Code for physician services only.

3. Sequencing is not considered in scoring for diagnoses or procedures in Part II of the examination. Review the procedures for coding that are supplied in Appendix B of the examination guidebook.

4. Modifiers and linking diagnoses to procedures are tested in Part I of the examination only and are not required for the coding cases.

5. Code for professional services only for the physician designated on the cover sheet of the case.

6. Assign CPT and/or HCPCS Level II codes for all appropriate procedures.

7. Confirm Evaluation and Management (E/M) codes based on the information provided for each case. The level of key components will be given so you will not be expected to assign the level of history, examinations, and medical decision making for the examination.

8. Assign CPT codes for
   - medical procedures based on current CPT guidelines.
   - anesthetic procedures listed in the anesthesia section if appropriate.
   - radiologic and laboratory procedures listed in the radiology and laboratory sections only when applicable.

9. Do not assign HCPCS Level III Local (alphanumerical) codes, ICD-9-CM E-codes, ICD-9-CM Morphology codes (M-codes), or ICD-9-CM procedure codes from Volume 3.

<u>Case Study 1</u>

Office Visit

Face Sheet

Patient's Name: Leon Kane

Date of Visit: 1/26/2010

Age: 55

Sex: Male

Insurance: Self-Pay

Case Study 1

Office Visit

This is a 55-year-old male returning to the office for palpitations. The patient reports what he describes as his "heart flipping about" and then experiences some pain. The episode lasted for just a few seconds. He states it is more likely to occur when he is stressed out. He has not noticed any association with exercise. He is quite concerned about the possibility of this being related to his heart. No other cardiovascular complaints. He also complains of excessive thirst and fatigue.

Allergies: None

Medications: None

Blood pressure is 100/60, and pulse 77. He is a well-developed, well-nourished male in no acute distress.

Neck:	Supple. No JVD or bruit.
Lungs:	Clear to auscultation.
Heart:	Rate & rhythm regular
	EKG was done; revealed normal sinus rhythm.
Abdomen:	No masses detected.

IMPRESSION AND PLAN:
1. Palpitations. Blood was drawn for cholesterol profile, which was sent to an outside lab. Stress test will be ordered for next week.
2. Rule out diabetes. Blood was drawn for glucose levels.
3. Fatigue. Blood was drawn for thyroid profile.
4. Patient is to follow-up in 2 weeks to discuss the stress test and all lab results.

History:	Expanded Problem-Focused
Examination:	Expanded Problem-Focused
Medical Complexity:	Low

Case Study 1

EKG RESULTS

A twelve-lead EKG machine was hooked up to a 55-year-old patient with leads placed in proper protocol. The vent rate was 62 BPM, PR interval was 156, QRS duration was 72, and P-R-T axes were 49, 50, and 49, respectively.

IMPRESSION:
1. Normal Sinus Rhythm
2. Normal EKG

Case Study 1

Answer Sheet   *99213   Est. Pat*

DIAGNOSES		ICD-9-CM CODES					
First listed DX *palpitations*		7	8	5	.	1	
DX 2 *polydipsia*		7	8	3	.	5	
DX 3 *fatigue*		7	8	0	.	7	9
DX 4					.		

PROCEDURES	CPT CODES					MODIFIERS (If Applicable)		
PR 1 *Est/Pat Office Visit*	9	9	2	1	3	-		
PR 2 *EKG Test/Drawn*	9	3	0	0	0	-		
PR 3 *Blood Test/Drawing Venapuncture*	3	6	4	1	5	-		
PR 4 *Lab/Blood Handling*	9	9	0	0	0	-		
PR 5						-		
PR 6						-		
PR 7						-		

specimen handling

Blood handling/Specimen 99000 - 99001

Case Study 2

Emergency Room Visit

Face Sheet

Patient's Name: Patience Cooper

Date of Visit: 1/14/2010

Age: 80

Sex: Female

Insurance: Medicare

Case Study 2

DATE OF ADMISSION: 1/14/2010

HISTORY:
This elderly female was brought to the emergency room today when she was out with some friends and developed nausea and vomiting. She also developed diarrhea last night. She has a slight fever and appears to be somewhat dehydrated. She has been started on an IV.

PAST MEDICAL HISTORY:
She has had the usual childhood diseases. She has a history of arthritis, and a history of cataract extraction of the left eye.

ALLERGIES: No apparent allergies.

MEDICATIONS: She is on no medications.

SOCIAL HISTORY: She is a widow who lives alone.

PHYSICAL EXAMINATION:

General:	Well-developed, well-nourished female in no acute distress. Blood pressure is 100/74, pulse 70, temperature of 101, respiration 18.
Head:	Normocephalic.
Eyes:	There is an opacity, right eye. Aphakia in the left.
Neck:	Supple. No bruits.
Skin:	Negative.
Chest:	Few scattered rhonchi.
Heart:	Normal rhythm. No murmurs appreciated.
Abdomen:	Slightly distended with tenderness. Bowel sounds present.
Extremities:	Negative.

IMPRESSION:
1. Gastroenteritis
2. Slight dehydration
3. Arthritis

The patient was discharged in good condition. No further nausea and vomiting. Patient was given a prescription for Flagyl 500 mg t.i.d. for 10 days.

LABORATORY EXAMINATION
Special Laboratory Examination: Stool.
Results: Stool shows moderate amount of Giardia Lamblia cysts.

History:	Expanded Problem-Focused
Examination:	Expanded Problem-Focused
Medical Decision:	Low

Case Study 2

Answer Sheet

DIAGNOSES	ICD-9-CM CODES					
First listed DX				.		
DX 2				.		
DX 3				.		
DX 4				.		

PROCEDURES	CPT CODES					MODIFIERS (If Applicable)		
PR 1						-		
PR 2						-		
PR 3						-		
PR 4						-		
PR 5						-		
PR 6						-		
PR 7						-		

Case Study 3

Office Visit

Face Sheet

Patient's Name: Lois Graham

Date of Visit: 1/03/2010

Age: 40

Sex: Female

Insurance: Government

Case Study 3

Office Visit

HISTORY OF PRESENT ILLNESS: This is a <u>first visit</u> for this 40-year-old female. She is complaining of <u>abnormal vaginal discharge and bleeding</u> on and off for approximately three weeks. She denies any trauma. Patient is sexually active and her LMP was a month ago. Period has not started this month. She denies any chest pain, shortness of breath, or urinary problems.

PAST MEDICAL HISTORY: Usual childhood diseases.
Two vaginal deliveries, one in 1977 and 1986.

ALLERGIES: None known.

MEDICATIONS: Birth control pills.

SOCIAL HISTORY: She does not smoke or drink. She is very active with jogging every day and playing tennis. She is married and lives with her husband and two children.

FAMILY HISTORY: Father died of an aneurysm seven years ago; mother is in good health. No history of breast or cervical cancer in the family.

PHYSICAL EXAMINATION:

Vital Signs:	BP 120/70; Pulse 85; Respirations 20. Height 5' 5", weight 135 lb. Well-developed, well-nourished female in no acute distress.
HEENT:	Pupils equal, round and reactive to light and accommodation. Extraocular muscles are intact: Trachea is midline.
Neck:	Thyroid not palpable. No jugular distention. Carotid pulses are present bilaterally.
Breasts:	No masses, tenderness or nipple discharge.
Lungs:	Clear to auscultation and percussion.
Heart:	Normal sinus rhythm. No murmurs appreciated.
Abdomen:	No masses or tenderness noted. No hernias appreciated. No enlargement of the liver or spleen.
Pelvic:	<u>Vaginal examination reveals</u> no lesions or masses. Discharge is noted and a <u>sample was collected</u> and sent to an <u>outside laboratory</u> for testing. No bleeding noted. External genitalia are normal. No lesions noted on cervix. Uterus is not enlarged.
Urinary:	Urethral meatus is normal. No masses noted for urethra or bladder.

PLAN: Patient is to follow-up in one week for lab results. Patient will be scheduled for abdominal x-ray tomorrow.

History:	Detailed
Examination:	Detailed
Medical Decision:	Low Complexity

Case Study 3

Answer Sheet

New Patient 99204

DIAGNOSES		ICD-9-CM CODES					
First listed DX *Vaginal discharge*		6	2	3	.	5	
DX 2 *Vaginal Bleeding* (Hemmorrhage)		6	2	3	.	8	
DX 3					.		
DX 4					.		

PROCEDURES		CPT CODES					MODIFIERS (If Applicable)	
PR 1 *New Pat*		9	9	2	0	3	-	
PR 2 *Lab - Handling specimen*		9	9	0	0	0	-	
PR 3							-	
PR 4							-	
PR 5							-	
PR 6							-	
PR 7							-	

Vag. discl.   623.5
Vag. Bleed.   623.8

? Pap Smear   88145-155
88164-167
88174-175

<u>Case Study 4</u>

Office Visit

Face Sheet

Patient's Name: Myles Springs

Date of Visit: 1/18/2010

Age: 17

Sex: Male

Insurance: Self-Pay

Case Study 4

Office Visit

HISTORY OF PRESENT ILLNESS: This is a recheck for a persistent toothache. Patient is a 17-year-old male with a bad tooth who was seen four days ago and started on penicillin and Percocet. He has run out of Percocet and his mother has not gotten him in to see the dentist. He has persistent pain.

PHYSICAL EXAMINATION:

HEENT:	The left lower second molar is viewed and found to be decaying with a large open cavity on the medial posterior aspect. He has persistent, severe pain; however, there is no significant inflammation of the gingiva, no active purulent discharge.
Head:	Normocephalic.
Lungs:	Clear.
IMPRESSION:	Odontalgia with dental decay. Patient was given a new prescription for Percocet and an appointment with a dental clinic for care.

History:	Problem-Focused
Examination:	Problem-Focused
Medical Decision:	Straightforward

Case Study 4

Answer Sheet

DIAGNOSES							ICD-9-CM CODES			
First listed DX	Odontalgia		5	2	5	.	9	
DX 2	Tooth decay – dental caries		5	2	1	.	0	0
DX 3						.		
DX 4						.		

PROCEDURES		CPT CODES					MODIFIERS (If Applicable)		
PR 1	Est Pat – Office Visit	9	9	2	1	2	-		
PR 2							-		
PR 3							-		
PR 4							-		
PR 5							-		
PR 6							-		
PR 7							-		

Tooth decay
dental caries

Case Study 5

Office Visit

Face Sheet

Patient's Name: Turk Joseph

Date of Visit: 1/08/2010

Age: 25

Sex: Male

Insurance: Prudential

Case Study 5

Office Visit

HISTORY OF PRESENT ILLNESS:
This is a first-time visit for this 25-year-old male. He is being seen on an emergency basis in the office due to the patient presenting with a lacerated hand. Patient stated that he cut his right hand while opening a can and just came to the closest physician. The wound does not involve any deep structures. Fingers do not have a decrease in movement.

PAST MEDICAL HISTORY: Non-contributory.

MEDICATIONS: None.

PHYSICAL EXAMINATION:

General:	Healthy-appearing male in mild distress. BP 130/75, Pulse 88, Respirations 16.
Skin:	Warm and dry. No lesions noted.
Lungs:	Clear to auscultation and percussion. No decreased breath sounds noted.
Extremities:	Normal range of motion times four. The dorsum part of the right hand has a 1.5-cm laceration that is superficial with no deep structure involvement.

The right hand was prepped with Betadine and anesthetized with 1% plain Xylocaine. The wound was irrigated with saline and explored. No evidence of foreign body or deep structure involvement. The wound was closed with interrupted sutures. A sterile dressing was applied.

IMPRESSION:
Right hand laceration. The patient was given a prescription for Erythromycin to prevent infection and he is to take Tylenol for pain.

Follow-up in office in three weeks for suture removal.

History:	Expanded problem
Examination:	Expanded problem
Medical Decision:	Straightforward

Case Study 5

Answer Sheet

DIAGNOSES		ICD-9-CM CODES					
First listed DX — *Open Wound (laceration) of hand w/o complication except fingers*		8	8	2	.	0	
DX 2					.		
DX 3					.		
DX 4					.		

PROCEDURES		CPT CODES					MODIFIERS (If Applicable)	
PR 1 *New Pat - Office Visit*		9	9	2	0	2	-	25
PR 2 *Emergency office Visit*		9	9	0	5	8	-	
PR 3 *Repair Wound - Simple* 2.5 cm or less		1	2	0	0	1	-	
PR 4							-	
PR 5							-	
PR 6							-	
PR 7							-	

?

Laceration > wound Repair > simple 12000 - 12021 (no comp)

Case Study 6

Office Visit

Face Sheet

Patient's Name: Dorothy Belle
Date of Visit: 1/06/2010
Age: 50
Sex: Female
Insurance: Commercial

Case Study 6

Office Visit

HISTORY OF PRESENT ILLNESS:
Patient presents to the office with a two-day history of a sore throat. Patient is also experiencing fever and difficulty with swallowing.

PAST HISTORY:
Patient has a history of asthma not under current management. Appendectomy two months ago. No known allergies.

PHYSICAL EXAMINATION:

General:	Alert and oriented. In no acute distress.
	T: 100.9; P: 128; R: 18; B/P: 102/60
Throat:	Tonsillar swelling with pharyngeal erythema.
Ears/Nose:	Normal.
Respiratory:	No respiratory distress.
Abdomen:	Surgical incision healing well.

Throat culture for strep screen taken and sent to an outside lab. Report came back positive.

IMPRESSION: Acute Tonsillitis   *Streptococcal*

Patient was given a prescription for Amox 400-mg p.o.

To return in one week.

History:	Expanded Problem-Focused
Examination:	Expanded Problem-Focused
Medical Decision:	Low

Case Study 6

Answer Sheet

DIAGNOSES		ICD-9-CM CODES					
First listed DX Tonsillitis (streptococcal)		O	3	4	.	0	
DX 2 Fever					.		
DX 3 dysphagia (difficulty swallowing)					.		
DX 4					.		

PROCEDURES	CPT CODES					MODIFIERS (If Applicable)		
PR 1 Est PAT - Office Visit	9	9	2	1	3	-		
PR 2 Lab - Strep screen	9	9	0	0	0	-		
PR 3						-		
PR 4						-		
PR 5						-		
PR 6						-		
PR 7						-		

Case Study 7

Emergency Room Visit

Face Sheet

Patient's Name: Steven Tam

Date of Visit: 1/16/2010

Age: 7

Sex: Male

Insurance: Government

Case Study 7

Emergency Room Report

HISTORY OF PRESENT ILLNESS:
This is a 7-year-old boy who was brought to the emergency room by his parents. He has been running an elevated temperature for the past 12 hours; the high was 103. He also complains of stomach pains and vomiting. The parents are very concerned.

PAST MEDICAL HISTORY: Negative.

ALLERGIES AND MEDICATIONS: None.

SOCIAL HISTORY: Patient lives with his parents. Attends elementary school where he is in the first grade.

PHYSICAL EXAMINATION:

General:	Well-developed, well-nourished child who is lethargic and pale. His temperature is 101. Pulse 110. Respirations 28. BP 99/72.
HEENT:	Eyes are normal. There is a minimal amount of inflammation of the tonsils. Ears, nose, and mouth are normal.
Neck:	Supple.
Skin:	Negative.
Chest:	Lungs sounds are normal.
Heart:	Normal rhythm with no murmurs appreciated.
Abdomen:	Diffuse tenderness. No masses or organomegaly noted.
Neurological:	Normal.
Extremities:	Normal.

EXAMINATIONS:
Abdominal x-ray was normal.
Labs normal except for UA, which was positive for E. coli > 100,000.

Hospital chges

IMPRESSION: Acute pyelonephritis.

DISPOSITION: Discharged with Bactrim and will follow-up with his physician.

History:	Expanded Problem-Focused
Examination:	Expanded Problem-Focused
Medical Decision:	Low

Hospital chges for x-ray & Labs

Case Study 7

ER Visit/Outpatient **Answer Sheet**

DIAGNOSES		ICD-9-CM CODES					
First listed DX _Acute pyelonephritis_	5	9	0	.		1	0
DX 2 _E. coli_ _Escherichia coli_	0	4	1	.		4	
DX 3				.			
DX 4				.			

PROCEDURES		CPT CODES				MODIFIERS (If Applicable)		
PR 1 _ER Visit_	9	9	2	8	2	-		
PR 2						-		
PR 3						-		
PR 4						-		
PR 5						-		
PR 6						-		
PR 7						-		

Code the Diagnoses using ICD-9-CM Codes and
Code the Emergency Room Physician Visit with CPT E/M Code(s)

Case Study 8

Emergency Room Report

Face Sheet

Patient's Name: Nancy Jean

Date of Visit: 1/16/2010

Age: 40

Sex: Female

Insurance: Commercial

Case Study 8

Emergency Room Report

DATE OF ADMISSION:	1/16/2010
CHIEF COMPLAINT:	Severe headaches, nausea, and vomiting.

HISTORY:

This 40-year-old female was seen in the emergency room for complaints of headaches, neck pain, nausea, and vomiting, with the possibility of viral meningitis. At the time, my impression was that it probably was a viral syndrome. A spinal tap was done by the hospital anesthesiologist to rule out viral meningitis. The spinal tap was unremarkable. A CT scan of the head was also performed by the hospital anesthesiologist and was also unremarkable.

PAST MEDICAL HISTORY:	Non-contributory.
Allergies:	None.
Medications:	None.
Social History:	Non-contributory.

PHYSICAL EXAMINATION:

General:	At present, examination reveals her to be in moderate distress due to her headaches.
HEENT:	Markedly photophobia. No gross lesions noted. Pupils round and reactive. Trachea midline.
Chest:	Lungs clear to auscultation and percussion.
Heart:	Murmurs not noted.
Abdomen:	Soft, no organomegaly.
Neurological:	Examination includes the cranial nerve, motor, sensory, gait and station, deep tendon reflexes, and cerebellum, which were unremarkable. No nuchal rigidity noted. No Brudzinski or Kernig's signs.
Extremities:	All pulses palpable.
PROCEDURE:	Spinal tap & CT of head performed by hospital anesthesiologist.
LABORATORY RESULTS:	CSF showed 1 WBC and 1 RBC, glucose 33, protein 27.

IMPRESSION:
1. Viral Syndrome
2. Headaches   *neck pain*

Patient is discharged from the emergency room and is to follow-up with her physician.
A prescription of Demerol 50 mg p.o. q.i.d. was given.

History:	Expanded Problem-Focused
Examination:	Expanded Problem-Focused
Medical Decision:	Moderate

No Labs @ ER

Case Study 8

Answer Sheet

DIAGNOSES	ICD-9-CM CODES					
First listed DX Viral Syndrome unspecified	0	7	9	.	9	9
DX 2 Headaches	7	8	4	.	0	
DX 3				.		
DX 4				.		

PROCEDURES	CPT CODES					MODIFIERS (If Applicable)		
PR 1 ER Visit	9	9	2	8	3	-		
PR 2						-		
PR 3						-		
PR 4						-		
PR 5						-		
PR 6						-		
PR 7						-		

Case Study 9

Emergency Room Visit

Face Sheet

Patient Name: Angela Miller

Date of Service: 01/09/2010

Age: 53

Sex: Female

Admitting Diagnosis: Abdominal pain

Discharge Diagnoses: Abdominal pain
Hemoptysis
Nausea and vomiting

Disposition: Home

Case Study 9

Emergency Room Visit

DATE OF VISIT: 01/09/2010

CHIEF COMPLAINT: Vomiting of blood.

HISTORY OF PRESENT ILLNESS: This female was seen in the emergency room today due to severe abdominal pain, nausea, and vomiting of blood. The patient does have a history of cholelithiasis with common bile duct obstruction. Cholecystectomy was done approximately 3 weeks prior to this admission without any complications.

PAST MEDICAL HISTORY: Cholecystectomy 3 weeks ago.

ALLERGIES: None.

MEDICATIONS: None.

SOCIAL HISTORY: Patient smokes 1/2 pack per day.

REVIEW OF SYSTEMS:
Cardiovascular System:	No dyspnea or pain.
Gastrointestinal:	Severe abdominal pain with nausea and vomiting of blood.
Genitourinary:	No dysuria.

PHYSICAL EXAMINATION:
General:	Well-nourished, well-developed female.
HEENT:	Pupils are equal, round, and reactive to light and accommodation. Extraocular muscles are intact.
Neck:	No masses or thyroidomegaly.
Chest:	Clear to auscultation bilaterally.
Heart:	Regular rate and rhythm.
Abdomen:	Soft, non-tender. No masses. Bowel sounds are present. There is a scar present secondary to cholecystectomy.
Neurological:	Normal
Extremities:	Normal

LABORATORY FINDINGS:
CBC 10/32; WBC 14; Na 140, K+ 4.5, Glu 115, BUN 2.0, Creatinine 0.5.

RADIOLOGY FINDINGS: Upper Abdominal and Gallbladder Ultrasound is normal.

PLAN:
Patient is discharged in stable condition and will follow-up with her physician.

She is to contact the emergency room if further symptoms occur.

History:	Expanded problem-focused
Physical:	Expanded problem-focused
Medical Decision Making:	Moderate Decision

No labs @ ER

Case Study 9

Radiology Report

DATE: 01/09/2010

PROCEDURE: Upper Abdominal and Gallbladder Ultrasound

The liver is normal in size, contour, and echogenicity. The pancreas is normal in size. Both kidneys are normal in size, shape, and position. The common bile duct is normal.

Case Study 9

Answer Sheet

DIAGNOSES	ICD-9-CM CODES					
First listed DX Abdominal Pain unspecified site	7	8	9	.	0	0
DX 2 Vomiting of Blood/Hematemesis	5	7	8	.	0	
DX 3 Nausea @ Vomiting	7	8	7	.	0	1
DX 4				.		

PROCEDURES	CPT CODES					MODIFIERS (If Applicable)		
PR 1 ER Visit	9	9	2	8	3	-		
PR 2						-		
PR 3						-		
PR 4						-		
PR 5						-		
PR 6						-		
PR 7						-		

Case Study 10

Ambulatory Surgery

Face Sheet

Patient Name: Cynthia Crossman

Date of Admission: 1/16/2010

Age: 45

Sex: Female

Admitting Diagnosis: Carpal tunnel syndrome, left wrist

Discharge Diagnosis: Carpal tunnel syndrome, left wrist

   Type 1 Diabetes Mellitus

   Hypertension

Procedure: Decompression of medial nerve, left wrist

Disposition: Home

Case Study 10

History and Physical

DATE OF ADMISSION: 1/16/2010

ADMITTING DIAGNOSIS: Carpal tunnel syndrome left wrist

HISTORY OF PRESENT ILLNESS:
This patient has been complaining of left wrist pain for approximately 1 year. She has been receiving physical therapy for 6 months, and it does not seem to be helping. She is a transcriptionist and does repetitive computer work. She has been wearing bilateral wrist supports, which have helped to some extent.

PAST MEDICAL HISTORY:
The patient has a history of T&A; hysterectomy 2 years ago; history of type 1 diabetes mellitus and hypertension. She does not complain of chest pain or shortness of breath.

ALLERGIES: No apparent allergies.

MEDICATIONS: Patient takes Humulin 70/30 and Zestril.

SOCIAL HISTORY: Non-contributory.

PHYSICAL EXAMINATION:

General:	This is a well-developed, well-nourished female in no acute distress.
Head:	Normocephalic.
Neck:	Supple. No masses. Carotid pulse is palpable. Trachea is in midline.
Skin:	Negative.
Chest:	Clear to auscultation and percussion.
Heart:	No murmurs, gallops, or rubs.
Abdomen:	Negative.
Extremities:	Left wrist has weakness. Unable to touch thumb and little finger together. There is a prominent mass on the palmar aspect of the left wrist.

PLAN:
Patient will be seen at the ambulatory surgery center for carpal tunnel surgery.

Case Study 10

Operative Report

Date of Operation:	1/16/2010
Preoperative Diagnosis:	Carpal tunnel syndrome left wrist
Postoperative Diagnosis:	Carpal tunnel syndrome left wrist
Operation:	Decompression of medial nerve, left wrist
Surgeon:	E.B. Mannion, MD
Anesthesia:	Bier block
Estimated Blood Loss:	Less than 500 cc

PROCEDURE:

Under Bier block anesthesia, preparation was done with Betadine scrub, Betadine solution and sterile draping was done. Curvilinear incision was made based on the lunar side of the longitudinal wrist crease and carried up to the proximal flexor wrist crease. This was carried through subcutaneous tissue. Range retractors were inserted. The median nerve was visualized at the proximal edge of the transverse carpal ligament. The nerve was protected and using curved dissecting scissors, the transverse carpal ligament was sectioned under direct vision. The nerve was quite compressed. After the ligament had been sectioned, the wound was closed with interrupted 5-0 nylon sutures and sterile dressings were applied. The patient tolerated the procedure well and circulation to the extremity was intact at the completion of the procedure.

Case Study 10

Progress Notes:

Patient was taken to the operating room for carpal tunnel repair. Patient tolerated the procedure well. No apparent complications are noted. Patient will be discharged when stable and will follow-up in my office in 2 weeks.

Case Study 10

Orders:

1. Standard post-operative orders.
2. Discharge patient from recovery room when stable.
3. Vital signs q 15 minutes × 4; then q 30 × 2; then q1h until discharge.
4. Tylenol 500 mg q 4 for pain.
5. Discharge when patient is stable.

Case Study 10

Answer Sheet

DIAGNOSES	*Carpal tunnel Syndrome -* *Lt wrist*	ICD-9-CM CODES					
First listed DX	Carpal tunnel Syndrome *not stated* Left wrist	3	5	4	.	0	
DX 2	Type 1 Diabetes mellitus *not stated as controlled*	2	5	0	.	0	1
DX 3	Hypertension (unspecified)	4	0	1	.	9	
DX 4					.		

PROCEDURES		CPT CODES					MODIFIERS (If Applicable)	
PR 1	Decompression of medial nerve - Left wrist	6	4	7	2	1	-	L T
PR 2							-	
PR 3							-	
PR 4							-	
PR 5							-	
PR 6							-	
PR 7							-	

Case Study 11

Ambulatory Surgery

Face Sheet

Patient Name: Timothy Johnson

Date of Service: 01/09/2010

Age: 61

Sex: Male

Admitting Diagnosis: Dyspepsia
                         Dysphagia

Discharge Diagnoses: Candidal esophagitis
                         Acute and chronic gastritis
                         Helicobacter

Procedure: Esophagogastroduodenoscopy with biopsies

Case Study 11

History and Physical

DATE OF ADMISSION: 1/09/2010

ADMITTING DIAGNOSIS: Dyspepsia and dysphagia.

HISTORY OF PRESENT ILLNESS:
This gentleman has been complaining of dyspepsia for the past month. Now he has developed difficulty swallowing. Patient was treated conservatively with Riopan. With the difficulty in swallowing, we will proceed with an esophagogastroduodenoscopy.

PAST MEDICAL HISTORY:
History of basal cell carcinoma of the back, hypertension now not treated, diabetes.

ALLERGIES: None.

MEDICATIONS: Riopan and Glucotrol.

SOCIAL HISTORY: Patient does not smoke; alcohol is minimal.

PHYSICIAL EXAMINATION:

General:	This is an obese male. Vital signs are within normal limits.
HEENT:	Extraocular movements are intact. No evidence of cataracts. Dysphagia and dyspepsia.
Neck:	Without bruits, masses, or adenopathy.
Chest:	Clear to auscultation bilaterally without any crackles or wheezes.
Heart:	Regular rate and rhythm. No murmurs or gallops.
Abdomen:	Without hernias, masses, or hepatosplenomegaly. Bowel sound present in all four quadrants.
Neurological:	Normal.
Extremities:	Unremarkable.

PLAN:
Patient will be admitted to one-day surgery for an esophagogastroduodenoscopy.

Case Study 11

Operative Report

Date of Operation:	1/09/2010
Preoperative Diagnosis:	1. Dyspepsia 2. Dysphagia
Postoperative Diagnosis:	1. Candidal esophagitis, biopsies taken for confirmation 2. Upper GI endoscopy was otherwise unremarkable. Gastric biopsies were taken to exclude Helicobacter pylori infection
Operation:	Esophagogastroduodenoscopy
Surgeon:	Rodney Verne, MD
Assistant:	V. G. Smith, MD
Anesthesia:	Demerol 50 mg intravenous, Versed 6 mg intravenous
Instrument:	Olympus video gastroscope

PROCEDURE:

The risks and benefits of the procedure were explained to the patient and informed consent was obtained. The patient was placed in the left lateral decubitus position. Flexible video endoscope was gently advanced through the circopharyngeus into the esophagus. There are typical changes of candidal esophagitis in the mid and distal esophagus. Photographs and biopsies were taken. The GE junction was located at 38 cm from the incisors. Retroflexed views in the cardia showed no fundic mass.

The endoscope was placed in the forward viewing position and advanced from the greater curvature to the antrum, and there was no evidence of ulceration or mass. The pylorus was patent. The duodenal bulb is non-deformed and free of ulceration. Postbulbar duodenum is unremarkable. The endoscope was then withdrawn back into the stomach. Gastric biopsies were taken to exclude Helicobacter pylori and the procedure was terminated. The patient tolerated the procedure well without evident complications.

RECOMMENDATIONS:
1. Await results of pathologic findings.
2. Diflucan therapy 100 mg daily x 3 weeks for treatment of Candidiasis.
3. The patient will follow-up with his primary physician.

Case Study 11

Pathology Report

Date:	1/09/2010
Physician:	Rodney Verne, MD
Preoperative Diagnosis:	Dyspepsia/dysphagia
Surgical Procedure:	EGD
Postoperative Diagnosis:	Candidal, esophagitis
Specimen(s):	1. Esophageal biopsy
	2. Gastric biopsy
GROSS:	There are two containers.

Container number one, labeled "biopsy esophagus," consists of fragments of gray-white soft tissue. In aggregate, these measure .3 × .3 × .2 cm and are submitted in cassette "1."

Container number two, labeled "biopsy gastric," consists of two fragments of gray-tan soft tissue in aggregate .3 × .2 × .2 cm. Submitted in cassette "2."

GROSS AND MICROSCOPIC EXAMINATION:
Biopsy of esophagus: Esophagitis

COMMENT:
Special stain for fungal organisms is positive, with fungal elements consistent with candidal esophagitis.

Gastric biopsies: Acute and chronic gastritis

COMMENT:
Special stain for Helicobacter organism is strongly positive.

Case Study 11

Progress Notes:

Patient has a history of dyspepsia and dysphagia for a month. Taken to endoscopy room where an esophagogastroscopy was performed. Biopsies showed esophagitis, acute and chronic gastritis with Helicobacter present. Patient tolerated the procedure well.

Orders:

1   Standard post-operative orders.
2. Vital signs q 15 minutes × 4; then q 30 × 2; then q 1 until discharge.
3. Start on soft diet.
4. Discharge when patient is stable.

Case Study 11

Answer Sheet

DIAGNOSES	ICD-9-CM CODES					
First listed DX *Candidal esophagitis*	1	1	2	.	8	4
DX 2 *Helicobacter pylori infection*	0	4	1	.	8	6
DX 3				.		
DX 4				.		

PROCEDURES	CPT CODES					MODIFIERS (If Applicable)		
PR 1 *Esophagogastroduodenoscopy* *with biopsies*	4	3	2	3	9	-		
PR 2						-		
PR 3						-		
PR 4						-		
PR 5						-		
PR 6						-		
PR 7						-		

Case Study 12

Emergency Room Visit

Face Sheet

Patient Name: Rose Spector

Date of Service: 01/08/2010

Age: 65

Sex: Female

Admitting Diagnosis: Nose bleed

Discharge Diagnosis: Recurrent nosebleed

Disposition: Home

Case Study 12

Emergency Room Visit

DATE OF SERVICE: 01/08/2010

HISTORY OF PRESENT ILLNESS:
Patient presents to the emergency room with a history of waking up with her nose bleeding. This is the second occurrence of epistaxis that she has had. She states that the bleeding has resolved. Denies that she takes any aspirin.

PHYSICAL EXAMINATION:

HEENT:	Normal tympanic membranes. The examination of the nares shows evidence of former bleeding site; it is now resolved. Oropharynx is normal.
Neck:	Supple, no bruits.
Lungs:	Clear.

IMPRESSION: Recurrent nosebleed.

The patient is to return to her primary physician if bleeding reoccurs.

History:	Problem-focused
Physical:	Problem-focused
Medical Decision Making:	Straightforward

Case Study 12

Answer Sheet

DIAGNOSES	ICD-9-CM CODES					
First listed DX *Epistaxis* Recurrent nosebleed	7	8	4	.	7	
DX 2				.		
DX 3				.		
DX 4				.		

PROCEDURES	CPT CODES					MODIFIERS (If Applicable)		
PR 1 *ER Visit*	9	9	2	8	1	-		
PR 2						-		
PR 3						-		
PR 4						-		
PR 5						-		
PR 6						-		
PR 7						-		

<u>Case Study 13</u>

Monthly Nursing Home Assessment

Face Sheet

Patient's Name: John Henning

Date of Visit: 1/01/2010

Age: 75

Sex: Male

Insurance: Medicare

Case Study 13

Monthly Nursing Home Assessment

DATE: 01/01/2010

This patient has been in the nursing home for the past 6 months and is being evaluated on a monthly basis. He has a previous history of left-sided cerebrovascular accident with right-sided paralysis. The patient has been demented since his stroke and has been seen by a psychiatrist, who diagnosed psychosis and placed him on risperidone and lorazepam. Patient will open his eyes to name only. Does not answer any questions. He has been having swallowing problems but has not developed any signs of choking.

GENERAL:	BP 125/78, P 78, Weight 108 with a loss of 5 lb. since last month.
HEENT:	Laxity of the lower jaw; cataracts bilaterally.
Lungs:	Clear to auscultation and percussion.
Heart:	Normal sinus rhythm. There is a 2/6 heart murmur.
Abdomen:	No mass, organomegaly, tenderness.
CNS:	The patient responds to name only; right-sided paralysis due to old CVA.
Skin:	Normal.

IMPRESSION:
1. Old left-sided cerebrovascular accident with right-sided paralysis
2. Malnutrition with weight loss
3. Psychosis

PLAN:
1. Speech pathologist to evaluate
2. Calorie count
3. The patient is a DNR.

History:	Detailed
Examination:	Detailed
Medical Decision:	Moderate complexity

<u>Case Study 13</u>

Answer Sheet

DIAGNOSES	ICD-9-CM CODES					
First listed DX *Cerebrovascular accident with right-sided paralysis*	4	3	8	.	2	1
DX 2 *malnutrition*	2	6	3	.	9	
DX 3 *Weight Loss*	7	8	3	.	2	1
DX 4 *Psychosis (unspecified)*	2	9	8	.	9	

PROCEDURES	CPT CODES					MODIFIERS (If Applicable)		
PR 1 *Nursing Home Visit/Subsequent*	9	9	3	0	7	-		
PR 2						-		
PR 3						-		
PR 4						-		
PR 5						-		
PR 6						-		
PR 7						-		

Case Study 14

Skilled Nursing Facility Visit

Face Sheet

Patient Name: Cora Wilkinson
Date of Visit: 1/15/2010
Age: 68
Sex: Female
Insurance: Medicare

Case Study 14

Skilled Nursing Facility Visit

Date of Visit: 1/15/2010

HISTORY OF PRESENT ILLNESS:
This is a follow-up visit for this 68-year-old female. She was admitted to Oakdale Nursing Home 10 days ago with cellulitis of the left foot. She was placed in Oakdale for IV therapy of her cellulitis. She is recovering well and the infection is almost gone. She has a history of type 1 diabetes.

Allergies: None

Medications: Insulin 70/30, IV vancomycin

REVIEW OF SYSTEMS: Normal.

PHYSICAL EXAMINATION:

General:	Well-developed, well-nourished female in no acute distress. BP 128/75. Pulse: 80, regular and strong. Respirations: 12, unlabored and regular. Temperature: Normal. Height: 5 foot.
HEENT:	Normal. No lesions noted.
Skin:	Left foot shows slight reddening on the upper surface. Infection had decreased significantly. All other areas are normal.

PLAN:
Patient is doing well and will be taken off IV vancomycin.

She will be discharged home tomorrow and will be given a prescription for penicillin.

She is to follow-up in my office in one week.

History:	Problem-focused
Examination:	Problem-focused
Medical Decision:	Straightforward

Case Study 14

Answer Sheet

DIAGNOSES		ICD-9-CM CODES					
First listed DX Cellulitis – LT foot (except toes)		6	8	2	.	7	
DX 2 Type 1 Diabetes w/o complication		2	5	0	.	0	1
DX 3					.		
DX 4					.		

PROCEDURES		CPT CODES					MODIFIERS (If Applicable)		
PR 1 Nursing Facility Visit		9	9	3	0	7	-		
PR 2							-		
PR 3							-		
PR 4							-		
PR 5							-		
PR 6							-		
PR 7							-		

PROVIDE ICD-9-CM DIAGNOSES CODES AND
CPT PROCEDURE CODE(S) ONLY

Case Study 15

Inpatient Face Sheet

Patient Name: Shauna Jones

Admit Date: 01/01/2010

Discharge Date: 01/04/2010

Sex: Female

Age: 27

Disposition: Home

Admitting Diagnoses:
1. Diarrhea, rule out infectious colitis, viral gastroenteritis, inflammatory bowel disease
2. Dehydration
3. Pregnancy
4. Thyroid goiter

Discharge Diagnoses:
1. Enteritis due to Clostridium difficile
2. Dehydration
3. Thyroid goiter
4. Pregnancy

Procedures:
1. Colonoscopy with biopsies

Case Study 15

Discharge Summary

Admitted: 01/01/2010

Discharged: 01/04/2010

DISCHARGE DIAGNOSES:
1. Infectious enteritis
2. Dehydration
3. Pregnant
4. Thyroid goiter

PROCEDURE PERFORMED: Colonoscopy on 1/3/2010.

HISTORY:
This is a 27-year-old pregnant female who is complaining of severe diarrhea with bowel movements every 10 minutes with watery stools and incontinence. This began early this morning. She does not feel it is caused by something she ate. She is also complaining of cramps and nausea. She is unable to keep liquids down.

PAST MEDICAL HISTORY: Positive for goiter.

PAST SURGICAL HISTORY: Negative

PHYSICAL EXAMINATION:

Vital Signs:	Blood pressure 110/60, temperature 98.6, pulse 88, respirations 16.
Neck:	Thyroid goiter.
Heart:	Regular rate and rhythm.
Lungs:	Clear to auscultation. No rales, rhonchi, or wheezing.
Abdomen:	Soft with good bowel sounds. No pain or masses. No hepatosplenomegaly. Some lower abdominal tenderness.
Extremities:	Within normal limits.

LABORATORY:
Hematology as of 1/1/2010 showed white blood count of 8,000, red blood cells 4.05, hemoglobin 12.9, hematocrit 39.3.

On 1/3/2010, the white blood count was 6,000, red blood cells 3.70, hemoglobin 12.3, and hematocrit 35.1.

Urinalysis on 1/1/2010 showed yellow-clear urine.

Chemistry levels on 1/1/2010 showed sodium 139, potassium 3, chloride 110, glucose 104, BUN 8, creatinine 0.5, total protein 6.8, albumin 3.9, globulin 2.9. Anion gap ratio 1.3. Calcium 9.3. Total bilirubin 0.2.

Chemistry profile on 1/3/2010 showed a sodium of 142, potassium 4, chloride 107, CO_2 22, glucose 85, BUN 3, creatinine 0.7, magnesium 1.6. HCG quantitative at 6,320, approximately 6-7 weeks. Stool culture was positive for Clostridium difficile and she was started on intravenous antibiotics.

Case Study 15

Discharge Summary

Continued:

RADIOLOGY:
Transabdominal and transvaginal obstetrical sonogram shows a normal single viable intrauterine pregnancy at 4.9 weeks gestational age.

HOSPITAL COURSE:
The patient was admitted with diarrhea to rule out underlying cause. Dr. Blessed saw her for pregnancy with gastrointestinal disturbance.

Recommendations were intravenous hydration and close monitoring. She was given Phenergan suppository for nausea and vomiting. The patient responded well to the treatment regime.

The patient was discharged in good condition. Activity and diet as tolerated. She will follow-up with me as needed and will follow-up with Dr. Blessed as instructed. The patient has been advised to have the goiter evaluated as an outpatient.

Case Study 15

History and Physical

CHIEF COMPLAINT:
This 27-year-old white female complains of severe diarrhea with bowel movements every 10 minutes and fecal incontinence, as well as nocturnal bowel movements. She complains of cramps with nausea and vomiting. She denies chronic diarrhea.

PAST MEDICAL HISTORY: Thyroid goiter.

PAST SURGICAL HISTORY: Negative

SOCIAL HISTORY: Non-smoker, non-drinker

FAMILY HISTORY: Negative for colitis or colon cancer

ALLERGIES: None known

MEDICATIONS: None

REVIEW OF SYSTEMS:

Cardiovascular:	Within normal limits.
Pulmonary:	Within normal limits.
Gastrointestinal:	Nausea and vomiting. Denies excessive aspirin or antacid use. Denies dysphagia, gallbladder disease, liver disease, or pancreatitis. No history of peptic ulcer disease.

PHYSICAL EXAMINATION:

Vital Signs:	Her temperature is 98.6, pulse 88, respiratory rate 16, blood pressure 110/60, weight 130, height 5 feet, 7 inches.
Neck:	Thyroid goiter
Heart:	Regular rate. No murmurs
Lungs:	Clear to auscultation. No rales, rhonchi, or wheezing.
Abdomen:	Soft. Good bowel sounds. No pain or masses. No hepatosplenomegaly. Some lower abdominal tenderness.
Rectal:	No stool. No masses.
Extremities:	Within normal limits.

IMPRESSIONS:
1. Severe diarrhea and dehydration secondary to infectious colitis versus Clostridium difficile infection versus viral gastroenteritis versus inflammatory bowel disease, less likely.
2. Thyroid goiter

PLAN:
1. IV hydration
2. Blood cultures
3. Stool cultures
4. Await CBC with differential to determine whether the patient needs IV antibiotics.

Case Study 15

Procedure Note

Date:	1/3/2010
Preoperative Diagnosis:	Refractory severe diarrhea with negative stool cultures
Postoperative Diagnosis:	1. No active colitis
	2. No pseudomembranes noted
	3. Normal terminal ileum that was visualized
	4. Internal hemorrhoids
Procedure:	Colonoscopy to the terminal ileum with random biopsies
Surgeon:	Robert Blessed, MD
Indications:	Refractory severe diarrhea with negative stool cultures.

DESCRIPTION OF PROCEDURE:

Following informed consent, the patient was brought to the endoscopy suite and given IV sedation. Colonoscope was inserted into the rectum and advanced to the left colon and beyond the splenic flexure, maneuvered through the hepatic flexure and moved down the ascending colon to the cecum. The appendiceal orifice was visualized. The ileocecal valve was entered and approximately 10 cm of terminal ileum were visualized and photographed and was within normal limits. The scope was withdrawn from the right colon, pulled back to the transverse, descending, sigmoid, and rectum; all adequately visualized and there was no active colitis and no pseudomembranes noted. There were no masses palpable or mucosal abnormalities. Random rectosigmoid biopsies were obtained and the scope was withdrawn.

PATHOLOGY REPORT

SPECIMENS: Tissue rectosigmoid biopsy

DIAGNOSIS:

Histologically unremarkable fragments of superficial colonic mucosa. No evidence of significant inflammation; no evidence of dysplasia.

Case Study 15

PROGRESS NOTES:

1/1:   Admit Note: Severe diarrhea, cramping, and nausea in a 27-year-old pregnant female. Patient is dehydrated due to the severe diarrhea. She is admitted for treatment and workup of gastrointestinal symptoms. Patient was unaware she was pregnant, so will have OB follow her also.

1/2:   S: Diarrhea less frequent; still complains of intestinal cramping
        O: Responding slowly to medications, vital signs good, blood cultures negative
        A: Still with GI symptoms and dehydration
        P: Will schedule colonoscopy to rule out colitis. Continue with IV hydration and repeat stool culture

1/3:   S: Feels better, still some cramping
        O: Stool positive for C. difficile
        A: Tolerated colonoscopy, normal colon
        P: Discontinue IVs, change to p.o. antibiotics

1/4:   S: Feels good, no diarrhea or cramping
        O: Labs within normal limits, vitals stable, tolerating full diet and activity
        A: Okay from GI standpoint. Will follow thyroid goiter as an outpatient
        P: Discharge home

Case Study 15

ORDERS:

1/1: 1. Admit patient to medical floor
2. Vital signs q. shift
3. Phenergan suppository for N/V
4. Blood and stool cultures
5. IV hydration
6. CBC, WBC, chemistry profile
7. Pregnancy test

1/2: 1. Transabdominal and transvaginal sonogram
2. Continue IV hydration
3. Colonoscopy in morning
4. Repeat stool culture

1/3: 1. Discontinue IVs, switch to p.o. antibiotics
2. Advance diet

1/4: 1. Discharge home

Case Study 15

Answer Sheet

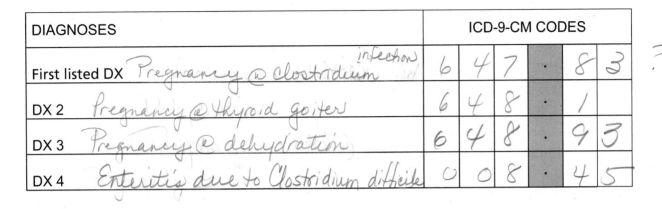

DIAGNOSES	ICD-9-CM CODES					
First listed DX Pregnancy @ clostridium _infection_	6	4	7	.	8	3
DX 2 Pregnancy @ thyroid goiter	6	4	8	.	1	
DX 3 Pregnancy @ dehydration	6	4	8	.	9	3
DX 4 Enteritis due to Clostridium difficile	0	0	8	.	4	5

PROCEDURES	CPT CODES					MODIFIERS (If Applicable)		
PR 1 Colonoscopy @ biopsies	4	5	3	8	0	-		
PR 2						-		
PR 3						-		
PR 4						-		
PR 5						-		
PR 6						-		
PR 7						-		

PROVIDE ICD-9-CM CODES FOR DIAGNOSES AND
CPT CODES FOR PROCEDURE(S)
Case Study 16

Inpatient Face Sheet

Patient Name: Kimberly Blackstone

Admit Date: 01/03/2010

Discharge Date: 01/08/2010

Sex: Female

Age: 62

Disposition: Home

ADMITTING DIAGNOSES:
1. Abdominal pain
2. Hypertension

DISCHARGE DIAGNOSES:
1. Acute and chronic cholecystitis and cholelithiasis
2. Hypertension
3. Hypokalemia
4. Urinary Tract Infection with E. coli

PROCEDURE:
1. Laparoscopic cholecystectomy

Case Study 16

Discharge Summary

Admitted: 01/03/2010

Discharged: 01/08/2010

ADMITTING DIAGNOSIS:
1. Abdominal pain
2. Hypertension

DISCHARGE DIAGNOSES:
1. Acute cholecystitis with cholelithiasis
2. Hypertension
3. Hypokalemia — low sodium
4. Urinary tract infection

PROCEDURES:
Laparoscopic cholecystectomy by Dr. Haley

HISTORY OF PRESENT ILLNESS:
See History and Physical

HOSPITAL COURSE:
Patient was admitted and given IV antibiotics and Demerol for pain. HIDA scan revealed complete blockage of the cystic duct, for which Dr. Haley performed a laparoscopic cholecystectomy without difficulty. Patient did very well post-operatively. Began ambulating post-op day one, and advanced to full diet on day two. She remained afebrile. Her potassium dropped to 2.7, and she was given IV potassium supplement with improvement.

LABORATORY DATA:
Admission chest x-ray was normal.

Hemoglobin and hematocrit 13.5/40 with post-op H/H at 12.1/37.

White count on admission was 16,000 with drop to 7,900 following surgery and IV antibiotics. Differential and platelets were normal.

Glucose 100, Na 135, BUN 9, SGOT 28.

Pathology report revealed gangrenous cholecystitis and cholelithiasis.

The patient was discharged on the fourth day post-operative.

She will resume her previous medications as prescribed.

She is also to take Cipro 500 mg. b.i.d. for 1 week.

Regular diet and activity as tolerated.

She will follow-up with Dr. Haley for staple removal in 1 week and follow-up with me in 2 weeks.

Case Study 16

History and Physical

REASON FOR ADMISSION: Abdominal pain and vomiting

HISTORY OF PRESENT ILLNESS: This is a 62-year-old woman with a history of back pain who is having increased epigastric abdominal pain with nausea for the past 4 days. She states the abdominal pain has since radiated to her back. She denies fever, chills, vomiting, or change in bowel habits.

ALLERGIES: Penicillin and morphine

PAST MEDICAL HISTORY: Hypertension, herniated lumbar and cervical discs requiring laminectomies, anxiety, and status post hysterectomy, reason unknown.

CURRENT MEDICATIONS: Procardia, Estrace, Relafen, Zantac, and quinine

SOCIAL HISTORY: Remote smoking history, social alcohol

REVIEW OF SYSTEMS:

General:	Well-developed, well-nourished woman in no acute distress
Vital Signs:	Stable, slightly febrile
Integument:	Slightly dry, decreased turgor
HEENT:	Clear, throat clear
Neck:	Supple
Chest:	A few rhonchi, otherwise clear to auscultation
Cardiac:	Regular rate and rhythm, no clicks, murmurs, or gallops
Abdomen:	Soft, tender in the right upper quadrant with no rebound or guarding. Normoactive bowel sounds
Rectal:	Heme negative with normal tone
Extremities:	No cyanosis or clubbing. Trace pedal edema
Neurological:	No deficits
Breasts:	Soft, symmetrical without discharge or masses
Genitalia:	Deferred

LABORATORY DATA:

Urinalysis shows positive bacteria, positive nitrates. Culture and sensitivity positive for E. coli.

White blood count 16,000, hemoglobin 13.5, hematocrit 40, platelet count 171,000. Sodium 135, Potassium 3.2, amylase 44.

Ultrasound of the gallbladder shows a 1.5-cm gallstone.

The hepatobiliary scan is positive for obstruction.

Electrocardiogram shows normal sinus rhythm with left anterior hemiblock, no acute ST-T changes.

ASSESSMENT:
1 Cholecystitis
2. Urinary tract infection

PLAN:
1. Start intravenous Ancef
2. Give patient pain control for gallbladder colic
3. Have surgery evaluate for acute abdomen

Case Study 16

Procedure Note

DATE OF PROCEDURE: 1/4/2010

PREOPERATIVE DIAGNOSIS: Acute cholecystitis *with lithiasis*

POSTOPERATIVE DIAGNOSIS: Acute and chronic cholecystitis with lithiasis

PROCEDURE: Laparoscopic cholecystectomy

SURGEON: Dr. Hailey

ANESTHESIA: General endotracheal anesthesia

ANESTHESIOLOGIST: Patricia Miller, MD

DESCRIPTION OF PROCEDURE:

Under general endotracheal anesthesia, with the patient in the supine position, the abdomen was prepped with Betadine and draped. The oral gastric tube and Foley catheter were inserted. An infraumbilical incision was made. A versus needle was inserted and the abdomen was insufflated to 15 millimeters of mercury with carbon dioxide. A 10–11 millimeter trocar was inserted and zero degree laparoscope was inserted. A 5 millimeter trocar was placed three finger breadths below the right costal margin in the anterior axillary line two finger breadths below the right costal margin in the mid clavicular line and three finger breadths below the xiphoid in the midline. The gallbladder was elevated superiorly and adhesions from the gallbladder to the hepatic flexure and omentum were reflected inferiorly. Dissection was carried out at the neck of the gallbladder and cystic duct. Silver clip was placed on the neck of the gallbladder to prevent stones from migrating down the cystic duct. The cystic duct was ligated times two with #0 chromic Endoloop approximately 4 millimeters from its junction with the common duct and a silver clip was placed between these two loops. The cystic artery was doubly silver clipped and divided. The gallbladder was removed from the liver fossa utilizing a hook cautery, placed in an Endopouch and retrieved through the umbilicus. During the course of the procedure, the abdomen was irrigated copiously with a solution of heparinized saline and Ancef. Once hemostasis was assured, air was evacuated and trocars were removed. Umbilical fascial defect was closed with a figure of eight suture of #0 Vicryl. The skin was closed with subcuticular #3-0 Vicryl. Steri-strips were applied. The patient tolerated the procedure well. The patient was transferred to the recovery room in satisfactory condition.

PATHOLOGY REPORT:

Specimen: Gallbladder

Microscopic Diagnosis: Acute and chronic gangrenous cholecystitis and cholelithiasis

Case Study 16

PROGRESS NOTES:

1/3: Admit note: This is a 62-year-old female who is admitted for evaluation of acute abdominal pain with nausea. The pain and nausea began 4 days ago and is now radiating to her back. Patient is started on antibiotics and Demerol for pain.

1/4: S: Complaining of abdominal pain and decreased appetite.
    O: HIDA scan positive for blockage of cystic duct secondary to gall stones. H/H okay at 13.5/40 and WBCs at 16,000. UA positive for E. coli; coverage with existing IV antibiotics.
    A: Cholecystitis with cholelithiasis
    P: Patient is scheduled for laparoscopic cholecystectomy.

1/5: S: Complaining of minimal pain at incision sites.
    O: H/H stable at 12.1/37, WBCs 7,900. Pathology positive for gangrenous acute and chronic cholecystitis and cholelithiasis.
    A: Good post-op course. Tolerating soft diet.
    P: Advance diet, continue IV fluids and antibiotics, repeat UA.

1/6: S: Feels good, hungry.
    O: K+ decreased to 2.7, add KCL to IV for replacement. Afebrile, vital signs stable, incisions clean and dry. Repeat UA clear.
    A: Progressing well.
    P: Advance to full diet, repeat K+ level following replacement. Change to p.o. medications when IVs finished.

1/7: S: Wants to go home.
    O: Electrolytes within normal limits, vitals stable, afebrile, incisions healing.
    A: Good post-op course
    P: Plan discharge.

1/8: S: No complaints.
    O: Vitals stable, bowel sounds present.
    A: Ready for discharge.
    P: Discharge home.

ORDERS:

1/3: 1. Admit patient.
    2. IV Ancef and Demerol for pain
    3. UA and culture if positive.
    4. Liquid diet
    5. HIDA scan
    6. CXR and EKG
    7. CBC, WBC, Chem Profile
    8. Continue with home meds.

1/4: 1. Prep for laparoscopic cholecystectomy.

1/5: 1. Repeat labs.
    2. Continue current IV medications.
    3. Advance to regular diet in morning.

1/6: 1. Replace K+ with KCL added to IV fluids.
    2. When IV fluids finished, switch to p.o. Cipro 500-mg b.i.d.

1/8: 1. Discharge home.

Case Study 16

Answer Sheet

DIAGNOSES		ICD-9-CM CODES					
First listed DX Acute cholecystitis with cholelithiasis		5	7	4	.	0	0
DX 2 ~~Chronic cholecystitis with cholelithiasis~~ ~~Hypertension~~		5	7	4	.	1	0
DX 3 Hypertension (unspecified)		4	0	1	.	9	
DX 4 Urinary Tract Infection		5	9	9	.	0	

E. Coli 041.4   Hypokalemia (low sodium)

PROCEDURES		CPT CODES					MODIFIERS (If Applicable)		
PR 1 Laparoscopic cholecystectomy		4	7	5	6	2	-		
PR 2							-		
PR 3							-		
PR 4							-		
PR 5							-		
PR 6							-		
PR 7							-		

47562 — 564
47600 — 620

PROVIDE ICD-9-CM CODES FOR DIAGNOSES

Case Study 17

Inpatient Face Sheet

Patient Name: Sarah Black

Admit Date: 1/06/2010

Discharge Date: 1/10/2010

Sex: Female

Age: 64

Disposition: Home

Admitting Diagnoses:
1. Neutropenic sepsis
2. Status post-chemotherapy for non-Hodgkin's lymphoma
3. Hypertension

Discharge Diagnoses:
1. Pancytopenia with neutropenic sepsis secondary to chemotherapy
2. Non-Hodgkin's lymphoma
3. Hypoalbuminemia
4. Hypertension

Case Study 17

Discharge Summary

Admitted: 1/06/2010

Discharge: 1/10/2010

ADMISSION DIAGNOSES:
1. Neutropenic sepsis
2. Status post-chemotherapy for non-Hodgkin's lymphoma
3. Hypertension

DISCHARGE DIAGNOSES:
1. Pancytopenia with neutropenic sepsis secondary to chemotherapy
2. Non-Hodgkin's lymphoma
3. Hypoalbuminemia
4. Hypertension   *Dehydration*

HISTORY: This is a 64-year-old female with non-Hodgkin's lymphoma, currently undergoing chemotherapy. The patient was evaluated by oncology in follow-up and found to be neutropenic as well as febrile.

PHYSICAL EXAMINATION:

Vital Signs: Blood pressure 132/90. Temperature was 102.

HEENT: Dry oral mucous membranes. No thrush or herpetic lesions.

Neck: Supple, no adenopathy.

Lungs: Clear.

Heart: Slightly tachycardiac, no murmur.

Abdomen: Soft, nontender.

Extremities: Pulses bilateral. Decreased muscle tone.

LABORATORY DATA: Chemistries revealed total protein 5.8, albumin 2.4. Calcium 7.3, 7.6.

The follow-up chem-7 revealed CO_2 of 25, chloride 111.

Admission white blood cell count was 0.1, hemoglobin 11.2, hematocrit 32.8, red cell indices were normal. The platelet count was 14,000. The last blood count revealed white blood cell count of 3,500. The hemoglobin was 11.4, hematocrit 34.3, red cell indices remained normal.

The urinalysis was pale in color and clear with trace protein noted, nitrite negative, leukocyte esterase negative. The urine culture showed no growth. Blood culture showed no growth.

RADIOLOGY: The chest x-ray showed no acute process.

HOSPITAL COURSE: The patient was admitted after follow-up with her oncologist. She was found to be febrile and neutropenic, rule out sepsis. The patient was admitted and placed in isolation. Cultures were obtained and the patient was placed on IV Fortaz as well as IV Gentamicin. The patient had pancytopenia with drop in her platelet count and the patient was given platelet transfusion and blood transfusions, as well as IV fluids for dehydration. The patient had a mild reaction to the transfusion and was given IV steroids as well as Benadryl.

Case Study 17

Discharge Summary

Continued:

The patient was started on Neupogen injections on 1/7/2010. The patient again received platelet and blood transfusion on 1/7/02010 and additional platelet transfusion on 1/9/2010. The patient's white blood cell count was increasing and she was less clinically septic. IV antibiotics were converted to oral Cipro. Her isolation was discontinued and she remained afebrile. The patient's platelets counts continued to be low. However, this will be managed as an outpatient.

DISCHARGE INFORMATION: Medications: Floxin 400 mg twice daily. Mycostatic swish and swallow 5 cc 3 times daily. Patient is discharged in improved condition. Diet and activity as tolerated. The patient will follow-up with me in my office in one week.

Case Study 17

History and Physical

CHIEF COMPLAINT: Neutropenic sepsis.

HISTORY OF PRESENT ILLNESS:
This is 64 year-old white female with a known history of non-Hodgkin's lymphoma. The patient has been treated with chemotherapy and, on evaluation by Oncology, was found to be febrile and neutropenic. She was felt to be clinically septic. There was also evidence of significant neutropenia. The patient was admitted to the Oncology floor for antibiotic therapy, monitoring of her blood counts, medications to raise her white and hemoglobin counts, and to be placed in reverse isolation.

PAST MEDICAL HISTORY: Non-Hodgkin's lymphoma, and hypertension.

SOCIAL HISTORY: Non-smoker, no alcohol use.

FAMILY HISTORY: Positive for cancer and heart disease.

REVIEW OF SYSTEMS: Negative

PHYSICAL EXAMINATION:
Vital Signs: Blood pressure 132/90, respirations 28, temperature 102.
HEENT: Negative except for dry oral mucous membranes.
              No thrush or herpetic lesions.
Neck: Supple, no carotid bruit. No evidence of adenopathy.
Lungs: Clear.
Cardiac: Slightly tachycardic, but no murmur.
Abdomen: Soft, non-tender, positive bowel sounds.
Extremities: Bilateral pulses. Poor muscle tone. No evidence of deep venous thrombosis or cellulitis.

ASSESSMENT:

1. Neutropenic sepsis, status post-chemotherapy
2. Non-Hodgkin's lymphoma

PLAN:

1. Admit and place in reverse isolation.
2. Intravenous hydration
3. Intravenous antibiotics
4. Continue present medications.
5. Follow blood counts.

Case Study 17

Progress Notes

1/6:   Admit Note: Patient with non-Hodgkin's lymphoma admitted to isolation for neutropenic sepsis secondary to chemotherapy.

1/7:   S: "Feel better today."
        O: Vital signs stable, WBCs 0.1, platelets 14,000, temperature 101.3, blood and urine cultures negative
        A: Responding to antibiotics, still dehydrated.
        P: Continue IV fluids and antibiotics. Transfuse platelets and PRBCs. Begin Neupogen injections.

1/8:   S: No complaints
        O: Vitals stable, temp 99.8, transfusion reaction last night requiring IV steroids and Benadryl
        A: Continued improvement, responded well to steroids and Benadryl for transfusion reaction.
        P: Continue current meds, transfuse PRBCs and platelets tomorrow.

1/9:   S: "I feel great."
        O: WBC at 3,500, platelets at 14,000, afebrile, vitals stable
        A: Less clinically septic, tolerated transfusions well with no adverse reaction.
        P: Discontinue isolation, change antibiotics to p.o. Discontinue IV fluids.

1/10:   S: "I want to go home."
        O: Afebrile, platelets still low
        A: Ready for discharge, will manage platelets as an outpatient.
        P: Discharge home.

Case Study 17

Orders:

1/6:
1. Admit to reverse isolation.
2. IV fluids at 83 cc/h with IV Fortaz and gentamicin
3. Urine and blood cultures
4. Chemistry profile
5. CBC, WBC
6. Type and cross 4 units
7. PA and lateral CXR
8. Vitals q shift

1/7:
1. Begin daily Neupogen injections.
2. Transfuse 2 units PRBCs and platelets.

1/8:
1. Continue with current treatment.

1/9:
1. Transfuse 2 units PRBCs and platelets.
2. Discontinue isolation.
3. Discontinue IV fluids when finished and switch to p.o. antibiotics.

1/10:
1. Discharge home.

Case Study 17

Answer Sheet

DIAGNOSES		ICD-9-CM CODES					
First listed DX	Pancytopenia @ Neutropenia Sepsis secondary to chemotherapy	0	3	8	.	9	
DX 2	Non-Hodgkin's lymphma	2	0	2	.	8	
DX 3	Hypertension	4	0	1	.	9	
DX 4	Adverse reaction to Chemotherapy	E9	3	3	.	1	

SIRS
995.93

Hypoalbunemia 273.8   Dehydration   276.

PROCEDURES	CPT CODES					MODIFIERS (If Applicable)	
PR 1						-	
PR 2						-	
PR 3						-	
PR 4						-	
PR 5						-	
PR 6						-	
PR 7							

**PROVIDE ICD-9-CM CODES FOR DIAGNOSES AND
CPT CODES FOR PROCEDURE(S)**

Case Study 18

Inpatient Face Sheet

Patient Name:	Jasmine Delaware
Admit Date:	1/11/2010
Discharge Date:	1/15/2010
Sex:	Female
Age:	50
Disposition:	Home

Admit Diagnoses:
1. Right upper lobe lesion
2. Asthmatic bronchitis
3. Depression

Discharge Diagnoses:
1. Non-small cell carcinoma right upper lobe
2. Metastasized to hilar and thoracic lymph nodes
3. Chronic obstructive pulmonary disease
4. Depression

Procedures:
1. Flexible bronchoscopy
2. Right upper lobe lobectomy

Case Study 18

Discharge Summary

Admitted: 1/11/2010

Discharged: 1/15/2010

DISCHARGE DIAGNOSES:
1. Non-small-cell carcinoma right upper lobe of lung with metastasis to hilar and thoracic lymph nodes
2. Chronic obstructive pulmonary disease
3. Depression

PROCEDURES PERFORMED:
1. Flexible bronchoscopy
2. Right upper lobe lobectomy

HISTORY OF PRESENT ILLNESS:
This is a 50-year-old female with a 3 cm lesion in the right upper lobe. She had an episode of bronchitis in January. Subsequent chest x-ray revealed a lesion in the right upper lobe. A CAT scan of the chest was performed and the presence of the lesion in the right upper lobe was confirmed.

HOSPITAL COURSE:
The patient underwent flexible bronchoscopy with right upper lobectomy on January 11, 2010. The findings were a 3-cm lesion in the right upper lobe with metastasis to the lymph nodes. The patient tolerated the procedure well. Vital signs remained stable. There was minimal chest tube drainage. She was advanced to a regular diet the second post-operative day.

LABORATORY DATA: Routine laboratory work on admission showed a potassium of 4.0, BUN 10, creatinine 0.6. WBCs 8.8, hemoglobin 13.7 and hematocrit 38.2. Platelet count 288,000. The urinalysis was negative. PT was 10.1. Discharge laboratory was unchanged with the exception of BUN 12, creatinine 0.9. Hemoglobin 11.3 and hematocrit 34.2

EKG: Sinus rhythm

IMAGING: The pre-operative chest x-ray showed a 3.0 cm suspicious nodule in the right upper lobe with chronic obstructive pulmonary disease. Post-operative chest x-ray showed good expansion of the right middle and lower lobes.

The patient was discharged on the fourth post-operative day in satisfactory condition. Regular diet as tolerated. She is to limit activity for the next 3 weeks. She will follow-up in my office in 1 week.

Discharge medications include: Vicodin 1 tablet P.O. q4h prn for pain. Elavil 150 mg h.s., Ventolin 2 puffs q.i.d.

Case Study 18

History and Physical

CHIEF COMPLAINT: Right upper lobe lesion.

HISTORY OF PRESENT ILLNESS:
This is a 50-year-old female with a 3 cm lesion in the right upper lobe. She had an episode of bronchitis in January. Subsequent chest x-ray revealed a lesion in the right upper lobe. A CAT scan of the chest was performed and the presence of the lesion in the right upper lobe was confirmed. The patient is admitted at this time for a bronchoscopy and right thoracotomy.

REVIEW OF SYSTEMS:
Patient denies hematemesis, melena, and angina pectoris. There are no complaints of syncope, claudication, or edema.

HEENT:	No masses, pupils equal, round, reactive to light. No oral cavity lesions. No evidence of JVD; thyroid is not enlarged. No carotid bruits.
Chest:	Symmetrical.
Lungs:	Clear to auscultation and percussion. No wheezing.
Heart:	No murmurs, no gallops, regular rhythm.
Abdomen:	No masses, no organomegaly.
Extremities:	No cyanosis, clubbing, or edema. Good peripheral pulses.

PAST MEDICAL HISTORY:
She has asthmatic bronchitis and has been hospitalized twice in the past for bronchitis. Patient is currently treated for depression. She has no history of diabetes mellitus, hypertension, myocardial infarction, or neurological deficits. She has had no surgeries.

MEDICATIONS: Elavil 150 mg h.s., Ventolin 2 puffs q.i.d.

ALLERGIES: None known

SOCIAL HISTORY: She smokes two packs of cigarettes per day and has smoked for 30 years.

FAMILY HISTORY: Non-contributory

IMPRESSION:
1. Right upper lobe lesion
2. Rule out bronchogenic carcinoma
3. Rule out benign lesion
4. Asthmatic bronchitis
5. Depression

PLAN: Patient is admitted for bronchoscopy and right thoracotomy with right upper lobectomy. The procedures and the risks involved were fully explained to the patient and all questions answered, and an informed consent was signed by the patient.

Case Study 18

Operative Report

DATE OF OPERATION:	1/11/2010
PREOPERATIVE DIAGNOSIS:	Right Upper Lobe Lesion
POSTOPERATIVE DIAGNOSIS:	Carcinoma of the right upper lobe with metastasis to hilar and thoracic lymph nodes
SURGEON:	Heather Schoonover, M.D.
OPERATIVE PROCEDURE:	1. Flexible bronchoscopy
	2. Right upper lobe lobectomy

INDICATIONS: Female patient with a 3-cm lesion centrally located in the right upper lobe.

FINDINGS:
The bronchoscopy was negative. On thoracotomy there was a 3-cm lesion centrally located in the right upper lobe. There were positive nodes in the hilar and thoracic lymph nodes.

DESCRIPTION OF PROCEDURE:
Under general anesthesia the flexible bronchoscope was introduced through both lumen of the endotracheal tube. The carina was normal. Both the right and left bronchial trees were visualized down to the subsegmental level. There was no evidence of endobronchial lesions. The bronchoscopy was negative.

After prepping and draping the operative area a right posterolateral thoracotomy was made. The incision was deepened through the skin, subcutaneous tissue, and latissimus dorsi muscle. The serratus anterior muscles were retracted anteriorly and the chest was entered through the fifth intercostal space. On exploration of the right lung there was a 3-cm lesion centrally located in the right upper lobe. A right total lobectomy was performed based upon the above findings. Surrounding lymph nodes were inspected and biopsies were obtained from both the hilar and surrounding thoracic nodes.

Frozen section was positive for non-small cell carcinoma. The bronchial resection margin was negative for tumor. The inferior pulmonary ligament was taken all of the way up to the inferior pulmonary vein. The bronchial stump was checked up to a pressure of 35 mmHg and there was no air leak. Hemostasis was again secured. A chest tube was placed through a separate stab wound and secured to the skin with 0 silk. The incision was closed using #2 Vicryl pericostal sutures, #1 Vicryl for the latissimus dorsi muscle, 2-0 Vicryl for the subcutaneous tissue, and staples for the skin.

The estimated blood loss was less than 200 cc. The patient tolerated the procedure very well and was taken to the recovery room in good condition with stable vital signs.

Case Study 18

PROGRESS NOTES:

1/11: Admit Note: A 50-year-old female found to have a 3 cm lesion in the right upper lobe. She is admitted at this time for flexible bronchoscopy and right thoracotomy.

1/12: S: Complains of incisional pain
O: Vital signs stable, labs within normal limits, minimal chest tube drainage
A: Post-op CXR shows good expansion of right middle and lower lobes.
P: Patient doing well from surgical standpoint, will remove chest tube in a.m.

1/13: S: Less pain, depressed with diagnosis
O: Vital remain stable, afebrile, good lung sounds
A: Progressing nicely.
P: Advance to full diet, increase ambulation.

1/14: S: Feels better today.
O: Afebrile, vital signs stable, labs look good
A: Incisions clean and dry with no redness
P: Possible discharge tomorrow

1/15: S: Ready to go home.
O: Discharge labs and CXR within normal limits
A: Incisions healing well.
P: Discharge patient.

ORDERS:

1/11: 1. Admit patient.
2. Have consents signed for flexible bronchoscopy and right thoracotomy.
3. Place pre-op diagnostics on chart.

1/12: 1. Ambulate patient.
2. Repeat CXR.
3. Repeat labs.

1/13: 1. Advance to full diet.
2. Increase ambulation.

1/14: 1. No new orders

1/15: 1. Discharge patient.

Case Study 18

Answer Sheet

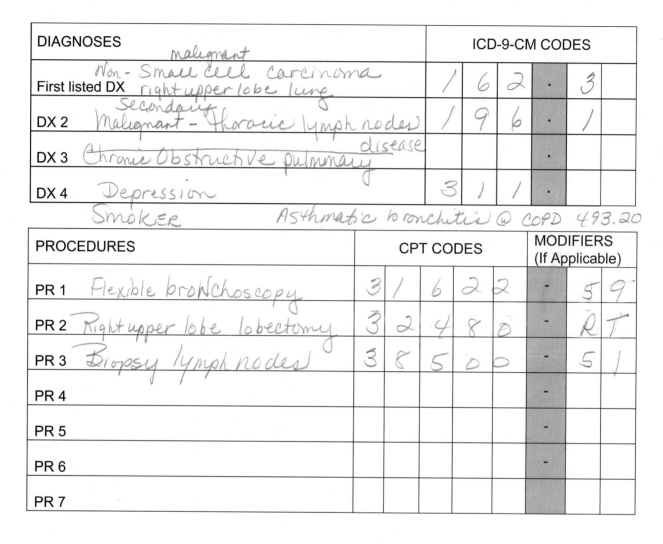

DIAGNOSES			ICD-9-CM CODES				
First listed DX *malignant* Non- Small Cell carcinoma right upper lobe lung			1	6	2	.	3
DX 2 *Secondary* Malignant - Thoracic lymph nodes			1	9	6	.	1
DX 3 Chronic Obstructive pulmonary *disease*						.	
DX 4 Depression			3	1	1	.	

Smoker   Asthmatic bronchitis @ COPD 493.20

PROCEDURES		CPT CODES					MODIFIERS (If Applicable)	
PR 1 Flexible bronchoscopy		3	1	6	2	2	-	5 9
PR 2 Right upper lobe lobectomy		3	2	4	8	0	-	R T
PR 3 Biopsy lymph nodes		3	8	5	0	0	-	5 1
PR 4							-	
PR 5							-	
PR 6							-	
PR 7								

32480 -482

PROVIDE CODES FOR DIAGNOSES AND
CPT CODES FOR PROCEDURE(S)

Case Study 19

Inpatient Face Sheet

Patient Name:	Sabrina Guimond
Admit Date:	1/15/2010
Discharge Date:	1/17/2010
Sex:	Female
Age:	46
Disposition:	Home

Admitting Diagnoses:
> Herniated cervical disc
> Neck and right arm pain
> Asthma

Discharge Diagnoses:
> Herniated C7-T1 disc
> Radiculopathy secondary to above
> Asthma
> Respiratory distress secondary to morphine

Procedure:
> Cervical fusion, anterior
> Excision of C7-T1

Case Study 19

History and Physical

CHIEF COMPLAINT: Neck and arm pain

HISTORY OF PRESENT ILLNESS:
This 46-year-old female is referred by her primary care physician, Dr. Adrianna Rose, due to neck and right arm pain that she attributes to a whiplash type injury sustained during a fall while using her inline skates in March of last year. She has been treated medically by her PCP without resolution of her symptoms. She was seen by Dr. Alexander Warren, who ordered EMG nerve conduction velocity testing and subsequent MRI. Patient describes her pain as radiating into the right shoulder, down the back of the arm with pain in the fingers. The pain is all on the right side and is made worse by moving her neck. Patient denies any other pain.

PAST MEDICAL HISTORY:

MEDICATIONS: Flexeril and Vicodin for pain and occasional inhaler for asthma.

ALLERGIES: None known

OPERATIONS: Appendectomy in 1979

REVIEW OF SYSTEMS:

Vital Signs: Temperature 98.7, pulse 73, respirations 18, blood pressure 117/78

HEENT: Unremarkable

Neck: Decreased range of motion due to pain

Heart: Regular rate and rhythm

Lungs: Clear

Abdomen: Soft, non-tender

Extremities: Decreased grip on the right as compared to the left.

SOCIAL HISTORY:
Single, non-drinker, non-smoker. Lives with two teen-aged children.

FAMILY HISTORY: Non-contributory

ASSESSMENT:
Review of MRI demonstrates herniated disc on the right at C7-T1
C8 radiculopathy secondary to C7-T1 herniated disc.

PLAN: Diskectomy

Case Study 19

Procedure Note

DATE:	1/15/2010
PREOPERATIVE DIAGNOSIS:	C7-T1 herniated disk, right
POSTOPERATIVE DIAGNOSIS:	C7-T1 herniated disk, right
PROCEDURE:	C7-T1 microdiskectomy and fusion with allograft and premier plate system.
SURGEON:	Dr. Stephanie Waldron
ASSISTANT:	Dr. Norma Millard
ANESTHESIA:	General

INDICATIONS: The patient is a 46-year-old female with neck and right arm pain, found to have a large herniated disk.

DESCRIPTION OF PROCEDURE: The patient was inducted with general anesthesia and placed supine on the operating table. The neck was prepped and draped in the usual manner. A transverse skin incision was made low in the neck from the sternocleidomastoid to the midline. The platysmas was cut sharply. Dissection was carried down to the space between carotid sheath laterally, esophagus and trachea medially. Prevertebral fascia was opened. Appropriate level was identified by x-ray. Longus colli muscles were cauterized, elevated, and retracted. Then, posts were drilled in the body of C7 and T1 and the disk space was distracted. It was opened initially with a #15 blade and interspace rongeurs. Microscope was brought into the field and a dissection was carried down to the posterior longitudinal ligament and the dura was exposed transversely. Herniated fragment was found in the right lateral gutter.

A foraminotomy was carried out, giving exposure to the initial part of the C8 nerve. Once this was accomplished, and it was felt to be well decompressed, the wound was irrigated out. An allograft was fashioned with slightly more height on the left than on the right, as this is where some extra bone was removed. This was tapped into place, the posts were removed, the holes were waxed, and an appropriate size 25-mm fusion premier plate was put into place and screwed into place. The compression devise was used to give some compression on the bone. Once this was accomplished, the wound was irrigated and closed with 3-0 coated Vicryl in the platysma and 4-0 coated Vicryl in the skin.

The patient tolerated the procedure well without complications.

ESTIMATED BLOOD LOSS: 100 cc

Case Study 19

Progress Notes

1/15:   Admit note: Patient admitted with complaint of neck pain radiating to the right arm. MRI revealed a herniated C7-T1 disc. Patient is admitted for elective diskectomy. The procedure, alternative therapy, and the accompanying risks have been discussed and she desires the procedure.

1/15:   Operative Note:

Pre-op: C7-T1 HNP
Post-op: Same
Operation: C7-T1 diskectomy
Surgeon: Dr. Waldron
Assistant: Dr. Millard
Anesthesia: General

Patient was given morphine post-operatively in the recovery room. Patient immediately suffered respiratory distress as a result of the morphine. Narcan was administered with immediate results. Patient was observed for an additional 2 hours post-recovery with no further adverse effects. She was transferred to the floor alert and oriented with no further signs of complications.

1/15:   S: Patient feeling well, only complaint of incisional pain.
         O: Respiratory rate normal with no signs of distress.
         A: Neurological stable.
         P: Patient advised of allergy to morphine and instructed to never allow administration of morphine.

1/16:   S: o complaints
         O: Afebrile, vital signs stable
         A: Upper extremity strength good, sutures intact without redness
         P: Discharge tomorrow

1/17:   Discharge Note: Patient admitted on 1/15/2010 for elective diskectomy C7-T1. Patient tolerated surgery well. Patient developed respiratory distress as a result of morphine given post-operatively in the recovery room. Respiratory distress quickly reversed with administration of Narcan. Patient's vital signs and laboratory values were within normal limits throughout hospitalization. Incision is healing well with sutures intact. Patient is stable from a neurological standpoint with good upper extremity strength. She is to follow-up with me in 3 weeks. Activity as tolerated; however, she is to do no lifting. Discharge home in good condition.

Case Study 19

Orders:

1/15: Pre-operative Orders:
1. Admit to Dr. Rose.
2. Complete following tests 2 days pre-op:
CBC
C/C UA
PT/PTT
Type and Screen
Chem basic
Chest x-ray
EKG
3. Pre-op per anesthesia
4. Start IV 1000CC D$_5$LR prior to surgery
5. Bilateral Thigh-High TED Hose
6. NPO

1/15: PACU Standing Orders
1. Vital signs every 5 minutes for 15 minutes, then every 15 minutes until discharged from PACU.
2. Oxygen via nasal cannula at 3-5 L/Minute.
3. May discontinue oxygen when stable.
4. Check operative site every 30 minutes.
5. Maintain IV with D5LR 500 cc while in PACU.
6. Discharge from PACU when discharge criteria met.

1/16: 1. Incentive spirometer q 2 hours.

1/17: 1. D/C home
2. F/U 3 weeks

Case Study 19

Answer Sheet

DIAGNOSES			ICD-9-CM CODES				
First listed DX Herniated cervical C7-T1 disks	7	2	2	.	0	
DX 2 Respiratory distress	2	8	6	.	0	9
DX 3 Abnormality				.		
DX 4 Adverse effect morphine in therapeutic use	9	3	5	.	2	

PROCEDURES		CPT CODES					MODIFIERS (If Applicable)		
PR 1 cervical Diskectomy C7-T1	2	2	5	5	4	-		
PR 2 Foraminotomy with Allograft & fusion premier plate	6	3	0	2	0	-	5	1
PR 3						-		
PR 4						-		
PR 5						-		
PR 6						-		
PR 7						-		

Excision Intervertebral Disk

PROVIDE ICD-9-CM CODES FOR DIAGNOSES AND
CPT CODES FOR PROCEDURE(S)

Case Study 20

Inpatient Face Sheet

Patient Name: Ronda Parker

Admit Date: 1/14/2010

Discharge Date: 1/15/2010

Sex: Female

Age: 24

Disposition: Home

Admitting Diagnosis: Pre-term Labor

Discharge Diagnosis: Pre-term Labor

Case Study 20

Labor and Delivery History and Physical

History: Patient is a 24-year-old female, gravida 2, para 0, abortus 0, who had her prenatal care at the Women's Clinic. She presented to labor and delivery with the complaint of abdominal pain and cramps. Her membrane is intact.

LMP: 05/20/07. EGA of 31.4 weeks. Ultrasound at 6 weeks. No complications during this pregnancy.

PAST MEDICAL HISTORY: Non-contributory

PAST SURGICAL HISTORY: None

MEDINCE: None during pregnancy

ALLERGIES: No known allergies

PRE-NATAL LABS: Rh +, Rubella BL, VDRL NR, GC -, Chlamydia -, Pap -, AB Screen 0, Hepatitis Screen -, Diabetic Screen 153

PHYSICAL EXAM:

Vital signs:	BP 135/82, Temp. 98.4, Pulse 102, Resp. 21, FHTs 145
General:	No acute diseases
HEENT:	No asymmetry
Neck:	No asymmetry
Heart:	Regular rate and rhythm
Lungs:	Clear to auscultation bilaterally
Abdomen:	Soft, non-tender, non-distended, + bowel sounds
Extremities:	No edema
Neuro:	No deficits
Cervix	1/th
Presenting Part	VTX/FFN +

Impression: 24-year-old G2P000 at 31.4 weeks with PTL.

Plan: 1. Admit
       2. U/S *Ultrasound*

History:	Detailed
Examination:	Detailed
Medical Decision:	Low complexity

Case Study 20

Progress Notes:

1/14:   Admit note: Patient admitted to labor and delivery with pre-term labor at 31.4 weeks' gestation. Patient immediately started on magnesium sulfate

      S: Patient denies HA/CP/SOB/CTX/RUQ pain.
      O: VS 121/73, P 87, FHT: 135-141, + accelerations
      A: 24-year-old at 31.4 weeks with PTL
      P: Follow Mg levels, perform US.

1/15:   S: Patient reports that pain is completely gone.
      O: PE, WNL. FHT: 150's, + accels, - decels.
      A: PTL with Mg tocolysis, US indicates fetus at 1,698 gm, cervix closed.
      P: DC today, strict bedrest with BRP, Follow-up at clinic in 1 week.

Orders:

1/14:   1. Admit to L&D with PTL at 31.4 weeks
      2. CBC and Clean Catch UA
      3. MgSo4 per protocol – 5 Gm loading dose/then 2 gms/hr
      4. Fetal Monitor
      5. US
      6. Strict bed rest
      7. Clear liquid diet

1/15:   1. DC MgSo4
      2. Transfer to antepartum.
      3. If patient remains stable throughout the day, may discharge this evening.

Case Study 20

Answer Sheet

31.4 wks

DIAGNOSES		ICD-9-CM CODES					
First listed DX Premature *Pre-Term* labor *antepartum*		6	4	4	.	0	3
DX 2					.		
DX 3					.		
DX 4					.		

PROCEDURES		CPT CODES					MODIFIERS (If Applicable)	
PR 1 Initial Hospital care		9	9	2	2	1	-	
PR 2							-	
PR 3							-	
PR 4							-	
PR 5							-	
PR 6							-	
PR 7								

PROVIDE ICD-9-CM CODES FOR DIAGNOSES AND
CPT CODES FOR PROCEDURE(S)

Case Study 21

Inpatient Face Sheet

Patient Name: Michael Wilson

Admit Date: 1/10/2010

Discharge Date: 1/15/2010

Sex: Male

Age: 55

Disposition: Home with Home Health Care

Admitting Diagnoses:
1. Diabetic ulcer
2. Uncontrolled diabetes
3. Chronic renal failure
4. Pneumonia

Discharge Diagnoses:
1. Diabetic ulcer
2. Uncontrolled diabetes with peripheral circulatory disease
3. Pneumonia
4. Anemia
5. Chronic renal failure

Procedure:
1. Excisional debridement of decubitus ulcer

Case Study 21

Discharge summary

Admitted: 1/10/2010
Discharged: 1/15/2010

ADMITTING DIAGNOSIS:
1. Diabetic ulcer
2. Uncontrolled diabetes
3. Chronic renal failure
4. Pneumonia

DISCHARGE DIAGNOSIS:
1. Diabetic ulcer
2. Uncontrolled diabetes with peripheral circulatory disease
3. Pneumonia
4. Anemia
5. Chronic renal failure

PROCEDURE:
1. Excisional debridement of decubitus ulcer

HISTORY:
This is a 55-year-old male who was admitted through the emergency room for elevated blood sugars, a necrotic heel ulcer of the left foot. The patient was admitted for control of his blood sugars and treatment of the heel ulcer.

PAST MEDICAL HISTORY:
This patient has a long history of type 1 diabetes, chronic renal failure, coronary artery disease with history of CABG, peripheral vascular disease with subsequent below knee amputation of the right leg.

HOSPITAL COURSE:
The patient was admitted to the hospital and started on intravenous antibiotic therapy. The patient was placed on sliding scale insulin therapy as well as wound care for the heel necrosis. The patient's left heel ulcer was debrided of all necrotic tissue on 1/11/2010. There was no cellulitis of the foot; however, there were multiple areas of skin breakdown on the foot. The patient had no feeling in his left foot, secondary to severe diabetic neuropathy. The patient was continued on local wound care and antibiotic therapy. The patient's renal failure was monitored and fluids restricted. The patient's chest x-ray was positive for left lower lobe pneumonia. Sputum culture was not ordered as the patient was already on intravenous antibiotic therapy for the skin ulcer.

LABORATORY DATA:
Hemoglobin 9.4, hematocrit 29.6, WBC 8,600, platelet count 336,000. Urinalysis was normal except for a small amount of bacteria, and proteinuria. Sodium was 130, potassium 4.1, chloride 92, CO_2 32, glucose 270, BUN 53, and creatinine 3.2.

DISCHARGE MEDICATIONS:
70/30 insulin in the morning and 20 units in the evening
Cardizem CD 180 mg once daily
Imdur 60 mg once a day

Case Study 21

Discharge summary

Continued:

Lasix 80 mg once a day
Pepcid 20 mg twice a day
Paxil 10 mg three times a day
Nitrostat prn.
Patient is prescribed Floxin once daily times 7 days

The patient was felt to have reached maximum benefit of hospitalization and was discharged home in fair condition. He will be followed by home health care for wound care and monitoring of his diabetes as well as chronic renal failure. He is to continue with an 1,800 ADA diet. His activity is limited due to his wheelchair. He is to have no weight bearing on his left foot. He will follow-up in my office in 10 days.

Case Study 21

History and Physical

CHIEF COMPLAINT: Diabetic ulcer left foot, elevated blood sugars.

HISTORY OF PRESENT ILLNESS:
This is a 55-year-old white male who presented to the emergency room because of high blood sugars. This patient has a long history of type 1 diabetes. He also has chronic renal failure due to his diabetes. This gentleman also has a history of coronary artery disease, CABG, and myocardial infarction in 1996. He has diabetic peripheral vascular disease with a history of below the knee amputation of his right leg. He presently has an open necrotic area on the left foot, most likely due to PVD.

PAST MEDICAL HISTORY:
He denies hypertension, shortness of breath. Significant past history is detailed above.

PAST SURGICAL HISTORY: See above.

ALLERGIES: None known.

MEDICATIONS:
70/30 insulin in the morning and 20 units in the evening, Cardizem CD 180 mg once daily, Imdur 60 mg once a day, Lasix 80 mg once a day, Pepcid 20 mg twice a day, Paxil 10 mg three times a day, Nitrostat as needed.

SOCIAL HISTORY:
Patient lives with his wife. He does not smoke or drink. Patient is disabled due to his chronic illness.

FAMILY HISTORY: Non-contributory

PHYSICAL EXAMINATION:
Vital Signs:	Temperature 97.7, pulse 77, respirations 20, blood pressure 146/62
HEENT:	Unremarkable
Neck:	Carotid bruit. The neck is supple
Heart:	Regular rate and rhythm
Lungs:	Clinically clear
Abdomen:	Soft, non-tender, no organomegaly
Extremities:	Right below the knee amputation. There is a necrotic area on the left heel and an open ulcer on the left foot.

Case Study 21

History and Physical

Continued:

DIAGNOSTIC DATA:

The patient's labs show a hemoglobin of 9.4, hematocrit of 29.6, white blood count 8.6, platelet count 336,000. Urinalysis is abnormal with 25-50 RBCs, 50-100 WBCs, small amount of bacteria, glycosuria, and proteinuria. Chemistry: sodium 130, potassium 4.1, chloride 92, CO_2 31, anion gap is 11, glucose 260. BUN 53 and creatinine 3.2. Blood cultures and urine cultures have been ordered. The patient has been started on Floxin 400 twice a day. He had a CT scan of the head, which is negative.

His EKG reveals right bundle branch block with right axis deviation, bifascular block, right bundle branch block with left posterior fascicular block.

IMPRESSION:
1. Uncontrolled diabetes
2. Atherosclerotic cardiovascular heart disease
3. Diabetic peripheral vascular disease with left heel and foot ulcer and neuropathy
4. Carotid stenosis
5. Status post right below the knee amputation
6. End-stage renal disease

Case Study 21

Progress Notes

1/10: Admit Note: 55-year-old diabetic male admitted for elevated blood sugars and necrotic heel ulcer of left foot. Patient has a long history of type 1 diabetes, PVD with BKA right in 1995. Patient has CRF, not yet requiring dialysis.

1/11:   S: Complains only of chest pain from coughing.
         O: Glucose under better control with sliding scale coverage, last Accucheck is 203, renal stable, BUN 57 and creatinine 3.8
         A: Foot ulcers debrided at bedside of necrotic tissue
         P: Continue IV antibiotics and wound care for ulcers.

1/12:   S: Feeling better
         O: BS at 189, BUN/Creatinine at 54/3.6, CXR shows clearing of infiltrates
         A: Foot healing nicely, respiratory status improving.
         P: Continue current treatment plan.

1/13   S: No complaints
        O: BS leveling, now at 160. Renal status is stable.
        A: Patient is improving, foot ulcer is healing well.
        P: DC IV fluids when completed and start on P.O. meds.

1/14:   S: Patient is ready to go home.
         O: Wounds look good, BS now in good control, renal status stable.
         A: Patient can be discharged tomorrow, reaching maximum medical improvement.
         P: Will plan discharge tomorrow.

1/15: Discharge note: Patient will be followed by home health care for wound care and monitoring of diabetes and renal failure.

Case Study 21

Orders:

1/10: 1.   Admit patient
     2.   CBC, WBC, Chem profile, CXR, EKG
     3.   IV antibiotics
     4.   Sliding scale insulin, accuchecks q2h
     5.   Whirlpool therapy for ulcers

1/11: 1.   Debridement tray at bedside
     2.   Continue with wound care treatment.

1/12: 1.   Adjust sliding scale.
     2.   Repeat labs and CXR.

1/13: 1.   DC IVs when finished.
     2.   Switch to Floxin 400 mg twice daily.

1/14: 1.   Repeat labs.

1/15: 1.   Discharge home with home health care.

Case Study 21

Answer Sheet

DIAGNOSES	ICD-9-CM CODES					
First listed DX				.		
DX 2				.		
DX 3				.		
DX 4				.		

PROCEDURES	CPT CODES					MODIFIERS (If Applicable)		
PR 1						-		
PR 2						-		
PR 3						-		
PR 4						-		
PR 5						-		
PR 6						-		
PR 7						-		

**PROVIDE ICD-9-CM CODES FOR DIAGNOSES AND
CPT CODES FOR PROCEDURE(S)**

Case Study 22

Inpatient Face Sheet

Patient Name:	Maureen Pranger
Admit Date:	1/07/2010
Discharge Date:	1/10/2010
Sex:	Female
Age:	72
Disposition:	Home

Admitting Diagnosis:
1. Chest pain, rule out acute coronary artery disease

Discharge Diagnoses:
1. Coronary Artery Disease
2. Unstable Angina
3. Atrial Fibrillation
4. Secondary Degree AV Block
5. Status Post Percutaneous Transluminal Coronary Angioplasty

Procedures:
1. Diagnostic left heart catheterization, percutaneous transluminal coronary angioplasty, coronary angiograms

Case Study 22

Discharge Summary

Admitted: 1/07/2010

Discharged: 1/10/2010

ADMITTING DIAGNOSES

1. Chest pain, rule out acute coronary artery disease

DISCHARGE DIAGNOSES:

1. Chest pain, acute intermediate coronary syndrome
2. History of arteriosclerosis of the native coronary vessels
3. Atrial fibrillation
4. Second degree atrioventricular block

PROCEDURE PERFORMED:

1. Left heart catheterization, selective coronary angiography, percutaneous transluminal coronary angioplasty.

HOSPITAL COURSE:

This is a 72-year-old female with a history of coronary artery disease, status post percutaneous transluminal coronary angioplasty several months ago. She came in with acute intermediate coronary syndrome. A myocardial infarction was ruled out. In view of these events, it was decided to perform a diagnostic heart catheterization and possible percutaneous transluminal coronary angioplasty versus bypass surgery.

A diagnostic heart catheterization was performed and showed the following: the left main coronary artery was open; the left anterior descending artery was open. There was a previous stent in the circumflex system, which had no obstruction. There was a totally occluded distal right coronary artery. There was some collateral circulation filling the right coronary artery. In view of this, it was felt that the patient would benefit from percutaneous transluminal coronary angioplasty, so the patient received IV Heparin, ReoPro and intracoronary nitroglycerin and we were able to open the distal right coronary artery with balloon angioplasty.

The patient began ambulation the day after the above procedure. The patient is stable at discharge. Discharge to home on Atenolol 25 mg once a day, Monopril 10 mg once a day, and aspirin. She will follow a low-cholesterol, low-fat diet. She is to follow-up in my office in 1 week.

Case Study 22

History and Physical

CHIEF COMPLAINT: Chest pain.

HISTORY OF PRESENT ILLNESS:
This is a 72-year-old white female with a history of coronary artery disease, status post percutaneous transluminal coronary angioplasty and stent implantation last summer, who has been taking Tenormin 50 mg once a day, Monopril 10 mg once a day, one aspirin a day, and nitroglycerin prn. She experienced an episode of palpitation and lightheadedness last night, and this morning she started having chest pain. The patient called 911 and the EMS staff found her with a very fast rhythm, heart rate of 160 per minute accompanied with atrial fibrillation. She denied any prior history of palpitations and denies chest pains prior to this episode. The patient denies diabetes mellitus or high blood pressure. She denies history of myocardial infarction in the past. She has a strong family history of coronary artery disease. She denies alcohol or smoking.

PAST MEDICAL HISTORY: The past history is only pertinent for coronary artery disease and low HDL, post-menopausal.

PAST SURGICAL HISTORY: History of back surgery

ALLERGIES: Sulfa

REVIEW OF SYSTEMS: See history of present illness. Patient denies paroxysmal nocturnal dyspnea, orthopnea, leg swelling, fatigue, or loss of consciousness.

PHYSICAL EXAMINATION:

General Appearance:	Patient is alert, cooperative, and in no acute distress.
Vital Signs:	Her heart rhythm is in regular. Telemetry shows a second-degree atrioventricular block, Mobitz type I, with beats 2 and 4, 2:3 conduction. No electrocardiogram evidence of ischemia.
Head and Neck:	Neck is supple. No jugular venous distention, no carotid bruits.
Lungs:	Clear
Heart:	Irregular rate and rhythm. No murmur, gallop or rub.
Abdomen:	Soft, non-tender. Bowel sounds present. No tenderness on rebound.
Extremities:	No cyanosis or edema. Bilateral peripheral pulses.

ASSESSMENT:
1. Prolonged chest pain, rule out acute coronary artery disease
2. Mobitz type I second degree atrioventricular block
3. Coronary artery disease, status post stent implantation eight months ago

PLAN:
1. Admit to telemetry. Obtain cardiac enzymes and serial electrocardiograms.
2. Hold Tenormin and place on Norvasc and nitrates.
3. Cardiac catheterization and electrophysiology study.

Case Study 22

Procedure Note

Date: 1/07/2010

Procedure: Left Heart Catheterization

Selective Coronary Angiography

PTCA of Distal Right Coronary Artery

Pre-Operative Diagnosis: Unstable angina r/o CAD

Post-Operative Diagnosis: CAD

Surgeon: Anthony C. Stamper, MD

Procedure Note:
A diagnostic left heart catheterization was performed and showed the following: the left main coronary artery was open. The left anterior descending artery was open. There was a previous stent in the circumflex system, which had no obstruction. There was a totally occluded distal right coronary artery. There was some collateral circulation filling the right coronary artery. In view of this, it was felt that the patient would benefit from percutaneous transluminal coronary angioplasty, so the patient received IV Heparin, ReoPro, and intracoronary nitroglycerin and we were able to open the distal right coronary artery with balloon angioplasty. There was no clot formation or dissection. The patient returned to the floor in stable condition.

Case Study 22

Progress Notes

1/07:   S: Chest pain
            O: EKG and enzymes negative for AMI
            A: Unstable angina, probable coronary occlusion
            P: Heart catheterization and possible PTCA

1/09:   S: Patient feels great, no chest pain.
            O: Labs within normal limits, EKG stable; patient ambulating.
            A: CAD
            P: Observe a few more days.

1/09:   S: No chest pain, wants to go home.
            O: Vitals stable, heart sounds good, regular rhythm.
            A: Patient is stable, continues to do well.
            P: Plan discharge for a.m.

1/10:   S: "Never felt better."
            O: CXR clear, labs and vitals within normal limits.
            A: Patient stable for discharge.
            P: Discharge now.

Orders

1/07:   1. Admit patient to telemetry.

          2. Vitals q4h.
          3. Prepare for Left Heart Catheterization and possible PTCA
          4. Continue home medications.
          5. Serial EKGs
          6. Cardiac enzymes
          7. Cardiac diet
          8. Hold Tenormin; place on Norvasc and IV nitrates.

1/09:   1. Ambulate.

1/09:   1. Discontinue all IVs.

1/10:   1: Discharge patient.

Case Study 22

Answer Sheet

DIAGNOSES	ICD-9-CM CODES					
First listed DX				.		
DX 2				.		
DX 3				.		
DX 4				.		

PROCEDURES	CPT CODES					MODIFIERS (If Applicable)	
PR 1						-	
PR 2						-	
PR 3						-	
PR 4						-	
PR 5						-	
PR 6						-	
PR 7						-	

PROVIDE ICD-9-CM CODES FOR DIAGNOSES AND
CPT CODES FOR PROCEDURE(S)

Case Study 23

Inpatient Face Sheet

Patient Name: Gladys Thomson

Admit Date: 1/04/2010

Discharge Date: 1/11/2010

Sex: Female

Age: 70

Disposition: Home

Admitting Diagnoses:
1.   Acute abdominal pain, rule out diverticular disease
2.   History of hypertension

Discharge Diagnoses:
1.   Perforated sigmoid colon secondary to diverticulitis
2.   Dense intra-abdominal adhesions
3.   Hypertension
4.   Post-operative atelectasis
5.   Acute pharyngitis
6.   Small bowel defect requiring resection

Procedures Performed:
1.   Hartmann's procedure, lysis of adhesions, small bowel resection, colostomy
2.   Flexible sigmoidoscopy

Case Study 23

Discharge Summary

Admitted: 1/04/2010

Discharged: 1/11/2010

ADMITTING DIAGNOSES:

1. Acute abdominal pain, probably due to diverticular disease
2. History of hypertension

DISCHARGE DIAGNOSIS:

1. Perforated sigmoid colon secondary to diverticulitis
2. Dense intra-abdominal adhesions
3. Hypertension
4. Pulmonary atelectasis, persistent post-operative
5. Acute pharyngitis

PROCEDURES:

1. Hartmann's procedure, lysis of adhesions, small bowel resection
2. Flexible sigmoidoscopy

HISTORY OF PRESENT ILLNESS:
This is a 70-year-old white woman who had, on the day of admission, undergone an outpatient colonoscopy. The physician was unable to advance the scope past the sigmoid colon and felt she had a perforated bowel secondary to diverticulitis. She has had a history of numerous episodes of diverticulitis.

PAST MEDICAL HISTORY: Hypertension, hysterectomy, appendectomy

MEDICATIONS ON ADMISSION: Inderal-LA and aspirin

ALLERGIES: None known

PHYSICAL EXAMINATION:
Reveals an elderly white woman with tenderness in the left lower quadrant of the abdomen.

LABORATORY DATA:
The admission laboratory data were within normal limits, with the exception of low hematocrit of 34, hemoglobin 11.8, and elevated globulin 3.9. Post-operatively, white count was over 19,000, transiently returning to normal in 2 days. The hemoglobin dropped to 10.1 with hematocrit of 29.7.

RADIOLOGY REPORTS:
Gastrografin enema findings were suggestive of perforation at the level of the rectosigmoid, at a point where the patient had extensive diverticula.

Case Study 23

Discharge Summary

Continued:

Chest x-ray revealed pneumomediastinum and subcutaneous emphysema, but no pneumothorax. There was air in the retroperitoneum. The follow-up chest x-rays showed nasogastric tube in satisfactory position with decreased subcutaneous emphysema within the neck and decreased pericardial air collection since the prior study, and development of small bilateral effusions on 1/08/2010. The abdominal x-rays showed a large amount of free retroperitoneal air and air in the mediastinum.

HOSPITAL COURSE:
The patient was admitted and started on intravenous antibiotics with Unasyn and Tobramycin combination.

The patient was seen in consult by Gastrology, who felt she probably had an acute sigmoid perforation secondary to diverticular disease. He felt she would benefit from Gastrografin enema, especially to determine whether she could be treated conservatively or not. The procedure was completed with the findings as mentioned above. It was felt she would require resection.

She was taken to the operating room, where the above procedures were performed. The patient tolerated the procedure well under general anesthesia. The estimated blood loss was less than 100 cc with no replacement. The pathology report revealed diverticulosis with diverticulitis and perforation of the small bowel.

Post-operatively, the wound was healing nicely. The colostomy was noted to be viable. She was transferred to the surgical floor on 1/05/2010. She was having the expected amount of abdominal discomfort post-surgery. She also complained of sore throat and was started on Cepacol throat lozenges. The intravenous fluids and medications were continued.

The colostomy was not functioning over the first few days. There was minimal drainage from the nasogastric tube. Reglan was added. Breath sounds were decreased over the right lower lobe on 1/08/2010. The chest x-ray revealed atelectasis. CXRs were done daily and the RLL was re-expanded on 1/10/2010.

The colostomy began functioning on 1/09/2010. Intravenous fluids were discontinued. Intravenous Lasix was given. Her diet was increased with toleration. Activity was increased and medications were changed to p.o.

The patient improved significantly in the next several days and she was stable enough to be discharged. She will be followed in the office in 1 week. She is discharged on Duricef 500-mg b.i.d. and Tylox one q4h prn. Soft diet and activity as tolerated.

Case Study 23

History and Physical

CHIEF COMPLAINT: Abdominal pain

HISTORY OF PRESENT ILLNESS:
The patient is a 70-year-old white female who has undergone attempted colonoscopy this morning. There was difficulty in negotiating the sigmoid colon and the patient developed tenderness post-colonoscopy. Abdominal x-rays revealed free air as well as mediastinal air.

PAST MEDICAL HISTORY: Hypertension, hysterectomy, appendectomy

MEDICATIONS ON ADMISSION: Inderal-LA and aspirin

ALLERGIES: None known

PHYSICAL EXAMINATION:
Well-developed, well-nourished, 70-year-old white female in moderate distress.

REVIEW OF SYSTEMS:

Cardiac:	Normal sinus rhythm
Pulmonary:	Clear
HEENT:	Within normal limits
Abdomen:	Soft with left lower quadrant pain and some distention
Extremities:	Bilateral pedal pulses

Patient will be admitted for conservative management in hopes of avoiding surgery. She will receive intravenous antibiotic and bowel rest.

Case Study 23

Procedure Note

DATE OF PROCEDURE: 1/04/2010

PROCEDURE: Attempted full colonoscopy

SURGEON: Alexander Glenn, MD

INDICATION: Abdominal pain with history of diverticular disease

DESCRIPTION OF PROCEDURE:
With the patient in the left lateral position under direct luminal vision, a complete colonoscopy was attempted, but the Olympus colonoscope was only advanced up to 30 cm inside the sigmoid. The findings were as follows:

1. Rectum and anal canal: Internal hemorrhoids are seen in circumferential fashion, not bleeding at the time. No evidence of masses, lesions, angioma, or polyps seen in the rectal area.
2. Rectosigmoid junction, sigmoid, and descending colon: Extensive sigmoid diverticulosis with significant peridiverticulitis and spasm appreciated in a highly redundant sigmoid.

In view of the fact that the diverticular process was so extensive and the sigmoid extremely redundant, the advancement of the scope beyond this area was difficult and hence the procedure was terminated.

The patient returned to the floor in stable condition.

FINAL IMPRESSION:
1. Extensive sigmoid diverticulosis with diverticulitis and spasm
2. Redundant sigmoid
3. Internal hemorrhoids

Case Study 23

Procedure Note

DATE OF PROCEDURE: 1/04/2010

PREOPERATIVE DIAGNOSIS: Perforated sigmoid colon

POSTOPERATIVE DIAGNOSIS:
1. Perforated sigmoid colon
2. Dense intra-abdominal adhesions

PROCEDURE:
1. Hartmann's procedure
2. Lysis of adhesions
3. Small bowel resection

SURGEON: Eric Worton, MD

FINDINGS: Moderately large perforation of the sigmoid colon, approximately 2 cm in diameter, with pelvic phlegmon. Dense intra-abdominal adhesions requiring extensive lysis, taking 2 hours.

DESCRIPTION OF PROCEDURE:

The patient was taken to the operating suite and placed in the supine position. After adequate induction of general anesthesia the patient was prepped and draped in sterile fashion.

A midline incision was made and the abdomen was entered. Dense adhesions were encountered, requiring extensive sharp dissection.

The area of transection in the proximal sigmoid was dissected out circumferentially. The mesentery was taken down between Kelly clamps. Rectosigmoid was mobilized. The distal sigmoid was dissected out circumferentially and a roticulator placed across this. A stapler was fired, the bowel was transected.

Small bowel adhesions were lysed. One area was extremely thin, resulting in a serosal defect, which required resection. An area in the mid jejunum was dissected out circumferentially both proximally and distally. The intervening mesentery was serially cross-clamped between Kelly clamps. The vessels were ligated with 2-0 silks. G.A. was fired across both sides. Functional end-to-end anastomosis was then performed.

The abdomen was irrigated with copious amounts of fluid. A Jackson-Pratt drain was placed in the pelvis.

Attention was then directed toward closure. The proximal defect was made in the left lower quadrant. Transected colon was brought out through the colostomy defect without difficulty. Upon adequate sponge, needle, lap, and instrument count, the abdominal wound was closed with running # 2 Prolene suture.

The subcutaneous tissue was irrigated with copious amounts of antibiotic solution. The cautery was utilized for hemostasis. The skin was loosely approximated. Jackson-Pratt drain was secured with 3-0 Nylon. A sterile dressing was applied and attention turned toward maturation of the colostomy.

Case Study 23

Procedure Note

Continued:

The colon was secured to the fascia with three interrupted 3-0 Vicryl sutures. The colon was than transected and the colostomy matured in the usual fashion with interrupted 3-0 Vicryl sutures. The colostomy appliance was placed and the patient was taken to the recovery room, having tolerated the procedure well.

Case Study 23

PROGRESS NOTES:

1/04:   Admit Note: Patient admitted following attempted colonoscopy. Physician was unable to advance the scope past the sigmoid colon and felt she had perforated bowel secondary to diverticulitis. This patient has a long history of diverticulitis. Laboratory data is within normal limits with the exception of H/H of 11.8/34. Patient was taken to surgery for resection of bowel. She tolerated the procedure well with minimal blood loss. The pathology report revealed diverticulitis and bowel perforation.

1/05:   S: Incisional pain
         O: H/H dropped to 10.1/29.7, WBC 19,000, vital signs stable
         A: Good post-operative course so far
         P: Continue present treatment

1/06:   S: Less surgical pain.
         O: WBCs coming down, now at 14,000, vitals stable, incisions clean and dry.
         A: Continues to improve.
         P: Begin ambulation, maintain liquid diet.

1/07:   S: Complaining of sore throat
         O: WBCs normal, incisions healing nicely, colostomy still not functioning, but Viable.
         A: Acute pharyngitis
         P: Continue all meds; add Cepacol lozenges for sore throat.

1/09:   S: Throat still sore, some surgical pain
         O: Minimal NG drainage, decreased breath sounds RLL
         A: Wound healing nicely, possible atelectasis.
         P: Get CXR to evaluate atelectasis.

1/09:   S: Feels better, throat less sore.
         O: CXR shows persistent post-op atelectasis RLL, colostomy beginning to function.
         A: Good post-op course.
         P: Advance diet; remove NG tube, CXR daily.

1/10:   S: More comfortable with NG tube out
         O: CXR improved, RLL expanded, tolerating diet.
         A: Continues to improve, colostomy functioning nicely.
         P: Plan for discharge tomorrow.

1/11:   S: Ready to go home.
         O: Wounds clean and dry, afebrile, tolerating diet
         A: Good post-op recovery
         P: Discharge today.

Case Study 23

ORDERS:

1/04:   1.   Admit patient and prep for bowel resection.
          2.   Transfer to SICU following surgery.
          3.   Follow unit protocol.
          4.   Vitals q4h
          5.   IV Unasyn and Tobramycin

1/05:   1.   Transfer to surgical floor.
          2.   Continue all current meds and treatment.
          3.   Cepacol throat lozenges for sore throat.

1/06:   1.   Portable CXR.
          2.   Continue all orders.

1/07:   1.   CXR daily.

1/09:   1.   Advance diet.

1/09:   1.   Remove NG tube.

1/10:   1.   Discontinue IVs.

1/11:   1.   Discharge.

Case Study 23

Answer Sheet

DIAGNOSES	ICD-9-CM CODES					
First listed DX				.		
DX 2				.		
DX 3				.		
DX 4				.		

PROCEDURES	CPT CODES					MODIFIERS (If Applicable)		
PR 1						-		
PR 2						-		
PR 3						-		
PR 4						-		
PR 5						-		
PR 6						-		
PR 7						-		

PROVIDE ICD-9-CM CODES FOR DIAGNOSES AND
CPT CODES FOR PROCEDURE(S)

Case Study 24

Inpatient Face Sheet

Patient Name: Joleen Barker

Admitted: 1/14/2010

Discharged: 1/17/2010

Sex: Female

Age: 35

Disposition: Home

Admitting Diagnosis:
1. Ovarian cyst

Discharge Diagnoses:
1. Ovarian cyst dense adhesions
2. Post-operative blood loss
3. Urinary tract infection

Procedures:
1. Total abdominal hysterectomy
2. Bilateral salpingo-oophorectomy
3. Exploratory laparotomy

Case Study 24

Discharge Summary

Admitted: 1/14/2010
Discharged: 1/17/2010

DISCHARGE DIAGNOSES:
1. Ovarian cyst
2. Uterine dense adhesions
3. Urinary tract infection
4. Post-operative anemia

PROCEDURES PERFORMED:
1. Exploratory laparotomy
2. Hysterectomy
3. Bilateral salpingo-oophorectomy

HISTORY:
This 35-year-old female has experienced pelvic pain for 3 months duration. Pelvic ultrasound revealed a right ovarian cystic mass. She was admitted for elective surgery.

PAST MEDICAL HISTORY:
Refer to History and Physical for complete history.

HOSPITAL COURSE:
Patient underwent exploratory laparotomy that revealed a benign cyst of the right ovary and adhesions of the uterus requiring hysterectomy and bilateral salpingo-oophorectomy. She tolerated the surgery without complication. Post-operative course was significant for post-operative anemia, requiring transfusion of PRBCs. She also was noted to have elevated temperature, and cultures indicated a urinary tract infection. She was already on IV antibiotics post-surgery that would also cover the UTI. She progressed well, in spite of the anemia and the UTI, and was discharged in good condition on 1/17/2010. She was given a prescription for antibiotics and iron pills. Activity as tolerated; however, no driving for 2 weeks. Diet as tolerated. She is to see me in 3 days for post-operative follow-up and staple removal.

Case Study 24

History and Physical

CHIEF COMPLAINT: Pelvic pain

HISTORY OF PRESENT ILLNESS:
This 35-year-old gravida 3, para 3, has complained of pelvic pain for 3 months duration. Pelvic ultrasound revealed her right ovary to be enlarged with a large cystic mass. She is admitted today for elective exploratory laparotomy. The patient understands that she may require a hysterectomy and possible salpingo-oophorectomy.

PAST MEDICAL HISTORY: Negative, except for childbirth.

PAST SURGICAL HISTORY: No surgeries.

SOCIAL HISTORY: Non-smoker, non-drinker

FAMILY HISTORY: Non-contributory.

ALLERGIES: Penicillin

MEDICATIONS: None

REVIEW OF SYSTEMS:
HEENT: Within normal limits
Neck: Supple. No lymphadenopathy.
Heart: Regular rhythm, no murmurs
Lungs: Clear to auscultation
Abdomen: Soft. Good bowel sounds. Pelvic pain on palpation.
Rectal: Deferred
Extremities: Within normal limits.

IMPRESSION:
1. Ovarian cyst

PLAN:
1. Exploratory laparotomy

Case Study 24

Procedure Note

Date of Procedure:	1/14/2010
Preoperative Diagnosis:	Ovarian cyst, right
Postoperative Diagnosis:	Right ovarian cyst
Surgeon:	Dr. Hollie Schoonover
Anesthesiologist:	Dr. Layne Allen
Procedure:	Exploratory laparotomy Hysterectomy, Bilateral salpingo-oophorectomy

DESCRIPTION OF PROCEDURE:
Following administration of general anesthesia, the patient's abdomen was prepped and draped in sterile manner. A midline incision was done below the umbilicus to the pubis symphysis and then taken down to the fascia. The muscles were separated and the peritoneum was cut, taking care to avoid the bladder and bowel. There was a large cystic mass on the right ovary measuring 6 x 8 centimeters. The right ovary and tube with the cyst intact were removed. The left tube and ovary were removed in similar fashion. The decision was made to perform a hysterectomy and this was carried out without complications. All bleeders were ligated using 0-Vicryl. The pelvic cavity was irrigated with saline. The abdomen was then closed using 2-0 Dexon, and the skin was closed using staples. The patient tolerated the procedure and was discharged to the recovery room in good condition.

Estimated blood loss: 400 cc

Pathology Report

Specimens:
1. Uterus
2. Left ovary and fallopian tube
3. Right ovary and fallopian tube with cystic mass

Microscopic Diagnosis:
1. Uterus:
   Mild chronic cervicitis
2. Left fallopian tube and ovary:
   Atrophic ovary with normal fallopian tube
3. Right fallopian tube and ovary:
   Normal right tube and benign cyst of the ovary

Case Study 24

Progress Notes:

1/14: Patient admitted to surgical floor following exploratory laparotomy, hysterectomy, and bilateral salpingo-oophorectomy. Patient tolerated the procedure well. Is fully awake and complains of moderate surgical pain. Patient will remain NPO until the evening meal and then will have a soft diet. Ambulate upon full recovery from anesthesia.

1/14:
- S: Moderate pain
- O: Incision clean and dry, vital signs good. H/H 9.8/35.4. Was 12.9/42.3 on admission. Temp elevated to 101.2.
- A: Probable post-op anemia
- P: Monitor H/H, continue with present pain medication.

1/15:
- S: Feels okay.
- O: Incision clean and dry, vitals good. H/H dropped to 8.10/32.2. Temp still elevated, 100.1.
- A: Possible occult infection.
- P: Will culture to r/o infection. Continue to monitor H/H.

1/16:
- S: Complains of minor pain at operative site.
- O: Vital signs good. H/H at 10.9/39.8 after transfusion. Temperature 99.9
- A: Urine culture revealed UTI. Treated with antibiotics. Ambulating freely, progressing well.
- P: Change to p.o. antibiotics, monitor H/H, probable discharge tomorrow.

1/17:
- S: Feels well, ready to go home.
- O: Incision healing well, vital signs good. H/H at 11.2/42.1. Temperature normal.
- A: Ready for discharge.
- P: Discharge home; follow-up in office in 1 week.

Orders:

1/14:
1. Admit patient to surgical floor from recovery
2. Standard post-operative orders
3. Vital signs q 6 hours

1/15:
1. Blood and urine cultures to rule out infection.
2. Transfuse two units PRBCs.
3. Continue with IV antibiotics.

1/16:
1. Change IV antibiotics to p.o.
2. Continue to monitor H/H.

1/17:
1. Discharge home.

Case Study 24

Answer Sheet

DIAGNOSES	ICD-9-CM CODES					
First listed DX				.		
DX 2				.		
DX 3				.		
DX 4				.		

PROCEDURES	CPT CODES					MODIFIERS (If Applicable)		
PR 1						-		
PR 2						-		
PR 3						-		
PR 4						-		
PR 5						-		
PR 6						-		
PR 7						-		

Case Study 25

Emergency Room Visit

Face Sheet

Patient Name: Elizabeth Colter

Date of Service: 01/01/2010

Age: 25

Sex: Female

Admitting Diagnosis: Injury to left wrist

Discharge Diagnosis: Sprain left wrist

Disposition: Home

Case Study 25

Emergency Room Visit

DATE OF SERVICE: 1/01/2010

HISTORY OF PRESENT ILLNESS:
A 25-year-old female was at work today when a bread tray fell on her left wrist. She has persistent pain in the area, which is exacerbated with moving the wrist and hand. She describes the pain as very severe.

PAST MEDICAL HISTORY: Non-contributory.

ALLERGIES: None.

PHYSICAL EXAMINATION:

General:	Well-developed, well-nourished female in moderate distress. Vitals are stable.
Skin:	Warm and dry.
HEENT:	Unremarkable.
Chest:	Symmetrical.
Extremities:	The left wrist is tender and mildly swollen especially over the distal ulna with no gross deformity. Normal range of motion against resistance with moderate pain. No abrasions or lacerations. Normal distal neurosensory examination. The remainder of the extremity examination is within normal limits.
Neurological:	She is awake, alert, and oriented times three with no focal neurologic deficits.

RADIOLOGY EXAMINATION:
The patient was taken to the x-ray room where the wrist was x-rayed. No acute fractures appreciated in the AP and lateral views.

IMPRESSION: Left wrist sprain.

The patient was placed in a padded splint and was given a prescription for Darvocet. She will follow-up with her physician next week.

History:	Expanded problem-focused
Examination:	Detailed
Medical Decision Making:	Low decision

Case Study 25

Answer Sheet

DIAGNOSES	ICD-9-CM CODES					
First listed DX				.		
DX 2				.		
DX 3				.		
DX 4				.		

PROCEDURES	CPT CODES					MODIFIERS (If Applicable)		
PR 1						-		
PR 2						-		
PR 3						-		
PR 4						-		
PR 5						-		
PR 6						-		
PR 7						-		

PROVIDE ICD-9-CM CODES FOR DIAGNOSES AND
CPT CODE(S) FOR PHYSICIAN VISIT (E/M CODE)

Case Study 26

Inpatient Face Sheet

Patient Name: Caroline Delaney

Admit Date: 1/12/2010

Discharge Date: 1/18/2010

Sex: Female

Age: 75

Disposition: Home

Admitting Diagnoses:
1. Asthmatic bronchitis
2. Pneumonia
3. Supraventricular tachycardia
4. Chronic diastolic heart failure

Discharge Diagnoses:
1. Pneumonia
2. Asthmatic bronchitis
3. Supraventricular tachycardia
4. Chronic diastolic heart failure
5. Tobacco use

Procedures:
None

Code E/M Visit for Dr. Magee's Initial Hospital Care

History: Comprehensive
Examination: Comprehensive
Medical Decision Making: Moderate Complexity

Case Study 26

DISCHARGE SUMMARY

ADMTTED: 1/12/2010

DISCHARGED: 1/18/2010

ADMITTING DIAGNOSES:
1. Asthmatic bronchitis, rule out pneumonia
2. Supraventricular tachycardia

DISCHARGE DIAGNOSES:
1. Pneumonia
2. Asthmatic bronchitis.
3. Supraventricular tachycardia.
4. Chronic diastolic heart failure

CHIEF COMPLAINT: Shortness of breath, history of asthma, possible pneumonia, fever.

HISTORY OF PRESENT ILLNESS: A 75-year-old female presented to the emergency room with the above complaints. She had been treated as an outpatient by her primary care physician, Dr. Nicholas Magee. She failed to improve with Zithromax. The patient has a past history of bronchial asthma, supraventricular arrhythmia, and chronic diastolic heart failure. Her cardiologist is Dr. Benjamin William and her pulmonologist is Dr. Victoria Stamper. On 3/23/06, the patient had a cardiac catheterization with findings of minimal coronary artery disease.

PHYSICAL EXAMINATION: On exam today, the patient is short of breath with congestion noted in the head and chest, expiratory wheezing, rales, and rhonchi throughout. No edema. For complete physical details, please see history and physical.

HOSPITAL COURSE: The patient was admitted and given intravenous fluids, placed on telemetry monitoring, started on intravenous steroids, which were subsequently tapered; pan cultured, and had a pulmonary medicine consult. Chest x-ray shows and pneumonia.

Consultation with Dr. Stamper of pulmonary medicine was performed.

RADIOLOGY REPORTS:
PA and lateral chest x-ray of January 12, showed left lower lobe pneumonia. Follow-up PA and lateral chest x-ray on 1/15 showed clear, but hyperexpanded lungs compatible with the patient's clinical history of asthma, no evidence of focal consolidation pneumonia compared to the chest x-ray of 1/13, which showed slight improvement of left lower lobe pneumonia and hiatal hernia.

Continued:

LABORATORY DATA: On admission glucose 116, sodium 135, potassium 3.5, blood urea nitrogen 11, creatinine 1.4, calcium 8.4. On 1/15 glucose 125, sodium 137, potassium 3.9, blood urea nitrogen 19, creatinine 1.5, calcium 8.5. On admission, white blood cell count was 22,300 with a hemoglobin 13.9, hematocrit 42.0, platelets 210,000. White blood cell count had decreased on 1/15 to 12,900 with hemoglobin of 12.7, hematocrit 37.7, platelets 266,000. Blood culture negative.

HOSPITAL COURSE: The patient presented with shortness of breath, cough and congestion, following outpatient care for respiratory infection. She has a history of asthma. She was admitted and placed on intravenous antibiotics, supplemental oxygen, nebulizer therapy with bronchodilators, and intravenous steroids. She also was found to have sinusitis and pneumonia.

The patient was felt to have reached maximum medical improvement on 1/17 and was cleared for discharge. The patient was given instructions and advice and will go home with the medications and the nebulizer treatments of Albuterol and saline four times a day.

DISCHARGE MEDICATIONS:
1. Levaquin 250 mg once a day for 7 days.
2. Claritin 10 mg, one tablet daily.
3. Nasonex nasal spray, two sprays each nostril daily.
4. Potassium chloride spray, three or four times four times a day.
5. Lanoxin 0.125 mg daily
6. Lasix

Case Study 26

History and Physical

ADMISSION DATE: 1/12/2010

CHIEF COMPLAINT: Shortness of breath, history of asthma, possible pneumonia, fever.

HISTORY: This 75-year-old female presented to the emergency room with the above complaints. She was initially seen by her primary care physician, who prescribed Zithromax, which failed to improve her symptoms. The patient was found to have possible infiltrate on chest x-ray, pyrexia, and was admitted for further evaluation and treatment.

The past medical history includes bronchial asthma, history of supraventricular arrhythmia, and palpitation.

PREVIOUS CONSULTANTS: Dr. Benjamin William and Dr. Victoria Stamper

PROCEDURES: On 04/23/2005, the patient had cardiac catheterization with findings of minimal coronary artery disease with recommendation for medical management.

PRESENT MEDICATIONS: The present medications include Lanoxin .25 milligrams daily, Nasonex nasal spray, and Claritin D 24 hour tablet.

Additional medical history includes asthmatic bronchitis, and respiratory allergies.

PAST SURGERY: cataracts

SOCIAL HISTORY: The patient admits to cigarette smoking. She has never been married and has no children.

ALLERGIES: None known.

SYSTEMS REVIEW:
INTEGUMENT: Denies rashes, seborrhea, or psoriasis.
HEENT: Denies any problems chewing, tasting, hearing, or swallowing.
RESPIRATORY: Admits to shortness of breath, asthma, and dyspnea on exertion
GASTROINTESTINAL: Unremarkable

FAMILY HISTORY: The family history includes two brothers and two sisters. One brother deceased. One brother has asthma. Parents are deceased. Mother died at age 82 from a stroke and father died at age 85 from a stroke.

PHYSICAL EXAMINATION: The physical examination reveals a well-nourished, well-hydrated, Caucasian female with no complaints, alert and cooperative, mild respiratory stridor.

Continued:

LUNGS:	Full aeration, expiratory wheezing bilaterally.
CARDIOVASCULAR:	S1 and S2 regular. No palpitations perceived at this time. No irregular rhythm noted on auscultation by this examiner. There is no jugular venous distention.
ABDOMEN:	The abdomen is soft, non-tender. No guarding, rebound, or rigidity.

IMPRESSION AT THIS TIME: Asthmatic bronchitis, rule out pneumonia.

RECOMMENDATION: Intravenous fluids, intravenous steroids, intravenous Levaquin, panculture, pulmonary medicine consult.

CONDITION AT THIS TIME: Guarded.

Case Study 26

Consultation

DATE: 1/12/2010

REQUESTING PHYSICIAN: Dr. Magee

CONSULTING PHYSICIAN: Dr. Stamper

This is a 75-year-old female who has a long-standing history of asthma since the age of eight who was not doing well for the past few days with increased shortness of breath, cough, and congestion. She saw Dr. Magee, who gave her Zithromax, which did not help her symptoms. Then she developed increased fever, cough, and congestion, so she came to the emergency room, where she was noted to have questionable pneumonia and bronchitis and bronchospasm. She was admitted to the hospital for further treatment.

PAST MEDICAL HISTORY: The past medical history is positive for long-standing asthma, COPD exacerbation requiring recurrent hospitalization, and history of allergic rhinitis. She also has a history of postnasal drip, chronic wheezing, shortness of breath, and tachycardia.

SOCIAL HISTORY: Past history of smoking. Does not abuse alcohol. She lives alone.

FAMILY HISTORY: Parents died of stroke in their eighties. One brother had asthma.

MEDICATIONS PRIOR TO ADMISSION: The patient's medications prior to admission included Vioxx 25 milligrams once a day, Ablution inhaler, Claritin 10 milligrams once a day, Serevent inhaler, Flonase inhaler, and nasal spray.

ALLERGIES: None known
REVIEW OF SYSTEMS: Otherwise negative.

PHYSICAL EXAMINATION: Alert white female who is in acute distress, tachycardic and tachypneic, she is short of breath. Temperature 100.4, pulse 120, respirations 20, blood pressure 140/98, saturation 88 percent, on admission. Last vitals: temperature 97, pulse 99, respirations 20, blood pressure 150/80.

HEENT:	Negative except some sinus tenderness and postnasal drip.
NECK:	No jugular venous distention.
LUNGS:	Bilateral diffuse rhonchi and wheezes.
HEART:	Regular rhythm, tachycardia, no gallops or murmur.
ABDOMEN:	The abdomen is soft, non-tender.
EXTREMITIES:	No edema.

Chest x-ray was reviewed; there is no definite infiltrate except some basilar atelectasis, early infiltrate cannot be ruled out. Arterial blood gas – pH 7.45, pCO_2 30, pO_2 73 on two liters nasal cannula. White blood count 18.1, hemoglobin 13.9. Comprehensive metabolic panel essentially unremarkable. Bilirubin 1.67. Digoxin .49.

Continued:

ASSESSMENT:
1. Bronchial asthma.
2. Bronchitis.
3. No definite pneumonia; however, it cannot be ruled out.
4. Basilar atelectasis.
5. Tachycardia due to above

RECOMMENDATION: Intravenous Solu-Medrol, intravenous antibiotics, oxygen, nebulizer treatment, sinus x-rays and follow closely.

Case Study 26

Answer Sheet

DIAGNOSES	ICD-9-CM CODES				
First listed DX				.	
DX 2				.	
DX 3				.	
DX 4				.	

PROCEDURES	CPT CODES				MODIFIERS (If Applicable)	
PR 1					-	
PR 2					-	
PR 3					-	
PR 4					-	
PR 5					-	
PR 6					-	
PR 7					-	

PROVIDE ICD-9-CM CODES FOR DIAGNOSES

Case Study 27

INPATIENT FACE SHEET

Patient Name: Jeremy Denton

Admit Date: 1/15/2010

Discharge Date: 1/21/2010

Age: 78

Sex: Male

Disposition: Home

Admit Diagnoses:

1. Dyspnea, rule out pulmonary embolism
2. History of deep venous thrombosis
3. Chronic renal insufficiency
4. Dizziness, possibly benign positional vertigo, rule out other causes

Discharge Diagnoses:

1. Dyspnea on exertion, confirmed secondary to pulmonary embolism
2. Mild congestive heart failure, chronic systolic
3. History of chronic renal failure
4. Diabetes mellitus type I
5. Diabetic neuropathy

Procedure Performed:

None

Case Study 27

DISCHARGE SUMMARY

ADMITTED: 1/15/2010

DISCHARGED: 1/21/2010

ADMITTING DIAGNOSES:
1. Dyspnea, rule out pulmonary embolism
2. History of deep venous thrombosis
3. Chronic renal insufficiency
4. Dizziness, possibly benign positional vertigo, rule out other causes

DISCHARGE DIAGNOSES:
1. Dyspnea on exertion, confirmed secondary to pulmonary embolism
2. Mild congestive heart failure, chronic systolic
3. History of chronic renal failure
4. Type I diabetes mellitus
5. Diabetic neuropathy
6. Chronic obstructive pulmonary disease
7. Dizziness: etiology likely multifactorial, patient started on Meclezine

HISTORY: This is a 78-year-old gentleman with the above-mentioned medical problems who came to the emergency room at this time with light-headedness, dizziness, wooziness, drunk feeling, not sure of his steps. He was having increasing shortness of breath and does have a history of deep venous thrombosis and pulmonary emboli.

PERTINENT EXAM: Blood pressure 123/80, pulse rate 109, respirations 16, temperature 96.

HEENT: Unremarkable.

NECK: No jugular venous distention.

LUNGS: A few crepitations, no wheezing.

HEART: Regular. No murmur.

ABDOMEN: Distended, soft, non-tender.

EXTREMITIES: 2-3 + edema.

LABORATORY: White blood cell account 11,500, left shift differential. Other counts were normal. Follow-up hemoglobin 11.1, hematocrit 32.9. Baseline INR normal. Chemistries: sodium 135, blood urea nitrogen 35, creatinine 1.8, alkaline phosphatase 80. AST/ALT levels initially normal. Follow-up blood sugar 198–200. Urinalysis: yellow and hazy appearance, microscopic blood noted, protein noted, nitrite negative, a small amount of leukocyte esterase detected. Urine culture suggested a contaminated specimen.

Chest film revealed some prominent interstitial markings and possible congestive heart failure.

Continued:

Computed tomography brain scan: mild atrophy. Ventilation perfusion lung scan revealed an intermediate probability for pulmonary embolism. Electrocardiogram: sinus rhythm, sinus tachycardia. Arterial blood gases on two liters nasal cannula, pH 7.41, pCO_2 33.1, pO_2 98.8, bicarb 20.8, and saturation is 97.5%.

HOSPITAL COURSE: The patient admitted with increasing weakness, dyspnea, and hypoxemia and dizziness at this time as well. There is no evidence of acute cerebrovascular accident. Computed tomography brain scan revealing chronic changes, nothing acute.

Ultimately the patient was found to have a pulmonary embolism and started on subcutaneous Lovenox injection, 1 mg/kg subcutaneous every 12 hours and then Coumadin started as well. Daily prothrombin time, INR evaluations were obtained, and Coumadin doses were titrated accordingly. We were able to confirm the suspicion with a computed tomography scan and pulmonary angiogram. The patient was continued on anticoagulation, as well as treatment for heart failure with Ace inhibitor therapy. He had reached the maximal hospital benefit and was discharged 1/21/2010.

MEDICATIONS ON DISCHARGE:

1. Humulin 75/25 15 units twice daily
2. Xanax .25 mg three times a day
3. Celexa 30 mg a daily
4. Coumadin 10 mg daily
5. Protonex 40 mg a day
6. Prinivil 40 mg daily
7. Meclezine

DIET: 1,800 ADA, low fat, low salt

OTHER THERAPEUTIC MEASURES: The patient reached maximum therapeutic benefit from his hospital admission. He was discharged with his medications and diet as listed.

ACTIVITY: As tolerated.

Case Study 27

HISTORY & PHYSICAL

ADMITTED: 1/15/2010

CHIEF COMPLAINT: Dizziness, lightheadedness, and shortness of breath on exertion.

HISTORY OF PRESENT ILLNESS: This is 78-year-old gentleman who has a history of multiple medical problems. He came into the emergency room because he was feeling dizzy, lightheaded, woozy, and kind of drunk. He could not be sure of his steps. He has also been complaining of increased shortness of breath on exertion. He does have chronic dyspnea on exertion due to multiple medical problems including obesity and deep venous thrombosis; however, he feels that his symptoms are worse than before.

PAST MEDICAL HISTORY: His history is positive for multiple medical problems. He has history of hypertension, diabetes mellitus type 1, deep venous thrombosis. He has been on Coumadin for quite some time because of deep venous thrombosis.

SOCIAL HISTORY: He smoked cigarettes, but quit smoking 25 years ago. He does not drink alcohol. He is married and lives with his wife.

ALLERGIES: None.

REVIEW OF SYSTEMS: As mentioned earlier; other than that, is unremarkable. He does not have any chest pain, denies any shortness of breath on exertion. He has no cough, hemoptysis, fever, or chills. No nausea or vomiting, abdominal pain, diarrhea, or urinary burning or hematuria at this time.

MEDICATIONS: Protonix 40 milligrams once a day, and insulin 75/25 Humalog 35 units in the morning and 35 units in the evening.

PHYSICIAL EXAMINATION:

GENERAL APPEARANCE: Elderly white gentleman who is in no respiratory distress, but gets short of breath on exertion.

VITAL SIGNS: Blood pressure 123/80 on admission, pulse 109, respirations 16, temperature 96, oxygen saturation 98%.

HEENT:	Head, ears, eyes, nose, and throat was negative.
NECK:	No jugular venous distention.
LUNGS:	There are a few crepitations, no wheezing, rhonchi, or rales.
HEART:	Regular rhythm, no gallops or murmur.
ABDOMEN:	The abdomen is distended, soft, non-tender.
EXTREMITIES:	There is 2-3 + edema.

LABORATORY DATA: The pertinent laboratories include on admission, urinalysis positive for white blood cells and 2+ bacteria. White blood cell count 11.5, hemoglobin 12.4. Comprehensive metabolic panel is unremarkable, except blood urea nitrogen 35, creatinine 1.8. Troponin I 0.05. Prothrombin time and partial thromboplastin time normal, partial thromboplastin time 54. D-dimer positive. Chest x-ray: Basal atelectasis, otherwise unremarkable. There is some interstitial marking. Computerized tomography scan of the brain was unremarkable. Urine culture: multiple species, could be contaminated.

Continued:

ASSESMENT:

1. Shortness of breath on exertion, which could be related to obesity, chronic obstructive pulmonary disease, asthma, bronchitis, rule out pulmonary emboli, especially with the history of deep venous thrombosis.
2. History of deep venous thrombosis and renal insufficiency.
3. Dizziness, rule out benign positional vertigo, orthostatic hypotension, rule out bleeding, cerebrovascular accident, etc.

RECOMMENDATIONS:

1. Computerized tomography scan of brain.
2. Neurology consultation.
3. Orthostatic check of blood pressure and pulse.
4. Check complete blood count, chemistry, other laboratories.
5. Get pulmonary CT angiogram to rule out pulmonary emboli.
6. Check oxygen saturation on exertion.
7. Give nebulizer treatment and oxygen, insulin, and other medications as before.

Case Study 27

CONSULTATION

DATE: 1/16/2010

REQUESTING PHYSICIAN: Dr. Chase William

CONSULTING PHYSICIAN: Dr. Lynn Pagano

HISTORY OF PRESENT ILLNESS: The patient is a 78-year-old white male with history of diabetes mellitus type 1, history of hypertension, who was admitted to the hospital with dizziness. He denied any fall, any loss of consciousness, denied any slurring of the speech, he denied any weakness focally.

PAST MEDICAL HISTORY: Hypertension, diabetes mellitus type I.

MEDICATIONS: He is on clonidine, Norvasc, Protonix, and insulin.

NEUROLOGICAL EXAMINATION:

GENERAL APPEARANCE: On examination, the patient is pleasant, awake, alert, oriented times three.

VITAL SIGNS: Temperature 98 degrees, blood pressure 133/74, pulse is 94 beats per minute.

HEENT:	There is equal eye movement, reactive to light. No nystagmus, no carotid bruit. The left visual field is normal. No neck rigidity, no Kernig or Brudzinski sign.
CRANIAL NERVES:	The cranial nerves are unremarkable. Palatal movement is intact with tongue midline. Corneal and gag reflexes are intact.
MOTOR SYSTEM:	Normal tone and power, 5/5 in all four extremities proximally and distally. There is decreased pinprick and touch in bilateral upper and lower extremities distally, with decreased position and vibration. Deep tendon reflexes +2 in the lower extremities, +1 knee jerk, and absent ankle jerk, and absent ankle jerk. Plantar is both down going.
CEREBELLAR:	Finger-to-nose, heel-to-shin normal. Speech is clear, alert, with normal naming, normal comprehensions, normal reading.
LABORATORY DATA:	Urinalysis: Hazy and many bacteria 2+, Chemistry: Sodium 135, potassium 4.8, blood urea nitrogen 35, creatinine 0.8, sugar 149, alkaline phosphatase 580, globulin 4.5. White blood cell count 11.5, hemoglobin 12.5, hematocrit 36.5, platelet count 268.

IMPRESSION:
The patient has hypertension, diabetes mellitus type 1, with severe peripheral neuropathy with complaints of feeling dizziness, lightheaded, without any acute focal motor or sensory deficit, without any nystagmus:

1. Rule out benign positional vertigo.
2. Rule out cardiac arrhythmia versus gastrointestinal, which is unlikely.
3. Rule out orthostatic hypotension.

Continued:

RECOMMENDATIONS:

1. Computerized tomography scan of the head
2. Meclezine 25 milligrams p.o. b.i.d.
3. Physical therapy, occupational therapy for gait training
4. Diabetic control
5. Check for orthostatic blood pressure every 6 hours.

Case Study 27

Answer Sheet

DIAGNOSES	ICD-9-CM CODES					
First listed DX				.		
DX 2				.		
DX 3				.		
DX 4				.		

PROCEDURES	CPT CODES					MODIFIERS (If Applicable)		
PR 1						-		
PR 2						-		
PR 3						-		
PR 4						-		
PR 5						-		
PR 6						-		
PR 7						-		

PROVIDE ICD-9-CM CODES FOR DIAGNOSES AND CPT CODES FOR PROCEDURE(S)

Case Study 28

Inpatient Face Sheet

Patient Name: Sally Kramer

Admit Date: 1/05/2010

Discharge Date: 1/09/2010

Sex: Female

Age: 35

Disposition: Home

Admitting Diagnoses:
1. Induction of labor
2. Severe pre-eclampsia
3. Intrauterine growth retardation

Discharge Diagnoses:
1. Severe pre-eclampsia
2. Accelerated hypertension
3. Intrauterine growth retardation
4. Pre-term at 36 weeks

Procedure:
1. Primary low transverse c-section

Case Study 28

Discharge Summary

Admitted: 1/05/2010
Discharged: 1/09/2010

ADMITTING DIAGNOSES:
1. Induction of labor
2. Severe pre-eclampsia
3. IUGR

DISCHARGE DIAGNOSES:
1. Severe pre-eclampsia
2. Accelerated hypertension
3. IUGR

Patient is a 35-year-old, gravida 3, para 2, admitted for induction due to severe pre-eclampsia and late decelerations. She was admitted for induction and began on Pitocin. However, due to persistent late decelerations, patient underwent a primary low flap transverse cesarean section with delivery of a 4 pound 12 ounce liveborn male with 6, 9 Apgars.

There were no post-operative problems other than accelerated hypertension, for which the patient was started on Apresoline and Aldomet. Last blood pressure reading was 180/90. Discharge hemoglobin and hematocrit were 11.3 and 32.4 and platelet count was 122. The platelet count had been as low as 94,000. The patient's magnesium levels when she was on magnesium ranged between 4.5 and 4.0, her electrolytes were normal, alkaline phosphatase 262 and 304. The hemoglobin and hematocrit on admission were 13 and 37, platelet count was 158,000. The PT and PTT were normal. The urinalysis was negative.

The patient was discharged in satisfactory condition with diet and activity as tolerated. Patient will continue to take Aldomet and Apresoline. I will see the patient in my office in 1 week for staple removal.

Case Study 28

History and Physical

HISTORY OF PRESENT ILLNESS:

The patient is a 35-year-old gravida 3, para 2, due date 1/05/2010, whom I saw in my office with blood pressure of 154/104, 150/98, 2+ protein. She was immediately sent to the hospital for admission for induction of labor.

ANTEPARTUM HISTORY:

She has had two vaginal deliveries in the past. Her ultrasound was consistent with dates. Her group B Strep was negative. She has a history of hypertension.

PAST MEDICAL HISTORY: Usual childhood diseases.

FAMILY HISTORY: Non-contributory

ALLERGIES: None known

PHYSICAL EXAMINATION:

Vital Signs:	Blood pressure ranged from 154/90 to 168/104
HEENT:	Within normal limits
Chest:	Clear to percussion and auscultation
Heart:	Normal sinus rhythm
Breasts:	Without masses or discharge
Abdomen:	Gravid
Extremities:	Without clubbing or cyanosis. There was +1 edema. Reflexes were +2.
Cervical:	Cervical examination revealed she was 1 cm.

She was admitted and Pitocin was started. Decreased variability and occasional late decelerations were noted. The Pitocin was once again stopped. She began having contractions on her own with recurrent late decelerations. Oxygen was started. She was turned on her side and the late decels continued. Magnesium was started at 6 g and then 1 g an hour for the pre-eclampsia. There was no response to the medication; consequently the patient will undergo a primary low transverse c-section.

Case Study 28

Procedure Note

DATE:	1/05/2010
PREOPERATIVE DIAGNOSES:	Intrauterine pregnancy 36 weeks, pre-eclampsia, fetal distress
POSTOPERATIVE DIAGNOSES:	Intrauterine pregnancy 36 weeks, severe pre-eclampsia, persistent late decelerations with intrauterine growth retardation
PROCEDURE:	Primary low transverse c-section
SURGEON:	Nicolas Todd, M.D.
ANESTHESIA:	Spinal

The patient was taken to the operating room. After adequate level of spinal anesthesia, Foley catheter was inserted. She was prepped and draped in the usual sterile fashion.

A Pfannenstiel incision was made taken down through the subcutaneous tissue to the fascia. The fascia was scored and taken transversely. Rectus muscle was split. The peritoneum was opened.

The uterus was incised in a low transverse manner with delivery of 6–9 Apgar liveborn male. The cord was noted to be thin. The placenta was delivered. It was noted to be small. Uterus, tubes, and ovaries were noted to be normal. The uterus was closed in two separate layers with running locked 0 chromic. Posterior peritoneum was closed with 0 chromic. The uterus was placed back into the abdomen; anterior peritoneum was closed with 0 chromic. The fascia was closed with running 0 Vicryl and the skin was closed with staples.

ESTIMATED BLOOD LOSS: 600 cc

FLUIDS RECEIVED: Ringer's lactate

The patient tolerated the procedure well and left the recovery room in satisfactory condition.

Case Study 28

PROGRESS NOTES:

1/05: Admit note: Gravida 3, para 2, 35-year-old white female admitted for induction of labor due to severe pre-eclampsia. Patient was admitted directly from my office. She is at 36 weeks' gestation by dates. There is evidence of IUGR also. Patient has had a benign prenatal course with the exception of hypertension. Patient was started on Pitocin without success. There were persistent late decelerations noted and patient was transferred to surgical suite for immediate c-section. Patient delivered a 4 pound, 12 ounce liveborn male infant.

1/06: S: Feels well, other than surgical pain.
     O: BP 160/95
     A: Incision clean and dry, no redness or tenderness.
     P: Continue BP meds, advance diet and activity.

1/07: S: Feeling well
     O: Good post-op course, BP 168/104
     A: Accelerated hypertension
     P: Continue meds.

1/09: S: No pain, ambulating
     O: BP better, but still high at 150/98
     A: Continues with elevated BP.
     P: Doing well, will discharge.

1/09: S: Ready for home.
     O: Vitals stable, except BP, afebrile, incisions healing
     A: Hypertension
     P: Discharge, follow hypertension as outpatient.

ORDERS:

1/05: 1. Admit patient to obstetrics.
     2. IV Pitocin for induction
     3. Monitor BP q 15 min
     4. CBC, WBC, Chem profile
     5. Magnesium IV

1/05: 1. Prep for c-section.

1/06: 1. Continue IV fluids.
     2. Start patient on Apresoline and Aldomet for BP control.
     3. Advance diet.

1/07: 1. Continue BP meds.
     2. Discontinue IVs.

1/09: 1. Continue meds.

1/09: 1. Discharge.

Case Study 28

Answer Sheet

DIAGNOSES	ICD-9-CM CODES					
First listed DX				.		
DX 2				.		
DX 3				.		
DX 4				.		

PROCEDURES	CPT CODES					MODIFIERS (If Applicable)	
PR 1						-	
PR 2						-	
PR 3						-	
PR 4						-	
PR 5						-	
PR 6						-	
PR 7						-	

PROVIDE ICD-9-CM CODES FOR DIAGNOSES ONLY

Case Study 29

Inpatient Face Sheet

Patient Name: Nadine Endicott

Admit Date: 1/13/2010

Discharge Date: 1/16/2010

Sex: Female

Age: 86

Disposition: Home with Home Health Care

Admitting Diagnoses:
1. Cellulitis, right lower extremity
2. Acute exacerbation of chronic obstructive pulmonary disease
3. Coronary artery disease
4. Hypothyroidism

Discharge Diagnoses:
1. Cellulitis right lower extremity
2. Acute exacerbation of chronic obstructive pulmonary disease
3. Coronary artery disease
4. Hypothyroidism
5. Gastroesophageal reflux disease
6. Depression
7. Degenerative joint disease

Case Study 29

Discharge Summary

Admitted: 1/13/2010
Discharged: 1/16/2010

DISCHARGE DIAGNOSES:
1. Cellulitis of the right lower extremity
2. Acute exacerbation of chronic obstructive pulmonary disease
3. Coronary artery disease
4. Hypothyroidism
5. Gastroesophageal reflux disease
6. Depression
7. Degenerative joint disease

HISTORY OF PRESENT ILLNESS:
Please see admission history and physical examination. This is an 86-year-old female with a 75 pack/year smoking history and severe chronic obstructive pulmonary disease who is seen for recurrent cellulitis in the right lower extremity, which has not responded to outpatient oral antibiotic and diuretic treatment.

HOSPITAL COURSE:
She was treated with intravenous Lasix, Aldactone, potassium supplement, bronchodilator treatment, Solu-Medrol, and intravenous Claforan. The inflammation of the right lower extremity resolved over the next few days. Her wheezing improved and at rest her lungs were clear. With minimal exertion, she was noted to have wheezing and desaturation with O_2 saturation dropping to 84% on room air. She was advised to have home oxygen therapy.

The edema of the lower extremities resolved and she will be continued on oral Lasix and Aldactone. The patient is discharged home with home health care to follow. Oxygen 2 liters via nasal cannula. Her condition is improved.

DISCHARGE MEDICATIONS:
1. Imdur 60 mg 1/2 tablet q a.m.
2. Synthroid 0.125 mg q.i.d.
3. Albuterol 2.5 mg plus Atrovent 500 mg via nebulizer q3h
4. K-Dur 20 mEq b.i.d.
5. Aldactone 25 mg b.i.d.
6. Lasix 80 mg q a.m. and noon
7. Flovent 220 4 puffs b.i.d. with aerochamber
8. Biaxin 250 mg b.i.d. times 3 days
9. Accolate 20 mg b.i.d.
10. Effexor XR 75 mg q.i.d. for depression

Diet: No added salt. Activity as tolerated.

Plan: She will follow-up in my office in 10 days.

Case Study 29

History and Physical

DATE: 1/13/2010

CHIEF COMPLAINT: Swelling, redness, and heat of the right lower extremity.

HISTORY OF PRESENT ILLNESS:
Patient was seen in my office for swelling, erythema, and heat of the right lower extremity and started on oral antibiotics and diuretics as an outpatient. She has not responded to outpatient treatment, therefore, is admitted for inpatient therapy.

PAST MEDICAL HISTORY:
Surgeries include thyroidectomy, total hip replacement, appendectomy. She also has severe COPD, hypothyroidism, peptic ulcer disease, diverticulosis, coronary artery disease, and mild congestive heart failure.

MEDICATIONS:
Current medications include Synthroid 0.125 mg q.i.d., Imdur 60 mg one-half tablet q.i.d., Azmacort 2 puffs q.i.d., potassium chloride 10 mEq t.i.d., Aldactone 25 mg b.i.d., Lasix 80 mg b.i.d., Colace 100 mg b.i.d., Accolate 20 mg b.i.d., Albuterol 2.5 mg plus Atrovent 500 mcg nebulizer q3h.

ALLERGIES: Iodine

FAMILY HISTORY: Non-contributory

SOCIAL HISTORY: Previous smoker, no tobacco currently. No alcohol.

REVIEW OF SYSTEMS:
History of gastroesophageal reflux disease, peptic ulcer disease, and osteoarthritis.

PHYSICAL EXAMINATION:

Vital Signs:	Blood pressure 168/70, pulse 96, temperature 99.5, respirations 30. She is wheezing and appears dyspneic
HEENT:	Unremarkable
Neck:	Thyroidectomy scar, carotids 2+. No JVD
Chest:	Wheezing bilaterally
Cardiovascular:	Regular rate and rhythm
Abdomen:	Benign
Extremities:	Pitting edema both lower extremities; right greater than left. Right anterior shin is hot, red, and indurated
Neurologic:	Unremarkable

Continued:

LABORATORY DATA:
Electrolytes are normal. Potassium 4.1. White count 9.5, hemoglobin 12.5. Urinalysis is clear. Chest x-ray shows slight atelectasis in the right base, chronic obstructive pulmonary disease. No acute infiltrates nor congestive heart failure noted. Electrocardiogram shows sinus rhythm, right bundle branch block, non-specific ST-T changes.

ASSESSMENT:
1. Cellulitis, right lower extremity
2. Acute exacerbation of COPD
3. Coronary artery disease
4. Hypothyroidism
5. Degenerative joint disease
6. Gastroesophageal reflux disease

PLAN:
Admit for intravenous antibiotics, diuresis, and pulmonary rehab.

Case Study 29

PROGRESS NOTES:

1/13:   Admit Note: 86-year-old female was seen in my office 1 week ago with recurrent cellulitis of her right leg. She was placed on antibiotics and diuretics, however, has had no response to outpatient therapy. She is now admitted for aggressive treatment.

1/14:   S: Complains only of leg pain and SOB.
           O: Afebrile, vital signs stable, wheezing with minimal exertion
           A: Leg looks better, less redness. COPD is severe; will probably require home O_2.
           P: Continue with present treatment.

1/15:   S: Feeling much better, able to ambulate some but easily tires.
           O: Labs within normal limits, vitals remain stable, still with SOB and wheezing on exertion.
           A: Leg has responded well to IV medications.
           P: DC IV and start on p.o. Biaxin.

1/16:   S: Patient desires discharge.
           O: Afebrile, vital signs stable.
           A: Leg looks much better.
           P: Discharge patient.

ORDERS:

1/13:   1. Admit patient to service of Sarah Stamper, M.D.
           2. IV Lasix and Claforan
           3. Respiratory treatments
           4. WBC, CBC, EKG, CXR

1/14:   1. Continue current treatment regime.

1/15:   1. Increase ambulation.
           2. DC IV fluids.
           3. Biaxin 500 mg p.o. twice daily.

1/16:   1. Discharge patient with home health care.

Case Study 29

Answer Sheet

DIAGNOSES	ICD-9-CM CODES					
First listed DX				.		
DX 2				.		
DX 3				.		
DX 4				.		

PROCEDURES	CPT CODES				MODIFIERS (If Applicable)		
PR 1					-		
PR 2					-		
PR 3					-		
PR 4					-		
PR 5					-		
PR 6					-		
PR 7					-		

PROVIDE ICD-9-CM CODE(S) FOR DIAGNOSES ONLY

Case Study 30

Inpatient Face Sheet

Patient Name: Juan Ruiz

Admit Date: 1/04/2010

Discharge Date: 1/07/2010

Sex: Male

Age: 84

Disposition: Expired

Admitting Diagnoses:
1. Pneumonia secondary to possible community-acquired Strep pneumonia
2. Respiratory failure and hypoxia secondary to pneumonia
3. New onset atrial fibrillation
4. History of liver cirrhosis with splenomegaly and some ascites
5. History of myeloproliferative disorder

Discharge Diagnoses:
1. Respiratory failure
2. Streptococcus pneumonia
3. Atrial fibrillation
4. Alcoholic liver cirrhosis
5. Hepatorenal syndrome
6. Streptococcal septicemia
7. Septic shock
8. Urinary Tract Infection, E. coli
9. Uremia
10. Hypertension
11. Hypoglycemia

Case Study 30

Discharge Summary

Admitted: 1/04/2010
Expired: 1/07/2010

ADMITTING DIAGNOSES:
1. Pneumonia secondary to possible community-acquired Strep pneumonia
2. Respiratory failure and hypoxia secondary to pneumonia
3. New onset atrial fibrillation
4. History of liver cirrhosis with splenomegaly and some ascites
5. History of myeloproliferative disorder

DISCHARGE DIAGNOSES:
1. Septic shock with multiorgan failure
2. Streptococcal pneumonia and respiratory failure
3. Escherichia coli urosepsis
4. Hypoglycemia secondary to sepsis and cirrhosis of the liver
5. New onset atrial fibrillation
6. Hepatorenal syndrome

HISTORY OF PRESENT ILLNESS AND HOSPITAL COURSE:
The patient is an 84-year-old Hispanic male who is admitted to the hospital after complaining of shortness of breath, cough with productive sputum, fever and chills, and pain below the breast area. In the emergency room his temperature was 98.3, blood pressure was 140/80, pulse was 140. Patient was noted to be in atrial fibrillation with rapid ventricular rate and required Digoxin intravenous push and Procainamide and cardioversion. Patient went into respiratory failure with hypoxia, requiring intubation and ventilator assistance. Patient was also noted to be severely neutropenic and acidotic in acute renal failure. Patient was seen in the emergency room by cardiology for new onset of atrial fibrillation and cardioverted for this.

The patient's white blood cell count remained 1,700 the day after admission and his echocardiogram Doppler studies showed that he had a left ejection fraction of 60%, mild mitral regurgitation, and tricuspid regurgitation. His prothrombin time was 12 and partial thromboplastic time was 41. His BUN and creatinine went up to 67/2.6 and his hemoglobin and hematocrit remains within normal limits. His calcium did drop to 7.8 along with a decreased albumin. His chest x-ray shows right-sided opacity secondary to his pneumonia. Blood cultures grew gram-positive cocci in chains.

Impression on 1/05/2010 the patient was having Streptococcus pneumonia with multiorgan failure. The patient did have a history of cirrhosis of the liver and splenomegaly and pancytopenia. Patient was started on intravenous dopamine and intravenous hydration because of decreased urine output and increasing renal functions and possible hepatorenal syndrome. The patient remained lethargic, responding to deep painful stimuli. The patient's urine grew Escherichia coli and blood cultures grew Streptococcal pneumonia. His white count increased to 23,900 with Neupogen. His BUN and creatinine went up to 86/4.4. The patient remained hypoglycemic and required D_5 and D_{10} drips. The patient continued to be hypertensive in renal failure and acidotic.

In spite of the aggressive treatment and continued ventilator assistance, the patient expired on 1/07/2010.

Case Study 30

History and Physical

CHIEF COMPLAINT:

The patient was admitted through the emergency room after complaining of increased shortness of breath and productive cough.

HISTORY OF PRESENT ILLNESS:

Patient was well until 2 days prior to admission when he began having shortness of breath, productive cough, fever, and chills. He also complained of pain beneath the breast area. The patient was brought to the emergency room by EMS. In the emergency room the patient's temperature was 98.3, blood pressure was 140/80, pulse was 140. Patient was in atrial fibrillation with rapid ventricular response and was treated with Digoxin 0.5 mg intravenous push and Procainamide. Patient also required cardioversion at 100–200 joules. The patient was also noted to be in acute respiratory distress with hypoxia, requiring intubation and ventilator assistance. The patient's blood work revealed severe neutropenia, acidosis, and renal failure.

At present, the patient is sedated and most of the history is taken from the wife and from previous charts.

PAST MEDICAL HISTORY:

Includes cirrhosis of the liver, likely secondary to excessive alcohol intake. There is also a history of myeloproliferative disorder and a history of ascites. There is no prior history of atrial fibrillation, heart disease, diabetes, gastrointestinal disease, or neurological symptoms.

SOCIAL HISTORY: History of excessive alcohol intake and former smoker.

FAMILY HISTORY: Strong history of colon cancer.

ALLERGIES: None known.

PHYSICAL EXAMINATION: Presently intubated, sedated, and unresponsive.
HEENT: Pupils equal and reactive to light, non-icterus, non-pallor. Orally intubated.
Neck: Supple, no lymphadenopathy, and no jugular venous distention.
Lungs: No rales, no rhonchi
Heart: S1 and S2, no murmur or gallop
Abdomen: Distended, possible ascites present
Extremities: Mild peripheral edema, no rash or ulcers noted

LABORATORY DATA:

Blood gas revealed pH 7.33, pCO_2 34, and pO_2 of 51 and saturation of 86%. The patient's urinalysis is consistent with leukocyte esterase small amount, nitrite negative. His white blood cell count is 0.8, hemoglobin 10.6, hematocrit 31.8, and platelet count 79,000. His sodium is 137, potassium 4.2, chloride 102, glucose is 88, BUN 60, creatinine 2.3, and CPK is 63. Alkaline phosphatase 142, SGOT 185, bilirubin 1.8. Prothrombin time is 13, INR is 1.1, and partial thromboplastin time is 42.

Continued:

IMPRESSION:
1. Pneumonia secondary to community-acquired Strep pneumonia
2. Respiratory failure secondary to pneumonia
3. New onset atrial fibrillation
4. History of cirrhosis of the liver with splenomegaly and ascites
5. History of myeloproliferative syndrome with pancytopenia

PLAN:
1. Patient is admitted to intensive care, intubated, and on ventilator.
2. Patient has already been started on broad-spectrum intravenous antibiotic.

Case Study 30

Progress Notes:

1/04: Admit Note: Elderly white gentleman admitted through the emergency room in acute respiratory failure, pneumonia, sepsis, and septic shock. He also has new onset of atrial fibrillation that required cardioversion in the ER. The patient was intubated and placed on the ventilator. The patient required Digoxin and Procainamide IV push in the ER.

1/05:   S: Unresponsive
       O: Lethargic, responds to deep, painful stimuli. UA positive for E. coli, blood positive for strep. BUN/creatinine 86/4.4, decreased urine output, BP 210/130
       A: Sepsis, UTI, acute renal failure, multiorgan failure, prognosis grave
       P: IV Dopamine and hydration, continue present vent settings

1/06:   S: Unresponsive
       O: White count increasing with Neupogen injections, renal labs worsening, patient less responsive; now hypoglycemic
       A: Respiratory and multiorgan failure, renal failure, hepatorenal syndrome
       P: Prognosis is poor

1/07:   S: Unresponsive
       O: Patient rapidly declining.
       A: Poor prognosis
       P: Continue supportive care.

Case Study 30

Orders:

1/04:   1. Admit patient to CCU.
      2. Follow CCU protocol.
      3. Respiratory services to maintain vent.
      4. Strict I&O.

1/05:   1. IV Dopamine and hydration.
      2. Add Neupogen injections.
      3. Continue present vent settings.
      4. Repeat all labs.

1/06   1. Add D_5 and D_{10} drips for hypoglycemia.
      2. Continue all previous orders.

<u>**Case Study 30**</u>

Answer Sheet

DIAGNOSES	ICD-9-CM CODES					
First listedDX				.		
DX 2				.		
DX 3				.		
DX 4				.		

PROCEDURES	CPT CODES				MODIFIERS (If Applicable)		
PR 1					-		
PR 2					-		
PR 3					-		
PR 4					-		
PR 5					-		
PR 6					-		
PR 7					-		

PROVIDE ICD-9-CM CODE(S) FOR DIAGNOSES ONLY

Case Study 31

Inpatient Face Sheet

Patient Name: Carmelita Sargento

Admit Date: 1/05/2010

Discharge Date: 1/10/2010

Sex: Female

Age: 82

Disposition: Skilled Nursing Facility for Rehab

Admitting Diagnoses:
1. Cerebral infarction
2. Hypertension
3. Atrial fibrillation
4. Osteoarthritis

Discharge Diagnoses:
1. Left middle cerebral artery occlusion with cerebral infarction
2. Atrial fibrillation
3. Mitral regurgitation
4. Urinary tract infection
5. Pacemaker in situ
6. Bilateral carotid artery disease
7. Hypertension
8. Osteoarthritis
9. Right hemiplegia

Case Study 31

Discharge Summary

Admitted: 1/05/2010

Discharge: 1/10/2010

DISCHARGE DIAGNOSES:
1. Left middle cerebral artery occlusion with cerebral infarction
2. Atrial fibrillation
3. Mitral regurgitation
4. Urinary tract infection
5. Pacemaker in situ
6. Bilateral carotid artery disease
7. Hypertension
8. Osteoarthritis

HISTORY OF PRESENT ILLNESS:
This is an 82-year-old Hispanic female who was found on the floor at her home. She had right-sided weakness, stool incontinence, and garbled speech. The CAT scan was positive for infarction with left basal ganglia hemorrhage.

HISTORY AND PHYSICAL: See H&P

MEDICATIONS: Lanoxin

ALLERGIES: Sulfa

PHYSICAL EXAMINATION:
Elderly white female, hypertensive 196/73. Pale subconjuntival and nail beds. Garbled speech with weakness on the right.

LABORATORY DATA:
The patient's admission laboratory data were within normal limits, with the exception of hemoglobin 16.5, hematocrit 48.8; 100 mg of protein, a large amount of occult blood and 5 to 9 red blood cells on urinalysis; elevated globulin of 4.2, alkaline phosphatase 161, CPK 346. The Lanoxin was subtherapeutic at 0.6. Drug screening was negative. During hospitalization there was a transient mild leukocytosis of 14,700 and hemoglobin returned to normal. Sedimentation rate was elevated at 39 on 1/12/2010. The PTT rose to therapeutic and vacillated throughout.

A repeat urinalysis revealed a large amount of leukocytes, continued occult blood, and red blood cells up to 50+ with 20 to 29 white blood cells and moderate bacteria. Urine culture revealed Escherichia coli.

The sodium dropped as low as 126, but rebounded to 132 by 1/08/2010. The globulin returned to normal. The albumin dropped slightly below normal. The alkaline phosphatase returned to normal. The CPK levels steadily decreased to 213 and 186, with CK-MB remaining within normal limits.

Continued:

RADIOLOGY REPORTS:
The chest x-ray revealed cardiomegaly, several calcified granuloma in the right upper, mid, and lower lung zones, left-sided pacemaker in satisfactory position and no acute changes.

The CAT scan of the brain, non-contrast, showed acute left middle cerebral artery infarction with hemorrhage within the left basal ganglia. A repeat CAT scan was unchanged.

A KUB showed nasogastric tube in satisfactory position, non-specific bowel gas pattern. A repeat KUB did reveal the nasogastric tube to be coiled in the stomach on 1/09/2010.

A carotid duplex Doppler examination showed moderate bilateral carotid occlusive disease with plaquing at the right carotid bifurcation, left common carotid, and carotid bifurcation, but no evidence of flow-restricting lesion, stenosis of less than 35%, external carotid stenosis approaching 40% to 50%, antegrade vertebral artery blood flow bilaterally, no change since January of last year.

An echocardiogram revealed hypokinetic septal and apical wall motion, aortic valve sclerosis, mitral annular calcification, and moderate mitral regurgitation.

An electrocardiogram revealed pacemaker rhythm with rate of 58 per minute, left ventricular hypertrophy, ST-T abnormalities, Q waves in V1 and V2, diffuse T wave abnormalities, consistent with ischemia. The subsequent repeats showed atrial fibrillation with transient rapid ventricular response and premature ventricular contractions.

HOSPITAL COURSE:
The patient was admitted on 1/05/2010. She was started on routine and intensive care unit orders, neuro checks, Lanoxin, Decadron intravenously, multivitamins, intravenous hydration.

It was noted by neurological consult that the patient had two cerebrovascular accidents, with the atrial fibrillation as the likely source. Anticoagulation was initiated cautiously after blood pressure was brought under control. Intravenous Nipride was begun for blood pressure control. Heparin was begun. Catapres was added for additional blood pressure control and Decadron was also added.

The patient remained afebrile other than intermittent temperatures of 100.

The patient was evaluated by speech pathology. She was noted to have severe receptive and fluent aphasia. Speech therapy will be initiated.

Nasogastric tube was inserted for administration of medications due to lack of poor oral intake and dysphagia, with some aspiration potential noted on video swallow study. Following improvement in the patient's condition, nasogastric tube was removed and diet was adjusted. Dysphagia cleared by discharge.

The patient began to improve, but remained aphasic and with right-sided hemiplegia. It was decided that she would require intensive rehab, so she was transferred to a rehab facility for continued physical, speech, and occupational therapy. Patient is to be continued on pureed diet.

DISCHARGE MEDICATIONS:

Catapres TTS Patch 0.4 mg patch q weekly
Lanoxin 0.125 mg daily
Norvasc 5 mg daily
Multivitamins one daily
Floxin 200 mg q12h times 5 days

Case Study 31

History and Physical

CHIEF COMPLAINT: Garbled speech and right-sided weakness.

HISTORY OF PRESENT ILLNESS:
This 82-year-old Hispanic female was found on the floor by her neighbors and brought to the emergency room via EMS. A CAT scan of the brain was completed, which revealed a left MCA infarct with hemorrhage into the left basal ganglia.

CURRENT MEDICATIONS: Lanoxin

PAST MEDICAL HISTORY:
Positive for hypertension, atrial fibrillation, and degenerative osteoarthritis.

SOCIAL HISTORY: Non-smoker, occasional alcohol

PHYSICAL EXAMINATION:
Elderly white female who is in acute distress. She has garbled speech.

REVIEW OF SYSTEMS:
Vital Signs: Blood pressure 199/73, pulse 78, respiratory rate of 18, afebrile
HEENT: Pupils equal and reactive to light, sclerae is not icteric. Subconjunctival is pale
Lungs: Clear
Heart: Regular sinus rhythm with an irregular rate
Abdomen: Soft, benign. No organomegaly or mass to palpation
Extremities: No edema, no varicosity. Nail beds are pale
Neuro: Good DTR, negative Babinski

IMPRESSION: Acute cerebrovascular accident

PLAN:
1. Admit to intensive care.
2. Serial electrocardiograms and cardiac enzymes
3. Neuro checks q2h
4. Carotid duplex
5. Echo to heart. EEG

Case Study 31

Progress Notes:

1/05:   Admit Note: Patient admitted with left MCA infarction. Patient also has severe hypertension. Please see H&P for complete details.

1/06:   S: Non-communicative.
          O: Sed rate elevated to 39, rest of lab data within normal limits. Carotid Doppler revealed bilateral occlusive disease, but not of any clinical significance.
          A: Patient still aphasic with right-sided paralysis.
          P: Repeat CT of brain and do KUB, ECHO.

1/07:   S: Remains aphasic.
          O: BP remains high, but slowly coming under control. NG tube in good position per KUB. Repeat CT of brain unchanged from admission CT. ECHO revealed moderate mitral regurgitation.
          A: Patient is slowly improving.
          P: Transfer to neuro floor. Add Catapres for additional BP control.

1/08:   S: Feels better after transfer out of ICU.
          O: BP better controlled. Repeat UA positive for E. coli. Some strength returning on right. Sodium dropped to 126.
          A: UTI, hyponatremia, dysphagia clearing.
          P: Remove NG tube and advance diet. Start Cipro p.o. 500 mg for UTI. Monitor sodium level.

1/09:   S: No new complaints
          O: Labs improving, vitals stable
          A: Tolerating advanced diet.
          P: Discharge planning for intensive rehab, patient agreeable.

1/10:   S: Ready for transfer to rehab.
          O: Patient's condition is stable. BP better controlled. Sodium level normal.
          A: Patient will continue with speech and physical therapy at rehab center.
          P: Transfer patient.

Case Study 31

Orders:

1/05: 1. Admit to ICU
     2. Neuro checks q2h
     3. Serial EKGs and cardiac enzymes
     4. CXR
     5. ICU protocol
     6. Carotid Doppler
     7. IV Decadron, Lanoxin, Nipride, and fluids at 83 cc/h

1/06: 1. Repeat CT brain.
     2. KUB, ECHO.
     3. Continue present meds.
     4. Repeat UA.

1/07: 1. Add Catapres.
     2. Have speech pathology evaluated.

1/08: 1. Remove NG tube, advance diet.
     2. Cipro for UTI.

1/09: 1. Case management for discharge planning.

1/10: 1. Transfer to rehab.

Case Study 31

Answer Sheet

DIAGNOSES	ICD-9-CM CODES					
First listed DX				.		
DX 2				.		
DX 3				.		
DX 4				.		

PROCEDURES	CPT CODES				MODIFIERS (If Applicable)		
PR 1					-		
PR 2					-		
PR 3					-		
PR 4					-		
PR 5					-		
PR 6					-		
PR 7					-		

PROVIDE ICD-9-CM CODE(S) FOR DIAGNOSES ONLY

Case Study 32

Inpatient Face Sheet

Patient Name: Juanita Horton

Admit Date: 1/10/2010

Discharge Date: 1/13/2010

Sex: Female

Age: 79

Disposition: ACLF

Admitting Diagnoses:
1. Syncope
2. Hypertension
3. Chronic obstructive pulmonary disease (COPD)
4. Hyperlipidemia
5. Congestive heart failure (CHF)

Discharge Diagnoses:
1. Syncope, undetermined etiology
2. Chronic obstructive pulmonary disease (COPD)
3. Congestive heart failure (CHF)
4. Hypertension
5. Hyperlipidemia

Case Study 32

Discharge Summary

ADMITTED: 1/10/2010

DISCHARGED: 1/13/2010

DISCHARGE DIAGNOSES:
1. Syncope, undetermined etiology
2. Malnourishment
3. CHF
4. COPD
5. Hypertension
6. Hyperlipidemia

PROCEDURES: None

HISTORY OF PRESENT ILLNESS:
Patient presented to the emergency department with complaint of weakness and feeling of passing out for 2 days' duration. Patient was admitted to telemetry to rule out cardiac origin of syncope. Patient is also under current treatment for COPD, CHF, hypertension, and hyperlipidemia.

HOSPITAL COURSE:
Patient was continued on home medications for treatment of chronic illnesses as documented above. Lab values were within normal limits, with the exception of low protein and albumin indicative of mild malnourishment. In addition, the lipids were elevated. Patient was started on Ensure to address the malnourishment and Pravacol was increased to 40 mg per day to bring the lipids under control. EKG and ECHO were insignificant in determining a cause of the syncope. The patient's hypertension, COPD, and CHF remained under control while the patient was in the hospital. In light of not finding a cause of the syncope and the patient's weakened state from the malnourishment, it was recommended that she enter an ACLF temporarily until her strength returned and she was able to return to her own home. She was in agreement with this and arrangements were made for discharge to an ACLF. She is to follow a high-protein, low-fat diet and continue with Ensure. Activity as tolerated.

<u>Case Study 32</u>

History & Physical

Date: 1/10/2010

CHIEF COMPLAINT: Weakness and syncope

HISTORY OF PRESENT ILLNESS:
This 79-year-old woman presented to the emergency room with complaints of weakness and syncope. She was accompanied by a friend, who provided most of the current history. The friend states that the patient has had several episodes of "passing out" in the last 2 days. The patient has not fallen during these episodes, so there has been no injury as a result of these syncopal episodes.

PAST MEDICAL HISTORY:
Significant for COPD, for which she uses inhalers and nebulizer treatment. Also is treated for hypertension, CHF, and high cholesterol. Patient has had a hysterectomy and cholecystectomy.

FAMILY HISTORY:
Mother deceased at 82 years of age with a myocardial infarction. Father deceased at 45 due to coal miner's disease. Patient has no siblings.

SOCIAL HISTORY: 100 pack/year smoking history, quit in 1995. No alcohol use.

MEDICATIONS: Lasix, Pravacol, potassium, and Cardizem

ALLERGIES: None known

PHYSICAL EXAMINATION: Blood pressure 110/75, pulse 88, respirations 18, temperature 98.2. Patient appears malnourished.

REVIEW OF SYSTEMS:
HEENT: Pupils equal and reactive to light. Pale conjunctiva. Moist mucous membranes.
NECK: Supple without masses.
LUNGS: Decreased breath sounds.
HEART: Regular rate and rhythm.
ADOMEN: Soft, non-tender. Bowel sounds present.
EXTREMITIES: No cyanosis or clubbing.

IMPRESSION:
1. Syncope, etiology to be determined
2. Hypertension
3. COPD
4. Hyperlipidemia
5. CHF

PLAN:
1. Admit to telemetry.
2. Continue with home meds.

Case Study 32

Progress Notes:

1/10:   Admit Note: Patient admitted via emergency room to telemetry for syncope, undetermined etiology. Patient to continue with home meds for CHF, COPD, hypertension, and hyperlipidemia.

1/11:   S: No syncope while here.
O: EKG showed sinus rhythm with RBBB. ECHO WNL Chest x-ray, no CHF, known COPD. Hypertension under control. Vital signs good. Chem profile significant for low
protein and albumin with HDL of 281.
A: No cardiac reason for syncope. Patient is malnourished.
P: Continue with current treatment. Add Ensure to diet as a supplement.

1/12:   S: No complaints. No further syncopal episodes.
O: Rhythm remains unchanged. Condition stable.
A: Repeat labs within normal limits, except for protein and albumin, which are still low.
P: Case management to arrange transfer to ACLF until patient can return home.

1/13:   Discharge Note: No cardiac or chemical explanation for syncope. Patient to be discharged to an ACLF until she can return to her own home. Continue with dietary supplement in light of mild malnourishment.

Orders:

1/10:   1. Admit patient to service of Dr. James Mitchell, per Dr. Lyle Douglas, emergency room physician.
2. Place patient on telemetry.
3. Chem profile, CBC.
4. Continue with patient's home medications.
5. EKG, chest x-ray, ECHO.

1/11:   1. Repeat labs.
2. Provide patient with Ensure.
3. Case management to assist with discharge plans.

1/12:   1. Discontinue telemetry.
2. Arrange transfer to ACLF tomorrow.

1/13:   1. Discharge today to ACLF.

Case Study 32

Answer Sheet

DIAGNOSES	ICD-9-CM CODES					
First listed DX				.		
DX 2				.		
DX 3				.		
DX 4				.		

PROCEDURES	CPT CODES					MODIFIERS (If Applicable)	
PR 1						-	
PR 2						-	
PR 3						-	
PR 4						-	
PR 5						-	
PR 6						-	
PR 7						-	

**PROVIDE ICD-9-CM CODES FOR DIAGNOSES AND
CPT CODE(S) FOR PROCEDURE(S)**

Case Study 33

Inpatient Face Sheet

Patient Name:	Carl Jenkins
Admit Date:	1/3/2010
Discharge Date:	1/6/2010
Sex:	Male
Age:	60
Disposition:	Home with Home Health Care

Admit Diagnoses:
1. Fracture right hip
2. Ascites
3. Decubitus ulcer

Discharge Diagnoses:
1. Intertrochanteric fracture right hip
2. Decubitus ulcer
3. Ascites in alcoholic liver cirrhosis
4. Hyperammonemia
5. Chronic obstructive pulmonary disease (COPD)
6. Right lower quadrant abdominal mass, etiology unknown

Procedures:
1. Closed reduction with internal fixation of fracture right hip
2. Paracentesis

Case Study 33

DISCHARGE SUMMARY

ADMITTED: 1/03/2010
DISCHARGED: 1/06/2010

DISCHARGE DIAGNOSES:
1. Intertrochanteric fracture right hip
2. Severe COPD
3. Chronic alcoholic cirrhosis with massive ascites
4. Right lower quadrant abdominal mass, etiology unknown

PROCEDURES:
1. Closed reduction with internal fixation of fracture of right hip
2. Paracentesis

HOSPITAL COURSE:
This elderly gentleman had a fall at home resulting in an intertrochanteric fracture of the right hip. He was transported to the emergency room and placed in Buck's traction. The patient was typed and crossed for six units of blood. He received two units pre-operatively. On post-operative day two, he underwent paracentesis for removal of 2.5 liters of ascites. The post-operative course was complicated by a rise in ammonia. This came down with Lactulose. The patient also has two open areas, stage II decubitus on his coccyx and buttock. The bases are clean and dry. These are being treated with Duoderm.

On the day of discharge his ammonia was 47. He is comfortable and ambulating with a walker. His abdomen is less tense. He is afebrile and vital signs are stable. The hip wound is healing. He is discharged on Percodan, and routine medications of Lasix 40 mg b.i.d., Aldactone 100 mg q.i.d. wit K-Dur 20 mEq in the morning and 10 mEq in the evening.

He is discharged on a low-salt diet with moderate fluid restriction. He will be seen by home health care. The patient will see me in my office in 10 days and will undergo a colonoscopy in 4 to 6 weeks to investigate the abdominal mass.

Case Study 33

History and Physical

CHIEF COMPLAINT: Fell at home, presents now with hip pain

HISTORY OF PRESENT ILLNESS:
This is a 60-year-old male who fell at home this morning with immediate pain in the right hip. There was no loss of consciousness. In the emergency room he was found to have an intertrochanteric fracture. He is admitted to the hospital for definitive evaluation and treatment.

PAST MEDICAL HISTORY:
Significant for long-standing alcoholic liver disease with cirrhosis and ascites. He was found to have a right lower quadrant mass by his gastroenterologist.

ALLERGIES: Tylenol PM

MEDICATIONS:
Lasix 40 mg b.i.d., Aldactone 100 mg q.i.d. with K-Dur 10 mEq b.i.d., low-salt diet, moderate fluid restriction to 1200 cc q.i.d.

SOCIAL HISTORY:
No alcohol in the past 5 years. One pack of tobacco per day. Patient is retired.

PHYSICAL EXAMINATION: Blood pressure 110/70, pulse 88, marked muscle wasting.

REVIEW OF SYSTEMS:
HEENT:	Within normal limits.
Neck:	Supple, no adenopathy
Chest:	Clear
Abdomen:	Marked ascites, liver spans about 2-3 fingers below costal margin and is firm.
Extremities:	Patient is in Buck's traction with foreshortening of the right leg.

LABORATORY DATA:
Random blood sugar 145, alkaline phosphatase 179. Bilirubin and SGOT are normal. The white blood cell count is 15,400, hemoglobin of 8.8 with a hematocrit of 26.2, MCV is 72, MCH is 23.9.

IMPRESSION:
1. Fall resulting in an intertrochanteric fracture right hip
2. Chronic cirrhosis
3. COPD, with tobacco dependency
4. Right lower quadrant abdominal mass, will work up

PLAN:
1. Type and cross 6 units, transfuse 2
2. Gastrointestinal consult regarding paracentesis
3. Closed reduction with internal fixation of fracture of right hip

<u>Case Study 33</u>

PROCEDURE NOTE

DATE OF PROCEDURE: 1/03/2010

PREOPERATIVE DIAGNOSIS: Intertrochanteric fracture, right hip

POSTOPERATIVE DIAGNOSIS: Intertrochanteric fracture, right hip

SURGEON: Alexander Warren, M.D.

ANESTHESIA: Spinal

ANESTHESIOLOGIST: Norma Jean, M.D.

ESTIMATED BLOOD LOSS: 350 cc
                                No replacement

DESCRIPTION OF PROCEDURE:

After satisfactory induction of spinal anesthesia with the patient lying on the fracture table, traction applied to the right lower extremity with internal rotation, reducing the fracture. The left leg abducted to allow the image intensifier to come into view in both AP and lateral positions.

Standard lateral incision was made, taken through the skin and subcutaneous tissue, the fascia slit longitudinally. The vastus lateralis split longitudinally, coming along the proximal aspect of the femur. Guide wire inserted in good position, both AP and lateral. This was then reamed to accept the 95 mm barrel screw. A 135-degree four-hole plate was attached. The titanium cortical side screws were inserted. Good fixation was obtained.

The area was irrigated with saline and antibiotic solution. A medium set screw was put in place. Constavac drain was inserted through a separate puncture site. Vastus lateralis was closed with interrupted 0 Vicryl suture, the fascia with interrupted 0 Vicryl suture, the subcutaneous tissue with 00 Vicryl and the skin with staples. Neosporin, Adaptic, bulky 4 x 4s, ABDs and Mefix dressing applied.

The patient tolerated the procedure well and left the operating room in good condition.

Case Study 33

PROGRESS NOTES

1/6:   Admit Note: Patient is admitted via the emergency room after suffering a fall at home, resulting in intertrochanteric fracture of the right femur. Patient was a former drinker, now has liver cirrhosis and ascites. Patient is also a smoker with COPD. Patient is admitted for definitive treatment of hip fracture. Admitting H/H is 10.8/37.2, will T&C six units and transfuse two prior to surgery.

1/7:   S: Only complaint is surgical pain.
       O: H/H is stable, will not require blood transfusions. Abdomen is very tense. Stable respiratory status. No shortness of breath and good lung sounds.
       A: Ascites, stable from surgical standpoint.
       P: Begin ambulation with minimal weight bearing, will do paracentesis tomorrow.

1/8:   S: No complaints
       O: Vital signs stable, afebrile, incision clean and dry, ammonia elevated
       A: Paracentesis with removal of 2.5 liters ascitic fluid
       P: Continue ambulation, give Lactulose for elevated ammonia

1/9:   S: Doing well.
       O: Vitals stable, ammonia level within normal limits, abdomen less tense, afebrile
       A: Good post-operative recovery
       P: Will plan discharge for tomorrow.

1/10: Patient to be discharged home with home health care

ORDERS:

1/6:   1.   Admit patient.
       2.   Continue Buck's traction.
       3.   Prepare for surgery this afternoon.
       4.   Cross and type six units, transfuse two prior to surgery.
       5.   Respiratory treatments prior to surgery
       6.   CBC, WBC, Chem profile

1/7:   1.   Incentive spirometer q4h
       2.   Begin ambulation
       3.   Ammonia level

1/8:   1.   Paracentesis tray to bedside
       2.   Lactulose for elevated ammonia level

1/9:   1.   Continue with current orders.

1/10: 1.   Discharge home with home health care.

Case Study 33

Answer Sheet

DIAGNOSES	ICD-9-CM CODES					
First listed DX				.		
DX 2				.		
DX 3				.		
DX 4				.		

PROCEDURES	CPT CODES					MODIFIERS (If Applicable)	
PR 1						-	
PR 2						-	
PR 3						-	
PR 4						-	
PR 5						-	
PR 6						-	
PR 7						-	

PROVIDE ICD-9-CM CODES FOR DIAGNOSES ONLY

Case Study 34

Inpatient Face Sheet

Patient Name: Holly Blaize

Admit Date: 1/02/2010

Discharge Date: 1/05/2010

Sex: Female

Age: 42

Disposition: Transfer to Psychiatric Facility

Admitting Diagnoses:
1. Drug overdose
2. Diet-controlled diabetes
3. Peripheral vascular disease

Discharge Diagnoses:
1. Accidental overdose of Haldol and Xanax
2. Diet controlled diabetes
3. Peripheral vascular disease

Case Study 34

Discharge Summary

Admitted: 1/02/2010
Discharged: 1/05/2010

Discharge Diagnoses:
1. Accidental poisoning of Haldol and Xanax
2. Type 2 diabetes
3. Peripheral vascular disease
4. Depression

HISTORY:
This 42-year-old female was admitted to intensive care following overdose of Haldol and Xanax. Patient is currently treated for depression. See history and physical for complete details.

HOSPITAL COURSE:
This patient was admitted to the intensive care unit following ingestion of Haldol and Xanax. Patient was given IV fluids and Narcan to counteract the overdose of medication. She responded well to the Narcan and the day following admission was more alert and less confused. She remained in the ICU for one additional day until she was transferred to the medical floor. Her laboratory results were within normal limits on transfer to the medical unit. The patient denied a suicide attempt; however, in light of her ongoing depression she is being transferred to the psychiatric facility for continued treatment. Her condition from a medical standpoint was stable upon transfer.

Case Study 34

History & Physical

CHIEF COMPLAINT:
This patient was brought to my office by her friend who had stopped by her home because she was unable to reach her by phone. The friend states that the patient was exhibiting inappropriate behavior and told her that she had taken some pills. I sent the patient to the hospital as a direct admission because of her mental status changes and possible drug overdose.

HISTORY OF PRESENT ILLNESS:
Upon presentation to my office, the patient had become lethargic and was becoming difficult to arouse. She has a known history of depression and was treated with antidepressants. It is unknown at this time if she has overmedicated herself with the antidepressants. This patient has a history of peripheral vascular disease and diet controlled diabetes.

ALLERGIES: None

PAST MEDICAL HISTORY: As indicated above.

CURRENT MEDICATIONS: Haldol and Xanax

SOCIAL HISTORY: Lives alone. No tobacco or alcohol use.

REVIEW OF SYSTEMS:
GENERAL:	Well-developed, somewhat unkempt woman. She is confused. Somewhat lethargic and difficult to arouse and then becomes combative.
VITAL SIGNS:	Temperature of 99.9, blood pressure 120/90. Pulse 118. Respirations at 21.
HEENT:	Within normal limits.
NECK:	No lymphadenopathy.
CARDIAC:	Sinus tachycardia.
LUNGS:	Clear to auscultation
ABDOMEN:	No masses, bowel sounds present
EXTREMITIES:	No cyanosis, edema or clubbing
SKIN:	Unremarkable

IMPRESSION: 1. Drug overdose, Haldol and Xanax
                 2. Peripheral vascular disease
                 3. Type 2 diabetes

PLAN: 1. Admit patient to intensive care
           2. Standing ICU orders
           3. Drug screen

Case Study 34

Progress Notes:

1/2:   Admit Note: Patient admitted to intensive care for suspected drug overdose of Haldol and Xanax. Prescriptions had been issued 2 days ago. Multiple dosages were missing from the bottles and drug screen is positive for antidepressants. Patient has been under treatment for depression. Monitor patient in ICU.

1/3:   S: Patient does not recall what brought her to the hospital.
       O: Patient awake, less confused, vital signs improved, labs improving.
       A: Patient somewhat improved.
       P: Continue ICU monitoring and with current meds and IVs. Case management to arrange transfer to psychiatric facility when medically stable.

1/4:   S: Feels much better, but admits to feeling depressed. Denied suicide attempt.
       O: Patient more alert today. Vital signs good. All labs WNL.
       A: Transfer out of ICU today.
       P: Transfer to psych hospital in the morning.

1/5:   Discharge Note: Patient is medically stable for transfer to psychiatric facility following overdose of Haldol and Xanax.

Case Study 34

Orders:

1/2: 1. Admit to ICU
2. Standing ICU orders
3. IV NS at 125 cc/h
4. Narcan IV
5. Accuchecks q 4 hours
6. Drug screen

1/3: 1. Decrease IV rate to 75 cc/h

2. Case management for discharge planning

1/4: 1. Transfer to medical floor.
2. DC IVs.

1/5: 1. Transfer to psychiatric facility under the care of Dr. Sierra Seybolt.

Case Study 34

Answer Sheet

DIAGNOSES	ICD-9-CM CODES					
First listed DX				.		
DX 2				.		
DX 3				.		
DX 4				.		

PROCEDURES	CPT CODES					MODIFIERS (If Applicable)		
PR 1						-		
PR 2						-		
PR 3						-		
PR 4						-		
PR 5						-		
PR 6						-		
PR 7						-		

> **PROVIDE ICD-9-CM CODES FOR DIAGNOSES AND
> CPT CODE(S) FOR PROCEDURE(S)**

Case Study 35

INPATIENT FACE SHEET

Patient Name:	Elmer Miller
Admit Date:	1/01/2010
Discharge Date:	1/13/2010
Age:	79
Sex:	Male
Disposition:	Home with Home Health Care

Admission Diagnoses:

1. Acute bronchial asthma in exacerbation
2. Hypoxemia, hypercapnia
3. Suspected chronic obstructive pulmonary disease
4. Rule out pulmonary embolism.
5. Hypertension
6. Hyperlipidemia

Discharge Diagnoses:

1. Acute bronchial asthma with acute exacerbation
2. Tracheobronchitis
3. Chronic hypoxemia
4. Suspect underlying chronic obstructive pulmonary disease
5. History of hypertension
6. Hyperlipidemia

Procedures Performed:

1. Broncoscopy with biopsies and lavage

Case Study 35

DISCHARGE SUMMARY

ADMITTED: 1/1/2010

DISCHARGED: 1/13/2010

DISCHARGE DIAGNOSES:

1. Acute bronchial asthma with acute exacerbation
2. Tracheobronchitis
3. Chronic hypoxemia
4. Suspect underlying chronic obstructive pulmonary disease
5. History of hypertension
6. Hyperlipidemia

ADMITTING DIAGNOSES:

1. Acute bronchial asthma in exacerbation
2. Hypoxemia, hypercapnia
3. Suspected chronic obstructive pulmonary disease
4. Rule out pulmonary embolism
5. Hypertension
6. Hyperlipidemia

PROCEDURE:

1. Bronchoscopy with lavage and biopsy

HISTORY OF PRESENT ILLNESS:
This is a 79-year-old male patient with above-mentioned medical problems who now presents with increasing shortness of breath, cough, wheezing, and respiratory distress. He has been on multiple bronchodilators and inhaled steroids, including Flovent, nebulizer, theophylline, and a small dose of prednisone.

HOSPITAL COURSE:
This patient was admitted with increasing shortness of breath. He was not responding to outpatient medical therapy. He was placed on Albuterol nebulized respiratory treatment and started on a short course of pulse intravenous steroids, given mucolytics expectorants and continued on theophylline. He was cultured and placed on intravenous Claforan initially, empirically; he was otherwise continued on treatment for hypertension. A therapeutic bronchoscopy was performed with evidence of thick, purulent mucous plugs widespread on both sides, some narrowing of the left lower lobe bronchus also noted with some inflammation. Biopsies were negative for malignancy. He was continued on Mucomyst at this point, nebulized respiratory treatments, chest physiotherapy, and intravenous Solu-Medrol.

Following several days of aggressive treatment, he started to improve and was less short of breath; bronchospasm was resolving and was discharged on January 13.

Case Study 35

DISCHARGE SUMMARY

Continued:

PERTINENT EXAM:	Audible wheezing, coughed continuously, tachycardic, tachypneic, afebrile.
VITAL SIGNS:	Blood pressure stable.
HEENT:	Revealed postnasal drip.
NECK:	No jugular venous distention.
LUNGS:	Diffuse wheezing, rhonchi, and rales.
HEART:	Regular.
ABDOMEN:	Soft.
EXTREMITIES:	No edema.

REVIEW OF LABORATORY DATA:
The bronchoscopy cytology revealed no malignancy. The arterial blood gases on room air: pH 7.48, pCO_2 36, pO_2 56, bicarb 26.4, and saturation 92.3%. Complete blood count: white blood cell count 9,800. Hemoglobin 15, hematocrit 47.1, and platelet count normal. Follow–up complete blood count remained stable. Chemistries: blood urea nitrogen 17, creatinine 1.4. Troponin I normal on a serial basis. Albumin 2.4 to 3.3. Liver functions normal. theophylline level 19.2. Urinalysis: yellow and clear; microscopic blood noted, protein negative, nitrite negative, leukocyte esterase a small amount detected. Sputum revealed Candida. Urine culture: no growth. Sputum for acid-fast bacilli: test still pending at this time although smears were negative. The chest revealed a new hazy opacity of the left mid lung, in the lower lung area, possibly fusion or atelectasis. This persisted on follow-up.

Electrocardiogram: sinus rhythm, sinus tachycardia. While on telemetry the patient was in sinus rhythm.

MEDICATIONS ON DISCARGE:

1. Prednisone 30 mg daily for 4 days, then 20 mg daily for 4 days, then 10 mg daily
2. Flovent 220 mcg three puffs twice daily
3. Albuterol treatments four times daily
4. Norvasc 5 mg daily
5. Lasix 40 mg half tablet daily
6. Potassium 10 mEq daily
7. Nasonex spray two puffs daily
8. theophylline 200 mg twice daily

ACITIVITY: As tolerated.

Case Study 35

HISTORY AND PHYSICIAL

ADMISSION DATE: 1/01/2010

CHIEF COMPLAINT: Shortness of breath, wheezing, cough, and chest congestion.

HISTORY OF PRESENT ILLNESS:
This is a 79-year-old male with multiple admissions for respiratory problems and exacerbation of asthma. Presented to the emergency room because of increasing shortness of breath, cough, wheezing, and respiratory distress. Apparently he has been on multiple bronchodilators and inhaled steroids, including Flovent, nebulizer, theophylline, and a small dose of Prednisone a day. In spite of the outpatient treatment, his symptoms continued to worsen. He was admitted to the hospital for further treatment.

PAST MEDICAL HISTORY:
Past medical history is positive for long-standing bronchial asthma with chronic exacerbation, steroid-dependent asthma. He also had history of tracheobronchitis, hypertension, and hyperlipidemia.

MEDICATIONS AT HOME:
Flovent 220 micrograms 2 puffs twice a day, but he is not using regularly. Nebulizer 4 times a day, Norvasc 5 milligrams once a day, Lasix 40 milligrams ½ tablet once a day, potassium 10 milliequivalent once a day, calcium t.i.d., theophylline 200 milligrams b.i.d., and Prednisone 5 milligrams once a day.

ALLERGIES: None.

SOCIAL HISTORY: Does not smoke. Never smoked.

REVIEW OF SYSTEMS:

HEENT:	Revealed postnasal drip.
NECK:	No jugular venous distension.
LUNGS:	Bilateral diffuse wheezing, rhonchi, and rales.
HEART:	Regular rhythm.
ABDOMEN:	Soft.
EXTREMITIES:	No edema.
GASTROINTESTINAL:	No gastritis, gastroesophageal reflux, occasional indigestion; no ulcer.
RESPIRATORY:	As mentioned in the history.
CARDIAC:	History of hypertension, but no history of angina, coronary artery disease. Does not have any chest pain. He had an echocardiogram in 2001, which was normal with ejection fraction of 60 percent.
MUSCULOSKELETAL:	Negative.
NEUROLOGIC:	Negative for stroke, transient ischemic attack, headache, dizziness, or syncope.
GENITOURINARY:	Negative. The rest of review of systems is negative.

Case Study 35

HISTORY AND PHYSICIAL

Continued:

PHYSICAL EXAMINATION:
Elderly male who is in acute distress with audible wheeze. He coughs continuously. He is tachycardiac, tachypneic, afebrile. Vitals stable otherwise.

The labs, x-rays, etc., were reviewed.

IMPRESSION:
1. Acute bronchial asthma and exacerbation.
2. Severe hypoxemia, hypercapnia. Rule out due to chronic obstructive pulmonary disease, bronchospasm. Rule out other causes, like pulmonary embolism.

PLAN: Will give IV steroids, IV antibiotics, nebulizer treatment, and oxygen.
          Get a spiral CT scan to rule out pulmonary emboli.
          Continue other treatment, and will follow him closely.

Case Study 35

PROCEDURE REPORT

DATE: 1/02/2010

ENDOSCOPIST: Dr. Brandon Douglas

PROCEDURE: Bronchoscopy

INDICATION: Left lower lobe collapse, due to mucous plug

ANESTHESIA: Dr. Jeffrey Cottrell

DESCRIPTION OF PROCEDURE:
After the anesthesiologist anesthetized the patient, the Olympus bronchoscope was introduced through the bite block into the oral cavity. The upper airway was seen and was unremarkable. Cords were sprayed with Xylocaine. The scope was passed through the cords into the trachea, which was free of lesion. Carina was sharp. The scope was passed into the right mid stem bronchus. The upper lobe and middle lobe segments were seen. They are remarkable for thick, purulent mucous plugging of all the bronchial segments. Aggressive lavage with saline and Mucomyst were done. In spite of that, mucous plugs were quite thick and required manual removal through the scope. Subsequently the scope was withdrawn back to the left main stem, and left upper lobe, lingual lobe, and sub segments were seen. They were also remarkable for severe mucous plugs, which were removed manually. After complete evacuation of mucous plugs was done, bronchial segments were visualized again and there was some narrowing of left lower segment with some inflamed, swollen mucosa. Biopsies were done from that segment. Bronchial washings were done and sent for cytology and culture.

The patient tolerated the procedure well.

FINDINGS: Thick, purulent mucous pluggings were widespread on both sides. There was some narrowing of left lower lobe bronchus with inflamed, swollen mucosa with smooth margin.

SPECIMENS: Biopsies were done from left lobe bronchus. Washing was done. Bronchoscopic lavage was done using saline and Mucomyst, and all the mucous plugs were removed.

Case Study 35

PATHOLOGY REPORT

DATE: 1/02/2010

SPECIMEN TYPE: CYTO

SURGICAL PATHOLOGY / CYTOPATHOLOGY REPORT

PRE – OP DIAGNOSIS: Left lower lobe collapse: inflamed swollen bronchial mucosa left lower lobe

POST-OP DIAGNOSIS: Left lower lobe collapse: inflamed swollen bronchial mucosa left lower lobe

SPECIMEN(S)

BRONCHIAL WASHING MATERIAL:

GROSS DESCRIPTION:
Received 8 cc of hemorrhagic fluid in the laboratory. 2 smears and 1 cell block are prepared for cytological evaluation.

MICROSCOPIC DESCRIPTION:
Microscopic examination of the specimen reveals groups of and single epithelial cells that appear poorly preserved, displaying nuclear enlargement, hyperchromasia, increased N/C bronchial columnar, metaplastic, and reserve cells: pulmonary macrophages, mixed inflammatory cells, necrotic debris, and fungal elements.

CYTOPATHOLOGICAL DIAGNOSIS:

BRONCHIAL WASHING: Poorly preserved dysplastic epithelial cells present.

Candida species identified.

Case Study 35

SURGICAL PATHOLOGY / CYTOPATHOLOGY REPORT

PRE–OP Diagnosis: Left lower lobe collapse: inflamed swollen bronchial mucosa left lower lobe

POST-OP Diagnosis: Left lower lobe collapse: inflamed swollen bronchial mucosa left lower lobe

SPECIMEN(S)

     LUNG LEFT LOWER LOBE – BIOPSY X4

GROSS DESCRIPTION:
The specimen consists of four fragments of tan tissue ranging from 0.1 up to 0.6 cm in greatest dimension. Entirely submitted.

MICROSCOPIC DIAGNOSIS:

BIOPSY OF LEFT LOWER LOBE: Mild non-specific chronic bronchitis with hypertrophy of the submucosal glands and thickening of the subepithelial basement membrane.

No tumor present.

FINAL DIAGNOSIS

BIOPSY OF LEFT LOWER LOBE:

Minute detached fragment of dysplastic epithelium.

Mild non-specific chronic bronchitis with hypertrophy of submucosal glands and thickened subepithelial basement membrane.

Case Study 35

Answer Sheet

DIAGNOSES	ICD-9-CM CODES					
First listed DX				.		
DX 2				.		
DX 3				.		
DX 4				.		

PROCEDURES	CPT CODES					MODIFIERS (If Applicable)		
PR 1						-		
PR 2						-		
PR 3						-		
PR 4						-		
PR 5						-		
PR 6						-		
PR 7						-		

PROVIDE ICD-9-CM CODES FOR DIAGNOSES AND CPT CODE(S) FOR PROCEDURE(S)

Case Study 36

INPATIENT FACE SHEET

Patient Name: Samual Horn

ADMIT DATE: 01/02/2010

DISCHARGE DATE: 01/10/2010

AGE: 47

SEX: Male

DISPOSITION: Home

ADMISSION DIAGNOSES:

1. Low back pain
2. L5-S1 radiculopathy

DISCHARGE DIAGNOSIS:

1. Herniated nucleus pulposus right-sided at L5-S1

OPERATION/PROCEDURE:

1. Lumbar laminectomy at L5 and S1
2. Right-sided L5-S1 micro-diskectomy
3. Use of operating microscope

Case Study 36

HISTORY & PHYSICAL

ADMISSION DATE: 01/02/2010

REASON FOR ADMISSION: The patient is a 47-year-old gentleman who presented with severe back pain.

HISTORY OF PRESENT ILLNESS:
The patient is a 47-year-old gentleman seen in my office in a severe state of pain. It was suspected that the patient had radiculopathy. The patient was sent for an MRI. The radiologist reported a very large disc herniation with right-sided disc protrusion and early extrusion of the disc material at L5-S1 with compression of the thecal sac.

MEDICATIONS PRIOR TO ADMISSION:
The patient's medications prior to admission included Tylenol #3, Decadron, and Vicodin.

ALLERGIES: The patient has no known allergies.

SOCIAL HISTORY:
The patient is married and lives with his wife. The patient has a history of smoking one pack of cigarettes per day. The patient has a history of drinking alcoholic beverages occasionally.

REVIEW OF SYSTEMS:
The patient denied a history of chest pain. The patient denied a history of chest pressure. The patient denied a history of chest tightness. The patient denied a history of difficulty breathing.

PHYSICAL EXAMINATION:

VITAL SIGNS:	The patient's vital signs on admission were stable.
NECK:	The neck was supple. There was no jugular venous distention. There were no carotid bruits.
LUNGS:	The lungs were clear to auscultation and percussion. There were no signs of consolidation.
HEART:	The heart was normal.
ABDOMEN:	The abdomen was soft and non-tender. The bowel sounds were positive.
EXTREMITIES:	The examination of the extremities was negative for cyanosis, clubbing, or edema.
NEUROLOGICAL:	The cranial nerves II through XII appeared to be intact. The tone was normal. The power was five by five in the upper extremities. The power was decreased in the right lower extremity secondary to maybe being in pain. The sensation on the right side revealed only one plus at the knee and ankle jerks. The straight leg raising was positive.

PLAN: Consultation with neurology and surgical consultation will be requested.

Case Study 36

CONSULTATION

REQUESTING PHYSICIAN: Dr. Rosie Wags

DATE: 01/02/2010

CONSULTING PHYSICIAN: Dr. Zachary Service

CHIEF COMPLAINT: Right lower extremity pain

HISTORY OF PRESENT ILLNESS: This is a 47-year-old gentleman who has a past medical history significant for bulging disc at L5-L1. The patient was having this pain and was ultimately relieved with medication, as well as chiropractic manipulation. The patient had magnetic resonance imaging done yesterday, which showed he had a bulging disc at L5-S1 on the right side. At the time of the examination, the patient is awake, alert, and oriented x 4. He denied any lower extremity weakness, but complained of right lower extremity pain at the L5-S1 nerve root distribution. He denied any bowel or bladder dysfunction.

PAST MEDICAL HISTORY: No significant past medical history.

MEDICATIONS: Vicodin, Tylenol #3, Soma, Decadron.

SOCIAL HISTORY: Smokes one pack of cigarettes per day. Denies any alcohol use.

REVIEW OF SYSTEMS: Completely reviewed and was negative.

PHYSICAL EXAMINATION: This is a 47-year-old gentleman lying in bed in no acute distress.

HEAD: Norma cephalic, traumatic.

ENT: Within normal limits.

NECK: Supple. No bruits are auscultated. No adenopathy.

CHEST: Clear to auscultation.

HEART: Regular rate and rhythm. No murmurs, rubs, or gallops.

ABDOMEN: Positive bowel sounds, non-tender, no distended. No organomegaly.

EXTREMITIES: No cyanosis, edema, or clubbing.

NEUROLOGIC: The patient is alert and oriented x 3. Cranial nerves II-XII are grossly intact. Pupils are equal, round, and react to light and accommodation. Extraocular movements are intact. Cerebellar function is intact. Motor/sensory exam is intact.

There is negative Babinski. No pronator drift. Strength is 5/5 in all extremities in all ranges of motion. There was a positive straight-leg raise on the right. There was evidence of a decreased reflex knee jerk on the right, which was 1+. MRI scan of the lumbar spine revealed L5-S1 right-sided disc herniation.

IMPRESSION: Low back pain. L5-S1 radiculopathy.

RECOMMENDATIONS:

1. The patient is stable.
2. Continue current care.
3. Suggest an epidural steroid injection, as well as physical therapy at this time.

Case Study 36

Consultation

REQUESTING PHYSICIAN: Dr. Rosie Wags

DATE: 01/02/2010

CONSULTING PHYSICIAN: Dr. Liza Gaige

REASON FOR CONSULTATION:

The patient is a 47-year-old gentleman who presented with lower back pain.

HISTORY OF PRESENT ILLNESS:

The patient is a 47-year-old gentleman whose past medical history was significant for a history of a bulging disc in 1994 at L5 and S1. He subsequently had a MRI that revealed L5 and S1, herniated disc. The patient was then admitted to the hospital for further management. A neurological consultation was then requested. At this time the patient is still having lower back pain with some pain radiating to the right lower extremity, all the way to the toes. The patient denied a history of chest pain. The patient denied a history of shortness of breath. There is no history of nausea or vomiting. The patient denied a history of dysphagia.

PAST MEDICAL AND SURGICAL HISTORY:

The patient has a history of a fall with lower back pain.

MEDICATIONS PRIOR TO ADMISSION:

The patient's medications prior to admission included Vicodin and Tylenol #3 and Soma and Decadron.

ALLERGIES: The patient has no known allergies.

SOCIAL HISTORY:

The patient has a history of smoking approximately one pack of cigarettes per day. The patient has a history of drinking alcoholic beverages occasionally.

PHYSICAL EXAMINATION:

GENERAL APPEARANCE: On examination the patient is awake, alert and oriented times three.

NEUROLOGICAL: Extraocular movements were intact. Pupils are equal, round, and reactive to light and accommodation. There was no nystagmus. There were no carotid bruits. The visual fields were within normal limits. There was no Kernig sign. There was no Brudzinski sign. The cranial nerves II through XII appeared to be intact. The tongue was midline. The corneal reflex was intact. The gag reflex was intact. Motor system revealed tone was normal. Power was five by five in left upper extremity and the right upper extremity. The power in the lower extremities was five by five distally but three plus to four by five because of the severe pain proximally. The sensory examination revealed normal pinprick, touch, and temperature. Normal position. Normal vibration. The reflexes were plus one at the right knee jerk and ankle jerk. The straight leg raising was a stronger positive in the right lower extremity than in the left lower extremity. The patient can walk but with a limp. The patient cannot walk on heel and tiptoes.

Case Study 36

Consultation

Continued:

LABORATORY INVESTIGATIONS:

The Magnetic Resonance Imaging of the lumbar spine revealed L5-S1 central and right-side herniated disc.

IMPRESSION:

1. Severe lower back pain.
2. Severe radicular pain, mainly of the right lower extremity secondary to herniated disc.
3. L5-S1 radiculopathy.
4. Straight leg raising positive.
5. Right knee jerk plus one, decreased compared to the left knee jerk.

RECOMMENDATIONS:

1. Immediate lumbar laminectomy

Case Study 36

OPERATIVE REPORT

DATE:	01/03/2010
SURGEON:	Dr. Liza Gaige
PREOPERATIVE DIAGNOSIS:	Herniated nucleus pulposus right-sided at L5-S1.
POSTOPERATIVE DIAGNOSIS:	Herniated nucleus pulposus right-sided at L5-S1.
OPERATION/PROCEDURE:	Lumbar laminectomy at L5 and S1, right-sided. L5-S1 diskectomy.
ASSISTANT:	Dr. Jeff Cottrell
COMPLICATIONS:	There were no complications.
ANESTHESIA:	General endotracheal anesthesia.

ESTIMATED BLOOD LOSS: Less than 50cc.

INDICATIONS FOR THE PROCEDURE:
This is a young gentleman with intractable right sciatica of 8 years duration who has failed conservative treatment. The patient is now being taken to surgery for decompression and removal of the disc. The risks of the surgery and the limitations of the surgery were explained to the patient and the patient's wife at length. They understand the risks and wish to proceed with procedure.

DESCRIPTION OF THE OPERATION:
Intravenous lines were started. Thigh-high TED and compression boots were placed on the lower extremities. The patient received general endotracheal anesthesia. The patient was placed in the prone position resting on the Wilson frame. All the pressure points were appropriately padded. The area in the lumbar spine was shaved, prepped, and draped in the usual sterile manner. An incision was made in the spinous process of L5 to S1 inclusive using the subperiosteal dissection. The lamina of right L5 and S1 were exposed. Intra-operative x-ray confirmed our level. Using the Anspach drill we thinned out the lamina arch to the level of the ligamentum flavum. We then proceeded to do the laminotomy of L5 on the right side of the inferior two thirds and superior two thirds of S1. This exposed the nerve root going out. The nerve root was retracted slightly medially. There was a large anterior compression of the nerve root pushing the nerve root posteriorly. Slightly moving the nerve root medially, we exposed the big rent in the angelus fibrosis, entered this big defect, and the diskectomy was performed.

Case Study 36

OPERATIVE REPORT

Continued:

There was a large disc herniation that had broken through the angelus and into the posterior part of the vertebral body of L5-S1. Once the diskectomy was performed, the wound was irrigated thoroughly using antibiotic solution. With a small nerve hook we went ahead and looked for any residual fragments and there were none. The wound was then irrigated thoroughly using a copious amount of antibiotic solution. The wound was closed in serial layers using #0-Vicryl in an interrupted fashion on the muscle and fascial layers. We used #2-0 Vicryl sutures to close the subcutaneous tissues. We used #2-0 Nurolon vertical and multi-locking sutures for the skin. All the sponge and needle counts were reported correct at the end of the procedure. The patient tolerated the procedure well. The patient was extubated in the operating room and was taken to the recovery room in stable condition, moving all extremities.

SURGICAL PATHOLOGY REPORT

ACUTE HERNIATED DISC L5-S1

SPECIMENS(S)   DISC. NOS – L5-S1

GROSS DESCRIPTION:

The specimen consists of multiple irregular fragments of fibrocartilaginous tissue weighing approximately 5 grams in aggregate.

Representative sections are submitted in a single cassette for decalcification and processing.

MICROSCOPIC DIAGNOSIS:
Degenerated fibrocartilaginous tissue consistent with intervertebral disc. Clinically herniated disc L5-S1.

Case Study 36

Answer Sheet

DIAGNOSES	ICD-9-CM CODES					
First listed DX				.		
DX 2				.		
DX 3				.		
DX 4				.		

PROCEDURES	CPT CODES					MODIFIERS (If Applicable)		
PR 1						-		
PR 2						-		
PR 3						-		
PR 4						-		
PR 5						-		
PR 6						-		
PR 7						-		

**PROVIDE ICD-9-CM CODES FOR DIAGNOSES AND
CPT CODE(S) FOR PROCEDURE(S)**

Case Study 37

INPATIENT FACE SHEET

Patient Name: Matilda Winters

Admit Date: 1/14/2010

Discharge Date: 1/16/2010

Age: 89

Sex: Female

Disposition: Home

ADMIT DIAGNOSES:

Lower abdominal pain and nausea possibly due to partial small bowel obstruction.

History of colon resection for cancer with elevated CEA of 23.1. Rule out recurrence of cancer.

DISCHARGE DIAGNOSES:

1.   Diverticulosis
2.   Benign colon polyp

PROCEDURE:

1.   Colonoscopy with polypectomy and biopsy

Case Study 37

HISTORY AND PHYSICAL

ADMITTED: 1/14/2010

CHIEF COMPLAINT: Abdominal pain, nausea, and vomiting.

HISTORY OF PRESENT ILLNESS: This is an 89-year-old woman who has been complaining of abdominal pains, vomiting, and nausea for several weeks. She is admitted at this time for further evaluation, including colonoscopy. The patient has a history of colon cancer with an elevated CEA, suggesting recurrence of cancer.

PAST HISTORY: The patient had colon resection in June 2001 for colon cancer. She had her left lung resected in July 1995 for carcinoma. In addition, she has had coronary artery bypass graft in 1999 for severe coronary artery disease. She has known hypertension and osteoporosis with L1 compression fracture.

MEDICATIONS: Metoprolol 100 milligrams b.i.d., Cardizem 180 milligrams daily, and Cardura.

ALLERGIES: No known allergies.

SOCIAL HISTORY: The patient is widowed and lives alone. She does not smoke cigarettes or drink alcohol.

FAMILY HISTORY: There is a strong family history of arteriosclerotic heart disease and myocardial infarction.

REVIEW OF SYSTEMS: The patient has had intermittent diarrhea over the past years, since the time of her colon surgery. She has had episodes where her abdomen becomes distended and hard.

PHYSICAL EXAMINATION:

GENERAL: On physical examination the patient is a pleasant, alert, 89-year-old woman in no distress.

HEENT: Shows capillary reflexes. Her extraocular movements are normal. There is no pallor, icterus. Ears and throat are unremarkable. Neck is supple and free of masses. There is no jugular venous distension in the neck.

CHEST: Symmetrical.

LUNGS: Lung fields are clear.

HEART: Heart sounds are regular with no significant murmurs.

ABDOMEN: Firm. Bowel sounds are active. There is some diffuse low abdominal tenderness, most noted in the right lower quadrant. There is no rebound tenderness. There are no apparent masses.

EXTREMITIES: Show 2 plus edema.

ASSESSMENT: The patient is an 89-year-old woman with known colon cancer and recurrent episodes of abdominal pain and vomiting over the past several weeks. The case has been discussed with her gastroenterologist, Dr. Angela Gaige. She is admitted at this time for continued intravenous fluid hydration, colonoscopy, and diagnostic workup.

Case Study 37

CONSULTATION

DATE: 1/14/2010

REQUESTING PHYSICIAN: Dr. Bronwyn Mills

CONSULTING PHYSICIAN: Dr. David Clark

REASON FOR CONSULTATION: Evaluation of patient with lower abdominal pain, nausea, and vomiting.

HISTORY: This 89-year-old woman is referred for further evaluation of lower abdominal pain, nausea, and vomiting. Her bowel movements are erratic and range from being constipated with no bowel movement for several days to loose bowel movements. She has lost about 3 pounds over the past month.

She underwent outpatient CT scan of the abdomen and pelvis on 1/13/2010, revealing a dilated bile duct. Her liver enzymes, however, were normal and HIDA scan revealed no evidence of obstruction, and thus it was felt that the dilation of the bile duct was physiologic and did not represent obstruction. She had a CEA of 23.1 on 1/13/2010.

PAST MEDICAL HISTORY:
Colon resection for cancer of the colon in June 2001.
Coronary artery bypass graft in 1995.

MEDICATIONS IN THE HOSPITAL: Pepcid 20 mg IV q12h; nitroglycerin q.i.d.; atenolol 25 mg p.o. b.i.d.

ALLERGIES: None known.

SOCIAL HISTORY: Cigarettes: smoked up until 1989.

FAMILY HISTORY: Negative for cancer.

PHYSICAL EXAMINATION:

GENERAL APPEARANCE: Pleasant cooperative woman, who appears to be in moderate distress due to her abdominal symptoms.

HEENT:	Normocephalic, traumatic. No scleral icterus.
NECK:	Supple. No lymphadenopathy or thyromegaly.
LUNGS:	Clear.
HEART:	Regular rate and rhythm. No murmurs, rubs, or gallops.
ABDOMEN:	Moderately tender and moderately distended in the lower abdomen. No hepatosplenomegaly.
RECTAL:	No masses. Firm stool. Negative for occult blood.
EXTREMITIES:	No cyanosis, clubbing, or edema.
NEUROLOGIC:	Alert and oriented x 3. Grossly non-focal.

LABORATORY: 1/14/2010, glucose 113, BUN 25, creatinine 1.3. The remainder of the CMP, amylase, and lipase are within normal range. CBC within normal range.

Case Study 37

CONSULTATION

Continued:

Abdominal series on 1/14/2010 reveals possible partial small bowel obstruction and possible persistent pleural effusion.

IMPRESSION:
Lower abdominal pain and nausea possibly due to partial small bowel obstruction.
History of colon resection for cancer with elevated CEA of 23.1. Rule out recurrence of cancer.
Dilated common bile duct, but normal liver enzymes and HIDA scan on recent admission suggesting no physiological obstruction.

PLAN:

Colonoscopy advised.

Repeat CEA.

Clear liquid diet.

Case Study 37

PROCEDURE NOTE

Date of Procedure: 1/15/2010

Preoperative Diagnoses: Abdominal pain, nausea, vomiting, history of colon cancer

Postoperative Diagnoses: Marked diverticulosis

Small internal hemorrhoid

Benign polyp

Surgeon: Dr. David Clark

Procedure: Colonoscopy with biopsy

DESCRIPTION OF PROCEDURE:
Following IV sedation, the colonoscope was inserted into the rectum and advanced to the left colon and beyond to the splenic flexure and into the ascending colon and into the cecum. A five mm polyp at the level of previous anastomosis was removed with snare and additional biopsies were taken at the sigmoid level. The patient tolerated the procedure well.

Case Study 37

Answer Sheet

DIAGNOSES	ICD-9-CM CODES					
First listed DX				.		
DX 2				.		
DX 3				.		
DX 4				.		

PROCEDURES	CPT CODES					MODIFIERS (If Applicable)		
PR 1						-		
PR 2						-		
PR 3						-		
PR 4						-		
PR 5						-		
PR 6						-		
PR 7						-		

Case Study 38

Office Visit

Patient's Name: Eunice Freeman

Date of Visit: 1/31/2010

Age: 17

Sex: Female

Insurance: Commercial

Case Study 38

Office Visit

HISTORY OF PRESENT ILLNESS:
This is a first-time visit for this 17-year-old female who was referred to me from the Rosedale Hospital emergency room. The patient was seen in the emergency room on Sunday with neck and back discomfort due to an automobile accident. The patient was a restrained driver. The car received front-end damage that occurred at a moderate rate of speed. According to the emergency room report, there was no loss of consciousness. There is no evidence of hearing disorder, headaches, or blurry vision. No initial neurologic complaints. She is wearing a neck brace.

PAST MEDICAL HISTORY: Negative.

PHYSICAL EXAMINATION:

Vital Signs:	Blood pressure: 120/70, Temperature normal. Pulse 68. Respiration 20.
General:	Well-developed, well-nourished female in no acute distress, but has mild discomfort in the neck and lower back.
HEENT:	Pupils are equal and reactive. Fundoscopic is normal. Negative Battle sign.
Neck:	Mildly tender in the paracervical muscles, but no deformity is noted. No hematoma noted.
Back:	Lower back is minimally tender in the paralumbar muscles.
Chest:	The chest wall is non-tender.
Lungs:	Clear bilaterally with no rales, rhonchi, or wheezes.
Abdomen:	Soft and non-tender.
Extremities:	No clubbing, cyanosis, or edema. Range of motion is intact.
Neurological:	Cranial nerves II-XII are intact. Plantar reflexes are downward going bilaterally.

MEDICAL DECISION:
Patient brought the x-rays taken in the emergency room and they were reviewed. C-spine is unremarkable. Lumbosacral spine shows evidence of transitional vertebral body with partial lumbarization of S1, with no evidence of acute fracture or subluxation.

IMPRESSION: Neck and lumbar back strain secondary to automobile accident.

She was given instructions for rest for the next 24 hours. Prescriptions for Darvocet N100 q.i.d., p.r.n. for pain and Robaxin 750 q.i.d. for spasms p.r.n. She is to continue wearing the neck brace to help keep the neck area still. She is to follow-up with me in 1 week.

History:	Detailed
Examination:	Detailed
Medical Decision:	Low complexity

Case Study 38

Answer Sheet

DIAGNOSES	ICD-9-CM CODES					
First listed DX				.		
DX 2				.		
DX 3				.		
DX 4				.		

PROCEDURES	CPT CODES					MODIFIERS (If Applicable)		
PR 1						-		
PR 2						-		
PR 3						-		
PR 4						-		
PR 5						-		
PR 6						-		
PR 7						-		

Case Study 39

Ambulatory Surgery

Face Sheet

Patient's Name: Bonnie Bonn

Date of Visit: 1/06/2010

Age: 71

Sex: Female

Insurance: Medicare

Case Study 39

History and Physical

DATE OF ADMISSION: 01/06/2010

HISTORY OF PRESENT ILLNESS:
This 71-year-old female has been hospitalized for symptomatic slow heart rate and atrial fibrillation. Echocardiogram did show evidence of enlarged left atrium and the patient has been taking Coumadin for over a month. Patient has also had electrocardioversion and was converted, but did revert back into atrial fibrillation. Patient is not taking any medications for the complete AV block, and it was felt that a pacemaker would be the best option for the patient.

PAST MEDICAL HISTORY: Non-contributory.

SOCIAL HISTORY: Patient is married and lives with her husband. Does not smoke or drink alcohol.

PHYSICAL EXAMINATION:
General:	Well-developed female in no acute distress.
HEENT:	Within normal limits.
Heart:	Complete AV block and atrial fibrillation. No murmurs noted.
Lungs:	Clear to auscultation.
Abdomen:	Soft, non-tender.
Urogenital:	Denies problems.
Extremities:	Within normal limits. Full range of motion.

PLAN: Patient will be admitted for a pacemaker.

Case Study 39

Operative Report

Date of Operation:	1/06/2010
Preoperative Diagnosis:	AV Block
	Atrial Fibrillation
Postoperative Diagnosis:	AV Block
	Atrial Fibrillation
Operation:	Implantation of a DDIR mode-switching permanent pacemaker and leads
Surgeon:	David Pool, MD
Assistant:	Kent David, MD
Anesthesia:	Versed 6 mg IV, 1% Xylocaine

PROCEDURE:

The left infraclavicular area was prepped and draped in the usual manner and the area was infused with 1% Xylocaine. A pacemaker pocket was formed with the incision made parallel to the left clavicle, down to the level of the prepectoral fascia. The left subclavian vein was then easily cannulated and over a guide wire, two 7-French sheaths were passed without difficulty. Through these sheaths, a Medtronic model lead was fastened to the right ventricular apex and fixed into position. Through the other sheath, a Medtronic model lead was passed to the right atrial appendage and fixed into position. After adequate endocardiac anchoring was assured, threshold testing on these leads were performed.

R waves measured 10.2 mV. Ventricular capture occurred down to an amplitude of 0.4 volts, and a pulse width of 0.5 msec, measuring a current of 0.7 MA. The 5-volt resistance was measured at 707 ohms. On the atrial lead, atrial fibrillation waves measured 1.5 to 3.8 mV. Atrial impedance measured 536 ohms. We could not test capture due to the presence of the atrial fibrillation. Once in these positions, the leads were anchored using the anchoring sleeves with two 2-Ethibond sutures, then a purse string suture was placed around the leads to prevent back bleeding.

The patient tolerated the procedure well without any complications.

<u>Case Study 39</u>

Progress Note:

The patient was admitted for a permanent pacemaker for a complete AV block and atrial fibrillation. The patient was taken to the operating room, where a pacemaker was inserted. No complications from the procedure were noted. The patient is to be discharged when discharge criteria has been met and will follow-up in my office in a week.

Physician Orders:

Routine vital signs

Place on cardiac monitor until discharge.

Diet as tolerated

Up with assistance

IV D_5RL@83 cc/h. Change to heparin lock with flush when tolerating p.o. fluids well.

M.S. 4–10 mg IM for severe pain q 3–4 h p.r.n.

Discharge when patient is stable.

Case Study 39

Answer Sheet

DIAGNOSES	ICD-9-CM CODES					
First listed DX				.		
DX 2				.		
DX 3				.		
DX 4				.		

PROCEDURES	CPT CODES					MODIFIERS (If Applicable)		
PR 1						-		
PR 2						-		
PR 3						-		
PR 4						-		
PR 5						-		
PR 6						-		
PR 7						-		

Case Study 40

Ambulatory Care

Face Sheet

Date of Admission:	1/16/2010
Date of Discharge:	1/16/2010
Age:	46
Sex:	Female
ADMITTING DIAGNOSIS:	Nasal obstruction
DISCHARGE DIAGNOSES:	1. Bilateral hypertrophic turbinates
	2. Nasoseptal spur
PROCEDURE:	Functional internal nasal reconstruction
DISPOSITION:	Home

Case Study 40

History and Physical

DATE OF ADMISSION: 1/16/2010

ADMITTING DIAGNOSIS: Nasal obstruction

HISTORY OF PRESENT ILLNESS:
This patient has been complaining of nasal obstruction for several months. She also had a left nasal polyp and a Caldwell-Luc done many years ago. She has been given antihistamines and decongestants, but they have not rectified her condition.

PAST MEDICAL HISTORY:

Caldwell-Luc many years ago. No other significant problems.

ALLERGIES: None.

MEDICATIONS: Antihistamine and decongestant

SOCIAL HISTORY:

Patient smokes 1/2 pack per day; alcohol, social. Hobbies include gardening, reading, and sailing.

PHYSICAL EXAMINATION:

General:	Well-developed, well-nourished female in no acute distress.
HEENT:	Head is normocephalic. She has a spur on the right in the inferior turbinates bilaterally, which are obstructed and hypertrophic.
Chest:	Clear to auscultation and percussion.
Heart:	Normal rhythm.
Abdomen:	Negative.
Neurological:	Normal.
Extremities:	Normal.

PLAN:

The patient will be admitted to one-day surgery for functional intranasal surgery for bilateral hypertrophic turbinates and nasoseptal spur.

Case Study 40

Operative Report

Date of Operation:	1/16/2010
Preoperative Diagnoses:	1. Bilateral hypertrophic turbinates
	2. Nasoseptal spur
Postoperative Diagnoses:	Same
Operation:	Functional internal nasal reconstruction
Surgeon:	Carlos Earl, III, MD
Anesthesia:	General
Anesthesiologist:	C.V. Wilkinson, MD
Estimated Blood Loss:	Less than 500 cc
Complications:	None

PROCEDURE:

The patient was taken to the surgical suite and prepped and draped in the usual fashion. General anesthesia was given, both nasal cavities were packed, and the anterior aspect of the septum and both inferior turbinates were infiltrated with 1% Xylocaine with 1:40,000 epinephrine solution.

The nose was inspected and the patient was found to have a septal spur on the right side, which was obstructing her nasal passages. Both interior turbinates were hypertrophic.

An incision was made along the caudal end of the septum and was carried down to the perichondrium and dissected posteriorly and inferiorly. The second incision was then made 1.5 cm beyond the first one, and the mucoperichondrium on the opposite side was dissected posteriorly and inferiorly. The septal cartilage was not detached from the maxillary crest and the nasal process of the palatine bone on that side was removed. The vomer was fractured and left intact.

With the obstructing cartilaginous and bony portion corrected, the septal mucosa was placed back and was closed. A left inferior turbinoplasty was then carried out, making an incision from the anterior superior aspect down to the anterior inferior. The turbinate bone was dissected medially and laterally and was removed. The nasal cavity was packed and attention was turned to the other side, where an incision was made and the turbinate bone was dissected medially and posteriorly. Some of the bone was removed.

Bilateral nasal splints were placed and bilateral nasal packing was placed inferiorly. The patient was transferred to the recovery room in satisfactory condition. No apparent complications noted.

Case Study 40

Progress Notes:

Patient was taken to the operating room for functional internal nasal reconstruction. Patient tolerated the procedure well. Nasal packs are in place. No apparent complication from the surgery or anesthesia is noted. Patient will be discharged when stable and is to follow-up in my office tomorrow.

Orders:

1. Standard postoperative orders.
2. Discharge patient from recovery room when stable.
3. Vital signs q 15 minutes x 4; then q 30 x 2; then q1h until discharge.
4. Urinary catheterization x 1 if patient unable to void.
5. Start on soft diet.
6. Check nasal packings prior to leaving for excessive bleeding.
7. Discharge when patient is stable.

Case Study 40

Answer Sheet

DIAGNOSES	ICD-9-CM CODES					
First listed DX				.		
DX 2				.		
DX 3				.		
DX 4				.		

PROCEDURES	CPT CODES					MODIFIERS (If Applicable)	
PR 1						-	
PR 2						-	
PR 3						-	
PR 4						-	
PR 5						-	
PR 6						-	
PR 7						-	

Case Study 41

Ambulatory Surgery

Face Sheet

Patient's Name: Bill Penn

Date of Visit: 1/19/2010

Age: 40

Sex: Male

Insurance: Commercial

Case Study 41

Ambulatory Surgery

History and Physical

DATE OF ADMISSION: 01/09/2010

CHIEF COMPLAINT: Left elbow pain.

HISTORY OF PRESENT ILLNESS:
The patient has been complaining of left elbow pain for approximately 6 months. MRI was positive for torn ulnar collateral ligament. Patient underwent left ulnar collateral ligament repair approximately 5 months ago. The patient has sharp pain in the elbow with ulnar nerve palsy. He denies feeling a pop in the elbow.

ALLERGIES: None.

MEDICATIONS: None.

PAST SURGICAL HISTORY: Left ulnar collateral ligament reconstruction.

PHYSICAL EXAMINATION:
General: Vital signs are within normal limits.
HEENT: Extraocular movements are intact.
Chest: Clear to auscultation bilaterally without any crackles or wheezes.
Extremities: Tender over the medial aspect of the elbow. Hitchhiker's test is positive. He has decreased sensation along the 5th finger and on the 4th finger; he is intact to light touch on the radial border. On the ulnar border, 2-point discrimination is intermittent.

PLAN: Patient will be admitted to local hospital for ulnar nerve transposition.

Case Study 41

Ambulatory Surgery

Operative Report

DATE OF OPERATION:	1/09/2010
PREOPERATIVE DIAGNOSIS:	Left ulnar nerve entrapment
POSTOPERATIVE DIAGNOSIS:	Left ulnar nerve entrapment
PROCEDURE:	Ulnar nerve transposition
SURGEON:	Rodney Verne, MD
ASSISTANT:	V.G. Smith, MD

PROCEDURE:
The patient was taken to the operating room, where general anesthesia was administered without complications. The left arm was prepped and draped in the usual sterile manner.

The previous incision was used and dissected down. The medial cutaneous nerve was identified, protected, and retracted out of harm's way. The ulnar nerve was identified proximally and the intermuscular septum was excised. The ulnar nerve was followed into the cubital tunnel and the tunnel was released. The ulnar nerve was encased in scar tissue over the ulnar collateral ligament reconstruction. We released the cubital tunnel and released the scar tissue at the ulnar nerve. We then followed the ulnar nerve down as it split into the two heads of the flexor carpi ulnaris. The FCU is split at four fingerbreadths below the joint surface. The inferior fascia is clearly identified and released. The superior fascia from the FCU is clearly identified and released.

The nerve was then stimulated, and it did respond to the stimulation distal to the area of compression. Satisfied with the decompression, we then went to transport the nerve. The ulnar nerve is elevated using vessel loops and transposed anteriorly. After the nerve is transposed, a limited neurolysis is performed. After the neurolysis, the fascicles are clearly seen to be intact. A sling is made using the fascia of the flexor wad and is tied down with ample room for the ulnar nerve.

The nerve is irrigated and the tourniquet is released. No excessive bleeding is noted. The subcu is closed with #1 and 2-0. Dry sterile dressing is applied. The patient tolerated the procedure well.

Case Study 41

Ambulatory Surgery

Progress Notes and Orders

PROGRESS NOTES

Patient admitted to the ambulatory surgery suite where the patient was prepped for surgery. The patient received education on the procedure to be performed.

Taken to the operating room where an ulnar nerve transposition was performed and the patient returned to the room in satisfactory condition.

ORDERS

Ancef 1 g IVPB 1 hour pre-op

NPO

Clip, prep, scrub op site with Betadine Solution

Postoperative Orders

Discharge when alert and stable.
IV orders per anesthesia.
Tylenol #3 q4h p.r.n.

Case Study 41

Answer Sheet

DIAGNOSES				ICD-9-CM CODES		
First listed DX				.		
DX 2				.		
DX 3				.		
DX 4				.		

PROCEDURES	CPT CODES					MODIFIERS (If Applicable)		
PR 1						-		
PR 2						-		
PR 3						-		
PR 4						-		
PR 5						-		
PR 6						-		
PR 7						-		

Case Study 42

Ambulatory Surgery

Face Sheet

Patient's Name: Georgia Phillips

Date of Visit: 1/17/2010

Age: 52

Sex: Female

Insurance: Medicare

Case Study 42

History and Physical

DATE OF ADMISSION: 1/17/2010

HISTORY OF PRESENT ILLNESS:
The patient has a history of bilateral breast cysts and in a follow-up mammogram a mass was discovered in the left breast. Patient also has some dimpling in the area, demonstrated on mammogram in the upper outer quadrant.

PAST MEDICAL HISTORY: Patient has a history of mitral valve prolapse.

ALLERGIES: Demerol and Biaxin.

MEDICATIONS: V-Tabs prior to procedures for her mitral valve prolapse.

PHYSICAL EXAMINATION:

Vital signs: BP 146/80; Respirations 17; Pulse 77; Temperature 99.0

Skin: Warm and dry.

Eyes: The pupils are equal, round, reactive to light and accommodation.

Sclera is clear.

Neck: Supple. No masses, scars, or bruits.

Lungs: Clear to auscultation and percussion.

Heart: Normal sinus rhythm. No murmurs or gallops.

Breasts: Breasts are symmetrical. There is an area of slight skin retraction on the upper outer quadrant of the left breast. There is some thickness in the area. No other masses felt. No axillary lymphadenopathy.

Extremities: Good distal pulses.

PLAN:

Patient will be brought to the ambulatory surgical center for a left breast biopsy.

Case Study 42

Operative Report

Date of Operation:	1/17/2010
Preoperative Diagnosis:	Left breast mass
Postoperative Diagnosis:	Infiltrating ductal cell carcinoma left breast.
Procedure Performed:	Excision of left breast mass.
Surgeon:	Cheryl Bottom, MD
Assistant:	Jon Actor, MD

PROCEDURE:

The patient was placed in the supine position where anesthesia was administered. The left breast was prepped and draped in the usual sterile manner.

A transverse incision was made along the mass and was carried down through the skin and subcutaneous tissue. A firm mass was identified and was sharply excised from the surrounding breast tissue. Bleeding was controlled with electrocautery.

The wound was closed using interrupted sutures of 3-0 Vicryl for the deep layer. The subcutaneous tissue was closed with interrupted suture of 3-0 Vicryl and the skin was closed 4-0 Monocryl. Dressing was applied. The patient tolerated the procedure well.

Case Study 42

Pathology Report

Date:	1/17/2010
Physician:	Cheryl Bottom, MD
Preoperative Diagnosis:	Left breast mass
Surgical Procedure:	Excision left breast mass
Postoperative Diagnosis:	Infiltrating ductal carcinoma
Specimen(s):	Left breast mass

GROSS:

Received directly from the operating room is a 4 x 3 x 3 cm ovoid pink-tan to yellow fibroadipose tissue, which is firm.

GROSS AND MICROSCOPIC EXAMINATION:

Excisional biopsy of left breast:

Invasive ductal carcinoma, 2.3 cm, histologic grade 2, nuclear grade 2, mitotic grade 1. Focal lymph vascular space invasion is noted.

Diffuse fibrocystic changes are also noted.

Case Study 42

PROGRESS NOTES:

Patient has a left breast mass and was taken to the operating room, where an excisional biopsy of the mass was performed. Pathology report is pending final determination, but preliminary report is ductal carcinoma.

PHYSICIAN ORDERS:

<u>Pre-Operative Orders</u>

Diet: NPO

Consent to read: Excision left breast mass

Ancef 1 g IV before surgery

<u>Post-Operative Orders</u>

Vicodin 1 q6h p.r.n.

Liquids as tolerated.

Discharge when criteria are met.

Case Study 42

Answer Sheet

DIAGNOSES	ICD-9-CM CODES					
First listed DX				.		
DX 2				.		
DX 3				.		
DX 4				.		

PROCEDURES	CPT CODES					MODIFIERS (If Applicable)		
PR 1						-		
PR 2						-		
PR 3						-		
PR 4						-		
PR 5						-		
PR 6						-		
PR 7						-		

X. CCS-P Case Study Coding Review Answer Key

Although E-codes are not coded on the examination, we wanted to remind you that all adverse effects must be coded as per coding guidelines. This may be covered in the multiple-choice question in the first part of the examination, also.

CCS-P Case Study Answer Key

Case 1

Diagnoses	ICD-9-CM Codes					
First listed DX Palpitations	7	8	5	.	1	
DX 2 Fatigue	7	8	0	.	7	9
DX 3 Thirst	7	8	3	.	5	
DX 4				.		

Procedures	CPT Codes					Modifier (If Applicable)	
PR1 Office visit	9	9	2	1	3	-	
PR2 EKG - 12 Lead	9	3	0	0	0	-	
PR3 Blood draw	3	6	4	1	5	-	
PR4 Lab handling	9	9	0	0	0	-	
PR5						-	
PR6						-	
PR7						-	

Case 2

Diagnoses	ICD-9-CM Codes					
First listed DX Giardiasis	0	0	7	.	1	
DX 2 Dehydration (volume depletion)	2	7	6	.	5	1
DX 3 Arthropathy, unspecified site	7	1	6	.	9	0
DX 4				.		

Procedures	CPT Codes					Modifier (If Applicable)	
PR1 ER visit	9	9	2	8	2	-	
PR2						-	
PR3						-	
PR4						-	
PR5						-	
PR6						-	
PR7						-	

CCS-P Case Study Answer Key

Case 3

Diagnoses	ICD-9-CM Codes					
First listed DX Vaginal discharge	6	2	3	.	5	
DX 2 Vaginal bleeding	6	2	3	.	8	
DX 3				.		
DX 4				.		

Procedures	CPT Codes					Modifier (If Applicable)		
PR1 Office visit	9	9	2	0	3	-		
PR2 Lab handling	9	9	0	0	0	-		
PR3						-		
PR4						-		
PR5						-		
PR6						-		
PR7						-		

Case 4

Diagnoses	ICD-9-CM Codes					
First listed DX Odontalgia	5	2	5	.	9	
DX 2 Dental caries	5	2	1	.	0	0
DX 3				.		
DX 4				.		

Procedures	CPT Codes					Modifier (If Applicable)		
PR1 Office visit	9	9	2	1	2	-		
PR2						-		
PR3						-		
PR4						-		
PR5						-		
PR6						-		
PR7						-		

CCS-P Case Study Answer Key

Case 5

Diagnoses	ICD-9-CM Codes					
First listed DX Open wound of hand except finger(s) alone, without mention of complication	8	8	2	.	0	
DX 2				.		
DX 3				.		
DX 4				.		

Procedures	CPT Codes					Modifier (If Applicable)		
PR1 Office visit, new patient	9	9	2	0	2	.		
PR2 Office visit - emergency basis	9	9	0	5	8	.		
PR3 Simple repair of superficial wound 2.5 cm or less	1	2	0	0	1	.		
PR4						.		
PR5						.		
PR6						.		
PR7						.		

Case 6

Diagnoses	ICD-9-CM Codes					
First listed DX Streptococcal tonsillitis	0	3	4	.	0	
DX 2				.		
DX 3				.		
DX 4				.		

Procedures	CPT Codes					Modifier (If Applicable)		
PR1 Office visit	9	9	2	1	3	.		
PR2 Culture handling	9	9	0	0	0	.		
PR3						.		
PR4						.		
PR5						.		
PR6						.		
PR7						.		

CCS-P Case Study Answer Key

Case 7

Diagnoses	ICD-9-CM Codes					
First listed DX Acute pyelonephritis, without lesion	5	9	0	.	1	0
DX 2 E. Coli	0	4	1	.	4	
DX 3				.		
DX 4				.		

Procedures	CPT Codes					Modifier (If Applicable)		
PR1 Emergency Room visit	9	9	2	8	2	-		
PR2						-		
PR3						-		
PR4						-		
PR5						-		
PR6						-		
PR7						-		

Case 8

Diagnoses	ICD-9-CM Codes					
First listed DX Unspecified viral infection	0	7	9	.	9	9
DX 2 Headaches	7	8	4	.	0	
DX 3				.		
DX 4				.		

Procedures	CPT Codes					Modifier (If Applicable)		
PR1 Emergency Room visit	9	9	2	8	3	-		
PR2						-		
PR3						-		
PR4						-		
PR5						-		
PR6						-		
PR7						-		

CCS-P Case Study Answer Key

<u>**Case 9**</u>

Diagnoses	ICD-9-CM Codes					
First listed DX Abdominal pain, unspecified site	7	8	9	.	0	0
DX 2 Hematemesis	5	7	8	.	0	
DX 3 Nausea with vomiting	7	8	7	.	0	1
DX 4				.		

Procedures	CPT Codes					Modifier (If Applicable)		
PR1 Emergency Room visit	9	9	2	8	3	-		
PR2						-		
PR3						-		
PR4						-		
PR5						-		
PR6						-		
PR7						-		

<u>**Case 10**</u>

Diagnoses	ICD-9-CM Codes					
First listed DX Carpal tunnel syndrome	3	5	4	.	0	
DX 2 Type I diabetes mellitus, without mention of complication, not stated as uncontrolled	2	5	0	.	0	1
DX 3 Essential hypertension, unspecified	4	0	1	.	9	
DX 4				.		

Procedures	CPT Codes					Modifier (If Applicable)		
PR1 Decompression of medial nerve, left wrist	6	4	7	2	1	-	L	T
PR2						-		
PR3						-		
PR4						-		
PR5						-		
PR6						-		
PR7						-		

CCS-P Case Study Answer Key

Case 11

Diagnoses	ICD-9-CM Codes					
First listed DX Candidal esophagitis	1	1	2	.	8	4
DX 2 Acute gastritis, without hemorrhage	5	3	5	.	0	0
DX 3 Atrophic gastritis, without hemorrhage	5	3	5	.	1	0
DX 4 Helicobacter pylori (bacterial infection)	0	4	1	.	8	6

Procedures	CPT Codes					Modifier (If Applicable)		
PR1 Esophagogastroduodenoscopy with biopsies	4	3	2	3	9	-		
PR2						-		
PR3						-		
PR4						-		
PR5						-		
PR6						-		
PR7						-		

Case 12

Diagnoses	ICD-9-CM Codes					
First listed DX Epistaxis	7	8	4	.	7	
DX 2				.		
DX 3				.		
DX 4				.		

Procedures	CPT Codes					Modifier (If Applicable)		
PR1 Emergency Room visit	9	9	2	8	1	-		
PR2						-		
PR3						-		
PR4						-		
PR5						-		
PR6						-		
PR7						-		

CCS-P Case Study Answer Key

<u>Case 13</u>

Diagnoses	ICD-9-CM Codes					
First listed DX CVA with paralysis	4	3	8	.	2	0
DX 2 Malnutrition	2	6	3	.	9	
DX 3 Weight loss	7	8	3	.	2	1
DX 4 Psychosis	2	9	8	.	9	

Procedures	CPT Codes					Modifier (If Applicable)		
PR1 Nursing Home visit	9	9	3	0	9	-		
PR2						-		
PR3						-		
PR4						-		
PR5						-		
PR6						-		
PR7						-		

<u>Case 14</u>

Diagnoses	ICD-9-CM Codes					
First listed DX Other cellulitis and abscess, foot, except toes	6	8	2	.	7	
DX 2 Type 1 diabetes mellitus, without mention of complication, not stated as uncontrolled	2	5	0	.	0	1
DX 3				.		
DX 4				.		

Procedures	CPT Codes					Modifier (If Applicable)		
PR1 Nursing Home visit	9	9	3	0	7	-		
PR2						-		
PR3						-		
PR4						-		
PR5						-		
PR6						-		
PR7						-		

CCS-P Case Study Answer Key

Case 15

Diagnoses	ICD-9-CM Codes					
First listed DX Pregnancy with clostridium infection	6	4	7	.	8	3
DX 2 Pregnancy with thyroid goiter	6	4	8	.	1	3
DX 3 Pregnancy with dehydration	6	4	8	.	9	3
DX 4 Enteritis due to clostridium difficile	0	0	8	.	4	5

Procedures	CPT Codes					Modifier (If Applicable)		
PR1 Colonoscopy with biopsy	4	5	3	8	0	-		
PR2						-		
PR3						-		
PR4						-		
PR5						-		
PR6						-		
PR7						-		

Case 16

Diagnoses	ICD-9-CM Codes					
First listed DX Acute cholecystitis with cholelithiasis	5	7	4	.	0	0
DX 2 Chronic cholecystitis with cholelithiasis	5	7	4	.	1	0
DX 3 Urinary tract infection	5	9	9	.	0	
DX 4 E. Coli	0	4	1	.	4	

Procedures	CPT Codes					Modifier (If Applicable)		
PR1 Laparoscopic cholecystectomy	4	7	5	6	2	-		
PR2						-		
PR3						-		
PR4						-		
PR5						-		
PR6						-		
PR7						-		

CCS-P Case Study Answer Key

Case 17

Diagnoses	ICD-9-CM Codes					
First listed DX Unspecified septicemia	0	3	8	.	9	
DX 2 SIRS	9	9	5	.	9	3
DX 3 Non-Hodgkin's lymphoma	2	0	2	.	8	0
DX 4 Adverse effect of chemotherapy	E9	3	3	.	1	

Procedures	CPT Codes					Modifier (If Applicable)		
PR1						-		
PR2						-		
PR3						-		
PR4						-		
PR5						-		
PR6						-		
PR7						-		

Case 18

Diagnoses	ICD-9-CM Codes					
First listed DX Malignant neoplasm right upper lobe, lung	1	6	2	.	3	
DX 2 Secondary malignancy thoracic lymph nodes	1	9	6	.	1	
DX 3 Asthmatic bronchitis	4	9	3	.	2	0
DX 4 Depression, NOS	3	1	1	.		

Procedures	CPT Codes					Modifier (If Applicable)		
PR1 Lobectomy of right upper lobe	3	2	4	8	0	-	R	T
PR2 Flexible bronchoscopy	3	1	6	2	2	-	5	9
PR3 Biopsy lymph nodes	3	8	5	0	0	-	5	1
PR4						-		
PR5						-		
PR6						-		
PR7						-		

CCS-P Case Study Answer Key

Case 19

Diagnoses	ICD-9-CM Codes					
First listed DX Displacement of cervical intervertebral disc without myelopathy	7	2	2	.	0	
DX 2 Dyspnea & respiratory abnormality	7	8	6	.	0	9
DX 3 Opiates/narcotics causing adverse effects in therapeutic use	E9	3	5	.	2	
DX 4 Asthma, unspecified	4	9	3	.	9	0

Note: Although E-codes are not coded on the examination, we wanted to remind you that all adverse effects must be coded as per coding guidelines. This may be covered in the multiple-choice question in the first part of the examination, also.

Procedures	CPT Codes					Modifier (If Applicable)		
PR Arthrodesis, anterior, including diskectomy; cervical	2	2	5	5	4	-		
PR2 Laminotomy, foraminotomy and/or excision of herniated intervertebral disk, cervical	6	3	0	2	0	-	5	1
PR3						-		
PR4						-		
PR5						-		
PR6						-		
PR7						-		

Case 20

Diagnoses	ICD-9-CM Codes					
First listed DX Threatened premature labor, antepartum	6	4	4	.	0	3
DX 2					.	
DX 3					.	
DX 4					.	

Procedures	CPT Codes					Modifier (If Applicable)		
PR1 Initial hospital care	9	9	2	2	1	-		
PR2						-		
PR3						-		
PR4						-		
PR5						-		
PR6						-		
PR7						-		

CCS-P Case Study Answer Key

<u>Case 21</u>

Diagnoses	ICD-9-CM Codes					
First listed DX Diabetes mellitus, type I with peripheral circulatory disorder, uncontrolled	2	5	0	.	7	3
DX 2 Diabetic ulcer of heel and midfoot	7	0	7	.	1	4
DX 3 Chronic renal failure	5	8	5	.	9	
DX 4 Pneumonia	4	8	6	.		

Procedures	CPT Codes					Modifier (If Applicable)		
PR 1 Excisional debridement	1	1	0	4	0	-		
PR 2						-		
PR 3						-		
PR 4						-		
PR 5						-		
PR 6						-		
PR7						-		

<u>Case 22</u>

Diagnoses	ICD-9-CM Codes					
First listed DX Coronary artery disease, native artery	4	1	4	.	0	1
DX 2 Unstable angina	4	1	1	.	1	
DX 3 Atrial fibrillation	4	2	7	.	3	1
DX 4 Second-degree atrioventricular block	4	2	6	.	1	3

Procedures	CPT Codes					Modifier (If Applicable)		
PR 1 PTCA, single vessel	9	2	9	8	2	-	R	C
PR 2 Left heart catheterization	9	3	5	1	0	-		
PR 3 Coronary angiography	9	3	5	4	5	-		
PR 4 Supervision and interpretation	9	3	5	5	6	-		
PR 5						-		
PR 6						-		
PR7						-		

CCS-P Case Study Answer Key

Case 23

Diagnoses	ICD-9-CM Codes					
First listed DX Diverticulitis of colon	5	6	2	.	1	1
DX 2 Post-operative atelectasis	9	9	7	.	3	9
DX 3 Atelectasis	5	1	8	.	0	9
DX 4 Peritoneal adhesions	5	6	8	.	0	

Procedures	CPT Codes					Modifier (If Applicable)		
PR 1 Hartman's Procedure	4	4	1	4	3	-		
PR 2 Lysis of adhesion	4	4	0	0	5	-	2	2
PR 3 Flexible sigmoidoscopy	4	5	3	7	8	-	5	2
PR 4 Small bowel resection	4	4	1	2	0	-	5	1
PR 5						-		
PR 6						-		
PR 7						-		

Case 24

Diagnoses	ICD-9-CM Codes					
First listed DX Ovarian cyst	6	2	0	.	2	
DX 2 Acute blood loss anemia	2	8	5	.	1	
DX 3 Urinary tract infection	5	9	9	.	0	
DX 4 Intrauterine synechiae	6	2	1	.	5	

Procedures	CPT Codes					Modifier (If Applicable)		
PR 1 Hysterectomy with bilateral salpingo-oophorectomy	5	8	1	5	0	-		
PR 2						-		
PR 3						-		
PR 4						-		
PR 5						-		
PR 6						-		
PR7						-		

CCS-P Case Study Answer Key

Case 25

Diagnoses				ICD-9-CM Codes		
First listed DX Sprain, wrist, unspecified site	8	4	2	.	0	0
DX 2				.		
DX 3				.		
DX 4				.		

Procedures	CPT Codes					Modifier (If Applicable)		
PR 1 Application of short arm splint (forearm to hand)	2	9	1	2	5	-	L	T
PR 2 Evaluation and Management (ER visit)	9	9	2	8	2	-		
PR 3 X-ray, wrist, two views	7	3	1	0	0	-	L	T
PR 4						-		
PR 5						-		
PR 6						-		
PR7						-		

Case 26

Diagnoses				ICD-9-CM Codes		
First listed DX Pneumonia	4	8	6	.		
DX 2 Asthmatic bronchitis with acute exacerbation	4	9	3	.	9	2
DX 3 Supraventricular tachycardia	4	2	7	.	8	9
DX 4 Chronic diastolic heart failure	4	2	8	.	3	2
Additional diagnosis DX 5 Tobacco use disorder	3	0	5		1	

Note: Although the instruction guides you to code only four diagnoses, we have added additional DX for your study convenience.

Procedures	CPT Codes					Modifier (If Applicable)		
PR 1 Initial hospital visit	9	9	2	2	2	-		
PR 2						-		
PR 3						-		
PR 4						-		
PR 5						-		
PR 6						-		
PR7						-		

CCS-P Case Study Answer Key

<u>Case 27</u>

Diagnoses	ICD-9-CM Codes					
First listed DX Pulmonary embolism	4	1	5	.	1	9
DX 2 Chronic systolic congestive heart failure	4	2	8	.	2	2
DX 3 Hypertensive renal disease with failure	4	0	3	.	9	0
DX 4 Type 1 diabetes with neurological manifestations	2	5	0	.	6	1
*Diabetic neuropathy	3	5	7	.	2	
Additional DX Deep vein thrombophlebitis	4	5	3		4	0
Additional DX Dizziness	7	8	0		4	
Additional DX Chronic obstructive pulmonary disease	4	9	6			
Additional DX Chronic kidney disease, unspecified	5	8	5		9	
Additional DX Obesity	2	7	8		0	0
Additional DX Long term (current) use of insulin	V	5	8		6	7
Additional DX History of tobacco use	V	1	5		8	2

Note: As per instructions, only four DX will be coded. The additional DX were added for your study convenience.

*Both the diabetes code and the diabetic neuropathy must be used.

Procedures	CPT Codes					Modifier (If Applicable)		
PR1						.		
PR2						.		
PR3						.		
PR4						.		
PR5						.		
PR6						.		
PR7						.		

CCS-P Case Study Answer Key
Case 28

Diagnoses	ICD-9-CM Codes					
First listed DX Abnormality in fetal heart rate, delivered	6	5	9	.	7	1
DX 2 Pre-eclampsia or eclampsia superimposed on pre-existing hypertension, delivered	6	4	2	.	7	1
DX 3 Malignant hypertension	4	0	1	.	0	
DX 4 Poor fetal growth, affecting management of mother, delivered	6	5	6	.	5	1
Additional DX Mother with single Liveborn	V	2	7	.	0	
Additional DX Early onset of delivery, delivered	6	4	4	.	2	1
Additional DX Elderly multigravida, delivered	6	5	9	.	6	1

Note: As per instructions, only four DX will be coded. The additional DX were added for your study convenience.

Procedures	CPT Codes					Modifier (If Applicable)		
PR 1 Low cervical cesarean section	5	9	5	1	0	-		
PR 2						-		
PR 3						-		
PR 4						-		
PR 5						-		
PR 6						-		
PR 7						-		

CCS-P Case Study Answer Key

Case 29

Diagnoses	ICD-9-CM Codes					
First listed DX Cellulitis and abscess of leg, except foot	6	8	2	.	6	
DX 2 Acute exacerbation of chronic obstructive pulmonary disease	4	9	1	.	2	1
DX 3 Congestive heart failure, unspecified	4	2	8	.	0	
DX 4 Coronary atherosclerosis, of native coronary artery	4	1	4	.	0	1
Additional DX Hypothyroidism, post-surgical	2	4	4	.	0	
Additional DX Osteoarthrosis, unspecified whether generalized or localized, site unspecified	7	1	5	.	9	0
Additional DX Gastroesophageal reflux	5	3	0	.	8	1
Additional DX Depressive disorder, not elsewhere classified	3	1	1	.		
Additional DX History of tobacco use	V	1	5	.	8	2

Note: As per instructions, only four DX will be coded. The additional DX were added for your study convenience.

Procedures	CPT Codes					Modifier (If Applicable)		
PR1						-		
PR2						-		
PR3						-		
PR4						-		
PR5						-		
PR6						-		
PR7						-		

CCS-P Case Study Answer Key

Case 30

Diagnoses	ICD-9-CM Codes					
First listed DX Acute respiratory failure	5	1	8	.	8	1
DX 2 Streptococcus pneumonia	4	8	1	.		
DX 3 Atrial fibrillation	4	2	7	.	3	1
DX 4 Alcoholic liver cirrhosis	5	7	1	.	2	
Additional DX Systemic inflammatory response syndrome	9	9	5	.	9	2
Additional DX Septic shock	7	8	5	.	5	2
Additional DX Hepatorenal syndrome	5	7	2	.	4	
Additional DX Urinary tract infection	5	9	9	.	0	
Additional DX Bacterial infection in conditions classified elsewhere and of unspecified site, E.coli	0	4	1	.	4	
Additional DX Alcohol dependence	3	0	3	.	9	0
Additional DX Acute renal failure	5	8	4	.	9	
Additional DX Essential hypertension, unspecified	4	0	1	.	9	
Additional DX Hypoglycemia	2	5	1	.	2	

Note: As per instructions, only four DX will be coded. The additional DX were added for your study convenience.

Procedures	CPT Codes					Modifier (If Applicable)		
PR1						-		
PR2						-		
PR3						-		
PR4						-		
PR5						-		
PR6						-		
PR7						-		

CCS-P Case Study Answer Key

Case 31

Diagnoses	ICD-9-CM Codes					
First listed DX Unspecified cerebral artery occlusion with cerebral infarction	4	3	4	.	9	1
DX 2 Urinary tract infection	5	9	9	.	0	
DX 3 Atrial fibrillation	4	2	7	.	3	1
DX 4 Mitral regurgitation, not otherwise specified	4	2	4	.	0	
Additional DX Hyposmolality and/or hyponatremia	2	7	6	.	1	
Additional DX Occlusion and stenosis of precerebral arteries, multiple and bilateral, without mention of cerebral infarction	4	3	3	.	3	0
Additional DX Hemiplegia, unspecified, affecting unspecified site	3	4	2	.	9	0
Additional DX Essential hypertension, unspecified	4	0	1	.	9	
Additional DX Aphasia	7	8	4	.	3	
Additional DX Bacterial infection in conditions classified elsewhere and of unspecified site, E. Coli	0	4	1	.	4	
Additional DX Pacemaker (other post procedural status)	V	4	5		0	1

Note: As per instructions, only four DX will be coded. The additional DX were added for your study convenience.

Procedures	CPT Codes					Modifier (If Applicable)		
PR1						-		
PR2						-		
PR3						-		
PR4						-		
PR5						-		
PR6						-		
PR7						-		

CCS-P Case Study Answer Key

Case 32

Diagnoses	ICD-9-CM Codes					
First listed DX Syncope, and collapse	7	8	0	.	2	
DX 2 Malnourishment of mild degree	2	6	3	.	1	
DX 3 Congestive heart failure, unspecified	4	2	8	.	0	
DX 4 Chronic obstructive pulmonary disease	4	9	6	.		
Additional DX Essential hypertension, unspecified	4	0	1	-	9	
Additional DX Hyperlipidemia, unspecified	2	7	2	-	4	
Additional DX History of tobacco use	V	1	5	-	8	2

Note: As per instructions, only four DX will be coded. The additional DX were added for your study convenience.

Procedures	CPT Codes					Modifier (If Applicable)		
PR1						-		
PR2						-		
PR3						-		
PR4						-		
PR5						-		
PR6						-		
PR7						x		

Case 33

Diagnoses	ICD-9-CM Codes					
First listed DX Closed fracture of neck of femur, intertrochanteric section	8	2	0	.	2	1
DX 2 Decubitus ulcer, buttock	7	0	7	.	0	5
DX 3 Chronic obstructive pulmonary disease	4	9	6	.		
DX 4 Alcoholic liver cirrhosis	5	7	1	.	2	
Additional DX Ascites	7	8	9	.	5	9
Additional DX Tobacco use disorder	3	0	5	.	1	
Additional DX Hyperammonemia	2	7	0	.	6	
Additional DX Abdominal mass, right lower quadrant	7	8	9	.	3	3
Additional DX Decubitus ulcer, other site (coccyx)	7	0	7	.	.0	.9
Additional DX Pressure ulcer, stage II	7	0	7	.	2	2

Note: As per instructions, only four DX will be coded. The additional DX were added for your study convenience.

Procedures	CPT Codes					Modifier (If Applicable)		
PR1 Closed reduction, internal fixation femur	2	7	2	4	4	-	R	T
PR2 Paracentesis	4	9	0	8	0	-	5	1
PR3 Transfusions, whole blood	3	6	4	3	0	-	5	1
PR4						-		
PR5						-		
PR6						-		
PR7						-		

CCS-P Case Study Answer Key

Case 34

Diagnoses	ICD-9-CM Codes					
First listed DX Poisoning, Haldol	9	6	9	.	2	
DX 2 Accidental poisoning	E8	5	3	.	1	
DX 3 Poisoning, Xanax	9	6	9	.	4	
DX 4 Accidental poisoning	E8	5	3	.	2	
Additional DX Depressive disorder	3	1	1	.		
Additional DX Type 2 diabetes	2	5	0	.	0	0
Additional DX Peripheral vascular disease, unspecified	4	4	3	.	9	

Note: As per instructions, only four DX will be coded. The additional DX were added for your study convenience.

Procedures	CPT Codes					Modifier (If Applicable)	
PR1						-	
PR2						-	
PR3						-	
PR4						-	
PR5						-	
PR6						-	
PR7						-	

CCS-P Case Study Answer Key

Case 35

Diagnoses	ICD-9-CM Codes					
First listed DX Acute bronchial asthma with exacerbation	4	9	3	.	2	2
DX 2 Tracheobronchitis, not specified as acute or chronic	4	9	0	.		
DX 3 Hypertension	4	0	1	.	9	
DX 4 Hyperlipidemia, unspecified	2	7	2	.	4	

Procedures	CPT Codes					Modifier (If Applicable)		
PR1 Bronchoscopy with closed (endoscopic) biopsy	3	1	6	2	5	-		
PR2 Bronchial lavage	3	1	6	2	4	-	5	1
PR3						-		
PR4						-		
PR5						-		
PR6						-		
PR7						-		

Case 36

Diagnoses	ICD-9-CM Codes					
First listed DX Herniated lumbar intervertebral disc, without myelopathy	7	2	2	.	1	0
DX 2				.		
DX 3				.		
DX 4				.		

Procedures	CPT Codes					Modifier (If Applicable)		
PR1 Excision, intervertebral disc	6	3	0	3	0	-		
PR2 Operating microscope	6	9	9	9	0	-		
PR3						-		
PR4						-		
PR5						-		
PR6						-		
PR7						-		

CCS-P Case Study Answer Key

Case 37

Diagnoses	ICD-9-CM Codes					
First listed DX Diverticulosis of colon	5	6	2	.	1	0
DX 2 Benign neoplasm, colon	2	1	1	.	3	
DX 3 Personal history of colon cancer	V	1	0	.	0	5
DX 4 Osteoporosis, unspecified	7	3	3	.	0	0
Additional DX Post-coronary artery bypass status	V	4	5	.	8	1
Additional DX Personal history of lung carcinoma	V	1	0	.	1	1
Additional DX Essential hypertension, unspecified	4	0	1	.	9	

Note: As per instructions, only four DX will be coded. The additional DX were added for your study convenience.

Procedures	CPT Codes					Modifier (If Applicable)		
PR1 Colonoscopy with removal of polyp	4	5	3	8	5	-		
PR2 Colonoscopy with closed (endoscopic) biopsy of large intestine	4	5	3	8	0	-	5	1
PR3						-		
PR4						-		
PR5						-		
PR6						-		
PR7						-		

Case 38

Diagnoses	ICD-9-CM Codes				
First listed DX Neck strain	8	4	7	.	0
DX 2 Lumbar back strain	8	4	7	.	2
DX 3				.	
DX 4				.	

Procedures	CPT Codes					Modifier (If Applicable)		
PR 1 Office visit	9	9	2	0	3	-		
PR 2						-		
PR 3						-		
PR 4						-		
PR 5						-		
PR 6						-		
PR7						-		

CCS-P Case Study Answer Key

Case 39

Diagnoses	ICD-9-CM Codes					
First listed DX Atrioventricular block, complete	4	2	6	.	0	
DX 2 Atrial fibrillation	4	2	7	.	3	1
DX 3				.		
DX 4				.		

Procedures	CPT Codes					Modifier (If Applicable)		
PR 1 Insertion of pacemaker with dual leads	3	3	2	0	8	-		
PR 2						-		
PR 3						-		
PR 4						-		
PR 5						-		
PR 6						-		
PR 7						-		

Case 40

Diagnoses	ICD-9-CM Codes					
First listed DX Hypertrophy of nasal turbinates	4	7	8	.	0	
DX 2 Other diseases of nasal cavity and sinuses	4	7	8	.	1	9
DX 3				.		
DX 4				.		

Although it is not mandatory, you could also code for "smoking."

Procedures	CPT Codes					Modifier (If Applicable)		
PR 1 Nasal reconstruction	3	0	5	2	0	-		
PR 2 Excision, nasoseptal spur	3	0	1	3	0	-	5	1
PR 3						-		
PR 4						-		
PR 5						-		
PR 6						-		
PR 7						-		

CCS-P Case Study Answer Key

Case 41

Diagnoses	ICD-9-CM Codes					
First listed DX Ulnar nerve entrapment	3	5	4	.	2	
DX 2				.		
DX 3				.		
DX 4				.		

Procedures	CPT Codes					Modifier (If Applicable)		
PR 1 Ulnar nerve transposition	6	4	7	1	8	-		
PR 2						-		
PR 3						-		
PR 4						-		
PR 5						-		
PR 6						-		
PR7						-		

Case 42

Diagnoses	ICD-9-CM Codes					
First listed DX Malignant neoplasm of female breast, upper-outer quadrant	1	7	4	.	4	
DX 2 Mitral valve disorder	4	2	4	.	0	
DX 3				.		
DX 4				.		

Procedures	CPT Codes					Modifier (If Applicable)		
PR 1 Excision, breast mass	1	9	1	2	0	-	L	T
PR 2						-		
PR 3						-		
PR 4						-		
PR 5						-		
PR 6						-		
PR7						-		

XI. CCS-P Mock Examination

CCS-P MOCK EXAMINATION

This mock examination follows the basic format and time constraints that are used in the certification examination. The mock examination contains 60 multiple-choice questions and a total of 16 coding cases.

The CCS-P examination is in a computer-based format. Carefully read your Candidate Handbook for the CCS-P examination and continue to monitor AHIMA's Web site to look for updated information on the examination.

Part I of the CCS-P Mock Examination has 60 multiple-choice questions. You are allotted 90 minutes to complete them. The timing you are striving for is about one minute to one and one half (1 to 1½) minutes per question so that you will be able to complete this part of the "real" examination in the 90 minutes allotted. These questions cover physician-based competencies, ICD-9-CM diagnostic coding, CPT, and HCPCS (Level II) procedural coding across all specialties. You will not be allowed to use your codebooks for Part I of the examination.

Part II of the examination consists of 16 coding cases testing your knowledge of ICD-9-CM Volumes 1–2 and HCPCS Level II (including E/M and all sections of CPT Coding). You are allowed 150 minutes to complete Part II of the examination. That gives you between nine and nine and one half (9 to 9½) minutes per case.

By following the time constraints on this mock examination, we hope you will get an idea of how much time you need and how much time is allotted for both the multiple-choice questions and the cases to code on the CCS-P Certification Examination.

Scoring in the CCS-P Examination:
- Points will be deducted for incorrect and/or unnecessary codes.
- Points will be deducted for any inappropriate codes.
- Sequencing the diagnoses and operative codes are not considered in scoring.

Do not use facility, regional, or insurance standards that differ from the procedures given for the examination.

NOTE: See procedures for coding that appear in Appendix B of the AHIMA Candidate Handbook for the CCS-P Examination.

1. As part of a concurrent record review, you need to locate the initial plan of action based on the attending physician's initial assessment of the patient. You can expect to find this documentation either within the body of the history and physical or in the

    A. doctor's admitting progress note.
    B. nurse's admit note.
    C. review of systems.
    D. discharge summary.

2. In the CPT coding system, when there is no code to properly represent the work performed by the provider, the coder must use the code

    A. not otherwise specified.
    B. not elsewhere classifiable.
    C. unlisted procedure.
    D. miscellaneous code.

3. You would expect to find documentation regarding the assessment of an obstetric patient's lochia, fundus, and perineum on the

    A. prenatal record.
    B. labor record.
    C. delivery room record.
    D. postpartum record.

4. A patient is admitted through the emergency department. Three days after admission, the physician documents uncontrolled diabetes mellitus. What is the "present on admission" (POA) indicator for uncontrolled diabetes mellitus?

    A. "Y"
    B. "U"
    C. "W"
    D. "N"

5. Your facility would like to improve physician documentation in order to allow improved coding. As coding supervisor, you have found it very effective to provide the physicians with

    A. a copy of the facility coding guidelines, along with written information on improved documentation.
    B. the UHDDS and information on where each data element is collected and/or verified in your facility.
    C. regular in-service presentations on documentation, including its importance and tips for improvement.
    D. feedback on specific instances when improved documentation would improve coding.

6. The special form that plays the central role in planning and providing care at nursing, psychiatric, and rehabilitation facilities is the

    A. interdisciplinary care plan.
    B. medical history and review of systems.
    C. interval summary.
    D. problem list.

7. Which diagnostic technique records the patient's heart rates and rhythms over a 24-hour period?

    A. echocardiography
    B. electrocardiography
    C. Holter monitor
    D. angiocardiography

8. Which of the following is considered late effects regardless of time?

    A. congenital defect
    B. non-union
    C. non-healing fracture
    D. poisoning

9. Patient is admitted for elective cholecystectomy for treatment of chronic cholecystitis with cholelithiasis. Prior to administration of general anesthesia, patient suffers cerebral thrombosis. Surgery is subsequently canceled. Code and sequence the diagnoses codes.

> 434.00   Cerebral thrombosis without cerebral infarction
> 574.10   Chronic cholecystitis with cholelithiasis
> V64.1   Surgery canceled, contraindication
> 997.02   Iatrogenic cerebrovascular infarction or hemorrhage

A. 997.02, 574.10
B. 574.10, 434.00, V64.1
C. 997.02, 434.00, V64.1
D. 434.00, V64.1

10. According to CPT, a biopsy of the breast that involves removal of only a portion of the lesion for pathological examination is:

A. percutaneous.
B. incisional.
C. excisional.
D. punch.

11. The practice of using a code that results in a higher payment to the provider than the code that more accurately reflects the service provided is known as

A. unbundling.
B. upcoding.
C. optimizing.
D. downcoding.

12. When coding multiple wound repairs in CPT,

A. only the most complex repair is reported.
B. only the least complex repair is reported.
C. up to nine individual repair codes may be reported.
D. all wound repairs are coded, with the most complex reported first.

13. Four people were seen in your emergency department yesterday. Which one will be coded as a poisoning?

> - Robert: diagnosed with digitalis intoxication
> - Gary: had an allergic reaction to a dye administered for a pyelogram
> - David: developed syncope after taking Contac pills with a double scotch
> - Brian: had an idiosyncratic reaction between two properly administered prescription drugs

A. Robert
B. Gary
C. David
D. Brian

14. A PAR physician is one who

A. can bill 115% above the Medicare Fee Schedule.
B. signs an agreement to participate in the Medicare program and agrees to accept whatever Medicare pays for a provider or service.
C. receives 5% less than other non-PAR physicians.
D. submits claim forms using ICD-9-CM procedure codes.

15. Which of the following scenarios identifies a pathologic fracture?

A. greenstick fracture secondary to fall from a bed
B. compression fracture of the skull after being hit with a baseball bat
C. vertebral fracture with cord compression following a car accident
D. compression fracture of the vertebrae as a result of bone metastasis

16. A patient is seen in the emergency department following an accident. The physician documents that the wound required multiple layers and extensive undermining. According to CPT definitions, this type of repair would be classified as:

    A. complex.   C. simple.
    B. intermediate.   D. advancement flap.

17. The patient sees a PAR provider and has a procedure performed after meeting the annual deductible. If the Medicare-approved amount is $200, how much is the patient's out-of-pocket expense?

    A. $0   C. $40
    B. $20   D. $100

18. Ensuring that data have been modified or accessed only by individuals who are authorized to do so is a function of data

    A. accuracy.   C. integrity.
    B. validity.   D. quality.

19. Security devices that form barriers between routers of a public network and a private network to protect access by unauthorized users are called

    A. data translators.   C. data manipulation engines.
    B. passwords.   D. firewalls.

20. You are conducting an educational session on benchmarking. You tell your audience that the key to benchmarking is to use the comparison to

    A. implement your QI process.
    B. make recommendations for improvement to the other department or organization.
    C. improve your department's processes.
    D. compare your department with another.

21. Which of the following procedures can be identified as "destruction" of lesions?

    A. removal of skin tags   C. laser removal of condylomata
    B. shaving of skin lesion   D. paring of hyperkeratotic lesion

22. Which of the following would NOT require HCPCS/CPT codes?

    A. hospital ambulatory surgery visit C. clinic visit
    B. hospital outpatient visit   D. hospital inpatient visit

23. Patient was seen in the emergency department with lacerations on the left arm. Two lacerations, one 7 cm and one 9 cm, were closed with layered sutures.

12002	Simple repair of superficial wounds of scalp, neck, axillae, external genitalia, trunk and/or extremities (including hands and feet); 2.6 cm to 7.5 cm
12004	Simple repair of superficial wounds of scalp, neck, axillae, external genitalia, trunk, and/or extremities (including hands and feet); 7.6 cm to 12.5 cm
12035	Layer closure of wounds of scalp, axillae, trunk and/or extremities (excluding hands and feet); 12.6 cm to 20.0 cm
12045	Layer closure of wounds of neck, hands, feet, and/or external genitalia; 12.6 cm to 20.0 cm

    A. 12045   C. 12002, 12004
    B. 12035   D. 12004

24. Patient was seen for excision of two interdigital neuromas from the left foot.

28080	Excision, interdigital (Morton) neuroma, single, each
64774	Excision of neuroma; cutaneous nerve, surgically identifiable
64776	Excision of neuroma; digital nerve, one or both, same digit

A. 64774   C. 28080
B. 64776   D. 28080, 28080

25. Patient was seen today for regular hemodialysis. No problems reported. Patient tolerated procedure well.

90935	Hemodialysis procedure with single physician evaluation
90937	Hemodialysis procedure requiring repeated evaluations(s) with or without substantial revision of dialysis prescription
90945	Dialysis procedure other than hemodialysis (eg, peritoneal dialysis, hemofiltration, or other continuous renal replacement therapies), with single physician evaluation
+99354	Prolonged physician service in the office or other outpatient setting requiring direct (face-to-face) contact beyond the usual service, first hour (List separately in addition to code for office or other outpatient Evaluation and Management service.)

A. 90937   C. 90945
B. 99354   D. 90935

26. Office visit for 43-year-old male, new patient, with no complaints. Patient is applying for life insurance and requests a physical examination. A detailed health and family history was obtained and a basic physical was done. Physician completed life insurance physical form at patient's request. Blood and urine were collected.

99381	Initial comprehensive preventive medicine evaluation and management of an individual including an age and gender appropriate history, examination, counseling/anticipatory guidance/risk factor reduction interventions, and the ordering of appropriate laboratory/diagnostic procedures, new patient; infant (age under 1 year)
99386	Initial comprehensive preventive medicine evaluation and management of an individual including an age- and gender-appropriate history examination, counseling/anticipatory guidance/risk factor reduction interventions, and the ordering of appropriate laboratory/diagnostic procedures, new patient; 40–64 years
99396	Periodic comprehensive preventive medicine reevaluation and management of an individual including an age and gender appropriate history, examination, counseling/anticipatory guidance/risk factor reduction interventions and the ordering of appropriate laboratory/diagnostic procedures, established patient; 40–64 years
99450	Basic life and/or disability examination that includes completion of a medical history following a life insurance pro forma

A. 99450   C. 99396
B. 99386   D. 99381

27. A quantitative drug assay was performed for a patient to determine digoxin level.

80050	General health panel
80101	Drug screen, qualitative; single drug class method (eg, immunoassay, enzyme assay), each drug class
80162	Digoxin (therapeutic drug assay, quantitative examination)
80166	Doxepin (therapeutic drug assay, quantitative examination)

A. 80101   C. 80166
B. 80050   D. 80162

28. Provide the CPT code for anesthesia services for the transvenous insertion of a pacemaker.

00530	Anesthesia for permanent transvenous pacemaker insertion
00560	Anesthesia for procedures on heart, pericardial sac, and great vessels of chest; without pump oxygenator
33202	Insertion of epicardial electrode(s); by open incision
33206	Insertion or replacement of permanent pacemaker with transvenous electrode(s); atrial

A. 00560   C. 00530
B. 33202, 00530   D. 33206, 00560

29. A 4-year-old had a repair of an incarcerated inguinal hernia. This is the first time this child has been treated for this condition.

49496	Repair initial inguinal hernia full-term infant, under age 6 months, or preterm infant over 50 weeks post-conception age and under 6 months at the time of surgery with or without hydrocelectomy; incarcerated or strangulated
49501	Repair initial inguinal hernia, age 6 months to under 5 years, with or without hydrocelectomy; incarcerated or strangulated
49521	Repair recurrent inguinal hernia, any age; incarcerated or strangulated
49553	Repair initial femoral hernia, any age; incarcerated or strangulated

A. 49553   C. 49521
B. 49496   D. 49501

30. The patient had a thrombectomy, without catheter, of the peroneal artery, by leg incision.

34203	Embolectomy or thrombectomy, with or without catheter; popliteal-tibio-peroneal artery, by leg incision
35226	Repair blood vessel, direct; lower extremity
35302	Thromboendarterectomy, including patch graft, if performed superficial femoral artery
37799	Unlisted procedure, vascular surgery

A. 34203   C. 35302
B. 37799   D. 35226

31. A patient with lung cancer and bone metastasis is seen for complex treatment planning by a radiation oncologist.

77263	Therapeutic radiology treatment planning; complex
77290	Therapeutic radiology simulation-aided field setting; complex
77315	Teletherapy, isodose plan (whether hand or computer calculated); complex (mantle or inverted Y, tangential ports, the use of wedges, compensators, complex blocking, rotational beam, or special beam considerations)
77334	Treatment devices, design and construction; complex (irregular blocks, special shields, compensators, wedges, molds, or casts)

A. 77315　　　　　　　　　　C. 77290
B. 77263　　　　　　　　　　D. 77334

32. An established patient was seen by physician in her office for DtaP vaccine and Hib.

90471	Immunization administration (includes percutaneous, intradermal, subcutaneous, or intramuscular injections); one vaccine (single or combination vaccine/toxoid)
90700	Diptheria, tetanus toxoids, and acellular pertussis vaccine (DTaP), when administered to individuals younger than 7 years, for intramuscular use
90720	Diphtheria, tetanus toxoids, and whole cell pertussis vaccine and Hemophilus influenza B vaccine (DTP-Hib), for intramuscular use
90721	Diptheria, tetanus toxoids, and acellular pertussis vaccine and Hemophilus influenza B vaccine (DtaP-Hib), for intramuscular use
90748	Hepatitis B and Hemophilus influenza B vaccine (Hep B-Hib), for intramuscular use
99211	Office or other outpatient visit for the evaluation and management of an established patient which may not require the presence of a physician. Usually, the presenting problem(s) are minimal. Typically, 5 minutes are spent performing or supervising these services.

A. 90721　　　　　　　　　　C. 90700, 90748, 99211
B. 90720, 90471　　　　　　　D. 90471, 90721

33. The purpose of the Correct Coding Initiative is to

A. increase fines and penalties for bundling services into comprehensive CPT codes.
B. restrict Medicare reimbursement to hospitals for ancillary services.
C. teach coders how to unbundle codes.
D. detect and prevent payment for improperly coded services.

34. If the same condition is described as both acute and chronic, and separate subentries exist in the ICD-9-CM alphabetic index at the same indentation level,

A. they should both be coded, acute sequenced first.
B. they should both be coded, chronic sequenced first.
C. only the acute condition should be coded.
D. only the chronic condition should be coded.

35. A patient was sent to the surgeon's office as requested by the patient because the insurance company requires a second opinion regarding surgery. The patient has been complaining of lower back pain for over a year due to a herniated disk. The patient presents to the surgeon's office, where a detailed history and physical examination was performed. Medical records from the primary care physician and the physical therapist were reviewed along with the tests performed in the office. Low medical decision making was made. A copy of the surgeon's reports was sent to the insurance company.

99203　　Office or other outpatient visit for the evaluation and management of a new patient that requires these three key components
* A detailed history;
* A detailed examination; and
* Medical decision making of low complexity

Counseling and/or coordination of care with other providers or agencies are provided consistent with the nature of the problem(s) and the patient's and/or family's needs.

Usually, the presenting problem(s) are of moderate severity. Physicians typically spend 30 minutes face to face with the patient and/or family.

99242　　Office consultation for a new or established patient that requires three key components:
* An expanded problem focused history;
* An expanded problem focused examination; and
* Straight-forward medical decision making.

Counseling and/or coordination with other providers or agencies are provided consistent with the nature of the problem(s) and the patient's and/or family's needs.

Usually the presenting problem(s) are of low severity. Physicians typically spend 30 minutes face to face with the patient and/or family.

99243　　Office consultation for a new or established patient that requires these three components:
* A detailed history;
* A detailed examination; and
* Medical decision making of low complexity.

Counseling and/or coordination with other providers or agencies are provided consistent with the nature of the problem(s) and the patient's and/or family's needs.

Usually the presenting problem(s) are of moderate severity. Physicians typically spend 40 minutes face to face with the patient and/or family.

99253　　Inpatient consultation for a new or established patient that requires these three key components: detailed history, detailed examination, and medical decision making of low complexity
* A detailed history;
* A detailed examination; and
* Medical decision making of low complexity.

Counseling and/or coordination with other providers or agencies are provided consistent with the nature of the problem(s) and the patient's and/or family's needs.

Usually the presenting problem(s) are of moderate severity. Physicians typically spend 55 minutes at the bedside and on the patient's hospital floor or unit.

-32　　Mandated services.

A.　99242-32　　　　　　　　C.　99253-32
B.　99243　　　　　　　　　　D.　99203-32

36. Patient arrives in the emergency room via a medical helicopter. The patient has sustained multiple life-threatening injuries due to a multiple car accident. The patient goes into cardiac arrest upon arrival. An hour and 30 minutes of critical care time is spent trying to stabilize the patient.

99282   Emergency department visit for the evaluation and management of a patient that requires these three key components:
- An expanded problem focused history;
- An expanded problem focused examination; and
- Medical decision making of low complexity.

Counseling and/or coordination of acre with other providers or agencies are provided consistent with the nature of the problem(s) and the patient's and/or family's needs.
Usually, the presenting problem(s) are of low to moderate severity.

99285   Emergency department visit for the evaluation and management of a patient that requires these three key components within the constraints imposed by the urgency clinical condition and/or mental status:
- A comprehensive history;
- A comprehensive examination; and
- Medical decision making of high complexity.

Counseling and/or coordination of acre with other providers or agencies are provided consistent with the nature of the problem(s) and the patient's and/or family's needs.
Usually, the presenting problem(s) are of high severity and pose an immediate significant threat to life or physiological function.

99288   Physician direction of emergency medical systems (EMS) emergency care, advanced life support.

99291   Critical care, evaluation and management of the critically ill or critically injured patient; first 30–74 minutes.

+99292 Each additional 30 minutes (list separately in addition to code for primary service).

A. 99285; 99288; 99291
B. 99291; +99292
C. 99291;+ 99292; 99285
D. 99282

37. Patient presents with a diabetic ulcer that needs to be debrided. The patient was taken to the operating room where debridement of the muscle took place.

11011   Debridement including removal of foreign material associated with open fracture(s) and, or dislocation(s); skin, subcutaneous tissue, muscle fascia, and muscle.
11043   Debridement; skin, subcutaneous tissue and muscle.
11400   Excision, benign lesion including margins, except skin tag (unless listed elsewhere), trunk, arms or legs; excised diameter 0.5 centimeter or less.
15999   Unlisted procedure, excision pressure ulcer (for free skin graft to close ulcer or donor site, see 15002 et seq).

A. 15999
B. 11400
C. 11011
D. 11043

38. Excision, soft tissue lipoma of the back: (Code for diagnoses using ICD-9-CM. Code for procedure using CPT)

214.1	Lipoma of other skin and subcutaneous tissue
216.5	Benign neoplasm of the skin of the trunk except scrotum
216.9	Benign neoplasm of the skin, site unspecified
11600	Excision, malignant lesion, trunk, arms, or legs, lesion diameter 0.5 cm or less
21556	Excision, tumor, soft tissue of neck or anterior thorax; subfascial (e.g. intramuscular) less than 5 cm
21925	Biopsy, soft tissue of back or flank; deep
21930	Excision, tumor, soft tissue of back or flank, subcutaneous; less than 3 cm

A. 216.5, 11600
B. 214.1, 21925
C. 216.9, 21556
D. 214.1, 21930

39. Patient presents to the hospital and undergoes a posterior L1–L5 spinal fusion for scoliosis with placement of a Harrington rod.

22612	Arthrodesis, posterior or posterolateral technique, single level; lumbar (with or without) lateral transverse technique.
22800	Arthrodesis, posterior, for spinal deformity, with or without cast; up to 6 vertebral segments.
+22840	Posterior non-segmental instrumentation (eg, Harrington rod technique, pedicle fixation across one interspace, atlantoaxial transarticular screw fixation, sublaminar wiring at C1, facet screw fixation) (list separately in addition to code for primary procedure).
+22841	Internal spinal fixation by wiring spinous processes (list separately in addition to code for primary procedure).
+22842	Posterior segmental instrumentation (eg, pedicle fixation, dual rods with multiple hooks and sublaminar wires); 3–6 vertebral segments (list separately in addition to code for primary procedure).
+22846	Anterior instrumentation; 4 to 7 vertebral segments (list separately in addition to code for primary procedure).

A. 22800; 22846
B. 22800; 22842
C. 22800; 22840
D. 22612; 22800; 22841

40. Patient has tear of the medial meniscus with loose bodies in the medial compartment of the left knee that was repaired by arthroscopic medial meniscectomy, shaving and trimming of meniscal rim, resection of synovium and removal of the loose bodies.

27331	Arthrotomy, knee; including joint exploration, biopsy, or removal of loose or foreign bodies.
27333	Arthrotomy, knee; medial and lateral.
29800	Arthroscopy, temporomandibular joint, diagnostic, with or without synovial biopsy (separate procedure).
29804	Arthroscopy, temporomandibular joint, surgical; (for open procedures, use 21010)
29819	Arthroscopy, shoulder, surgical; with removal of loose body or foreign body (for open procedure, see 23040-23044, 23107).
29874	Arthroscopy, knee, surgical; for removal of loose body or foreign body (eg, osteochondritis dissecans fragmentation, chondral fragmentation).
29881	Arthroscopy, knee, surgical; with meniscectomy (medial OR lateral, including any meniscal shaving).
LT	Left.

A. 29804

B. 27333-LT; 27331-LT

C. 29800-LT; 29819-LT

D. 29881-LT

41. Single lung transplant without cardiopulmonary bypass:

32652	Thoracoscopy, surgical; with total pulmonary decortication, including intrapleuaral pneumonolysis
32850	Donor pneunomectomy(s) (including cold preservation), from cadaver donor
32851	Lung transplant, single; without cardiopulmonary bypass
32852	Lung transplant, single; with cardiopulmonary bypass

A. 32850

B. 32852

C. 32852

D. 32851

42. Patient has a year history of mitral valve regurgitation and now presents for a mitral valve replacement with bypass.

33425	Valvuloplasty, mitral valve, with cardiopulmonary bypass
33430	Replacement, mitral valve, with cardiopulmonary bypass
33460	Valvectomy, tricuspid valve, with cardiopulmonary bypass
35231	Repair blood vessel with vein graft; neck

A. 33430

B. 33460

C. 33425

D. 35231

43. Patient has breast carcinoma and is now undergoing complete axillary lymphadenectomy.

38525	Biopsy or excision of lymph nodes; open, deep axillary node(s)
38562	Limited lymphadenectomy for staging (separate procedure; pelvic and para-aortic
38740	Axillary lymphadenectomy; superficial
38745	Axillary lymphadenectomy; complete

A. 38525

B. 38740

C. 38562

D. 38745

44. Patient presents to the GI lab for a colonoscopy. During the colonoscopy, polyps were discovered in the ascending colon and in the transverse colon. Polyps in the ascending colon were removed via hot biopsy forceps and the polyps in the transverse colon were removed by snare technique.

211.3	Benign neoplasm of colon
44392	Colonoscopy through stoma; with removal of polyps, hot biopsy forceps
44394	Colonoscopy through stoma; with removal of polyps, snare technique
45355	Colonoscopy, transabdominal via colotomy
45383	Colonoscopy, with ablation of polyps, not by hot biopsy forceps or snare technique
45384	Colonoscopy with removal of polyps, hot biopsy forceps
45385	Colonoscopy with removal of polyps, snare technique
-59	Distinct procedural service

A. 211.3, 45355   C. 211.3, 44392, 44394 -59

B. 211.3, 45384, 45385 -59   D. 211.3, 45355, 45383 -59

45. Patient came to the hospital ambulatory surgical center for repair of incisional hernia. This is the second time the patient has developed this problem. The hernia was repaired with Gore-Tex graft. Choose the appropriate ICD-9-CM and CPT codes.

550.10	Inguinal hernia, with obstruction, without gangrene, unilateral or unspecified
553.20	Ventral hernia, unspecified without obstruction or gangrene
553.21	Incisional hernia, without obstruction or gangrene
49520	Repair recurrent inguinal hernia, any age, reducible
49560	Repair initial incisional or ventral hernia, reducible
49565	Repair recurrent incisional or ventral hernia, reducible
+49568	Implantation of mesh or other prosthesis for incisional or ventral hernia repair, or mesh for closure of debridement for necrotizing soft tissue infection (List separately in addition to code for the incisional or ventral hernia repair.)

A. 553.21, 49565, 49568   C. 550.10, 49565

B. 553.20, 553.21, 49520, 49568   D. 550.10, 553.20, 49560, 49568

46. Female with six (6) months of stress incontinence. Laparoscopic urethral suspension was completed. Choose the appropriate ICD-9-CM and CPT codes.

625.6	Urinary stress incontinence, female
788.30	Urinary incontinence, unspecified
788.32	Urinary stress incontinence, male
51840	Anterior vesicourethropexy or urethropexy (eg, Marshall-Marchetti-Krantz, Burch); simple
51845	Abdomino-vaginal vesical neck suspension with or without endoscopic control
51990	Laparoscopy, surgical; urethral suspension for stress incontinence
51992	Laparoscopy, surgical; sling operation for stress incontinence

A. 788.30; 51992   C. 788.32; 51840

B. 625.6; 51990   D. 788.30; 51845

47. Male patient has been diagnosed with benign prostatic hypertrophy and undergoes a transurethral destruction of the prostate by radiofrequency thermotherapy. (Code ICD-9-CM for diagnoses and CPT for procedures.)

600.00	Hypertrophy (benign of prostate) without urinary obstruction and other lower urinary tract symptoms (LUTS)
52601	Transurethral electrosurgical resection of prostate including control of postoperative bleeding, complete (vasectomy, meatotomy, cystourethroscopy, urethral calibration and/or dilation, and internal urethrotomy are included)
52648	Laser vaporization of prostate, including control of postoperative bleeding, complete (vasectomy, meatotomy, cystourethroscopy, urethral calibration and/or dilation, internal urethrotomy, and transurethral transection of the prostate are included if performed)
53850	Transurethral destruction of prostate tissue; by microwave thermotherapy
53852	Transurethral destruction of prostate tissue; by radiofrequency thermotherapy

A. 600.00, 52648
B. 600.00, 53852
C. 600.00, 52601
D. 600.00, 53850

48. Hysteroscopy with D&C and polypectomy:

58100	Endometrial sampling biopsy with or without endocervical sampling biopsy, without cervical dilation, any method (separate procedure)
58120	Dilation and curettage, diagnostic and/or therapeutic (nonobstetrical)
58555	Hysteroscopy, diagnostic (separate procedure)
58558	Hysteroscopy, surgical; with sampling (biopsy) of endometrium and/or polypectomy, with or without D&C
58563	Hysteroscopy, surgical; with endometrial ablation (eg, endometrial resection, electrosurgical ablation, thermoablation)

A. 58563
B. 58558
C. 58120, 58100, 58555
D. 58558, 58120

49. Cesarean delivery with antepartum and postpartum care:

59400	Routine obstetric care, including antepartum care, vaginal delivery (with or without episiotomy and/or forceps), and postpartum care (vaginal delivery)
59510	Routine obstetric care, including antepartum care, cesarean delivery, and postpartum care
59514	Cesarean delivery only
59610	Routine obstetric care, including antepartum care, vaginal delivery (with or without episiotomy and/or forceps) and postpartum care, after previous cesarean delivery

A. 59610
B. 59514
C. 59400
D. 59510

50. D&C for missed abortion, first trimester:

59820	Treatment of missed abortion, completed surgically; first trimester
59840	Induced abortion, by dilation and curettage
59850	Induced abortion, by one or more intra-amniotic injections, (amniocentesis -injections) including hospital admission and visits, delivery of fetus, and secundines
59855	Induced abortion, by one or more vaginal suppositories (eg, prostaglandin), with or without cervical dilation, (eg, laminaria), including hospital admission and visits, delivery of fetus and secundines

A. 59840   C. 59855

B. 59850   D. 59820

51. Total transcervical thymectomy:

60200	Excision of cyst or adenoma of thyroid, or transection of isthmus
60240	Thyroidectomy, total or complete
60520	Thymectomy, partial or total; transcervical approach (separate procedure)
60540	Adrenalectomy, partial or complete, or exploration of adrenal gland with or without biopsy, transabdominal, lumbar, or dorsal (separate procedure)

A. 60520   C. 60240

B. 60540   D. 60200

52. Patient with carpal tunnel comes in for an open carpal tunnel release. (Code ICD-9-CM for diagnoses and CPT for procedures.)

354.0	Carpal tunnel syndrome
64721	Neuroplasty and/or transposition; median nerve at carpal tunnel
64892	Nerve graft (includes obtaining graft), single strand, arm or leg; up to 4 cm length
64905	Nerve pedicle transfer; first stage
64999	Unlisted procedure, nervous system

A. 354.0, 64999   C. 354.0, 64905

B. 354.0, 64721   D. 354.0, 64892

53. Lumbar laminectomy (one segment) for decompression of spinal cord: (Code CPT for procedures.)

62263	Percutaneous lysis of epidural adhesions using solution injection (eg, hypertonic saline, enzyme) or mechanical means (eg, catheter) including radiologic localization (includes contrast when administered), multiple adhesiolysis sessions; 2 or more days.
63005	Laminectomy, with exploration and/or decompression of spinal cord and/or cauda equina, without facetectomy, foraminotomy or diskectomy (eg, spinal stenosis), one or two vertebral segments; lumbar except for spondylolisthesis
63030	Laminotomy (hemilaminectomy), with decompression of nerve roots, including partial facetectomy, foraminotomy, and/or excision of herniated intervertebral disk including open and/or endoscopically-assisted approaches); one interspace, lumbar.
63170	Laminectomy with myelotomy (eg, Bischof or DREZ type) cervical, thoracic, or thoracolumbar

A. 63005   C. 63170

B. 62263   D. 63030

54. Phacoemulsification of left cataract with IOL implant and subconjunctival injection. (Code ICD-9-CM for procedures and CPT for procedures.)

366.9	Unspecified cataract
66940	Removal of lens material; extracapsular
66983	Intracapsular cataract extraction with insertion of intraocular lens prosthesis (one stage procedure)
66984	Extracapsular cataract removal with insertion of intraocular lens prosthesis (one-stage procedure), manual or mechanical technique (eg, irrigation and aspiration or phacoemulsification)
68200	Subconjunctival injection

A. 366.9, 66940-LT
B. 366.9, 66983, 68200
C. 366.9, 66984-LT
D. 366.9, 66984-LT, 68200-LT

55. Chronic otitis media with bilateral myringotomy and tube insertion, using local anesthesia. (Code ICD-9-CM for diagnoses and CPT for procedures.)

381.00	Acute nonsuppurative otitis media, unspecified
381.05	Acute allergic mucoid otitis media
382.9	Unspecified otitis media
69400	Eustachian tube inflation, transnasal with catheterization
69405	Eustachian tube catheterization, transtympanic
69420	Myringotomy including aspiration and/or eustachian tube inflation
69433	Tympanostomy (requiring insertion of ventilating tube), local or topical anesthesia

A. 382.9, 69420, 69420
B. 382.9, 69433, 69433
C. 381.05, 69405, 69405
D. 381.00, 69400, 69400

56. A document that acknowledges patient responsibility for payment if Medicare denies the claim is a(n)

A. explanation of benefits.
B. remittance advice.
C. advance beneficiary notice.
D. CMS-1500 claim form.

57. A(n) _____ form is used to record the patient's diagnoses and the services performed for a particular visit. It also includes codes (CPT, HCPCS, and ICD-9-CM) used specifically by that physician's office.

A. authorization
B. ABN (Advance Beneficiary Notice)
C. superbill
D. EOB (Explanation of Benefits)

58. What is the term used to describe the adjusting of the dollar amount due from the patient or insurance company to reflect a zero balance due on the claim?

A. authorization
B. write off
C. rebill
D. outstanding

59. Your organization is sending confidential patient information across the Internet using technology that will transform the original data into unintelligible code that can be re-created by authorized users. This technique is called

A. a firewall.
B. validity processing.
C. a call-back process.
D. data encryption.

60. What legal term is used in describing sexual harassment in reference to unwelcome sexual advances, request for sexual favors, and verbal or physical conduct of a sexual nature made in return for job benefits.

A. res ipsa loquitur

B. qui tam

C. quid pro quo

D. respondeat superior

CCS-P Mock Exam Answer Key
 ANSWER EXPLANATION

1. A   A clinical impression and an intended course of action are either entered in the physical examination or provided in the admission note. The admission note provides an overview of the patient and adds any relevant information that is not included in the history and physical examination.

REFERENCE: Green and Bowie, p 136–137

2. C

REFERENCE: AMA CPT (2010), p xii
 AMA, p 29, 323
 Eid, p 28
 Green, p 430

3. D   The postpartum data records information about the condition of the mother after delivery and includes an assessment of the lochia and conditions of the breasts, fundus, and perineum.

REFERENCE: Abdelhak, p 111
 Green and Bowie, p 170, 174

4. D

REFERENCE: McWay, p 132
 LaTour and Eichenwald-Maki, p 54, 400, 615
 Johns, 2006, p 803–804

5. D

REFERENCE: Green, p 13–15
 Abdelhak, p 183–184

6. A   The interdisciplinary care plan is the foundation around which patient care is organized. It contains input from the unique perspective of each discipline involved. It includes an assessment, statement of goals, identification of specific activities or strategies to achieve those goals, and periodic assessment of goal attainment.

REFERENCE: Abdelhak, p 107
 Johns, p 83
 LaTour and Eichenwald-Maki, p 203

7. C

REFERENCE: Jones, p 385–386
 Scott and Fong, p 270
 Sormunen, p 197

CCS-P Mock Exam Answer Key
      ANSWER   EXPLANATION

8. B

REFERENCE: Bowie and Shaffer (2010), p 61–63
                  Brown, p 59, 354
                  Johnson and McHugh, p 72–73
                  Schraffenberger, p 314–315

9. B

REFERENCE: Bowie and Shaffer (2010), p 624
                  Brown, p 72–73
                  Green, p 185
                  Johnson and McHugh, p 24
                  Schraffenberger, p 40–41

10. B

REFERENCE: Bowie and Schaffer (2008), p 114
                  Green, p 455–456
                  Johnson and McHugh, p 240–241
                  Smith, p 70–71

11. B
REFERENCE: Green and Rowell, p 91
                  Johnson and McHugh, p 559, 604
                  Green and Bowie, p 312
                  Bowie and Schaffer (2008), p 91–93
                  Green, p 12–13

12. D

REFERENCE: Bowie and Schaffer (2008), p 101–102
                  Eid, p 57–58
                  Green, p 442–448
                  Johnson and McHugh, p 227

13. C   The condition should be coded as a poisoning when there is an interaction of an over-the-
         counter drug and alcohol. Answers A, B, and D are adverse effects of a correctly
         administered prescription drug.
REFERENCE: Brown, p 435–437
                  Eid, p 262–263
                  Frisch, p 149–150
                  Green, p 164–167, 170–171
                  Johnson and McHugh, p 68–69
                  Schraffenberger, p 289–290

CCS-P Mock Exam Answer Key
    ANSWER   EXPLANATION

14. B

REFERENCE: Eid, p 269–270
                Green, p 782
                Hazelwood and Venable, p 288–290
                Green and Rowell, p 401–402
                Rizzo, p 188

15. D

REFERENCE: Bowie and Shaffer (2010), p 281–282
                Brown, p 255, 318, 379, 409
                Green, p 157
                Hazelwood and Venable, p 239
                Johnson and McHugh, p 252–253

16. A

REFERENCE: Bowie and Schaffer (2008), p 100–102
                Eid, p 55–58
                Green, p 442–445
                Johnson and McHugh, p 226–228
                Smith, p 60

17. C   Medicare pays 80% or $160 and the patient pays 20%, or $40.

REFERENCE: Eid, p 269–270
                Green, p 782
                Green and Rowell, p 401–402
                Rizzo, p 187–188
                Hazelwood and Venable, p 288–290

18. C

REFERENCE: Green and Bowie, p 271
                LaTour and Eichenwald-Maki, p 134, 250–251

19. D

REFERENCE: LaTour and Eichenwald-Maki, p 79, 252
                McWay, p 312, 422

20. C   Benchmarking involves comparing your department to other departments or organizations known to be excellent in one or more areas. The success of benchmarking involves finding out how the other department functions and then incorporating their ideas into your department.

REFERENCE: LaTour and Eichenwald-Maki, p 691
                McWay, p 148, 153, 1571

21. C

REFERENCE: Johnson and McHugh, p 219, 237–239
                Green, p 438–439

CCS-P Mock Exam Answer Key
     ANSWER   EXPLANATION

22. D   The hospital inpatient procedure would not be coded using HCPCS/CPT codes. Hospital inpatient visit diagnoses and procedures are coded using ICD-9-CM codes.

REFERENCE: Green, p 210–211
                  Johnson and McHugh, p 24, 577
                  Schraffenberger (2010), p xi-xii
                  Smith, p 1

23. B   The sizes of the layered wound repairs of the same body area are added together in order to select the correct CPT code.

REFERENCE: Bowie and Schaffer (2008), 100–102
                  Green, p 442–445
                  Johnson and McHugh, p 226–228
                  Smith, p 60–61
                  AMA, 131–132

24. D   Look up in CPT code book under foot, neuroma.

REFERENCE: AMA CPT (2010)

25. D   "Dialysis" is the main term to be referenced in the CPT manual index.

REFERENCE: Bowie and Schaffer (2008), p 346–349
                  Green, p 798
                  Johnson and McHugh, p 414–415
                  Smith, p 214

26. A   The codes in this subsection are used to report evaluations for life or disability insurance baseline information.

REFERENCE: Bowie and Schaffer (2008), p 74–75
                  AMA CPT (2010). 34
                  Green, p 365
                  Johnson and McHugh, p 180
                  AMA, 88–90

27. D

REFERENCE: Bowie and Schaffer (2008), p 235–236
                  Green, p 706–707
                  AMA, p 362–365
                  Johnson and McHugh, p 400–402
                  Smith, p 163

28. C

REFERENCE: Bowie and Schaffer (2008), p 81–822
                  Green, p 400–401
                  AMA, p 99–103
                  Johnson and McHugh, p 182–183

CCS-P Mock Exam Answer Key
ANSWER   EXPLANATION

29. D

REFERENCE: Bowie and Schaffer (2008), p 226
                  Green, p 576–577
                  Johnson and McHugh, p 196–197
                  AMA, p 229–230
                  Smith, p 110–111

30. A

REFERENCE: Bowie and Schaffer (2008), p 172–173
                  Eid, p 97
                  Green, p 525–526
                  Johnson and McHugh, p 301

31. B

REFERENCE: Bowie and Schaffer (2008), p 327–328
                  AMA CPT (2010), p 373
                  Eid, p 163
                  Green, p 679–683
                  Johnson and McHugh, p 391
                  Smith, p 154–155
                  AMA, p 269, 282, 344–345

32. D   If the immunization is the only service that the patient receives, two codes are used to report the service: the immunization administration code is first and then the code for the vaccine/toxoid.

REFERENCE: Bowie and Schaffer (2008), p 342
                  AMA CPT (2010), p 435–439
                  Eid, p 184–185
                  AMA, p 394–395, 398
                  Green, p 732–733
                  Johnson and McHugh, p 411,413
                  Smith, p 200

33. D

REFERENCE: Bowie and Schaffer (2008), p 91–93
                  Frisch, p 235–240
                  Green, p 12, 317–318, 806
                  Hazelwood and Venable, p 292
                  Johnson and McHugh, p 556–557
                  Smith, p 53

CCS-P Mock Exam Answer Key
       ANSWER   EXPLANATION

34. A

REFERENCE: Bowie and Schaffer (2010), p 59
              Brown, p 57–58
              Frisch, p 133
              Green, p 101
              Johnson and McHugh, p 75
              Schraffenberger, p 442, 508

35. D

REFERENCE: AMA (2010), p 20–22
              Eid, p 30–31
              Frisch, p 16, 49–53
              Green, p 307, 347
              Johnson and McHugh, p 116, 126–127
              AMA, p 53, 491
              Smith, p 190–191
              Bowie and Schaffer (2008), p 15, 57

36. B

REFERENCE: Bowie and Schaffer (2008), p 58–61
              AMA CPT (2010), p 18–19
              AMA, p 37, 68–71, 92–93, 115
              Eid, p 39
              Frisch, p 27–32
              Green, p 357–359
              Johnson and McHugh, p 170–172
              Smith, p 200–201

37. D

REFERENCE: Bowie and Schaffer (2008), 96–97
              Johnson and McHugh, p 219–220
              AMA, p 120–122
              Green, p 444

38. D   Excision of lipomas: code to excision of soft tissue.

REFERENCE: Bowie and Schaffer (2010), p 83–84
              AMA CPT (2010), p 98
              Green, p 477
              Smith, p 57
              Brown, p 476–477

CCS-P Mock Exam Answer Key
     ANSWER   EXPLANATION

39. C

REFERENCE: Bowie and Schaffer (2008), 127
                 AMA CPT (2010), 104
                 Green, p 481–482
                 Johnson and McHugh, 268–269
                 AMA, p 160–162

40. D If debridement or shaving of articular cartilage and mensectomy are performed in the same compartment of the knee, then code only 298.81

REFERENCE: Bowie and Schaffer (2008), p 137
                 CPT Assistant, April 2001, p 5–7, 12
                 CPT Assistant, April 2003, p 12, 14
                 Green, p 488–489
                 AMA, p 171–172
                 Johnson and McHugh, p 263–264

41. D

REFERENCE: Bowie and Schaffer (2008), p 157–158
                 CPT Assistant, Winter 1993, p 2
                 AMA, p 182
                 Green, p 500–501
                 Johnson and McHugh, p 300–301

42. A Valvuloplasty is a plastic repair of a valve.

REFERENCE: Bowie and Schaffer (2008), p 168
                 Green, 518–519
                 Johnson and McHugh, p 275
                 AMA, p 195

43. D

REFERENCE: Bowie and Schaffer (2008), 191–192
                 Green, p 543
                 Johnson and McHugh, p 191

44. B According to *CPT Assistant,* when a colonoscopy with polypectomy is performed by two different techniques, both techniques are coded.

REFERENCE: Bowie and Schaffer (2008), p 221
                 Green, p 571–573
                 Johnson and McHugh, p 193
                 Smith, p 104–106
                 Bowie and Schaffer (2010), p 78–79

CCS-P Mock Exam Answer Key
    ANSWER   EXPLANATION

45. A   The mesh is reported as an additional code. The hernia is considered recurrent because this
        documentation states this is the second hernia.

REFERENCE: Bowie and Schaffer (2008), p 226
                 MA, p 121, 229– 230
                 AMA CPT (2010), p 244–245
                 Green, p 576–577
                 Johnson and McHugh, p 196–197
                 Smith, p 110–111
                 Bowie and Schaffer (2010), p 183
                 Schraffenberger, p 183

46. B   There are two different ICD-9-CM codes for stress incontinence: one for males and one for
        females.

REFERENCE: Bowie and Schaffer (2008), p 242
                 Brown, p 219
                 Green, p 578–579
                 Johnson and McHugh, p 198–200
                 AMA, p 245
                 Schraffenberger, p 197
                 Johnson and McHugh, p 198–200

47. B

REFERENCE: Bowie and Schaffer (2010), p 238
                 Bowie and Schaffer (2008), p 244
                 Brown, p 225–226
                 Eid, p 134–135
                 Green, p 598–299
                 Johnson and McHugh, p 198–201
                 AMA, p 241–242

48. B

REFERENCE: Bowie and Schaffer (2008), p 262
                 Green, p 601–605
                 Johnson and McHugh, p 370–371
                 AMA, p 250

49. D

REFERENCE: Bowie and Schaffer (2008), p 271
                 Eid, p 139
                 Green, p 606–610
                 Johnson and McHugh, p 344
                 AMA, p 256

CCS-P Mock Exam Answer Key
ANSWER   EXPLANATION

50. D

REFERENCE: Bowie and Schaffer (2008), p 272
Green, p 610
Johnson and McHugh, p 352
AMA, p 258–259

51. A

REFERENCE: Bowie and Schaffer (2008), p 278–279
Green, p 612

52. B

REFERENCE: Bowie and Schaffer (2008), p 293
Green, p 624–625
AMA, p 492

53. A

REFERENCE: Bowie and Schaffer (2008), p 292–193
Green, p 621–622
Johnson and McHugh, p 203
AMA, p 154, 163

54. C   Subconjunctival injections are included in 66984.

REFERENCE: Bowie and Schaffer (2008), p 301
Bowie and Schaffer (2010), p 172–173
AMA, p 297, 302
CPT Assistant, Fall 1992, p 5, 8
CPT Assistant, February 2001, p 7
CPT Assistant, November 2003, p 11
Green, p 626–632
Johnson and McHugh, p 204–205
Brown, p 172
Schraffenberger, p 132

55. B   Because the procedure is bilateral, either code twice or use the modifier -50.

REFERENCE: Bowie and Schaffer (2006), p 313
Green, p 633–634
AMA, p 308
Schraffenberger, p 133

56. C

REFERENCE: Frisch, p 90, 169–177
Green, p 314–314
Green and Rowell, p 16, 69–71, 73

CCS-P Mock Exam Answer Key
    ANSWER   EXPLANATION

57. C

REFERENCE: Frisch, p 247
              Green, p 799, 801
              Johnson and McHugh, p 435–436, 535–538
              Rimmer, p 37

58. B

REFERENCE: Rimmer, p 209

59. D

REFERENCE: McWay, p 321
              Krager and Krager, p 99–100
              Green and Bowie, p 286

60. B

REFERENCE: McWay, p 294
              Green and Bowie, p 286

REFERENCES

Abdelhak, M., Grostick, S., Hanken, M. A., and Jacobs, E. (Eds.) (2007). *Health information: Management of a strategic resource* (3rd ed.). Philadelphia: Saunders Elsevier.

American Hospital Association. *Coding Clinic for ICD-9-CM.* Chicago: American Hospital Association (AMA)

American Medical Association. (2010). *Physicians' current procedural terminology (CPT) professional edition.* Chicago: American Medical Association (AMA).

American Medical Association. (2010). *Principles of CPT coding.* Chicago: American Medical Association (AMA).

Bowie, M., and Schaffer, L. (2010). *Understanding ICD-9-CM, worktext.* Clifton Park, NY: Delmar Cengage Learning.

Bowie, M., and Schaffer, L. (2008). *Understanding procedural coding: A worktext.* Clifton Park, NY: Delmar Cengage Learning.

Brown, F. (2009). *ICD-9-CM coding handbook 2010 with answers.* Chicago: American Hospital Association (AHA) Press.

Eid, D. (2008). *Applying coding concepts: Encoder workbook.* Clifton Park, NY: Delmar Cengage Learning.

Frisch, B. (2007). *Correct coding for Medicare, compliance, and reimbursement.* Clifton Park, NY: Delmar Cengage Learning.

Green, M. (2010). *3-2-1 Code It* (2nd ed.). New York: Delmar Cengage Learning.

Green, M. A., and Bowie, M. J. (2005). *Essentials of health information management: Principles and practices.* Clifton Park, NY: Delmar Cengage Learning.

Green, M., and Rowell. (2008). *Understanding health insurance a guide to billing and reimbursement* (9th ed.). Delmar Cengage Learning.

ICD-9-CM Code Books

    Channel Publishing, Ltd. *The educational annotation of ICD-9-CM (2010).* Reno, NV: Author.

    INGENIX. *ICD-9-CM code book, professional edition 2010.* Salt Lake City, UT: Author.

Johns, M. (2006). *Health information technology: An applied approach* (2nd ed.). Chicago: American Health Information Management Association (AHIMA).

Johnson, S. L., and McHugh, C. S. (2006). *Understanding medical coding: A comprehensive guide* (2nd ed.). Clifton Park, NY: Delmar Cengage Learning.

Jones, B. D. (2008). *Comprehensive medical terminology* (3rd ed.). Clifton Park, NY: Delmar Cengage Learning.

Koch, G. (2008). *Basic allied health statistics and analysis* (3rd ed.). Clifton Park, NY: Delmar Cengage Learning.

LaTour, K., and Eichenwald-Maki, S. (2010). *Health information management concepts: Principles and practice* (3rd ed.). Chicago: American Health Information Management Association (AHIMA).

McWay, D. C. (2008). *Today's health information management: An integrated approach.* Clifton Park, NY: Delmar Cengage Learning.

Neighbors, M., and Tannehill-Jones, R. (2006). *Human diseases* (2nd ed.). Clifton Park, NY: Delmar Cengage Learning.

Schraffenberger, L. A. (2010). *Basic ICD-9-CM coding.* Chicago: American Health Information Management Association (AHIMA).

Schraffenberger, L. A., and Keuhn, L. (2007). *Effective management of coding services* (3rd ed.). Chicago: American Health Information Management Association (AHIMA).

Smith, G. (2009). *Basic current procedure terminology and HCPCS coding*. Chicago: American Health Information Management Association (AHIMA).

Competencies for the CCS-P Mock Examination Part 1

Question	CCS-P Domain						
	1	2	3	4	5	6	7
1					X		
2			X				
3	X						
4		X					
5					X		
6	X						
7	X						
8		X					
9		X					
10			X				
11				X			
12			X				
13		X					
14					X		
15	X						
16			X				
17				X			
18							X
19						X	
20					X		
21			X				
22		X					
23			X				
24			X				
25			X				
26			X				
27			X				

Question	CCS-P Domain							
	1	2	3	4	5	6	7	
28			X					
29			X					
30			X					
31			X					
32			X					
33							X	
34		X						
35			X					
36			X					
37			X					
38		X						
39			X					
40			X					
41			X					
41			X					
42			X					
43			X					
44			X					
45			X					
46			X					
47			X					
48			X					
49			X					
50			X					
51			X					
52			X					
53			X					
54			X					
55			X					
56					X			

Question	CCS-P Domain							
	1	2	3	4	5	6	7	
57					X			
58					X			
59						X		
60							X	

XII. CCS-P Mock Examination Coding Cases

CCS-P MOCK EXAMINATION Part II
CODING INSTRUCTIONS

Part II of the CCS-P examination is for medical record coding. You will be performing ICD-9-CM coding (diagnostic coding), CPT coding, and HCPCS coding for procedural coding for physician services. There will be 16 records to code:

- Six cases from the CPT Evaluation and Management chapter
- Six cases from the CPT Surgery chapter
- Three cases from the CPT Medicine chapter
- One additional case from any of the remaining chapters of CPT or and HCPCS II

Refer to the latest AHIMA Candidate handbook for updated coding instructions for Part II of the CCS-P Certification Examination. Visit AHIMA online at www.AHIMA.org for additional information on the electronic testing process.

1. You will record up to four ICD-9-CM diagnoses and seven CPT and/or HCPCS Level II procedural codes in the spaces provided on screen at the end of each coding case. Do not forget that, on the certification examination, points are deducted for inappropriate codes and failure to list a required code. You will be typing the codes on an answer form screen on the computer.

2. Select diagnoses, conditions, problems, or other reasons for care that require ICD-9-CM coding in a physician-based encounter/visit, either in a physician's office, clinic, outpatient area, emergency room, ambulatory surgery, or other ambulatory care setting. Apply ICD-9-CM instructional notations and conventions and current approved "Basic Coding Guidelines for Outpatient Services" and "Diagnostic Coding and Reporting Requirements for Physician Billing" (*Coding Clinic for ICD-9-CM*, Fourth Quarter, 1995). In addition, the latest updated Coding Guidelines for Outpatient Services are in the back of this book. Code for physician services only.

3. Sequencing is not considered in scoring for diagnoses or procedures in Part II of the examination. Review the procedures for coding that are supplied in Appendix B of the examination guidebook.

4. Modifiers and linking diagnoses to procedures are tested in Part I of the examination only and are not required for the coding cases.

5. Code for professional services only for the physician designated on the cover sheet of the case.

6. Assign CPT and/or HCPCS Level II codes for all appropriate procedures.

7. Confirm Evaluation and Management (E/M) codes based on the information provided for each case. The level of key components will be given so you will not be expected to assign the level of history, examinations, and medical decision making for the examination.

8. Assign CPT codes for:
   - medical procedures based on current CPT guidelines.
   - anesthetic procedures listed in the anesthesia section if appropriate.
   - radiologic and laboratory procedures listed in the radiology and laboratory sections only when applicable..

9. Do not assign HCPCS Level III Local (alphanumerical) codes, ICD-9-CM E-codes, ICD-9-CM Morphology codes (M-codes), or ICD-9-CM procedure codes from Volume 3.

Mock Examination

Part II Case 1

Office Visit

Face Sheet

Patient's Name: Fern Bishop

Date of Visit: 1/05/2010

Age: 65

Sex: Female

Insurance: Medicare

CCS-P Mock Examination
Part II Case 1
Office Visit

HISTORY OF PRESENT ILLNESS: This is the third office visit for this 65-year-old female. For the past 4–5 weeks she has been having significant sharp, stabbing pains in her anterior chest, primarily with movement, especially when lying down or sitting up. She does not have any palpitations or any significant shortness of breath, cough, wheezing, fever, or chills. She does have a history of COPD with chronic mild exertional dyspnea.

PAST MEDICAL HISTORY: Pacemaker.

ALLERGIES: NKA.

MEDICATIONS: Lanoxin q day, inhaler as needed.

SOCIAL HISTORY: She quit smoking after 40 years. She is retired and lives with her husband.

FAMILY HISTORY: Father died of old age. Mother died from complications of open heart surgery. Siblings are alive and well. One sister has diabetes and one brother has hypertension.

REVIEW OF SYSTEMS:
HEENT: No diplopia or new visual disturbance. No tinnitus, otalgia, or sore throat.
Cardiac: No sustained chest pain or palpitations.
Pulmonary: COPD with chronic mild exertional dyspnea.
Gastrointestinal: No melena, hematochezia, vomiting, or diarrhea.
Musculoskeletal: As per history of present illness.
The remaining systems are negative.

PHYSICAL EXAMINATION:
General: Well-developed, well-nourished female in mild distress. Blood pressure 120/70. Temperature normal. Respirations 16. Pulse 68.
Skin: No gross abnormalities.
HEENT: Pupils are equal, round, and reactive to light. Extraocular movements intact. Sclerae are clear. Conjunctivae are pink. Ears are normal. Pharynx is clear. Good occlusion of the teeth.
Neck: Supple, no bruits.
Chest: Anterior chest wall tenderness, primarily from the mid and lower left sternal border, extending laterally across the costal chondral cartilage. No associated deformity, swelling, erythema. No gross abnormalities.
Lungs: Mildly diminished breath sounds bilaterally with no prominent rales, wheezing, rales, or rhonchi. No rubs.
Heart: Regular rate and rhythm. No murmurs, clicks, or rubs.
Abdomen: Soft and non-tender. Bowel sounds are normal. No masses.
Back: Appears normal with no tenderness.
Extremities: Good color and warmth.
Vascular: Pulses are present and symmetrical.
Neurological: Alert, responds to questions. Cranial nerves grossly intact. Symmetrical strength and grasp bilaterally. No acute focal deficits.
Psychiatric: No acute psychosis.
Pelvic/Genitalia: Deferred as inappropriate.
Rectal: Deferred as inappropriate

CCS-P Mock Examination

Part II Case 1

Office Visit

Continued:

ELECTROCARDIOGRAM: Dual-chamber pacemaker, rate of 60. Rhythm, sinus. No significant ectopy noted.

IMPRESSION:

Chest wall pain. We will be placing her on anti-inflammatory drugs and will start her on the first dose of Motrin here. It is recommended that she start taking regular Motrin and limit activities that exacerbate her discomfort. Follow-up office visit is scheduled for 2 weeks from today.

History:	Comprehensive
Examination:	Comprehensive
Medical Decision:	Moderate Complexity

Answer Sheet

CCS-P Mock Examination

<u>**Part II Case 1**</u>

DIAGNOSES	ICD-9-CM CODES					
First listed DX				.		
DX 2				.		
DX 3				.		
DX 4				.		

PROCEDURES	CPT CODES					MODIFIERS (If Applicable)		
PR 1						-		
PR 2						-		
PR 3						-		
PR 4						-		
PR 5						-		
PR 6						-		
PR 7						-		

CCS-P Mock Examination

<u>**Part II Case 2**</u>

Office Visit

Face Sheet

Patient's Name:	Alice Snook
Date of Visit:	1/06/2010
Age:	25
Sex:	Female
Insurance:	Worker's Compensation

CCS-P Mock Examination

<u>**Part II Case 2**</u>

Office Visit

HISTORY OF PRESENT ILLNESS:
First visit for this 25-year-old female who was at home when she accidentally punched a door. She has had persistent pain in the left hand since yesterday. She describes the pain as severe. Left hand is swollen and sore to the touch in the knuckle area of the 5th digit.

PAST MEDICAL HISTORY: Non-contributory.

ALLERGIES: None.

PHYSICAL EXAMINATION:

General:	Well-developed, well-nourished female in moderate distress. BP: 121/85 P: 88; R: 18;
Skin:	Warm and dry.
HEENT:	Unremarkable.
Chest:	Symmetrical.
Extremities:	The left hand is tender and mildly swollen with no gross deformity. Normal range of motion against resistance with moderate pain. No abrasions or lacerations. Normal distal neurosensory examination. The remainder of the extremity examination is within normal limits.
Neurological:	She is awake, alert, and oriented times three with no focal neurologic deficits.

RADIOLOGY EXAMINATION:
The patient was taken to the office x-ray room where the left hand was x-rayed.
Boxer's fracture shaft 5th finger appreciated in the AP and lateral views.

IMPRESSION:
Left 5th finger Boxer's fracture.
The patient was placed in an ulnar splint and was given a prescription for Darvocet p.r.n. pain and Motrin 800 mg t.i.d. She will follow up with me next week.

History:	Expanded Problem-Focused
Examination:	Expanded Problem-Focused
Medical Decision:	Straightforward

Answer Sheet

CCS-P Mock Examination

Part II Case 2

DIAGNOSES	ICD-9-CM CODES					
First listed DX				.		
DX 2				.		
DX 3				.		
DX 4				.		

PROCEDURES	CPT CODES					MODIFIERS (If Applicable)		
PR 1						-		
PR 2						-		
PR 3						-		
PR 4						-		
PR 5						-		
PR 6						-		
PR 7						-		

CCS-P Mock Examination

Part II Case 3

Office Visit

Face Sheet

Patient's Name: Sadie Phillips

Date of Visit: 1/03/2010

Age: 70

Sex: Female

Insurance: Medicare and AARP

CCS-P Mock Examination
Part II Case 3
Office Visit

HISTORY OF PRESENT ILLNESS:

Patient has complaints of right-sided abdominal pain for 1 day. Experienced some dizziness today. No nausea/vomiting/diarrhea. No dysuria, but has experienced frequent urination. Patient does have a history of UTIs, which was documented in last office visit notes 4 years ago.

PAST MEDICAL HISTORY: Negative.

MEDICATIONS: None.

ALLERGIES: None known.

PHYSICAL EXAMINATION:

Vitals:	BP: 96/69; P: 62; R: 18; T: 97.9
HEENT:	ENT is normal. Pharynx is normal.
Neck:	Normal. Thyroid is normal.
Abdomen:	Normal bowel sounds. Non-tender and no organomegaly. Mild pain in right groin area.
Rectum:	Normal.
Urogenital:	Within normal limits.

Automated microscopic urinalysis was performed in the office.
WBC: 11-25; RBC: 0; epithelial cells: Moderate; Bacteria: > 100,000.

IMPRESSION AND PLAN:
1. UTI
2. Bactrim 1 tab p.o. bid x 7 days.
3. Follow-up in office in 1 week.

History: Expanded Problem-Focused
Examination: Expanded Problem-Focused
Medical Decision: Straightforward

Answer Sheet

CCS-P Mock Examination

Part II Case 3

DIAGNOSES	ICD-9-CM CODES					
First listed DX				.		
DX 2				.		
DX 3				.		
DX 4				.		

PROCEDURES	CPT CODES					MODIFIERS (If Applicable)		
PR 1						-		
PR 2						-		
PR 3						-		
PR 4						-		
PR 5						-		
PR 6						-		
PR 7						-		

CCS-P Mock Examination

Part II Case 4

Office Visit

Face Sheet

Patient's Name: James Phillips

Date of Visit: 1/13/2010

Age: 44

Sex: Male

Insurance: Government

CCS-P Mock Examination

Part II Case 4

Office Visit

DATE OF OFFICE VISIT: 1/13/2010

HISTORY OF PRESENT ILLNESS

This is an established patient who complains of left elbow pain. The pain started about a month ago and has progressively gotten worse. It is exacerbated by rotation and flexion and extension of the elbow. Denies any trauma to the area. The patient is an avid tennis player and it seems that the pain is aggravated during play. He is in a tournament next week and is requesting help with pain relief. He has been on NSAIDs with very little effect.

PHYSICAL EXAMINATION:

General: Blood pressure 120/65. Pulse 68. Respirations 16. Temperature normal.

Extremities: The left elbow has no swelling or ecchymosis. There is tenderness over the lateral epicondyle. Left shoulder and wrist are normal. Right upper extremity is normal.

CNS: Intact sensation with equal strength. Ulnar and radial pulses are normal.

IMPRESSION: Left lateral epicondylitis

The patient was given an injection of 10 mg Aristospan and 4.0 cc of 2% Lidocaine into the area of tenderness on the left elbow. He was told to use ibuprofen 600 mg q.i.d. Patient to follow-up in 1 week.

History:	Expanded problem-focused
Examination:	Expanded problem-focused
Medical Decision:	Low complexity

Answer Sheet

CCS-P Mock Examination

Part II Case 4

DIAGNOSES	ICD-9-CM CODES					
First listed DX				.		
DX 2				.		
DX 3				.		
DX 4				.		

PROCEDURES	CPT CODES					MODIFIERS (If Applicable)		
PR 1						-		
PR 2						-		
PR 3						-		
PR 4						-		
PR 5						-		
PR 6						-		
PR 7						-		

CCS-P Mock Examination

Part II Case 5

Office Visit

Face Sheet

Patient's Name: Lafayette Wilkinson

Date of Visit: 1/15/2010

Age: 50

Sex: Male

Insurance: Self-Pay

CCS-P Mock Examination

Part II Case 5
Office Visit

HISTORY OF PRESENT ILLNESS:

Patient returns to the office 1 week following appendectomy. Patient is doing well and has no complaints of pain, bleeding, nausea, or vomiting. Patient is taking Ampicillin 500 mg p.o. q6h and Tylenol for pain as needed. There are no complaints of chest pain, shortness of breath, or difficulty urinating.

ALLERGIES: No known allergies.

PHYSICAL EXAMINATION:

Vital Signs:	Blood pressure 110/70. Temperature normal. Respirations 20. Pulse 66.
HEENT:	Normal. No masses. Eyes are equal and reactive. No thyroidomegaly.
Lungs:	Clear to auscultation and percussion.
Abdomen:	There is a healing surgical scar in the right lower quadrant. No redness or tenderness in that area noted.

PLAN:

Patient is doing well after his surgery. To continue on Ampicillin for 1 more week and continue Tylenol for pain as needed. To follow up with us in 2 weeks.

History:	Expanded Problem-focused
Examination:	Expanded Problem-focused
Medical Decision:	Straightforward

CCS-P Answer Sheet

Mock Examination

Part II Case 5

DIAGNOSES	ICD-9-CM CODES					
First listed DX				.		
DX 2				.		
DX 3				.		
DX 4				.		

PROCEDURES	CPT CODES					MODIFIERS (If Applicable)		
PR 1						-		
PR 2						-		
PR 3						-		
PR 4						-		
PR 5						-		
PR 6						-		
PR 7						-		

CCS-P Mock Examination

Part II Case 6

Ambulatory Surgery

Face Sheet

Patient's Name: Cora Law

Date of Visit: 1/04/2010

Age: 58

Sex: Female

Insurance: Commercial

CCS-P Mock Examination

<u>**Part II Case 6**</u>

History and Physical

DATE OF ADMISSION: 1/4/2010

ADMITTING DIAGNOSIS: Scalp mass.

HISTORY OF PRESENT ILLNESS:
Patient is returning for recurrent scalp masses. She had one removed approximately 1 year ago and now has two more.

PAST MEDICAL HISTORY:
Scalp mass, 1 year ago. Patient has a history of hypertension and COPD.

ALLERGIES: Sulfa.

MEDICATIONS: Tenormin and Alupent.

SOCIAL HISTORY:
She smokes 1/2 pack a day; alcohol, social. She is retired and her hobbies include reading, gardening, and bingo.

PHYSICAL EXAMINATION:

General	Patient weighs 185. She is 5' 6" tall. BP 148/78. Pulse 80. Patient appears generally in good health, considering her weight and history of COPD.
Head:	Mass on the vertex of the scalp with another mass located in the right posterior occipital region.
HEENT:	Pupils are equal, round, and reactive to light and accommodation. Extraocular muscles are intact. Fundi are poorly visualized.
Neck:	Thyroid not palpable. No jugular venous distention.
Chest:	Lungs showed resonant breath sounds equally with left basilar rales.
Heart:	Regular rate and rhythm, no murmurs.
Abdomen:	No masses or rebound tenderness.
Extremities:	Normal with good reflexes.

PLAN:
Admit to day surgery for removal of scalp masses.

CCS-P Mock Examination

Part II Case 6
Operative Report

Date of Operation:	1/04/2010
Pre-Operative Diagnosis:	Scalp mass × 2
Post-Operative Diagnosis:	Scalp mass × 2
Operation:	Excision of scalp mass × 2
Surgeon:	Fairuza Padma, MD
Anesthesia:	Monitored anesthesia care
Anesthesiologist:	James Allen, MD
Estimated Blood Loss:	Minimal
Drains:	None
Complications:	None

PROCEDURE:

Patient is taken to the operating room with her informed consent. She is prepped and draped in the usual manner. IV sedation is administered, and then local, using one percent lidocaine.

The first mass measuring 2.0 cm was on the vertex of the scalp. There is a scar here from a previous excision and a mass just posterior to it. The scar was excised through a 2 cm transverse incision with an elliptical incision, and she was found to have a sebaceous cyst, which was adherent to the scar and also tracking posteriorly. This was excised in its entirety. The wound was closed with 2-0 Prolene in an interrupted fashion.

Next, a 2.5 cm mass is located in the right posterior occipital region, and this area was anesthetized with one percent lidocaine and a 2.5 cm transverse incision made over this through the skin and subcutaneous tissue, and the mass was circumferentially dissected and excised.

The wound was closed with 3-0 Vicryl in interrupted fashion for the subcutaneous tissue, and we had a good skin closure with this. Steri-Strips and Benzoin applied.

The patient tolerated the procedure well. She was written a prescription for Vicodin one q4h p.r.n. for pain.

CCS-P Mock Examination

Part II Case 6
PATHOLOGY REPORT:

Date:	1/04/2010
Physician:	Linda Lee, MD
Pre-Operative Diagnosis:	Scalp mass × 2
Post-Operative Diagnosis:	Scalp mass × 2
Surgical Procedure:	Excision of scalp masses × 2
Specimen(s):	1. Scalp Mass
	2. Scalp Mass
GROSS:	There are two containers.

Container number one, labeled "scalp mass," consists of an ovoid firm mass of smooth surfaced tissue with overall dimensions of 2 × 1.5 × .5 cm. The specimen is marked with India ink, bisected, and entirely submitted in cassette A1.

Container number two, labeled "scalp mass," consists of multiple portions of yellow-gray-white soft tissue in aggregate 3 × 1.5 × .3 cm and entirely submitted in cassette A2.

GROSS AND MICROSCOPIC EXAMINATION:

Mass from scalp:	(Specimen #1)	Sebaceous Cyst
Mass from scalp:	(Specimen #2)	Sebaceous Cyst

CCS-P Mock Examination

Part II Case 6

Progress Notes:

Patient had removal of two scalp lesions. Tolerated procedure well. No complications. Will follow up in my office in 2 weeks. Normal diet, regular activities.

Physician Orders:

STANDARD POST-OPERATIVE ORDERS:

Discharge from recovery room when stable.
Urinary catheterization if patient unable to void postop × 1; then call physician.
Vital signs q 15 minutes × 4; then q 30 minutes × 2; then q one × hour until discharge.
Tylenol 500 mg q4h for pain.
Start on soft diet.

Discharge when patient is stable.

CCS-P Answer Sheet

Mock Examination

<u>**Part II Case 6**</u>

DIAGNOSES	ICD-9-CM CODES					
First listed DX				.		
DX 2				.		
DX 3				.		
DX 4				.		

PROCEDURES	CPT CODES				MODIFIERS (If Applicable)		
PR 1					-		
PR 2					-		
PR 3					-		
PR 4					-		
PR 5					-		
PR 6					-		
PR 7					-		

CCS-P Mock Examination

<u>Part II Case 7</u>

Emergency Room Visit

Face Sheet

Patient's Name: Kris Keuren

Date of Visit: 1/09/2010

Age: 35

Sex: Female

Insurance: Commercial

CCS-P Mock Examination

Part II Case 7

Emergency Room Visit

DATE OF ADMISSION: 1/09/2010

HISTORY:

This 35-year-old female presents to the emergency room complaining of right wrist pain. Patient states she slipped and fell on an ice patch and used her right hand to break the fall. Right wrist is painful to the touch and quite painful with any movement. She has a contusion on her right hip.

PAST MEDICAL HISTORY: Non-contributory.

ALLERGIES: None.

PHYSICAL EXAMINATION:
General: Well-developed female in acute distress.
HEENT: Nose and throat clear.
Heart: Regular rhythm.
Extremities: Moves 3 extremities well. The right wrist is painful to touch. Unable to move wrist. Contusion, right hip.

PLAN:

Due to a massive accident, the radiological equipment is unavailable. Patient was given the option of waiting or going to a local orthopedic physician, who has agreed to x-ray and treat the patient. The patient has opted to go to the physician's office. Wrist was wrapped in an ACE bandage and patient was discharged to the orthopedics' office.

IMPRESSION:
Sprain, right wrist. R/O fracture.

History:	Expanded Problem-focused
Examination:	Expanded Problem-focused
Medical Decision:	Low

CCS-P Mock Examination

Part II Case 7

Answer Sheet

DIAGNOSES	ICD-9-CM CODES					
First listed DX				.		
DX 2				.		
DX 3				.		
DX 4				.		

PROCEDURES	CPT CODES					MODIFIERS (If Applicable)		
PR 1						-		
PR 2						-		
PR 3						-		
PR 4						-		
PR 5						-		
PR 6						-		
PR 7						-		

CCS-P Mock Examination

Part II Case 8

Nursing Home Visit

Face Sheet

Patient's Name: Sheik Billy

Date of Visit: 1/14/2010

Age: 35

Sex: Male

Insurance: Commercial

CCS-P Mock Examination

Part II Case 8

Nursing Home Visit

HISTORY OF PRESENT ILLNESS:

This 35-year-old male patient is new to the Oakdale Nursing Home. He was admitted to this facility on 1/13/2010 with the diagnoses of bilateral lower amputee, ruptured spleen, lacerated liver, and fractured pelvis sustained from a motor vehicle accident. The patient is admitted for therapy.

PAST MEDICAL HISTORY:

Patient was healthy prior to the accident. No history of diabetes, hypertension, cardiac, or respiratory disease.

PAST SURGICAL HISTORY:

Patient has had both legs amputated below the knee. Splenectomy. Liver repair.

ALLERGIES:

No known allergies.

SOCIAL HISTORY:

Patient does not smoke or drink. Patient was an avid runner prior to the accident.

FAMILY HISTORY:

Non-contributory.

REVIEW OF SYSTEMS:

HEENT:	Normal.
Respiratory:	Normal.
Cardiovascular:	Normal.
Hematologic:	Normal except for splenectomy and repair of lacerated liver.
Musculoskeletal:	Bilateral lower amputee. Healing pelvic fracture. Otherwise normal.
Neurological:	Normal.
Psychiatric:	Depressed.

CCS-P Mock Examination
Part II Case 8
Nursing Home Visit

Continued:

PHYSICAL EXAMINATION:

General: Well-developed, well-nourished, depressed male in no acute distress. BP 128/75. Pulse: 80, regular and strong. Respirations: 12, unlabored and regular. Temperature: Normal. Height 5 foot 10 inches.

HEENT: Pupils are reactive to light and accommodation. No vessel changes, exudates, or hemorrhages noted. Oral mucosa is normal. No lesions noted.

Neck: Supple. No masses. Trachea is midline.

Respiratory: Normal. No wheezes or rubs appreciated.

Cardiovascular: Normal sinus rhythm. No murmurs.

Abdomen: Laparotomy scar is healing well. No signs of infection. No evidence of masses or hernias.

Lymphatic: No lymphadenopathy.

Genitourinary: Normal.

Rectal Examination: Deferred.

Musculoskeletal: Patient is a bilateral lower amputee. Currently confined to wheelchair. Pelvic fracture is healing according to x-rays. Lower leg muscles have not been used since accident and are flaccid. Upper body is within normal limits. Range of motion is good.

Neurological: Cranial nerves are intact. Moves all upper extremities on command without difficulty. Hand grips strong bilaterally. Lower extremities are flaccid and it is unsure if patient is unable to move stumps or will not move stumps.

Psychiatric: Patient is depressed and this will be a concern that might hinder him in therapy. Patient is orientated to person, place, and time. Judgment is impaired due to depression. Patient does have phantom leg syndrome.

PLAN:

Patient will begin therapy to strengthen his lower stumps. He will be fitted with prostheses and will begin rehabilitative therapy. Psychologist will be obtained to help patient deal with depression and therapy.

Patient is on no special diet. Needs to become interactive with residents.

History:	Comprehensive
Examination:	Comprehensive
Medical Decision:	Moderate Complexity

CCS-P Answer Sheet
Mock Examination
Part II Case 8

DIAGNOSES	ICD-9-CM CODES					
First listed DX				.		
DX 2				.		
DX 3				.		
DX 4				.		

PROCEDURES	CPT CODES					MODIFIERS (If Applicable)		
PR 1						-		
PR 2						-		
PR 3						-		
PR 4						-		
PR 5						-		
PR 6						-		
PR 7						-		

CCS-P Mock Examination

<u>**Part II Case 9**</u>

OFFICE VISIT

Face Sheet

Patient's Name: J.W. Goldie

Date of Visit: 1/07/2010

Age: 56

Sex: Male

Insurance: Medicare

CCS-P Mock Examination

Part II Case 9

Office Visit

DATE OF OFFICE VISIT: 1/07/2010

This is a repeat visit for this patient. He has complaints of indigestion for the past month. The indigestion occurs after eating heavy meals and/or physical exertion. The duration of pain lasts about 20 minutes. He states that he has had a previous cholecystectomy approximately 2 years ago.

There is no shortness of breath, nausea, vomiting, bloody stools, or sweating. There is a family history of heart disease, with his father having bypass surgery in his 60s. His mother died of an MI 3 years ago. The patient has a history of smoking, but is currently on the patch to help him stop. He does not exercise regularly. He denies any chest pains or cough. GU, Musc, Neuro, Skin, Eyes are negative.

ALLERGIES: PCN and sulfa
MEDICATIONS: Smoking patch.

PHYSICAL EXAMINATION:

General:	Blood pressure 140/80, P 76, Resp. 16. Temperature is normal.
HEENT:	Head is normocephalic. No masses or lesions noted on the eyes. Oral mucosa is normal. Throat is normal.
Neck:	No distention of jugular vein.
Lungs:	Clear bilaterally to auscultation and percussion. No rubs, rales, or wheezing noted.
Heart:	Normal sinus rhythm. No rubs, gallops, or murmurs. Carotid arteries, abdominal artery and femoral arteries are normal. No bruits noted. Pedal pulses normal. No peripheral edema noted.
Abdomen:	No masses, tenderness, organomegaly.
Neurological:	Normal.
Extremities:	No clubbing, cyanosis, ischemia, or edema noted. Gait is steady. Good range of motion in all extremities.

Patient was taken to the office stress laboratory and the patient was placed on the treadmill.

PLAN:
Blood was drawn for cardiac profile and was sent to an outside lab. At this point, the patient will not be placed on prescriptions. It was suggested that he take an over-the-counter antacid such as Pepcid or Axid to help prevent heartburn. It was recommended that the patient make an appointment with a gastroenterologist to rule out GI problems.

History:	Detailed
Examination:	Detailed
Medical Decision:	Moderate Complexity

CCS-P Mock Examination

Part II Case 9

Stress Test Report

The patient arrived in the stress lab and was placed on the ECG monitor and activated the treadmill. The patient was able to tolerate the treadmill for approximately 10 minutes and reached his desired heart rate. He did not develop any chest pains or signs of indigestion. There were no ECG changes.

RESULTS: Normal.

CCS-P Mock Examination

Part II Case 9

Answer Sheet

DIAGNOSES	ICD-9-CM CODES					
First listed DX				.		
DX 2				.		
DX 3				.		
DX 4				.		

PROCEDURES	CPT CODES					MODIFIERS (If Applicable)		
PR 1						-		
PR 2						-		
PR 3						-		
PR 4						-		
PR 5						-		
PR 6						-		
PR 7						-		

CCS-P Mock Examination

Part II Case 10

Ambulatory Surgery

Face Sheet

Patient's Name: Sally Hunter

Date of Visit: 1/16/2010

Age: 45

Sex: Female

Insurance: Commercial

CCS-P Mock Examination

Part II Case 10

Ambulatory Surgery

History and Physical

DATE OF ADMISSION: 1/16/2010

ADMITTING DIAGNOSIS: Eyes turn out.

HISTORY OF PRESENT ILLNESS:
This is the first visit for this patient, who is being admitted for ambulatory surgery. Patient will undergo eye muscle surgery in hopes of recapturing and maintaining binocular function.

PAST MEDICAL HISTORY:
The patient's eyes began to turn out in early childhood; patient underwent surgery for correction at the age of seven. Progression of the disease has now resulted in the patient only being able to use one eye at a time.

ALLERGIES: None.
MEDICATIONS: None.
FAMILY HISTORY: No familial disorders known.

REVIEW OF SYSTEMS:
Review of systems is unremarkable.

PHYSICAL EXAMINATION:

General: Patient is alert, cooperative, and in no acute distress. BP 120/80; Respirations 17; Pulse 77.

HEENT: Head is normocephalic. Tympanic membranes clear. Nose, throat, and mouth are normal. No inflammation is noted.

Neck: Supple with no masses palpated.

Eyes: Visual acuity 20/20 OU with correction. Fundus is normal. Exotropia 30 prism diopters at distance, 20 prism diopters at near. Sensory testing reveals binocular function when the amount of strabismus is corrected with prisms, otherwise suppression OS.

Chest: Clear to auscultation and percussion.

Heart: Normal sinus rhythm without murmur, gallop, or rub.

Skin: Clear.

Extremities: Full range of motion. Normal peripheral pulses.

Neurological: Cranial nerves II through XII and deep tendon reflexes equal and symmetrical.

PLAN: Strabismus surgery under general anesthesia.

CCS-P Mock Examination

Part II Case 10

Ambulatory Surgery

Operative Report

DATE OF OPERATION:	1/16/2010
PRE-OPERATIVE DIAGNOSIS:	Exotropia
POST-OPERATIVE DIAGNOSIS:	Exotropia
PROCEDURE PERFORMED:	Recession, lateral rectus muscle, 6 mm O.U.
SURGEON:	E.B. Mannion, MD
ASSISTANT SURGEON:	Carlos Earl, III, MD
ANESTHESIOLOGIST:	Jim Wilkins, MD

PROCEDURE:

Under general endotracheal anesthesia, the patient's adnex were prepped with Betadine. The patient was draped under sterile conditions. Forced ductions were performed and found to be negative, OU. A small wire lid speculum with solid teeth was applied OD. The right eye was rotated superonasally and an inferotemporal incision was made at the conjunctiva and tendon capsule in the cul-de-sac region with Westcott scissors. The right lateral rectus muscle was isolated on a muscle hook and brought out through the incision site. A double-arm suture of 6-0 Vicryl on a #29 spatula needle was placed through the muscle at its insertion and locked at both ends. The muscle was removed from the globe and reinserted into the sclera 6.0 mm from the original insertion site as measured with calipers. The conjunctiva was repositioned in its original position without suturing.

The lid speculum was transferred to the patient's left eye for an identical technique. The left lateral rectus muscle was recessed 6.0 mm.

At the completion of the surgery, several drops of Maxitrol were instilled OU and the patient left the operating room in good condition. No apparent complications noted.

CCS-P Mock Examination

Part II Case 10

Ambulatory Surgery

Progress Notes and Orders

PROGRESS NOTES:

Patient was taken to the operating room for strabismus surgery. Patient tolerated the procedure well and no apparent complications were noted. The patient will be discharged when stable and when discharge criteria have been met. The patient is to follow up in my office tomorrow.

PHYSICIAN ORDERS:

A.M. admit on 1/16/2010.
Patient to sign for permission to operate

POST-OPERATIVE ORDERS:

Discharge when alert and stable.
IV orders per anesthesia
Tylenol #3 q4h p.r.n.
Vistaril 50 mg q4h for nausea
Cold moist compress to both eyes p.r.n. drainage

CCS-P Mock Examination

Part II Case 10

Answer Sheet

DIAGNOSES	ICD-9-CM CODES					
First listed DX				.		
DX 2				.		
DX 3				.		
DX 4				.		

PROCEDURES	CPT CODES					MODIFIERS (If Applicable)		
PR 1						-		
PR 2						-		
PR 3						-		
PR 4						-		
PR 5						-		
PR 6						-		
PR 7						-		

CCS-P Mock Examination

Part II Case 11

Ambulatory Surgery

Face Sheet

Patient's Name: John Brown

Date of Visit: 1/08/2010

Age: 22

Sex: Male

Insurance: Self-Pay

CCS-P Mock Examination

Part II Case 11

History and Physical

DATE OF ADMISSION: 1/08/2010

ADMITTING DIAGNOSIS: Twisting injury, right knee.

HISTORY OF PRESENT ILLNESS:
This patient was playing baseball 2 weeks ago when he sustained an injury to his right knee while sliding into a base. Patient was seen in the emergency room, where x-rays were negative for any fractures. Patient has been keeping his leg elevated and keeping weight off of it as much as possible.

PAST MEDICAL HISTORY: Negative.

ALLERGIES: None.

MEDICATIONS: None.

SOCIAL HISTORY: Patient smokes 1 pack a day; alcohol, none.

PHYSICAL EXAMINATION:
General: Well-developed, well-nourished male. BP 120/70; Respirations 16; Pulse 75.
HEENT: No gross lesions noted. Pupils round and equal. No icterus. No masses or thyroidomegaly. Oropharynx negative. Neck no masses or thyroidomegaly.
Chest: Clear to auscultation and percussion.
Heart: Normal sinus rhythm.
Abdomen: No masses or rebound tenderness.
Extremities: Right knee with recurrent swelling, locking, and catching. 2+ effusion. Left knee is normal.

PLAN:
Patient will be admitted for one-day surgery for arthroscopy of the right knee.

CCS-P Mock Examination

Part II Case 11

Operative Report

Date of Operation:	1/08/2010
Pre-Operative Diagnosis:	Right knee medial meniscus tear
Post-Operative Diagnosis:	Right knee medial meniscus tear
Operation:	Arthroscopic medial meniscectomy
Surgeon:	Edmundo Diego, MD
Anesthesia:	General
Anesthesiologist:	Branden Godfrey, MD

INDICATIONS:
This patient has a twisting injury to the right knee. He has had swelling, locking, catching, and involving the knee, 2+ effusion.

PROCEDURE:
The patient was taken to the operating room and general anesthesia was induced without complications. A well-padded pneumatic tourniquet was placed to the right upper thigh. The right leg was prepped and draped in the normal fashion. Diagnostic arthroscopy was performed. The findings are as listed below.

Under direct visualization, a medial portal was established. The posterior horn of the medial meniscus was debrided. A shaver was then introduced and taken back to a stable rim. The rest of the knee was then probed and the findings are listed below.

The scope was then withdrawn and the wound closed with #4-0 Vicryl. The patient tolerated the procedure well and was transferred to the recovery room.

FINDINGS:
1. Patello-femoral joint: No articular cartilage change.
2. Medial compartment: Grade 1 changes of the mediofemoral condyle, posterior horn meniscus tear.
3. Anterior cruciate ligament and posterior cruciate ligament intact.
4. Lateral compartment, no articular cartilage changes noted. Lateral meniscus is intact.

CCS-P Mock Examination

Part II Case 11

PROGRESS NOTES

Patient has a twisting injury to the right knee with swelling, locking, and catching.

Patient was taken to the operating room, where an arthroscopic medial meniscectomy was performed.

Patient will be discharged with crutches and will make a follow-up appointment in 2 weeks.

STANDARD POST-OPERATIVE ORDERS

1. Discharge from recovery room when stable.
2. Urinary catheterization if patient unable to void post-op × 1; then call physician.
3. Elevate right knee 20 degrees. Ice packs for 15 minutes then discontinue. Repeat × 1 hour.
4. Vital signs q 15 minutes × 4; then q 30 minutes × 2; then q1h until discharge.
5. Tylenol 500 mg q4h for pain
6. Start on soft diet.
7. Discharge when patient is stable.

CCS-P Mock Examination

Part II Case 11

Answer Sheet

DIAGNOSES	ICD-9-CM CODES					
First listed DX				.		
DX 2				.		
DX 3				.		
DX 4				.		

PROCEDURES	CPT CODES					MODIFIERS (If Applicable)		
PR 1						-		
PR 2						-		
PR 3						-		
PR 4						-		
PR 5						-		
PR 6						-		
PR 7						-		

CCS-P Mock Examination

Part II Case 12

Ambulatory Care

Face Sheet

Patient Name: Juan Summers

Date of Service: 1/05/2010

Age: 62

Sex: Male

Admitting Diagnoses: Urinary retention

Post Operative Diagnoses: Benign prostatic hypertrophy

Procedure: 1. Cystoscopy

                           2. Transurethral resection of the prostate

Discharge Disposition: Home

CCS-P Mock Examination

Part II Case 12

History and Physical

DATE OF ADMISSION: 1/05/2010

ADMITTING DIAGNOSIS: Urinary retention

HISTORY OF PRESENT ILLNESS:
This is a 62-year-old male who has been experiencing increasing signs of urinary retention with urgency and difficulty with urination.

PAST MEDICAL HISTORY:
Positive for severe COPD, requiring home oxygen at 2.5 liters. Patient is also on steroids for COPD. Past history of myocardial infarction with coronary artery disease. Patient underwent cardiac catheterization, but is not considered a surgical candidate.

ALLERGIES: None known.

MEDICATIONS:
Albuterol one dose four times a day; Theo-Dur 200 mg twice a day; Cardizem CD 120 mg once a day.

SOCIAL HISTORY: Significant for smoking two packs a day for 45 years. Occasional alcohol use.

FAMILY HISTORY: Non-contributory.

PHYSICAL EXAMINATION:
General:	The patient is awake, alert, and oriented.
HEENT:	Pupils are equal and react to light and accommodation. Extraocular muscles are intact.
Respiratory:	Prolonged expiratory phase. Scattered wheezes.
Cardiovascular:	Regular rate and rhythm. No murmurs, rubs, or gallops.
Abdomen:	Soft, non-tender. Bowel sounds are present. No organomegaly.
Extremities:	No edema, cyanosis, or clubbing.
Neurologic:	Non-focal.

PLAN:
Patient is admitted to ambulatory surgery for cystoscopy and possible transurethral resection of the prostate.

CCS-P Mock Examination

Part II Case 12

Operative Report

Date of Operation:	1/05/2010
Pre-Operative Diagnosis:	Urinary retention
Post-Operative Diagnosis:	Benign Prostatic Hypertrophy Incomplete Bladder Emptying
Operation:	Laser Coagulation of the Prostate
Surgeon:	Christopher Magee, Jr., MD
Anesthesiologist:	Leeland Kenna, MD
Anesthesia:	Spinal

DESCRIPTION OF PROCEDURE:

The patient was placed on the operating table in the lithotomy position after spinal anesthesia was given. External genitalia was prepped and draped in the sterile manner.

A 21-French cystoscope was introduced within the bladder. The bladder was carefully inspected and there was no evidence of tumor. There was mild trabeculations in both ureteral orifices. At this time, the resectoscope was introduced and resection of the lateral lobes of the prostate was done, allowing complete opening of the prostatic urethra. All of the prostatic chips were removed from the bladder. The bladder was coagulated and completely smoothed out with the VaporTrode. An 18-French Foley catheter was inserted into the bladder and left indwelling.

The patient tolerated the procedure well and was sent to the recovery room in satisfactory condition.

The patient will be discharged home when fully recovered, with Foley in place. Patient will see me in my office tomorrow for removal of the Foley.

CCS-P Mock Examination

Part II Case 12

PATHOLOGY REPORT

TISSUES: Prostate tissue

PRE-OPERATIVE DIAGNOSIS: Urinary retention

POST-OPERATIVE DIAGNOSIS: Benign prostatic hypertrophy

GROSS DESCRIPTION:

Specimen received in formalin labeled "prostate tissue" consists of 9.0 × 9.0 × 2.5 cm. 40 gram aggregate of multiple irregular rubbery gray-white, tan-yellow, and tan-pink tissue. Representative sections (40 chips) are submitted.

MICROSCOPIC DIAGNOSIS:

Prostate tissue: Benign hyperplasia in 36 chips
Foci of adenocarcinoma in 4 chips

CCS-P Mock Examination

Part II Case 12

PROGRESS NOTE:

The patient was taken to the operating room where, under spinal anesthesia, a cystoscopy and transuretheral resection of the prostate was performed. The patient tolerated the procedure well and was transferred to the recovery room in satisfactory condition. Pathology report showed BPH and foci of adenocarcinoma in 4 chips.

STANDARD POST-OPERATIVE ORDERS:

Discharge from the recovery room when stable.

Vital signs q 15 minutes × 4, q 30 minutes × 2, then q 1 hour until discharge.

Vicodin, 40 mg one tablet p.r.n. for pain.

Macrobid b.i.d. for 1 week.

Discharge patient home when fully recovered and stable, with Foley indwelling.

Patient is to return to my office tomorrow for follow-up and Foley removal.

CCS-P Mock Examination

Part II Case 12

Answer Sheet

DIAGNOSES	ICD-9-CM CODES					
First listed DX				.		
DX 2				.		
DX 3				.		
DX 4				.		

PROCEDURES	CPT CODES					MODIFIERS (If Applicable)		
PR 1						-		
PR 2						-		
PR 3						-		
PR 4						-		
PR 5						-		
PR 6						-		
PR 7						-		

CCS-P Mock Examination

<u>**Part II Case 13**</u>

Ambulatory Care

Face Sheet

Patient Name: George Johnson

Date of Service: 1/7/2010

Age: 52

Sex: Male

Admitting Diagnosis: Chest pain

Discharge Diagnoses: Coronary artery disease, native artery
                                 Angina
                                 History of coronary aorta bypass grafting

Procedures: Left heart catheterization

Disposition: Home

CCS-P Mock Examination

Part II Case 13

History and Physical

DATE OF ADMISSION: 1/07/2010

HISTORY OF PRESENT ILLNESS:

This is a 52-year-old male with a history of angina, for which he underwent four-vessel coronary surgical revascularization. This was performed last December. He had a left internal mammary artery graft to the left anterior descending coronary artery, sequential saphenous vein graft to the obtuse marginal and diagonal vessels, and a saphenous vein graft to the right coronary artery. His left ventricular function was normal.

More recently he has been having problems with chest pain. For this reason he is now brought back to the cardiac catheterization laboratory for re-evaluation.

ALLERGIES: Demerol and Biaxin.

LABORATORY DATA:

His laboratory studies reveal normal electrolytes, BUN, creatinine and a mildly depressed hemoglobin and hematocrit of 13 and 38.8, respectively, with normochromic, normocytic indices. The platelet count is normal. PT and PTT are normal.

ELECTROCARDIOGRAM: Demonstrates sinus bradycardia and otherwise is normal.

PHYSICAL EXAMINATION:

Vital signs:	Stable.
General:	Well-developed, well-nourished male in no acute distress. Patient is oriented times three. Skin is warm and dry. Pupils round and equal. Neck supple; trachea is midline.
Chest:	Clear to auscultation and percussion.
Heart:	Normal sinus rhythm. No rubs, gallops appreciated.
Abdomen:	Soft without distention. There is no guarding or rebound. No organomegaly.
Extremities:	Unremarkable.

Further decisions will be based on cardiac catheterization test results. He is agreeable to proceed. He is aware of the risks that include bleeding, infection, heart attack, rhythm disturbance, death, stroke, reaction to dye, or damage to nerve or blood vessel.

He is aware of the alternatives of cardiac catheterization, which would include medical therapy and possibly stress testing. He is agreeable to catheterization.

CCS-P Mock Examination

Part II Case 13
Cardiac Catheterization Report

Date of Catheterization:	1/07/2010
Procedure:	Cardiac catheterization
Pre-operative Diagnosis:	Chest pain History of angina
Post-operative Diagnosis:	Coronary artery disease
Surgeon:	Cheryl Bottom, MD
Assistant:	Sadie Phillips, MD

CARDIAC CATHETERIZATION PROCEDURE:
The patient was brought to the cardiac catheterization laboratory n.p.o. with a peripheral intravenous line in place. The right groin was prepped and draped in the usual fashion. Local anesthesia was obtained with xylocaine 2%.

Utilizing a modified Seldinger technique, the right femoral artery was entered percutaneously and a #5 French side-arm sheath was placed. Utilizing Judkins technique and left and right 4 bend Judkins catheters and a #5 French 110-cm pigtail catheter, left heart catheterization was completed.

Upon completion, the arterial catheter and sheath were removed and hemostasis was achieved by direct pressure applied to the right groin. The patient tolerated the procedure well and left in stable condition.

IMPRESSION:
1. Severe native multi-vessel coronary arterial disease. Total occlusion of the proximal left anterior descending coronary artery after the first septal and first diagonal vessels.
2. Anatomically obstructive stenosis in the obtuse marginal vessel - 3 in its proximal and midportions.
3. Total occlusion of the mid right coronary artery.
4. Patent LIMA graft to the left anterior descending coronary artery.
5. Patent sequential saphenous vein graft to the diagonal vessel and OM-3 vessel. Small diseased diagonal vessel demonstrated.
6. Patent saphenous vein graft to the distal right coronary artery. Approximate 60%-70% stenosis in the midportion of the posterior descending coronary artery.
7. Normal left ventricular size and systolic contractile pattern.
8. Mildly elevated left ventricular end-diastolic pressure 16 mmHg.

CCS-P Mock Examination

Part II Case 13

PROGRESS NOTE

1/07   Patient admitted for left heart catheterization. Aware of risks and benefits. Agreeable to proceed.

1/07   LHC completed via right femoral approach. Tolerated well. SVG to Diag./OM patent. Stenosis at level of Diagonal at SVG. SVG - RCA patent. LIMA to LAD patent. Normal LV. Severe native CAD. Films to be reviewed. D/C home today.

PHYSICIAN ORDERS:

1/07
1. NPO - after MN except for meds
2. D_5 1/2 NSS with 10 mEq KCL/l at 75 cc/hr on admit
3. Pre op meds
4. Benadryl 50 mg p.o.
5. Tagamet 300 mg
6. Consent for right and left heart catheterization
7. Diet: Cardiac

POST-OPERATIVE ORDERS

1/07
1. Darvocet –100 tab p.o. q 4-6h PRN pain.
2. Tylenol #3 one tab p.o. q4h PRN pain if unrelieved by Darvocet.
3. Maintain IV at 150 cc/h × 4 h, then Heplock.
4. Resume diet.
5. Bed rest for 3 hours, then bathroom privileges.
6. Blood pressure in right arm, pulse, respirations q 15 minutes × 2; q 30 minutes × 2; q1h × 2 or until stable; the q4h. Call physician if heart rate 50 or > 100 systolic B/P.
7. Check pulses distal to catheterization site q 15 minutes × 2; q 30 minutes × 2; q1h × 2; then q4h. Notify physician of loss of palpable pulse, complaint, or pain or coldness in distal extremity.
8. Check dressing for bleeding and hematoma q 15 minutes × 2; q 30 minutes × 2; then q1h × 2 and PRN.
9. Discharge when patient is stable.

CCS-P Mock Examination

Part II Case 13

Answer Sheet

DIAGNOSES	ICD-9-CM CODES					
First listed DX				.		
DX 2				.		
DX 3				.		
DX 4				.		

PROCEDURES	CPT CODES					MODIFIERS (If Applicable)		
PR 1						-		
PR 2						-		
PR 3						-		
PR 4						-		
PR 5						-		
PR 6						-		
PR 7						-		

CCS-P Mock Examination

Part II Case 14

Ambulatory Surgery

Face Sheet

Patient Name: Nathan Jenkins

Date of Visit: 1/7/2010

Age: 45

Insurance: HMO

CCS-P Mock Examination

Part II Case 14

History & Physical

DATE: 1/07/2010

CHIEF COMPLAINT: Palpitations

PRESENT ILLNESS: This is a 45-year-old male, who had visited the emergency room at Sun City Hospital on January 4 for rapid palpitations. He has had three episodes of sudden, rapid palpitations. Usually they break on their own. The last episode lasted 18 hours. Patient was given Cardizem, without any response. He usually is completely asymptomatic, although he feels poorly the day after.

The arrhythmia seen on the electrocardiogram at Sun City Hospital was most consistent with classical flutter. Holter monitor was performed, which was normal. Ablation was recommended to the patient.

PAST MEDICAL HISTORY: Borderline hypertension, but he is not treated for it. No history of diabetes or pulmonary disease.

FAMILY HISTORY: Negative.

SOCIAL HISTORY: Denies cigarette use.

PHYSICAL EXAMINATION:

General: Overweight male in no acute distress. Blood pressure is high at 138/80; pulse is regular at 160 beats per minute.
Neck: Neck is supple without evidence of bruits. There is no thyromegaly.
Chest: Clear to auscultation.
Heart: Cardiac examination revealed a normal S1 S2 without murmurs.
Abdomen: Benign.
Extremities: No evidence of clubbing, cyanosis, or edema.

His electrocardiogram at Sun City Hospital showed classical atrial flutter at 104 beats per minute.

IMPRESSION: The patient's arrhythmia is fairly classic for atrial flutter.

PLAN: Patient is to be admitted as an outpatient for ablation.

CCS-P Mock Examination

Part II Case 14

Operative Report

Date of Operation:	1/07/2010
Pre-Operative Diagnosis:	Atrial Flutter
Post-Operative Diagnosis:	1. Typical atrioventricular re-entrant tachycardia 2. Classic type I atrial flutter
Operation:	1. Full electrophysiologic study with coronary sinus catheter 2. Follow-up programmed stimulation with isoproterenol 3. Electrical cardioversion of atrial flutter 4. Radiofrequency catheter ablation of the slow A-V nodal pathway 5. Radiofrequency catheter ablation of the atrial flutter
Medications given:	Heparin 1,000 units per hour Isoproterenol 2 mcg per minute

Findings:

1. Baseline normal sinus nodal and His-Purkinje function. Ventricular function was not completely studied. The corrected sinus nodal recovery time measured 154 milliseconds at baseline. The H-V interval measured 53 milliseconds at baseline.

2. On isoproterenol 2 mcg per minute, reproducible induced typical AV nodal reentrant tachycardia with a cycle length of 260 milliseconds (231 beats per minute) was induced by double atrial electric stimuli at the high right atrium. This produces systolic blood pressure of 83 mmHg. The arrhythmia was terminated with ventricular burst pacing at 230 milliseconds. Dual AV nodal pathways were evident at baseline with a fast AV nodal effective refractory period measuring 500/310; the slow AV nodal effective refractory period measured 500/350/220.

3. Successful radiofrequency catheter ablation of the slow A-V nodal pathway was accomplished after 3 applications of radiofrequency energy of 50 watts/60 degrees centigrade to the roof of the coronary sinus os. Junctional tachycardia occurred within 6 seconds of radiofrequency application.

4. After slow AV nodal pathway ablation, antegrade AV nodal block measured 300 milliseconds. The AV nodal effective refractory period measured 400/240 and no slow AV nodal conduction could be seen. No inducible A-V nodal reentrant tachycardia, despite double atrial electric stimuli on isoproterenol 2 mcg per minute AV nodal refractoriness.

5. Induced atrial fibrillation with rapid atrial pacing at 230 milliseconds at the high right atrium on isoproterenol 2 mcg per minute. This organized to classic type I atrial flutter.

6. Successful creation of bidirectional conduction block was accomplished across the isthmus of the tricuspid annulus and inferior vena cava, coronary sinus os of the inferior vena cava, coronary sinus os of the tricuspid annulus. Conduction block was proven using coronary sinus os and low right atrial pacing.

Impression:

1. Inducible typical atrioventricular nodal re-entrant tachycardia.
2. Inducible atrial flutter, classic type I

CCS-P Mock Examination

Part II Case 14

Progress Notes:

Feels good
BP 140/84
Groins healing well
Cardiac - normal
Will discharge home

Physician Orders:

1. Supine bed rest for 4 hours, keeping left and right legs straight.
2. May elevate HOB no greater than 30 degrees
3. Vital signs every 15 minutes × 4, every 30 minutes × 4, every hour × 4.
4. Change IV to Heplock.
5. 12 lead EKG
6. Percocet 1–2 p.o. q 6

POST-OPERATIVE ORDERS:

1. Discharge home when stable.
2. ASA 325 mg QD
3. Follow up with me in 1 month.
4. Regular diet and activity

CCS-P Mock Examination
<u>Part II Case 14</u>
Answer Sheet

DIAGNOSES	ICD-9-CM CODES					
First listed DX				.		
DX 2				.		
DX 3				.		
DX 4				.		

PROCEDURES	CPT CODES					MODIFIERS (If Applicable)		
PR 1						-		
PR 2						-		
PR 3						-		
PR 4						-		
PR 5						-		
PR 6						-		
PR 7						-		

CCS-P Mock Examination

Part II Case 15

Emergency Room

Face Sheet

Name: Charles Teal

Date: 1/04/2010

Age: 50

Insurance: HMO

CCS-P Mock Examination

Part II Case 15
Emergency Room Visit

DATE: 1/4/2010

CHIEF COMPLAINT: Cyst on groin area for several days

HISTORY OF PRESENT ILLNESS: Patient complains of a tender swollen spot in the perirectal region. This has occurred for several days. It is painful and it is getting worse as time progresses.

PAST MEDICAL HISTORY: Negative for diabetes or hypertension.

MEDICATIONS: None

ALLERGIES: ASA

SOCIAL HISTORY: Patient smokes one pack per day.

REVIEW OF SYSTEMS: All negative.

PHYSICAL EXAMINATION:

General: Patient is alert and oriented × 3. Patient is in moderate distress.

Vitals: BP: 130/80; P: 111; R: 21; T: 100

Skin: There is a fluctuant abscess in the scrotal area, which needs to be drained.

PROCEDURE: Skin was prepped with Betadine and lidocaine 1% was given. The abscess was incised with a #11 knife and a large amount of pus drained. The area was irrigated with saline and packed with gauze.

IMPRESSION: Abscess of the scrotal wall.

DISCHARGE INSTRUCTIONS: Patient is to follow up in 3 days for removal of the gauze. Patient is to take Tylenol if needed for pain.

History:	Problem-focused
Physical Exam:	Problem-focused
Medical Decision:	Straightforward

CCS-P Mock Examination

Part II Case 15

Answer Sheet

DIAGNOSES	ICD-9-CM CODES					
First listed DX				.		
DX 2				.		
DX 3				.		
DX 4				.		

PROCEDURES	CPT CODES					MODIFIERS (If Applicable)		
PR 1						-		
PR 2						-		
PR 3						-		
PR 4						-		
PR 5						-		
PR 6						-		
PR 7						-		

CCS-P Mock Examination

Part II Case 16

Ambulatory Surgery

Face Sheet

Name: Elizabeth Cooper

Date: 1/03/2010

Age: 72

Insurance: Medicare

CCS-P Mock Examination

Part II Case 16

HISTORY AND PHYSICAL

DATE : 01/03/2010

HISTORY OF PRESENT ILLNESS:
Mrs. Cooper is returning to our office for follow-up of lightheadedness. The patient has been doing well since her last visit. She has not experienced any syncope or near syncope. No chest pain or pressure, PND, orthopnea, or dyspnea on exertion.

MEDICATIONS: She is taking aspirin 81 mg q.d. and Celexa 10 mg q.d.

Review of Systems: General: No fevers or chills. Respiratory: No wheezing, cough, or shortness of breath. GI: No complaints. GU: No complaints. Extremities: No edema or other problems.

PREVIOUS TESTING RESULTS: Stress nuclear study showed an area of septal and also apical thinning with improvements in counts on delay. There was some motion artifact; however, one has to be concerned about the possibility of ischemia in this region, which would appear to be, if present, LAD. LV function was normal and there appears to be LVH. Of concern, the patient did not exercise a great distance, got about 3 minutes on Bruce protocol, and had a dip near her starting blood pressure at peak exercise.

Holter monitor showed short runs of paroxysmal SVT versus atrial fibrillation up to 150 beats per minute. Echocardiogram showed normal LV function, mild to moderate MR, mild TR. I am concerned with the stress nuclear study showing a question of LAD ischemia and the fact that her blood pressure at peak exercise dropped back near starting level.

PHYSICAL EXAMINATION:

Vital signs:	BP: 144/60; P: 72 and regular.
Neck:	No JVD.
Lungs:	Clear bilaterally.
Cardiac:	Regular rate and rhythm. Grade 1/6 right upper sternal border systolic murmur and a positive S4.
Abdomen:	Soft, non-tender and benign.
Extremities:	Femoral pulses appear to be 2+ without bruits. Distal extremities unremarkable. No significant edema.
Neurologic:	Alert and oriented, grossly appears non-focal.

IMPRESSION:
1. Coronary artery disease. Based on nuclear described above, I suspect there may be LAD coronary artery disease.
2. Mild to moderate MR by echo.
3. Probable hypertension.

PLAN:
1. Patient will be scheduled for outpatient cardiac catheterization.
2. Continue aspirin at this point.

CCS-P Mock Examination

Part II Case 16

PROCEDURE

Date of Procedure:	1/03/2010
Pre-Operative Diagnosis:	Coronary artery disease
Post-Operative Diagnosis:	Coronary artery disease of mid lateral anterior descending artery
Procedure:	Left heart catheterization Coronary arteriograms Left ventriculography PTCA with stent

Patient was taken to the cardiac catheterization lab and was prepped and draped in the usual sterile manner. The right femoral artery was entered using the percutaneous technique. Left coronary arteriograms were performed using 6 fr, JL4 catheters. Left ventriculography was performed using 6 fr, JR4 catheters. Right coronary arteriograms were performed using 6 fr JR4.

#6 French sheath was sutured to right groin. Heparinized NaCl via pressure bag attached to 6 French sheath. The injection fraction was 79%.

Then 6 French RFA & FRV flex sheaths were placed. GFXB 3.5 guide & PT Graphix wire was used to cross lesion. IV NTG given. ACT baseline = 133. IV Heparin 3 units given. Mid left anterior descending lesion was predilated with 2.5 × 20 mm Maverick balloon. Stented with 2.5 × 18 mm Bx Velocity stent immediately distal to diagonal. Post dilated with 2.75 × 15 mm Maverick balloon with 14 bars with good opposition.

Results: Residual 0%-5%. Side branch: Diagonal not jeopardized.

Complications: None.

CCS-P Mock Examination

Part II Case 16

Progress Notes

1/3   Heart catheterization showed 90% stenosis of LAD. PTCA was performed with insertion of 2.5 × 18 mm BX Velocity stent. Patient tolerated procedure well.

1/4   No problems or complications from catheterization. Pulses OK. Abdomen soft. No bleeding from femoral site.

Physician Orders:

January 3
1. Right groin check, right DP pulse q 15 min × 4, then q 30 min × 4; then q4h.
2. Monitor femoral artery line, Swan if applicable.
3. NPO until fully alert, then liquids, then advance as tolerated to cardiac diet.
4. Bed rest with right leg extended; loose protective device on right ankle. May elevate HOB 30 degrees while sheaths in.
5. Bed rest × 8 hours after sheaths out, then out of bed with assistance.
6. IV D_5 1/2 NS at 125 mL/h × 8 hours.
7. Tridil 10 mcg/min per standard concentration. Wean at 6 a.m.
8. Uncoated ASA 325 mg PO q A.M.
9. O_2 at 2 L/min via nasal cannula prn, SOB, or O_2 sats < 90%. Oximeter if O_2 in use.

January 4
1. Discharge patient.
2. Script for Plavix 75 mg po OD × 1 month.
3. Follow up with me in 2 weeks.

CCS-P Mock Examination

Part II Case 16

Answer Sheet

DIAGNOSES	ICD-9-CM CODES					
First listed DX				.		
DX 2				.		
DX 3				.		
DX 4				.		

PROCEDURES	CPT CODES					MODIFIERS (If Applicable)		
PR 1						-		
PR 2						-		
PR 3						-		
PR 4						-		
PR 5						-		
PR 6						-		
PR 7						-		

XIII. CCS-P Mock Examination Coding Cases Answer Key

CCS-P Mock Examination Answer Key

Case 1

Diagnoses	ICD-9-CM Codes					
First listed DX Painful respiration	7	8	6	.	5	2
DX 2 Pacemaker status	V	4	5	.	0	1
DX 3 Chronic airway obstruction	4	9	6	.		
DX 4 History of tobacco use	V	1	5	.	8	2

Procedures	CPT Codes						
PP 1 Office visit	9	9	2	1	5	-	
PP 2 EKG - 12 Lead	9	3	0	0	0	-	
PP 3						-	
PP 4						-	
PP 5						-	
PP 6						-	
PP 7							

Case 2

Diagnoses	ICD-9-CM Codes					
First listed DX Closed fracture, shaft or metacarpal bone	8	1	5	.	0	3
DX 2				.		
DX 3				.		
DX 4				.		

Procedures	CPT Codes						
PP 1 Radiology on hand, 2 views	7	3	1	2	0	-	
PP 2 Office visit	9	9	2	0	2	-	
PP 3 Splint (supplies)	A	4	5	7	0	-	
PP 4 Application of short arm splint	2	9	1	2	5	-	
PP 5						-	
PP 6						-	
PP 7							

CCS-P Mock Examination Answer Key

Case 3

Diagnoses	ICD-9-CM Codes					
First listed DX Urinary tract infection	5	9	9	.	0	
DX 2				.		
DX 3				.		
DX 4				.		

Procedures	CPT Codes						
PP 1 Office visit	9	9	2	0	2	-	
PP 2 Automated microscopic urinalysis	8	1	0	0	1	-	
PP 3						-	
PP 4						-	
PP 5						-	
PP 6						-	
PP 7							

Case 4

Diagnoses	ICD-9-CM Codes					
First listed DX Left lateral epicondylitis	7	2	6	.	3	2
DX 2				.		
DX 3				.		
DX 4				.		

Procedures	CPT Codes						
PP 1 Arthrocentesis, aspiration or injection, small joint or bursa	2	0	6	0	5	-	
PP 2 Injection Aristospan 5 mg	J	3	3	0	3	-	
PP 3 Injection Aristospan 5 mg	J	3	3	0	3	-	
PP 4 Office visit	9	9	2	1	3	-	
PP 5						-	
PP 6						-	
PP 7							

CCS-P Mock Examination Answer Key

Case 5

Diagnoses	ICD-9-CM Codes					
First listed DX Postoperative follow-up surgery	V	6	7	.	0	9
DX 2				.		
DX 3				.		
DX 4				.		

Procedures	CPT Codes							
PP 1 Office visit (postoperative period)	9	9	0	2	4	-		
PP 2						-		
PP 3						-		
PP 4						-		
PP 5						-		
PP 6						-		
PP 7						-		

Case 6

Diagnoses	ICD-9-CM Codes					
First listed DX Sebaceous cyst	7	0	6	.	2	
DX 2 Hypertension	4	0	1	.	9	
DX 3 Chronic airway obstruction	4	9	6	.		
DX 4 Tobacco use disorder	3	0	5	.	1	

Procedures	CPT Codes							
PP 1 Excision of cyst 2.0 cm	1	1	4	2	2	-		
PP 2 Excision of cyst 2.5 cm	1	1	4	2	3	-	5	1
PP 3						-		
PP 4						-		
PP 5						-		
PP 6						-		
PP 7						-		

CCS-P Mock Examination Answer Key

Case 7

Diagnoses	ICD-9-CM Codes					
First listed DX Wrist sprain	8	4	2	.	0	0
DX 2 Hip contusion	9	2	4	.	0	1
DX 3				.		
DX 4				.		

Procedures	CPT Codes							
PP 1 ER visit	9	9	2	8	2	-		
PP 2						-		
PP 3						-		
PP 4						-		
PP 5						-		
PP 6						-		
PP 7						-		

Case 8

Diagnoses	ICD-9-CM Codes					
First listed DX Rehabilitation	V	5	7	.	8	9
DX 2 Status post amputee	V	4	9	.	7	5
DX 3 Depression	3	1	1	.		
DX 4 Wheelchair dependence	V	4	6	.	3	

Procedures	CPT Codes							
PP 1 Rehab visit	9	9	3	0	5	-		
PP 2						-		
PP 3						-		
PP 4						-		
PP 5						-		
PP 6						-		
PP 7								

CCS-P Mock Examination Answer Key

Case 9

Diagnoses	ICD-9-CM Codes					
First listed DX Dyspepsia	5	3	6	.	8	
DX 2 Family history of ischemic heart disease	V	1	7	.	3	
DX 3				.		
DX 4				.		

Procedures	CPT Codes						
PP 1 Office visit	9	9	2	1	4	-	
PP 2 Stress test	9	3	0	1	5	-	
PP 3 Blood draw	G	0	0	0	1	-	
PP 4 Lab handling	9	9	0	0	0	-	
PP 5						-	
PP 6						-	
PP 7							

Case 10

Diagnoses	ICD-9-CM Codes					
First listed DX Exotropia, unspecified	3	7	8	.	1	0
DX 2				.		
DX 3				.		
DX 4				.		

Procedures	CPT Codes							
PP 1 Strabismus surgery, recession, lateral rectus muscle	6	7	3	1	1	-	5	0
PP 2						-		
PP 3						-		
PP 4						-		
PP 5						-		
PP 6						-		
PP 7								

CCS-P Mock Examination Answer Key

Case 11

Diagnoses	ICD-9-CM Codes					
First listed DX Medial meniscus tear	8	3	6	.	0	
DX 2 Tobacco use disorder	3	0	5	.	1	
DX 3				.		
DX 4				.		

Procedures	CPT Codes							
PP 1 Arthroscopic medial meniscectomy	2	9	8	8	1	-	R	T
PP 2						-		
PP 3						-		
PP 4						-		
PP 5						-		
PP 6						-		
PP 7								

Case 12

Diagnoses	ICD-9-CM Codes					
First listed DX Benign prostatic hypertrophy	6	0	0	.	0	1
DX 2 Malignant neoplasm of prostate	1	8	5	.		
DX 3 Coronary artery disease, native artery	4	1	4	.	0	1
DX 4 Chronic airway obstruction	4	9	6	.		
Additional DX Retention of urine, unspecified	7	8	8		2	0
Additional DX Incomplete bladder emptying	7	8	8		2	1
Additional DX Supplemental oxygen	V	4	6		2	

Note: As per instructions, only 4 DX will be coded. These additional DX were added for your study convenience.

Procedures	CPT Codes							
PP 1 Laser coagulation of prostate	5	2	6	4	7	-		
PP 2						-		
PP 3						-		
PP 4						-		
PP 5						-		
PP 6						-		
PP 7						-		

CCS-P Mock Examination Answer Key

Case 13

Diagnoses	ICD-9-CM Codes					
First listed DX Coronary artery disease of native artery	4	1	4	.	0	1
DX 2 Angina pectoris	4	1	3	.	9	
DX 3 History of coronary artery bypass graft	V	4	5	.	8	1
DX 4				.		

Procedures	CPT Codes							
PP 1 Left heart catheterization	9	3	5	1	0	-		
PP 2 Injection during heart catheterization	9	3	5	3	9	-		
PP 3 Injection for grafts	9	3	5	4	0	-		
PP 4 Left ventriculogram	9	3	5	4	3	-		
PP 5 Imaging supervision, interpretation, and report for injection procedure(s) during cardiac catheterization; ventricular	9	3	5	5	5	-		
PP 6 Imaging supervision, interpretation, and report for injection procedure(s) during cardiac catheterization; selective coronary angiography	9	3	5	5	6	-		
PP 7						-		

Case 14

Diagnoses	ICD-9-CM Codes					
First listed DX Other specified cardiac dysrhythmias	4	2	7	.	8	9
DX 2 Atrial flutter	4	2	7	.	3	2
DX 3				.		
DX 4				.		

Procedures	CPT Codes							
PP 1 Comprehensive EPS	9	3	6	2	0	-		
PP 2 Ablation	9	3	6	5	0	-		
PP 3 Programmed stimulation and pacing	9	3	6	2	3	-		
PP 4						-		
PP 5						-		
PP 6						-		
PP 7						-		

CCS-P Mock Examination Answer Key

Case 15

Diagnoses	ICD-9-CM Codes					
First listed DX Inflammatory disorders of male genital organs	6	0	8	.	4	
DX 2				.		
DX 3				.		
DX 4				.		

Procedures	CPT Codes							
PP 1 Incision and drainage, scrotal wall	5	5	1	0	0	-		
PP 2 ER visit	9	9	2	8	1	-	2	5
PP 3						-		
PP 4						-		
PP 5						-		
PP 6						-		
PP 7						-		

Case 16

Diagnoses	ICD-9-CM Codes					
First listed DX Coronary artery disease of native artery	4	1	4	.	0	1
DX 2 Mitral valve disorder	4	2	4	.	0	
DX 3				.		
DX 4				.		

Procedures	CPT Codes							
PP 1 LD Stent placement	9	2	9	8	0	-	L	D
PP 2 Left heart catheterization	9	3	5	1	0	-	5	1
PP 3 Coronary angiograms	9	3	5	4	5	-		
PP 4 Left ventriculogram	9	3	5	4	3	-		
PP 5 Imaging supervision, interpretation, and report for injection procedure(s), ventricular angiography	9	3	5	5	5	-		
PP 6 Imaging supervision, interpretation and report for selective coronary angiography	9	3	5	5	6	-		
PP 7						-		

APPENDIX A
PHARMACOLOGY

The most common prescription drugs with examples of diagnoses

Analgesics

Acetaminophen w/codeine (Tylenol #2, #3, #4) mild to moderate pain

Advil (ibuprofen) mild to moderate pain

Aspirin, enteric coated (salisilate) reduce fever, relieve mild to moderate pain

Darvon (propoxyphene N/APAP) mild to moderate pain

Dilaudid (hydromorphine HC1) moderate to severe pain

Feldene (piroxicam) NSAID

hydrocodone w/APAP (Lortab 2.5) pain, moderate to severe; antitussives/expectorants, back
   pain

ibuprofen (Advil, Motrin) NSAID, arthritis, osteoarthritis; rheumatoid arthritis, dysmenorrhea;
   mild to moderate pain, fever; gout

Lortab (hydrocodone w/APAP) moderate to severe pain, expectorant

Motrin (ibuprofen) mild to moderate pain

Oxycodone pain

Piroxicam (Feldene) NSAID

propoxyphene N/APAP (Darvon) pain, narcotic

tramadol (Ultram) moderate to severe pain

Tylenol #2, #3, #4 (acetaminophen w/codeine) mild to moderate pain

Ultram (tramadol) short term pain

Antibacterial

amoxicillin (AMOXIL) antibiotic; broad-spectrum antibacterial drug, urinary tract infections, strep
   throat

Amoxil (amoxicillin) antibiotic; broad spectrum antibacterial drug

Augmentin (amoxicilln with clavulante potassium) treat certain bacterial infections of the ears,
   lungs, sinus, skin, and urinary tract.

Avelox (moxifloxacin hydrochloride) for susceptible strains of designated micro-organisms

Bactroban (mupirocin) topical antibiotic

Cephalexin, USP (Keflex) antibiotic – antibacterial

ciprofloxacin (Cipro) antibacterial (drug-resistant bacteria)

Cipro (ciprofloxacin) antibacterial (drug-resistant bacteria)

Clindamycin (Cleocin) antibacterial

doxycycline hyclate (Vibra-Tabs) antibacterial (drug-resistant bacteria)

erythromycin (Ery-Tab, Erythrocin) macrolide antibotic

Fabyl (metronidazole) trichomoniasis

Keflex (Cephalixin, USP) antibacterial antibiotic

levofloxacin (Levaquin) antibacterial (drug-resistant bacteria)

Levaquin (levofloxacin) antibacterial (drug-resistant bacteria), acute bacterial sinusitis

metronidazole Tabs (Fagyl) trichomoniasis

mupirocin (bactroban) topical antibiotic

Omnicef (cefdinir) drug-resistant bacteria

Penicillin VK infections

tetracycline HCI (Sumycin, Panmycin) antibiotic

Vibra-Tabs (doxycycline hyclate, USP) antibacterial (drug-resistant bacteria)

Anti-inflammatory

Anaprox (naproxen) relieve pain and swelling
Asacol (mesalamine) GI anti-inflammatory (5-aminosalicylic acid derivate)
Celebrex (celecoxib) osteoarthritis, rheumatoid arthritis
celecoxib (Celebrex) osteoarthritis and rheumatoid arthritis, adenomatous colorectal polyps
diclofenac (Voltaren) osteoarthritis, rheumatoid arthritis
Indocin (indomethacin) relieve pain, swelling, and joint stiffness
Lidoderm (lidocaine-transdermal) topical analgesic
Lortab (hydrocodone bitartrate and acetaminophren) relieve moderate to moderately severe pain
Medrol (methylprednisolone) reduces swelling and redness
methylprednisolone (Medrol) inflammatory disorders
Motrin (ibuprofen) relieves pain and swelling
Nalfon (fenoprofen calcium) reduces pain, swelling, and joint stiffness from arthritis
naproxen (Anaprox) NSAID, mild to moderate pain, osteoarthritis, rheumatoid arthritis, dysmenorrhea, gout, ankylosing spondylitis, fever
prednisone (Deltasone) inflammatory disorders, adrenal insufficiency, MS relapsing, pneumocystic pneumonia, asthma, inflammatory bowel disease
Mobic (meloxicam) osteoarthritis and rheumatoid arthritis
Ultram (tramadol hydrochloride) juvenile rheumatoid arthritis, rheumatoid arthritis, chronic fatigue syndrome
Voltaren (diclofenac) osteoarthritis, rheumatoid arthritis

Antifungal

Nystatin (Nystatin oral) antifungal agent
Nystatin (Nystop) topical antifungal cream

Antineoplastic

Arimidex (anastrozole) treat breast cancer
Nolvadet (tamoxifen citrate) antineoplastic agent, SERM, Estrogen receptor antagonist

Antiviral

Acyclovir (zovirax) decrease pain and speed healing of sores or blisters from varicella (chicken pox), herpes zoster (shingles), and outbreaks of genital herpes.
Tamiflu (oseltamivir phosphate) antiviral

Cardiovascular

Accupril (quinapril) HTN
Aldomet (methyldopa) HTN
Altace (ramipril) reduce risk of MI, stroke, hypertension
Amodarone (cordarone,pacerone) anti arrhythmic
amlodipidine (Norvasc) angina, essential HTN, (calcium channel blocker)
Atacand (candesartan cilexetil) antihypertensive
atenolol (Tenomin) angina pectoris, essential HTN, myocardial infarction
atorvastatin (Lipitor) hypercholesterolemia, hyperlipidemia; dysbetalipoproteinemia
Avalide (irbesartan-hydrochlorothiazide) hypertension
Avapro (irbesartan) hypertension
benazepril (Lotensin) HTN, CHF
Benicar (olmesartan medoxomil) hypertension
Caduet (amlodipine besylate with atorvastatin) anti-hypertensive
Cardura (doxazosin) HTN
Catapres (clonidine HC1) HTN
Clonidine high blood pressure
clopidogrel bisulfate (Plavix) reduction of atherothrombotic events

Cardiovascular (continued)

Coreg (carvedilol) congestive heart failure
Coumadin (warfarin sodium) anticoagulant venous thrombosis, pulmonary embolism
Cozaar (losartan potassium) hypertension

Crestor (rosuvastatin calcium) cholesterol
Digoxin (lanoxin) heart failure, irregular heart beat (chronic atrial fibrillation)
Digitek heart failure
Diovan (valsartan) hypertension, heart failure, post-myocardial infarction
Doxazosin (Cardura) HTN, BPH
Dyazide (triamterene/HCTZ) diuretic, hypertension
Enalapril maleate (vasotec) hypertension
enalapril (Vasotec) HTN, CHF, acute MI, nephropathy, asymptomatic left ventricular dysfunction
furosemide (Lasix) diuretic, peripheral and pulmonary edema, hypercalcemia, kidney failure
Gemfibrozil high serum triglyceride
Hyzaar (losartan potassium-hydrochlorithiazide) hypertension
Imdur (isosorbide mononitrate) angina
Inderal (propranolol HCI) beta-blocker, antihypertensive
isosorbide mononitrate (Imdur, ISMO) angina
ISMO (isosorbide mononitrate) angina
lanoxin (Digoxin) CHF, atrial fibrillation/flutter, paroxysmal atrial tachycardia
Lasix (furosemide) CHF, HTN, diuretic
Lipitor (atorvastatin) high cholesterol
lisinopril (Prinivil, Zestril) hypertension (HTN), congestive heart failure (CHF), acute MI
Lopressor (metoprolol) hypertension
Lotensin (benazepril) HTN
Lotrel (amlodipine besylate and benazepril HCI) HTN
Lovaza (omega-3-acid ethyl esters) antihyperlipidemic
metoprolol tartrate (Lopressor, Toprol XL) HTN, CHF, acute MI, angina
Mevacor (lovastatin) cholesterol-lowering agent
Miscardis HCT (telmisartan with hydrochlorothiazide)
Minipress (prazosin HC1) HTN
nifedipine ER (Procardia, Adalat) angina
Nitrostat (nitroglycerine) angina pectoris due to coronary artery disease
Norvasc (amlodipine besylate) hypertension
Plavix (clopidogrel bisulfate) reduction of atherothrombotic events, heart attack, stroke, peripheral vascular disease
Pravachol (pravastatin sodium) hypercholesterolemia, hyperlipidemia, dysbetalipoproteinemia
Prinivil (lisinopril) HTN
quinapril (Accupril) hypertension, CHF
ramipril (Altace) reduce risk of MI, stroke, hypertension
simvastatin (Zocor) hypercholesterolemia, hypertriglyceridemia, dysbetalipoproteinemia
Toprol XL (metoprolol) HTN
triamterene/HCTZ (Dyazide) diuretic, hypertension, peripheral edema
Tricor (penofibrate) hypercholesterolemia
Trizac (dilitiazem hydrochloride) hypertension
Valsartan (Diovan) hypertension
Vasotec (enalapril) HTN
verapamil angina, hypertension, supraventricular arrhythmia, atrial fibrillation/flutter, migraine prophylaxis
Vytorin (ezetimibe with simvastatin) cholesterol

Cardiovascular (continued)

Warfarin (Coumadin) anticoagulation
Zestril (lisinopril) HTN
Zetia (ezetimibe) primary hypercholesterolemia
Zocor (simvastatin) high cholesterol

Electrolytes

K-Dur (potassium chloride) hypokalemia, prevention of hypokalemia
Klor-Con (potassium chloride) hypokalemia, prevention of hypokalemia
potassium chloride (K-Dur, Klor-Con) hypokalemia, prevention of hypokalemia

Endocrinology

Actos (pioglitazone hydrochloride) DM type 2
Aldactone (spironolactone) hyperaldosteronism
Allopurinol (Zyloprim) gout
Avandia (rosiglitazone maleate) DM type 2
Byetta (exenatide) anti-diabetic (incretin mimetic)
DiaBeta (glyburide) DM type 2
Estrace (estrogen) reduces menopausal symptoms
glipizide (Glucotrol XL) DM type 2
Glucophage XR (metformin hydrochloride) diabetes
Glucotrol XL (glipizide) DM type 2
glyburide (DiaBeta, Micronase) DM type 2
Humalog (insulin lispro, rDNA origin) diabetes
Januvia (sitagliptin) DM type 2
Lantus (insulin glargine [rDNA origin] injection) DM type 1
Levothroid (levothyroxine) hypothyroidism
levothyroxine (Levoxyl, Synthyroid Levothroid) hypothyroidism, myxedema coma, thyroid cancer
Levoxyl (levothyroxine sodium) hypothyroidism, pituitary TSH suppression
metformin (Glucophage) DM, type II2
Methylprednisolone endocrine disorders, rheumatic disorders
Micronase (glyburide) DM type II 2
NovoLog (insulin) antidiabetic
Synthroid (levothyroxine) hypothyroidism

Gastrointestinal

Aciphex (rabeprazole sodium) erosive or ulcerative GERD
esomeprazole magnesium (Nexium) GERD
Lomotil (diphenoxylate) diarrhea
Metoclopramide (Reglan) GERD
NEXIUM (esomeprazole magnesium) GERD
omeprazole (Prilosec) GERD, erosive esophagitis, gastric/duodenal ulcer, H. Pylori treatment
pantoprazole sodium (Protonix) GERD
Pepcid (famotidine) GERD, duodenal ulcer
Prevacid (lansoprazole) GERD
Prilosec (omeprazole) GERD
Protonix (pantoprazole sodium) GERD, stomach ulcers, heartburn
Xantac (ranitidine Hcl) duodenal ulcer, gastric ulcer

Genitourinary

allopurinol (Zyloprim) prophylaxis for gout, urate nephropathy, calcium oxalate calculi
Aviane contraceptive
Avodart (dutasteride) prostate anti-inflammatory
azithromycin (Zithromax) chlamydia
Cialis (tadalifil) erectile dysfunction
conjugated estrogens (Premarin, Prempro) antineoplastics; cancer of breast and prostate,
  menopause; osteoporosis prevention; ovarian failure; primary atrophic vaginitis
Detrol (tolterodine tartrate) overactive bladder, urinary incontinence
Diflucan (fluconazole) vaginal yeast infections
Ditropan (oxybutynin chloride) urinary antispasmodic agent
Estrace (estradiol) reduces menopausal symptoms
estradiol (Estrace) vasomotor symptoms, atrophic vaginitis, osteoporosis prevention, palliative
  treatment for breast cancer and prostate cancer
Flomax (tamsulosin hydrochloride) benign prostatic hyperplasia
fluconazole (Diflucan) vaginal candidiasis, oropharyngeal and esophageal candidiasis,
  cryptococcal meningitis
Demadex (torsemide) loop diuretic
Levitra (vardenafil HCI) erectile dysfunction
medroxyprogesterone (Provera) HRT, amenorrhea, dysfunctional uterine bleeding
norgestimate/ethinyl estradiol (Ortho Tri-Cyclen) oral contraceptive
Nuvaring (etonogestrel/ethinyl estradiol vaginal ring) contraceptive
Ortho Evra (norelgestromin/ethinyl estradiol) contraceptive
Ortho Tri-Cyclen (norgestimate/ethinyl estradiol) contraceptive
Premarin (conjugated estrogens) vasomotor symptoms and vaginal atrophy due to menopause,
  breast cancer, prostate cancer
Prempro (conjugated estrogens/medroxyprogesterone) reduces menopausal symptoms
Provera (medroxyprogesterone) restores normal menstrual periods
Pyridium (phenazopyridine HCI) urinary tract analgesic
Septra (trimethoprim/sulfametoxazole) antibacterial bladder infections
sildenafil citrate (Viagra) erectile dysfunction
trimethoprim/sulfametoxazole (Septra) antibacterial bladder infections
Trisprintec (Ortho Tri-Cyclen) (norgestimate/ethinyl estradiol) contraceptive
Valtrex (valacyclovir hydrochloride) herpes zoster, genital herpes
Vesicare (solifenacin succinate) anticoholinergic agent (urinary bladder modifier)
Viagra (sildenafil citrate) erectile dysfunction
Yasmin (drospirenone and ethinyl estradiol) contraceptive
Zithromax (azithromycin) treat STD (chlamydia)
Zyloprim (allopurinol) gout, kidney stones

Immunology and Allergy

Adrenalin (epinephrine) allergies
Allegra (fexofenadine hydrochloride) allergies, hay fever
Astelin (azelastine hydrochloride) allergic rhinitis
Cetirizine (Zyrtec) allergies
Chlor-Trimeton (chlorapheneramine maleate) allergies
Clarinex (desloratadine) seasonal allergic rhinitis
Dimetane (brompheniramine maleate) allergies
fexofenadine (Allegra) allergic rhinitis, chronic urticaria
Flonase (fluticasone propionate) allergic rhinitis, sleep apnea
fluticasone proprionate (Flonase) allergic rhinitis, sleep apnea
momentasone nasal (Nasonex) seasonal and year-round allergy symptoms of the nose
Nasacort (triamcinolone acetonide, USP) seasonal and perennial allergic rhinitis

Immunology and Allergy (continued)

Nasonex (mometasone nasal) seasonal and year-round allergy symptoms of the nose
Rhinocort Aqua (budensoide nasal spray) anti allergy
Promethazine (Phenergan) allergic symptoms, nausea, motion sickness
Singular (montelukast sodium) allergic rhinitis
Tussionex (chlorpheniramine with hydrocodone) antihistime/antitussive
Zyrtec (cetirizine) allergic rhinitis, chronic urticaria

Musculoskeletal

Actonel (risedronate sodium) osteoporosis
alendronate (Fosamax) osteoporosis, Paget's disease
Baclofen (lioresal, kemstro) skeletal muscle relaxant
Boniva (ibandronate sodium) osteoporosis in postmenopausal women
carisoprodol (Soma) muscle spasm
cyclobenzaprine (Flexeril) muscle spasm
Evista (raloxifene hydrochloride) osteoporosis
Flexeril (cyclobenzaprine) muscle spasm, sciatica
Fosamax (alendronate sodium) osteoporosis
Skelaxin (metaxalone) acute, painful musculoskeletal conditions
Soma (carisoprodol) treat pain and discomfort from muscle injuries

Neurological

Aricept (donepezil hydrochloride) mild to moderate dementias of the Alzheimer's type
Benztropine mesylate (cognentine) treats tremors, symtoms of Parkenson's disease
clonazepam (Klonopin) neuralgia, absence seizures, epilepsy, panic attacks
Depakote (divalproex) seizure disorders, psychiatric conditions, prevents migraines
Dilantin (phenytoin sodium) seizures
divalproex (Depakote) seizure disorder, mania, migraine prophylaxis
gabapentin (Neurontin) partial seizures, neuropathic pain, postherpetic neuralgia in adults, epilepsy
Imitrex (sumatriptan succinate) hemiplegic or basilar migraine
Keppra (levetiracetam) partial onset seizures due to epilepsy
Klonopin (clonazepam) seizure disorders and panic attacks
Lamictal (lamotrigine) epilepsy
Lyrica (pregablalin) neurolopathic pain, postherpetic neuralgia, partial onset seizures, fibromyalgia
Mirapex (pramipexol dihydrochloride) anti-Parkinson's agent –dopamine agonist
Namenda (memantine HCI) agent for Alzheimer's dementia (NMDA receptor antagonist)
Neurontin (gabapentin) control seizures, nerve pain
Requip (ropinirole HCI) anti-parkinson's agent –dopamine agonist
Trileptal (oxcarbazepin) antiepileptic
Topamax (topiramate) epilepsy

Optical

Alphagan-P (brimonidine tartrate) glaucoma
Cosopt (dorzolamide hydrochloride and timolol maleate) reduce intraocular pressure in ocular hypertension, glaucoma
Lumigan (bimatoprost) glaucoma
Patanol (olopatadine) allergic conjunctivitis
Vigamox (moxifloxacin hydrochloride) bacterial conjunctivitis
TobraDex (tobramycin and dexamethasone) antibiotic ophthalmic corticosteroid
Travatan (travoprost) antiglaucoma agent (ophthalmic prostagladin)
Xalatan (latanoprost) reduce intraocular pressure, glaucoma

Psychiatric

Abilify (aripiprazole) schizophrenia
Adderall ADHD
alprazolam (Xanax) anxiety, panic disorder
Ambien (zolpidem tartrate) sleep disorders, insomnia
amitriptyline (Elavil, Endep) depression, chronic pain
Ativan (lorazepam) anxiety
bupropion HCL (Wellbutrin SR) major depressive disorder
Budisol (butabarbital sodium) sedative or hypnotic, insomnia
Celexa (citalopram) depression
Citalopram (Celexa) depression
Concerta (methylphenidate HCI extended release) ADHD
Cymbalta (duloxetine hydrochloride) suicidal tendencies and depression
Desyrel (trazodone) depression
Diazepam (Valium) anxiety, alcohol withdrawal stress, muscle spasm, seizure disorder, status epilepticus
Effexor XR (venlafaxine hydrochloride) major depressive disorder
Elavil (amitriptyline) depression, fibromyalgia
Endep (amitriptyline) depression
escitapropram oxalate (Lexapro) antidepressant
fluoxetine hydrochloride (Prozac) bulimia nervosa, depression, obsessive-compulsive disorder, social anxiety disorder
Focalin XR (dexmethylphenidate HCI) ADHD
Haldol (haloperidol) treat mental/mood disorders
Hydroxyzine (Atarax) anxiety, psychoneurosis
Lexapro (escitapropram oxalate) antidepressant, anxiety
Lorazepam (Ativan) anxiety, panic attacks, depression
Lunesta (eszopiclone) non-BZD (non benzodiazepines drug)hypnotic
modafinil (Provigil) sleep disorders
Nortriptyline (Pamelor) depression
Privigil (modafinil) sleep disorders
paroxetine (Paxil) anxiety, panic disorder, depression, obsessive-compulsive disorder
Paxil (paroxetine) panic attacks, depression, obsessive-compulsive disorder, post-traumatic stress disorder (PTSD)
Prozac (fluoxetine) depression, obsessive-compulsive disorder, panic attacks, bulimia, premenstrual syndrome
Restoril (temazepam) insomnia
Risperdal (risperidone) schizophrenia
Seroquel (quetiapine funarate) treatment of bipolar mania
sertraline (Zoloft) anxiety, panic disorder, depression, obsessive-compulsive disorder
Strattera (atomoxetine HCI) ADHD
trazodone (Desyrel) depression
Valium (diazepam) anxiety
venlafaxine (Effexor EX) depression, anxiety
Wellbutrin SR (bupropion HCL) major depressive disorder
Xanax (alprazolam) anxiety and panic disorders
Zoloft (sertraline hydrochloride) depression, panic attacks, post-traumatic stress disorder (PTSD)
zolpidem (Ambien) insomnia
Zyprexa (olanzapine) dementia-related psychosis

Respiratory

Advair Diskus (fluticasone propionate) treatment of asthma
albuterol (Proventil, Ventolin) asthma
Budenoside (plumicort) anti-asthmatic
Combivent Flovent (fluticasone propionate) asthma
fluticasone propionate (Flovent) asthma
montelukast (Singular) asthma
Proair FHA (Albuterol sulfate inhalation aerosol) asthma
Proventil (albuterol) asthma
Singulair (montelukast) asthma
Spiriva (tiotropium bromide inhalation powder) bronchospasm associated with COPD
Tussionex (pennkinetic) cough and upper respiratory symptoms associated with allergy or cold
Ventolin (albuterol) asthma
Xopenex (levalbuterol HCI) anti-asthmatic (beta 2 agonist)

Smoking Cessation

Chantix (varenicline) aid to smoking cessation

Common Abbreviations

Always use with caution! Abbreviations may have multiple meanings.

a	before
ac, a.c.	before meals
AD	right ear
ad lib	as desired
alt dieb	alternate days
alt hr	alternate hours
alt noc	alternate nights
am, AM	morning
amt	amount
ante	before
aq	aqueous (water)
AS	left ear
AU	both ears
Ba	barium
bid, b.i.d.	two times a day
bin	two times a night
C	100
c, w/	with
cap(s)	capusle(s)
cc	cubic centimeter
CHF	congestive heart failure
d	day
Dx	diagnosis
D₅W	5% dextrose in water
D/C, dc	discontinue
dil	dilute
disp	dispense
DM	diabetes mellitus
dr	dram
elix	elixir
emul	emulsion
et	and
ext	extract/external
FDA	Food and Drug Administration
Fe	iron
Fl	fluid
G	gauge
g, GM, gm, gr	gram(s)
gal	gallon
gt, gtt	drop(s)
H	hour/hypodermic
HRT	hormone replacement therapy
Hs, h.s.	hour of sleep (bedtime)
HTN	hypertension
HRT	hormone replacement therapy
IM	intramuscular
Inj	injection
IU	international units
IV	intravenous
IVPB	IV piggyback (2nd line)
K	potassium
kg	kilogram
L	liter
Liq	liquid
mcg	microgram
mg	milligram(s)
ml, mL	milliliter(s)
mm	millimeter
NaCl 0.9%	normal saline
NKA	no known allergy
NKDA	no known drug allergy
noc, noct	night
non rep	do not repeat
NPO	nothing by mouth
NS	normal saline
NSAID	non-steroidal anti-inflammatory drug(s)
O	pint
od	once day/daily
OD	right eye
om	every morning
OTC	over the counter
Oz, oz	ounce
Pc, p.c.	after meals
PCA	patient-controlled analgesia, patient controlled administration
PCN	penicillin
PDR	Physician's Desk Reference
per	with
PM, pm	evening
PRN, prn	as needed as necessary
PO, po, p.o.	by mouth
pt	pint, patient
pulv	powder
Q, q	every
q2h	every two hours
qAm	every morning
qd, q.d.	every day
qh, q.h.	every hour
qhs	every bedtime
qid, q.i.d.	four times a day
qns	quantity not sufficient
qPM	every evening
qs, q.s.	as much as needed, sufficient quantity
Rx	prescription

Common Abbreviations (continued)

SC, sc, sq, subc, subq.	Subcutaneous
Sig, sig	let be labeled as follows, directions
SL	sublingual
SOB	shortness of breath

susp .... suspension
T, tbsp .... tablespoon
tab .... tablet

tid, t.i.d. .... three times a day
TO .... telephone order
Top, top ....apply topically
tsp .... teaspoon
TX .... treatment
ut, diet, UD .... as directed
wt .... weight

BE ALERT FOR SOUND ALIKES

Drug names may be similar in sound as well as spelling. It is important to be alert when referring to drugs. For example:

Celebrex .... NSAID
       vs
Cerebyx........... anticonvulsant

DiaBeta ...... oral hypoglycemic
      vs
Zebeta beta-adrenergic blocker

Paxil............... .antidepressant
      vs
Taxol…………………..antineoplastic

REFERENCES FOR PHARMACOLOGY

Nobles, S. (2002). *Delmar's drug reference for health care professionals.* Clifton Park, NY: Delmar Cengage Learning.

Woodrow, R. (2007). *Essentials of pharmacology for health occupations* (5th ed). Clifton Park, NY: Delmar Cengage Learning.

Web sites for Pharmacology: http://www.rxlist.com/script/main/hp.asp
                         http://www.epocrates.com/
                         http://www.fda.gov/
                         http://pdr.net/login/Login.aspx
                         http://mayoclinic.com/

HEMATOLOGY/COAGULATION

Complete Blood Count

Use: basic blood evaluation
AKA: CBC, CBC with differential
Note: usually includes Hct, Hgb, WBC counts and differential, platelet count, and often RBC count

Erythrocyte Count

AKA: RBC count (red blood cell)
High: acute hepatitis, acute MI, PID, rheumatoid arthritis
Low: anemias, leukemias, and following severe hemorrhage

Hematocrit

Use: determines the percent of whole blood composed of red blood cells
AKA: Hct, HCT, PVC
High: dehydration, Addison's disease, polycythemia due to dehydration, and shock
Low: anemia, severe hemorrhage

Hemoglobin

Use: measures Hgb in the blood
AKA: Hb, Hgb
High: dehydration, pernicious anemia, sickle cell anemia, thalassemia, polycythemia, obstructive pulmonary diseases, CHF
Low: excessive fluid intake, iron-deficiency anemia, pregnancy

Hemoglobin, Glycated

Use: monitors blood sugar control
AKA: HbA1C, GHb, DM control index
Note: Abnormal results over time indicate inadequate control.

Leukocyte Count

AKA: WBC Count (white blood cell)
High: acute infections, leukemias, acute hemorrhage
Low: chemotherapy, shock, cachexia

Partial Thromboplastin Time

Use: measures intrinsic clotting time
AKA: APTT, activated
High: cirrhosis, leukemia, vitamin K deficiency, hemophilia
Low: extensive ca, early stages of disseminated intravascular coagulation

Platelet Count

Use: dx a bleeding disorder or bone marrow disease

High: iron-deficiency anemia, postop patients, malignancies, polycythemia
Low: acute leukemia, aplastic anemia, thrombocytopenic purpura

Prothrombin Time

Use: monitor blood-thinning medications used to prevent blood clots
AKA: PT, Pro Time
Prolonged: severe liver damage, heparin use, low vitamin K diet, colitis, chronic diarrhea

Reticulocyte Count

Use: measures percent of reticulocytes (slightly immature red blood cells)
High: need for RBCs, hemolytic anemias, acute or severe bleeding
Low: bone marrow failure (toxicity, tumor, fibrosis, infection), cirrhosis, iron-deficiency, radiation therapy

Sedimentation Rate

Use: monitors inflammatory and malignant diseases, and acute MI
AKA: erythrocyte sedimentation rate, sed rate, ESR
High: pregnancy, menstruation, infectious diseases, tissue damage

SERUM ELECTROLYTES

Note: essential to normal metabolism, exists as acids, bases, and salts
AKA: "Lytes"

Calcium, Total

Use: blood test to screen/monitor diseases of bone or calcium regulation (diseases of parathyroid and kidneys)
AKA: $Ca+2$, $Ca++$, serum calcium
High: metastatic ca of bone, lung, breast, Paget's disease, hyperparathyroidism, excess vitamin D
Low: severe pancreatitis, renal insufficiency, uremia, malabsorption, osteomalacia, hypoparathyroidism

SERUM ELECTROLYTES (continued)

Chloride

AKA: Cl

High: renal insufficiency, necrosis, dehydration, renal tubular acidosis, Cushing's syndrome, hyperventilation
Low: CHF, chronic renal failure, diabetic acidosis, diarrhea, excessive sweating, emphysema

Magnesium
AKA: Mg+2
High: renal insufficiency, use of antacids with magnesium
Low: chronic alcoholism, chronic diarrhea, hepatic insufficiency

Phosphorus
AKA: PO4
High: renal insufficiency, healing fx, hypoparathyroidism, excess vitamin D
Low: chronic alcoholism, ketoacidosis, hyperalimentation, hyperparathyroidism

Potassium
AKA: K
High: renal insufficiency, adrenal insufficiency, Addison's disease, hypoventilation
Low: chronic diarrhea, vomiting or malabsorption syndrome, diabetic acidosis, chronic kidney disease, use of thiazide diuretics

Sodium
AKA: NA
High: (hypernatremia) excessive dietary intake, Cushing's disease, excessive sweating, diabetes insipidus
Low: (hyponatremia): ascites, CHF, insufficient intake, diarrhea, vomiting, SIADH (syndrome of inappropriate diuretic hormone), diuretic use, chronic renal insufficiency, excessive water intake, peripheral edema, pleural effusion

SERUM/URINE/STOOL

Acid Phosphatase

High: metastatic ca of bone, prostatic ca, some liver diseases, MI, pulmonary embolism, hepatobiliary diseases, hyperparathyroidism

Alanine Aminotransferase
Use: screens for liver disease
AKA: ALT, SGPT
High: acute hepatitis, liver necrosis

Albumin
Use: screen for liver or kidney disease or evaluate nutritional status
AKA: ALB
Note: Albumin is a protein.
High: shock, dehydration, multiple myeloma
Low: malnutrition, malabsorption, acute or chronic glomerulonephritis, cancers, leukemia, hepatitis, cirrhosis, hepatocellular necrosis

Alkaline Phosphatase
Use: screen/monitor treatment for liver or bone disorders
AKA: ALP, alk phos
High: biliary duct obstruction, hyperparathyroidism, healing fx, rickets, osteomalacia, neoplastic bone disorders, liver diseases

Ammonia
AKA: NH4+
Note: particularly toxic to the brain; can cause confusion and lethargy
High: CHF, liver failure, GI bleed, leukemia, pericarditis

Amylase
Use: blood test to diagnose/monitor pancreatic disease (blood)
Note: amylase is an enzyme that helps digest glycogen and starch
High: acute pancreatitis, ca of the pancreas, ovaries, or lungs, mumps, intestinal obstruction
Low: acute and chronic hepatitis, cirrhosis, toxemia of pregnancy

Anion Gap
Use: dx and tx of acidosis
High: lactic acidosis, diabetic ketoacidosis, alcoholic ketoacidosis, starvation, renal failure
Low: multiple myeloma, chronic vomiting, hyperaldosteronism

SERUM/URINE/STOOL (continued)
Arterial Blood Gases
AKA: ABGs
Abnormal Results: respiratory, metabolic or renal diseases, trauma
Aspartate Aminotransferase
Use: detect liver damage
AKA: AST, SGOT

High: acute MI, liver disease, diseases of skeletal muscles

Bilirubin, Total
Use: screen/monitor liver disorders
Note: bilirubin is a product of hemoglobin breakdown, causes jaundice
High: acute/chronic hepatitis, gallstones, toxic reaction to drugs/chemicals, infectious mononucleosis

Blood Urea Nitrogen
Use: evaluate kidney function and dialysis effectiveness
AKA: BUN
High: GI hemorrhage, dehydration, renal insufficiency
Low: hepatic failure, cachexia

Carbon Dioxide, Total
AKA: CO_2
High: respiratory diseases, vomiting, intestinal obstruction
Decreased: acidosis, nephritis, diarrhea

Carcinoembryonic Antigen
Use: dx cancer and monitor tx
AKA: CEA
High: colon, breast, lung, pancreatic, thyroid ca, also heavy smoking

Cholesterol, Total
Use: screen for heart disease
High: MI, uncontrolled DM, hypothyroidism, atherosclerosis, hypercholesterolemia, hyperlipidemia
Low: acute MI, pernicious anemia, malnutrition, liver disease, sepsis, malabsorption.

Creatinine
Use: evaluate kidney function and tx
High: dehydration, diabetic nephropathy, kidney disease

Creatine (Phospho) kinase
Use: evaluate muscle damage
AKA: CPK, CK
High: acute MI, muscular dystrophies, muscle injury, CNS trauma, and stroke

Globulin
Use: protein evaluation
AKA: CPK, CK
High: hepatic disease, plasma cell neoplasms, lupus, malaria

Glucose
Use: diagnose and manage DM
AKA: GTT glucose tolerance test
High: DM, IV therapy, hyperthyroidism, hyperpituitarism, liver diseases, nephritis
Low: hyperinsulinism, hyperthyroidism, Addison's disease

Iron
AKA: Fe
High: anemias, liver disease
Low: iron-deficiency anemia, excessive fluid intake, pregnancy

Lactose Dehydrogenase
AKA: LDH
High: acute MI, infectious hepatitis, malignant tumors and widespread ca, hemolytic and pernicious anemias, acute leukemias
Low: x-ray irradiation

Oxygen Saturation
AKA: oximetry, O_2
High: hyperventilation
Low: inadequate O_2 inspiration, hypoxic lung diseases, hypoxic cardiac diseases, severe hypoventilation

Prostate-Specific Antigen
AKA: PSA
High: BPH, prostate ca, prostatism

Stool Guaiac Test
Use: detect hidden blood in stool
AKA: hemoccult
Abnormal Results: NSAIDs, colon polyps, colon ca, GI tumors, esophagitis, gastritis, inflammatory bowel disease, peptic ulcer

Thyrotropin
AKA: THS
Abnormal Findings: hyperthyroidism, hypothyroidism, depression, acute starvation, pregnancy, old age

Thyroxine
AKA: T_4
High: Graves' disease, toxic thyroid adenoma, acute thyroiditis
Low: cretinism, myxedema, pituitary or iodine insufficiency, hypothalamic failure, renal failure, Cushing's disease, cirrhosis, advanced cancer

Triglycerides
AKA: TG

High: hyperlipidemias, hypothyroidism, poorly controlled DM, nephrotic syndrome, hypertension, alcoholic cirrhosis, pregnancy, MI

Low: malabsorption syndrome, malnutrition, hyperthyroidism

Uric Acid

High: gout, leukemia, renal insufficiency, polycythemia, pneumonia

Low: acute hepatitis

Viral Load

Use: severity of immune system damage, monitor HIV status and treatment

AKA: CD4 lymphocyte count

Low below 350 ml: herpes simplex, herpes zoster, TB

Low below 200 ml: pneumocystis carinii pneumonia,

Low below 100 ml: AIDS dementia

Low below 50 ml: cytomegalovirus

COMMON ABBREVIATIONS

AKA ....also known as
ca, Ca ....cancer, calcium
CHF ....congestive heart failure
DM..............................diabetes mellitus
Dx ....diagnosis
fx ....fracture
GI................................ gastrointestinal
HIV.......... human immunodeficiency virus
IV.. intravenous
MI .... myocardial infarction
NIDDM ....non-insulin-dependent DM
NSAID ....non-steroidal anti-inflammatory
tx ....treatment

REFERENCES FOR LAB TESTING

Mosisio, M.A., & Moisio, E.W. (1998). *Understanding Laboratory and Diagnostic Tests*. Clifton Park, NY: Delmar Cengage Learning.

Estridge, B.H., & Reynolds, A.P. (2008). *Basic Clinical Laboratory Techniques* (5th ed.). Clifton Park, NY: Delmar Cengage Learning.

Lab Tests Online
     http://www.labtestsonline.org/

ICD-9-CM Official Guidelines for Coding and Reporting

Effective October 1, 2009
Narrative changes appear in bold text
Items underlined have been moved within the guidelines since October 1, 2008

The Centers for Medicare and Medicaid Services (CMS) and the National Center for Health Statistics (NCHS), two departments within the U.S. Federal Government's Department of Health and Human Services (DHHS) provide the following guidelines for coding and reporting using the International Classification of Diseases, 9th Revision, Clinical Modification (ICD-9-CM). These guidelines should be used as a companion document to the official version of the ICD-9-CM as published on CD-ROM by the U.S. Government Printing Office (GPO).

These guidelines have been approved by the four organizations that make up the Cooperating Parties for the ICD-9-CM: the American Hospital Association (AHA), the American Health Information Management Association (AHIMA), CMS, and NCHS. These guidelines are included on the official government version of the ICD-9-CM, and also appear in *"Coding Clinic for ICD-9-CM"* published by the AHA.

These guidelines are a set of rules that have been developed to accompany and complement the official conventions and instructions provided within the ICD-9-CM itself. **The instructions and conventions of the classification take precedence over guidelines.** These guidelines are based on the coding and sequencing instructions in Volumes I, II and III of ICD-9-CM, but provide additional instruction. Adherence to these guidelines when assigning ICD-9-CM diagnosis and procedure codes is required under the Health Insurance Portability and Accountability Act (HIPAA). The diagnosis codes (Volumes 1-2) have been adopted under HIPAA for all healthcare settings. Volume 3 procedure codes have been adopted for inpatient procedures reported by hospitals. A joint effort between the healthcare provider and the coder is essential to achieve complete and accurate documentation, code assignment, and reporting of diagnoses and procedures. These guidelines have been developed to assist both the healthcare provider and the coder in identifying those diagnoses and procedures that are to be reported. The importance of consistent, complete documentation in the medical record cannot be overemphasized. Without such documentation accurate coding cannot be achieved. The entire record should be reviewed to determine the specific reason for the encounter and the conditions treated.

The term encounter is used for all settings, including hospital admissions. In the context of these guidelines, the term provider is used throughout the guidelines to mean physician or any qualified health care practitioner who is legally accountable for establishing the patient's diagnosis. Only this set of guidelines, approved by the Cooperating Parties, is official.

The guidelines are organized into sections. Section I includes the structure and conventions of the classification and general guidelines that apply to the entire classification, and chapter-specific guidelines that correspond to the chapters as they are arranged in the classification. Section II includes guidelines for selection of principal diagnosis for non-outpatient settings. Section III includes guidelines for reporting additional diagnoses in non-outpatient settings. Section IV is for outpatient coding and reporting.

Section I. Conventions, general coding guidelines and chapter specific guidelines

The conventions, general guidelines and chapter-specific guidelines are applicable to all health care settings unless otherwise indicated. **The conventions and instructions of the classification take precedence over guidelines.**

A. Conventions for the ICD-9-CM

The conventions for the ICD-9-CM are the general rules for use of the classification independent of the guidelines. These conventions are incorporated within the index and tabular of the ICD-9-CM as instructional notes. The conventions are as follows:

1. Format:

The ICD-9-CM uses an indented format for ease in reference

2. Abbreviations

a. Index abbreviations

NEC   "Not elsewhere classifiable"
This abbreviation in the index represents "other specified" when a specific code is not available for a condition the index directs the coder to the "other specified" code in the tabular.

b. Tabular abbreviations

NEC   "Not elsewhere classifiable"
This abbreviation in the tabular represents "other specified". When a specific code is not available for a condition the tabular includes an NEC entry under a code to identify the code as the "other specified" code.
(See Section I.A.5.a. "Other" codes").

NOS   "Not otherwise specified"
This abbreviation is the equivalent of unspecified.
(See Section I.A.5.b., "Unspecified" codes)

3. Punctuation

[ ]   Brackets are used in the tabular list to enclose synonyms, alternative wording or explanatory phrases. Brackets are used in the index to identify manifestation codes.
(See Section I.A.6. "Etiology/manifestations")

( )   Parentheses are used in both the index and tabular to enclose supplementary words that may be present or absent in the statement of a disease or procedure without affecting the code number to which it is assigned. The terms within the parentheses are referred to as nonessential modifiers.

: Colons are used in the Tabular list after an incomplete term which needs one or more of the modifiers following the colon to make it assignable to a given category.

4. Includes and Excludes Notes and Inclusion terms

Includes: This note appears immediately under a three-digit code title to further define, or give examples of, the content of the category.

Excludes: An excludes note under a code indicates that the terms excluded from the code are to be coded elsewhere. In some cases the codes for the excluded terms should not be used in conjunction with the code from which it is excluded. An example of this is a congenital condition excluded from an acquired form of the same condition. The congenital and acquired codes should not be used together. In other cases, the excluded terms may be used together with an excluded code. An example of this is when fractures of different bones are coded to different codes. Both codes may be used together if both types of fractures are present.

Inclusion terms: List of terms is included under certain four and five digit codes. These terms are the conditions for which that code number is to be used. The terms may be synonyms of the code title, or, in the case of "other specified" codes, the terms are a list of the various conditions assigned to that code. The inclusion terms are not necessarily exhaustive. Additional terms found only in the index may also be assigned to a code.

5. Other and Unspecified codes

a. "Other" codes

Codes titled "other" or "other specified" (usually a code with a 4th digit 8 or fifth-digit 9 for diagnosis codes) are for use when the information in the medical record provides detail for which a specific code does not exist. Index entries with NEC in the line designate "other" codes in the tabular. These index entries represent specific disease entities for which no specific code exists so the term is included within an "other" code.

b. "Unspecified" codes

Codes (usually a code with a 4th digit 9 or 5th digit 0 for diagnosis codes) titled "unspecified" are for use when the information in the medical record is insufficient to assign a more specific code.

6. **Etiology/manifestation convention ("code first", "use additional code" and "in diseases classified elsewhere" notes)**

Certain conditions have both an underlying etiology and multiple body system manifestations due to the underlying etiology. For such conditions, the ICD-9-CM has a coding convention that requires the underlying condition be sequenced first followed by the manifestation. Wherever such a combination exists, there is a "use additional code" note at the etiology code, and a "code first" note at the manifestation code. These instructional notes indicate the proper sequencing order of the codes, etiology followed by manifestation.

In most cases the manifestation codes will have in the code title, "in diseases classified elsewhere." Codes with this title are a component of the etiology/ manifestation convention. The code title indicates that it is a manifestation code. "In diseases classified elsewhere" codes are never permitted to be used as first listed or principal diagnosis codes. They must be used in conjunction with an underlying condition code and they must be listed following the underlying condition.

There are manifestation codes that do not have "in diseases classified elsewhere" in the title. For such codes a "use additional code" note will still be present and the rules for sequencing apply.

In addition to the notes in the tabular, these conditions also have a specific index entry structure. In the index both conditions are listed together with the etiology code first followed by the manifestation codes in brackets. The code in brackets is always to be sequenced second.

The most commonly used etiology/manifestation combinations are the codes for Diabetes mellitus, category 250. For each code under category 250 there is a use additional code note for the manifestation that is specific for that particular diabetic manifestation. Should a patient have more than one manifestation of diabetes, more than one code from category 250 may be used with as many manifestation codes as are needed to fully describe the patient's complete diabetic condition. The category 250 diabetes codes should be sequenced first, followed by the manifestation codes.

"Code first" and "Use additional code" notes are also used as sequencing rules in the classification for certain codes that are not part of an etiology/ manifestation combination.
See - Section I.B.9. "Multiple coding for a single condition".

7. **"And"**

The word "and" should be interpreted to mean either "and" or "or" when it appears in a title.

8. **"With"**

The word "with" in the alphabetic index is sequenced immediately following the main term, not in alphabetical order.

9. **"See" and "See Also"**

The "see" instruction following a main term in the index indicates that another term should be referenced. It is necessary to go to the main term referenced with the "see" note to locate the correct code.

A "see also" instruction following a main term in the index instructs that there is another main term that may also be referenced that may provide additional index entries that may be useful. It is not necessary to follow the "see also" note when the original main term provides the necessary code.

B. General Coding Guidelines

1. **Use of Both Alphabetic Index and Tabular List**

Use both the Alphabetic Index and the Tabular List when locating and assigning a code. Reliance on only the Alphabetic Index or the Tabular List leads to errors in code assignments and less specificity in code selection.

2. **Locate each term in the Alphabetic Index**

Locate each term in the Alphabetic Index and verify the code selected in the Tabular List. Read and be guided by instructional notations that appear in both the Alphabetic Index and the Tabular List.

3. **Level of Detail in Coding**

Diagnosis and procedure codes are to be used at their highest number of digits available.

ICD-9-CM diagnosis codes are composed of codes with 3, 4, or 5 digits. Codes with three digits are included in ICD-9-CM as the heading of a category of codes that may be further subdivided by the use of fourth and/or fifth digits, which provide greater detail.

A three-digit code is to be used only if it is not further subdivided. Where fourth-digit subcategories and/or fifth-digit subclassifications are provided, they must be assigned. A code is invalid if it has not been coded to the full number of digits required for that code. For example, Acute myocardial infarction, code 410, has fourth digits that describe the location of the infarction (e.g., 410.2, Of inferolateral wall), and fifth digits that identify the episode of care. It would be incorrect to report a code in category 410 without a fourth and fifth digit.

ICD-9-CM Volume 3 procedure codes are composed of codes with either 3 or 4 digits. Codes with two digits are included in ICD-9-CM as the heading of a category of codes that may be further subdivided by the use of third and/or fourth digits, which provide greater detail.

4. Code or codes from 001.0 through V89.09

The appropriate code or codes from 001.0 through **V89.09** must be used to identify diagnoses, symptoms, conditions, problems, complaints or other reason(s) for the encounter/visit.

5. Selection of codes 001.0 through 999.9

The selection of codes 001.0 through 999.9 will frequently be used to describe the reason for the admission/encounter. These codes are from the section of ICD-9-CM for the classification of diseases and injuries (e.g., infectious and parasitic diseases; neoplasms; symptoms, signs, and ill-defined conditions, etc.).

6. Signs and symptoms

Codes that describe symptoms and signs, as opposed to diagnoses, are acceptable for reporting purposes when a related definitive diagnosis has not been established (confirmed) by the provider. Chapter 16 of ICD-9-CM, Symptoms, Signs, and Ill-defined conditions (codes 780.0 - 799.9) contain many, but not all codes for symptoms.

7. Conditions that are an integral part of a disease process

Signs and symptoms that are associated routinely with a disease process should not be assigned as additional codes, unless otherwise instructed by the classification.

8. Conditions that are not an integral part of a disease process

Additional signs and symptoms that may not be associated routinely with a disease process should be coded when present.

9. Multiple coding for a single condition

In addition to the etiology/manifestation convention that requires two codes to fully describe a single condition that affects multiple body systems, there are other single conditions that also require more than one code. "Use additional code" notes are found in the tabular at codes that are not part of an etiology/manifestation pair where a secondary code is useful to fully describe a condition. The sequencing rule is the same as the etiology/manifestation pair - "use additional code" indicates that a secondary code should be added.

For example, for infections that are not included in chapter 1, a secondary code from category 041, Bacterial infection in conditions classified elsewhere and of unspecified site, may be required to identify the bacterial organism causing the infection. A "use additional code" note will normally be found at the infectious disease code, indicating a need for the organism code to be added as a secondary code.

"Code first" notes are also under certain codes that are not specifically manifestation codes but may be due to an underlying cause. When a "code first" note is present and an underlying condition is present the underlying condition should be sequenced first.

"Code, if applicable, any causal condition first", notes indicate that this code may be assigned as a principal diagnosis when the causal condition is unknown or not applicable. If a causal condition is known, then the code for that condition should be sequenced as the principal or first-listed diagnosis.

Multiple codes may be needed for late effects, complication codes and obstetric codes to more fully describe a condition. See the specific guidelines for these conditions for further instruction.

10. Acute and Chronic Conditions

If the same condition is described as both acute (subacute) and chronic, and separate subentries exist in the Alphabetic Index at the same indentation level, code both and sequence the acute (subacute) code first.

11. Combination Code

A combination code is a single code used to classify:
Two diagnoses, or
A diagnosis with an associated secondary process (manifestation)
A diagnosis with an associated complication

Combination codes are identified by referring to subterm entries in the Alphabetic Index and by reading the inclusion and exclusion notes in the Tabular List.

Assign only the combination code when that code fully identifies the diagnostic conditions involved or when the Alphabetic Index so directs. Multiple coding should not be used when the classification provides a combination code that clearly identifies all of the elements documented in the diagnosis. When the combination code lacks necessary specificity in describing the manifestation or complication, an additional code should be used as a secondary code.

12. Late Effects

A late effect is the residual effect (condition produced) after the acute phase of an illness or injury has terminated. There is no time limit on when a late effect code can be used. The residual may be apparent early, such as in cerebrovascular accident cases, or it may occur months or years later, such as that due to a previous injury. Coding of late effects generally requires two codes sequenced in the following order: The condition or nature of the late effect is sequenced first.   The late effect code is sequenced second.

An exception to the above guidelines are those instances where the code for late effect is followed by a manifestation code identified in the Tabular List and title, or the late effect code has been expanded (at the fourth and fifth-digit levels) to include the manifestation(s). The code for the acute phase of an illness or injury that led to the late effect is never used with a code for the late effect.

13.   Impending or Threatened Condition

Code any condition described at the time of discharge as "impending" or "threatened" as follows:
> If it did occur, code as confirmed diagnosis.
> If it did not occur, reference the Alphabetic Index to determine if the condition has a subentry term for "impending" or "threatened" and also reference main term entries for "Impending" and for "Threatened."
> If the subterms are listed, assign the given code.
> If the subterms are not listed, code the existing underlying condition(s) and not the condition described as impending or threatened.

14.   Reporting Same Diagnosis Code More than Once

Each unique ICD-9-CM diagnosis code may be reported only once for an encounter. This applies to bilateral conditions or two different conditions classified to the same ICD-9-CM diagnosis code.

15.   Admissions/Encounters for Rehabilitation

When the purpose for the admission/encounter is rehabilitation, sequence the appropriate V code from category V57, Care involving use of rehabilitation procedures, as the principal/first-listed diagnosis. The code for the condition for which the service is being performed should be reported as an additional diagnosis.

Only one code from category V57 is required. Code V57.89, Other specified rehabilitation procedures, should be assigned if more than one type of rehabilitation is performed during a single encounter.   A procedure code should be reported to identify each type of rehabilitation therapy actually performed.

16.   Documentation for BMI and Pressure Ulcer Stages

For the Body Mass Index (BMI) and pressure ulcer stage codes, code assignment may be based on medical record documentation from clinicians who are not the patient's provider (i.e., physician or other qualified healthcare practitioner legally accountable for establishing the patient's diagnosis), since this information is typically documented by other clinicians involved in the care of the patient (e.g., a dietitian often documents the BMI and nurses often documents the pressure ulcer stages). However, the associated diagnosis (such as overweight, obesity, or pressure ulcer) must be documented by the patient's provider. If there is conflicting medical record documentation, either from the same clinician or different clinicians, the patient's attending provider should be queried for clarification.

The BMI and pressure ulcer stage codes should only be reported as secondary diagnoses. As with all other secondary diagnosis codes, the BMI and pressure ulcer stage codes should only be assigned when they meet the definition of a reportable additional diagnosis (see Section III, Reporting Additional Diagnoses).

17. Syndromes

Follow the Alphabetic Index guidance when coding syndromes. In the absence of index guidance, assign codes for the documented manifestations of the syndrome.

C. Chapter-Specific Coding Guidelines

In addition to general coding guidelines, there are guidelines for specific diagnoses and/or conditions in the classification. Unless otherwise indicated, these guidelines apply to all health care settings. Please refer to Section II for guidelines on the selection of principal diagnosis.

1. Chapter 1: Infectious and Parasitic Diseases (001-139)

a. Human Immunodeficiency Virus (HIV) Infections

1) Code only confirmed cases

Code only confirmed cases of HIV infection/illness. This is an exception to the hospital inpatient guideline Section II, H.

In this context, "confirmation" does not require documentation of positive serology or culture for HIV; the provider's diagnostic statement that the patient is HIV positive, or has an HIV-related illness is sufficient.

2) Selection and sequencing of HIV codes

(a) Patient admitted for HIV-related condition

If a patient is admitted for an HIV-related condition, the principal diagnosis should be 042, followed by additional diagnosis codes for all reported HIV-related conditions.

(b) **Patient with HIV disease admitted for unrelated condition**

If a patient with HIV disease is admitted for an unrelated condition (such as a traumatic injury), the code for the unrelated condition (e.g., the nature of injury code) should be the principal diagnosis. Other diagnoses would be 042 followed by additional diagnosis codes for all reported HIV-related conditions.

(c) **Whether the patient is newly diagnosed**

Whether the patient is newly diagnosed or has had previous admissions/encounters for HIV conditions is irrelevant to the sequencing decision.

(d) **Asymptomatic human immunodeficiency virus**

V08 Asymptomatic human immunodeficiency virus [HIV] infection, is to be applied when the patient without any documentation of symptoms is listed as being "HIV positive," "known HIV," "HIV test positive," or similar terminology. Do not use this code if the term "AIDS" is used or if the patient is treated for any HIV-related illness or is described as having any condition(s) resulting from his/her HIV positive status; use 042 in these cases.

(e) **Patients with inconclusive HIV serology**

Patients with inconclusive HIV serology, but no definitive diagnosis or manifestations of the illness, may be assigned code 795.71, Inconclusive serologic test for Human Immunodeficiency Virus [HIV].

(f) **Previously diagnosed HIV-related illness**

Patients with any known prior diagnosis of an HIV-related illness should be coded to 042. Once a patient has developed an HIV-related illness, the patient should always be assigned code 042 on every subsequent admission/encounter. Patients previously diagnosed with any HIV illness (042) should never be assigned to 795.71 or V08.

(g) **HIV Infection in Pregnancy, Childbirth and the Puerperium**

During pregnancy, childbirth or the puerperium, a patient admitted (or presenting for a health care encounter) because of an HIV-related illness should receive a principal diagnosis code of 647.6X, Other specified infectious and parasitic diseases in the mother classifiable elsewhere, but complicating the pregnancy, childbirth or the puerperium, followed by 042 and the code(s) for the HIV-related illness(es). Codes from Chapter 15 always take sequencing priority.

Patients with asymptomatic HIV infection status admitted (or presenting for a health care encounter) during pregnancy, childbirth, or the puerperium should receive codes of 647.6X and V08.

(h) **Encounters for testing for HIV**

If a patient is being seen to determine his/her HIV status, use code V73.89, Screening for other specified viral disease. Use code V69.8, Other problems related to lifestyle, as a secondary code if an asymptomatic patient is in a known high risk group for HIV. Should a patient with signs or symptoms or illness, or a confirmed HIV related diagnosis be tested for HIV, code the signs and symptoms or the diagnosis. An additional counseling code V65.44 may be used if counseling is provided during the encounter for the test.

When a patient returns to be informed of his/her HIV test results use code V65.44, HIV counseling, if the results of the test are negative.

If the results are positive but the patient is asymptomatic use code V08, Asymptomatic HIV infection. If the results are positive and the patient is symptomatic use code 042, HIV infection, with codes for the HIV related symptoms or diagnosis. The HIV counseling code may also be used if counseling is provided for patients with positive test results.

b. Septicemia, Systemic Inflammatory Response Syndrome (SIRS), Sepsis, Severe Sepsis, and Septic Shock

1) **SIRS, Septicemia, and Sepsis**

(a) The terms *septicemia* and *sepsis* are often used interchangeably by providers, however they are not considered synonymous terms. The following descriptions are provided for reference but do not preclude querying the provider for clarification about terms used in the documentation:

(i) Septicemia generally refers to a systemic disease associated with the presence of pathological microorganisms or toxins in the blood, which can include bacteria, viruses, fungi or other organisms.

(ii) Systemic inflammatory response syndrome (SIRS) generally refers to the systemic response to infection, trauma/burns, or other insult (such as cancer) with symptoms including fever, tachycardia, tachypnea, and leukocytosis.

(iii)Sepsis generally refers to SIRS due to infection.

(iv)Severe sepsis generally refers to sepsis with associated acute organ dysfunction.

(b) **The Coding of SIRS, sepsis and severe sepsis**

The coding of SIRS, sepsis and severe sepsis requires a minimum of 2 codes: a code for the underlying cause (such as infection or trauma) and a code from subcategory 995.9 Systemic inflammatory response syndrome (SIRS).

(i) The code for the underlying cause (such as infection or trauma) must be sequenced before the code from subcategory 995.9 Systemic inflammatory response syndrome (SIRS).

(ii) Sepsis and severe sepsis require a code for the systemic infection (038.xx, 112.5, etc.) and either code 995.91, Sepsis, or 995.92, Severe sepsis. If the causal organism is not documented, assign code 038.9, Unspecified septicemia.

(iii) Severe sepsis requires additional code(s) for the associated acute organ dysfunction(s).

(iv) If a patient has sepsis with multiple organ dysfunctions, follow the instructions for coding severe sepsis.

(v) Either the term sepsis or SIRS must be documented to assign a code from subcategory 995.9.

See Section I.C.17.g), Injury and poisoning, for information regarding systemic inflammatory response syndrome (SIRS) due to trauma/burns and other non-infectious processes.

(c) Due to the complex nature of sepsis and severe sepsis, some cases may require querying the provider prior to assignment of the codes.

2) **Sequencing sepsis and severe sepsis**

(a) **Sepsis and severe sepsis as principal diagnosis**

If sepsis or severe sepsis is present on admission, and meets the definition of principal diagnosis, the systemic infection code (e.g., 038.xx, 112.5, etc) should be assigned as the principal diagnosis, followed by code 995.91, Sepsis, or 995.92, Severe sepsis, as required by the sequencing rules in the Tabular List. Codes from subcategory 995.9 can never be assigned as a principal diagnosis. A code should also be assigned for any localized infection, if present.

If the sepsis or severe sepsis is due to a postprocedural infection, see Section I.C.1.b.10 for guidelines related to sepsis due to postprocedural infection.

(b) **Sepsis and severe sepsis as secondary diagnoses**

When sepsis or severe sepsis develops during the encounter (it was not present on admission), the systemic infection code and code 995.91 or 995.92 should be assigned as secondary diagnoses.

(c) **Documentation unclear as to whether sepsis or severe sepsis is present on admission**

Sepsis or severe sepsis may be present on admission but the diagnosis may not be confirmed until sometime after admission. If the documentation is not clear whether the sepsis or severe sepsis was present on admission, the provider should be queried.

3) **Sepsis/SIRS with Localized Infection**

If the reason for admission is both sepsis, severe sepsis, or SIRS and a localized infection, such as pneumonia or cellulitis, a code for the systemic infection (038.xx, 112.5, etc) should be assigned first, then code 995.91 or 995.92, followed by the code for the localized infection. If the patient is admitted with a localized infection, such as pneumonia, and sepsis/SIRS doesn't develop until after admission, see guideline I.C.1.b.2.b).

If the localized infection is postprocedural, *see Section I.C.1.b.10 for guidelines related to sepsis due to postprocedural infection.*

Note: The term urosepsis is a nonspecific term. If that is the only term documented then only code 599.0 should be assigned based on the default for the term in the ICD-9-CM index, in addition to the code for the causal organism if known.

4) **Bacterial Sepsis and Septicemia**

In most cases, it will be a code from category 038, Septicemia, that will be used in conjunction with a code from subcategory 995.9 such as the following:

(a) **Streptococcal sepsis**

If the documentation in the record states streptococcal sepsis, codes 038.0, Streptococcal septicemia, and code 995.91 should be used, in that sequence.

(b) **Streptococcal septicemia**

If the documentation states streptococcal septicemia, only code 038.0 should be assigned, however, the provider should be queried whether the patient has sepsis, an infection with SIRS.

5) **Acute organ dysfunction that is not clearly associated with the sepsis**

If a patient has sepsis and an acute organ dysfunction, but the medical record documentation indicates that the acute organ dysfunction is related to a medical condition other than the sepsis, do not assign code 995.92, Severe sepsis. An acute organ dysfunction must be associated with the sepsis in order to assign the severe sepsis code. If the documentation is not clear as to whether an acute organ dysfunction is related to the sepsis or another medical condition, query the provider.

6) **Septic shock**

(a) **Sequencing of septic shock**

Septic shock generally refers to circulatory failure associated with severe sepsis, and, therefore, it represents a type of acute organ dysfunction.

For all cases of septic shock, the code for the systemic infection should be sequenced first, followed by codes 995.92 and 785.52. Any additional codes for other acute organ dysfunctions should also be assigned. As noted in the sequencing instructions in the Tabular List, the code for septic shock cannot be assigned as a principal diagnosis.

(b) **Septic Shock without documentation of severe sepsis**

Septic shock indicates the presence of severe sepsis.

Code 995.92, Severe sepsis, must be assigned with code 785.52, Septic shock, even if the term severe sepsis is not documented in the record. The "use additional code" note and the "code first" note in the tabular support this guideline.

7)   Sepsis and septic shock complicating abortion and pregnancy

Sepsis and septic shock complicating abortion, ectopic pregnancy, and molar pregnancy are classified to category codes in Chapter 11 (630-639).
See section I.C.11.i.7. for information on the coding of puerperal sepsis.

8)   Negative or inconclusive blood cultures

Negative or inconclusive blood cultures do not preclude a diagnosis of septicemia or sepsis in patients with clinical evidence of the condition, however, the provider should be queried.

9)   Newborn sepsis

See Section I.C.15.j for information on the coding of newborn sepsis.

10)   Sepsis due to a Postprocedural Infection

(a)   Documentation of causal relationship

As with all postprocedural complications, code assignment is based on the provider's documentation of the relationship between the infection and the procedure.

(b)   Sepsis due to postprocedural infection

In cases of postprocedural sepsis, the complication code, such as code 998.59, Other postoperative infection, or 674.3x, Other complications of obstetrical surgical wounds should be coded first followed by the appropriate sepsis codes (systemic infection code and either code 995.91or 995.92). An additional code(s) for any acute organ dysfunction should also be assigned for cases of severe sepsis.

11)   External cause of injury codes with SIRS

Refer to Section I.C.19.a.7 for instruction on the use of external cause of injury codes with codes for SIRS resulting from trauma.

12)   Sepsis and Severe Sepsis Associated with Non-infectious Process

In some cases, a non-infectious process, such as trauma, may lead to an infection which can result in sepsis or severe sepsis. If sepsis or severe sepsis is documented as associated with a non-infectious condition, such as a burn or serious injury, and this condition meets the definition for principal diagnosis, the code for the non-infectious condition should be sequenced first, followed by the code for the systemic infection and either code 995.91, Sepsis, or 995.92, Severe sepsis. Additional codes for any associated acute organ dysfunction(s) should also be assigned for cases of severe sepsis. If the sepsis or severe sepsis meets the definition of principal diagnosis, the systemic infection and sepsis codes should be sequenced before the non-infectious condition. When both the associated non-infectious condition and the sepsis or severe sepsis meet the definition of principal diagnosis, either may be assigned as principal diagnosis.

See Section I.C.1.b.2.a. for guidelines pertaining to sepsis or severe sepsis as the principal diagnosis.

Only one code from subcategory 995.9 should be assigned. Therefore, when a non-infectious condition leads to an infection resulting in sepsis or severe sepsis, assign either code 995.91 or 995.92. Do not additionally assign code 995.93, Systemic inflammatory response syndrome due to non-infectious process without acute organ dysfunction, or 995.94, Systemic inflammatory response syndrome with acute organ dysfunction.

See Section I.C.17.g for information on the coding of SIRS due to trauma/burns or other non-infectious disease processes.

c.   Methicillin Resistant *Staphylococcus aureus* (MRSA) Conditions

1)   Selection and sequencing of MRSA codes

(a)   Combination codes for MRSA infection

When a patient is diagnosed with an infection that is due to methicillin resistant *Staphylococcus aureus* (MRSA), and that infection has a combination code that includes the causal organism (e.g., septicemia, pneumonia) assign the appropriate code for the condition (e.g., code 038.12, Methicillin resistant Staphylococcus aureus septicemia or code 482.42, Methicillin resistant pneumonia due to Staphylococcus aureus). Do not assign code 041.12, Methicillin resistant Staphylococcus aureus, as an additional code because the code includes the type of infection and the MRSA organism. Do not assign a code from subcategory V09.0, Infection with microorganisms resistant to penicillins, as an additional diagnosis.

See Section C.1.b.1 for instructions on coding and sequencing of septicemia.

(b) **Other codes for MRSA infection**

When there is documentation of a current infection (e.g., wound infection, stitch abscess, urinary tract infection) due to MRSA, and that infection does not have a combination code that includes the causal organism, select the appropriate code to identify the condition along with code 041.12, Methicillin resistant Staphylococcus aureus, for the MRSA infection. Do not assign a code from subcategory V09.0, Infection with microorganisms resistant to penicillins.

(c) **Methicillin susceptible Staphylococcus aureus (MSSA) and MRSA colonization**

The condition or state of being colonized or carrying MSSA or MRSA is called colonization or carriage, while an individual person is described as being colonized or being a carrier. Colonization means that MSSA or MSRA is present on or in the body without necessarily causing illness. A positive MRSA colonization test might be documented by the provider as "MRSA screen positive" or "MRSA nasal swab positive".

Assign code V02.54, Carrier or suspected carrier, Methicillin resistant Staphylococcus aureus, for patients documented as having MRSA colonization. Assign code V02.53, Carrier or suspected carrier, Methicillin susceptible Staphylococcus aureus, for patient documented as having MSSA colonization.

Colonization is not necessarily indicative of a disease process or as the cause of a specific condition the patient may have unless documented as such by the provider.

Code V02.59, Other specified bacterial diseases, should be assigned for other types of staphylococcal colonization (e.g., S. *epidermidis, S. saprophyticus*). Code V02.59 should not be assigned for colonization with any type of *Staphylococcus aureus* (MRSA, MSSA).

(d)   MRSA colonization and infection

If a patient is documented as having both MRSA colonization and infection during a hospital admission, code V02.54, Carrier or suspected carrier, Methicillin resistant *Staphylococcus aureus*, and a code for the MRSA infection may both be assigned.

2.   Chapter 2: Neoplasms (140-239)

General guidelines

Chapter 2 of the ICD-9-CM contains the codes for most benign and all malignant neoplasms. Certain benign neoplasms, such as prostatic adenomas, may be found in the specific body system chapters. To properly code a neoplasm it is necessary to determine from the record if the neoplasm is benign, in-situ, malignant, or of uncertain histologic behavior. If malignant, any secondary (metastatic) sites should also be determined.

The neoplasm table in the Alphabetic Index should be referenced first. However, if the histological term is documented, that term should be referenced first, rather than going immediately to the Neoplasm Table, in order to determine which column in the Neoplasm Table is appropriate. For example, if the documentation indicates "adenoma," refer to the term in the Alphabetic Index to review the entries under this term and the instructional note to "see also neoplasm, by site, benign." The table provides the proper code based on the type of neoplasm and the site. It is important to select the proper column in the table that corresponds to the type of neoplasm. The tabular should then be referenced to verify that the correct code has been selected from the table and that a more specific site code does not exist. *See Section I. C. 18.d.4. for information regarding V codes for genetic susceptibility to cancer.*

a. Treatment directed at the malignancy

If the treatment is directed at the malignancy, designate the malignancy as the principal diagnosis.

The only exception to this guideline is if a patient admission/encounter is solely for the administration of chemotherapy, immunotherapy or radiation therapy, assign the appropriate V58.x code as the first-listed or principal diagnosis, and the diagnosis or problem for which the service is being performed as a secondary diagnosis.

b. Treatment of secondary site

When a patient is admitted because of a primary neoplasm with metastasis and treatment is directed toward the secondary site only, the secondary neoplasm is designated as the principal diagnosis even though the primary malignancy is still present.

c. Coding and sequencing of complications

Coding and sequencing of complications associated with the malignancies or with the therapy thereof are subject to the following guidelines:

1) Anemia associated with malignancy

When admission/encounter is for management of an anemia associated with the malignancy, and the treatment is only for anemia, the appropriate anemia code (such as code 285.22, Anemia in neoplastic disease) is designated as the principal diagnosis and is followed by the appropriate code(s) for the malignancy.

Code 285.22 may also be used as a secondary code if the patient suffers from anemia and is being treated for the malignancy.

Code 285.22, Anemia in neoplastic disease, and code 285.3, Antineoplastic chemotherapy induced anemia, may both be assigned if anemia in neoplastic disease and anemia due to antineoplastic chemotherapy are both documented.

2) Anemia associated with chemotherapy, immunotherapy and radiation therapy

When the admission/encounter is for management of an anemia associated with chemotherapy, immunotherapy or radiotherapy and the only treatment is for the anemia, the anemia is sequenced first. The appropriate neoplasm code should be assigned as an additional code.

3) **Management of dehydration due to the malignancy**

When the admission/encounter is for management of dehydration due to the malignancy or the therapy, or a combination of both, and only the dehydration is being treated (intravenous rehydration), the dehydration is sequenced first, followed by the code(s) for the malignancy.

4) **Treatment of a complication resulting from a surgical procedure**

When the admission/encounter is for treatment of a complication resulting from a surgical procedure, designate the complication as the principal or first-listed diagnosis if treatment is directed at resolving the complication.

d. **Primary malignancy previously excised**

When a primary malignancy has been previously excised or eradicated from its site and there is no further treatment directed to that site and there is no evidence of any existing primary malignancy, a code from category V10, Personal history of malignant neoplasm, should be used to indicate the former site of the malignancy. Any mention of extension, invasion, or metastasis to another site is coded as a secondary malignant neoplasm to that site. The secondary site may be the principal or first-listed with the V10 code used as a secondary code.

e. **Admissions/Encounters involving chemotherapy, immunotherapy and radiation therapy**

1) **Episode of care involves surgical removal of neoplasm**

When an episode of care involves the surgical removal of a neoplasm, primary or secondary site, followed by adjunct chemotherapy or radiation treatment during the same episode of care, the neoplasm code should be assigned as principal or first-listed diagnosis, using codes in the 140-198 series or where appropriate in the 200-203 series.

2) **Patient admission/encounter solely for administration of chemotherapy, immunotherapy and radiation therapy**

If a patient admission/encounter is solely for the administration of chemotherapy, immunotherapy or radiation therapy assign code V58.0, Encounter for radiation therapy, or V58.11, Encounter for antineoplastic chemotherapy, or V58.12, Encounter for antineoplastic immunotherapy as the first-listed or principal diagnosis. If a patient receives more than one of these therapies during the same admission more than one of these codes may be assigned, in any sequence.

The malignancy for which the therapy is being administered should be assigned as a secondary diagnosis.

3) Patient admitted for radiotherapy/chemotherapy and immunotherapy and develops complications

When a patient is admitted for the purpose of radiotherapy, immunotherapy or chemotherapy and develops complications such as uncontrolled nausea and vomiting or dehydration, the principal or first-listed diagnosis is V58.0, Encounter for radiotherapy, or V58.11, Encounter for antineoplastic chemotherapy, or V58.12, Encounter for antineoplastic immunotherapy followed by any codes for the complications.

f. Admission/encounter to determine extent of malignancy

When the reason for admission/encounter is to determine the extent of the malignancy, or for a procedure such as paracentesis or thoracentesis, the primary malignancy or appropriate metastatic site is designated as the principal or first-listed diagnosis, even though chemotherapy or radiotherapy is administered.

g. Symptoms, signs, and ill-defined conditions listed in Chapter 16 associated with neoplasms

Symptoms, signs, and ill-defined conditions listed in Chapter 16 characteristic of, or associated with, an existing primary or secondary site malignancy cannot be used to replace the malignancy as principal or first-listed diagnosis, regardless of the number of admissions or encounters for treatment and care of the neoplasm.

h. Admission/encounter for pain control/management

See Section I.C.6.a.5 for information on coding admission/encounter for pain control/management.

i. Malignant neoplasm associated with transplanted organ

A malignant neoplasm of a transplanted organ should be coded as a transplant complication. Assign first the appropriate code from subcategory 996.8, Complications of transplanted organ, followed by code 199.2, Malignant neoplasm associated with transplanted organ. Use an additional code for the specific malignancy.

3. **Chapter 3: Endocrine, Nutritional, and Metabolic Diseases and Immunity Disorders (240-279)**

a. **Diabetes mellitus**

Codes under category 250, Diabetes mellitus, identify complications/manifestations associated with diabetes mellitus. A fifth-digit is required for all category 250 codes to identify the type of diabetes mellitus and whether the diabetes is controlled or uncontrolled.

See I.C.3.a.7 for secondary diabetes

1) **Fifth-digits for category 250:**

The following are the fifth-digits for the codes under category 250:

0 type II or unspecified type, not stated as uncontrolled
1 type I, [juvenile type], not stated as uncontrolled
2 type II or unspecified type, uncontrolled
3 type I, [juvenile type], uncontrolled

The age of a patient is not the sole determining factor, though most type I diabetics develop the condition before reaching puberty. For this reason type I diabetes mellitus is also referred to as juvenile diabetes.

2) **Type of diabetes mellitus not documented**

If the type of diabetes mellitus is not documented in the medical record the default is type II.

3) **Diabetes mellitus and the use of insulin**

All type I diabetics must use insulin to replace what their bodies do not produce. However, the use of insulin does not mean that a patient is a type I diabetic. Some patients with type II diabetes mellitus are unable to control their blood sugar through diet and oral medication alone and do require insulin. If the documentation in a medical record does not indicate the type of diabetes but does indicate that the patient uses insulin, the appropriate fifth-digit for type II must be used. For type II patients who routinely use insulin, code V58.67, Long-term (current) use of insulin, should also be assigned to indicate that the patient uses insulin. Code V58.67 should not be assigned if insulin is given temporarily to bring a type II patient's blood sugar under control during an encounter.

4)   **Assigning and sequencing diabetes codes and associated conditions**

When assigning codes for diabetes and its associated conditions, the code(s) from category 250 must be sequenced before the codes for the associated conditions. The diabetes codes and the secondary codes that correspond to them are paired codes that follow the etiology/manifestation convention of the classification *(See Section I.A.6., Etiology/manifestation convention)*. Assign as many codes from category 250 as needed to identify all of the associated conditions that the patient has. The corresponding secondary codes are listed under each of the diabetes codes.

(a)   **Diabetic retinopathy/diabetic macular edema**

Diabetic macular edema, code 362.07, is only present with diabetic retinopathy. Another code from subcategory 362.0, Diabetic retinopathy, must be used with code 362.07. Codes under subcategory 362.0 are diabetes manifestation codes, so they must be used following the appropriate diabetes code.

5)   **Diabetes mellitus in pregnancy and gestational diabetes**

(a)   For diabetes mellitus complicating pregnancy, see Section I.C.11.f., Diabetes mellitus in pregnancy.

(b)   For gestational diabetes, see Section I.C.11, g., Gestational diabetes.

6)   **Insulin pump malfunction**

(a)   **Underdose of insulin due insulin pump failure**

An underdose of insulin due to an insulin pump failure should be assigned 996.57, Mechanical complication due to insulin pump, as the principal or first listed code, followed by the appropriate diabetes mellitus code based on documentation.

(b)   **Overdose of insulin due to insulin pump failure**

The principal or first listed code for an encounter due to an insulin pump malfunction resulting in an overdose of insulin, should also be 996.57, Mechanical complication due to insulin pump, followed by code 962.3, Poisoning by insulins and antidiabetic agents, and the appropriate diabetes mellitus code based on documentation.

7)   Secondary Diabetes Mellitus

Codes under category 249, Secondary diabetes mellitus, identify complications/manifestations associated with secondary diabetes mellitus. Secondary diabetes is always caused by another condition or event (e.g., cystic fibrosis, malignant neoplasm of pancreas, pancreatectomy, adverse effect of drug, or poisoning).

(a)   Fifth-digits for category 249:

A fifth-digit is required for all category 249 codes to identify whether the diabetes is controlled or uncontrolled.

(b)   Secondary diabetes mellitus and the use of insulin

For patients who routinely use insulin, code V58.67, Long-term (current) use of insulin, should also be assigned. Code V58.67 should not be assigned if insulin is given temporarily to bring a patient's blood sugar under control during an encounter.

(c)   Assigning and sequencing secondary diabetes codes and associated conditions

When assigning codes for secondary diabetes and its associated conditions (e.g. renal manifestations), the code(s) from category 249 must be sequenced before the codes for the associated conditions. The secondary diabetes codes and the diabetic manifestation codes that correspond to them are paired codes that follow the etiology/manifestation convention of the classification. Assign as many codes from category 249 as needed to identify all of the associated conditions that the patient has. The corresponding codes for the associated conditions are listed under each of the secondary diabetes codes. For example, secondary diabetes with diabetic nephrosis is assigned to code 249.40, followed by 581.81.

(d)   Assigning and sequencing secondary diabetes codes and its causes

The sequencing of the secondary diabetes codes in relationship to codes for the cause of the diabetes is based on the reason for the encounter, applicable ICD-

9-CM sequencing conventions, and chapter-specific guidelines.

If a patient is seen for treatment of the secondary diabetes or one of its associated conditions, a code from category 249 is sequenced as the principal or first-listed diagnosis, with the cause of the secondary diabetes (e.g. cystic fibrosis) sequenced as an additional diagnosis.

If, however, the patient is seen for the treatment of the condition causing the secondary diabetes (e.g., malignant neoplasm of pancreas), the code for the cause of the secondary diabetes should be sequenced as the principal or first-listed diagnosis followed by a code from category 249.

(i) Secondary diabetes mellitus due to pancreatectomy

For postpancreatectomy diabetes mellitus (lack of insulin due to the surgical removal of all or part of the pancreas), assign code 251.3, Postsurgical hypoinsulinemia. **Assign a code from subcategory 249 and code V45.79, Other acquired absence of organ, as additional codes.** Code also any diabetic manifestations (e.g. diabetic nephrosis 581.81).

(ii) Secondary diabetes due to drugs

Secondary diabetes may be caused by an adverse effect of correctly administered medications, poisoning or late effect of poisoning.
See section I.C.17.e for coding of adverse effects and poisoning, and section I.C.19 for E code reporting.

4. Chapter 4: Diseases of Blood and Blood Forming Organs (280-289)

a. Anemia of chronic disease

Subcategory 285.2, Anemia in chronic illness, has codes for anemia in chronic kidney disease, code 285.21; anemia in neoplastic disease, code 285.22; and anemia in other chronic illness, code 285.29. These codes can be used as the principal/first listed code if the reason for the encounter is to treat the anemia. They may also be used as secondary codes if treatment of the anemia is a component of an encounter, but not the primary reason for the encounter. When using a code from subcategory 285 it is also necessary to use the code for the chronic condition causing the anemia.

1) Anemia in chronic kidney disease

When assigning code 285.21, Anemia in chronic kidney disease, it is also necessary to assign a code from category 585, Chronic kidney disease, to indicate the stage of chronic kidney disease.

See I.C.10.a. Chronic kidney disease (CKD).

2) Anemia in neoplastic disease

When assigning code 285.22, Anemia in neoplastic disease, it is also necessary to assign the neoplasm code that is responsible for the anemia. Code 285.22 is for use for anemia that is due to the malignancy, not for anemia due to antineoplastic chemotherapy drugs. **Assign code 285.3 for anemia due to antineoplastic chemotherapy.**

See I.C.2.c.1 Anemia associated with malignancy.
See I.C.2.c.2 Anemia associated with chemotherapy, immunotherapy and radiation therapy.

5. Chapter 5: Mental Disorders (290-319)

Reserved for future guideline expansion

6. Chapter 6: Diseases of Nervous System and Sense Organs (320-389)

a. Pain - Category 338

1) General coding information

Codes in category 338 may be used in conjunction with codes from other categories and chapters to provide more detail about acute or chronic pain and neoplasm-related pain, unless otherwise indicated below.

If the pain is not specified as acute or chronic, do not assign codes from category 338, except for post-thoracotomy pain, postoperative pain, neoplasm related pain, or central pain syndrome.

A code from subcategories 338.1 and 338.2 should not be assigned if the underlying (definitive) diagnosis is known, unless the reason for the encounter is pain control/ management and not management of the underlying condition.

(a)   Category 338 Codes as Principal or First-Listed Diagnosis

Category 338 codes are acceptable as principal diagnosis or the first-listed code:

- When pain control or pain management is the reason for the admission/encounter (e.g., a patient with displaced intervertebral disc, nerve impingement and severe back pain presents for injection of steroid into the spinal canal). The underlying cause of the pain should be reported as an additional diagnosis, if known.

- When an admission or encounter is for a procedure aimed at treating the underlying condition (e.g., spinal fusion, kyphoplasty), a code for the underlying condition (e.g., vertebral fracture, spinal stenosis) should be assigned as the principal diagnosis. No code from category 338 should be assigned.

- When a patient is admitted for the insertion of a neurostimulator for pain control, assign the appropriate pain code as the principal or first listed diagnosis. When an admission or encounter is for a procedure aimed at treating the underlying condition and a neurostimulator is inserted for pain control during the same admission/encounter, a code for the underlying condition should be assigned as the principal diagnosis and the appropriate pain code should be assigned as a secondary diagnosis.

(b)   Use of Category 338 Codes in Conjunction with Site Specific Pain Codes

(i) Assigning Category 338 Codes and Site-Specific Pain Codes

Codes from category 338 may be used in conjunction with codes that identify the site of pain (including codes from chapter 16) if the category 338 code provides additional information. For example, if the code describes the site of the pain, but does not fully describe whether the pain is acute or chronic, then both codes should be assigned.

(ii) Sequencing of Category 338 Codes with Site-Specific Pain Codes

The sequencing of category 338 codes with site-specific pain codes (including chapter 16 codes), is dependent on the circumstances of the encounter/admission as follows:

- If the encounter is for pain control or pain management, assign the code from category 338 followed by the code identifying the specific site of pain (e.g., encounter for pain management for acute neck pain from trauma is assigned code 338.11, Acute pain due to trauma, followed by code 723.1, Cervicalgia, to identify the site of pain).

- If the encounter is for any other reason except pain control or pain management, and a related definitive diagnosis has not been established (confirmed) by the provider, assign the code for the specific site of pain first, followed by the appropriate code from category 338.

2) Pain due to devices, implants and grafts

Pain associated with devices, implants or grafts left in a surgical site (for example painful hip prosthesis) is assigned to the appropriate code(s) found in Chapter 17, Injury and Poisoning. Use additional code(s) from category 338 to identify acute or chronic pain due to presence of the device, implant or graft (338.18-338.19 or 338.28-338.29).

3) Postoperative Pain

Post-thoracotomy pain and other postoperative pain are classified to subcategories 338.1 and 338.2, depending on whether the pain is acute or chronic. The default for post-thoracotomy and other postoperative pain not specified as acute or chronic is the code for the acute form.

Routine or expected postoperative pain immediately after surgery should not be coded.

(a)   **Postoperative pain not associated with specific postoperative complication**

Postoperative pain not associated with a specific postoperative complication is assigned to the appropriate postoperative pain code in category 338.

(b)   **Postoperative pain associated with specific postoperative complication**

Postoperative pain associated with a specific postoperative complication (such as painful wire sutures) is assigned to the appropriate code(s) found in Chapter 17, Injury and Poisoning. If appropriate, use additional code(s) from category 338 to identify acute or chronic pain (338.18 or 338.28). If pain control/management is the reason for the encounter, a code from category 338 should be assigned as the principal or first-listed diagnosis in accordance with *Section I.C.6.a.1.a above*.

(c)   **Postoperative pain as principal or first-listed diagnosis**

Postoperative pain may be reported as the principal or first-listed diagnosis when the stated reason for the admission/encounter is documented as postoperative pain control/management.

(d)   **Postoperative pain as secondary diagnosis**

Postoperative pain may be reported as a secondary diagnosis code when a patient presents for outpatient surgery and develops an unusual or inordinate amount of postoperative pain.

The provider's documentation should be used to guide the coding of postoperative pain, as well as *Section III. Reporting Additional Diagnoses* and *Section IV. Diagnostic Coding and Reporting in the Outpatient Setting*.

See Section II.I.2 for information on sequencing of diagnoses for patients admitted to hospital inpatient care following post-operative observation.

See Section II.J for information on sequencing of diagnoses for patients admitted to hospital inpatient care from outpatient surgery.

See Section IV.A.2 for information on sequencing of diagnoses for patients admitted for observation.

4)   Chronic pain

Chronic pain is classified to subcategory 338.2. There is no time frame defining when pain becomes chronic pain. The provider's documentation should be used to guide use of these codes.

5)   Neoplasm Related Pain

Code 338.3 is assigned to pain documented as being related, associated or due to cancer, primary or secondary malignancy, or tumor. This code is assigned regardless of whether the pain is acute or chronic.

This code may be assigned as the principal or first-listed code when the stated reason for the admission/encounter is documented as pain control/pain management. The underlying neoplasm should be reported as an additional diagnosis.

When the reason for the admission/encounter is management of the neoplasm and the pain associated with the neoplasm is also documented, code 338.3 may be assigned as an additional diagnosis.

See Section I.C.2 for instructions on the sequencing of neoplasms for all other stated reasons for the admission/encounter (except for pain control/pain management).

6)   Chronic pain syndrome

This condition is different than the term "chronic pain," and therefore this code should only be used when the provider has specifically documented this condition.

7.   **Chapter 7: Diseases of Circulatory System (390-459)**

a.   **Hypertension**

Hypertension Table

The Hypertension Table, found under the main term, "Hypertension", in the Alphabetic Index, contains a complete listing of all conditions due to or associated with hypertension and classifies them according to malignant, benign, and unspecified.

1)   **Hypertension, Essential, or NOS**

Assign hypertension (arterial) (essential) (primary) (systemic) (NOS) to category code 401 with the appropriate fourth digit to indicate malignant (.0), benign (.1), or unspecified (.9). Do not use either .0 malignant or .1 benign unless medical record documentation supports such a designation.

2)   **Hypertension with Heart Disease**

Heart conditions (425.8, 429.0-429.3, 429.8, 429.9) are assigned to a code from category 402 when a causal relationship is stated (due to hypertension) or implied (hypertensive). Use an additional code from category 428 to identify the type of heart failure in those patients with heart failure. More than one code from category 428 may be assigned if the patient has systolic or diastolic failure and congestive heart failure.

The same heart conditions (425.8, 429.0-429.3, 429.8, 429.9) with hypertension, but without a stated causal relationship, are coded separately. Sequence according to the circumstances of the admission/encounter.

3)   **Hypertensive Chronic Kidney Disease**

Assign codes from category 403, Hypertensive chronic kidney disease, when conditions classified to category 585 are present. Unlike hypertension with heart disease, ICD-9-CM presumes a cause-and-effect relationship and classifies chronic kidney disease (CKD) with hypertension as hypertensive chronic kidney disease.

Fifth digits for category 403 should be assigned as follows:

- 0 with CKD stage I through stage IV, or unspecified.
- 1 with CKD stage V or end stage renal disease.

The appropriate code from category 585, Chronic kidney disease, should be used as a secondary code with a code from category 403 to identify the stage of chronic kidney disease.

See Section I.C.10.a for information on the coding of chronic kidney disease.

4) Hypertensive Heart and Chronic Kidney Disease

Assign codes from combination category 404, Hypertensive heart and chronic kidney disease, when both hypertensive kidney disease and hypertensive heart disease are stated in the diagnosis. Assume a relationship between the hypertension and the chronic kidney disease, whether or not the condition is so designated. Assign an additional code from category 428, to identify the type of heart failure. More than one code from category 428 may be assigned if the patient has systolic or diastolic failure and congestive heart failure.

Fifth digits for category 404 should be assigned as follows:
- 0 without heart failure and with chronic kidney disease (CKD) stage I through stage IV, or unspecified
- 1 with heart failure and with CKD stage I through stage IV, or unspecified
- 2 without heart failure and with CKD stage V or end stage renal disease
- 3 with heart failure and with CKD stage V or end stage renal disease

The appropriate code from category 585, Chronic kidney disease, should be used as a secondary code with a code from category 404 to identify the stage of kidney disease.

See Section I.C.10.a for information on the coding of chronic kidney disease.

5) Hypertensive Cerebrovascular Disease

First assign codes from 430-438, Cerebrovascular disease, then the appropriate hypertension code from categories 401-405.

6) Hypertensive Retinopathy

Two codes are necessary to identify the condition. First assign the code from subcategory 362.11, Hypertensive retinopathy, then the appropriate code from categories 401-405 to indicate the type of hypertension.

7) Hypertension, Secondary

Two codes are required: one to identify the underlying etiology and one from category 405 to identify the hypertension.

Sequencing of codes is determined by the reason for admission/encounter.

8)   Hypertension, Transient

Assign code 796.2, Elevated blood pressure reading without diagnosis of hypertension, unless patient has an established diagnosis of hypertension. Assign code 642.3x for transient hypertension of pregnancy.

9)   Hypertension, Controlled

Assign appropriate code from categories 401-405. This diagnostic statement usually refers to an existing state of hypertension under control by therapy.

10) Hypertension, Uncontrolled

Uncontrolled hypertension may refer to untreated hypertension or hypertension not responding to current therapeutic regimen. In either case, assign the appropriate code from categories 401-405 to designate the stage and type of hypertension. Code to the type of hypertension.

11) Elevated Blood Pressure

For a statement of elevated blood pressure without further specificity, assign code 796.2, Elevated blood pressure reading without diagnosis of hypertension, rather than a code from category 401.

b.   Cerebral infarction/stroke/cerebrovascular accident (CVA)

The terms stroke and CVA are often used interchangeably to refer to a cerebral infarction. The terms stroke, CVA, and cerebral infarction NOS are all indexed to the default code 434.91, Cerebral artery occlusion, unspecified, with infarction. Code 436, Acute, but ill-defined, cerebrovascular disease, should not be used when the documentation states stroke or CVA.

See Section I.C.18.d.3 for information on coding status post administration of tPA in a different facility within the last 24 hours.

c.   Postoperative cerebrovascular accident

A cerebrovascular hemorrhage or infarction that occurs as a result of medical intervention is coded to 997.02, Iatrogenic cerebrovascular infarction or hemorrhage. Medical record documentation should clearly specify the cause- and-effect relationship between the medical intervention and the cerebrovascular accident in order to assign this code. A secondary code from the code range 430-432 or from a code from subcategories 433 or 434 with a fifth digit of "1" should also be used to identify the type of hemorrhage or infarct.

This guideline conforms to the use additional code note instruction at category 997. Code 436, Acute, but ill-defined, cerebrovascular disease, should not be used as a secondary code with code 997.02.

d. Late Effects of Cerebrovascular Disease

1) Category 438, Late Effects of Cerebrovascular disease

Category 438 is used to indicate conditions classifiable to categories 430-437 as the causes of late effects (neurologic deficits), themselves classified elsewhere. These "late effects" include neurologic deficits that persist after initial onset of conditions classifiable to 430-437. The neurologic deficits caused by cerebrovascular disease may be present from the onset or may arise at any time after the onset of the condition classifiable to 430-437.

2) Codes from category 438 with codes from 430-437

Codes from category 438 may be assigned on a health care record with codes from 430-437, if the patient has a current cerebrovascular accident (CVA) and deficits from an old CVA.

3) Code V12.54

Assign code V12.54, Transient ischemic attack (TIA), and cerebral infarction without residual deficits (and not a code from category 438) as an additional code for history of cerebrovascular disease when no neurologic deficits are present.

e. Acute myocardial infarction (AMI)

1) ST elevation myocardial infarction (STEMI) and non ST elevation myocardial infarction (NSTEMI)

The ICD-9-CM codes for acute myocardial infarction (AMI) identify the site, such as anterolateral wall or true posterior wall. Subcategories 410.0-410.6 and 410.8 are used for ST elevation myocardial infarction (STEMI). Subcategory 410.7, Subendocardial infarction, is used for non ST elevation myocardial infarction (NSTEMI) and nontransmural MIs.

2) **Acute myocardial infarction, unspecified**

Subcategory 410.9 is the default for the unspecified term acute myocardial infarction. If only STEMI or transmural MI without the site is documented, query the provider as to the site, or assign a code from subcategory 410.9.

3) **AMI documented as nontransmural or subendocardial but site provided**

If an AMI is documented as nontransmural or subendocardial, but the site is provided, it is still coded as a subendocardial AMI. If NSTEMI evolves to STEMI, assign the STEMI code. If STEMI converts to NSTEMI due to thrombolytic therapy, it is still coded as STEMI.

See Section I.C.18.d.3 for information on coding status post administration of tPA in a different facility within the last 24 hours.

8. Chapter 8: Diseases of Respiratory System (460-519)

See I.C.17.f. for ventilator-associated pneumonia.

a. Chronic Obstructive Pulmonary Disease [COPD] and Asthma

1) **Conditions that comprise COPD and Asthma**

The conditions that comprise COPD are obstructive chronic bronchitis, subcategory 491.2, and emphysema, category 492. All asthma codes are under category 493, Asthma. Code 496, Chronic airway obstruction, not elsewhere classified, is a nonspecific code that should only be used when the documentation in a medical record does not specify the type of COPD being treated.

2) **Acute exacerbation of chronic obstructive bronchitis and asthma**

The codes for chronic obstructive bronchitis and asthma distinguish between uncomplicated cases and those in acute exacerbation. An acute exacerbation is a worsening or a decompensation of a chronic condition. An acute exacerbation is not equivalent to an infection superimposed on a chronic condition, though an exacerbation may be triggered by an infection.

3) Overlapping nature of the conditions that comprise COPD and asthma

Due to the overlapping nature of the conditions that make up COPD and asthma, there are many variations in the way these conditions are documented. Code selection must be based on the terms as documented. When selecting the correct code for the documented type of COPD and asthma, it is essential to first review the index, and then verify the code in the tabular list. There are many instructional notes under the different COPD subcategories and codes. It is important that all such notes be reviewed to assure correct code assignment.

4) Acute exacerbation of asthma and status asthmaticus

An acute exacerbation of asthma is an increased severity of the asthma symptoms, such as wheezing and shortness of breath. Status asthmaticus refers to a patient's failure to respond to therapy administered during an asthmatic episode and is a life threatening complication that requires emergency care. If status asthmaticus is documented by the provider with any type of COPD or with acute bronchitis, the status asthmaticus should be sequenced first. It supersedes any type of COPD including that with acute exacerbation or acute bronchitis. It is inappropriate to assign an asthma code with 5th digit 2, with acute exacerbation, together with an asthma code with 5th digit 1, with status asthmatics. Only the 5th digit 1 should be assigned.

b. Chronic Obstructive Pulmonary Disease [COPD] and Bronchitis

1) Acute bronchitis with COPD

Acute bronchitis, code 466.0, is due to an infectious organism. When acute bronchitis is documented with COPD, code 491.22, Obstructive chronic bronchitis with acute bronchitis, should be assigned. It is not necessary to also assign code 466.0. If a medical record documents acute bronchitis with COPD with acute exacerbation, only code 491.22 should be assigned. The acute bronchitis included in code 491.22 supersedes the acute exacerbation. If a medical record documents COPD with acute exacerbation without mention of acute bronchitis, only code 491.21 should be assigned.

c.   Acute Respiratory Failure

1)   Acute respiratory failure as principal diagnosis

Code 518.81, Acute respiratory failure, may be assigned as a principal diagnosis when it is the condition established after study to be chiefly responsible for occasioning the admission to the hospital, and the selection is supported by the Alphabetic Index and Tabular List. However, chapter-specific coding guidelines (such as obstetrics, poisoning, HIV, newborn) that provide sequencing direction take precedence.

2)   Acute respiratory failure as secondary diagnosis

Respiratory failure may be listed as a secondary diagnosis if it occurs after admission, or if it is present on admission, but does not meet the definition of principal diagnosis.

3)   Sequencing of acute respiratory failure and another acute condition

When a patient is admitted with respiratory failure and another acute condition, (e.g., myocardial infarction, cerebrovascular accident, aspiration pneumonia), the principal diagnosis will not be the same in every situation. This applies whether the other acute condition is a respiratory or nonrespiratory condition. Selection of the principal diagnosis will be dependent on the circumstances of admission. If both the respiratory failure and the other acute condition are equally responsible for occasioning the admission to the hospital, and there are no chapter-specific sequencing rules, the guideline regarding two or more diagnoses that equally meet the definition for principal diagnosis *(Section II, C.)* may be applied in these situations.

If the documentation is not clear as to whether acute respiratory failure and another condition are equally responsible for occasioning the admission, query the provider for clarification.

d.   Influenza due to *certain* identified *viruses*

Code only confirmed cases of avian influenza **(code 488.0, Influenza due to identified avian influenza virus) or novel H1N1 influenza virus (H1N1 or swine flu, code 488.1).** This is an exception to the hospital inpatient guideline Section II, H. (Uncertain Diagnosis).

In this context, "confirmation" does not require documentation of positive laboratory testing specific for avian **or novel H1N1** influenza. However, coding should be based on the provider's diagnostic statement that the patient has avian **or novel H1N1 (H1N1 or swine flu)** influenza.

If the provider records "suspected or possible or probable avian **or novel H1N1** influenza **(H1N1 or swine flu)**," the appropriate influenza code from category 487 should be assigned. **A code from category** 488, Influenza due to **certain** identified influenza virus**es**, should not be assigned.

9. Chapter 9: Diseases of Digestive System (520-579)

Reserved for future guideline expansion

10. Chapter 10: Diseases of Genitourinary System (580-629)

a. Chronic kidney disease

1) Stages of chronic kidney disease (CKD)

The ICD-9-CM classifies CKD based on severity. The severity of CKD is designated by stages I-V. Stage II, code 585.2, equates to mild CKD; stage III, code 585.3, equates to moderate CKD; and stage IV, code 585.4, equates to severe CKD. Code 585.6, End stage renal disease (ESRD), is assigned when the provider has documented end-stage-renal disease (ESRD).

If both a stage of CKD and ESRD are documented, assign code 585.6 only.

2) Chronic kidney disease and kidney transplant status

Patients who have undergone kidney transplant may still have some form of CKD, because the kidney transplant may not fully restore kidney function. Therefore, the presence of CKD alone does not constitute a transplant complication. Assign the appropriate 585 code for the patient's stage of CKD and code V42.0. If a transplant complication such as failure or rejection is documented, see section I.C.17.f.**2**.b for information on coding complications of a kidney transplant. If the documentation is unclear as to whether the patient has a complication of the transplant, query the provider.

3) Chronic kidney disease with other conditions

Patients with CKD may also suffer from other serious conditions, most commonly diabetes mellitus and hypertension. The sequencing of the CKD code in relationship to codes for other contributing conditions is based on the conventions in the tabular list.

See I.C.3.a.4 for sequencing instructions for diabetes.
See I.C.4.a.1 for anemia in CKD.
See I.C.7.a.3 for hypertensive chronic kidney disease.
See I.C.17.f.2.b, Kidney transplant complications, for instructions on coding of documented rejection or failure.

11. Chapter 11: Complications of Pregnancy, Childbirth, and the Puerperium (630-679)

a. General Rules for Obstetric Cases

1) Codes from chapter 11 and sequencing priority

Obstetric cases require codes from chapter 11, codes in the range 630-679, Complications of Pregnancy, Childbirth, and the Puerperium. Chapter 11 codes have sequencing priority over codes from other chapters. Additional codes from other chapters may be used in conjunction with chapter 11 codes to further specify conditions. Should the provider document that the pregnancy is incidental to the encounter, then code V22.2 should be used in place of any chapter 11 codes. It is the provider's responsibility to state that the condition being treated is not affecting the pregnancy.

2) Chapter 11 codes used only on the maternal record

Chapter 11 codes are to be used only on the maternal record, never on the record of the newborn.

3) Chapter 11 fifth-digits

Categories 640-648, 651-676 have required fifth-digits, which indicate whether the encounter is antepartum, postpartum and whether a delivery has also occurred.

4) Fifth-digits, appropriate for each code

The fifth-digits, which are appropriate for each code number, are listed in brackets under each code. The fifth-digits on each code should all be consistent with each other. That is, should a delivery occur all of the fifth-digits should indicate the delivery.

b. Selection of OB Principal or First-listed Diagnosis

1) Routine outpatient prenatal visits

For routine outpatient prenatal visits when no complications are present codes V22.0, Supervision of normal first pregnancy, and V22.1, Supervision of other normal pregnancy, should be used as the first-listed diagnoses. These codes should not be used in conjunction with chapter 11 codes.

2) Prenatal outpatient visits for high-risk patients

For **routine** prenatal outpatient visits for patients with high-risk pregnancies, a code from category V23, Supervision of high-risk pregnancy, should be used as the first-listed diagnosis. Secondary chapter 11 codes may be used in conjunction with these codes if appropriate.

3) Episodes when no delivery occurs

In episodes when no delivery occurs, the principal diagnosis should correspond to the principal complication of the pregnancy, which necessitated the encounter. Should more than one complication exist, all of which are treated or monitored, any of the complications codes may be sequenced first.

4) When a delivery occurs

When a delivery occurs, the principal diagnosis should correspond to the main circumstances or complication of the delivery. In cases of cesarean delivery, the selection of the principal diagnosis **should be the condition established after study that was responsible for the patient's admission. If the patient was admitted with a condition that resulted in the performance of a cesarean procedure, that condition should be selected as the principal diagnosis.** If the reason for **the** admission/encounter was unrelated to the condition resulting in the cesarean delivery, **the condition related to the reason for the admission/encounter should be selected as the principal diagnosis, even if a cesarean was performed.**

5) Outcome of delivery

An outcome of delivery code, V27.0-V27.9, should be included on every maternal record when a delivery has occurred. These codes are not to be used on subsequent records or on the newborn record.

c. Fetal Conditions Affecting the Management of the Mother

1) Codes from category 655

Known or suspected fetal abnormality affecting management of the mother, and category 656, Other fetal and placental problems affecting the management of the mother, are assigned only when the fetal condition is actually responsible for modifying the management of the mother, i.e., by requiring diagnostic studies, additional observation, special care, or termination of pregnancy. The fact that the fetal condition exists does not justify assigning a code from this series to the mother's record.

See I.C.18.d. for suspected maternal and fetal conditions not found

2) In utero surgery

In cases when surgery is performed on the fetus, a diagnosis code from category 655, Known or suspected fetal abnormalities affecting management of the mother, should be assigned identifying the fetal condition. Procedure code 75.36, Correction of fetal defect, should be assigned on the hospital inpatient record.

No code from Chapter 15, the perinatal codes, should be used on the mother's record to identify fetal conditions. Surgery performed in utero on a fetus is still to be coded as an obstetric encounter.

d. HIV Infection in Pregnancy, Childbirth and the Puerperium

During pregnancy, childbirth or the puerperium, a patient admitted because of an HIV-related illness should receive a principal diagnosis of 647.6X, Other specified infectious and parasitic diseases in the mother classifiable elsewhere, but complicating the pregnancy, childbirth or the puerperium, followed by 042 and the code(s) for the HIV-related illness(es).

Patients with asymptomatic HIV infection status admitted during pregnancy, childbirth, or the puerperium should receive codes of 647.6X and V08.

e. **Current Conditions Complicating Pregnancy**

Assign a code from subcategory 648.x for patients that have current conditions when the condition affects the management of the pregnancy, childbirth, or the puerperium. Use additional secondary codes from other chapters to identify the conditions, as appropriate.

f. **Diabetes mellitus in pregnancy**

Diabetes mellitus is a significant complicating factor in pregnancy. Pregnant women who are diabetic should be assigned code 648.0x, Diabetes mellitus complicating pregnancy, and a secondary code from category 250, Diabetes mellitus, or category 249, Secondary diabetes to identify the type of diabetes.

Code V58.67, Long-term (current) use of insulin, should also be assigned if the diabetes mellitus is being treated with insulin.

g. **Gestational diabetes**

Gestational diabetes can occur during the second and third trimester of pregnancy in women who were not diabetic prior to pregnancy. Gestational diabetes can cause complications in the pregnancy similar to those of pre-existing diabetes mellitus. It also puts the woman at greater risk of developing diabetes after the pregnancy. Gestational diabetes is coded to 648.8x, Abnormal glucose tolerance. Codes 648.0x and 648.8x should never be used together on the same record.

Code V58.67, Long-term (current) use of insulin, should also be assigned if the gestational diabetes is being treated with insulin.

h. **Normal Delivery, Code 650**

1) **Normal delivery**

Code 650 is for use in cases when a woman is admitted for a full-term normal delivery and delivers a single, healthy infant without any complications antepartum, during the delivery, or postpartum during the delivery episode. Code 650 is always a principal diagnosis. It is not to be used if any other code from chapter 11 is needed to describe a current complication of the antenatal, delivery, or perinatal period. Additional codes from other chapters may be used with code 650 if they are not related to or are in any way complicating the pregnancy.

2) Normal delivery with resolved antepartum complication

Code 650 may be used if the patient had a complication at some point during her pregnancy, but the complication is not present at the time of the admission for delivery.

3) V27.0, Single liveborn, outcome of delivery

V27.0, Single liveborn, is the only outcome of delivery code appropriate for use with 650.

i. The Postpartum and Peripartum Periods

1) Postpartum and peripartum periods

The postpartum period begins immediately after delivery and continues for six weeks following delivery. The peripartum period is defined as the last month of pregnancy to five months postpartum.

2) Postpartum complication

A postpartum complication is any complication occurring within the six-week period.

3) Pregnancy-related complications after 6 week period

Chapter 11 codes may also be used to describe pregnancy-related complications after the six-week period should the provider document that a condition is pregnancy related.

4) Postpartum complications occurring during the same admission as delivery

Postpartum complications that occur during the same admission as the delivery are identified with a fifth digit of "2." Subsequent admissions/encounters for postpartum complications should be identified with a fifth digit of "4."

5) Admission for routine postpartum care following delivery outside hospital

When the mother delivers outside the hospital prior to admission and is admitted for routine postpartum care and no complications are noted, code V24.0, Postpartum care and examination immediately after delivery, should be assigned as the principal diagnosis.

6) **Admission following delivery outside hospital with postpartum conditions**

A delivery diagnosis code should not be used for a woman who has delivered prior to admission to the hospital. Any postpartum conditions and/or postpartum procedures should be coded.

7) **Puerperal sepsis**

Code 670.2x, Puerperal sepsis, should be assigned with a secondary code to identify the causal organism (e.g., for a bacterial infection, assign a code from category 041, Bacterial infections in conditions classified elsewhere and of unspecified site). A code from category 038, Septicemia, should not be used for puerperal sepsis. Do not assign code 995.91, Sepsis, as code 670.2x describes the sepsis. If applicable, use additional codes to identify severe sepsis (995.92) and any associated acute organ dysfunction.

j. **Code 677, Late effect of complication of pregnancy**

1) **Code 677**

Code 677, Late effect of complication of pregnancy, childbirth, and the puerperium is for use in those cases when an initial complication of a pregnancy develops a sequelae requiring care or treatment at a future date.

2) **After the initial postpartum period**

This code may be used at any time after the initial postpartum period.

3) **Sequencing of Code 677**

This code, like all late effect codes, is to be sequenced following the code describing the sequelae of the complication.

k. **Abortions**

1) **Fifth-digits required for abortion categories**

Fifth-digits are required for abortion categories 634-637. **Fifth digit assignment is based on the status of the patient at the beginning (or start) of the encounter.** Fifth-digit 1, incomplete, indicates that all of the products of conception have not been expelled from the uterus. Fifth-digit 2, complete, indicates that all products of conception have been expelled from the uterus.

2)   Code from categories 640-648 and 651-659

A code from categories 640-648 and 651-659 may be used as additional codes with an abortion code to indicate the complication leading to the abortion.

Fifth digit 3 is assigned with codes from these categories when used with an abortion code because the other fifth digits will not apply. Codes from the 660-669 series are not to be used for complications of abortion.

3)   Code 639 for complications

Code 639 is to be used for all complications following abortion. Code 639 cannot be assigned with codes from categories 634-638.

4)   Abortion with Liveborn Fetus

When an attempted termination of pregnancy results in a liveborn fetus assign code 644.21, Early onset of delivery, with an appropriate code from category V27, Outcome of Delivery. The procedure code for the attempted termination of pregnancy should also be assigned.

5)   Retained Products of Conception following an abortion

Subsequent admissions for retained products of conception following a spontaneous or legally induced abortion are assigned the appropriate code from category 634, Spontaneous abortion, or 635 Legally induced abortion, with a fifth digit of "1" (incomplete). This advice is appropriate even when the patient was discharged previously with a discharge diagnosis of complete abortion.

12. Chapter 12: Diseases Skin and Subcutaneous Tissue (680-709)

a. Pressure ulcer stage codes

1) Pressure ulcer stages

Two codes are needed to completely describe a pressure ulcer: A code from subcategory 707.0, Pressure ulcer, to identify the site of the pressure ulcer and a code from subcategory 707.2, Pressure ulcer stages.

The codes in subcategory 707.2, Pressure ulcer stages, are to be used as an additional diagnosis with a code(s) from subcategory 707.0, Pressure Ulcer. Codes from 707.2, Pressure ulcer stages, may not be assigned as a principal or first-listed diagnosis. The pressure ulcer stage codes should only be used with pressure ulcers and not with other types of ulcers (e.g., stasis ulcer).

The ICD-9-CM classifies pressure ulcer stages based on severity, which is designated by stages I-IV and unstageable.

2) Unstageable pressure ulcers

Assignment of code 707.25, Pressure ulcer, unstageable, should be based on the clinical documentation. Code 707.25 is used for pressure ulcers whose stage cannot be clinically determined (e.g., the ulcer is covered by eschar or has been treated with a skin or muscle graft) and pressure ulcers that are documented as deep tissue injury but not documented as due to trauma. This code should not be confused with code 707.20, Pressure ulcer, stage unspecified. Code 707.20 should be assigned when there is no documentation regarding the stage of the pressure ulcer.

3) Documented pressure ulcer stage

Assignment of the pressure ulcer stage code should be guided by clinical documentation of the stage or documentation of the terms found in the index. For clinical terms describing the stage that are not found in the index, and there is no documentation of the stage, the provider should be queried.

4) Bilateral pressure ulcers with same stage

When a patient has bilateral pressure ulcers (e.g., both buttocks) and both pressure ulcers are documented as being the same stage, only the code for the site and one code for the stage should be reported.

5) Bilateral pressure ulcers with different stages

When a patient has bilateral pressure ulcers at the same site (e.g., both buttocks) and each pressure ulcer is documented as being at a different stage, assign one code for the site and the appropriate codes for the pressure ulcer stage.

6) Multiple pressure ulcers of different sites and stages

When a patient has multiple pressure ulcers at different sites (e.g., buttock, heel, shoulder) and each pressure ulcer is documented as being at different stages (e.g., stage 3 and stage 4), assign the appropriate codes for each different site and a code for each different pressure ulcer stage.

7) Patients admitted with pressure ulcers documented as healed

No code is assigned if the documentation states that the pressure ulcer is completely healed.

8) Patients admitted with pressure ulcers documented as healing

Pressure ulcers described as healing should be assigned the appropriate pressure ulcer stage code based on the documentation in the medical record. If the documentation does not provide information about the stage of the healing pressure ulcer, assign code 707.20, Pressure ulcer stage, unspecified.

If the documentation is unclear as to whether the patient has a current (new) pressure ulcer or if the patient is being treated for a healing pressure ulcer, query the provider.

9) Patient admitted with pressure ulcer evolving into another stage during the admission

If a patient is admitted with a pressure ulcer at one stage and it progresses to a higher stage, assign the code for highest stage reported for that site.

13. Chapter 13: Diseases of Musculoskeletal and Connective Tissue (710-739)

a. Coding of Pathologic Fractures

1) Acute Fractures vs. Aftercare

Pathologic fractures are reported using subcategory 733.1, when the fracture is newly diagnosed. Subcategory 733.1 may be used while the patient is receiving active treatment for the fracture. Examples of active treatment are: surgical treatment, emergency department encounter, evaluation and treatment by a new physician.

Fractures are coded using the aftercare codes (subcategories V54.0, V54.2, V54.8 or V54.9) for encounters after the patient has completed active treatment of the fracture and is receiving routine care for the fracture during the healing or recovery phase. Examples of fracture aftercare are: cast change or removal, removal of external or internal fixation device, medication adjustment, and follow up visits following fracture treatment.

Care for complications of surgical treatment for fracture repairs during the healing or recovery phase should be coded with the appropriate complication codes.

Care of complications of fractures, such as malunion and nonunion, should be reported with the appropriate codes.

See Section I. C. 17.b for information on the coding of traumatic fractures.

14. Chapter 14: Congenital Anomalies (740-759)

a. Codes in categories 740-759, Congenital Anomalies

Assign an appropriate code(s) from categories 740-759, Congenital Anomalies, when an anomaly is documented. A congenital anomaly may be the principal/first listed diagnosis on a record or a secondary diagnosis.

When a congenital anomaly does not have a unique code assignment, assign additional code(s) for any manifestations that may be present.

When the code assignment specifically identifies the congenital anomaly, manifestations that are an inherent component of the anomaly should not be coded separately. Additional codes should be assigned for manifestations that are not an inherent component.

Codes from Chapter 14 may be used throughout the life of the patient. If a congenital anomaly has been corrected, a personal history code should be used to identify the history of the anomaly. Although present at birth, a congenital anomaly may not be identified until later in life. Whenever the condition is diagnosed by the physician, it is appropriate to assign a code from codes 740-759.

For the birth admission, the appropriate code from category V30, Liveborn infants, according to type of birth should be sequenced as the principal diagnosis, followed by any congenital anomaly codes, 740-759.

15.   Chapter 15: Newborn (Perinatal) Guidelines (760-779)

For coding and reporting purposes the perinatal period is defined as before birth through the 28th day following birth. The following guidelines are provided for reporting purposes. Hospitals may record other diagnoses as needed for internal data use.

a.   General Perinatal Rules

1)   Chapter 15 Codes

They are <u>never</u> for use on the maternal record. Codes from Chapter 11, the obstetric chapter, are never permitted on the newborn record. Chapter 15 code may be used throughout the life of the patient if the condition is still present.

2)   Sequencing of perinatal codes

Generally, codes from Chapter 15 should be sequenced as the principal/first-listed diagnosis on the newborn record, with the exception of the appropriate V30 code for the birth episode, followed by codes from any other chapter that provide additional detail. The "use additional code" note at the beginning of the chapter supports this guideline. If the index does not provide a specific code for a perinatal condition, assign code 779.89, Other specified conditions originating in the perinatal period, followed by the code from another chapter that specifies the condition. Codes for signs and symptoms may be assigned when a definitive diagnosis has not been established.

3) **Birth process or community acquired conditions**

If a newborn has a condition that may be either due to the birth process or community acquired and the documentation does not indicate which it is, the default is due to the birth process and the code from Chapter 15 should be used. If the condition is community-acquired, a code from Chapter 15 should not be assigned.

4) **Code all clinically significant conditions**

All clinically significant conditions noted on routine newborn examination should be coded. A condition is clinically significant if it requires:

- clinical evaluation; or
- therapeutic treatment; or
- diagnostic procedures; or
- extended length of hospital stay; or
- increased nursing care and/or monitoring; or
- has implications for future health care needs

Note: The perinatal guidelines listed above are the same as the general coding guidelines for "additional diagnoses", except for the final point regarding implications for future health care needs. Codes should be assigned for conditions that have been specified by the provider as having implications for future health care needs. Codes from the perinatal chapter should not be assigned unless the provider has established a definitive diagnosis.

b. **Use of codes V30-V39**

When coding the birth of an infant, assign a code from categories V30-V39, according to the type of birth. A code from this series is assigned as a principal diagnosis, and assigned only once to a newborn at the time of birth.

c. **Newborn transfers**

If the newborn is transferred to another institution, the V30 series is not used at the receiving hospital.

d. **Use of category V29**

1) **Assigning a code from category V29**

Assign a code from category V29, Observation and evaluation of newborns and infants for suspected conditions not found, to identify those instances when a healthy newborn is evaluated for a suspected condition that is determined after study not to be present. Do not use a code from category V29 when the patient has identified signs or symptoms of a suspected problem; in such cases, code the sign or symptom.

A code from category V29 may also be assigned as a principal code for readmissions or encounters when the V30 code no longer applies. Codes from category V29 are for use only for healthy newborns and infants for which no condition after study is found to be present.

2) V29 code on a birth record

A V29 code is to be used as a secondary code after the V30, Outcome of delivery, code.

e. Use of other V codes on perinatal records

V codes other than V30 and V29 may be assigned on a perinatal or newborn record code. The codes may be used as a principal or first-listed diagnosis for specific types of encounters or for readmissions or encounters when the V30 code no longer applies.
See Section I.C.18 for information regarding the assignment of V codes.

f. Maternal Causes of Perinatal Morbidity

Codes from categories 760-763, Maternal causes of perinatal morbidity and mortality, are assigned only when the maternal condition has actually affected the fetus or newborn. The fact that the mother has an associated medical condition or experiences some complication of pregnancy, labor or delivery does not justify the routine assignment of codes from these categories to the newborn record.

g. Congenital Anomalies in Newborns

For the birth admission, the appropriate code from category V30, Liveborn infants according to type of birth, should be used, followed by any congenital anomaly codes, categories 740-759. Use additional secondary codes from other chapters to specify conditions associated with the anomaly, if applicable.
Also, see Section I.C.14 for information on the coding of congenital anomalies.

h. **Coding Additional Perinatal Diagnoses**

    1) **Assigning codes for conditions that require treatment**

Assign codes for conditions that require treatment or further investigation, prolong the length of stay, or require resource utilization.

    2) **Codes for conditions specified as having implications for future health care needs**

Assign codes for conditions that have been specified by the provider as having implications for future health care needs.

Note: This guideline should not be used for adult patients.

    3) **Codes for newborn conditions originating in the perinatal period**

Assign a code for newborn conditions originating in the perinatal period (categories 760-779), as well as complications arising during the current episode of care classified in other chapters, only if the diagnoses have been documented by the responsible provider at the time of transfer or discharge as having affected the fetus or newborn.

i. **Prematurity and Fetal Growth Retardation**

Providers utilize different criteria in determining prematurity. A code for prematurity should not be assigned unless it is documented. The 5th digit assignment for codes from category 764 and subcategories 765.0 and 765.1 should be based on the recorded birth weight and estimated gestational age.

A code from subcategory 765.2, Weeks of gestation, should be assigned as an additional code with category 764 and codes from 765.0 and 765.1 to specify weeks of gestation as documented by the provider in the record.

j. **Newborn sepsis**

Code 771.81, Septicemia [sepsis] of newborn, should be assigned with a secondary code from category 041, Bacterial infections in conditions classified elsewhere and of unspecified site, to identify the organism. A code from category 038, Septicemia, should not be used on a newborn record. Do not assign code 995.91, Sepsis, as code 771.81 describes the sepsis. If applicable, use additional codes to identify severe sepsis (995.92) and any associated acute organ dysfunction.

16. Chapter 16: Signs, Symptoms and Ill-Defined Conditions (780-799)

Reserved for future guideline expansion

17. Chapter 17: Injury and Poisoning (800-999)

a. **Coding of Injuries**

When coding injuries, assign separate codes for each injury unless a combination code is provided, in which case the combination code is assigned. Multiple injury codes are provided in ICD-9-CM, but should not be assigned unless information for a more specific code is not available. These **traumatic injury** codes are not to be used for normal, healing surgical wounds or to identify complications of surgical wounds.

The code for the most serious injury, as determined by the provider and the focus of treatment, is sequenced first.

1) **Superficial injuries**

Superficial injuries such as abrasions or contusions are not coded when associated with more severe injuries of the same site.

2) **Primary injury with damage to nerves/blood vessels**

When a primary injury results in minor damage to peripheral nerves or blood vessels, the primary injury is sequenced first with additional code(s) from categories 950-957, Injury to nerves and spinal cord, and/or 900-904, Injury to blood vessels. When the primary injury is to the blood vessels or nerves, that injury should be sequenced first.

b. **Coding of Traumatic Fractures**

The principles of multiple coding of injuries should be followed in coding fractures. Fractures of specified sites are coded individually by site in accordance with both the provisions within categories 800-829 and the level of detail furnished by medical record content. Combination categories for multiple fractures are provided for use when there is insufficient detail in the medical record (such as trauma cases transferred to another hospital), when the reporting form limits the number of codes that can be used in reporting pertinent clinical data, or when there is insufficient specificity at the fourth-digit or fifth-digit level. More specific guidelines are as follows:

1) Acute Fractures vs. Aftercare

Traumatic fractures are coded using the acute fracture codes (800-829) while the patient is receiving active treatment for the fracture. Examples of active treatment are: surgical treatment, emergency department encounter, and evaluation and treatment by a new physician.

Fractures are coded using the aftercare codes (subcategories V54.0, V54.1, V54.8, or V54.9) for encounters after the patient has completed active treatment of the fracture and is receiving routine care for the fracture during the healing or recovery phase. Examples of fracture aftercare are: cast change or removal, removal of external or internal fixation device, medication adjustment, and follow up visits following fracture treatment.

Care for complications of surgical treatment for fracture repairs during the healing or recovery phase should be coded with the appropriate complication codes.

Care of complications of fractures, such as malunion and nonunion, should be reported with the appropriate codes.

Pathologic fractures are not coded in the 800-829 range, but instead are assigned to subcategory 733.1. *See Section I.C.13.a for additional information.*

2) Multiple fractures of same limb

Multiple fractures of same limb classifiable to the same three-digit or four-digit category are coded to that category.

3) Multiple unilateral or bilateral fractures of same bone

Multiple unilateral or bilateral fractures of same bone(s) but classified to different fourth-digit subdivisions (bone part) within the same three-digit category are coded individually by site.

4) Multiple fracture categories 819 and 828

Multiple fracture categories 819 and 828 classify bilateral fractures of both upper limbs (819) and both lower limbs (828), but without any detail at the fourth-digit level other than open and closed type of fractures.

5) **Multiple fractures sequencing**

Multiple fractures are sequenced in accordance with the severity of the fracture. The provider should be asked to list the fracture diagnoses in the order of severity.

c. **Coding of Burns**

Current burns (940-948) are classified by depth, extent and by agent (E code). Burns are classified by depth as first degree (erythema), second degree (blistering), and third degree (full-thickness involvement).

1) **Sequencing of burn and related condition codes**

Sequence first the code that reflects the highest degree of burn when more than one burn is present.

a. When the reason for the admission or encounter is for treatment of external multiple burns, sequence first the code that reflects the burn of the highest degree.

b. When a patient has both internal and external burns, the circumstances of admission govern the selection of the principal diagnosis or first-listed diagnosis.

c. When a patient is admitted for burn injuries and other related conditions such as smoke inhalation and/or respiratory failure, the circumstances of admission govern the selection of the principal or first-listed diagnosis.

2) **Burns of the same local site**

Classify burns of the same local site (three-digit category level, 940-947) but of different degrees to the subcategory identifying the highest degree recorded in the diagnosis.

3) **Non-healing burns**

Non-healing burns are coded as acute burns.
Necrosis of burned skin should be coded as a non-healed burn.

4) **Code 958.3, Posttraumatic wound infection**

Assign code 958.3, Posttraumatic wound infection, not elsewhere classified, as an additional code for any documented infected burn site.

5)   **Assign separate codes for each burn site**

When coding burns, assign separate codes for each burn site. Category 946 Burns of Multiple specified sites, should only be used if the location of the burns are not documented. Category 949, Burn, unspecified, is extremely vague and should rarely be used.

6)   **Assign codes from category 948, Burns**

Burns classified according to extent of body surface involved, when the site of the burn is not specified or when there is a need for additional data. It is advisable to use category 948 as additional coding when needed to provide data for evaluating burn mortality, such as that needed by burn units. It is also advisable to use category 948 as an additional code for reporting purposes when there is mention of a third-degree burn involving 20 percent or more of the body surface.

In assigning a code from category 948:

Fourth-digit codes are used to identify the percentage of total body surface involved in a burn (all degree).

Fifth-digits are assigned to identify the percentage of body surface involved in third-degree burn.

Fifth-digit zero (0) is assigned when less than 10 percent or when no body surface is involved in a third-degree burn.

Category 948 is based on the classic "rule of nines" in estimating body surface involved: head and neck are assigned nine percent, each arm nine percent, each leg 18 percent, the anterior trunk 18 percent, posterior trunk 18 percent, and genitalia one percent. Providers may change these percentage assignments where necessary to accommodate infants and children who have proportionately larger heads than adults and patients who have large buttocks, thighs, or abdomen that involve burns.

7)   **Encounters for treatment of late effects of burns**

Encounters for the treatment of the late effects of burns (i.e., scars or joint contractures) should be coded to the residual condition (sequelae) followed by the appropriate late effect code (906.5-906.9). A late effect E code may also be used, if desired.

8)   **Sequelae with a late effect code and current burn**

When appropriate, both a sequelae with a late effect code, and a current burn code may be assigned on the same record (when both a current burn and sequelae of an old burn exist).

d.   **Coding of Debridement of Wound, Infection, or Burn**

Excisional debridement involves surgical removal or cutting away, as opposed to a mechanical (brushing, scrubbing, washing) debridement.

For coding purposes, excisional debridement is assigned to code 86.22.

Nonexcisional debridement is assigned to code 86.28.

e.   **Adverse Effects, Poisoning and Toxic Effects**

The properties of certain drugs, medicinal and biological substances or combinations of such substances, may cause toxic reactions. The occurrence of drug toxicity is classified in ICD-9-CM as follows:

1)   **Adverse Effect**

When the drug was correctly prescribed and properly administered, code the reaction plus the appropriate code from the E930-E949 series. Codes from the E930-E949 series must be used to identify the causative substance for an adverse effect of drug, medicinal and biological substances, correctly prescribed and properly administered. The effect, such as tachycardia, delirium, gastrointestinal hemorrhaging, vomiting, hypokalemia, hepatitis, renal failure, or respiratory failure, is coded and followed by the appropriate code from the E930-E949 series.

Adverse effects of therapeutic substances correctly prescribed and properly administered (toxicity, synergistic reaction, side effect, and idiosyncratic reaction) may be due to (1) differences among patients, such as age, sex, disease, and genetic factors, and (2) drug-related factors, such as type of drug, route of administration, duration of therapy, dosage, and bioavailability.

2) Poisoning

(a) Error was made in drug prescription

Errors made in drug prescription or in the administration of the drug by provider, nurse, patient, or other person, use the appropriate poisoning code from the 960-979 series.

(b) Overdose of a drug intentionally taken

If an overdose of a drug was intentionally taken or administered and resulted in drug toxicity, it would be coded as a poisoning (960-979 series).

(c) Nonprescribed drug taken with correctly prescribed and properly administered drug

If a nonprescribed drug or medicinal agent was taken in combination with a correctly prescribed and properly administered drug, any drug toxicity or other reaction resulting from the interaction of the two drugs would be classified as a poisoning.

(d) Interaction of drug(s) and alcohol

When a reaction results from the interaction of a drug(s) and alcohol, this would be classified as poisoning.

(e) Sequencing of poisoning

When coding a poisoning or reaction to the improper use of a medication (e.g., wrong dose, wrong substance, wrong route of administration) the poisoning code is sequenced first, followed by a code for the manifestation. If there is also a diagnosis of drug abuse or dependence to the substance, the abuse or dependence is coded as an additional code.
See Section I.C.3.a.6.b. if poisoning is the result of insulin pump malfunctions and Section I.C.19 for general use of E-codes.

3) Toxic Effects

(a) Toxic effect codes

When a harmful substance is ingested or comes in contact with a person, this is classified as a toxic effect. The toxic effect codes are in categories 980-989.

(b) Sequencing toxic effect codes

A toxic effect code should be sequenced first, followed by the code(s) that identify the result of the toxic effect.

(c) External cause codes for toxic effects

An external cause code from categories E860-E869 for accidental exposure, codes E950.6 or E950.7 for intentional self-harm, category E962 for assault, or categories E980-E982, for undetermined, should also be assigned to indicate intent.

f. Complications of care

1) Complications of care

(a) Documentation of complications of care

As with all procedural or postprocedural complications, code assignment is based on the provider's documentation of the relationship between the condition and the procedure.

2) Transplant complications

(a) Transplant complications other than kidney

Codes under subcategory 996.8, Complications of transplanted organ, are for use for both complications and rejection of transplanted organs. A transplant complication code is only assigned if the complication affects the function of the transplanted organ. Two codes are required to fully describe a transplant complication, the appropriate code from subcategory 996.8 and a secondary code that identifies the complication.

Pre-existing conditions or conditions that develop after the transplant are not coded as complications unless they affect the function of the transplanted organs.

See I.C.18.d.3) for transplant organ removal status

See I.C.2.i for malignant neoplasm associated with transplanted organ.

(b)   **Chronic kidney disease and kidney transplant complications**

Patients who have undergone kidney transplant may still have some form of chronic kidney disease (CKD) because the kidney transplant may not fully restore kidney function. Code 996.81 should be assigned for documented complications of a kidney transplant, such as transplant failure or rejection or other transplant complication. Code 996.81 should not be assigned for post kidney transplant patients who have chronic kidney (CKD) unless a transplant complication such as transplant failure or rejection is documented. If the documentation is unclear as to whether the patient has a complication of the transplant, query the provider.

For patients with CKD following a kidney transplant, but who do not have a complication such as failure or rejection, *see section I.C.10.a.2, Chronic kidney disease and kidney transplant status*.

3)   **Ventilator associated pneumonia**

(a)   **Documentation of Ventilator associated Pneumonia**

As with all procedural or postprocedural complications, code assignment is based on the provider's documentation of the relationship between the condition and the procedure.

Code 997.31, Ventilator associated pneumonia, should be assigned only when the provider has documented ventilator associated pneumonia (VAP). An additional code to identify the organism (e.g., Pseudomonas aeruginosa, code 041.7) should also be assigned. Do not assign an additional code from categories 480-484 to identify the type of pneumonia.

Code 997.31 should not be assigned for cases where the patient has pneumonia and is on a mechanical ventilator but the provider has not specifically stated that the pneumonia is ventilator-associated pneumonia.

If the documentation is unclear as to whether the patient has a pneumonia that is a complication attributable to the mechanical ventilator, query the provider.

(b)   **Patient admitted with pneumonia and develops VAP**

A patient may be admitted with one type of pneumonia (e.g., code 481, Pneumococcal pneumonia) and subsequently develop VAP. In this instance, the principal diagnosis would be the appropriate code from categories 480-484 for the pneumonia diagnosed at the time of admission. Code 997.31, Ventilator associated pneumonia, would be assigned as an additional diagnosis when the provider has also documented the presence of ventilator associated pneumonia.

g.   SIRS due to Non-infectious Process

The systemic inflammatory response syndrome (SIRS) can develop as a result of certain non-infectious disease processes, such as trauma, malignant neoplasm, or pancreatitis. When SIRS is documented with a noninfectious condition, and no subsequent infection is documented, the code for the underlying condition, such as an injury, should be assigned, followed by code 995.93, Systemic inflammatory response syndrome due to noninfectious process without acute organ dysfunction, or 995.94, Systemic inflammatory response syndrome due to non-infectious process with acute organ dysfunction. If an acute organ dysfunction is documented, the appropriate code(s) for the associated acute organ dysfunction(s) should be assigned in addition to code 995.94. If acute organ dysfunction is documented, but it cannot be determined if the acute organ dysfunction is associated with SIRS or due to another condition (e.g., directly due to the trauma), the provider should be queried.

When the non-infectious condition has led to an infection that results in SIRS, *see Section I.C.1.b.12 for the guideline for sepsis and severe sepsis associated with a non-infectious process.*

18. **Classification of Factors Influencing Health Status and Contact with Health Service (Supplemental V01-V89)**

Note: The chapter specific guidelines provide additional information about the use of V codes for specified encounters.

a. **Introduction**

ICD-9-CM provides codes to deal with encounters for circumstances other than a disease or injury. The Supplementary Classification of Factors Influencing Health Status and Contact with Health Services (V01.0 - V89.09) is provided to deal with occasions when circumstances other than a disease or injury (codes 001-999) are recorded as a diagnosis or problem.

There are four primary circumstances for the use of V codes:

1) A person who is not currently sick encounters the health services for some specific reason, such as to act as an organ donor, to receive prophylactic care, such as inoculations or health screenings, or to receive counseling on health related issues.

2) A person with a resolving disease or injury, or a chronic, long-term condition requiring continuous care, encounters the health care system for specific aftercare of that disease or injury (e.g., dialysis for renal disease; chemotherapy for malignancy; cast change). A diagnosis/symptom code should be used whenever a current, acute, diagnosis is being treated or a sign or symptom is being studied.

3) Circumstances or problems influence a person's health status but are not in themselves a current illness or injury.

4) Newborns, to indicate birth status

b. **V codes use in any healthcare setting**

V codes are for use in any healthcare setting. V codes may be used as either a first listed (principal diagnosis code in the inpatient setting) or secondary code, depending on the circumstances of the encounter. Certain V codes may only be used as first listed, others only as secondary codes.
See Section I.C.18.e, **V Codes That May Only be Principal/First-Listed Diagnosis.**

c.   V Codes indicate a reason for an encounter

They are not procedure codes. A corresponding procedure code must accompany a V code to describe the procedure performed.

d.   Categories of V Codes

1)   Contact/Exposure

Category V01 indicates contact with or exposure to communicable diseases. These codes are for patients who do not show any sign or symptom of a disease but have been exposed to it by close personal contact with an infected individual or are in an area where a disease is epidemic. These codes may be used as a first listed code to explain an encounter for testing, or, more commonly, as a secondary code to identify a potential risk.

2)   Inoculations and vaccinations

Categories V03-V06 are for encounters for inoculations and vaccinations. They indicate that a patient is being seen to receive a prophylactic inoculation against a disease. The injection itself must be represented by the appropriate procedure code. A code from V03-V06 may be used as a secondary code if the inoculation is given as a routine part of preventive health care, such as a well-baby visit.

3)   Status

Status codes indicate that a patient is either a carrier of a disease or has the sequelae or residual of a past disease or condition. This includes such things as the presence of prosthetic or mechanical devices resulting from past treatment. A status code is informative, because the status may affect the course of treatment and its outcome. A status code is distinct from a history code. The history code indicates that the patient no longer has the condition.

A status code should not be used with a diagnosis code from one of the body system chapters, if the diagnosis code includes the information provided by the status code. For example, code V42.1, Heart transplant status, should not be used with code 996.83, Complications of transplanted heart. The status code does not provide additional information. The complication code indicates that the patient is a heart transplant patient.

The status V codes/categories are:

V02   Carrier or suspected carrier of infectious diseases
Carrier status indicates that a person harbors the specific organisms of a disease without manifest symptoms and is capable of transmitting the infection.

V07.5X   Prophylactic use of agents affecting estrogen receptors and estrogen level
This code indicates when a patient is receiving a drug that affects estrogen receptors and estrogen levels for prevention of cancer.

V08   Asymptomatic HIV infection status
This code indicates that a patient has tested positive for HIV but has manifested no signs or symptoms of the disease.

V09   Infection with drug-resistant microorganisms
This category indicates that a patient has an infection that is resistant to drug treatment.
Sequence the infection code first.

V21   Constitutional states in development

V22.2   Pregnant state, incidental
This code is a secondary code only for use when the pregnancy is in no way complicating the reason for visit. Otherwise, a code from the obstetric chapter is required.

V26.5x   Sterilization status

V42   Organ or tissue replaced by transplant

V43   Organ or tissue replaced by other means

V44   Artificial opening status

V45   Other postsurgical states
Assign code V45.87, Transplant organ removal status, to indicate that a transplanted organ has been previously removed. This code should not be assigned for the encounter in which the transplanted organ is removed. The complication necessitating removal of the transplant organ should be assigned for that encounter.

See section I.C17.f.2. for information on the coding of organ transplant complications.

Assign code V45.88, Status post administration of tPA (rtPA) in a different facility within the last 24 hours prior to admission to the current facility, as a secondary diagnosis when a patient is received by transfer into a facility and documentation indicates they were administered tissue plasminogen activator (tPA) within the last 24 hours prior to admission to the current facility.

This guideline applies even if the patient is still receiving the tPA at the time they are received into the current facility.

The appropriate code for the condition for which the tPA was administered (such as cerebrovascular disease or myocardial infarction) should be assigned first.

Code V45.88 is only applicable to the receiving facility record and not to the transferring facility record.

V46	Other dependence on machines
V49.6	Upper limb amputation status
V49.7	Lower limb amputation status

Note: Categories V42-V46, and subcategories V49.6, V49.7 are for use only if there are no complications or malfunctions of the organ or tissue replaced, the amputation site or the equipment on which the patient is dependent.

V49.81	Postmenopausal status
V49.82	Dental sealant status
V49.83	Awaiting organ transplant status
V58.6x	Long-term (current) drug use

Codes from this subcategory indicate a patient's continuous use of a prescribed drug (including such things as aspirin therapy) for the long-term treatment of a condition or for prophylactic use. It is not for use for patients who have addictions to drugs. This subcategory is not for use of medications for detoxification or maintenance programs to prevent withdrawal symptoms in patients with drug dependence (e.g., methadone maintenance for opiate dependence). Assign the appropriate code for the drug dependence instead.

Assign a code from subcategory V58.6, Long-term (current) drug use, if the patient is receiving a medication for an extended period as a prophylactic measure (such as for the prevention of deep vein thrombosis) or as treatment of a chronic condition (such as arthritis) or a disease requiring a lengthy course of treatment (such as cancer). Do not assign a code from subcategory V58.6 for medication being administered for a brief period of time to treat an acute illness or injury (such as a course of antibiotics to treat acute bronchitis).

V83 Genetic carrier status
Genetic carrier status indicates that a person carries a gene, associated with a particular disease, which may be passed to offspring who may develop that disease. The person does not have the disease and is not at risk of developing the disease.

V84 Genetic susceptibility status
Genetic susceptibility indicates that a person has a gene that increases the risk of that person developing the disease.

Codes from category V84, Genetic susceptibility to disease, should not be used as principal or first-listed codes. If the patient has the condition to which he/she is susceptible, and that condition is the reason for the encounter, the code for the current condition should be sequenced first. If the patient is being seen for follow-up after completed treatment for this condition, and the condition no longer exists, a follow-up code should be sequenced first, followed by the appropriate personal history and genetic susceptibility codes. If the purpose of the encounter is genetic counseling associated with procreative management, a code from subcategory V26.3, Genetic counseling and testing, should be assigned as the first-listed code, followed by a code from category V84. Additional codes should be assigned for any applicable family or personal history.

See Section I.C. 18.d.14 for information on prophylactic organ removal due to a genetic susceptibility.

V85 Body Mass Index (BMI)
V86 Estrogen receptor status
V88 Acquired absence of other organs and tissue

4) History (of)

There are two types of history V codes, personal and family. Personal history codes explain a patient's past medical condition that no longer exists and is not receiving any treatment, but that has the potential for recurrence, and therefore may require continued monitoring. The exceptions to this general rule are category V14, Personal history of allergy to medicinal agents, and subcategory V15.0, Allergy, other than to medicinal agents. A person who has had an allergic episode to a substance or food in the past should always be considered allergic to the substance.

Family history codes are for use when a patient has a family member(s) who has had a particular disease that causes the patient to be at higher risk of also contracting the disease.

Personal history codes may be used in conjunction with follow-up codes and family history codes may be used in conjunction with screening codes to explain the need for a test or procedure. History codes are also acceptable on any medical record regardless of the reason for visit. A history of an illness, even if no longer present, is important information that may alter the type of treatment ordered.

The history V code categories are:

V10	Personal history of malignant neoplasm
V12	Personal history of certain other diseases
V13	Personal history of other diseases
	Except: V13.4, Personal history of arthritis, and V13.6, Personal history of congenital malformations. These conditions are life-long so are not true history codes.
V14	Personal history of allergy to medicinal agents
V15	Other personal history presenting hazards to health
	Except: V15.7, Personal history of contraception.
V16	Family history of malignant neoplasm
V17	Family history of certain chronic disabling diseases
V18	Family history of certain other specific diseases
V19	Family history of other conditions
V87	Other specified personal exposures and history presenting hazards to health

5) **Screening**

Screening is the testing for disease or disease precursors in seemingly well individuals so that early detection and treatment can be provided for those who test positive for the disease. Screenings that are recommended for many subgroups in a population include: routine mammograms for women over 40, a fecal occult blood test for everyone over 50, an amniocentesis to rule out a fetal anomaly for pregnant women over 35, because the incidence of breast cancer and colon cancer in these subgroups is higher than in the general population, as is the incidence of Down's syndrome in older mothers.

The testing of a person to rule out or confirm a suspected diagnosis because the patient has some sign or symptom is a diagnostic examination, not a screening. In these cases, the sign or symptom is used to explain the reason for the test.

A screening code may be a first listed code if the reason for the visit is specifically the screening exam. It may also be used as an additional code if the screening is done during an office visit for other health problems. A screening code is not necessary if the screening is inherent to a routine examination, such as a pap smear done during a routine pelvic examination.

Should a condition be discovered during the screening then the code for the condition may be assigned as an additional diagnosis.

The V code indicates that a screening exam is planned. A procedure code is required to confirm that the screening was performed.

The screening V code categories:
V28   Antenatal screening
V73-V82   Special screening examinations

6)   **Observation**

There are three observation V code categories. They are for use in very limited circumstances when a person is being observed for a suspected condition that is ruled out. The observation codes are not for use if an injury or illness or any signs or symptoms related to the suspected condition are present. In such cases the diagnosis/symptom code is used with the corresponding E code to identify any external cause.

The observation codes are to be used as principal diagnosis only. The only exception to this is when the principal diagnosis is required to be a code from the V30, Live born infant, category. Then the V29 observation code is sequenced after the V30 code. Additional codes may be used in addition to the observation code but only if they are unrelated to the suspected condition being observed.

Codes from subcategory V89.0, Suspected maternal and fetal conditions not found, may either be used as a first listed or as an additional code assignment depending on the case. They are for use in very limited circumstances on a maternal record when an encounter is for a suspected maternal or fetal condition that is ruled out during that encounter (for example, a maternal or fetal condition may be suspected due to an abnormal test result). These codes should not be used when the condition is confirmed. In those cases, the confirmed condition should be coded. In addition, these codes are not for use if an illness or any signs or symptoms related to the suspected condition or problem are present. In such cases the diagnosis/symptom code is used.

Additional codes may be used in addition to the code from subcategory V89.0, but only if they are unrelated to the suspected condition being evaluated.

Codes from subcategory V89.0 may not be used for encounters for antenatal screening of mother. *See Section I.C.18.d., Screening).*

For encounters for suspected fetal condition that are inconclusive following testing and evaluation, assign the appropriate code from category 655, 656, 657 or 658.

The observation V code categories:

V29   Observation and evaluation of newborns for suspected condition not found
        For the birth encounter, a code from category V30 should be sequenced before the V29 code.
V71   Observation and evaluation for suspected condition not found
V89   Suspected maternal and fetal conditions not found

7)   **Aftercare**

Aftercare visit codes cover situations when the initial treatment of a disease or injury has been performed and the patient requires continued care during the healing or recovery phase, or for the long-term consequences of the disease. The aftercare V code should not be used if treatment is directed at a current, acute disease or injury. The diagnosis code is to be used in these cases. Exceptions to this rule are codes V58.0, Radiotherapy, and codes from subcategory V58.1, Encounter for chemotherapy and immunotherapy for neoplastic conditions. These codes are to be first listed, followed by the diagnosis code when a patient's encounter is solely to receive radiation therapy or chemotherapy for the treatment of a neoplasm. Should a patient receive both chemotherapy and radiation therapy during the same encounter code V58.0 and V58.1 may be used together on a record with either one being sequenced first.

The aftercare codes are generally first listed to explain the specific reason for the encounter. An aftercare code may be used as an additional code when some type of aftercare is provided in addition to the reason for admission and no diagnosis code is applicable. An example of this would be the closure of a colostomy during an encounter for treatment of another condition.

Aftercare codes should be used in conjunction with any other aftercare codes or other diagnosis codes to provide better detail on the specifics of an aftercare encounter visit, unless otherwise directed by the classification. The sequencing of multiple aftercare codes is discretionary.

Certain aftercare V code categories need a secondary diagnosis code to describe the resolving condition or sequelae, for others, the condition is inherent in the code title.

Additional V code aftercare category terms include fitting and adjustment, and attention to artificial openings.

Status V codes may be used with aftercare V codes to indicate the nature of the aftercare. For example code V45.81, Aortocoronary bypass status, may be used with code V58.73, Aftercare following surgery of the circulatory system, NEC, to indicate the surgery for which the aftercare is being performed. Also, a transplant status code may be used following code V58.44, Aftercare following organ transplant, to identify the organ transplanted. A status code should not be used when the aftercare code indicates the type of status, such as using V55.0, Attention to tracheostomy with V44.0, Tracheostomy status.

See Section I. B.16 Admissions/Encounter for Rehabilitation

The aftercare V category/codes:
V51.0   Encounter for breast reconstruction following mastectomy
V52   Fitting and adjustment of prosthetic device and implant

V53	Fitting and adjustment of other device
V54	Other orthopedic aftercare
V55	Attention to artificial openings
V56	Encounter for dialysis and dialysis catheter care
V57	Care involving the use of rehabilitation procedures
V58.0	Radiotherapy
V58.11	Encounter for antineoplastic chemotherapy
V58.12	Encounter for antineoplastic immunotherapy
V58.3x	Attention to dressings and sutures
V58.41	Encounter for planned post-operative wound closure
V58.42	Aftercare, surgery, neoplasm
V58.43	Aftercare, surgery, trauma
V58.44	Aftercare involving organ transplant
V58.49	Other specified aftercare following surgery
V58.7x	Aftercare following surgery
V58.81	Fitting and adjustment of vascular catheter
V58.82	Fitting and adjustment of non-vascular catheter
V58.83	Monitoring therapeutic drug
V58.89	Other specified aftercare

8) Follow-up

The follow-up codes are used to explain continuing surveillance following completed treatment of a disease, condition, or injury. They imply that the condition has been fully treated and no longer exists. They should not be confused with aftercare codes that explain current treatment for a healing condition or its sequelae. Follow-up codes may be used in conjunction with history codes to provide the full picture of the healed condition and its treatment. The follow-up code is sequenced first, followed by the history code.

A follow-up code may be used to explain repeated visits. Should a condition be found to have recurred on the follow-up visit, then the diagnosis code should be used in place of the follow-up code.

The follow-up V code categories:

V24	Postpartum care and evaluation
V67	Follow-up examination

9) Donor

Category V59 is the donor codes. They are used for living individuals who are donating blood or other body tissue. These codes are only for individuals donating for others, not for self donations. They are not for use to identify cadaveric donations.

10) Counseling

Counseling V codes are used when a patient or family member receives assistance in the aftermath of an illness or injury, or when support is required in coping with family or social problems. They are not necessary for use in conjunction with a diagnosis code when the counseling component of care is considered integral to standard treatment.

The counseling V categories/codes:

V25.0	General counseling and advice for contraceptive management
V26.3	Genetic counseling
V26.4	General counseling and advice for procreative management
V61.**X**	Other family circumstances
V65.1	Person consulted on behalf of another person
V65.3	Dietary surveillance and counseling
V65.4	Other counseling, not elsewhere classified

11) Obstetrics and related conditions

See Section I.C.11., the Obstetrics guidelines for further instruction on the use of these codes.

V codes for pregnancy are for use in those circumstances when none of the problems or complications included in the codes from the Obstetrics chapter exist (a routine prenatal visit or postpartum care). Codes V22.0, Supervision of normal first pregnancy, and V22.1, Supervision of other normal pregnancy, are always first listed and are not to be used with any other code from the OB chapter.

The outcome of delivery, category V27, should be included on all maternal delivery records. It is always a secondary code.

V codes for family planning (contraceptive) or procreative management and counseling should be included on an obstetric record either during the pregnancy or the postpartum stage, if applicable.

Obstetrics and related conditions V code categories:

V22	Normal pregnancy
V23	Supervision of high-risk pregnancy Except: V23.2, Pregnancy with history of abortion. Code 646.3, Habitual aborter, from the OB chapter is required to indicate a history of abortion during a pregnancy.
V24	Postpartum care and evaluation
V25	Encounter for contraceptive management Except V25.0x *(See Section I.C.18.d.11, Counseling)*
V26	Procreative management Except V26.5x, Sterilization status, V26.3 and V26.4 *(See Section I.C.18.d.11., Counseling)*
V27	Outcome of delivery
V28	Antenatal screening *(See Section I.C.18.d.6., Screening)*

12)   Newborn, infant and child

See Section I.C.15, the Newborn guidelines for further instruction on the use of these codes.

Newborn V code categories:

V20	Health supervision of infant or child
V29	Observation and evaluation of newborns for suspected condition not found *(See Section I.C.18.d.7, Observation)*
V30-V39	Liveborn infant according to type of birth

13)   Routine and administrative examinations

The V codes allow for the description of encounters for routine examinations, such as, a general check-up, or examinations for administrative purposes, such as a pre-employment physical. The codes are not to be used if the examination is for diagnosis of a suspected condition or for treatment purposes. In such cases the diagnosis code is used. During a routine exam, should a diagnosis or condition be discovered, it should be coded as an additional code. Pre-existing and chronic conditions and history codes may also be included as additional codes as long as the examination is for administrative purposes and not focused on any particular condition.

Pre-operative examination **and pre-procedural laboratory examination** V codes are for use only in those situations when a patient is being cleared for **a procedure or** surgery and no treatment is given.

The V codes categories/code for routine and administrative examinations:

V20.2   Routine infant or child health check
        Any injections given should have a corresponding procedure code.
V70   General medical examination
V72   Special investigations and examinations
        Codes V72.5 **and V72.62** may be used if the reason for the patient encounter is for routine laboratory/radiology testing in the absence of any signs, symptoms, or associated diagnosis. If routine testing is performed during the same encounter as a test to evaluate a sign, symptom, or diagnosis, it is appropriate to assign both the V code and the code describing the reason for the non-routine test.

14)   Miscellaneous V codes

The miscellaneous V codes capture a number of other health care encounters that do not fall into one of the other categories. Certain of these codes identify the reason for the encounter, others are for use as additional codes that provide useful information on circumstances that may affect a patient's care and treatment.

Prophylactic Organ Removal

For encounters specifically for prophylactic removal of breasts, ovaries, or another organ due to a genetic susceptibility to cancer or a family history of cancer, the principal or first listed code should be a code from subcategory V50.4, Prophylactic organ removal, followed by the appropriate genetic susceptibility code and the appropriate family history code.

If the patient has a malignancy of one site and is having prophylactic removal at another site to prevent either a new primary malignancy or metastatic disease, a code for the malignancy should also be assigned in addition to a code from subcategory V50.4. A V50.4 code should not be assigned if the patient is having organ removal for treatment of a malignancy, such as the removal of the testes for the treatment of prostate cancer.

Miscellaneous V code categories/codes:

V07 Need for isolation and other prophylactic measures
Except V07.5, Prophylactic use of agents affecting estrogen receptors and estrogen levels

V50 Elective surgery for purposes other than remedying health states

V58.5 Orthodontics

V60 Housing, household, and economic circumstances

V62 Other psychosocial circumstances

V63 Unavailability of other medical facilities for care

V64 Persons encountering health services for specific procedures, not carried out

V66 Convalescence and Palliative Care

V68 Encounters for administrative purposes

V69 Problems related to lifestyle

15) **Nonspecific V codes**

Certain V codes are so non-specific, or potentially redundant with other codes in the classification, that there can be little justification for their use in the inpatient setting. Their use in the outpatient setting should be limited to those instances when there is no further documentation to permit more precise coding. Otherwise, any sign or symptom or any other reason for visit that is captured in another code should be used.

Nonspecific V code categories/codes:

V11 Personal history of mental disorder
A code from the mental disorders chapter, with an in remission fifth-digit, should be used.

V13.4 Personal history of arthritis

V13.6 Personal history of congenital malformations

V15.7 Personal history of contraception

V23.2 Pregnancy with history of abortion

V40 Mental and behavioral problems

V41 Problems with special senses and other special functions

V47 Other problems with internal organs

V48 Problems with head, neck, and trunk

V49   Problems with limbs and other problems
                 Exceptions:

V49.6	Upper limb amputation status
V49.7	Lower limb amputation status
V49.81	Postmenopausal status
V49.82	Dental sealant status
V49.83	Awaiting organ transplant status

V51.8   Other aftercare involving the use of plastic surgery

V58.2   Blood transfusion, without reported diagnosis

V58.9   Unspecified aftercare

See Section IV.K. and Section IV.L. of the Outpatient guidelines.

e. **V Codes That May Only be Principal/First-Listed Diagnosis**

The list of V codes/categories below may only be reported as the principal/first-listed diagnosis, except when there are multiple encounters on the same day and the medical records for the encounters are combined or when there is more than one V code that meets the definition of principal diagnosis (e.g., a patient is admitted to home healthcare for both aftercare and rehabilitation and they equally meet the definition of principal diagnosis). These codes should not be reported if they do not meet the definition of principal or first-listed diagnosis.

See Section II and Section IV.A for information on selection of principal and first-listed diagnosis.

See Section II.C for information on two or more diagnoses that equally meet the definition for principal diagnosis.

V20.X	Health supervision of infant or child
V22.0	Supervision of normal first pregnancy
V22.1	Supervision of other normal pregnancy
V24.X	Postpartum care and examination
V26.81	Encounter for assisted reproductive fertility procedure cycle
V26.82	**Encounter for fertility preservation procedure**
V30.X	Single liveborn
V31.X	Twin, mate liveborn
V32.X	Twin, mate stillborn
V33.X	Twin, unspecified
V34.X	Other multiple, mates all liveborn
V35.X	Other multiple, mates all stillborn
V36.X	Other multiple, mates live- and stillborn
V37.X	Other multiple, unspecified
V39.X	Unspecified
V46.12	Encounter for respirator dependence during power failure
V46.13	Encounter for weaning from respirator [ventilator]
V51.0	Encounter for breast reconstruction following mastectomy
V56.0	Extracorporeal dialysis
V57.X	Care involving use of rehabilitation procedures
V58.0	Radiotherapy
V58.11	Encounter for antineoplastic chemotherapy
V58.12	Encounter for antineoplastic immunotherapy
V59.X	Donors
V66.0	Convalescence and palliative care following surgery

V66.1	Convalescence and palliative care following radiotherapy
V66.2	Convalescence and palliative care following chemotherapy
V66.3	Convalescence and palliative care following psychotherapy and other treatment for mental disorder
V66.4	Convalescence and palliative care following treatment of fracture
V66.5	Convalescence and palliative care following other treatment
V66.6	Convalescence and palliative care following combined treatment
V66.9	Unspecified convalescence
V68.X	Encounters for administrative purposes
V70.0	Routine general medical examination at a health care facility
V70.1	General psychiatric examination, requested by the authority
V70.2	General psychiatric examination, other and unspecified
V70.3	Other medical examination for administrative purposes
V70.4	Examination for medicolegal reasons
V70.5	Health examination of defined subpopulations
V70.6	Health examination in population surveys
V70.8	Other specified general medical examinations
V70.9	Unspecified general medical examination
V71.X	Observation and evaluation for suspected conditions not found

19. **Supplemental Classification of External Causes of Injury and Poisoning (E-codes, E800-E999)**

Introduction: These guidelines are provided for those who are currently collecting E codes in order that there will be standardization in the process. If your institution plans to begin collecting E codes, these guidelines are to be applied. The use of E codes is supplemental to the application of ICD-9-CM diagnosis codes.

External causes of injury and poisoning codes (**categories E000 and E800-E999**) are intended to provide data for injury research and evaluation of injury prevention strategies. **Activity codes (categories E001-E030) are intended to be used to describe the activity of a person seeking care for injuries as well as other health conditions, when the injury or other health condition resulted from an activity or the activity contributed to a condition.** E codes capture how the injury, **poisoning, or adverse effect** happened (cause), the intent (unintentional or accidental; or intentional, such as suicide or assault), **the person's status (e.g. civilian, military), the associated activity** and the place where the event occurred.

Some major categories of E codes include:
transport accidents
poisoning and adverse effects of drugs, medicinal substances and biologicals
accidental falls
accidents caused by fire and flames
accidents due to natural and environmental factors
late effects of accidents, assaults or self injury
assaults or purposely inflicted injury
suicide or self inflicted injury

These guidelines apply for the coding and collection of E codes from records in hospitals, outpatient clinics, emergency departments, other ambulatory care settings and provider offices, and nonacute care settings, except when other specific guidelines apply.

a. **General E Code Coding Guidelines**

1) **Used with any code in the range of 001-V89**

An E code **from categories E800-E999** may be used with any code in the range of 001-V89, which indicates an injury, poisoning, or adverse effect due to an external cause.

An activity E code (categories E001-E030) may be used with any code in the range of 001-V89 that indicates an injury, or other health condition that resulted from an activity, or the activity contributed to a condition.

2) **Assign the appropriate E code for all initial treatments**

Assign the appropriate E code for the initial encounter of an injury, poisoning, or adverse effect of drugs, not for subsequent treatment.

External cause of injury codes (E-codes) may be assigned while the acute fracture codes are still applicable. *See Section I.C.17.b.1 for coding of acute fractures.*

3) **Use the full range of E codes**

Use the full range of E codes **(E800 – E999)** to completely describe the cause, the intent and the place of occurrence, if applicable, for all injuries, poisonings, and adverse effects of drugs.

See a.1.), j.), and k.) in this section for information on the use of status and activity E codes.

4) **Assign as many E codes as necessary**

Assign as many E codes as necessary to fully explain each cause.

5) **The selection of the appropriate E code**

The selection of the appropriate E code is guided by the Index to External Causes, which is located after the alphabetical index to diseases and by Inclusion and Exclusion notes in the Tabular List.

6) **E code can never be a principal diagnosis**

An E code can never be a principal (first listed) diagnosis.

7) **External cause code(s) with systemic inflammatory response syndrome (SIRS)**

An external cause code is not appropriate with a code from subcategory 995.9, unless the patient also has **another condition for which an E code would be appropriate (such as** an injury, poisoning, or adverse effect of drugs.

8) **Multiple Cause E Code Coding Guidelines**

More than one E-code is required to fully describe the external cause of an illness, injury or poisoning. The assignment of E-codes should be sequenced in the following priority:

If two or more events cause separate injuries, an E code should be assigned for each cause. The first listed E code will be selected in the following order:

E codes for child and adult abuse take priority over all other E codes.
See Section I.C.19.e., Child and Adult abuse guidelines.

E codes for terrorism events take priority over all other E codes except child and adult abuse.

E codes for cataclysmic events take priority over all other E codes except child and adult abuse and terrorism.

E codes for transport accidents take priority over all other E codes except cataclysmic events, child and adult abuse and terrorism.

Activity and external cause status codes are assigned following all causal (intent) E codes.

The first-listed E code should correspond to the cause of the most serious diagnosis due to an assault, accident, or self-harm, following the order of hierarchy listed above.

9) If the reporting format limits the number of E codes

If the reporting format limits the number of E codes that can be used in reporting clinical data, report the code for the cause/intent most related to the principal diagnosis. If the format permits capture of additional E codes, the cause/intent, including medical misadventures, of the additional events should be reported rather than the codes for place, activity or external status.

b.   Place of Occurrence Guideline

Use an additional code from category E849 to indicate the Place of Occurrence. The Place of Occurrence describes the place where the event occurred and not the patient's activity at the time of the event.

Do not use E849.9 if the place of occurrence is not stated.

c.   Adverse Effects of Drugs, Medicinal and Biological Substances Guidelines

1)   Do not code directly from the Table of Drugs

Do not code directly from the Table of Drugs and Chemicals. Always refer back to the Tabular List.

2) **Use as many codes as necessary to describe**

Use as many codes as necessary to describe completely all drugs, medicinal or biological substances.

If the reporting format limits the number of E codes, and there are different fourth digit codes in the same three digit category, use the code for "Other specified" of that category of drugs, medicinal or biological substances. If there is no "Other specified" code in that category, use the appropriate "Unspecified" code in that category.

If the reporting format limits the number of E codes, and the codes are in different three digit categories, assign the appropriate E code for other multiple drugs and medicinal substances.

3) **If the same E code would describe the causative agent**

If the same E code would describe the causative agent for more than one adverse reaction, assign the code only once.

4) **If two or more drugs, medicinal or biological substances**

If two or more drugs, medicinal or biological substances are reported, code each individually unless the combination code is listed in the Table of Drugs and Chemicals. In that case, assign the E code for the combination.

5) **When a reaction results from the interaction of a drug(s)**

When a reaction results from the interaction of a drug(s) and alcohol, use poisoning codes and E codes for both.

6) **Codes from the E930-E949 series**

Codes from the E930-E949 series must be used to identify the causative substance for an adverse effect of drug, medicinal and biological substances, correctly prescribed and properly administered. The effect, such as tachycardia, delirium, gastrointestinal hemorrhaging, vomiting, hypokalemia, hepatitis, renal failure, or respiratory failure, is coded and followed by the appropriate code from the E930-E949 series.

d. **Child and Adult Abuse Guideline**

1) **Intentional injury**

When the cause of an injury or neglect is intentional child or adult abuse, the first listed E code should be assigned from categories E960-E968, Homicide and injury purposely inflicted by other persons, (except category E967). An E code from category E967, Child and adult battering and other maltreatment, should be added as an additional code to identify the perpetrator, if known.

2) Accidental intent

In cases of neglect when the intent is determined to be accidental E code E904.0, Abandonment or neglect of infant and helpless person, should be the first listed E code.

e. Unknown or Suspected Intent Guideline

1) If the intent (accident, self-harm, assault) of the cause of an injury or poisoning is unknown

If the intent (accident, self-harm, assault) of the cause of an injury or poisoning is unknown or unspecified, code the intent as undetermined E980-E989.

2) If the intent (accident, self-harm, assault) of the cause of an injury or poisoning is questionable

If the intent (accident, self-harm, assault) of the cause of an injury or poisoning is questionable, probable or suspected, code the intent as undetermined E980-E989.

f. Undetermined Cause

When the intent of an injury or poisoning is known, but the cause is unknown, use codes: E928.9, Unspecified accident, E958.9, Suicide and self-inflicted injury by unspecified means, and E968.9, Assault by unspecified means.

These E codes should rarely be used, as the documentation in the medical record, in both the inpatient outpatient and other settings, should normally provide sufficient detail to determine the cause of the injury.

g. Late Effects of External Cause Guidelines

1) Late effect E codes

Late effect E codes exist for injuries and poisonings but not for adverse effects of drugs, misadventures and surgical complications.

2) Late effect E codes (E929, E959, E969, E977, E989, or E999.1)

A late effect E code (E929, E959, E969, E977, E989, or E999.1) should be used with any report of a late effect or sequela resulting from a previous injury or poisoning (905-909).

3) Late effect E code with a related current injury

A late effect E code should never be used with a related current nature of injury code.

4) Use of late effect E codes for subsequent visits

Use a late effect E code for subsequent visits when a late effect of the initial injury or poisoning is being treated. There is no late effect E code for adverse effects of drugs.

Do not use a late effect E code for subsequent visits for follow-up care (e.g., to assess healing, to receive rehabilitative therapy) of the injury or poisoning when no late effect of the injury has been documented.

h.   Misadventures and Complications of Care Guidelines

1) Code range E870-E876

Assign a code in the range of E870-E876 if misadventures are stated by the provider. **When applying the E code guidelines pertaining to sequencing, these E codes are considered causal codes.**

2) Code range E878-E879

Assign a code in the range of E878-E879 if the provider attributes an abnormal reaction or later complication to a surgical or medical procedure, but does not mention misadventure at the time of the procedure as the cause of the reaction.

i.   Terrorism Guidelines

1) Cause of injury identified by the Federal Government (FBI) as terrorism

When the cause of an injury is identified by the Federal Government (FBI) as terrorism, the first-listed E-code should be a code from category E979, Terrorism. The definition of terrorism employed by the FBI is found at the inclusion note at E979. The terrorism E-code is the only E-code that should be assigned. Additional E codes from the assault categories should not be assigned.

2) **Cause of an injury is suspected to be the result of terrorism**

When the cause of an injury is suspected to be the result of terrorism a code from category E979 should not be assigned. Assign a code in the range of E codes based circumstances on the documentation of intent and mechanism.

3) **Code E979.9, Terrorism, secondary effects**

Assign code E979.9, Terrorism, secondary effects, for conditions occurring subsequent to the terrorist event. This code should not be assigned for conditions that are due to the initial terrorist act.

4) **Statistical tabulation of terrorism codes**

For statistical purposes these codes will be tabulated within the category for assault, expanding the current category from E960-E969 to include E979 and E999.1.

j. **Activity Code Guidelines**

Assign a code from category E001-E030 to describe the activity that caused or contributed to the injury or other health condition.

Unlike other E codes, activity E codes may be assigned to indicate a health condition (not just injuries) resulted from an activity, or the activity contributed to the condition.

The activity codes are not applicable to poisonings, adverse effects, misadventures or late effects.

k. **External cause status**

A code from category E000, External cause status, should be assigned whenever any other E code is assigned for an encounter, including an Activity E code, except for the events noted below. Assign a code from category E000, External cause status, to indicate the work status of the person at the time the event occurred. The status code indicates whether the event occurred during military activity, whether a non-military person was at work, whether an individual including a student or volunteer was involved in a non-work activity at the time of the causal event.

A code from E000, External cause status, should be assigned, when applicable, with other external cause codes, such as transport accidents and falls. The external cause status codes

are not applicable to poisonings, adverse effects, misadventures or late effects.
Do not assign a code from category E000 if no other E codes (cause, activity) are applicable for the encounter.

Do not assign code E000.9, Unspecified external cause status, if the status is not stated.

Section II. Selection of Principal Diagnosis

The circumstances of inpatient admission always govern the selection of principal diagnosis. The principal diagnosis is defined in the Uniform Hospital Discharge Data Set (UHDDS) as "that condition established after study to be chiefly responsible for occasioning the admission of the patient to the hospital for care."

The UHDDS definitions are used by hospitals to report inpatient data elements in a standardized manner. These data elements and their definitions can be found in the July 31, 1985, Federal Register (Vol. 50, No, 147), pp. 31038-40.

Since that time the application of the UHDDS definitions has been expanded to include all non-outpatient settings (acute care, short term, long term care and psychiatric hospitals; home health agencies; rehab facilities; nursing homes, etc).

In determining principal diagnosis the coding conventions in the ICD-9-CM, Volumes I and II take precedence over these official coding guidelines.
(See Section I.A., Conventions for the ICD-9-CM)

The importance of consistent, complete documentation in the medical record cannot be overemphasized. Without such documentation the application of all coding guidelines is a difficult, if not impossible, task.

A. Codes for symptoms, signs, and ill-defined conditions

Codes for symptoms, signs, and ill-defined conditions from Chapter 16 are not to be used as principal diagnosis when a related definitive diagnosis has been established.

B. Two or more interrelated conditions, each potentially meeting the definition for principal diagnosis.

When there are two or more interrelated conditions (such as diseases in the same ICD-9-CM chapter or manifestations characteristically associated with a certain disease) potentially meeting the definition of principal diagnosis, either condition may be sequenced first, unless the circumstances of the admission, the therapy provided, the Tabular List, or the Alphabetic Index indicate otherwise.

C. Two or more diagnoses that equally meet the definition for principal diagnosis

In the unusual instance when two or more diagnoses equally meet the criteria for principal diagnosis as determined by the circumstances of admission, diagnostic workup and/or therapy provided, and the Alphabetic Index, Tabular List, or another coding guidelines does not provide sequencing direction, any one of the diagnoses may be sequenced first.

D. Two or more comparative or contrasting conditions.

In those rare instances when two or more contrasting or comparative diagnoses are documented as "either/or" (or similar terminology), they are coded as if the diagnoses were confirmed and the diagnoses are sequenced according to the circumstances of the admission. If no further determination can be made as to which diagnosis should be principal, either diagnosis may be sequenced first.

E. A symptom(s) followed by contrasting/comparative diagnoses

When a symptom(s) is followed by contrasting/comparative diagnoses, the symptom code is sequenced first. All the contrasting/comparative diagnoses should be coded as additional diagnoses.

F. Original treatment plan not carried out

Sequence as the principal diagnosis the condition, which after study occasioned the admission to the hospital, even though treatment may not have been carried out due to unforeseen circumstances.

G. Complications of surgery and other medical care

When the admission is for treatment of a complication resulting from surgery or other medical care, the complication code is sequenced as the principal diagnosis. If the complication is classified to the 996-999 series and the code lacks the necessary specificity in describing the complication, an additional code for the specific complication should be assigned.

H. Uncertain Diagnosis

If the diagnosis documented **at the time of discharge** is qualified as "probable", "suspected", "likely", "questionable", "possible", or "still to be ruled out", or other similar terms indicating uncertainty, code the condition as if it existed or was established. The bases for these guidelines are the diagnostic workup, arrangements for further workup or observation, and initial therapeutic approach that correspond most closely with the established diagnosis.

Note: This guideline is applicable only to inpatient admissions to short-term, acute, long-term care and psychiatric hospitals.

I.   Admission from Observation Unit

1.   Admission Following Medical Observation

When a patient is admitted to an observation unit for a medical condition, which either worsens or does not improve, and is subsequently admitted as an inpatient of the same hospital for this same medical condition, the principal diagnosis would be the medical condition which led to the hospital admission.

2. Admission Following Post-Operative Observation

When a patient is admitted to an observation unit to monitor a condition (or complication) that develops following outpatient surgery, and then is subsequently admitted as an inpatient of the same hospital, hospitals should apply the Uniform Hospital Discharge Data Set (UHDDS) definition of principal diagnosis as "that condition established after study to be chiefly responsible for occasioning the admission of the patient to the hospital for care."

J. Admission from Outpatient Surgery

When a patient receives surgery in the hospital's outpatient surgery department and is subsequently admitted for continuing inpatient care at the same hospital, the following guidelines should be followed in selecting the principal diagnosis for the inpatient admission:

- If the reason for the inpatient admission is a complication, assign the complication as the principal diagnosis.
- If no complication, or other condition, is documented as the reason for the inpatient admission, assign the reason for the outpatient surgery as the principal diagnosis.
- If the reason for the inpatient admission is another condition unrelated to the surgery, assign the unrelated condition as the principal diagnosis.

Section III. Reporting Additional Diagnoses

GENERAL RULES FOR OTHER (ADDITIONAL) DIAGNOSES

For reporting purposes the definition for "other diagnoses" is interpreted as additional conditions that affect patient care in terms of requiring:

clinical evaluation; or
therapeutic treatment; or
diagnostic procedures; or
extended length of hospital stay; or
increased nursing care and/or monitoring.

The UHDDS item #11-b defines Other Diagnoses as "all conditions that coexist at the time of admission, that develop subsequently, or that affect the treatment received and/or the length of stay. Diagnoses that relate to an earlier episode which have no bearing on the current hospital stay are to be excluded." UHDDS definitions apply to inpatients in acute care, short-term, long term care and psychiatric hospital setting. The UHDDS definitions are used by acute care short-term hospitals to report inpatient data elements in a standardized manner. These data elements and their definitions can be found in the July 31, 1985, Federal Register (Vol. 50, No, 147), pp. 31038-40.

Since that time the application of the UHDDS definitions has been expanded to include all non-outpatient settings (acute care, short term, long term care and psychiatric hospitals; home health agencies; rehab facilities; nursing homes, etc).

The following guidelines are to be applied in designating "other diagnoses" when neither the Alphabetic Index nor the Tabular List in ICD-9-CM provide direction. The listing of the diagnoses in the patient record is the responsibility of the attending provider.

A. Previous conditions

If the provider has included a diagnosis in the final diagnostic statement, such as the discharge summary or the face sheet, it should ordinarily be coded. Some providers include in the diagnostic statement resolved conditions or diagnoses and status-post procedures from previous admission that have no bearing on the current stay. Such conditions are not to be reported and are coded only if required by hospital policy.

However, history codes (V10-V19) may be used as secondary codes if the historical condition or family history has an impact on current care or influences treatment.

B. Abnormal findings

Abnormal findings (laboratory, x-ray, pathologic, and other diagnostic results) are not coded and reported unless the provider indicates their clinical significance. If the findings are outside the normal range and the attending provider has ordered other tests to evaluate the condition or prescribed treatment, it is appropriate to ask the provider whether the abnormal finding should be added.

Please note: This differs from the coding practices in the outpatient setting for coding encounters for diagnostic tests that have been interpreted by a provider.

C. Uncertain Diagnosis

If the diagnosis documented at the time of discharge is qualified as "probable", "suspected", "likely", "questionable", "possible", or "still to be ruled out" or other similar terms indicating uncertainty, code the condition as if it existed or was established. The bases for these guidelines are the diagnostic workup, arrangements for further workup or observation, and initial therapeutic approach that correspond most closely with the established diagnosis.

Note: This guideline is applicable only to inpatient admissions to short-term, acute, long-term care and psychiatric hospitals.

Section IV. Diagnostic Coding and Reporting Guidelines for Outpatient Services

These coding guidelines for outpatient diagnoses have been approved for use by hospitals/ providers in coding and reporting hospital-based outpatient services and provider-based office visits.

Information about the use of certain abbreviations, punctuation, symbols, and other conventions used in the ICD-9-CM Tabular List (code numbers and titles), can be found in Section IA of these guidelines, under "Conventions Used in the Tabular List." Information about the correct sequence to use in finding a code is also described in Section I.

The terms encounter and visit are often used interchangeably in describing outpatient service contacts and, therefore, appear together in these guidelines without distinguishing one from the other.

Though the conventions and general guidelines apply to all settings, coding guidelines for outpatient and provider reporting of diagnoses will vary in a number of instances from those for inpatient diagnoses, recognizing that:

> The Uniform Hospital Discharge Data Set (UHDDS) definition of principal diagnosis applies only to inpatients in acute, short-term, long-term care and psychiatric hospitals.

> Coding guidelines for inconclusive diagnoses (probable, suspected, rule out, etc.) were developed for inpatient reporting and do not apply to outpatients.

A. Selection of first-listed condition

> In the outpatient setting, the term first-listed diagnosis is used in lieu of principal diagnosis.

> In determining the first-listed diagnosis the coding conventions of ICD-9-CM, as well as the general and disease specific guidelines take precedence over the outpatient guidelines.

> Diagnoses often are not established at the time of the initial encounter/visit. It may take two or more visits before the diagnosis is confirmed.

> The most critical rule involves beginning the search for the correct code assignment through the Alphabetic Index. Never begin searching initially in the Tabular List as this will lead to coding errors.

1. Outpatient Surgery

When a patient presents for outpatient surgery, code the reason for the surgery as the first-listed diagnosis (reason for the encounter), even if the surgery is not performed due to a contraindication.

2. Observation Stay

When a patient is admitted for observation for a medical condition, assign a code for the medical condition as the first-listed diagnosis.

When a patient presents for outpatient surgery and develops complications requiring admission to observation, code the reason for the surgery as the first reported diagnosis (reason for the encounter), followed by codes for the complications as secondary diagnoses.

B. Codes from 001.0 through V89

The appropriate code or codes from 001.0 through **V89** must be used to identify diagnoses, symptoms, conditions, problems, complaints, or other reason(s) for the encounter/visit.

C. Accurate reporting of ICD-9-CM diagnosis codes

For accurate reporting of ICD-9-CM diagnosis codes, the documentation should describe the patient's condition, using terminology which includes specific diagnoses as well as symptoms, problems, or reasons for the encounter. There are ICD-9-CM codes to describe all of these.

D. Selection of codes 001.0 through 999.9

The selection of codes 001.0 through 999.9 will frequently be used to describe the reason for the encounter. These codes are from the section of ICD-9-CM for the classification of diseases and injuries (e.g. infectious and parasitic diseases; neoplasms; symptoms, signs, and ill-defined conditions, etc.).

E. Codes that describe symptoms and signs

Codes that describe symptoms and signs, as opposed to diagnoses, are acceptable for reporting purposes when a diagnosis has not been established (confirmed) by the provider. Chapter 16 of ICD-9-CM, Symptoms, Signs, and Ill-defined conditions (codes 780.0 - 799.9) contain many, but not all codes for symptoms.

F. Encounters for circumstances other than a disease or injury

ICD-9-CM provides codes to deal with encounters for circumstances other than a disease or injury. The Supplementary Classification of factors Influencing Health Status and Contact with Health Services (V01.0- **V89**) is provided to deal with occasions when circumstances other than a disease or injury are recorded as diagnosis or problems. *See Section I.C. 18 for information on V-codes.*

G. Level of Detail in Coding

1. ICD-9-CM codes with 3, 4, or 5 digits

ICD-9-CM is composed of codes with either 3, 4, or 5 digits. Codes with three digits are included in ICD-9-CM as the heading of a category of codes that may be further subdivided by the use of fourth and/or fifth digits, which provide greater specificity.

2. Use of full number of digits required for a code

A three-digit code is to be used only if it is not further subdivided. Where fourth-digit subcategories and/or fifth-digit subclassifications are provided, they must be assigned. A code is invalid if it has not been coded to the full number of digits required for that code.

See also discussion under Section I.b.3., General Coding Guidelines, Level of Detail in Coding.

H. ICD-9-CM code for the diagnosis, condition, problem, or other reason for encounter/visit

List first the ICD-9-CM code for the diagnosis, condition, problem, or other reason for encounter/visit shown in the medical record to be chiefly responsible for the services provided. List additional codes that describe any coexisting conditions. In some cases the first-listed diagnosis may be a symptom when a diagnosis has not been established (confirmed) by the physician.

I. Uncertain diagnosis

Do not code diagnoses documented as "probable", "suspected," "questionable," "rule out," or "working diagnosis" or other similar terms indicating uncertainty. Rather, code the condition(s) to the highest degree of certainty for that encounter/visit, such as symptoms, signs, abnormal test results, or other reason for the visit.

Please note: This differs from the coding practices used by short-term, acute care, long-term care and psychiatric hospitals.

J. Chronic diseases

Chronic diseases treated on an ongoing basis may be coded and reported as many times as the patient receives treatment and care for the condition(s)

K. Code all documented conditions that coexist

Code all documented conditions that coexist at the time of the encounter/visit, and require or affect patient care treatment or management. Do not code conditions that were previously treated and no longer exist. However, history codes (V10-V19) may be used as secondary codes if the historical condition or family history has an impact on current care or influences treatment.

L. Patients receiving diagnostic services only

For patients receiving diagnostic services only during an encounter/visit, sequence first the diagnosis, condition, problem, or other reason for encounter/visit shown in the medical record to be chiefly responsible for the outpatient services provided during the encounter/visit. Codes for other diagnoses (e.g., chronic conditions) may be sequenced as additional diagnoses.

For encounters for routine laboratory/radiology testing in the absence of any signs, symptoms, or associated diagnosis, assign V72.5 and **a code from subcategory V72.6**. If routine testing is performed during the same encounter as a test to evaluate a sign, symptom, or diagnosis, it is appropriate to assign both the V code and the code describing the reason for the non-routine test.

For outpatient encounters for diagnostic tests that have been interpreted by a physician, and the final report is available at the time of coding, code any confirmed or definitive diagnosis(es) documented in the interpretation. Do not code related signs and symptoms as additional diagnoses.

Please note: This differs from the coding practice in the hospital inpatient setting regarding abnormal findings on test results.

M. Patients receiving therapeutic services only

For patients receiving therapeutic services only during an encounter/visit, sequence first the diagnosis, condition, problem, or other reason for encounter/visit shown in the medical record to be chiefly responsible for the outpatient services provided during the encounter/visit. Codes for other diagnoses (e.g., chronic conditions) may be sequenced as additional diagnoses.

The only exception to this rule is that when the primary reason for the admission/encounter is chemotherapy, radiation therapy, or rehabilitation, the appropriate V code for the service is listed first, and the diagnosis or problem for which the service is being performed listed second.

N. Patients receiving preoperative evaluations only

For patients receiving preoperative evaluations only, sequence first a code from category V72.8, Other specified examinations, to describe the pre-op consultations. Assign a code for the condition to describe the reason for the surgery as an additional diagnosis. Code also any findings related to the pre-op evaluation.

O. Ambulatory surgery

For ambulatory surgery, code the diagnosis for which the surgery was performed. If the postoperative diagnosis is known to be different from the preoperative diagnosis at the time the diagnosis is confirmed, select the postoperative diagnosis for coding, since it is the most definitive.

P. Routine outpatient prenatal visits

For routine outpatient prenatal visits when no complications are present, codes V22.0, Supervision of normal first pregnancy, or V22.1, Supervision of other normal pregnancy, should be used as the principal diagnosis. These codes should not be used in conjunction with chapter 11 codes.

Appendix I
Present on Admission Reporting Guidelines

Introduction

These guidelines are to be used as a supplement to the *ICD-9-CM Official Guidelines for Coding and Reporting* to facilitate the assignment of the Present on Admission (POA) indicator for each diagnosis and external cause of injury code reported on claim forms (UB-04 and 837 Institutional).

These guidelines are not intended to replace any guidelines in the main body of the *ICD-9-CM Official Guidelines for Coding and Reporting*. The POA guidelines are not intended to provide guidance on when a condition should be coded, but rather, how to apply the POA indicator to the final set of diagnosis codes that have been assigned in accordance with Sections I, II, and III of the official coding guidelines. Subsequent to the assignment of the ICD-9-CM codes, the POA indicator should then be assigned to those conditions that have been coded.

As stated in the Introduction to the ICD-9-CM Official Guidelines for Coding and Reporting, a joint effort between the healthcare provider and the coder is essential to achieve complete and accurate documentation, code assignment, and reporting of diagnoses and procedures. The importance of consistent, complete documentation in the medical record cannot be overemphasized. Medical record documentation from any provider involved in the care and treatment of the patient may be used to support the determination of whether a condition was present on admission or not. In the context of the official coding guidelines, the term "provider" means a physician or any qualified healthcare practitioner who is legally accountable for establishing the patient's diagnosis.

These guidelines are not a substitute for the provider's clinical judgment as to the determination of whether a condition was/was not present on admission. The provider should be queried regarding issues related to the linking of signs/symptoms, timing of test results, and the timing of findings.

General Reporting Requirements

All claims involving inpatient admissions to general acute care hospitals or other facilities that are subject to a law or regulation mandating collection of present on admission information.

Present on admission is defined as present at the time the order for inpatient admission occurs -- conditions that develop during an outpatient encounter, including emergency department, observation, or outpatient surgery, are considered as present on admission.

POA indicator is assigned to principal and secondary diagnoses (as defined in Section II of the Official Guidelines for Coding and Reporting) and the external cause of injury codes.

Issues related to inconsistent, missing, conflicting or unclear documentation must still be resolved by the provider.

If a condition would not be coded and reported based on UHDDS definitions and current official coding guidelines, then the POA indicator would not be reported.

Reporting Options

Y - Yes
N - No
U - Unknown
W – Clinically undetermined
Unreported/Not used (or "1" for Medicare usage) – (Exempt from POA reporting)

Reporting Definitions

Y = present at the time of inpatient admission
N = not present at the time of inpatient admission
U = documentation is insufficient to determine if condition is present on admission
W = provider is unable to clinically determine whether condition was present on admission or not

Timeframe for POA Identification and Documentation

There is no required timeframe as to when a provider (per the definition of "provider" used in these guidelines) must identify or document a condition to be present on admission. In some clinical situations, it may not be possible for a provider to make a definitive diagnosis (or a condition may not be recognized or reported by the patient) for a period of time after admission. In some cases it may be several days before the provider arrives at a definitive diagnosis. This does not mean that the condition was not present on admission. Determination of whether the condition was present on admission or not will be based on the applicable POA guideline as identified in this document, or on the provider's best clinical judgment.

If at the time of code assignment the documentation is unclear as to whether a condition was present on admission or not, it is appropriate to query the provider for clarification.

Assigning the POA Indicator

Condition is on the "Exempt from Reporting" list
Leave the "present on admission" field blank if the condition is on the list of ICD-9-CM codes for which this field is not applicable. This is the only circumstance in which the field may be left blank.

POA Explicitly Documented
Assign Y for any condition the provider explicitly documents as being present on admission.

Assign N for any condition the provider explicitly documents as not present at the time of admission.

Conditions diagnosed prior to inpatient admission

Assign "Y" for conditions that were diagnosed prior to admission (example: hypertension, diabetes mellitus, asthma)

Conditions diagnosed during the admission but clearly present before admission

Assign "Y" for conditions diagnosed during the admission that were clearly present but not diagnosed until after admission occurred.

Diagnoses subsequently confirmed after admission are considered present on admission if at the time of admission they are documented as suspected, possible, rule out, differential diagnosis, or constitute an underlying cause of a symptom that is present at the time of admission.

Condition develops during outpatient encounter prior to inpatient admission

Assign Y for any condition that develops during an outpatient encounter prior to a written order for inpatient admission.

Documentation does not indicate whether condition was present on admission

Assign "U" when the medical record documentation is unclear as to whether the condition was present on admission. "U" should not be routinely assigned and used only in very limited circumstances. Coders are encouraged to query the providers when the documentation is unclear.

Documentation states that it cannot be determined whether the condition was or was not present on admission

Assign "W" when the medical record documentation indicates that it cannot be clinically determined whether or not the condition was present on admission.

Chronic condition with acute exacerbation during the admission

If the code is a combination code that identifies both the chronic condition and the acute exacerbation, see POA guidelines pertaining to combination codes.

If the combination code only identifies the chronic condition and not the acute exacerbation (e.g., acute exacerbation of CHF), assign "Y."

Conditions documented as possible, probable, suspected, or rule out at the time of discharge

If the final diagnosis contains a possible, probable, suspected, or rule out diagnosis, and this diagnosis was **based on signs, symptoms or clinical findings** suspected at the time of inpatient admission, assign "Y."

If the final diagnosis contains a possible, probable, suspected, or rule out diagnosis, and this diagnosis was based on **signs,** symptoms or clinical findings that were not present on admission, assign "N".

Conditions documented as impending or threatened at the time of discharge

If the final diagnosis contains an impending or threatened diagnosis, and this diagnosis is based on symptoms or clinical findings that were present on admission, assign "Y".

If the final diagnosis contains an impending or threatened diagnosis, and this diagnosis is based on symptoms or clinical findings that were not present on admission, assign "N".

Acute and Chronic Conditions

Assign "Y" for acute conditions that are present at time of admission and N for acute conditions that are not present at time of admission.

Assign "Y" for chronic conditions, even though the condition may not be diagnosed until after admission.

If a single code identifies both an acute and chronic condition, see the POA guidelines for combination codes.

Combination Codes

Assign "N" if any part of the combination code was not present on admission (e.g., obstructive chronic bronchitis with acute exacerbation and the exacerbation was not present on admission; gastric ulcer that does not start bleeding until after admission; asthma patient develops status asthmaticus after admission)

Assign "Y" if all parts of the combination code were present on admission (e.g., patient with diabetic nephropathy is admitted with uncontrolled diabetes)

If the final diagnosis includes comparative or contrasting diagnoses, and both were present, or suspected, at the time of admission, assign "Y".

For infection codes that include the causal organism, assign "Y" if the infection (or signs of the infection) was present on admission, even though the culture results may not be known until after admission (e.g., patient is admitted with pneumonia and the provider documents pseudomonas as the causal organism a few days later).

Same Diagnosis Code for Two or More Conditions

When the same ICD-9-CM diagnosis code applies to two or more conditions during the same encounter (e.g. bilateral condition, or two separate conditions classified to the same ICD-9-CM diagnosis code):

Assign "Y" if all conditions represented by the single ICD-9-CM code were present on admission (e.g. bilateral fracture of the same bone, same site, and both fractures were present on admission)

Assign "N" if any of the conditions represented by the single ICD-9-CM code was not present on admission (e.g. dehydration with hyponatremia is assigned to code 276.1, but only one of these conditions was present on admission).

Obstetrical conditions

Whether or not the patient delivers during the current hospitalization does not affect assignment of the POA indicator. The determining factor for POA assignment is whether the pregnancy complication or obstetrical condition described by the code was present at the time of admission or not.

If the pregnancy complication or obstetrical condition was present on admission (e.g., patient admitted in preterm labor), assign "Y".

If the pregnancy complication or obstetrical condition was not present on admission (e.g., 2nd degree laceration during delivery, postpartum hemorrhage that occurred during current hospitalization, fetal distress develops after admission), assign "N".

If the obstetrical code includes more than one diagnosis and any of the diagnoses identified by the code were not present on admission assign "N".
> (e.g., Code 642.7, Pre-eclampsia or eclampsia superimposed on pre-existing hypertension).

If the obstetrical code includes information that is not a diagnosis, do not consider that information in the POA determination.
> (e.g. Code 652.1x, Breech or other malpresentation successfully converted to cephalic presentation should be reported as present on admission if the fetus was breech on admission but was converted to cephalic presentation after admission (since the conversion to cephalic presentation does not represent a diagnosis, the fact that the conversion occurred after admission has no bearing on the POA determination).

Perinatal conditions

Newborns are not considered to be admitted until after birth. Therefore, any condition present at birth or that developed in utero is considered present at admission and should be assigned "Y". This includes conditions that occur during delivery (e.g., injury during delivery, meconium aspiration, exposure to streptococcus B in the vaginal canal).

Congenital conditions and anomalies

Assign "Y" for congenital conditions and anomalies. Congenital conditions are always considered present on admission.

External cause of injury codes

Assign "Y" for any E code representing an external cause of injury or poisoning that occurred prior to inpatient admission (e.g., patient fell out of bed at home, patient fell out of bed in emergency room prior to admission)

Assign "N" for any E code representing an external cause of injury or poisoning that occurred during inpatient hospitalization (e.g., patient fell out of hospital bed during hospital stay, patient experienced an adverse reaction to a medication administered after inpatient admission)

Categories and Codes
Exempt from
Diagnosis Present on Admission Requirement

Note: "Diagnosis present on admission" for these code categories are exempt because they represent circumstances regarding the healthcare encounter or factors influencing health status that do not represent a current disease or injury or are always present on admission

137-139, Late effects of infectious and parasitic diseases

268.1, Rickets, late effect

326, Late effects of intracranial abscess or pyogenic infection

412, Old myocardial infarction

438, Late effects of cerebrovascular disease

650, Normal delivery

660.7, Failed forceps or vacuum extractor, unspecified

677, Late effect of complication of pregnancy, childbirth, and the puerperium

905-909, Late effects of injuries, poisonings, toxic effects, and other external causes

V02, Carrier or suspected carrier of infectious diseases

V03, Need for prophylactic vaccination and inoculation against bacterial diseases

V04, Need for prophylactic vaccination and inoculation against certain viral diseases

V05, Need for other prophylactic vaccination and inoculation against single diseases

V06, Need for prophylactic vaccination and inoculation against combinations of diseases

V07, Need for isolation and other prophylactic measures

V10, Personal history of malignant neoplasm

V11, Personal history of mental disorder

V12, Personal history of certain other diseases

V13, Personal history of other diseases

V14, Personal history of allergy to medicinal agents

V15.01-V15.09, Other personal history, Allergy, other than to medicinal agents

V15.1, Other personal history, Surgery to heart and great vessels

V15.2, Other personal history, Surgery to other major organs

V15.3, Other personal history, Irradiation

V15.4, Other personal history, Psychological trauma

V15.5, Other personal history, Injury

V15.6, Other personal history, Poisoning

V15.7, Other personal history, Contraception

V15.80, Other personal history, History of failed moderate sedation

V15.81, Other personal history, Noncompliance with medical treatment

V15.82, Other personal history, History of tobacco use

V15.83, Other personal history, Underimmunization status

V15.84, Other personal history, Contact with and (suspected) exposure to asbestos

V15.85, Other personal history, Contact with and (suspected) exposure to potentially hazardous body fluids

V15.86, Other personal history, Contact with and (suspected) exposure to lead

V15.88, Other personal history, History of fall

V15.89, Other personal history, Other

V15.9 Unspecified personal history presenting hazards to health

V16, Family history of malignant neoplasm

V17, Family history of certain chronic disabling diseases

V18, Family history of certain other specific conditions

V19, Family history of other conditions

V20, Health supervision of infant or child

V21, Constitutional states in development

V22, Normal pregnancy

V23, Supervision of high-risk pregnancy

V24, Postpartum care and examination

V25, Encounter for contraceptive management

V26, Procreative management

V27, Outcome of delivery

V28, Antenatal screening

V29, Observation and evaluation of newborns for suspected condition not found

V30-V39, Liveborn infants according to type of birth

V42, Organ or tissue replaced by transplant

V43, Organ or tissue replaced by other means

V44, Artificial opening status

V45, Other postprocedural states

V46, Other dependence on machines

V49.60-V49.77, Upper and lower limb amputation status

V49.81-V49.84, Other specified conditions influencing health status

V50, Elective surgery for purposes other than remedying health states

V51, Aftercare involving the use of plastic surgery

V52, Fitting and adjustment of prosthetic device and implant

V53, Fitting and adjustment of other device

V54, Other orthopedic aftercare

V55, Attention to artificial openings

V56, Encounter for dialysis and dialysis catheter care

V57, Care involving use of rehabilitation procedures

V58, Encounter for other and unspecified procedures and aftercare

V59, Donors

V60, Housing, household, and economic circumstances

V61, Other family circumstances

V62, Other psychosocial circumstances

V64, Persons encountering health services for specific procedures, not carried out

V65, Other persons seeking consultation

V66, Convalescence and palliative care

V67, Follow-up examination

V68, Encounters for administrative purposes

V69, Problems related to lifestyle

V70, General medical examination

V71, Observation and evaluation for suspected condition not found

V72, Special investigations and examinations

V73, Special screening examination for viral and chlamydial diseases

V74, Special screening examination for bacterial and spirochetal diseases

V75, Special screening examination for other infectious diseases

V76, Special screening for malignant neoplasms

V77, Special screening for endocrine, nutritional, metabolic, and immunity disorders

V78, Special screening for disorders of blood and blood-forming organs

V79, Special screening for mental disorders and developmental handicaps

V80, Special screening for neurological, eye, and ear diseases

V81, Special screening for cardiovascular, respiratory, and genitourinary diseases

V82, Special screening for other conditions

V83, Genetic carrier status

V84, Genetic susceptibility to disease

V85, Body Mass Index

V86 Estrogen receptor status

V87.32, Contact with and (suspected) exposure to algae bloom

V87.4, Personal history of drug therapy

V88, Acquired absence of cervix and uterus

V89, Suspected maternal and fetal conditions not found

E000, External cause status

E001-E030, Activity

E800-E807, Railway accidents

E810-E819, Motor vehicle traffic accidents

E820-E825, Motor vehicle nontraffic accidents

E826-E829, Other road vehicle accidents

E830-E838, Water transport accidents

E840-E845, Air and space transport accidents

E846-E848, Vehicle accidents not elsewhere classifiable

E849.0-E849.6, Place of occurrence

E849.8-E849.9, Place of occurrence

E883.1, Accidental fall into well

E883.2, Accidental fall into storm drain or manhole

E884.0, Fall from playground equipment

E884.1, Fall from cliff

E885.0, Fall from (nonmotorized) scooter

E885.1, Fall from roller skates

E885.2, Fall from skateboard

E885.3, Fall from skis

E885.4, Fall from snowboard

E886.0, Fall on same level from collision, pushing, or shoving, by or with other person, In sports

E890.0-E890.9, Conflagration in private dwelling

E893.0, Accident caused by ignition of clothing, from controlled fire in private dwelling

E893.2, Accident caused by ignition of clothing, from controlled fire not in building or structure

E894, Ignition of highly inflammable material

E895, Accident caused by controlled fire in private dwelling

E897, Accident caused by controlled fire not in building or structure

E898.0-E898.1, Accident caused by other specified fire and flames

E917.0, Striking against or struck accidentally by objects or persons, in sports without subsequent fall

E917.1, Striking against or struck accidentally by objects or persons, caused by a crowd, by collective fear or panic without subsequent fall

E917.2, Striking against or struck accidentally by objects or persons, in running water without subsequent fall

E917.5, Striking against or struck accidentally by objects or persons, object in sports with subsequent fall

E917.6, Striking against or struck accidentally by objects or persons, caused by a crowd, by collective fear or panic with subsequent fall

E919.0-E919.1, Accidents caused by machinery

E919.3-E919.9, Accidents caused by machinery

E921.0-E921.9, Accident caused by explosion of pressure vessel

E922.0-E922.9, Accident caused by firearm and air gun missile

E924.1, Caustic and corrosive substances

E926.2, Visible and ultraviolet light sources

E928.0-E928.8, Other and unspecified environmental and accidental causes

E929.0-E929.9, Late effects of accidental injury

E959, Late effects of self-inflicted injury

E970-E978, Legal intervention

E979, Terrorism

E981.0-E981.8, Poisoning by gases in domestic use, undetermined whether accidentally or purposely inflicted

E982.0-E982.9, Poisoning by other gases, undetermined whether accidentally or purposely inflicted

E985.0-E985.7, Injury by firearms, air guns and explosives, undetermined whether accidentally or purposely inflicted

E987.0, Falling from high place, undetermined whether accidentally or purposely inflicted, residential premises

E987.2, Falling from high place, undetermined whether accidentally or purposely inflicted,

natural sites

E989, Late effects of injury, undetermined whether accidentally or purposely inflicted

E990-E999, Injury resulting from operations of war

POA Examples

The POA examples have been removed from the guidelines.

EVALUATION FORM FOR THE BOOK AND INTERACTIVE CD-ROM

As we have learned through quality improvement concepts, there is always the opportunity to do something better. Therefore, if you have suggestions for improving the book and CD-ROM, please let us know. We invite your input and feedback.

Please rate each of the following aspects of this book on a scale of 1 to 5, where: **5 is excellent, 4 is above average, 3 is average, 2 is below average, and 1 is poor.**

Depth/completeness of coverage	5	4	3	2	1
Organization of material	5	4	3	2	1
Study tips	5	4	3	2	1
Appropriate level of writing	5	4	3	2	1
Cover design and attractiveness	5	4	3	2	1
Overall design and layout of book	5	4	3	2	1
Overall satisfaction with book	5	4	3	2	1

Would you recommend this book and CD-ROM to future graduates studying for the CCS-P examination?

What can we do to make these products better for you to use? _____

_____
_____
_____
_____
_____
_____
_____

Please attach additional comments if you have further suggestions. Thank you!

Attention: Patricia J. Schnering
c/o Cengage Delmar Learning
Executive Woods
5 Maxwell Drive
Clifton Park, NY 12065

Email your comments and questions to the author at: *PJSPRG@AOL.COM*

CENGAGE LEARNING HAS PROVIDED YOU WITH THIS PRODUCT FOR YOUR REVIEW AND, TO THE EXTENT THAT YOU ADOPT THE ASSOCIATED TEXTBOOK FOR USE IN CONNECTION WITH YOUR COURSE, YOU AND YOUR STUDENTS WHO PURCHASE THE TEXTBOOK MAY USE THE MATERIALS AS DESCRIBED BELOW.

IMPORTANT! READ CAREFULLY: This End User License Agreement ("Agreement") sets forth the conditions by which Cengage Learning will make electronic access to the Cengage Learning-owned licensed content and associated media, software, documentation, printed materials, and electronic documentation contained in this package and/or made available to you via this product (the "Licensed Content"), available to you (the "End User"). BY CLICKING THE "I ACCEPT" BUTTON AND/OR OPENING THIS PACKAGE, YOU ACKNOWLEDGE THAT YOU HAVE READ ALL OF THE TERMS AND CONDITIONS, AND THAT YOU AGREE TO BE BOUND BY ITS TERMS, CONDITIONS, AND ALL APPLICABLE LAWS AND REGULATIONS GOVERNING THE USE OF THE LICENSED CONTENT.

1.0   SCOPE OF LICENSE

1.1   Licensed Content. The Licensed Content may contain portions of modifiable content ("Modifiable Content") and content which may not be modified or otherwise altered by the End User ("Non-Modifiable Content"). For purposes of this Agreement, Modifiable Content and Non-Modifiable Content may be collectively referred to herein as the "Licensed Content." All Licensed Content shall be considered Non-Modifiable Content, unless such Licensed Content is presented to the End User in a modifiable format and it is clearly indicated that modification of the Licensed Content is permitted.

1.2   Subject to the End User's compliance with the terms and conditions of this Agreement, Cengage Learning hereby grants the End User, a nontransferable, nonexclusive, limited right to access and view a single copy of the Licensed Content on a single personal computer system for noncommercial, internal, personal use only, and, to the extent that End User adopts the associated textbook for use in connection with a course, the limited right to provide, distribute, and display the Modifiable Content to course students who purchase the textbook, for use in connection with the course only. The End User shall not (i) reproduce, copy, modify (except in the case of Modifiable Content), distribute, display, transfer, sublicense, prepare derivative work(s) based on, sell, exchange, barter or transfer, rent, lease, loan, resell, or in any other manner exploit the Licensed Content; (ii) remove, obscure, or alter any notice of Cengage Learning's intellectual property rights present on or in the Licensed Content, including, but not limited to, copyright, trademark, and/or patent notices; or (iii) disassemble, decompile, translate, reverse engineer, or otherwise reduce the Licensed Content. Cengage reserves the right to use a hardware lock device, license administration software, and/or a license authorization key to control access or password protection technology to the Licensed Content. The End User may not take any steps to avoid or defeat the purpose of such measures. Use of the Licensed Content without the relevant required lock device or authorization key is prohibited. UNDER NO CIRCUMSTANCES MAY NON-SALEABLE ITEMS PROVIDED TO YOU BY CENGAGE (INCLUDING, WITHOUT LIMITATION, ANNOTATED INSTRUCTOR'S EDITIONS, SOLUTIONS MANUALS, INSTRUCTOR RESOURCE'S MATERIALS AND/OR TEST MATERIALS) BE SOLD, AUCTIONED, LICENSED OR OTHERWISE REDISTRIBUTED BY THE END USER.

2.0   TERMINATION

2.1   Cengage Learning may at any time (without prejudice to its other rights or remedies) immediately terminate this Agreement and/or suspend access to some or all of the Licensed Content, in the event that the End User does not comply with any of the terms and conditions of this Agreement. In the event of such termination by Cengage Learning, the End User shall immediately return any and all copies of the Licensed Content to Cengage Learning.

3.0   PROPRIETARY RIGHTS

3.1   The End User acknowledges that Cengage Learning owns all rights, title and interest, including, but not limited to all copyright rights therein, in and to the Licensed Content, and that the End User shall not take any action inconsistent with such ownership. The Licensed Content is protected by U.S., Canadian and other applicable copyright laws and by international treaties, including the Berne Convention and the Universal Copyright Convention. Nothing contained in this Agreement shall be construed as granting the End User any ownership rights in or to the Licensed Content.

3.2   Cengage Learning reserves the right at any time to withdraw from the Licensed Content any item or part of an item for which it no longer retains the right to publish, or which it has reasonable grounds to believe infringes copyright or is defamatory, unlawful, or otherwise objectionable.

4.0   PROTECTION AND SECURITY

4.1   The End User shall use its best efforts and take all reasonable steps to safeguard its copy of the Licensed Content to ensure that no unauthorized reproduction, publication, disclosure, modification, or distribution of the Licensed Content, in whole or in part, is made. To the extent that the End User becomes aware of any such unauthorized use of the Licensed Content, the End User shall immediately notify Cengage Learning. Notification of such violations may be made by sending an e-mail to infringement@cengage.com.

5.0 MISUSE OF THE LICENSED PRODUCT

5.1 In the event that the End User uses the Licensed Content in violation of this Agreement, Cengage Learning shall have the option of electing liquidated damages, which shall include all profits generated by the End User's use of the Licensed Content plus interest computed at the maximum rate permitted by law and all legal fees and other expenses incurred by Cengage Learning in enforcing its rights, plus penalties.

6.0 FEDERAL GOVERNMENT CLIENTS

6.1 Except as expressly authorized by Cengage Learning, Federal Government clients obtain only the rights specified in this Agreement and no other rights. The Government acknowledges that (i) all software and related documentation incorporated in the Licensed Content is existing commercial computer software within the meaning of FAR 27.405(b)(2); and (2) all other data delivered in whatever form, is limited rights data within the meaning of FAR 27.401. The restrictions in this section are acceptable as consistent with the Government's need for software and other data under this Agreement.

7.0 DISCLAIMER OF WARRANTIES AND LIABILITIES

7.1 Although Cengage Learning believes the Licensed Content to be reliable, Cengage Learning does not guarantee or warrant (i) any information or materials contained in or produced by the Licensed Content, (ii) the accuracy, completeness or reliability of the Licensed Content, or (iii) that the Licensed Content is free from errors or other material defects. THE LICENSED PRODUCT IS PROVIDED "AS IS," WITHOUT ANY WARRANTY OF ANY KIND AND CENGAGE LEARNING DISCLAIMS ANY AND ALL WARRANTIES, EXPRESSED OR IMPLIED, INCLUDING, WITHOUT LIMITATION, WARRANTIES OF MERCHANTABILITY OR FITNESS FOR A PARTICULAR PURPOSE. IN NO EVENT SHALL CENGAGE LEARNING BE LIABLE FOR: INDIRECT, SPECIAL, PUNITIVE OR CONSEQUENTIAL DAMAGES INCLUDING FOR LOST PROFITS, LOST DATA, OR OTHERWISE. IN NO EVENT SHALL CENGAGE LEARNING'S AGGREGATE LIABILITY HEREUNDER, WHETHER ARISING IN CONTRACT, TORT, STRICT LIABILITY OR OTHERWISE, EXCEED THE AMOUNT OF FEES PAID BY THE END USER HEREUNDER FOR THE LICENSE OF THE LICENSED CONTENT.

8.0 GENERAL

8.1 <u>Entire Agreement</u>. This Agreement shall constitute the entire Agreement between the Parties and supercedes all prior Agreements and understandings oral or written relating to the subject matter hereof.

8.2 <u>Enhancements/Modifications of Licensed Content</u>. From time to time, and in Cengage Learning's sole discretion, Cengage Learning may advise the End User of updates, upgrades, enhancements and/or improvements to the Licensed Content, and may permit the End User to access and use, subject to the terms and conditions of this Agreement, such modifications, upon payment of prices as may be established by Cengage Learning.

8.3 <u>No Export</u>. The End User shall use the Licensed Content solely in the United States and shall not transfer or export, directly or indirectly, the Licensed Content outside the United States.

8.4 <u>Severability.</u> If any provision of this Agreement is invalid, illegal, or unenforceable under any applicable statute or rule of law, the provision shall be deemed omitted to the extent that it is invalid, illegal, or unenforceable. In such a case, the remainder of the Agreement shall be construed in a manner as to give greatest effect to the original intention of the parties hereto.

8.5 <u>Waiver</u>. The waiver of any right or failure of either party to exercise in any respect any right provided in this Agreement in any instance shall not be deemed to be a waiver of such right in the future or a waiver of any other right under this Agreement.

8.6 <u>Choice of Law/Venue</u>. This Agreement shall be interpreted, construed, and governed by and in accordance with the laws of the State of New York, applicable to contracts executed and to be wholly preformed therein, without regard to its principles governing conflicts of law. Each party agrees that any proceeding arising out of or relating to this Agreement or the breach or threatened breach of this Agreement may be commenced and prosecuted in a court in the State and County of New York. Each party consents and submits to the nonexclusive personal jurisdiction of any court in the State and County of New York in respect of any such proceeding.

8.7   Acknowledgment. By opening this package and/or by accessing the Licensed Content on this Web site, THE END USER ACKNOWLEDGES THAT IT HAS READ THIS AGREEMENT, UNDERSTANDS IT, AND AGREES TO BE BOUND BY ITS TERMS AND CONDITIONS. IF YOU DO NOT ACCEPT THESE TERMS AND CONDITIONS, YOU MUST NOT ACCESS THE LICENSED CONTENT AND RETURN THE LICENSED PRODUCT TO CENGAGE LEARNING (WITHIN 30 CALENDAR DAYS OF THE END USER'S PURCHASE) WITH PROOF OF PAYMENT ACCEPTABLE TO CENGAGE LEARNING, FOR A CREDIT OR A REFUND. Should the End User have any questions/comments regarding this Agreement, please contact Cengage Learning at Delmar.help@cengage.com.